D0215292

Wisdom With
Understanding
is Better
Than Rubies
Lurine Karon Greenberg
Fine Arts Collection

Satchmo

Armstrong in 1933. (Louis Armstrong House and Archives at Queens College/CUNY)

SATCHMO

THE LOUIS ARMSTRONG ENCYCLOPEDIA

Michael Meckna

GREENWOOD PRESS
Westport, Connecticut • London

Library of Congress Cataloging-in-Publication Data

Meckna, Michael.
Satchmo : the Louis Armstrong encyclopedia / Michael Meckna.
p. cm.
Includes bibliographical references (p.), chronology (p.), discography (p.), list of web sites (p.), filmography (p.), and index.
ISBN 0-313-30137-9 (alk. paper)
1. Armstrong, Louis, 1901–1971—Encyclopedias. I. Title: Louis Armstrong encyclopedia. II. Title.
ML419.A75M45 2004
781.65'092—dc22 2003064260

British Library Cataloguing in Publication Data is available.

Copyright © 2004 by Michael Meckna

All rights reserved. No portion of this book may be reproduced, by any process or technique, without the express written consent of the publisher.

Library of Congress Catalog Card Number: 2003064260
ISBN: 0-313-30137-9

First published in 2004

Greenwood Press, 88 Post Road West, Westport, CT 06881
An imprint of Greenwood Publishing Group, Inc.
www.greenwood.com

Printed in the United States of America

The paper used in this book complies with the Permanent Paper Standard issued by the National Information Standards Organization (Z39.48–1984).

10 9 8 7 6 5 4 3 2 1

To Eva

CONTENTS

PREFACE

Louis "Satchmo" Armstrong (1901–1971) was undoubtedly the most famous American musician of his time and possibly of his century. His renown, furthermore, was not limited to his country, as he became one of the most celebrated musicians in the world. Almost single-handedly he invented swing style, scat singing, and modern jazz trumpet playing. He was the first jazz soloist, a role that cannot be underestimated in its impact not only on jazz but on all popular music. In his spare time, he appeared in some twenty-eight full-length feature films, moderated the temperature of U.S.–Soviet relations in the 1950s, and helped create a new respect for African Americans.

While writing *Twentieth-Century Brass Soloists,* I became fascinated by Louis Armstrong—how he became more than a trumpet player, more than a jazz musician, and how he influenced so many performers. Once a trumpet player myself, I was well aware of his impact on music and musicians. Therefore, a suggestion from Greenwood Press's Alicia S. Merritt that I make Armstrong the subject of a monograph fell on sympathetic ears. After a survey of the literature, I concluded that there was a great need for a reference book with detailed yet user-friendly entries on topics such as Armstrong's influences, musical style, legacy, friends, family, critics, hobbies, movies, tours, writings, and recordings. These and other subjects, organized alphabetically, constitute most of the encyclopedia. Also included are four appendices: an annotated list of Armstrong's best recordings available on compact disc, a detailed chronology, a complete film list, and an annotated webography. A selected bibliography and an index round out the volume. Finally, since sometimes a picture is worth a thousand words, there is a selection of photos, some never before published, from the Louis Armstrong House and Archives.

Armstrong's is an American success story, as he overcame numerous nearly insurmountable difficulties, both personal and societal. Toward the end of his life, mail could find him without an address, or even without his name. A reader interested in these and other phenomena can find details in several extended entries, such as "childhood," "awards," "firsts," "singing style," and "mail." There are also analytical entries on Armstrong's mentors (e.g., "Oliver, Joe 'King' "), contemporaries (e.g., "Ellington, Edward Kennedy 'Duke' "), and heirs (e.g., "Marsalis, Wynton"). Although this book is an encyclopedia, there are several discernible themes that surface throughout—the nature of genius, the development and acceptance of jazz, the ingredients of swing music, the progress of race relations in the United States, the African American in film, the influence of the Great Depression on jazz musicians, and others.

Armstrong's recording career spanned almost fifty years, from 1923 to 1971. His name was on the charts intermittently for over sixty years, from 1926 with

"Muskrat Ramble" to 1988 with "What a Wonderful World." In all he recorded nearly a thousand songs, many more than once. There are nearly a hundred different recordings of "When It's Sleepy Time Down South," and more than fifty of "When the Saints Go Marching In" and "Basin Street Blues." He recorded "(Back Home Again in) Indiana," "Muskrat Ramble," "Struttin' with Some Barbecue," and "Mack the Knife" over forty times each. Wherever possible each musical entry includes composer(s), lyricist(s), performers, date and place of the earliest recording (or an early recording, or a preferred recording), and in most cases some commentary. The "CD" number refers to Appendix 1 of this book, where a recording (though not always the one discussed in the music entry) may be found.

Names, terms, and places that themselves appear as entries are in **boldface** on first mention in a given entry, while musical titles, owing to their great number, remain unbolded. The terms "cornet" and "trumpet" are also too frequent to appear in boldface, although there is an entry on each instrument. The same applies to "critic," and moreover that entry focuses narrowly on Armstrong's detractors.

Mention above of the Armstrong Archives prompts me to acknowledge that invaluable resource and its indefatigable director Michael Cogswell. For details on the Archives' holdings, see the entry titled "Louis Armstrong House and Archives." In addition, there are entries on two other jazz archives that also house some valuable Armstrong materials, the "Institute of Jazz Studies" (Rutgers University) and the "William Ransom Hogan Jazz Archive" (Tulane University). Among the many archivists and/or administrative assistants at these institutions, I'd like in particular to thank Peggy Alexander, George Arevalo, Baltsar Beckeld, Peter Hirsch, Bruce Boyd Raeburn, Matt Sohn, and Alma D. Williams. To visit these archives, I am most grateful for a grant from Texas Christian University (TCU).

There are a good many other people to thank as well: TCU librarians and staff members Marianne Bobich, Judy Castillo, Kay Edmondson, Susan D. Hawk, Jill Kendle, Joyce Martindale, Sheila Madden, Sandy Schrag, and Karen Weber; student assistants Lance Beaumont, Andrea Helm, Amy Pummill, Hannah Smith, and Kathy Veale; and my School of Music friend and colleague Blaise Ferrandino. Among Armstrong friends and scholars, Joshua Berrett, Jack Bradley, Thomas Brothers, Håkan Forsberg, Gary Giddins, Scott Johnson, and Jos Willems deserve special mention, as does John Martin, founder of Black Sparrow Press, for his Satchmo-like generosity of spirit. At Greenwood Press (or, like Alicia Merritt, formerly associated with Greenwood), I'd like to single out Pamela St. Clair, Eric Levy, and Rob Kirkpatrick, and at Westchester Book Services, John Donohue and Susan E. Badger.

Finally, I am most profoundly grateful to my wife, Eva, without whose help this book simply could not have been written.

A

ABC. See **Associated Booking Corporation.**

abstract art. Armstrong's music has inspired many abstract artworks, perhaps because of the ambiguous nature of jazz. The dark *Swing Music (Louis Armstrong),* painted in 1938 by the American artist Arthur Dove (1880–1946), was suggested by the hit song "Public Melody Number One" and now hangs in the Art Institute of Chicago. Jazz lover and modernist Misha Reznikoff (1905–1971) did several jazz-related paintings, including *Cornet Chop Suey* (1938) and *Swing That Music* (1942). Other artists influenced by Armstrong include Stuart Davis (1892–1964) and George Wettling (1907–1968). Reproductions of these and other artists' work can be found in *Louis Armstrong: A Cultural Legacy* (1994), a catalog that accompanied the Smithsonian's traveling exhibit of objects chronicling Armstrong's accomplishments.

"Accentuate the Positive." By **Harold Arlen** and **Johnny Mercer;** rec. February 13, 1945, in New York City by Louis Armstrong and His Orchestra; CD #49.

Accra. See **Ghana.**

"Adam and Eve Had the Blues." By **Hociel Thomas;** rec. November 11, 1925, in Chicago by vocalist Hociel Thomas with Louis Armstrong's Jazz Four; CDs #10 and #36. The recordings made with this blues singer are interesting mostly for Armstrong's inventive playing.

Addison, Bernard (1905–1990). In the 1920s Addison played banjo in the Washington, D.C., area, then moved to New York where he recorded on guitar with Armstrong in 1930. Thereafter, guitar became his principal instrument, and he went on to distinguished career with **Fletcher Henderson, Jelly Roll Morton,** Bubber Miley, **Coleman Hawkins,** the **Mills Brothers,** and the Ink Spots. In 1940 he again linked up with Armstrong and made some memorable records for **Decca.** Addison can be heard on "My Sweet" and "I Can't Believe That You're in Love with Me."

African tours. Armstrong captured worldwide attention with his tours to Africa in the 1950s and 1960s, and he also favorably impressed fellow African Americans. These tours attracted record-breaking audiences (some conservatively estimated at 100,000 people), and they made for wonderful publicity. Pictures of Armstrong mingling with scantily clad though dignified African chiefs and playing his trumpet while exotically dressed locals danced in the street appeared back home in ***Life,*** *Look,* and ***Time*** magazines. His repertory included not only the expected upbeat tunes such as "When the Saints Go Marching In," but also a good many selections with dark overtones. At a 1956 concert in recently independent **Ghana,** for example, he sang "Black and Blue" and brought tears to the eyes of President Kwame Nkrumah. This and other moving moments can be seen in the Edward R. Murrow/Fred Friendly documentary ***Satchmo the Great.***

"After You've Gone." By Henry Creamer and Turner Layton; rec. November 26, 1929, in New York City by Louis Armstrong and His Orchestra; CDs #20, #23, and #46.

Agee, James (1909–1955). This Pulitzer Prize-winning writer negatively criticized many of Armstrong's film and musical performances. In his ***Time*** review of ***Cabin in the Sky,*** for example, he lamented the demeaning roles of the black actors and the film's "Sambo-style" direction. He expanded this and other ideas later in a *Partisan Review* article titled "Pseudo-Folk," in which he also developed the criticism, shared by many at the time (see **Baldwin, James; Blesh, Rudi;** and **Finkelstein, Sidney**), that Armstrong's swing music in the 1940s was a corruption of true jazz.

"Ain't It the Truth?" By **Harold Arlen** and E.Y. "Yip" Harburg; rec. August 28, 1942, in Los Angeles by Louis Armstrong and a studio orchestra; CD #45. This song was performed by Armstrong and **Lena Horne** for the 1943 **movie *Cabin in the Sky,*** but it was cut from the final version.

"Ain't Misbehavin'." By **Thomas "Fats" Waller,** Andy Razaf, and Harry Brooks; rec. July 19, 1929, in New York City by Louis Armstrong and His Orchestra; CDs #12, #13, #14, #17, #18, #36, #40, #41, #45, #47, #48, #56, #57, and #61. Armstrong thought highly of Waller, and fortunately their paths crossed numerous times. In the orchestra of the 1929 hit review ***Connie's Hot Chocolates,*** Armstrong had a big hit with "Ain't Misbehavin'." At first he performed it from the pit, but by popular demand he was soon moved to center stage. He later reprised it in the 1944 **movie *Atlantic City.*** As well as Armstrong sells this song, many feel that the definitive version is Waller's own in the 1943 film *Stormy Weather.*

airport. See **Louis Armstrong New Orleans International Airport.**

"Alabamy Bound." By Bud DeSylva, Bud Green, and Ray Henderson; rec. February 2, 1925, in New York City by **Fletcher Henderson** and His Orchestra. Armstrong made over a dozen recordings with Henderson, and although handicapped by the bandleader's procrustean style and arrangements, his inventive solos shone out and paved the way for the phenomenon of the featured soloist, an achievement that cannot be underestimated in its impact not only on jazz but on all popular music.

Albert, Mary. See **Armstrong, Mary Ann Albert "Mayann."**

Albertson, Chris. A record producer for the Riverside, Prestige, and **Columbia** labels, Albertson was also a freelance writer and contributing editor to *Stereo Review*. In addition to an excellent biography of **Bessie Smith,** he wrote extensive and genial liner notes to accompany the three-disc set of Armstrong recordings that Time-Life put out in 1972. Albertson knew **Lil Armstrong** well toward the end of her life and wrote movingly about how she still wore the rings her husband had given her and how she preserved his old cornet, letters, and photographs with the devotion of a museum curator. "She spoke of him with an indifference belied by the spark in her eyes," Albertson reflected in the September 25, 1971, issue of *Saturday Review*.

Alexander, Charles "Charlie" (c. 1904–1970). This Cincinnati-born and -bred pianist was active in Chicago until the spring of 1931, when he joined the Armstrong big band for one memorable year. "Now there's a band that really deserved a whole lot of credit that they didn't get," Armstrong wrote in **"The Goffin Notebooks"** (Brothers, p. 108).

"Alexander's Ragtime Band." By **Irving Berlin;** rec. July 7, 1937, in New York City by Louis Armstrong and His Orchestra; CD #34.

Alix, May (1904–1984). The Chicago-born vocalist worked with **Jimmie Noone, Carroll Dickerson,** and **Ollie Powers** and in 1926 recorded "Big Butter and Egg Man" and "Sunset Cafe Stomp" with Armstrong's **Hot Five.** She performed in Chicago and New York, then in the 1940s retired because of ill health. Although not a great singer, she is said to have been good-looking and a fine dancer.

"All of Me." By Seymour Simons and Gerald Marks; rec. January 27, 1932, in Chicago by Louis Armstrong and His Orchestra; CDs #1, #16, #42, #57, and #58. Armstrong made this hit an enduring jazz standard.

All Stars. Formally known as **Louis Armstrong and the All Stars,** this band was Armstrong's main performing and recording ensemble from 1947 to 1971.

"All That Meat and No Potatoes." By **Thomas "Fats" Waller** and Ed Kirkeby; rec. April 27, 1955, in New York City by Louis Armstrong and the All Stars; CD #56.

Allen, Henry "Red" (1908–1967). This New Orleans trumpeter's life followed a course similar in many ways to that of Armstrong, and for a time the two were even rivals. After learning his craft locally (his dad—Henry Allen, Sr.—led the New Orleans Allen Brass Band for over forty years), Allen left in 1927 to join **King Oliver,** then in St. Louis. He went on to play with **Fate Marable**'s Mississippi riverboat band, where he was approached by **Victor Records** to come to New York and record with **Luis Russell**'s band. The results rivaled the sensational successes of Armstrong on **Okeh Records** and established Allen as one of the leading soloists of the early swing era. After similar triumphs with **Fletcher Henderson** (1933–1934) and the **Mills Blue Rhythm Band** (1934–1937), Allen rejoined the Russell band and played second to Armstrong from 1937 to 1940. He then formed his own ensemble and went on to be a popular leader in New York. Like many young trumpet players in his day, Allen lived in the shadow of Armstrong.

A good place to hear their similarity is the joint solo on "I Ain't Got Nobody," which was recorded in 1929. One hears the same tone quality, technical fluency, slight anticipation of the beat, half-closed valve glissando, and little shake at the end of long notes. However, in the same year and without Armstrong in the room, Allen began to reveal a voice of his own. His best work can be heard in simple ballads. "Heartbreak Blues," "Body and Soul," and "There's a House in Harlem for Sale" all have a dark sound, blue notes, and long bittersweet tones that will remain among the memorable moments of music (for more, see Meckna, 1994, pp. 3–5).

Allen, Woody (b. 1935). The famous filmmaker is a devoted Armstrong fan and makes frequent use of Armstrong's music in his work. In *Stardust Memories* (1980), protagonist Sandy Bates (Allen) has a sweet moment of escape from anxiety and self-recrimination while listening to Armstrong's recording of **Hoagy Carmichael**'s "Star Dust," and in *Manhattan* (1979) the protagonist Isaac Davis (Allen again) has this to say about one of Armstrong's own compositions: "There are certain things that make [life] worthwhile. . . . I would say Groucho Marx, to name one thing, and Willie Mays, and the second movement of the Jupiter Symphony, and Louis Armstrong. . . . His recording of 'Potato Head Blues.' " Music prominently associated with Armstrong—"I'm Confessin' (That I Love You)," "You Made Me Love You," "That Old Feeling," and "Chinatown"—can be heard here and there in many of Allen's films. For example, his classic "West End Blues" cadenza is played by a flutist in *September* (1987). Allen is himself a musician who frequently plays the clarinet in traditional jazz ensembles. In *Sleeper* (1973), he used both his own original compositions and standards, which he performed with his New Orleans Funeral and Ragtime Orchestra and the Preservation Hall Jazz Band. *Wild Man Blues,* a 1998 documentary film about Allen's 1996 monthlong tour of Europe with the New Orleans Jazz Band, takes its name from a song that Armstrong is said (erroneously) to have cowritten with **Jelly Roll Morton** and recorded in 1927.

"Alligator Crawl." By **Thomas "Fats" Waller,** Andy Razaf, and Joe Davis; rec. May 10, 1927, in Chicago by Louis Armstrong and His **Hot Seven;** CD #10. Due to limited technology, drums were not employed in the recording studio until the mid-1920s. Therefore, up to this time Armstrong had had to help the ensemble keep the beat. Here **Baby Dodds** liberates him from this task. However, perhaps the freedom was too intoxicating because on the chromatic phrase in his solo Armstrong bobbles an attempt to jump octaves. The story behind the song's title can be found on several home-recorded tapes available at the **Louis Armstrong House and Archives** and on the 1997 rerelease of *Louis Armstrong Plays W.C. Handy* (CD #38). When he was a young boy, his mother sent him out to get some water. Armstrong came back some time later without water. When asked why he replied: "There's a big ol' rusty alligator there!" His mother scolded him with, "Oh, go on now, that alligator is as scared of you as you are of him," to which Armstrong retorted, "Well, if he's as scared of me as I am of him, then that water isn't fit to drink!"

"Alligator Hop." By **Joe Oliver** and **Alphonse Picou;** rec. October 5, 1923, in Richmond, Indiana, by King Oliver and His Creole Jazz Band; CD #35. Even at this relatively early date, Armstrong had been in the recording studio half a dozen times and recorded nearly two dozen numbers, albeit mostly in tandem with Oliver. Here, as so often in these sessions, Oliver dominates not only Armstrong but also the entire ensemble. Oliver's searing final chorus, though, is a good example of what must have attracted the young Armstrong. The group did such marvelous work together at the **Lincoln Gardens** from 1922 to 1923 that, remembered Armstrong, "all the white cats from downtown Chicago, **Bix** [**Beiderbecke**] and all of them boys, would come by after their work and sit up by the band and listen until the place shut. They didn't understand how we did it, without music or anything" (Jones and Chilton, p. 66).

alligator story. Among Armstrong's many standard jokes and stories was the tale about going to fetch some water as a little boy and being scared by an alligator. The story came up frequently in his conversation, and it appears in his correspondence and memoirs. A good place to hear him tell it is on the *Louis Armstrong Plays W.C. Handy* CD (CD #38). Originally released in October 1954, this CD was rereleased with bonus tracks in 1997, and the alligator story is one of the many extras. It goes roughly like this: One day when Armstrong was a little boy, his mother sent him down to the corner for a pail of water. He came back with an empty pail. When she asked where the water was, he responded that there was a big old alligator in that water. She told him to go on back and get the water. She said that the alligator was as afraid of him as he was of it. Louis replied that if the alligator was as afraid of him as he was of it, that water wouldn't be fit to drink.

"Almost Persuaded." By Glenn Sutton and Billy Sherrill; rec. August 1970 in New York City with the Nashville Group (guitarists Jack Eubanks, Stu Basore, and Billie Grammer, pianist Larry Butler, bass player Henry Strzelecki, and drummer Willie Ackerman). Armstrong's last album (his last recording was Clement Moore's classic Christmas poem **"The Night before Christmas"**) was a set of country and western songs, not exactly Armstrong's typical repertory, although he had recorded once with country music star **Jimmie Rodgers** ("Blue Yodel No. 9," 1930). "Almost Persuaded" is on *"Country and Western" Armstrong* (Avco Embassy AVE-33022), which was never reissued and is not available on CD.

"Alone at Last." By Ted Fiorito and Gus Kahn; rec. August 7, 1925, in New York City by The Southern Serenaders; CD #48. This used to be a hard-to-find recording, until it was included on the award-winning *Portrait of the Artist as a Young Man* compilation. Armstrong, playing with what was probably a **Fletcher Henderson** ensemble, takes only one chorus, but in it he varies the melodic line nicely and succeeds in getting his fellow musicians to **swing.**

Alvis, Hayes (Julian) (1907–1972). This outstanding bass player worked with Armstrong from 1940 to 1942. Previously he was a member of the **Duke Ellington** Orchestra, among other groups, and after

World War II he was the house bassist at Café Society in New York.

"Ambassador Satch." With his many tours in the 1950s and 1960s for the U.S. State Department, Armstrong became a diplomatic figure who took jazz (and by extension American culture) around the world. He was frequently photographed with heads of state or in politically sensitive areas, such as Berlin in the mid-1950s. An enduring image is the often reproduced studio portrait of him in a tuxedo, trumpet tucked under one arm and a suitcase in the other hand. Armstrong's success as an ambassador, as well as the appeal of jazz as a symbol of freedom, led to the U.S. State Department's hiring of other jazz artists (e.g., **Earl Hines** and **Dizzy Gillespie**) for goodwill tours. See also **African tours; European tours; nicknames;** CDs #1 and 55.

American Federation of Musicians. Founded in 1896, the AFM's membership is nearly half a million, which makes it the world's largest entertainment union. It's also one of the world's most powerful unions, entertainment or otherwise. As a member Armstrong worked both with and around the AFM throughout his career. For example, just before the AFM's two-year strike against the recording industry began in 1942, manager **Joe Glaser** cleverly had his client make four **soundies.** This exposure led to an offer to appear in ***Cabin in the Sky*** for $7,500 a week, which provided a handy war chest for enduring the strike.

"Among My Souvenirs." By Edgar Leslie and Horatio Nicholls; rec. April 17, 1942, in Chicago by Louis Armstrong and His Orchestra. It comes as a surprise to many fans that Armstrong liked the musical style of **Guy Lombardo**—the way he enriched rather than obscured a melody, adding little more than a tremulous vibrato, fleshing out the implied chords, and providing a clear, danceable beat. Like Lombardo, Armstrong also aimed for and reached the widest possible audience. There is a direct lineage from the Lombardo sound to Armstrong's performance of "Among My Souvenirs," "Sweethearts on Parade," and other songs.

Anatomy of a Performance. This reverential film documents the rehearsals leading up to the opening concert on July 10, 1970, of the seventeenth **Newport Jazz Festival,** which was billed as a tribute to Louis Armstrong. The New Orleans blueblood Eureka Brass Band was brought in for the occasion. Interspersed are clips from an interview done later with Armstrong at his home in **Corona.** Three other films (***The Antiquarians, Finale,*** and ***Trumpet Players' Tribute***) were made at the concert itself. Festifilm, Inc., 1970; color; 45 mins.; Dir. Sidney J. Stiber; Prod. George Wein.

"And the Angels Sing." By Ziggy Elman and **Johnny Mercer;** rec. January 30, 1957, in New York City with the **Sy Oliver** Orchestra; CD #26. Armstrong recorded an avowedly commercial album (*Louis and the Angels*) of a dozen songs, all with either "heaven" or "angel" in their title or lyrics. The result has a stronger appeal than it might have in less professional hands, as Armstrong not only succeeds in making music out of some unpromising material but also has fun doing so. In this number he is working with an excellent 1939 song by fellow trumpeter Ziggy Elman, who, with singer Martha Tilton, introduced it in the **Benny Goodman** Band.

Anderson, Eddie (1905–1977). This versatile actor, perhaps best known as Jack Benny's cocky "Rochester," played Little Joe in ***Cabin in the Sky*** (1943). In the movie Armstrong plays one of Lucifer, Jr.'s helpers in just one scene, contributing a short trumpet flourish and some lively dialogue in the Hotel Hades.

Anderson, Ernie. The overwhelming success of Armstrong's February 8, 1947, **Carnegie Hall concert** encouraged this savvy promoter immediately to set up a similar show at **Town Hall.** There was an important difference, however. At Carnegie the first half of the program featured a small jazz band and the second a big band. The small ensemble, however, clearly won greater critical and popular acclaim, and Anderson saw to it that only the small band played at Town Hall. The event took place on May 17, and its triumph underscored the waning of the big band movement. Armstrong, however, played out his remaining big band bookings and by the summer of 1947 had returned to the kind of small jazz band with which he'd first found success.

Anderson, Gene. Anderson was a Chicago pianist, and Armstrong worked with him there in the late 1920s when **Earl Hines** wasn't available. Anderson was a member of the band that Armstrong took to New York City in 1929, and he remained there for a time after the band broke up. "Gene was a First Class man—could read music perfect. And was also a good 'Swing' man," Armstrong wrote in **"The Goffin Notebooks"** (Brothers, p. 101).

Anderson, Marian (1897–1993). The famous African American contralto did not move in the same musical circles that Armstrong did, but their lives occasionally crossed paths, and both were similarly affected by racial prejudice. Like so many American performers, black or otherwise, Anderson was more celebrated abroad than at home. However, she is sometimes mistakenly listed as a member of the cast of the 1933 ***København, Kalundborg Og?*** (e.g., Collier, 1983, p. 264). Her 1935 triumph at New York City's Town Hall launched her career as one of the most in-demand concert singers in the United States. When in 1939 the Daughters of the American Revolution would not let her perform in Washington, D.C.'s Constitution Hall because of her color, she sang instead at the Lincoln Memorial for an audience of over 75,000. Nearly twenty years later, when Armstrong spoke out about school **segregation** in **Little Rock,** Arkansas, Anderson (in contrast to other black leaders such as statesman Adam Clayton Powell and entertainer **Sammy Davis, Jr.**) immediately voiced her support of his stance, firmly stating that she "will not from now on ever appear before a segregated audience" (*Variety,* September 25, 1957, p. 66). Just two years before Little Rock, she had become the first black soloist to sing with New York City's Metropolitan Opera. In 1958 Anderson was a U.S. delegate to the United Nations, and in 1977 she won the UN Peace Prize. Her autobiography *My Lord, What a Morning* (1956) makes fascinating reading.

Anderson, Tom. Anderson's New Cabaret and Restaurant, located at 122–6 No. Rampart Street, was one of the best-known nightclubs in New Orleans, and

Armstrong played cornet with a band there in the early 1920s before he left town to join **King Oliver** in Chicago. Armstrong wrote in ***Satchmo: My Life in New Orleans*** that rich racehorse owners frequented the place and gave big tips to the band for requests. They would also order fabulous meals and sometimes send them back mostly uneaten. The kindly waiters would save the "dead soldiers," or leftovers, for Armstrong. "I felt real important eating all those fine meals, meals I could not have possibly paid for then," Armstrong recalled (p. 215).

Andrews Coal Company. After young Louis left the **Colored Waif's Home** in June 1914, he made a little money playing his horn at night in one of the local honky-tonks. One of his day jobs was driving a coal cart for the C.A. Andrews Coal Company, at Ferret and Perdido Streets in New Orleans. His pay was fifteen cents a load, and he rarely hauled over five loads a day. "I loved it," he wrote in his **autobiography.** "I felt like a real man when I shoveled a ton of coal into my wagon" (1954, p. 59). Although he could earn $1.50 plus tips nightly in the honky-tonks, Armstrong continued to deliver coal (since it was a steady source of income) until Armistice Day, November 11, 1918. The end of World War I meant the reopening of dance halls and therefore the opportunity to play music full-time. Armstrong wrote that on hearing the news he immediately dropped his shovel, slowly put on his jacket, looked at his mule, Lady, and said: "So long, my dear. I don't think I'll ever see you again" (p. 144).

"Angel." By Peter DeRose and Mitchell Parish; rec. January 30, 1957, in New York City with the **Sy Oliver** Orchestra; CD #26. See comments on "And the Angels Sing."

"Angel Child." By Abner Silver, Benny Davis, and George Price; rec. January 29, 1957, in New York City with the **Sy Oliver** Orchestra; CD #26. See comments on "And the Angels Sing."

"Angela Mia." By Lew Pollack and Erno Rapee; rec. January 30, 1957, in New York City with the **Sy Oliver** Orchestra; CD #26. See comments on "And the Angels Sing."

Antiquarians, The. This film of performances by the Preservation Hall Jazz Band, the New Orleans Classic Ragtime Band, and the Eureka Brass Band was made at the opening concert of the **Newport Jazz Festival** on July 10, 1970. Armstrong does not play or sing here but is seen in clips from an interview at his **Corona** home in the fall of that year. Three other films were made in connection with this, Armstrong's last, Newport Festival (***Anatomy of a Performance, Finale,*** and ***Trumpet Players' Tribute***). Festifilm, Inc., 1970; color; 45 mins.; Dir. Sidney J. Stiber; Prod. George Wein.

"Anybody Here Want to Try My Cabbage?" By Andy Razaf, **Thomas "Fats" Waller,** and Edgar Dowell; rec. December 10, 1924, in New York City with vocalist **Maggie Jones** and pianist **Fletcher Henderson;** CDs #36 and #48. Armstrong made six recordings with Maggie Jones and pianist Fletcher Henderson in December 1924, and they nicely document Armstrong's growing invention and spontaneity. The bare-bones ensemble seems exactly right to portray the desolation of the blues. "Cabbage" is outstanding because of Armstrong's particularly arresting growls. Dan Morgenstern reports that decades after these recordings with Jones, someone played them for Armstrong, who was pleasantly surprised and said he liked them as well as his recordings with **Bessie Smith** (*Portrait,* 1994, p. 10).

"April in Paris." By E.Y. "Yip" Harburg and Vernon Duke; rec. August 16, 1956, in Los Angeles with vocalist **Ella Fitzgerald** and the **Oscar Peterson** Quartet; CD #9. Fitzgerald's voice, like Armstrong's, is one of that small handful that is immediately recognizable. She was a great fan of Armstrong's who recorded with him some in the 1940s. The two finally collaborated, though, in a big way with great success in the mid-1950s (see CD #9). There is a piquant contrast between Fitzgerald's polished and Armstrong's rugged voices, which shows up in their duets. While some critics have thought their work perhaps a little too stately, others have frankly called them models for aspiring jazz singers.

"April in Portugal." By Raul Ferrao and Jimmy Kennedy; rec. April 21, 1953, in New York City by Louis Armstrong and His Orchestra; CD #8. Despite the handicaps of inferior musical material and a head cold, Armstrong, ever the professional, sells the song completely.

archives. Like his music, Armstrong photographs, letters, recordings, newspaper clippings, ephemera, and memorabilia are seemingly everywhere. Fans far and wide have collected and treasured these materials, and they can sometimes be found concentrated in archives such as the Library of Congress (which has a collection of twenty-two letters, telegrams, and memos sent by Armstrong from 1955 to 1960 to his manager **Joe Glaser**) and locations abroad (e.g., **Hugues Panassié**'s collection of rare 78 rpm records at the Discothèque Municipale in Villefranche-de-Rouergue in southern France). Three archives stand out in particular: the **Louis Armstrong House and Archives** at Queens College, the **Institute of Jazz Studies** at Rutgers University, and the **William Ransom Hogan Jazz Archive** at Tulane University.

argot, jazz. See **slang.**

Arlen, Harold (1905–1986). This popular American composer's musical style had a strong affinity with black musical expression, and this may have accounted for Armstrong's attraction to his work. Armstrong made memorable recordings of such Arlen songs as "Between the Devil and the Deep Blue Sea," "I Gotta Right to Sing the Blues," "I've Got the World on a String," "Kickin' the Gong Around," and "Let's Do It (Let's Fall in Love)" (all written in collaboration with lyricist Ted Koehler). Arlen's blues influence can be heard in "Blues in the Night" (lyricist **Johnny Mercer**), a Dinah Shore specialty, which Armstrong recorded with **Oscar Peterson.**

Arlen wrote frequently for the movies (e.g., *The Wizard of Oz*), and he contributed "Public Melody Number One" to the 1937 film ***Artists and Models.*** Here Armstrong and a skin-darkened Martha Raye appetizingly portray the irresistibility of jazz. In the 1943 film ***Cabin in the Sky,*** Armstrong's "Ain't It the Truth?" (which Arlen wrote with lyricist Yip Harburg) was to have been the big production number, but its depiction of devils suggestively dancing in Hell was deemed too risky and got cut. A hint of what might have been can be heard on the 1997 Rhino CD *Now You Has Jazz: Louis Armstrong at M-G-M* (CD #45).

Armstrong, Alpha Smith (1907–1943). Armstrong's third wife met him in 1925 at Chicago's **Vendome Theater** where she worked. In contrast to Armstrong's second wife, **Lil,** Alpha was relaxed and fun-loving. In fact, Armstrong began seeing Alpha while he was still married to Lil, who had ambitious plans for her husband. Lil and Louis were finally divorced on September 30, 1938, and he married Alpha on October 11. Their marriage lasted four years, during about half of which time they were separated. Alpha used to fine him $5 every time he came home late, according to biographers Jones and Chilton. Armstrong wrote in the August 1954 issue of ***Ebony*** that "her mind was on furs, diamonds and other flashy luxuries. . . . She went through my money and then walked out" (p. 61). Alpha's alimony payment was $250 per month, but she didn't collect it for long, dying shortly after they split up.

Armstrong, Beatrice "Mama Lucy" (1903–c. 1985). The result of a brief reconciliation between **Willie** and **Mayann Armstrong,** Louis's sister was three years old when his grandmother **Josephine** returned him to his mother in 1906. Young Louis did his best to take care of his sister and their ailing mother. All evidence suggests that Louis was very fond of Mama Lucy. He was troubled by her leaving New Orleans for a saw mill job in Florida but not terribly concerned on learning that she had established a gambling business. Later in life, she lived humbly in New Orleans and declined to take money from her brother. He left her $5,000 in his will.

Armstrong, Clarence Myles Hatfield (1915–1998). The illegitimate and retarded child of Armstrong's cousin **Flora Myles** and a white man, Clarence was adopted by Armstrong, who provided for him all his life. Armstrong may have felt guilty about Clarence's condition, since while he was babysitting and distracted, Clarence slipped from the porch and fell one story down, landing on his head. The terrified Armstrong rushed him to a doctor, who said that Clarence would never be quite the same. When Armstrong was later established in Chicago, he sent for Clarence, who lived with him and **Lil** after they married. Eventually, when Armstrong began to tour, he placed Clarence in a special home. "There he turned to be one of the Best 'Base Ball, 'Basket Ball and 'Foot Ball Players in the whole school," Armstrong bragged in **"The Goffin Notebooks"** (Brothers, p. 89). In addition to providing all his life for the "rather nervous" Clarence, Armstrong left him $5,000 in his will (Brothers, p. 89). Photographs and other documents at the **Louis Armstrong House and Archives** reveal Armstrong's pleasure in Clarence's achievements and pride in the fact that everyone called him "Little Louis Armstrong" (Giddins, 2003, p. 58).

Armstrong, Daisy Parker (c. 1897–1972). Daisy was Louis's first wife. He tells the story of their exotic courtship in ***Satchmo: My Life in New Orleans*** (p. 54 f): how they met (she a prostitute and he a band member) in a honky-tonk, his competiting for her attention, their marriage in

1918, his mother's reaction, their temporary separations, and their final split in 1922. In 1925 she made the long trip from New Orleans to Chicago to see if she could win him back, but Armstrong had since gotten a legal divorce and remarried (**Lil Hardin**). They spent perhaps more than a little time together, however. In **"The Goffin Notebooks"** Louis proudly tells a story about how her defense of his name led to a barroom brawl in which her face was scarred (Brothers, p. 91). When it was finally clear that they'd not be getting back together, Daisy returned home. She occasionally reappeared in his life, though, once in 1931 on Louis's first return to New Orleans, then in 1949 at a New Orleans Mardi Gras performance, where she was one of relatively few people in the audience. On this last occasion she asked to be admitted free since she was "Mrs. Louis Armstrong." **Lucille Wilson Armstrong,** Louis's fourth and last wife, was also on hand. Louis himself had to clear up the confusion. With Daisy in her seat, he went on with the show. It's not known whether or not the two Mrs. Armstrongs conversed.

Armstrong, "Daniel" Louis. For their February 21, 1949, cover story, ***Time*** magazine writers invented "Daniel" as Armstrong's first name. One supposes that the intention was to add greater dignity or to conform with their mock-heroic house style. The invention stuck, though, as compilers of reference works quickly adopted the fiction. "Daniel" appears neither on his baptismal certificate nor on contemporary census reports. "I was born Louis Armstrong," he wrote to Jones and Chilton. "The Daniel came later . . . out of clear skies, I guess, I don't remember **Mayann** (**Mary Ann**) ever calling me by Daniel" (p. 48). He seemed to enjoy the newly acquired name, as well as the **"Satchmo,"** which he was dubbed in England on arriving in 1932. In his 1954 ***Satchmo*** memoir, he exclaims: "If you ever tasted Mayann's jambalaya and did not lick your fingers my name is not Louis Satchmo Daniel Armstrong" (p. 85).

Armstrong, Gertrude. Armstrong's stepmother was his father **William**'s second wife, and the fourteen-year-old Louis went to live with them and their two boys when he was released from the **Colored Waif's Home.** Although Armstrong bravely wrote in his 1954 memoir ***Satchmo*** that Gertrude was "a very fine woman, and she treated me just as though I were her own child," it was hardly a satisfactory arrangement (p. 54). Louis was basically the cook/babysitter, while Gertrude earned the family a second salary. When she gave birth to a girl, Gertrude remained home and could watch the boys. Louis became simply another mouth to feed, so he was sent back to live with his biological mother and sister. He was now in a better situation, but he had to have been hurt by his father's rejection.

Armstrong, Henry and William, Jr. "Willie." Armstrong's two half-brothers were the children of his father and **Gertrude.** The fourteen-year-old Louis's duties in their household were to cook and to baby-sit them. Henry seems to have been the more agreeable of the two, since, as Louis wrote in his 1954 memoir ***Satchmo,*** they became good friends (p. 54). Willie was a different case, though, "about as ornery as they come," said Louis. Both "used to laugh like mad" when Louis, fresh from his **Colored Waif's Home** triumphs, played his cornet. Eventually their mother gave birth to a little sister, and not long afterward—Gertrude now not working and home to take care of her boys—Louis was sent to live with his mother and sister.

Armstrong, Josephine. "When I was born," Armstrong wrote in his **autobiography,** "my mother and father lived with my grandmother, Mrs. Josephine Armstrong (bless her heart!), but they did not stay with her long" (1954, p. 8). The quarrels were evidently frequent and intense, and eventually both parents went separate directions. Louis stayed, and Josephine basically raised him to the age of five. By all accounts, she was a strict but loving person. A practicing Catholic, she probably had Louis baptized and saw to it that he went both to school and to church. In the latter institution he seems to have first developed a love for singing. Louis also accompanied Josephine when she went out to do washing and housework, sometimes helping out and sometimes playing with the children of her white employers. Thus he began to feel comfortable with whites at an early age. In 1906 Louis was returned to his mother and a three-year-old sister **Beatrice** (eventually nicknamed **"Mama Lucy"**), the result of a brief reconciliation between **Willie** and **Mayann.** Throughout his life, though, Armstrong would always be grateful for his grandmother's influence. "Ever since I was a baby I have had great love for my grandmother," he continued in his autobiography. "She spent the best of her days raising me" (p. 10).

Armstrong, Lillian Hardin "Lil" (1898–1971). Before Lil Hardin met Louis Armstrong in 1922, she studied music at Fisk University in Nashville and then moved in 1917 to Chicago, where she worked as a song plugger in a music store. She also performed with numerous bands including **King Oliver**'s before Armstrong arrived. Pretty and talented, Lil had many admirers, including Louis, who when he first met her thought she was out of his league in every way. "Who was I to think that a Big High-powered Chick like Lillian Hardin" could be interested? he later wrote (Brothers, p. 86). However, Lil was indeed interested, and it didn't take long for them to become an item. They were married on February 5, 1924.

His ambitious second wife helped Louis develop his career in many ways. Lil encouraged him to move on from the King Oliver Band to New York and the **Fletcher Henderson** Orchestra, then brought him back to Chicago to headline her own group. She helped write songs for the **Hot Five,** in which she played piano. Lil may have pushed Louis a little too hard, because he began seeking the company of other women. The two separated in 1931 and divorced in 1938. Lil led bands in New York and Chicago in the 1930s, worked as a house pianist for **Decca,** toured, and recorded. Although Louis remarried twice more, Lil stayed single and continued to reside at her and Louis's Chicago home (421 East 44th Street). She died six weeks after he did while playing "St. Louis Blues" at his Chicago memorial concert.

Armstrong, Lucille Wilson (1914–1983). The fourth and final Mrs. Armstrong was working as a **Cotton Club** chorus girl (stage name: Brown Sugar) when Louis met her in 1939. "When I first saw her the glow of her deep-brown skin got me

Armstrong and the Hot Five in 1925. *Left to right:* Armstrong, Johnny St. Cyr, Johnny Dodds, Kid Ory, and Lil Hardin Armstrong. (Louis Armstrong House and Archives at Queens College/CUNY)

deep down," Louis affectionately recalled in the August 1954 issue of ***Ebony*** magazine. They married in 1942, shortly after his divorce from **Alpha.** Although Lucille often joined him on his tours, she insisted that they have a real home and instigated the purchase of one in **Corona,** a section of the New York City borough of Queens. Louis grew to love the place, and they lived there over twenty-eight years until his death in 1971. Lucille provided comfort and stability in other aspects of his life as well. For their first **Christmas** together, she bought a small tree for their hotel room, and this so entranced Louis that he prevailed on Lucille to take it down and put it up in at least a dozen different hotels, night after night, until well after the New Year.

It can't have been easy to have been the wife of Louis Armstrong, who put his horn first and foremost and who often gave in to extramarital sexual opportunities. Lucille's devotion was as extraordinary as her intelligence was keen. For example, she solved the potentially awkward problem of joining her husband on the road by calling him well in advance. Lucille died in Boston very shortly after a Brandeis University fund-raising event in honor of her late husband. She is buried beside Armstrong. See **funeral.**

Armstrong, Mary Ann Albert "Mayann" (c. 1885–1927). Louis Armstrong's mother was born in Boutte, Louisiana, and moved as a child to New Orleans. There she worked in the house of a white family whose children she took care of. She married **William Armstrong** at age fifteen. When shortly after the birth of Louis her husband left her for another woman, she placed the baby in the care of her mother-in-law, **Josephine,** and moved to cheaper housing near New Orleans' infamous **Storyville** red-light district. She found some work keeping house and watching children for white families, although it is highly likely that she also worked as a prostitute. "Whether my mother did any hustling, I cannot say," Armstrong later wrote in ***Satchmo: My Life in New Orleans.*** "If she did, she certainly kept it out of sight. One thing is certain: everybody from the churchfolks to the lowest roughneck treated her with the greatest respect" (p. 8). When Louis was five years old he was returned to his mother and a three-year-old sister **Beatrice** (eventually nicknamed **"Mama Lucy"**), the result of a brief reconciliation between Willie and Mayann. Since Mayann did not earn enough from her domestic work, and since the contributions from successive "stepfathers" were erratic, Louis supplemented the family income by doing odd jobs—running errands, selling coal, and cleaning graves.

Throughout his life Louis praised his mother unreservedly in memoirs, letters, and interviews. No one could match her cooking; her many folk remedies were cheap but effective; she warded off ill health with regular "physic" doses (i.e., **laxatives**); she had him and his sister say grace before meals and prayers every night (a habit that he more or less retained all his life); she couldn't afford Vaseline and cleverly substituted railroad axle grease. And so on. After Louis left for Chicago in 1922, he wrote her regularly and sent money. She once responded to a rumor of his illness with an immediate train trip north. Louis, who was not ill, was both surprised and delighted to see her and, finding her an impressive apartment, persuaded her to stay a while. She did so with evident pleasure until she began to miss her church congregation.

When Mrs. Armstrong took ill a few years later, Louis brought her back to Chicago so he could supervise her medical care. She died in 1927 and was buried at the Lincoln Cemetery just outside Chicago. Louis later recalled in **"The Goffin Notebooks"** that "I've never cried in my life before, even when Mayann was dying and grabbed my hand and said 'God bless you, my son, and thank God I lived to see my son grow up to be a big successful young man.' " But after the sermon and when her coffin was lowered, "I let out *plenty* of Tears—and I just couldn't stop Crying" (Brothers, p. 90).

Armstrong, William "Willie" (c. 1875–1933). Louis remembered his father as a very good-looking and well-built man. "He made the chicks swoon when he marched by as the grand marshal in the Odd Fellows parade," Louis wrote in his **autobiography** (1954, p. 29). Evidently the attractions were mutual. Shortly after Louis was born, Willie left his wife for another woman (**Gertrude**). Two years later Louis's parents reconciled long enough to have another child (**"Mama Lucy"**), but eventually they divorced and Willie remarried. Louis's stay in the **Colored Waif's Home** came to an end in

1914 when his father promised to watch over and provide for him, but the main motive seems to have been the acquisition of a cheap babysitter for his two young boys (**Henry** and **Willie**) by another woman.

Armstrong had mostly negative feelings about his father, whose indifference he perceived as having made life very difficult for himself, his sister, and his mother. After working for most of his life in a turpentine factory, Willie Armstrong died in 1933. Louis did not attend the funeral. It would have been a long trip, since he had just opened to enthusiastic crowds in London.

Armstrong, Willie, Jr. See **Armstrong, Henry and William, Jr. "Willie."**

Armstrong Airport. See **Louis Armstrong New Orleans International Airport.**

Armstrong bands. See **Hot Five; Hot Seven; Louis Armstrong and the All Stars; Savoy Ballroom Five.**

Armstrong nicknames. See **"Ambassador Satch"; "Little Louis"; nicknames; Satchmo.**

Armstrong Park. See **Louis Armstrong Park.**

"Armstrong Story, The." This incomplete sequel to the second volume of Armstrong's 1954 **autobiography, *Satchmo: My Life in New Orleans,*** is a fascinating account of Armstrong's early experiences in Chicago, along with some of his opinions about racial issues and a good deal of the kind of musical discussion that would not appeal to a lay readership. An insight into Armstrong's deep respect for music and for tradition can be found in a passage where he criticizes the trumpet player Bobby Williams, who played with one hand. "*That* I did not particularly care for. Because the old school where 'I' came from, the good old timers wouldn't *dare* to *insult* a good piece of music by holding the horn in one hand to play" (Brothers, p. 76). The entire document is published in Thomas Brothers's edition of Armstrong's writings.

Armstrong's Secret Nine. In June 1931 Armstrong's tour of the lower Midwest and South took him back to his hometown, New Orleans, for the first time in nine years. He was given a hero's welcome and stayed for three months, performing at places such as the all-white **Suburban Gardens.** He also visited the **Colored Waif's Home** and for a time sponsored a local baseball team, which he provided with new uniforms and gear. A polite way to describe how well they played might be to say that they kept their uniforms neat and clean. "Armstrong's Secret Nine" was made up mostly of members of the **Zulu Social Aid and Pleasure Club.**

art by Armstrong. Armstrong loved to create collages out of carefully cut photographs, newspaper articles, headlines, and other images. **All Stars** band member **Marty Napoleon** remembered that Louis was always "carrying a pair of scissors around with him and constantly cutting up newspapers. . . . It was a hobby of his. We'd see him in between sets—cutting and pasting these bits together" (Miller, p. 209). For over fifteen years Armstrong decorated reel-to-reel tape boxes, made scrapbooks, and sometimes decorated the walls and even the ceiling of the den in his home in **Corona,** New York. Some 500 of these collages survive, and they reveal a great deal about his personality. Many include images of his mentors (e.g., **King Oliver**), colleagues (**Bix Beiderbecke**), and fellow African American pioneers (**Jackie Robinson**). Others affectionately feature his wife **Lucille** or his manager **Joe Glaser.** He weaves aphorisms ("It is great to be Great. But it's greater to be Human.") and witty remarks (about **Bill "Bojangles" Robinson:** "That man was so sharp he was bleeding.") into the pictorial narrative. For those who cannot get to the **Louis Armstrong House and Archives** at Queens College and to these fascinating collages (plus an abundance of other materials), a liberal selection is reproduced in Marc Miller's *Louis Armstrong: A Cultural Legacy.*

Artists and Models. This movie, a sequence of vaudeville acts, loosely tells two stories: the selection of a charity ball queen and the efforts of an ad man to land a silverware company account. In addition to Jack Benny as the ad man, the cast includes Martha Raye, Ben Blue, Ida Lupino, Gail Patrick, Judy Canova, Connee Boswell, Peter Arno, and Rube Goldberg. In a specialty number Martha Raye dresses in a sexy outfit with her skin darkened. She and Armstrong perform the song "Public Melody Number One" about the thrill and allure of jazz. However, on the screen it seemed to many that Louis was trying to use jazz to seduce Ms. Raye. "This intermingling of the races isn't wise," declared the August 4, 1937, edition of *Variety.* The scene was cut in many southern states. Paramount, 1937; B&W; 97 mins.; Dir. Raoul Walsh.

Artzybasheff, Boris (1899–1965). One of the many high points in Armstrong's life was his appearance on the cover of ***Time,*** the weekly newsmagazine, on February 21, 1949. Although the honor was earned by a lifetime of achievement, the specific occasion was his serving as **King of the Zulus** in the New Orleans Mardi Gras parade. Boris Artzybasheff, one of the magazine's most prolific cover artists, depicted Armstrong's facial features faithfully even down to the groove in his **embouchure.** Artzybasheff also had a whimsical side to his style, and this comes out in Armstrong's crown of trumpets and audience of happily dancing notes, except for the one crying note (appropriately colored blue). All in all, the cover underscored and celebrated Armstrong's having become a popular culture icon.

Associated Booking Corporation. ABC, founded by **Joe Glaser** shortly after he became Armstrong's manager in 1935, eventually became one of the most prominent artist management companies ever. Armstrong was ABC's only client at first, but by 1940 Glazer had dozens of artists and soon booked more black musicians than any other agency. **Duke Ellington, Billie Holiday,** Miriam Makeba, Josh White, and others were on ABC's roster, along with white artists **Dave Brubeck, Benny Goodman,** Stan Kenton, the Kingston Trio, and **Barbra Streisand.**

Glaser died standing pat in 1969, and he left a thriving business to his employees. In answer to speculation that ABC prospered on Armstrong's back, the company line has always been that it collected no more than the standard 15 percent. Authoritative outside observers, including **Lucille Armstrong,** have estimated the percentage at closer to 50 percent, since Glaser managed Armstrong's personal budget (his mortgage, spending money, as well as cars and TVs for friends) in addition to his bookings. In the end, Armstrong's **estate** was valued at just over $500,000, while Glaser's was over $3 million.

"At the Jazz Band Ball." By Nick La Rocca, Larry Shields, and **Johnny Mercer;** rec. July 5, 1960, in New York City by Louis Armstrong, vocalist **Bing Crosby,** and a studio band and choir conducted by Billy May. Armstrong and Crosby were friends from 1930 to Armstrong's death in 1971. They influenced each other's musical style, recorded frequently, and appeared in half a dozen **movies** together. In 1960 Crosby and Armstrong made the popular album *Bing and Satchmo,* which concludes with this rousing number.

Atkins, Boyd. (c. 1900–c. 1960). Atkins was a Kentucky-born violinist/saxophonist who performed with Armstrong on the **Streckfus** Line riverboat **S.S.** ***Sidney*** (1919) and in Chicago at the **Sunset Cafe** in 1926–1927. He was also the composer of "Heebie Jeebies." Atkins recorded only once with Armstrong—"Chicago Breakdown" in 1927.

"Atlanta Blues." By W.C. Handy and Dave Elman; rec. July 13, 1954, in Chicago by **Louis Armstrong and the All Stars;** CD #38. Armstrong had a deep admiration for Handy's compositions and thoroughly enjoyed taking some time out in July 1954 to record an entire album of his work. It was also a welcome relief for many fans to have him turn from making so many commercial recordings to the kind of music with which he grew up and first established his fame.

Atlantic City. A musical about an entrepreneur and his girlfriend who build a thriving enterprise out of some useless swampland. It stars Constance Moore and Brad Taylor and features the orchestras of Paul Whiteman and Louis Armstrong. Dorothy Dandridge sings and dances a shortened "Harlem on Parade" to introduce Armstrong, who reprises his famous "Ain't Misbehavin'." Armstrong's appearance in this film exemplifies a shift in Hollywood's presentation of black characters. Formerly comic servants, they here and often hereafter play more intelligent and complex roles. Republic Films, 1944; B&W; 87 mins.; Dir. Ray McCarey.

"Auld Lang Syne." Traditional; rec. New Year's Eve 1954, live at the Club Hangover in San Francisco by **Louis Armstrong and the All Stars;** CD #22.

"Aunt Hagar's Blues." By W.C. Handy and J. Tim Bryan; rec. July 12, 1954, in Chicago by **Louis Armstrong and the All Stars;** CD #38. See comments on "Atlanta Blues."

Austin High Gang. Tenor saxophonist **Bud Freeman** (1906–1991), cornetist Jimmy McPartland (1907–1991), pianist **Joe Sullivan,** clarinetist Frank Teschemacher (1906–1932), drummer Dave Tough (1907–1948), and a few others made up this informal group, so called because of their association with Chicago's Austin High School in the early 1920s. Other Chicago natives such as **Benny Goodman** and Gene Krupa were also drawn into the Gang's orbit. Non-natives such as Eddie Condon and Pee Wee Russell have been linked with the Gang as well, as was **Bix Beiderbecke,** who spent relatively little time in Chicago. Drawing inspiration from New Orleans jazz in general and Armstrong in particular, the Austin High Gang contributed strongly to what came to be known as Chicago jazz. The decline of the Chicago speakeasies sent many of these Chicago musicians to New York, and several became important swing musicians in the 1930s.

autobiography. Armstrong was and remains the most prolific autobiographer in the jazz world. He followed his 1936 ***Swing That Music*** with ***Satchmo: My Life in New Orleans*** in 1954, and he also left many lengthy unpublished manuscripts—**"The Armstrong Story," "The Goffin Notebooks," "Louis Armstrong + the Jewish Family . . . ,"** and **"The Satchmo Story."**

Armstrong also recorded for producer **Milt Gabler** a *musical* autobiography between 1956 and 1957 with the **All Stars** (and some occasional supplementary personnel). On four long-play discs, he recreated his 1920s and 1930s masterpieces, reminiscing between cuts. While the new versions generally are not better than or even as good as the originals, Armstrong does seem to improve upon "I Can't Give You Anything But Love," "King of the Zulus," and "When You're Smiling." Highlights of this set are Armstrong's storytelling and reminiscences. *Satchmo: A Musical Autobiography* was reissued on three CDs in 2001 (CD #52), including six tracks from 1927's legendary **Hot Five** sessions.

"Autumn in New York." By Vernon Duke; rec. July 23, 1957, in Los Angeles with vocalist **Ella Fitzgerald** and the **Oscar Peterson** Quartet; CD #9. See comments on "April in Paris."

Aux frontières du jazz. Published in 1932, this wide-ranging, naive book by Belgian jazz critic **Robert Goffin** was dedicated "To Louis Armstrong, the Real King of Jazz in testimony of my high admiration." When Armstrong first arrived in Paris (October 1932), Goffin ceremoniously gave him a copy of the book and tagged along with him while he worked. Goffin continued to write about Armstrong, and when Goffin fled to the United States from World War II–torn Belgium, Armstrong chose him to write his official biography and provided him with copious notes (see **"The Goffin Notebooks"**). Unfortunately, Goffin's *Horn of Plenty* (1947) was a disaster. It revealed a woeful lack of knowledge about life in the United States, the writer's uneasy acquaintance with English, and skewed political views.

Avakian, George (b. 1919). Born to Armenian parents in Russia, the future record producer grew up in New York and had a long and varied career before his path fortuitously crossed Armstrong's. He studied piano as a boy and earned a B.A. in English literature at Yale in 1941. During his student days he began working as a jazz critic for *Tempo* magazine and went on to contribute to *Mademoiselle,* ***Down Beat,*** and other publications. Also as a student he began to produce jazz recordings and, after serving in World War II, became a jazz and popular record producer for **Columbia.** Throughout his career he worked as well with Warner Bros., RCA, and other companies. Among his many innovations were the issuing of live recordings (beginning with the 1954 **Newport Jazz Festival**) and the reissuing of jazz recordings on LP. He was one of the first to employ the techniques of tape splicing, multitrack recording, and stereophonic sound, and he came up with the now-common idea of the "concept" album (e.g., an album that focuses on the music of just one composer). Avakian had an excellent ear and high standards, and his recordings were marvels in their day.

A good example of Avakian's work is the early LP *Louis Armstrong Plays W.C. Handy* (1954; reissued on CD in 1997; CD #38). Handy himself was present at the editing and was moved to tears. Avakian had plans for a series of *Louis Armstrong Plays*... albums (e.g., **Jelly Roll Morton**), but, so the story goes, Armstrong's manager **Joe Glaser** asked for too much money. However, it was probably Avakian's idea that Armstrong record "Mack the Knife," which he did on September 28, 1955—so well that it stayed on the ***Billboard* chart** from February to May 1956. (Bobby Darin later made the song his own but not before Armstrong had sold over a million copies.) A few months later, on July 14, 1956, Avakian organized a concert at Lewisohn Stadium in New York City after Armstrong's return from a triumphant tour in Africa (see **African tours**). With the Stadium Symphony Orchestra conducted by **Leonard Bernstein,** the event underscored the acceptance of traditional jazz into America's musical mainstream. Although the evening didn't end until shortly before midnight, the "still quivering" audience (so described by the *New York Times* reporter [p. A64] the following day), willingly remained to be extras in a series of sequences for the film documentary ***Satchmo the Great.***

Armstrong was very comfortable with Avakian, even discussing upsetting situations with him openly, as evidenced by a transcribed conversation between them that took place on November 11, 1953, about Armstrong's scurrilous manager **Johnny Collins** (see the excerpt in Berrett, 1999, pp. 85–86). Armstrong listened attentively to Avakian when he made musical suggestions during the taping of the Armstrong-Handy recording, as one can hear on the 1997 reissue, which includes some such studio banter. Finally, Avakian's gentle, intelligent demeanor can be both heard and seen in the film ***Satchmo: Louis Armstrong.***

In addition to his work with Armstrong, Avakian was also responsible for the artistic and commercial success of albums by Erroll Garner and **Benny Goodman,** and he facilitated the early careers of **Dave Brubeck, Miles Davis,** Keith Jarrett, and Sonny Rollins.

"Avalon." By Al Jolson and Vincent Rose; rec. May 24 or 25, 1960, in New York City with the **Dukes of Dixieland;** CD #53. When Armstrong and the Dukes finally got together in 1959, they responded warmly and generously to each other. "They... were sensational from the first day that they left New Orleans," Armstrong wrote in 1969. "You can see how happy I am to know that I finally had a chance to *blow* with White Boys *at last*" (Brothers, p. 35). On "Avalon" he takes four choruses, including a thrilling high "G." This popular song from 1920 was a standard for **Louis Armstrong and the**

All Stars and a feature number for trombonist **Tyree Glenn,** who would temporarily set aside his trombone to play it sweetly on the vibraphone. (Glenn, as well as Armstrong and the other All Stars, can be seen as well as heard playing this piece on the **television** film ***Solo.***)

Aventure du jazz, L'. This wide-ranging documentary features a fifteen-minute interview with Armstrong at his home in **Corona** in October 1969. It also focuses on **Duke Ellington, Lionel Hampton,** and others. The Armstrong segment is interspersed with footage of New Orleans brass bands, an interview with **Zutty Singleton,** and selections by the Buddy Tate Orchestra. Armstrong is heard playing his famous **stop-time** solo and final chorus from "Cornet Chop Suey" and also singing unaccompanied "Do You Know What It Means to Miss New Orleans?" and "Cabaret." Unfortunately, the film never received general distribution and seems to have survived only in bits and pieces held by collectors. Filmed 1969–1970; rev. 1972; color; 98 mins.; Prod. and Dir. by Claudine and Louis Panassié (see Stratemann, 1996, pp. 561–562).

awards. Armstrong flourished in a day when awards were not as pervasive as they have since become. He did win quite a few, though—some 120 plaques and certificates during his nearly sixty-year career. (These were the subject of an exhibit titled *And the Award Goes to . . . ,* curated by Peggy Alexander at the **Louis Armstrong House and Archives,** Queens College, from September 19 to December 2, 2002.) While most of Armstrong's awards were for his work as a trumpet player, vocalist, recording artist, and entertainer, some were purely humanitarian, reflecting his kind nature and generosity of spirit.

One of his earliest awards was presented in 1929. As **Dave Peyton** reported in the *Chicago Defender,* "[T]he white musicians of New York tendered Louis a banquet . . . and presented him with a handsome wristwatch, engraved thusly: 'To Louis Armstrong, the World's Greatest Cornetist, from the Musicians of New York' " (Aug. 10, 1929). One of his favorite awards was given to him in September 1941, while on tour at Fort Barrancas (near Panama City, Florida), when he received a medal in the form of crossed cannons from the commanding officer. "When they pinned that Official Coast Artillery Insignia on my lapel," wrote Armstrong later to **Leonard Feather,** "I was almost in tears" (Berrett, 1999, p. 117). Armstrong also won numerous ***Down Beat*** and ***Esquire*** polls.

Also significant are the awards that Armstrong *turned down.* In the 1960s when **Howard University** wanted to give him an honorary doctorate, he declined, saying: "Where were they forty years ago when I needed them?" In 1969 the newly elected Richard Nixon invited Armstrong to the White House. Armstrong's response? "Fuck that shit. Why didn't they do it before? The only reason he would want me to play there now is to make some niggers happy" (Giddins, 1988, p. 168).

As an innovator Armstrong might have been honored for numerous advances in many areas. See **firsts** for a list of his enduring and award-worthy achievements.

"Azalea." By **Duke Ellington;** rec. April 4, 1961, in New York City by **Louis Armstrong and the All Stars** with Duke Ellington; CD #11. Armstrong and Ellington worked together occasionally but not to any great extent until after Armstrong had played Ellington's music in the film ***Paris Blues.*** The resulting album features Ellington pieces played by Armstrong and the All Stars, with Ellington taking **Billy Kyle**'s place at the keyboard. Even though the Ellington numbers were not in Armstrong's repertory, he gave them the **Satchmo** treatment, and Ellington liked the fresh approach to his music. As a bonus, the small combo allowed Ellington's lean, suave piano style to be heard more clearly. This number, which Ellington had written in 1942 with Armstrong in mind, closes their remarkable album.

B

"Ba-Ba-Bo-ZET!" Armstrong was, of course, famous for **scat singing,** which he was the first to record with commercial success ("Heebie Jeebies" in 1926) and subsequently to popularize. "Ba-Ba-Bo-ZET!" is a scat phrase that turns up again and again in his singing, in his conversation, and sometimes in his letters.

"Baby." By Dorothy Fields and Jimmy McHugh; rec. December 11, 1928, in Chicago by vocalist **Lillie Delk Christian** with Louis Armstrong and His **Hot Four;** CD #36. Christian is said to have had a magnetic stage presence, and that must have made up somewhat for her poor singing ability. At any rate, what distinguishes this recording is the marvelous ensemble work by Armstrong, pianist **Earl Hines,** and clarinetist **Jimmie Noone.**

"Baby, I Can't Use You No More." By M. Wallace and **Sippie Wallace;** rec. November 28, 1924, in New York City with vocalist Sippie Wallace and **Clarence Williams' Blue Five;** CD #36. A fine blues singer, Wallace came from a musical family and began to perform at an early age. Armstrong frequently accompanied her between 1924 and 1926, as he did so many other blues singers of the day (e.g., **Alberta Hunter, Ma Rainey,** and **Bessie Smith**). Some of the sessions with Wallace are distinguished by the piano playing of her brother Hersal Thomas, but here the pianist is **Clarence Williams.**

"Baby, It's Cold Outside." By Frank Loesser; rec. January 30, 1951, live at the Pasadena Civic Auditorium in California by **Louis Armstrong and the All Stars;** CDs #6, #7, and #28. Armstrong and vocalist **Velma Middleton** used to bring down the house with their flirtatious duet version of this 1949 Academy Award–winning song from the film *Neptune's Daughter* with Esther Williams.

"Baby, Won't You Please Come Home?" By **Clarence Williams** and Charles Warfield; rec. June 15, 1939, in New York City by Louis Armstrong and His Orchestra; CDs #8, #18, #32, and #54. This gem eventually became a **Jack Teagarden** specialty number at **Louis Armstrong and the All Stars** concerts, and he so nearly stole the show with it that one can see why in August 1951 he left to form his own All Stars. He and Armstrong remained good friends, though, and there were many happy musical reunions.

"Baby, Your Sleep Is Showing." By N. Simon and Charles Tobias; rec. April 25, 1955, in New York City by **Louis Armstrong and the All Stars;** CD #8. This is one of many wonderfully risqué Armstrong/**Velma Middleton** duets.

"(Back Home Again in) Indiana." See **"Indiana, (Back Home Again in)."**

Back o' Town. This is the section of New Orleans where Armstrong was born. See **birthplace.**

"Back o' Town Blues." By Louis Armstrong and **Luis Russell;** rec. January 18, 1944, in New York City at the ***Esquire*** All American Jazz Concert; CDs #5, #6, #12, #13, #16, #21, #22, #32, #47, #53, and #57. This number eventually developed into a regular **Louis Armstrong and the All Stars** feature in which Armstrong would trade mock insults with the trombonist—usually **Tyree Glenn, Jack Teagarden,** or **Trummy Young.** Armstrong would sing "I had a woman," and the reply would be something like, "So what? I had five." Once an audience member said something, and Armstrong shot back: "Shut up, Boy!" This got such a big laugh that it, too, was added. In the 1966 **movie *A Man Called Adam,*** in which Armstrong plays an old musician who is treated badly by an up-and-coming but troubled musician (played by **Sammy Davis, Jr.**), Armstrong performs a straight version of "Back o' Town Blues."

Bailey, Buster (1902–1967). This excellent clarinetist was born in Memphis and at age seventeen settled in Chicago, where he played with **King Oliver** and **Erskine Tate,** and then, like Armstrong, joined **Fletcher Henderson**'s band in New York in 1924. After a distinguished career with Henderson, John Kirby, **Red Allen,** and others, he spent the last two years of his life (June 1965 to mid-1967) with the **All Stars.** (Armstrong kept up a grueling tour schedule of up to 300 days a year, and Bailey, as well as All Star pianist **Billy Kyle** and singer **Velma Middleton,** died on the road.)

Bailey, Calvin (1909–1988). Armstrong loved the camera, and vice versa. His favorite portrait was one that **Anton Bruehl** did for the November 1935 issue of ***Vanity Fair,*** and it is still seen everywhere (e.g., on the cover of Bergreen's 1997 book). So much did Armstrong like the photo that in 1948 he commissioned the up-and-coming African American painter Calvin Bailey to make an oil-on-canvas version. The result is also widely circulated (e.g., the cover of Miller's 1994 book), and it had pride of place in Armstrong's living room. Bailey worked for a time as a caricaturist in the Los Angeles entertainment industry and probably met Armstrong on the set of ***Cabin in the Sky*** (1943).

Bailey, Pearl (May) (1918–1990). Although she was an honorary pallbearer at his **funeral** at the **Corona** Congregational Church on July 9, 1971, Pearl Bailey did not work all that much with Armstrong. Nevertheless, they had much in common. Both recorded Hughie Cannon's 1902 song "Bill Bailey, Won't You Please Come Home?" (Armstrong was the first to popularize it, and Bailey did a revival version in the 1950s.) Both also made memorable recordings of "It Takes Two to Tango" in 1952. In the 1960s they each won recognition for "Hello Dolly!" performances—Armstrong for being the first jazz artist to top the charts in the Beatle era with his 1964 recording, and Bailey with a 1968 Special Tony Award for her performance in an all-black Broadway version. Finally, both were represented by **Joe Glaser**'s **Associated Booking Corporation.**

Otherwise, they had parallel careers. Bailey worked with Count Basie and others until the mid-1940s, when she joined **Cab Calloway.** At this time she became famous for the comic patter with which she seasoned her singing. Two of her great successes were the 1946 recordings of "Legalize My Name" and "It's a Woman's Prerogative." She was also a Broadway star (e.g., *St. Louis Woman* in 1946) and appeared in several films (e.g., *Carmen Jones* in 1954). Later in her career, she was a member of the American delegation to the United Nations and a television personality. Armstrong made one of his last public appearances on Bailey's popular **television** show on January 23, 1971.

Baker, Josephine (1906–1975). Because of France's long-standing tendency to romanticize things African, Paris between the two world wars was a congenial place for black American performers. Artists such as **Sidney Bechet, Cab Calloway, Duke Ellington,** and **Coleman Hawkins** received there the respect they were denied at home, and Josephine Baker, **Arthur Briggs,** Bricktop (**Ada Smith**), Bobby Jones, and others settled there permanently. When in 1934 an exhausted Armstrong, suffering from **lip problems,** took a few months off in Paris, he was welcomed warmly by this latter group.

Baker's star was shining brightly at this time. Earlier she had created a sensation in *La Revue Négre* (1925), becoming the talk of the town with her jazz singing, rhythmic dancing, and exotic costumes. Before becoming a French citizen in 1937, Baker returned to the United States to perform in the Ziegfeld Follies of 1936. During the Nazi occupation of France, she worked for the Red Cross and the Resistance, and in 1956 she retired to devote more time to her family of adopted children. However, she often returned to the stage and silver screen, and she died in Paris after a triumphant run of the revue *Josephine,* which celebrated her life.

Balanchine, George (1904–1983). The great Russian-born American choreographer supervised the dance sequences in ***Cabin in the Sky,*** the 1943 **Vincente Minnelli** film in which Armstrong plays one of Lucifer, Jr.'s assistants at the Hotel Hades.

Baldwin, James (1924–1987). Many African American activist artists had ambivalent feelings about Armstrong, and the great writer James Baldwin was no exception. In his 1957 story "Sonny's Blues" (which appears in *Going to Meet the Man,* 1965), a young man tries to explain his desire to become a jazz musician to his older brother, who asks if he means a musician like Louis Armstrong. The answer is firm. "No. I'm not talking about none of that old-time, down home crap." The young man mentions Charlie Parker, and the difference between Parker and Armstrong comes to symbolize the generation gap both between the two brothers and post-World War II African Americans.

Baldwin nevertheless admired Armstrong, as Dan Morgenstern relates in his liner notes to the 1997 CD reissue of *The*

Great Chicago Concert, 1956 (CD #19). Morgenstern remembers how at the 1958 **Newport Jazz Festival** he sat with Baldwin, and Armstrong finished his set, as usual, with "The Star Spangled Banner." As the final notes were dying away, Baldwin said: "You know, that's the first time I've liked that song" (reprinted in Berrett, 1999, pp. 177–186).

Armstrong inspired many writers, including **Amiri Baraka** (a.k.a. LeRoi Jones), **Ralph Ellison,** and Ishmael Reed (see ***C above C above High C***).

"Ballad of Davy Crockett, The." By Tom Blackburn and George Bruns; rec. March 16, 1968, in Hollywood by **Louis Armstrong and the All Stars** with a studio orchestra and mixed choir; CD #15. One can easily have mixed feelings about this once very popular song from the 1956 Disney film *Davy Crockett,* but Armstrong seems to like it. Here he records one of his last trumpet solos and tells the story with enthusiasm.

"Ballin' the Jack." By Chris Smith; rec. on or shortly after September 11, 1946, in Los Angeles with a small ensemble for the sound track to the film ***New Orleans.***

Bankhead, Tallulah (1903–1968). The sophisticated, husky voiced actress—famous for her performances in the plays *The Little Foxes* (1939) and *The Skin of Our Teeth* (1942) and the film *Lifeboat* (1944)—was a devoted Armstrong fan. She compared his artistic range to that of both Charlie Chaplin and Wolfgang Amadeus Mozart. In particular, she liked Armstrong's "Potato Head Blues," once saying "it is one of the greatest things in life." She played the record every night "to alleviate the tedium of playing the same part for so long," during the three-year Broadway run of *Private Lives* in the late 1920s (Giddins, 1988, p. 92).

Baraka, Amiri (a.k.a. LeRoi Jones) (b. 1934). The African American poet, playwright, and political activist wrote about Armstrong in his 1963 book *Blues People.* Following on the heels of sharp criticism of Armstrong by intellectuals and activists, Baraka defended his hero as the "honored priest of his culture" (p. 154). Baraka's essay in fact marked the beginning of a change in attitude toward Armstrong. During the preceding years, Armstrong had increasingly been seen both as a once promising artist who had sold out to commercial interests and as an Uncle Tom figure who would do anything to please the white folks. Baraka's efforts contributed to the reconsideration of Armstrong, who thereafter began to be seen as a pioneer figure and one of the most admirable artists in the African American musical tradition. Baraka himself has written numerous plays, twelve volumes of poetry, a novel, another book about music (*Black Music,* 1967), and an autobiography.

Armstrong inspired many writers, including **James Baldwin, Ralph Ellison,** and Ishmael Reed. See ***C above C above High C.***

Barbarin, Isidore (1872–1960). This New Orleans alto horn player and member of several prestigious brass bands (the **Onward,** the **Tuxedo,** and the Excelsior) was highly respected by Armstrong, who wrote him a letter from Chicago on September 1, 1922, not long after arriving in that city so far from home. This 300-word letter is not particularly notable for its I'm-fine-how-are-you and say-hi-to-so-

and-so content but rather for being the earliest surviving piece of writing by Armstrong. It can be seen in the **William Ransom Hogan Jazz Archive** at Tulane University and is reprinted in Brothers (p. 42). Hundreds more letters to friends and fans followed over the years.

Barbarin had four sons who became musicians—**Paul,** Louis, Lucien, and William. His grandson was the guitarist and banjo player Danny Barker.

Barbarin, Paul (1899–1969). The career of this excellent drummer, the son of New Orleans jazz patriarch **Isidore Barbarin,** developed for a time somewhat in tandem with Armstrong's. Barbarin, who had worked a bit with **Joe Oliver** in Chicago before 1920, rejoined him in 1924 and then moved to New York in 1928 to work with the **Luis Russell** band. There between 1929 and 1939 he recorded frequently and toured widely with Armstrong, who was the star soloist with the group. He then returned to New Orleans, where he spent the rest of his life playing in small groups and brass bands, except for brief forays abroad with **Red Allen** and **Sidney Bechet.** Barbarin is the author of several tunes, including "Bourbon Street Parade," "The Second Line," and "Come Back, Sweet Papa." Taking a page from his father's book, Barbarin played in the **Onward Brass Band,** which he revived in 1960. He died leading this ensemble during a Mardi Gras parade.

Barbour, David Michael "Dave" (1912–1965). The great acoustic guitarist worked briefly with Armstrong in 1936 and 1938. He can be heard, for example, on the **Decca** remakes of "Ain't Misbehavin' " and "I Can't Give You Anything But Love." On both of these numbers, Barbour, a solid section man, does not take any solos, let alone the fluent kind for which he later became famous.

Barbour began on the banjo but soon changed to the guitar. He worked with **Teddy Wilson, Bunny Berigan,** and **Benny Goodman,** and he also led his own band in the mid-1940s. He was married to singer **Peggy Lee,** and the two worked together frequently. He also briefly tried his hand as an actor, appearing in the 1950 film *The Secret Fury.*

Barcelona, Daniel "Danny" (b. 1929). The future **All Stars** drummer cut his professional teeth in the Hawaii Dixie All-Stars, which he took over from **Trummy Young** when that trombonist joined Armstrong's All Stars in 1952. In April 1958 Barcelona also hooked up with All Stars and remained with them to the end in 1971. A good place to hear him is on the 1961 *The Complete Louis Armstrong and Duke Ellington Sessions* (CD #11). Here a smaller ensemble allows his crisp, clean style to show through. In "Cottontail," "The Beautiful American," and especially "In a Mellow Tone," he uses the ride cymbal extensively, and his occasional solos (e.g., "Drop Me Off at Harlem") demonstrate a unique use of asymmetrical phrasing.

"Bare Necessities, The." By Terry Gilkyson; rec. February 27, 1968, in New York City by **Louis Armstrong and the All Stars;** CD #15. Phil Harris may own this song from **Disney**'s *The Jungle Book,* but Armstrong adopted it with gusto. He opens with a rousing trumpet solo, one of his very last on record.

baseball. See **Armstrong's Secret Nine; Robinson, Jackie.**

"Basin Street Blues." By Spencer Williams; rec. December 4, 1928, in Chicago, with the **Hot Five;** CDs #6, #8, #10, #12, #17, #19, #21, #23, #24, #25, #28, #30, #32, #40, #44, #45, #48, #52, #59, and #61. This is an all-time masterpiece—Armstrong's or anyone's. After **Earl Hines**'s delicate celeste opening, Armstrong's trumpet emerges and then gives way to an internationally understood **scat** vocal. Armstrong went on to record this song over fifty times, including another classic version on January 27, 1933, in Chicago with a larger ensemble. Here an upcoming **Teddy Wilson** plays the heavenly celeste introduction, and the humming chorus of sidemen helps to evoke an otherworldly, solemn atmosphere. Armstrong also contributed a memorable "Basin Street" to the 1951 **movie *The Strip*** and the 1954 ***The Glenn Miller Story.***

"Battle Royal." By **Duke Ellington;** rec. December 14, 1960, in Paris with a French studio ensemble. This number is featured in the 1961 **movie *Paris Blues,*** in which Armstrong plays fictional jazz legend "Wild Man Moore," and Paul Newman and Sidney Poitier play American expatriate jazz musicians who fall for two lovely tourists, Joanne Woodward and Diahann Carroll.

"Be My Life's Companion." By Bob Hilliard and Milton Delugg; rec. April 18, 1964, in New York City by **Louis Armstrong and the All Stars.**

Beal, Charlie (1908–1991). Armstrong and this fine pianist first worked together in the **Les Hite** Band (1930), and they recorded together in 1933. In 1946 Beal was selected for the band used in the film ***New Orleans,*** and his playing, particularly on "Mahogany Hall Stomp," shines through on the sound track. Before the film, Beal worked both as a sideman (with **Erskine Tate, Carroll Dickerson,** Buster Bailey, and others) and as a leader/soloist. Later in his career he appeared frequently in Europe and in New York.

"Beale Street Blues." By W.C. Handy; rec. July 12, 1954, in Chicago by **Louis Armstrong and the All Stars;** CD #38. See comments on "Atlanta Blues."

Bearden, Romare (1912–1988). Having lived across from Harlem's **Lafayette Theatre** as a child, this African American visual artist frequently turned to jazz themes in his painting and collage work. A book collaboration with photographer **Sam Shaw** based on the popular film ***Paris Blues*** (1961) was unfortunately never completed, and neither was a 1980s collaboration on the history of jazz. However, several of their collages for these projects have survived and, along with other pieces, have since been featured in exhibitions, for example, *Louis Armstrong: A Cultural Legacy,* which toured the United States in 1994–1997. (Examples can be found nicely reproduced in Marc Miller's widely available catalog. See selected bibliography.) Armstrong was a frequently recurring Bearden subject in such works as *Showtime* (1974), which depicts Armstrong's trumpet and iconic handkerchief. More subtle is Bearden's attempt to find and exploit the similarities between music and art. A retrospective titled *Riffs and Takes: Music in the Art of Romare Bearden* was mounted by the North Carolina Museum of Art in Raleigh from January 23 to April 3 in the year of the artist's death. An excellent study of the man and his work can be found in Myron Schwartzman's *Romare Bearden: His Life and Art* (New York: Abrams, 1990).

Beat Generation, The. Steve Cochran, Mamie Van Doren, Day Spain, and Ray Danton star in this film, and Armstrong makes brief appearances with the **All Stars** playing the title song, his own "Someday You'll Be Sorry," and an unidentified blues. Set in Los Angeles and the Venice Beach area in particular, the story is not so much about beatniks as it is about the pursuit of a rapist/murderer (the Aspirin Kid, played by Ray Danton) by a disaffected detective (Steve Cochran). As so often was the case elsewhere (e.g., ***Jam Session, Hello Dolly!, Artists and Models, Here Comes the Groom***), Armstrong's performance adds musical color and atmosphere but has very little to do with the story line. However, as also so often happened, he enlivens an otherwise pretty dull film. Frankly, Armstrong's presence reveals Hollywood's unrealistic vision, since the Beat Generation tended to prefer the more understated, cooler jazz of Chet Baker, **Miles Davis,** and Shorty Rogers. M-G-M, 1959; Cinemascope, B&W; 95 mins.; Dir. Charles Haas.

Beatles, The. Armstrong traveled with a portable record player and about twenty LPs, mostly of his own music but also that of a few others including The Beatles. "It's music, and they swing," Armstrong told Jones and Chilton (p. 217). The Fab Four cut their teeth playing between sets for jazz bands that played music heavily influenced by Armstrong. As everyone knows, they went on to rule the world of popular music in the 1960s. An achievement unheard of before or since, at one point in 1964 they held the top five positions on the ***Billboard* chart,** except for six weeks, that is. From early May to mid-June, Armstrong took over the No. 1 spot with his recording of "Hello Dolly!"

Beatty, Josephine. See **Hunter, Alberta.**

"Beau Koo Jack." By Alex Hill, Louis Armstrong, Walter Melrose, and **Don Redman;** rec. December 5, 1928, in Chicago by Louis Armstrong and His **Savoy Ballroom Five;** CDs #10, #30, and #48. Alex Hill's excellent arrangement of this tune (whose title means "lots of money") helped inspire an Armstrong solo so skillful and imaginative that Gunther Schuller transcribed it in *Early Jazz* (p. 128).

"Beautiful American, The." By **Duke Ellington;** rec. April 3, 1961, in New York City by **Louis Armstrong and the All Stars** with Duke Ellington; CD #11. This jaunty, minor key sketch of Armstrong was created in the recording studio. In addition to the subject's three choruses, **Barney Bigard,** who played with Ellington for fourteen years, takes a winsome solo. See additional comments on "Azalea."

Beavers, Louise (1902–1962). That Armstrong had intimations of immortality is demonstrated by his request that actress Louise Beavers be cast as his mother if ever his life should be made into a movie. In a letter written on May 7, 1944, while on tour in Tucson, Arizona, Armstrong wrote his designated biographer, **Robert Goffin,** to correspond with him at Beavers's home (2219 Hobart Boulevard, Los Angeles), where he would be stopping next. "She could really play the part of my mother since she looks . . . and acts just like her," he wrote. He continued: "Sometimes it saves one a lot of worry as to whom to get to play some parts" (Brothers, p. 78).

Beavers was one of the most frequently employed African American Hollywood actresses in her day. At first a real-life maid of actress Leatrice Joy, she later played the role of a maid in many films. She is probably best remembered for her pancake making in *Imitation of Life* (1934), although she also appeared, usually as housekeeper or cook, in such films as *Blonde Bombshell* (1933), *Made for Each Other* (1939), *No Time for Comedy* (1940), *Shadow of the Thin Man* (1941), and *Tammy and the Bachelor* (1957). In the early days of television, she played the title role in the *Beulah* series (1952–1953).

bebop. See **bop.**

"Because of You." By Dudley Wilkinson and Arthur Hammerstein; rec. September 17, 1951, in New York City by **Louis Armstrong and the All Stars;** CD #32. Here in an early use of the technique of double tracking, Armstrong can be heard accompanying his singing with his own trumpet playing. "Because of You," a popular song dating from 1940, was also recorded by Tony Bennett and by **opera** singer Jan Peerce.

Bechet, Sidney (Joseph) (1897–1959). It's really not fair to claim, as many do, that Armstrong was the first jazz soloist. While he may more precisely be called the first major *influence* in jazz, the honor of being the first jazz soloist goes to clarinetist and soprano saxophonist Sidney Bechet, also a New Orleans native. "The first time I heard Sidney Bechet play that clarinet he stood me on my ear," Louis wrote in his 1954 **autobiography** (p. 134). Although Bechet left New Orleans around 1916 to tour the southern and midwestern United States, and worked in Europe during the 1920s, he made some memorable recordings with Armstrong between 1923 and 1925. (There is a wonderful 1981 Smithsonian collection of these on two LPs, and it includes excellent liner notes by Lewis Porter.) The two teamed up again in 1940 but with less success, probably owing to Bechet's thorny personality. Bechet eventually found the United States less congenial than France, where in 1951 he settled permanently. *Treat It Gentle* is the title of his fascinating autobiography, published the year after he died in Paris.

Bedou, Arthur P. (1882–1922). Bedou was one of two African American photographers (the other was **Villard Paddio,** his student) in early-twentieth-century New Orleans who did family portraits and commercial work for the city's African American clientele. Bedou's skill and artistry won him a gold medal at the 1907 Jamestown Exposition in Virginia, and he accompanied Booker T. Washington on his 1911–1912 farewell tour. Bedou took evocative photographs of numerous musical ensembles, including one often seen of Armstrong in the **Fate Marable** Band, circa 1920. While the originals are in collections such as the **William Ransom Hogan Jazz Archive** at Tulane University, they have been widely reproduced in such publications as Marc Miller's *Louis Armstrong: A Cultural Legacy.*

"Before Long." By **Sid Catlett** and Carl Sigman; rec. October 16, 1947, in Chicago by **Louis Armstrong and the All Stars;** CDs #12 and #47. Armstrong croons tenderly on this sweet breakup song by Catlett, his favorite drummer. There's also some outstanding trombone work by **Jack Teagarden.**

Beiderbecke, Leon "Bix" (1903–1931). Although many claim that Armstrong was the first jazz soloist to be widely imitated, Bix Beiderbecke came along at about the same time, almost to the very month. Generously overlooking any feelings of competition, Armstrong was very enthusiastic in his admiration of the younger, white cornetist. He dedicated the first volume of his **autobiography,** ***Swing That Music,*** to him (in addition to **Eddie Lang** and **King Oliver**), and he wrote in the second volume, ***Satchmo: My Life in New Orleans:*** "Every musician in the world knew and admired Bix. . . . We all respected him as though he had been a god" (p. 209).

The two first met late in the summer of 1920, when Armstrong was playing in **Fate Marable**'s band on the Mississippi riverboat **S.S. *Sidney,*** when it stopped in Davenport, Iowa. Though their careers moved in different orbits, Beiderbecke and the Wolverines in 1923 made recordings as legendary as those of Armstrong. Beiderbecke went on to play with the Goldkette band and, when it folded in 1927, with the Paul Whiteman band. Meanwhile, the cumulative effect of years of alcohol abuse undermined Beiderbecke's health and playing. In September 1929 he took a leave, and partly because of the stock market crash and subsequent depressed economic conditions, he never fully recovered his career. Dorothy Baker's 1938 novel *Young Man with a Horn,* which was made into a movie starring Kirk Douglas in 1950, is based loosely on Beiderbecke's life. (For more information see Meckna, 1994, pp. 25–27.)

Belair, Felix (1907–1978). This *New York Times* writer pointed out early on the turn taken in Armstrong's career when, after World War II, jazz became a symbol of freedom and liberation. Armstrong's international tours in the late 1940s, U.S. State Department-sponsored tours in the 1950s and 1960s, and **Voice of America** broadcasts beginning in the early 1950s all gave his music a political subtext. As the Cold War set in, Belair observed on the front page of the November 6, 1955, *Times:* "America's secret weapon is a blue note in a minor key. Right now its most effective ambassador is Louis (Satchmo) Armstrong. American jazz has now become a universal language. It knows no national boundaries, but everyone knows where it comes from and where to look for more." See **"Ambassador Satch."**

Berard, Madeleine. Before Mlle. Berard—a Swiss journalist, photographer, and aspiring dancer—became Mme. **Arvell Shaw** (i.e., the wife of Armstrong's good friend and regular **All Star** bassist), she was Armstrong's frequent interviewer and correspondent. The two met at New York's Roxy Theater and later wrote each other frequently. As with many of his correspondents, Armstrong opened up to Berard with lengthy missives, often written late at night. One such can be found in Joshua Berrett's *The Louis Armstrong Companion,* where Armstrong chats openly about touring, movie making (***New Orleans,*** in particular), reading and speaking French, his Boston terrier **"General,"** and other subjects (p. 128f).

He would have gone on and on, but, as he writes in closing: "there are such things as wearing your welcome out" (p. 133).

Berigan, Rowland Bernart "Bunny" (1908–1942). Berigan was one of many outstanding trumpeters (Harry James, **Rex Stewart,** and Cootie Williams come immediately to mind) who began their careers as Armstrong imitators. However, he quickly developed a distinctive voice. Even in early recordings such as "Keep Smiling at Trouble" and "Nothin' but the Blues," one can hear the supple tone, thrilling high note shakes, sensuous low note lyricism, and adventurous yet symmetrical solos that attracted listeners across the United States. His "King Porter Stomp," recorded in July 1935, marks for many the official beginning of the swing era. His 1936 "I Can't Get Started," though, is the song most closely associated with Berigan. The idea to open it with a cadenza was probably inspired by Armstrong's "West End Blues" of 1928, but the rest of the piece—the extreme contrasts in range, the sumptuous lyricism, the blue notes, the angst-ridden glissandos, the rich high tones, the dramatic high "D-flat" (his favorite note) at the end—is pure Berigan. Like **Bix Beiderbecke,** Bunny Berigan died in his prime, the victim of alcohol. Armstrong himself pronounced the eulogy: "I've always admired [him] for his tone, soul, technique—his sense of phrasing and all. To me, Bunny can't do no wrong in music!" (Meckna, 1994, p. 30).

Berlin, Irving (1888–1989). Like everyone else in his day, Armstrong fell in love listening to Irving Berlin songs. He therefore delighted in adding "Alexander's Ragtime Band," "Blue Skies," "Cheek to Cheek," "I've Got My Love to Keep Me Warm," "Isn't This a Lovely Day?," and other songs to his repertory. "Sittin' in the Sun" sounds like it was written especially for him. To these songs he of course brought his own style. "Top Hat, White Tie, and Tails" very nearly sounds like a different song when compared to Fred Astaire's version since Armstrong practically recomposes the melody, and his voice on "White Christmas" adds a world-weariness not heard in the classic **Bing Crosby** version. With **Ella Fitzgerald** and backed by the **Oscar Peterson** Quartet, he recorded in 1957 an energetic and ever fresh "I'm Putting All My Eggs in One Basket."

Bernstein, Leonard (1918–1990). This outstanding musician contributed memorably to both serious and popular music. He wrote and conducted symphonies as well as musical theater, and as a pianist he played both concertos and jazz. His career intersected with that of numerous jazz artists, especially Armstrong. In the documentary ***Satchmo the Great,*** CBS cameras followed Armstrong on his triumphal 1956 tour of Europe and Africa, then finally back home to a New York performance with Bernstein conducting the Stadium Symphony Orchestra at Lewisohn Stadium. For many the occasion implied that jazz had now been accepted into the musical tradition, and perhaps even more. Armstrong in his travels had shown that American jazz could be a cultural bond between nations and a curative tonic for strife. In any case, the day (July 14) was memorable. On the program was W.C. Handy's "St. Louis Blues," and Handy himself was there in the audience with his daughter. Armstrong later reported that Bernstein at first lacked confidence about the concert, but "after the performance he liked to shake my hand off" (Bergreen, p. 462).

Berton, Vic (Victor Cohen) (1896–1951). The accomplished white drummer's career intersected briefly with Armstrong's when, in November 1930, the two were arrested for smoking **marijuana.** Details are fuzzy, but according to Vic's brother Ralph and the account in the November 19, 1930, *Variety,* the two were arrested in the parking lot of **Sebastian's New Cotton Club** in Culver City during a break between sets. A rival bandleader or nightclub owner may very well have set them up. In any case, they were allowed to return to the bandstand to finish the performance, then taken to jail. Within twenty-four hours they were out on bail and eventually won a suspended sentence, due either to the efforts of Armstrong's new manager, **Johnny Collins,** or to Berton's bandleader Abe Lyman, who was well connected. The event shook Armstrong, who hadn't been in big trouble with the law since his arrest for shooting a gun on New Year's Eve 1912. However, he certainly didn't quit smoking marijuana, which he began doing shortly after arriving in Chicago in 1922 and continued enthusiastically for the rest of his life. Berton continued with a successful career, performing and recording widely with big-name commercial bands and later with symphony orchestras. He lived out his days in Hollywood as a music director and percussionist for several top film studios.

Bertrand, Jimmy (1900–1960). While under contract with **Okeh Records,** Armstrong used to quietly pick up a little extra cash by recording here and there for other labels. For **Vocalion** with drummer Jimmy Bertrand's Washboard Wizards on April 21, 1927, he did four sides—"Easy Come, Easy Go Blues," "The Blues Stampede," "I'm Goin' Huntin'," and "If You Wanna Be My Sugar Papa (You Gotta Be Sweet to Me)." Armstrong seems to be carefully disguising his style so as not to get caught moonlighting. For example, he plays with comparatively little invention, stays away from high notes, and never sings at all. Bertrand performed and recorded with others but mostly led his own band. He was also active as a teacher, and among his students were **Lionel Hampton** and **Sid Catlett.**

"Bess, You Is My Woman Now." By George Gershwin, DuBose Heyward, and Ira Gershwin; rec. August 18, 1957, in Los Angeles with vocalist **Ella Fitzgerald** and a studio orchestra and choir conducted by Russell Garcia; CD #9. Gershwin's **opera** has been popular with African American artists since its premiere in 1935, but no one has surpassed the poignant interpretation of Armstrong and Fitzgerald. Many fans and critics consider it to be their best work, and even the fussiest have to call these performances virtuoso. "Bess, You Is My Woman Now" comes from a pivotal moment in Act II.

"Bessie Couldn't Help It." By Byron H. Warner, J.L. Richmond, and Charles Bayha; rec. February 1, 1930, in New York City by Louis Armstrong and His Orchestra.

Best, Willie (1916–1962). This black comedian, active 1930s–1940s, was paired with Armstrong in both ***Cabin in the Sky*** (1943) and ***Pillow to Post*** (1945). In the former, he plays one of the six devil assistants (he's the one who sleeps through most of his scene), while in the latter, he is "Lucille," a motel porter. In both he portrays the stereotypical slow-witted, shuffling black man and provides a foil to Armstrong's energetic, musical persona. Best also dances with casual elegance in two of the four **soundies** that Armstrong made in 1942. He had a considerable range of talent, as can be seen in such films as *Vivacious Lady* (1938; with Ginger Rogers and James Stewart) and *High Sierra* (1941; with Humphrey Bogart).

Beth Israel Hospital (New York City). Armstrong spent a good deal of time in this distinguished hospital, beginning in 1964 when his health began to flag. In March of that year he was admitted for acute edema in the lower right leg. In September 1968—after filming ***Hello Dolly!,*** appearing at the New Orleans Jazz Festival, and touring England—he complained of shortness of breath and was diagnosed with acute heart failure. He spent over three months in Beth Israel and at home convalescing. He also suffered from ulcers and kidney problems at this time. Finally, on March 15, 1971, he suffered a heart attack after (and against doctor's advice) playing a two-week gig at the **Waldorf Astoria** Empire Room in New York. He was in intensive care until mid-April, and at last on May 6 he left to return to his home in **Corona.** While confined in the hospital, Armstrong managed to have some good times, trying to sell the hospital staff on the laxative **Swiss Kriss** and flirting with the nurses. "They would congregate in my room to *chat* with me while I was resting," he wrote in a June 1, 1970, "Open Letter to Fans." "They kept my cheeks Rosy Red" (Brothers, p. 182).

Betty Boop. In 1932 Max Fleischer used Armstrong in one of his Betty Boop cartoons. It featured the song "(I'll Be Glad When You're Dead) You Rascal, You." Armstrong first appears "live" with his band, then as a cartoon cannibal, then as a head only in the upper corner of the screen singing the title song, and lastly with the band performing "Chinatown, My Chinatown" and the finale. It is both a diverting trifle and a fascinating artifact of its time.

"Between the Devil and the Deep Blue Sea." By **Harold Arlen** and Ted Koehler; rec. January 25, 1932, in Chicago by Louis Armstrong and His Orchestra; CDs #44, #48, and #58. In the mid-1940s, Armstrong made some notes for **Robert Goffin** to use in a **biography,** and in them he pointed to this as one of his finest recordings (Brothers, p. 108). It is easy to agree. It is also instructive to compare it with a second take, which Dan Morgenstern discovered in the 1960s, from the same recording session. Slower, muted, more ornate, yet slightly flawed (several missed notes), this later version is Armstrong pointing the way toward cool modern jazz. See Schuller, 1989, pp. 178–179, for a transcription.

"Bibbidi-Bobbidi-Boo." By Jerry Livingston, Mack David, and Al Hoffman; rec. March 16, 1968, in Hollywood by **Louis Armstrong and the All Stars** with a studio orchestra and mixed choir; CD #15. Armstrong popularized **scat singing** over two decades before this song was written in 1948 for **Disney**'s *Cinderella,* and the nonsense syllables come naturally for him. The arrangement is lame and the chorus stiff, but Armstrong manages to work some magic. One of his last recorded trumpet solos can be heard here.

Biberman, Herbert (1900–1971). Later notorious as one of the "Hollywood Ten" (a group of film industry professionals who came under suspicion of having communist sympathies), Biberman was the screenwriter for ***New Orleans*** (United Artists, 1947). McCarthyism came to Hollywood during the making of this film, and the studio felt the need to soften the movie's liberal and idealistic intentions. As a result Biberman (and of course the director, Arthur Lubin) shifted the focus from the talented African American musicians who had created jazz to the white actors who treated jazz as an ornament to their rather silly lives. Biberman had previously earned fame as director of the thriller *Meet Nero Wolfe* (1936) and as a writer on the romantic comedy *Together Again* (1944). He went on to direct the social realist movie *Salt of the Earth* (1954).

Big Band All Stars, The. This short-lived group was put together in April 1953 for Armstrong and **Benny Goodman** (both of whom had the same manager, **Joe Glaser**) to take on a six-week tour. Excitement was high, and advance sales were over a million dollars. Unfortunately, the two musicians did not get along well, and their conflict eventually came to such a pitch that the tour had to be canceled. (See the Goodman entry for details.)

"Big Butter and Egg Man." By Percy Venable and Louis Armstrong; rec. November 16, 1926, in Chicago with the **Hot Five** and vocalist **May Alix;** CDs #6, #10, #13, #22, #44, and #48. The title refers to a small-time big spender, and this performance contains an Armstrong solo that, seemingly tossed off with ease, has often been cited as one of his best. In his *Early Jazz,* Gunther Schuller states that "no composer, not even a Mozart or a Schubert, composed anything more natural and simply inspired" (1968, p. 104).

"Big Daddy Blues." By Louis Armstrong and **Velma Middleton;** rec. January 30, 1951, live at the Pasadena Civic Auditorium by **Louis Armstrong and the All Stars;** CD #6. This was a feature number for All Star vocalist Velma Middleton.

"Big Fat Ma and Skinny Pa." By Richard M. Jones; rec. June 23, 1926, in Chicago by Louis Armstrong and His **Hot Five;** CD #10.

"Big Mama's Back in Town." By **Velma Middleton;** rec. on January 21, 1955, in Los Angeles by **Louis Armstrong and the All Stars;** CDs #6, #19, and #23. This was a feature number for All Star vocalist Velma Middleton.

Bigard, Albany Leon "Barney" (1906–1980). Of the eight clarinetists who played with the **All Stars,** Bigard stayed the longest—September 1947 to late 1952, 1953 to September 1955, and mid-1960 to mid-1961. Having played with **Duke Ellington** for some fourteen years, he brought a cool elegance to temper the All Stars' rambunctious style. Bigard earlier had taken many of the same paths that Armstrong did. He was born and raised in New Orleans, played for a time with **King Oliver** in Chicago, and even recorded with Armstrong in the late

1920s. Bigard's joining the All Stars, according to critical reaction at the time, added a certain legitimacy. For example, ***Down Beat*** magazine began to pay respectful attention in their articles and influential polls. Armstrong himself was fond not only of Bigard's playing but of his plain speaking. For example, during the controversy over the then new **bop** style in the late 1940s, Armstrong was worried that what he called "this modern malice" would hurt music. However, Bigard responded: "Who wants to play like those folks thirty years ago . . . you got to do something different, you got to move along with the times" (*Down Beat,* April 7, 1948, p. 2). After leaving the All Stars for the third time in 1961, Bigard semi-retired but continued to make occasional appearances at concerts and festivals and in recording studios. He is co-composer (with Duke Ellington and Irvine Mills) of "Mood Indigo" (1931). His feature number with the All Stars was "Just You, Just Me."

Bigard, Emile (c. 1892–1935). **Barney Bigard**'s uncle was another important player in the New Orleans mix. A violinist, he performed with the Magnolia Orchestra (whose cornetist was **King Oliver**) and with **Kid Ory**'s Creole Ragtime Band. Armstrong wrote in the second volume of his **autobiography** that Bigard was one of the best violinists in town (p. 216). After World War I, Bigard worked with the Maple Leaf Orchestra and then with cornetist Hypolite Charles. It was Uncle Emile who gave his nephew Barney his first basic music lessons.

"Bill Bailey, Won't You Please Come Home?" By Hughie Cannon; rec. on June 4, 1965, live at the Palais des Sports in Paris by **Louis Armstrong and the All Stars;** CDs #2 and #59. This 1902 song was first recorded by Arthur Collins, then popularized by Armstrong, who picked it up probably because of a revival recording made by **Pearl Bailey** in the 1950s. Audiences loved it, and so did Ed Sullivan, who had Armstrong do the number on his **television** show.

***Billboard* chart.** Founded in 1894 and published in one form or another to the present day, *Billboard* is the leading music industry trade magazine. One of its important functions has been regularly to publish recording sales rankings for numerous musical genres—mainstream popular music mostly but also including rhythm and blues, country and western, gospel and contemporary Christian, New Age, classical, "classical **crossover,**" and others. Naturally, Armstrong frequently showed up in *Billboard.* His 1955 *Satch Plays Fats* album (CD #56) reached No. 10, and he had a similar success the following year with *Ella and Louis* (CD #9), which held the No. 12 spot. His 1955 single "Mack the Knife" ranked high from February to May 1956, and in 1964 his "Hello Dolly!" bumped **The Beatles** from the No. 1 spot for six weeks in the spring. Armstrong showed up in other *Billboard* categories as well. For example, "I Wonder" (1945), "The Frim Fram Sauce" (1946), and "That Lucky Old Sun" (1949) all showed up on the rhythm and blues list. All in all, he spent an astonishing sixty-two years on *Billboard* charts—from 1926 with "Muskrat Ramble" to 1988 with "What a Wonderful World."

Billy Berg's Swing Club. One of the most important Los Angeles area nightclubs (located on Vine Street in Hollywood),

Billy Berg's had its heyday in the 1940s. Lester Young, Benny Carter, **Dizzy Gillespie,** and Charlie Parker were all heard there, and Armstrong too. In fact, it was at Billy Berg's on August 13, 1947, that **Louis Armstrong and the All Stars** officially debuted. In the audience were **Benny Goodman, Hoagy Carmichael,** Woody Herman, **Johnny Mercer,** and other celebs. It was a memorable premiere for an ensemble that lasted until March 1971.

biographies. In addition to Armstrong's **autobiographies** (1936 and 1954), there are numerous Armstrong biographies. The first (and unfortunately probably the worst) is *Horn of Plenty: The Story of Louis Armstrong* (1947) by **Robert Goffin,** whom Armstrong more or less appointed his biographer and to whom he supplied four big notebooks of raw material. Similar material (Armstrong's letters and transcribed interviews) received better treatment by John Chilton and Max Jones, whose *Louis: The Louis Armstrong Story 1900–1971* was the first full-length biography published after Armstrong's death in 1971. Where Chilton and Jones's work suffers from a lack of chronological organization, *Louis Armstrong: An American Genius* (1983) by James Lincoln Collier progresses in a more orderly fashion and develops the thesis that Armstrong was driven to audience approval by insecurities acquired in **childhood.** Gary Giddins's 1988 *Satchmo,* whose size and abundance of illustrations make it look like a coffee-table item, is probably the best Armstrong biography yet published, since he methodically, accurately, and gracefully develops the thesis that it was Armstrong's achievement to be both a consummate artist and a popular entertainer. *Louis Armstrong: An Extravagant Life* (1997) by Lawrence Bergreen is the first biography to draw on additional unpublished manuscripts, oral histories, and magazine articles, as well as previous biographies. Richard Meryman's *Louis Armstrong—a Self-Portrait* (1971) is a lightly edited reprint of the biographical 1966 ***Life*** magazine interview. Other monographs have been written by **Hugues Panassié** (1947, rev. 1971), Albert McCarthy (1959), and Mike Pinfold (1987). Although not a biography, Michel Boujut's lavishly illustrated *Louis Armstrong* (1998) features a useful chronology and, in school yearbook style, testimonials from those who loved Armstrong. Dan Morgenstern is a major writer on Armstrong, and if he were to collect his numerous ***Down Beat*** and other articles on Armstrong, reviews of Armstrong-related materials, and lengthy booklets accompanying Armstrong recordings, they would easily amount to a full-length biography. Finally, of the over two dozen books about Louis Armstrong for juvenile readers (see selected bibliography), Roxane Orgill's *If I Only Had a Horn: Young Louis Armstrong* (1997) and Jeanette Eaton's *Trumpeter's Tale: The Story of Young Louis Armstrong* (1955) are outstanding. See also **books** for Armstrong anthologies, discographies, and others.

birthday. The often-cited July 4, 1900, birthday would have been perfect for a man who was to become the most popular American musician of the twentieth century. However, according to his baptismal certificate and a subsequent census report, Louis Armstrong was born on August 4, 1901. (These documents were discovered by jazz scholar Tad Jones while helping Gary Giddins research his

1988 *Satchmo.*) The confusion arose because in the year 1918, when young Louis probably needed proof that he was not a minor in order to get gigs and get married, he sought the imprimatur of the local draft board. He more than likely did not know his exact birthdate, not having celebrated it annually. In any case it was customary then for poor African Americans to give July 4, December 25, January 1, or other honorary dates as their birthday. The year was also a matter of choice and susceptible to memory or desire. Proof that he was eighteen was certainly important to him, though, because, as he later wrote in his **autobiography:** "When I could feel that draft card in my hip pocket I sure was a proud fellow" (1954, p. 124).

birthplace. When Armstrong was born on August 4, 1901 (see **birthday**), his voice, which would later become world famous, was first heard in very modest circumstances. More a shack than anything, the Armstrong home was located in **Jane Alley,** between Poydras and Perdido Streets in the **Back o' Town** district of New Orleans. It was one room measuring twenty-six feet by twenty-four feet and divided by upright boards into two or three sections. According to biographers Jones and Chilton, a jazz enthusiast discovered it just before it was scheduled for demolition in 1964. He bought it for $50 and arranged for the New Orleans Jazz Museum to move it, but the deadline wasn't met and, described as being "in terrible condition," the building was burned down (pp. 46–47).

Bishop, Jim (1907–1987). The author of *The Day Lincoln Was Shot* (1955), *The Day Christ Died* (1957), and a regular column for the *New York Journal-American,* Bishop reacted very negatively to Armstrong's September 18, 1957, remarks about segregated schools in **Little Rock.** "I checked the newspaper files to see what Louis Armstrong had done for the people of his race," Bishop wrote. "I haven't found anything and now I ask the musician himself: What have you done for your people, except hurt them?" (Jan. 2, 1958, p. 17). Bishop advocated a boycott of Armstrong's shows, live and televised.

The incident eventually passed, and if anything, it enhanced Armstrong's career. Had Bishop's suggestion been taken seriously, Armstrong would not have gone on to record "Blueberry Hill," "Hello Dolly!," "Mack the Knife," "What a Wonderful World," and "Cabaret." Nor would he have appeared in a dozen more films (including ***The Five Pennies*** with **Danny Kaye; *Paris Blues*** with Paul Newman, Joanne Woodward, and Sidney Poitier; and ***Hello Dolly!*** with **Barbra Streisand**). Bishop went on to write *Go with God* (1958), *The Day Kennedy Was Shot* (1968), a memoir *Jim Bishop, Reporter* (1966), and other books.

Bisma Rex. Armstrong was a firm believer in **laxatives** and other alimentary canal products, such as Bisma Rex, which relieves gas and bloating. "Always carry a package in your pocket," he wrote in an entertaining document about diet and weight control. "It's great for overstuffed stomachs. . . . Yes—it's a 'Gassuh!' " (Berrett, 1999, pp. 100–101).

"Black and Blue?, (What Did I Do to Be So)." By **Thomas "Fats" Waller,** Harry Brooks, and Andy Razaf; rec. July 22, 1929, in New York City by Louis Armstrong and His Orchestra; CDs #19, #28,

#48, #54, #55, #56, and #57. This number, along with "Ain't Misbehavin'" and "That Rhythm Man," are from the 1929 revue ***Connie's Hot Chocolates.*** In the Broadway show, "Black and Blue" is the lovelorn lament that a dark-skinned woman sings about always losing out to fairer-skinned rivals. Armstrong's recording brings out a subtext of racial discrimination and protest. He tells a sad tale but without excessive whining, even bringing a touch of humor to the song in a line about a mouse running from his house. His *recitativo* vocal style underscores the song's plaintive quality, while his exuberantly embellished trumpet solos at the beginning and end tend to counteract despair. Novelist **Ralph Ellison,** himself an accomplished trumpet player, weaves "Black and Blue" into the prologue of his 1952 classic *Invisible Man,* a semiautobiographical story about the life of a young African American. By then the number was a staple in Armstrong's repertory, and he used it frequently on U.S. State Department tours. At a 1956 concert in recently independent **Ghana,** his performance of "Black and Blue" brought tears to the eyes of President Kwame Nkrumah, as can be seen in the documentary film ***Satchmo the Great.***

"Black and Tan Fantasy." By James "Bubber" Miley and **Duke Ellington;** rec. April 4, 1961, in New York City by **Louis Armstrong and the All Stars** with Duke Ellington; CD #11. This interpretation of the 1927 classic has the flavor of the New Orleans funeral music that Armstrong took in with his mother's milk. Trombonist **Trummy Young** does some excellent work with the plunger mute. See additional comments on "Azalea."

Black Benny. See **Williams, "Black Benny."**

"Black Cloud." Rec. August 1970 in New York City with the Nashville Group. See comments on "Almost Persuaded."

Black Storyville. Three blocks away from the infamous New Orleans **Storyville** district was a second Storyville designated for African Americans. It was here—in an area bounded by Perdido, Gravier, Locust, and Franklin Streets—that the six-year-old Armstrong delivered coal to prostitutes and heard early jazz (played by **Bunk Johnson, Jelly Roll Morton, Joe Oliver,** and others) in the many honky-tonks. Black Storyville was an even tougher version of its segregated counterpart. Created in 1898 by eponymous New Orleans politician Sidney Story, Storyville lasted until 1917 when the U.S. Navy had prostitution banned there. During the interim, the development of jazz took a quantum leap here in honky-tonks and dance halls such as **Funky Butt Hall,** where **Buddy Bolden** and others played the blues for hustlers and whores. It was here that Armstrong grew up and learned music.

Blackhawk Restaurant. This Chicago nightclub, located at 139 No. Wabash Avenue, began having jazz performances in the 1920s, and Armstrong was the first to break the color barrier there when he opened in July 1927. It was not a successful enterprise, however, as the management tried to get him to reduce his group from twelve to six. Armstrong stood firm, though, and as a compromise reduced his residency to two weeks.

Blesh, Rudi (1899–1985). Armstrong certainly had his **critics,** and several—such as **James Agee, James Baldwin, Sidney Finkelstein,** and Rudi Blesh—wrote eloquently of their dissatisfaction when in 1929 Armstrong turned from the traditional New Orleans style to a more commercial dance band popular song style. Blesh felt that Armstrong had in fact ceased playing jazz and lamented the "loss to music which has resulted from Louis' public and recording devotion to swing" (Blesh, p. 287). **"Swing"** to many critics of the day meant a departure from traditional "hot music" to an inferior hybridized form of jazz. Blesh was the most outspoken of them all and often wrote in apocalyptic terms; for example, Armstrong had failed to meet the "immemorial need of his own race to find a Moses to lead it out of Egypt" (p. 258). Eventually a record producer and broadcaster as well as a writer, he went to Dartmouth College and in 1944 settled in New York as jazz critic for the *New York Herald Tribune.* He wrote several books and became the leading authority on the subject of ragtime music, which he almost single-handedly revived.

"Blow Satchmo." By **Dave** and Iola **Brubeck;** rec. September 12, 1961, in New York City by **Louis Armstrong and the All Stars** with pianist Dave Brubeck and guests; CD #50. "Blow Satchmo" is a brief ensemble number from the jazz oratorio ***The Real Ambassadors.*** See additional comments on "Cultural Exchange."

"Blue Again." By Dorothy Fields and Jimmy McHugh; rec. April 28, 1931, in Chicago by Louis Armstrong and His Orchestra; CDs #14 and #48. The opening of this popular song (which is reminiscent of Armstrong's 1928 "West End Blues" cadenza) served as a model for both **Bunny Berigan**'s (1937) and **Dizzy Gillespie**'s (1956) introductions to "I Can't Get Started." The orchestra basically stays in the background, as Armstrong sings artfully just behind the beat and plays an inventive repeated single note solo, eventually ending with a dramatic assent to high "C." Gary Giddins reports that this is the recording that inspired jazz giant Gil Evans to become a musician (1988, p. 126).

Blue Five. See **Clarence Williams' Blue Five.**

"Blue Moon." By Richard Rodgers and Lorenz Hart; rec. July, 4, 1957, in Newport, Rhode Island, by **Louis Armstrong and the All Stars;** CD #43. Many have recorded this pensive 1934 song (e.g., Mel Tormé in 1949), but Armstrong did not get around to it until his putative fifty-seventh **birthday** concert at the **Newport Jazz Festival.**

Blue Note. Although the term refers to the slightly lowered third, fifth, or seventh degree of the scale used in blues and related music, it has also been used as the name of a record company founded in New York in 1939 and of nightclubs in Chicago, New York, Paris, and elsewhere. Of these clubs, the one in Chicago is the oldest, having hosted Doc Evans, **Muggsy Spanier,** and others in the 1940s. It was Count Basie's unofficial headquarters from 1949 to 1958. Armstrong was a frequent attraction here in the 1940s and early 1950s.

"Blue Skies." By **Irving Berlin;** rec. August, 1945, in Los Angeles by Louis Armstrong and His Orchestra; CD #49. Armstrong here pairs up memorably with **Frank Sinatra** on this Armed Forces Radio Service broadcast.

"Blue Turning Grey Over You." By **Thomas "Fats" Waller** and Andy Razaf; rec. February 1, 1930, in New York City by Louis Armstrong and His Orchestra and April 27, 1955, in New York City by **Louis Armstrong and the All Stars;** CD #56. This song was a hit the first time around, and Armstrong revisited it on the *Satch Plays Fats* album. On the second time around a quarter of a century later, he takes a slower tempo, using a straight mute. After the vocal, producer **George Avakian** experimented successfully with splicing in a solo from another take—a new technique in its day. See additional comments on "Ain't Misbehavin'."

"Blue Yodel No. 9." By **Jimmie Rodgers;** rec. July 16, 1930, in Hollywood with the composer and pianist **Lil Armstrong;** CDs #12 and #36. This recording represents several landmarks for Armstrong: his first **crossover** (a term that had not yet been invented and a practice that he pioneered), his first in California (where he had just arrived to be the featured performer at Frank **Sebastian's New Cotton Club**), his last as a blues accompanist (in a long series that he began in 1924 with **Ma Rainey**), and his last with Lil Hardin Armstrong (his second wife). The music itself is a landmark as well. Rodgers starts off this ninth in a series of "Blue Yodels" with a quote from "The Bridwell Blues," in tribute to Armstrong's visceral playing on a 1926 recording of this number. On "Blue Yodel No. 9" Armstrong provides an exquisitely restless trumpet commentary throughout.

"Blueberry Hill." By Al Lewis, Larry Stock, and Vincent Rose; rec. on September 6, 1949, in New York City with the Gordon Jenkins Orchestra and Choir; CDs #2, #4, #14, #16, #20, #23, #28, #32, #39, #40, #46, #57, #59, and #61. Armstrong's recording of this 1941 Gene Autry song made the ***Billboard* charts** in November 1949. Fats Domino later covered it with great success in 1956.

"Blues Are Brewing, The." By Eddie DeLange and Louis Alter; rec. October 17, 1946, in Los Angeles by Louis Armstrong and His Orchestra; CD #12. Five weeks earlier Armstrong had recorded this number with vocalist **Billie Holiday** for the sound track of the 1947 **movie *New Orleans.***

"Blues for Bass." By **Arvell Shaw;** rec. January 21, 1955, live at the Crescendo Club in Los Angeles by **Louis Armstrong and the All Stars;** CD #6. This was a feature number for the All Stars bassist who was also the composer.

"Blues for Yesterday." By Les Carr; rec. September 6, 1946, in Los Angeles by Louis Armstrong and His **Hot Seven;** CDs #12, #21, and #47. Right around the time of the filming of ***New Orleans*** in 1946, Armstrong and a small group of players from the film recorded this and several other numbers ("Blues in the South," "Sugar," and "I Want a Little Girl") at a session organized by his friend **Leonard Feather,** who plays the piano here.

"Blues in the Night." By **Harold Arlen** and **Johnny Mercer;** rec. October 14, 1957, in Los Angeles with the **Oscar Peterson** Quartet; CD #37. Armstrong added this fine song to his repertory not long after it was written in 1941, but he did not record it memorably until getting together with Oscar Peterson. Here Peterson and guitarist Herb Ellis provide an especially elegant backing for Armstrong's brief solo toward the end. In general, on this song and others from the *Louis Armstrong Meets Oscar Peterson* album, Armstrong does more singing than trumpet playing. Peterson proves to be a marvelous collaborator, sensitive in the same way Armstrong had been in accompanying blues singers in the 1920s.

"Blues in the South." By William Johnstone and Les Carr; rec. September 6, 1946, in Los Angeles by Louis Armstrong and His **Hot Seven;** CDs #12 and #47. See comments on "Blues for Yesterday."

"Blues Stampede, The." By Irving Mills; rec. April 21, 1927, in Chicago by **Jimmy Bertrand**'s Washboard Wizards. While under exclusive contract to **Okeh Records,** Armstrong surreptitiously cut four sides with Jimmy Bertrand for **Vocalion Records** (and immediately after that another four with **Johnny Dodds**'s Black Bottom Stompers). Trying hard not to sound like himself and thus be detected, Armstrong governed his volume, stayed away from high notes, and in general attempted to disguise himself as a lesser player. His model may have been **Joe Smith,** the preferred sideman of blues singer **Bessie Smith,** who did not want to be outshone by an accompanist. As for this particular cut, leader Bertrand did play a real washboard, substituted for drums. (At this early stage in the development of studio technology, it was nearly impossible to include drums in recordings. Most drummers solved the problem with wood blocks.)

Boat Nose. See **nicknames.**

"Body and Soul." By Johnny Green, Edward Heyman, Robert Sour, and Frank Eyton; rec. on October 9, 1930, in Los Angeles with Louis Armstrong and His **Sebastian New Cotton Club** Orchestra; CDs #6, #8, #28, #40, #42, #44, #52, and #54. This is one of the many commercial songs that Armstrong introduced into the jazz repertory. In later years (e.g., a 1956 recording with **Louis Armstrong and the All Stars**), he relaxed the tempo of this piece and heated up the already fervent ending.

"Boff Boff." By **Coleman Hawkins;** rec. on November 30, 1947, live at Symphony Hall, Boston, by **Louis Armstrong and the All Stars;** CD #54. This early All Star number features Armstrong's favorite drummer, **Sid Catlett.**

Bojangles. See **Robinson, Bill "Bojangles."**

Bolden, Charles Joseph "Buddy" (1877–1931). Armstrong was somewhat in awe of this early jazz cornet player and bandleader. "Old Buddy Bolden blew so hard that I used to wonder if I would ever have enough lung power to fill one of those cornets," he recalled in his 1954 **autobiography** (p. 23). Informally Armstrong also said that he felt Bolden blew his brains out, which was at least figuratively true. After performing in and around New Orleans for not much more than ten years, he was institutionalized in 1907 for mental deterioration and remained in custody for the rest of his life. He was a revered performer who played with an emotionally charged style and who influenced many subsequent New Orleans cornetists. Michael Ondaatje's 1976 novel *Coming Through Slaughter* is based on Bolden's life.

Bolton, "Redhead" "Happy" (c. 1900–1928). When the preteen Armstrong dropped out of school, he co-formed a vocal quartet with childhood pals "Happy" Bolton, "Big Nose" Sidney, and "Little Mack." They performed on the streets of New Orleans and then passed a hat. During their approximately two years together, they earned lots of pennies from passersby and substantially developed both their musical and acting talents. In their repertory were such songs as "Swanee River" and "Mr. Moon, Won't You Please Shine Down on Me?" Once a crowd had gathered, Armstrong might do a jig, and "Little Mack" would offer somersaults. Armstrong and Bolton also had a funny little skit in which Louis played a suitor and on bended knee sang of his love for his "girlfriend." Bolton was replaced later in the vocal quartet by Georgie Grey and went on to be a jazz drummer.

"Boog It." By **Cab Calloway,** Buck Ram, and Jack Palmer; rec. April 10, 1940, in New York City with the **Mills Brothers** and guitarist Norman Brown. See comments on "Carry Me Back to Old Virginny."

books. In addition to **autobiographies** and **biographies,** there are several kinds of books about and even by Armstrong. One of the most valuable is Hans Westerberg's *Boy from New Orleans: A Discography of Louis "Satchmo" Armstrong* (1981), a painstakingly thorough treatment that tells you everything you ever wanted to know, and then some, about Armstrong's recordings. Klaus Stratemann does the same for Armstrong's many films and **television** appearances in *Louis Armstrong on the Screen* (1996). *Louis Armstrong: A Cultural Legacy* (1994), edited by Marc Miller, is the 248-page catalog for a major exhibition of Armstrong artifacts that toured the United States from 1994 to 1997, and it contains many illustrations plus five scholarly essays. Michael Cogswell does something similar for the **Louis Armstrong House and Archives** in *Louis Armstrong: The Offstage Story of Satchmo* (2003), which is generously illustrated with materials from this definitive collection. Joshua Berrett's *The Louis Armstrong Companion: Eight Decades of Commentary* (1999) offers a generous selection of Armstrong's previously unpublished writings, other important yet hard-to-find materials, interviews, and contemporary research. In similar fashion, Thomas Brothers's *Louis Armstrong, in His Own Words* (1999) contains writings by Armstrong—nineteen items in all—of previously unpublished letters and autobiographical essays, as well as several not easily accessible magazine articles. Brothers judiciously introduces, arranges, and edits Armstrong's writing. He also takes care to preserve Armstrong's unique capitalizing, italicizing, and punctuating, which are comparable to the expressive inflections in his trumpet playing. For complete bibliographic information on these and other Armstrong books, please see the selected bibliography.

Boone, Lester (1904–1989). Born in Tuskegee, Alabama, this saxophonist and clarinetist made a name for himself in Chicago in 1927, where he hooked up with Armstrong. Boone was in "a Band that really deserved a *whole lot* of *credit* that they *didn't* get. . . . They made some of my finest recordings with me," Armstrong wrote later in **"The Goffin Notebooks"** (Brothers, p. 108). Boone takes a memorable solo on the 1931 "I Got Rhythm." Later in New York he worked in several groups including the **Mills Blue Rhythm Band.** He also put together a band of his own in 1940.

bop. When be**bop** or "bop," as it eventually came to be known, first showed up in the early 1940s, its rhythmic and harmonic complexity, its divergence from **swing** dance style, and its subtext of rebellious politics offended many including Armstrong. Uncharacteristically, he even spoke out. "You get all them weird chords which don't mean nothing . . . and you got no melody to remember and no beat to dance to," he said in the April 7, 1948, issue of ***Down Beat*** (p. 2). He called bop "jujitsu music" and "that modern malice." A ***Metronome*** article in this same vein by George T. Simon ("Bebop's the Easy Way Out, Claims Louis," March 1948) is reprinted in Berrett, 1999, pp. 141–144. Having grown up to please an audience, he could not understand the new aggressive music played by **Dizzy Gillespie,** Charlie Parker, Thelonious Monk, and others. They in turn considered Armstrong passé and, worse, saw him as an "Uncle Tom" who clowned for whites. The live-and-let-live Armstrong soon softened his stance, though, saying diplomatically in the February 21, 1949, issue of ***Time*** (which featured him as a cover story) that "bop is nice to listen to for a while, but not all night" (p. 56). He didn't exactly let go of the matter, however, because in the early 1950s he slyly derided bebopper behavior in a recorded version of "The Whiffenpoof Song," which he dedicated to Gillespie. To his credit, Gillespie took it as the very kind of puckish prank he himself might have played. The two gradually grew to like as well as respect each other. "If it weren't for him, there wouldn't be any of us," Gillespie eventually concluded (Miller, p. 63).

While some of the bop controversy can be attributed to generational differences (after all, Armstrong came up at a time when such militancy would have made his career impossible), the disagreement was exaggerated by Armstrong's manager, **Joe Glaser,** for publicity purposes. For example, the **Institute of Jazz Studies** at Rutgers University has a fascinating "Publicity Manual" from the late 1940s in which Glaser's **Associated Booking Corporation** provides such fill-in-the-blanks copy as the following: "The national jazz controversy, which began in *Time* magazine will be centered in ____ when Louis Armstrong arrives for his ____ [Date Here] concert at ____ [Name of Hall Here]."

"Boppenpoof Song, The." See "Whiffenpoof Song, The."

boppers. See **bop.**

botta e risposta, La. Armstrong and the **All Stars** contribute "Struttin' with Some Barbecue," "That's My Desire," and a boogie-woogie version of "St. Louis Blues" to this comedy named after a highly popular Italian radio quiz show whose name roughly translates as "Tit for Tat." The film tells a convoluted story about the theft and return of a dress. In the process many Roman nightclubs are visited. At one point the congenial and knowledgeable quiz master of "Botta e risposta" is consulted. He is first encountered challenging his studio audience to identify the "King of Jazz," who is of course Armstrong, heard performing behind a curtain. In this as in his other European films, such as ***Kaerlighedens Melodi*** and ***La route du bonheur,*** Armstrong plays the role of a famous visiting entertainer whose performance is the musical high point that begins the denouement. Teatri della Farnesina, 1951; B&W; 90 mins.; Dir. Mario Soldati.

Bottom. Armstrong was dressed in a bright red fireman's suit to play this beloved Shakespearean character in ***Swingin' the Dream,*** a 1939 Rockefeller Center Theater jazz version of Shakespeare's *A Midsummer Night's Dream,* set in Louisiana in the 1890s.

"Bourbon Street Parade." By **Paul Barbarin;** rec. May 24 or 25, 1960, in New York City with the **Dukes of Dixieland;** CD #53. Armstrong fit right in with the Dukes on this traditional number by an old friend of his. See additional comments on "Avalon."

" 'Bout Time." By Richard M. Sherman and Robert B. Sherman; rec. February 27, 1968, in New York City by **Louis Armstrong and the All Stars;** CD #15. This sentimental yet engaging song, written for the **Disney** film *The One and Only, Genuine, Original Family Band,* was one of Armstrong's last recordings, and it comes from the very last album on which he plays the trumpet. Nevertheless, he opens and closes with a rousing solo, and he delivers a mediocre text with playful enthusiasm.

Bowie, Lester (1941–1999). Bowie was considered one of the most original trumpeters, what with his wide vibrato, bending of notes, growls, half-valve effects, and playfully irreverent style. Nevertheless, he, like so many musicians, frequently expressed endless admiration for Armstrong, both for his having virtually created jazz and also for his social impact. Armstrong "was that sort of revolutionary, a true revolutionary," Bowie says in the video ***Satchmo: Louis Armstrong.*** Bowie grew up and learned his craft in St. Louis, then moved in 1965 to Chicago, where he founded the Association for the Advancement of Creative Musicians and cofounded the Art Ensemble of Chicago. He was known for his fusion of jazz, rock, and gospel music. His witty style can be heard in "Jazz Death?" (1968) and "The Great Pretender" (1981).

"Boy from New Orleans." By Bob Roberts, Bill Katz, and Bob Thiele; rec. May 29, 1970, in New York City with a studio orchestra and chorus conducted by Oliver Nelson; CD #31. By the time of this his next-to-last album, Armstrong is no longer playing the trumpet, but he still sings with ease, including this autobiographical **swing** tune.

Boy from New Orleans, The. This documentary film (titled after a song about Armstrong by Bob Roberts, Bill Katz, and Bob Thiele) was put together from footage shot in preparation for an October 29, 1970, benefit concert in London. Armstrong's longtime friend and colleague

Bing Crosby provides some narration, as Armstrong is seen strolling around London, jamming with **All Star** trombonist **Tyree Glenn** in the dressing room, and in rehearsal. In the concert itself, Armstrong is accompanied by either a large British concert orchestra or a small group including Glenn. CBS, 1970; color; 53 mins.; Dir. Phil Schultz; Prod. Finley Hunt.

"Brahms' Lullaby." By Johannes Brahms and an anonymous poet from the German anthology *Des Knaben Wunderhorn;* rec. on or shortly after September 11, 1946, in Los Angeles with a small ensemble. Brahms's familiar lullaby was recorded for, but not used in, the 1947 **movie *New Orleans*** with **Billie Holiday.**

brass band. Brass bands have a venerable place in American music, and after the Civil War they became a vital part of African American communities. By Armstrong's day, they consisted of somewhere between eight and fourteen instruments (cornets, trombones, alto or baritone horn, tuba, and both snare and bass drums with cymbal attached) and were most often associated with funerals. They played somber music on the way to a burial and lively music on the way back. Brass bands also provided music for dances, parades, and picnics.

Armstrong grew up hearing such music. By the age of five he was marching, dancing, and singing with other youngsters as they followed brass bands in parades, a practice known as second lining. It must have been thrilling, since the memory was still vividly with him thirty years later. He wrote in the first volume of his **autobiography:** "I was so crazy about **Perez'** brass band [the **Onward Brass Band**], I would follow them on the streets when they paraded with the Elks and Moose and other societies" (1936, p. 15). The earliest surviving photo of Armstrong dates from 1913, when he stands proudly with the **Colored Waif's Home** Brass Band. Five years later he reached a kind of nirvana when he joined **Oscar Celestin**'s sartorially splendid **Tuxedo Brass Band,** in which many famous musicians like **Jimmie Noone** and **Johnny Dodds** had played. The Onward and Tuxedo bands coexisted in an active and highly competitive environment along with others such as the Eureka, the Excelsior, and the Reliance.

Brecht, Bertolt. See **"Mack the Knife."**

Bricktop. See **Smith, Ada "Bricktop."**

"Bridwell Blues, The." By Nolan Welsh and Richard M. Jones; rec. June 16, 1928, in Chicago with vocalist Welsh and pianist Jones; CDs #36 and #48. Welsh, one of the few male vocalists whom Armstrong accompanied, here sings (perhaps autobiographically) of the infamous Illinois prison, and Armstrong takes a fine, earthy solo. "Bridwell Blues" was later quoted by **Jimmie Rodgers** in "Blue Yodel No. 9."

Briggs, Arthur (1899–1991). A cousin of **Peter Briggs,** this Charleston-born trumpeter was one of the first African American jazzmen to relocate in Europe. He was well respected and living comfortably in Paris when Armstrong hired him for his European groups in the early 1930s. When in 1934 the exhausted Armstrong, suffering from **lip problems,** took a few months off in Paris, he hung out with Briggs and other African American expatriates—**Josephine Baker,** Bricktop (**Ada Smith**), and Bobby Jones. Briggs was a founding member of the **Hot Club de France** (1932), and he performed frequently with **Django Reinhardt** and Stephane Grappelli. Briggs also led his own groups until the 1960s, then turned to teaching.

Briggs, Peter (b. c. 1904). Born in Charleston (as was his cousin **Arthur Briggs**), this tuba player first made a name for himself in Chicago, performing with the **Carroll Dickerson** Orchestra in 1926 and remaining when the ensemble became Louis Armstrong's Stompers the following year. It was Briggs, along with drummer **Baby Dodds,** who made the Armstrong **Hot Five** into the **Hot Seven,** and he can be heard in "Weary Blues" (1927). In 1929 Briggs moved to New York with Armstrong, and he played with others as well (e.g., **Jelly Roll Morton**). He later took up the double bass, then retired from the music business in the 1940s.

"Broken Busted Blues." By Edgar Dowell; rec. January 7, 1925, in New York City with vocalist **Clara Smith** and pianist **Fletcher Henderson;** CD #36. Billed as "Queen of the Moaners," Clara Smith spent most of her life in the shadow of **Bessie Smith.** However, she was a worthy exponent of the blues, and as can be heard here, she worked memorably with Armstrong.

"Brother Bill" (a.k.a. "Me and Brother Bill"). By Louis Armstrong; rec. April 25, 1939, in New York City by Louis Armstrong and His Orchestra; CDs #5, #6, #49, and #60. For a while this novelty number about a mock-frightening hunting trip was one of Armstrong's most requested tunes. The cute recording of it made with the **All Stars** live at the Crescendo Club in Los Angeles on January 21, 1955 (CD #6), is surpassed only by the hilarious duet version made with **Bing Crosby** in New York City on July 5, 1960.

Brown, Jewel (b. 1937). This talented singer joined the **All Stars** in 1961 to replace vocalist **Velma Middleton,** and she stayed with the group until 1968. Brown can be both heard and seen in the 1962 film ***Goodyear Jazz Concert: Louis Armstrong,*** in which she does a sensuous "Jerry" and nearly steals the show on "When the Saints Go Marching In." In the 1965 short film ***Solo,*** she sings an uptempo rhythm and blues version of "My Man." On a typical All Stars concert program, Brown would do two or three numbers, such as "Bill Bailey," "Lover, Come Back to Me," and "Can't Help Lovin' Dat Man."

Brown, Lawrence (1907–1988). When Armstrong opened in July 1930 at Frank **Sebastian's New Cotton Club** in Culver City in west Los Angeles, he was delighted with the house band and in particular trombonist Lawrence Brown (as well as then drummer, later vibraphonist, **Lionel Hampton**). After a brief association and several recordings, Brown, the son of a clergyman, was fired by Armstrong's scurrilous manager **Johnny Collins** for failing to make an Easter Sunday rehearsal. Brown moved on to the **Duke Ellington** orchestra, with which he was mainly associated for the rest of his life.

Brown v. Board of Education. In this famous 1954 school **segregation** case, the U.S. Supreme Court reversed the 1896

Plessy v. Ferguson "separate but equal" decision, finding that separate educational facilities were inherently unequal. The decision gave impetus to the growing **civil rights** movement, leading to the Montgomery bus boycott during the following year and the 1957 **Little Rock** crisis, in which Armstrong played a significant role.

Browne, Scoville "Toby" (1915–1994). This reed man was born in Atlanta and moved to Chicago, where he worked with Armstrong in the 1930s. His mellow tone and fluent technique can be heard on "Basin Street Blues" (1933). Browne toured with Armstrong and later vouched for his fluency in reading music, the likable character of his third wife (**Alpha**), the skill of his manager (**Joe Glaser**), the reports that Armstrong played as many as 250 high "Cs" in a row, the haphazard way in which they made records, and over all the great fun they had (Collier, 1983, passim). Browne later attended the Chicago Musical College, then, after serving in World War II, worked with such groups as **Teddy Wilson**'s and **Lionel Hampton**'s and led his own from 1948 to 1952 and 1958 to 1960.

Brubeck, Dave (b. 1920). The great pianist, composer, and bandleader crossed paths with the great trumpeter, singer, composer, and bandleader several times. For example, on one memorable occasion (July 14, 1956) Armstrong, freshly returned from a successful State Department–sponsored tour of Africa, participated in a concert produced by **George Avakian** at Lewisohn Stadium in New York City. Brubeck's "intellectual-experimental" jazz (so-called by the *New York Times* reporter on p. A64 the following day) started the program, and Armstrong, with **Leonard Bernstein** conducting the orchestra, ended it. In 1960 both artists had their southern United States tours canceled once the promoters discovered that their bands were racially mixed. It was this and other incidents like it, along with a general climate of racism, that influenced Brubeck and his lyricist wife Iola to write ***The Real Ambassadors,*** a kind of jazz oratorio that focuses on Armstrong himself. Although **Joe Glaser** (who managed both Armstrong and Brubeck) was unenthusiastic, the work was recorded in New York on September 12 and 13, 1961, and reprised the following year in September at the Monterey Jazz Festival. Brubeck, a classically trained pianist who studied composition with Darius Milhaud and Arnold Schoenberg, is the composer of such jazz classics as "Blue Rondo à la Turk," as well as several ballets, oratorios, cantatas, and piano pieces. The Dave Brubeck Quartet, which many consider the epitome of cool jazz, was popular on college campuses from 1951 to 1967 and had a memorable reunion in 1976.

Bruehl, Anton (1879–1945). Armstrong's favorite portrait was taken by this high-society New York photographer, and it first appeared in the November 1935 issue of ***Vanity Fair.*** The photo depicts him with trumpet in one hand and handkerchief in the other and is dimly lit and shot from below with celestial results. Armstrong liked the photo so much that in 1948 he commissioned the up-and-coming African American painter **Calvin Bailey** to make an oil version, which hung in Armstrong's living room until his death. Both the photo and the oil version of it continue to turn up, the latter on the cover of Miller's 1994 book and the former on the cover of Bergreen's 1997 book.

"Buddy Bolden Blues." By **Jelly Roll Morton;** rec. on or shortly after September 11, 1946, in Los Angeles with a small ensemble for the 1947 film ***New Orleans.***

"Buddy's Habit." By Arnett Nelson and Charles Straight; rec. between October 5 and 15, 1923, in Chicago, with **King Oliver**'s Jazz Band. This recording features Armstrong on the slide whistle. See additional comments on "Alligator Hop."

"Bugle Blues." By Bobby Williams; rec. January 30, 1951, live at the Pasadena Civic Auditorium by **Louis Armstrong and the All Stars;** CD #6. Armstrong thought very highly of Williams, whom he met shortly after moving to Chicago in 1922. However, it bothered Armstrong that Williams liked to play cornet with just one hand, "because where 'I' came from, the good old timers wouldn't *dare* to *insult* a good piece of music by holding the horn in one hand to play," he later wrote (Brothers, p. 76). "Bugle Blues" was composed around 1920, when Williams was in the army, and it was his feature number at the **Sunset Cafe.**

"Bugle Call Rag." By Jack Pettis, Billy Meyers, and Elmer Schoebel; rec. April 26 or 27, 1950, in New York City by **Louis Armstrong and the All Stars;** CD #8. This number incorporates elements of W.C. Handy's "Ole Miss Blues" and was a feature number for drummer **Cozy Cole.** Because of the new ten-inch LP technology, one can get a good idea of what Armstrong's contemporaneous concerts were like.

Burns, Ken (b. 1953). On January 8, 2001, PBS aired the first of Ken Burns's ten-part series called ***Jazz.*** Reflecting on production in an on-air interview, Burns had this to say: "I think the person who became our talisman, the sort of pole star for the series, just as Abraham Lincoln was in *The Civil War* [1989] series and **Jackie Robinson** was in *Baseball* [1994], was Louis Armstrong. . . . [We] discovered quite early in this process that this wasn't just a guy with a handkerchief and a winning smile, with one foot in a kind of uncomfortable minstrelsy and transformer of popular songs like 'Hello Dolly!,' but in fact the most important person in music. And I quite consciously did not say 'jazz' music. He is the most important person in music in America in the 20th century. . . . He single-handedly turned jazz into a soloist's art by the way he played his instrument, in a way that no one had ever played before. Then he turned around and transformed the way that everyone sang in America, utterly liberating American instrumental playing and American vocalizing in a way that no one had done beforehand. He stands as a pioneer."

Burr, Henry. See **"Louis Armstrong and Opera."**

Bushkin, Joe (b. 1916). Armstrong's elite **All Stars** sextet lasted, with relatively few personnel changes, from 1947 to 1971, and Bushkin was one of the six pianists. He filled the brief gap in the spring of 1953 between **Marty Napoleon** and **Billy Kyle.** Bushkin can be heard on the recordings of "April in Portugal" and "Ramona" in April, after which he went on the ill-fated Armstrong/**Benny Goodman** joint tour. Bushkin had a distinguished career before joining Armstrong, having accompanied **Billie Holiday** on "No Regrets" and "Summertime" (both 1936) and "Oh! Look at Me Now" (1941) with the Tommy Dorsey Orchestra. Bushkin formed his own groups in the 1950s and 1960s, toured with **Bing Crosby** in the 1970s, and remained active in New York in the 1980s.

Butterbeans and Susie. See **Edwards, Jody, and Susie Hawthorne.**

Butterfield, Charles William "Billy" (1917–1988). Unlike many trumpeters in Armstrong's thrall, Butterfield actually worked with the master on several occasions. His fine playing can be heard on "Blueberry Hill" (1949) and "You Won't Be Satisfied" (1946). The latter recording also involved **Ella Fitzgerald,** and Armstrong said of it: "[Butterfield] knows how to blow his horn right" (Berrett, 1999, p. 142). However, we all know this for ourselves, for it is Butterfield who plays one of the most famous trumpet solos ever, "Star Dust," recorded in 1940 with Artie Shaw. After a distinguished career, Butterfield settled in Florida in the 1960s, but he continued to work with the World's Greatest Jazz Band (1968–1972) and as a freelancer into the 1980s.

"By the Waters of Minnetonka." By Thurlow Lieurance and J.M. Cavanass; not recorded. This once popular song was the first that Armstrong rehearsed with the **Fletcher Henderson** band when he arrived at the **Roseland Ballroom** in New York in September 1924. "I had the 3rd Trumpet part—And was 'Thrilled at playing a part in such an All Star Band as Fletcher Henderson's Band," Armstrong later recalled (Brothers, p. 93). See additional comments on "Alabamy Bound."

"Bye and Bye." By Harry Pease, Ed G. Nelson, and Larry Vincent; rec. January 23, 1925, in New York City by **Fletcher Henderson** and His Orchestra; CD #53. Here Armstrong sings enthusiastically with the band, which doubles as a choir. Naturally, not every Armstrong recording was "a gassah" (an expression he often used), and here's a good example. Armstrong dominates this recording, as trombonist **J.C. Higginbotham** almost does on a December 18, 1939, remake with Louis Armstrong and His Orchestra. "Bye and Bye" received better treatment from the **All Stars** in New York City on November 3, 1964.

"Bye Bye Blues." By Fred Hamm, David Bennett, Bert Lowe, and Chauncey Gray; rec. July 5, 1960, in New York City by Louis Armstrong, vocalist **Bing Crosby,** and a studio band and choir conducted by Billy May. Armstrong and Crosby did many duets together, including this popular song from 1930, which they put on their *Bing and Satchmo* LP. Unfortunately, it did not get onto the CD reissue.

C

C above C above High C. In this provocative 1997 play, Ishmael Reed (b. 1938) takes on the subject of Armstrong's reaction to the September 1957 school desegregation crisis in **Little Rock.** Reed's Armstrong takes on both President **Dwight Eisenhower** and **J. Edgar Hoover,** and he contrasts two of Armstrong's wives, **Lil Hardin** and **Lucille Wilson,** with Mamie Eisenhower, whose husband has an affair with Kay Summersby. Excerpts of an interview with Reed appear in Berrett, 1999, pp. 246–250.

" 'C' Jam Blues." By **Duke Ellington:** rec. July 1, 1960, live at the **Newport Jazz Festival** by **Louis Armstrong and the All Stars;** CDs #20 and #54. This number, which had been in the All Stars' repertory from its very first year (e.g., it's on the live Symphony Hall, Boston, recording made November 30, 1947), became a feature for clarinetist **Barney Bigard,** who for fourteen years played in the composer's orchestra. (When supplied with lyrics, this number becomes "Duke's Place.")

"Cabaret." By John Kander and Fred Ebb; rec. August 25, 1966, in New York City by **Louis Armstrong and the All Stars;** CDs #2, #4, #16, #28, #40, #57, #59, #61, and #62. It is little wonder that this was a big hit for Armstrong since its mood and lyrics fit his life and attitude so neatly. He immediately took it into the All Stars repertory and played it to the nation on the *Ed Sullivan Show.*

"Cabin in the Pines." See **"There's a Cabin in the Pines."**

Cabin in the Sky. Ethel Waters and **Eddie Anderson** star in this excellent film based on the 1940 Broadway musical, in which heaven and hell fight for the soul of Little Joe Jackson. Armstrong plays one of the helpers of Lucifer, Jr., contributing a short trumpet flourish and some lively dialogue in an ensemble scene with Mantan Moreland, **Willie Best,** and Rex Ingram. Armstrong's character takes credit for the idea of offering the apple to Eve in the Garden of Eden. He is also distinguished from the other devils by his jive talk, for example, ending his sentences with "man." Other musical sequences include **Lena Horne, Duke Ellington,** the Hall Johnson Choir, and of course, Ethel Waters. Unfortunately, the Armstrong–Lena Horne performance of "Ain't It the Truth?" was cut from the final version, but, according to Klaus Stratemann, it was once included in Pete

Smith's short 1946 film ***Studio Visit*** (p. 143). M-G-M, 1943; sepia; 100 mins.; Dir. **Vincente Minnelli.**

"Cain and Abel." By T. Fensteck and A. Loman; rec. May 1, 1940, in New York City by Louis Armstrong and His Orchestra. Armstrong treated everything with care, even this novelty number on which he plays one of his thrilling repeated note solos. There is also some impressive drumming by **Sid Catlett.**

"Cake Walking Babies from Home." By **Clarence Williams,** Chris Smith, and Henry Troy; rec. December 22, 1924, in New York City with the Red Onion Jazz Babies; CDs #14, #35, #36, and #48. Armstrong was most able to unfurl all his musical sails in a small ensemble, especially when challenged by a master such as **Sidney Bechet,** who here trades his clarinet for a soprano sax. After the so-so vocal duet by **Alberta Hunter** and Clarence Todd, the two instrumentalists engage in a friendly competition in the last two choruses. Bechet "launches a volley of eighth-note arpeggios with a vigor and confidence that leaves his bandmates . . . in the background" (Harker, 2003, p. 150). Armstrong and Bechet recorded the tune again two weeks later (January 8, 1925) with vocalist **Eva Taylor,** and this time Armstrong overpowered everyone with his inventive, virtuosic playing, particularly in the **stop-time** passage toward the end.

Caldwell, Albert W. "Happy" (1903–1978). Caldwell, who started on the clarinet and soon began playing the tenor sax, was well established by the time he recorded with Armstrong in 1929. Their March 5 recording of "Knockin' a Jug" (with trombonist **Jack Teagarden,** pianist **Joe Sullivan,** guitarist **Eddie Lang,** and drummer **Kaiser Marshall**) can be said to be the first jazz recording in which black and white musicians shared musical material equally. However, there had been isolated incidents of interracial recording as early as 1923, when **Jelly Roll Morton** went into the studio with the New Orleans Rhythm Kings. In any case, Caldwell (who also worked with Morton in 1939) went on to form the Happy Pals in 1941 and work with a wide variety of musicians such as trombonist and singer Clyde Bernhardt (1972–1973).

Callender, George Sylvester "Red" (1916–1992). The versatile double bass and tuba player worked with Armstrong on the film ***New Orleans*** (1947). Unfortunately, because of Senator Joseph McCarthy's shadow spreading over Hollywood, much of their music was either cut or relegated to incidental music. Eventually not even an interracial handshake survived the cutting room. Nevertheless, Callender's genial contribution can be heard on recordings such as "Where the Blues Were Born in New Orleans" and "Mahogany Hall Stomp," made in October 1946, just after the filming. Callender's long career included work with Erroll Garner, Art Tatum, and many others. He was also an accomplished arranger and composer.

Calloway, Cabell "Cab" (1907–1994). Only **Duke Ellington** and Cab Calloway were as famous as Armstrong in the 1930s. The three were like comets whose paths now and then crossed. Armstrong and Calloway both worked in the 1929 revue ***Connie's Hot Chocolates,*** both appeared with great success at the **Cotton Club** in the 1930s, and both were featured in the 1937 M-G-M cartoon ***Swing Wedding,*** based on Calloway's 1931 hit record "Minnie the Moocher." All three toured England and the Continent separately in the early 1930s. Compared to Ellington, Calloway's performance style was more similar to Armstrong's in that he put on a show in addition to playing music. Dressed in his signature white tuxedo, he cultivated an active stage presence, rolling his eyes and smiling broadly. Called the "Hi-de-ho-Man" because of his interpretation of his own famous song "Minnie the Moocher," his singing, and especially his **scat singing,** owed a great deal to Armstrong. In the late 1940s, Calloway turned to musical theater, playing Sportin' Life in *Porgy and Bess* (a role that Gershwin had modeled on him) and doing other shows. He was active in the 1980s and played himself in the movie *The Blues Brothers.*

"Camp Meeting Blues." By **Joe Oliver;** rec. October 16, 1923, in Chicago with King Oliver's Jazz Band. See comments on "Alligator Hop."

"Can Anyone Explain?" By Bennie Benjamin and George David Weiss; rec. August 25, 1950, in New York City with vocalist **Ella Fitzgerald** and the **Sy Oliver** Orchestra. Armstrong and Fitzgerald worked together often before recording this 1950 Ames Brothers hit. See additional comments on "April in Paris."

"Canal Street Blues." By **Joe Oliver** and Louis Armstrong; rec. April 5 or 6, 1923, in Richmond, Indiana, with King Oliver's Creole Jazz Band; CDs #8, #35, and #52. In this very early recording, there are no Armstrong solos but a graceful duet with Oliver to some lyrical clarinet counterpoint by **Johnny Dodds.** Armstrong kept the number in his repertory, though, and revisited it in the studio on January 25, 1957, for his *Satchmo: A Musical Autobiography* (CD #52), this time shining out over the ensemble (which had been enhanced by auxiliary trumpeter Yank Lawson and an organist). Armstrong still had more to say in a final recording made August 25, 1966, in New York with the **All Stars.**

"Can't Help Lovin' Dat Man." By Jerome Kern and Oscar Hammerstein II; rec. June 5, 1965, live at the Palais des Sports in Paris by **Louis Armstrong and the All Stars;** CD #2. This was one of All Stars vocalist **Jewel Brown**'s feature numbers.

"Can't We Be Friends?" By Paul James and Kay Swift; rec. August 16, 1956, in Los Angeles with vocalist **Ella Fitzgerald** and the **Oscar Peterson** Quartet; CDs #9 and #28. This 1929 song gets a definitive performance by Armstrong and his close friend. See additional comments on "April in Paris."

Capone, Al (1899–1947). The famous gangster who led organized crime in Chicago in the 1920s and 1930s either owned, supplied, or "protected" several nightclubs in the Chicago area where Armstrong performed. Both Armstrong and, more important, his manager, **Joe Glaser,** got along well with Capone, who could be charming. In 1966 Armstrong looked back on the association: "Al Capone with his army . . . used to come to enjoy our music. He was a nice little cute fat boy—young—like some professor who had just come out of college to teach or something" (Meryman, 1966, p. 36). Capone and his fellow mobsters influenced Armstrong's career to the very end. Because of Glaser's obligations, Armstrong frequently had to perform at nightclubs owned by hoodlums. Glaser's name came up again and again in **FBI** files and congressional hearings. When Glaser died in 1969, mob lawyer Sidney Korshak took complete control of the **Associated Booking Corporation.**

Cara, Mancy. See **Carr, Mancy "Peck."**

"Careless Love Blues." By W.C. Handy; rec. May 26, 1925, in New York City with vocalist **Bessie Smith,** trombonist **Charlie Green,** and pianist Fred Longshaw; CD #36. Although Bessie Smith seems to have preferred trumpeter **Joe Smith** (no relation) as an accompanist, the best of her nearly 200 recordings were made with Armstrong, who gave her some beneficial competition. "Everything I did with her, I *like,*" Armstrong later told ***Life*** magazine's Richard Meryman (1971, p. 32).

Carey, Thomas "Mutt" (1891–1948). All through his life Armstrong admired "this little cornet player" who "played all them pretty little things" back in New Orleans circa 1914 (***Down Beat,*** April 7, 1948, p. 2). Carey began on drums and played guitar and alto horn before settling on the cornet. In 1917 he went on tour with **Kid Ory** (after Armstrong declined the invitation). In 1946 Carey worked with Armstrong in the film ***New Orleans*** but unfortunately on segments that were dropped from the final version. Carey led several groups of his own, too. In fact, his New Yorkers was a main force in the late 1940s revival of traditional jazz. Armstrong's high opinion of Carey was reciprocated. Carey recalled that when in 1914 Armstrong had just gotten out of the **Colored Waif's Home,** he sat in with the Kid Ory Band. "Now at that time I was the Blues King of New Orleans," Carey told an interviewer, "and when Louis played that day he played more blues than I ever heard in my life" (Shapiro and Hentoff, 1955, p. 46).

Carmichael, Hoagland Howard "Hoagy" (1899–1981). When this already fairly accomplished songwriter, singer, and pianist (in the company of **Bix Beiderbecke**) first heard Armstrong in the summer of 1923, he remembered (in his autobiography *The Stardust Road,* 1946): "I dropped my cigarette and gulped my drink. . . . Something as unutterably stirring as that deserved to be heard by the world" (p. 53). The two eventually developed a memorable working relationship. For example, in 1931 they share vocals on the first recording of Carmichael's "Rockin' Chair." During the same year, Armstrong made inspired recordings of Carmichael's "Star Dust," "Georgia on My Mind," and "Lazy River." Later, Armstrong made the definitive recordings of both "Ev'ntide" (1936) and "Jubilee" (1938). On August 13, 1947, Carmichael was in the audience at **Billy Berg's Swing Club** in Hollywood when his friend's **All Stars** officially debuted. He was also there on July 3, 1970 (the eve of Armstrong's unofficial birthday) to preside over an enormous party (some 6,700 fans) at the Shrine Auditorium in Los Angeles. In between and after, Carmichael of course had his own stellar career, appearing in fourteen films (e.g., *To Have and Have Not,* 1944), working in radio and television, and writing a second autobiography (*Sometimes I Wonder,* 1965).

Carnegie Hall concert. Just as **Benny Goodman** had brought big band **swing** music to that cathedral of classical music Carnegie Hall (on January 16, 1938), so did Armstrong bring traditional jazz on February 8, 1947. Although the promoters wanted to have him lead a small ensemble, Armstrong had become used to working with a big band. A compromise was reached whereby he played the first half of the show with a small group and the second half with the big one. The event was that rarity, both a critical and popular success. And everyone (or nearly) preferred the small group, that is, the kind in which Louis got his start a quarter of a century earlier. The event also signaled the imminent demise of the big band movement. Armstrong's subsequent triumph with only a small jazz band at the May 17, 1947, **Town Hall concert** solidified the new direction in his career and tapped the shovel on the big band grave.

"Carolina Stomp." By Rube Bloom and Bartley Costello; rec. October 21, 1925, in New York City by **Fletcher Henderson** and His Orchestra. One of Armstrong's early achievements was to extend the upward range of his instrument. High "C" was plenty for most, but on this tune he goes up to a "D" (and would continue far beyond that in the near future). Armstrong can also be heard here and elsewhere trying to get the Henderson Orchestra to **swing,** and in some measure he succeeded before leaving for Chicago a month after this recording. See additional comments on "Alabamy Bound."

Carr, Mancy "Peck." Born in Charleston, West Virginia, around the turn of the century, banjoist and guitarist Peck Carr (often misspelled "Cara") met Armstrong during the 1920s in the **Carroll Dickerson** Orchestra in Chicago, and he joined Armstrong's **Hot Four,** recording memorably with **Lillie Delk Christian,** example, "Too Busy" (1928). Since early recording techniques precluded drums, Carr's contribution was especially prominent. After Carr made more recordings with Armstrong in New York in 1929, he returned to Chicago, then moved back to West Virginia.

Carroll Dickerson Orchestra. See **Dickerson, Carroll.**

"Carry Me Back to Old Virginny." By James Bland; rec. April 7, 1937, in New York City with the **Mills Brothers.** The Mills Brothers were already popular by the time they first worked with Armstrong. **Joe Glaser** managed both acts, and they also had **Decca** recordings in common, so their teaming up seemed natural. In the later 1930s the hot new bands were trying to get some of the old nineteenth-century songs to **swing** (e.g., **Benny Goodman**'s "Loch Lomond"), but "Carry Me Back" does not turn out as well as other Armstrong/Mills Brothers efforts, such as "Old Folks at Home."

Carson, Johnny (b. 1925). Armstrong was a frequent guest on Johnny Carson's popular *Tonight Show,* which began airing in 1962. In fact, one of Armstrong's last **television** appearances was with Carson (March 1, 1971). On July 9, 1971, Carson served as an honorary pallbearer for Armstrong's **funeral** at the **Corona** Congregational Church.

cartoons. Armstrong's wide popularity can be seen in the fact that there were animated versions of him in many cartoons, such as *Clean Pastures* (1937), ***I'll Be Glad When You're Dead, You Rascal, You*** (1932), *Old Mill Pond* (1936), and ***Swing Wedding/Minnie the Moocher's Wedding Day*** (1937).

Caruso, Enrico. See **"Louis Armstrong and Opera."**

Cary, Richard Durant "Dick" (1916–1994). This versatile musician first achieved success on the violin, later switching to the piano but also playing and recording respectably on the alto horn, mellophone, trumpet, and trombone. He was as well an accomplished arranger and composer. His connection to Armstrong began with the historic May 17, 1947, **Town Hall concert,** which inaugurated the **All Stars.** On that occasion, Cary was responsible for an endearing mistake, playing the piano introduction to a "A Monday Date" when Armstrong had announced "Big Butter and Egg Man." Everyone including the audience had a good laugh and the incident underscored in this august venue the spontaneous nature of both this performance and of jazz itself. Cary was one of only six pianists to play with that ensemble during its twenty-four-year run. He left in 1948 (probably because of the shenanigans of manager **Joe Glaser**'s perverse road manager Pierre "Frenchy" Tallerie) to join the **Jimmy Dorsey** Orchestra, then went on to a wide variety of ensembles and performance venues.

"Cash for Your Trash." By **Thomas "Fats" Waller** and Ed Kirkeby; rec. April 17, 1942, in Chicago by Louis Armstrong and His Orchestra.

"Cast Away." By J. Brown, S. Easton, and J. Stewart; rec. March 4, 1925, in New York City with vocalist **Eva Taylor** and **Clarence Williams' Blue Five;** CD #36. Taylor belongs to a distinguished group of blues singers with whom Armstrong worked in the 1920s. She was married to pianist, composer, publisher, and promoter **Clarence Williams,** and she often recorded his songs. Here and elsewhere, despite excellent diction, Taylor is overshadowed by Armstrong's inventiveness.

Catlett, Elizabeth (b. 1919). This is the artist who created the eleven-foot, one-ton bronze statue of Louis Armstrong that since 1980 has presided over **Louis Armstrong Park** in New Orleans. The $30,000 project, backed by **Bing Crosby** and others, was begun in 1970 and had a stormy history. Before Catlett was selected, there was a debate over the statue's style: abstract or classical. Catlett reluctantly acquiesced to the classical but refused to depict a smiling Armstrong, feeling that any hint of clowning would be unseemly. Unveiled on July 4, 1976, in Jackson Square, the statue now presides over the thirty-one-acre park less than a mile from Armstrong's **birthplace.** See also **Jackson, Preston.**

Catlett, George James "Buddy" (b. 1933). The **All Stars** bassist from June 1965 to the end in 1971 came to his instrument after first studying the clarinet and then the saxophone. Before joining Armstrong, he performed with a wide variety of ensembles led by Cal Tjader, Chico

Hamilton, and Count Basie. A gifted and protean performer, he could perform both supportively in a large ensemble or with strong individuality in a small group.

Catlett, Sidney "Sid" (1910–1951). Armstrong's favorite drummer performed with Benny Carter, **Fletcher Henderson,** and others before settling in Armstrong's big band from 1938 to 1942. The two worked again when the **All Stars** was formed in 1947. Catlett had an unfortunate tendency to get into fights with fellow band members, not excluding Armstrong. Nevertheless, Armstrong thought so highly of Catlett that he had him ride on his **King of the Zulus** float in the February 1949 Mardi Gras in New Orleans. Catlett's health eventually began to fail, and he was replaced by the energetic if less sophisticated **Cozy Cole.** Catlett can be heard on numerous Armstrong recordings, example, "Boff Boff" and "Steak Face" (both 1947). His feature number with the All Stars was "Mop Mop," which Armstrong called "our be**bop** number, the only one in our files" (Giddins, 1988, p. 177). There's also a generous sample of Catlett's style in Warner Brothers' 1944 documentary *Jammin' the Blues.*

Cavalleria Rusticana. See **"Intermezzo" from *Cavalleria Rusticana.***

Cavett, Dick (b. 1936). The popular **television** host had Armstrong as a guest on his ABC television show numerous times beginning in 1968. In his last appearance on February 22, 1971, Armstrong sang "When It's Sleepy Time Down South." Five months later, on July 9, 1971, Cavett served as an honorary pallbearer for Armstrong's **funeral** at the **Corona** Congregational Church.

Celestin, Oscar Phillip "Papa" (1884–1954). Born in Napoleonville, Louisiana, Celestin moved to New Orleans in 1906 and eventually formed the popular **Tuxedo Brass Band.** Armstrong called him "a marvelous trumpeter and a very fine musician. He was also one of the finest guys who ever hit New Orleans" and very early in his career was pleased to play second cornet with Celestin (***Satchmo,*** 1954, pp. 179–180). With the onset of the **Depression,** Celestin sought other employment, then revived the Tuxedos at the end of World War II. In 1953 he was invited to play for President **Eisenhower,** and he appears in the 1955 film *Cinerama Holiday.*

"C'est si bon." By Henri Betti and Jerry Seelen; rec. June 26, 1950, in New York City with the **Sy Oliver** Orchestra; CDs #6, #23, and #28. Armstrong kept the **All Stars'** repertory fresh with hits he made with big studio ensembles, and this is a good example. The song was brand new in 1950, and Armstrong (with his fondness for a love song and affinity for the French language) gave it a big boost.

Chambers, Charles "Henderson" (1908–1967). Born in Alexandria, Louisiana, the trombonist went to Morehouse College in Atlanta, Georgia, where he got valuable band experience, then played in several territory bands (1934–1936). In New York, he worked with Armstrong from 1941 to 1943. His bold style can be heard on "Cash for Your Trash" and "I Never Knew," both from 1942.

"Changeable Daddy of Mine." By Sam Wooding and Bob Schaffer; rec. November 25, 1924, in New York City with vocalist **Margaret Johnson** and **Clarence Williams' Blue Five;** CDs #36 and #48. Armstrong was a much-sought-after blues accompanist, and the reasons can be heard here, as his energetic double-time work and imaginative improvisation raise the artistic level of the ensemble. Lewis Porter observes in his 1981 liner notes that an Armstrong break here foreshadows his opening cadenza to "West End Blues" (1928).

"Chant, The." By **Jelly Roll Morton.** Armstrong's recordings sold so well in the mid-1920s that the publisher Melrose had pianist Elmer Schoebel transcribe his solos, such as this one, for publication. See ***125 Jazz Breaks for Cornet*** and ***50 Hot Choruses for Cornet*** in the selected bibliography.

"Chantez les bas" ("Sing 'em Low"). By W.C. Handy; rec. July 14, 1954, in Chicago by **Louis Armstrong and the All Stars;** CD #38. See comments on "Atlanta Blues."

"Chattanooga Stomp." By **Joe Oliver** and **Alphonse Picou;** rec. October 15, 1923, in Chicago with King Oliver's Creole Jazz Band. See comments on "Alligator Hop."

"Cheek to Cheek." By **Irving Berlin;** rec. August 16, 1956, in Los Angeles with vocalist **Ella Fitzgerald** and the **Oscar Peterson** Quartet; CD #9. See comments on "April in Paris."

"Cheesecake." By I. Fields and Louis Armstrong; rec. April 1966 in New York City by **Louis Armstrong and the All Stars.** This playful number features the singing of trombonist **Tyree Glenn.**

"Cherry." By **Don Redman;** rec. April 11, 1940, in New York City with the **Mills Brothers.** This and "Darling Nellie Gray" are probably the best of the Armstrong–Mills Brothers collaborations. They had excellent chemistry, and, as French fan **Hugues Panassié** puts it, Armstrong's "trumpet chorus is full of serenity" (1971, p. 116). See additional comments on "Carry Me Back to Old Virginny."

"Chicago Breakdown." By **Jelly Roll Morton;** rec. May 9, 1927, in Chicago by the **Sunset Stompers;** CDs #10, #30, and #48. This is Armstrong's first recording as the leader of a big band and the only recording of the Stompers, a ten-piece ensemble with which he worked at Chicago's **Sunset Cafe** in 1927. Here, after a trumpet-style opening by co-leader and pianist **Earl Hines,** Armstrong takes two solos, the second a very tender one, muted, with guitar alone.

childhood. Abandoned by his father and left by his mother in the care of his paternal grandmother, young Louis Armstrong grew up in difficult circumstances. Luckily **Josephine Armstrong** was by all accounts an attentive and loving person. She raised Louis to the age of five, seeing to it that he went both to school and to church. In the latter institution he seems to have developed a love for singing. Louis also accompanied his grandmother when she did washing and housework, sometimes helping out and sometimes playing with the children of her white employers. In 1906 Louis was returned to his mother and three-year-old sister **Beatrice** (eventually nicknamed "Mama Lucy"), the result of a brief reconciliation between **Willie** and **Mayann.** Since Mayann did not earn enough from keeping house and watching children for white families, and since the contributions from successive "stepfathers" were erratic, Louis supplemented the family income by doing odd jobs—running errands, selling coal and rags, and cleaning graves. In his numerous autobiographical writings, a common theme is his pride in bringing home a pocket full of change, which often meant that the threesome could eat something more substantial than day-old bread.

His first taste of earning money from music came from a vocal quartet that he formed with friends. They would troll for an audience in the Rampart Street area, between Perdido and Gravier, and pass a hat after singing. The group usually did pretty well by the end of the night when they would divvy up their earnings. "Then," Louis recalled, "I would make a bee line for home [1303 Perdido Street] and dump my share into mama's lap" (***Satchmo,*** 1954, p. 34). Louis also began playing the cornet at this time, or at least he played an imitation of one. At the age of seven he went to work for the **Karnofsky family,** who from a wagon bought and sold junk as well as coal. Louis had a toy tin horn, which he would use to call out customers. When he expressed the desire for a real horn, the Karnofskys lent him five dollars for a pawn shop cornet, which he paid back in weekly installments of fifty cents. By watching such legendary players as **Buddy Bolden, Bunk Johnson,** and **Joe Oliver,** Louis worked out how to play "Home! Sweet Home!" and some blues tunes. Thus began one of the most stellar musical careers in all of music history. See **education.**

"Chim Chim Cher-ee." By Richard M. Sherman and Robert B. Sherman; rec. March 17, 1968, in Hollywood by **Louis Armstrong and the All Stars** with a studio orchestra and mixed choir; CD #15. This number from the 1964 movie *Mary Poppins* was recorded for a **Disney** album and is one of the few successes on it. Armstrong seems to have a special affinity for the underclass chimney sweep whose story he tells, and his raspy voice and inflection highlight the song's minor key mysteriousness. His two trumpet breaks, among his last on record, stay in the low register, which he was the first to explore some fifty years earlier.

"Chimes Blues." By **Joe Oliver;** rec. April 5, 1923, in Richmond, Indiana, with King Oliver's Creole Jazz Band; CDs #35 and #48. This is a landmark recording—Armstrong's first solo. According to musicologist Brian Harker, the arpeggiated figuration shows the influence of clarinetists (2003, p. 143). The solo also gives us a glimpse of Armstrong's emerging musical personality, especially toward the end when he teases the beat. Jones and Chilton put it nicely with their observation that here Armstrong "emphatically places his calling card in the hall of fame" (p. 248).

"Chinatown, My Chinatown." By William Jerome and Jean Schwartz; rec. November 3, 1931, in Chicago by Louis Armstrong and His Orchestra; CDs #14, #48, and #58. This was a technical display piece for Armstrong, whose speed and high notes inspired so many trumpeters. **Roy Eldridge,** for example, heard Armstrong play it live in 1932 at the **Layfayette Theatre** in New York City, and it changed his musical style. He developed his speed and range, although perhaps sometimes at the expense of melodic expression. Eldridge would later receive another lesson from the master, who helped polish off his rough edges with the advice that instead of always playing as fast as possible, a soloist should tell a story complete with introduction and conclusion.

"Chloe." By Gus Kahn and Neil Moret; rec. September 22, 1952, in Los Angeles with the Gordon Jenkins Orchestra; CD #39.

Christian, Lillie Delk. Armstrong worked with numerous blues singers, including Lillie Delk Christian, with whom in 1928 he recorded "You're a Real Sweetheart," "I Must Have That Man," "Too Busy," and others. He usually played a complementary trumpet obbligato, but in "Too Busy" he sang **scat** behind her in trumpet style. Delk, a rather mediocre singer, was very popular in the early twentieth century. See **Hot Four.**

Christian, Narcisse J. "Buddy" (c. 1895–c. 1958). This New Orleans pianist and banjo player worked with **King Oliver** at first, then around 1919 went to New York where he frequently recorded with **Clarence Williams.** In the **Clarence Williams' Blue Five** with Armstrong, Christian's banjo can be heard in "Coal Cart Blues," "Squeeze Me," "You Can't Shush Katie," and several others, all from 1925. Christian also worked with the Red Onion Jazz Babies, then formed his own band.

Christmas. Among her many gifts to him throughout their marriage, **Lucille** brought Christmas to Armstrong in 1942. On October 7 of that year, they were married in St. Louis. There was no time for a honeymoon, however, since he had six solid months of advance bookings. The new Mrs. Armstrong joined him on the road and in December bought a small Christmas tree for their hotel room. Louis was deeply moved by the decorations and colorful lights. As the story is told in Hentoff's *The Jazz Life,* Armstrong stared at the tree speechlessly, with childlike eyes (pp. 26–27). It was evidently his first Christmas tree. He asked Lucille to take it from one hotel to another, which she did until after New Year's. He even wanted her to mail it home. Armstrong went on to record a great deal of Christmas music (see CDs #7 and #33), and his very last recording (February 26, 1971) was a reading of Clement Moore's "The Night before Christmas" (CD #7).

"Christmas in New Orleans." By Robert B. Sherman and Joe Van Winkle; rec. September 8, 1955, in Los Angeles with the Benny Carter Orchestra; CDs #7 and #33. Armstrong fell in love with **Christmas** after being introduced to it in 1942 by his new, fourth, and final wife, **Lucille.** She set up a Christmas tree in their hotel room, and this so captivated him that he had her take it down and put it up in a dozen subsequent hotel rooms, well after the new year. In his recordings of Christmas music, such as this broadly swinging number, he conveys some of this childlike enthusiasm.

"Christmas Night in Harlem." By Raymond Scott and Maxwell Parish; rec. September 8, 1955, in Los Angeles with the Benny Carter Orchestra; CDs #7 and #33. Armstrong has fun with the clever lyrics and sprightly rhythm of this song. See additional comments on "Christmas in New Orleans."

"Circle of Your Arms, The." By Carolyn Leigh and J. Segal; rec. August 1965 in Hollywood by **Louis Armstrong and the All Stars.**

civil rights. Born at the turn of the twentieth century, Armstrong lived in an era when African Americans made significant progress in civil rights, and he himself did a great deal to help. His 1954 **autobiography** matter-of-factly records numerous examples of oppression and overt cruelty. In a May 1961 ***Ebony*** article titled "Daddy, How the Country Has Changed!" he recalled that in an earlier day, "We couldn't get into hotels. Our money wasn't even good. We'd play night clubs and spots which didn't have a little boy's room for Negroes. We'd have to go outside, often in the freezing cold, and in the dark" (p. 81). On tour in October 1931 an illustrative event took place in Memphis where the entire band was arrested simply because the only white person on the bus was a woman, manager **Johnny Collins**'s wife. During the 1930s, however, he began quietly stipulating in his contracts that he wouldn't perform where he couldn't stay. Without any fanfare in 1931, he led the first black band ever to play the Roof Garden of the Kentucky Hotel in Louisville. Later that same year he returned to his native New Orleans to play at the white-only **Suburban Gardens.** When the regular announcer refused to introduce "that nigger," Armstrong took the microphone and did so himself, thereby becoming the first African American to speak on the radio in that region. On his first **European tour** in 1932 he was the first black man to head a white European band and the first jazz artist of any color to appear as an individual star. Back in the United States, Armstrong went on in 1937 to become the first African American performer to host a sponsored national network radio program when he took over for Rudy Vallee on the **The Fleischmann's Yeast Hour.** He was the first black actor to be featured in mainstream movies, beginning in 1936 with ***Pennies from Heaven.***

During his long career, he regularly endured racial prejudice and even hate crimes. For example, in February 1957, he was playing a concert in Knoxville, Tennessee, before an audience of approximately 8,000 whites and 1,000 blacks. A stick of dynamite went off outside the auditorium. Louis kept everyone calm by joking, "That's all right, folks, it's just the phone" (Giddins, 1988, p. 160). He'd dealt with similar situations before, many many times. In September of the same year, though, he took a dramatic public stand on a school desegregation incident in **Little Rock,** Arkansas. "It's getting almost so bad that a colored man hasn't got any country," he told a reporter, then went on to say that he planned to cancel a government-sponsored trip to Russia. "The people over there ask me what's wrong with my country, what am I supposed to say?" (*New York Herald Tribune,* Sept. 19, 1957, p. A3). The effect of this incident on civil rights was dramatic. Although in 1954 the U.S. Supreme Court declared separate educational facilities illegal, it took people such as Armstrong speaking out and working in noncollusive tandem with others to make civil rights a reality.

Clarence Williams' Blue Five. This ensemble came into being in New York in 1923 as a savvy business move on the part of **Clarence Williams,** a pianist, composer, and publisher, who assembled some of the best musicians of the day to play his own music and to accompany singers such as **Eva Taylor,** his wife. The Blue Five created a substantial and widely respected body of early jazz recordings, comparable to that of **King Oliver**'s Creole Jazz Band. Armstrong recorded with the Blue Five and the similar Red Onion Jazz Babies during 1924–1925. He can be heard learning his craft and developing his style on such tunes as "Cake Walking Babies from Home." Virtuoso clarinetist and band member **Sidney Bechet** challenged Armstrong to get away from ragtime clichés, and Armstrong responded exuberantly. Particularly outstanding is "Texas Moaner Blues," where one gets a good taste of how the blues may have been played for slow drag dancing in New Orleans brothels. With the Blue Five, Armstrong had more freedom than he did with **Fletcher Henderson**'s bulky ensemble. He recorded "Everybody Loves My Baby" with both groups (and the Red Onion Jazz Babies as well, backing up **Alberta Hunter**). With Henderson it was Armstrong's first recorded vocal, but a subdued rendition it seems when compared with his lengthy and complex Blue Five cornet solo, which leaves Eva Taylor in the dust.

"Clarinet Marmalade." By Henry Ragas, E. Edwards, Nick La Rocca, T. Sparbaro, and Larry Shields; rec. December 19, 1955, in Milan, Italy, by **Louis Armstrong and the All Stars;** CD #19. This was a feature number for clarinetist **Edmond Hall.** During the All Stars' 1956 tour, Armstrong unwittingly broke protocol when, at Empress Hall in London, he acknowledged the presence of a member of the royal family. "We've got one of our special fans in the house," he said to the astonished audience, "and we're really going to lay this one on for the Princess [Margaret]." The princess smoothed things over by applauding heartily and even keeping time with her feet as the All Stars began "Clarinet Marmalade." The incident was big international news.

Clayton, Wilbur Dorsey "Buck" (1911–1991). Clayton was one of a great many trumpet players who were influenced by Armstrong, and not just musically. "His hair looked nice and shiny and he had on a pretty gray suit," Clayton later wrote in his memoirs about seeing Armstrong come out of a Los Angeles hotel in the early 1930s. "He wore a tie that looked like an ascot tie with an extra-big knot.... Soon all the hip cats were wearing big knots in their ties" (Clayton, p. 36). Clayton first approached his idol backstage to learn how to do a trombone-style glissando. (Push the valves partly down and tighten the lips.) Clayton went on to be one of the leading soloists in the Count Basie band, an accompanist for singers (**Billie Holiday** in particular), and a leading composer–arranger. He toured frequently, including a State Department trip to Africa (1977), another trail first blazed by Armstrong. Both players suffered from a problem common to trumpet players: the accumulation of scar tissue on the inside of the lips (see **lip problems**).

Cliburn, Van (b. 1934). In 1957, shortly after he made a public stand over segregated schools in **Little Rock,** Armstrong was scheduled to appear on *The Steve Allen Show* along with the celebrated pianist Van Cliburn. Allen wanted them to play a duet, but Cliburn's manager nixed the idea out of concern for his client's image. However, after the show the two men did play something together, "Melancholy Baby."

"Coal Cart Blues." By Louis Armstrong and **Lil Hardin Armstrong;** rec. October 8, 1925, in New York City with vocalist **Eva Taylor** and **Clarence Williams' Blue Five;** CDs #36 and #61. Legend has it that young Louis jotted down this number during a break from his job delivering coal. Whatever the truth is, this performance has an authentic New Orleans flavor with its group improvisation, even with several New Yorkers in the ensemble. Armstrong himself sings on a May 27, 1940, recording made in New York City. See additional comments on "Cast Away."

"Cocktails for Two." By Sam Coslow and Arthur Johnston; rec. June 4, 1965, live at the Palais des Sports in Paris by **Louis Armstrong and the All Stars.** This was a feature number for bassist **Buddy Catlett.**

"Cold in Hand Blues." By Fred Longshaw and Jack Gee; rec. January 14, 1925, in New York City with vocalist **Bessie Smith** and pianist Longshaw; CD #36. As is usual with this singer whose best recorded work was done with Armstrong, Smith responds warmly to her accompanists. Especially moving is her exchange with Armstrong on the line "I've tried hard to treat him kind." Later Armstrong gets to take a solo on which he uses a wa-wa mute, something he rarely did. (See also "Careless Love Blues"; "Reckless Blues"; "You've Been a Good Ole Wagon.") "I remember the first Louis record I ever heard, 'Cold in Hand Blues.' I was down in Texas and all the musicians stood and listened to it over and over again," remembered **Jack Teagarden** (Jones and Chilton, p. 116).

Cole, William Randolph "Cozy" (1906–1981). Cole was one of only five drummers to play with the **All Stars** during its twenty-four-year history. He joined in July 1949 and left in late 1953 to start a drum school in New York City with Gene Krupa. Before signing on with Armstrong, though, he had played with numerous bands and had initially established himself during a four-year stint (1938–1942) with **Cab Calloway.** Cole appeared in the movies *Make Mine Music* (1945) and ***The Glenn Miller Story*** (1953) and also played on the soundtrack of ***The Strip*** (1951), dubbing "drummer" Mickey Rooney. In 1958 Cole's recording "Topsy" was an international hit.

Collins, Johnny. Collins was Armstrong's manager from 1930 to 1933. Depending on the story, he was either sent by or replaced **Tommy Rockwell** (Armstrong's manager since 1929). Collins's first job was to get Armstrong out of a **marijuana** possession charge in Los Angeles in November 1930. Back in Chicago, rival mob gangs feuded over control of Armstrong, so Collins took his client on the road. However, he did little to make the ten-month tour comfortable for Armstrong. "We couldn't get into hotels," Armstrong later recalled. "Our money wasn't even good. We'd play night clubs and spots which didn't have a little boy's room for Negroes. We'd have to go outside, often in the freezing cold, and in the dark" (***Ebony,*** May 1961, p. 81). On that tour on October 10, 1931, the entire band was arrested simply because the only white person on the bus was a woman, Johnny Collins's wife. In July 1932 Collins accompanied Armstrong to Europe, where his boorish and avaricious behavior offended everyone. When they made the trip again the following year, Armstrong took the unusual step of firing Collins. By all accounts (and there were many witnesses), it was an ugly scene. The inebriated Collins "called me a nigger in the middle of the ocean," Armstrong later recollected with record producer and writer **George Avakian,** and then Collins proceeded to tell Armstrong what to play on an upcoming program (Berrett, 1999, p. 85). It was the straw that broke the camel's back. Collins took some mean-spirited revenge in walking off with Armstrong's passport. When in 1935 **Joe Glaser** took over as Armstrong's manager, he paid a $5,000 buyout fee to Collins, who then slithered out of Armstrong's life.

Colored Waif's Home for Boys. "The Waif's Home for Boys was sort of like a boy's jail, but they didn't have routines like a jail," wrote Armstrong in his memoir ***Swing That Music*** of this New Orleans institution in which he was placed at age eleven (1936, p. 6). His offense was delinquency in general. Specifically he had shot a pistol, which he had found among his mother's belongings, into the air on New Year's Eve 1912. He remained in the Home from January 1913 to June 1914. The experience did him good, and he remembered it affectionately. He learned the three "Rs" (in addition to what he'd picked up earlier at the **Fisk School**) and received his first formal training in music. Initially he played the tambourine, snare drum, alto horn, bass drum, bugle, and finally (as a reward for good behavior) the cornet. Band director **Peter Davis** gave Armstrong lessons, and eventually made him the leader of the group. "I was in seventh heaven," Armstrong recalled in ***Satchmo: My Life in New Orleans*** (p. 46). At discharge time Armstrong was ambivalent about leaving the Waif's. It's significant that the earliest surviving photo of him is not a family picture but a 1913 portrait of the proud-looking Colored Waif's Home Brass Band. Eighteen years later, in June 1931, Armstrong had a homecoming when a tour took him back to New Orleans for the first time since he had left in August 1922. He was given a hero's welcome throughout the city and was careful to set aside some time to visit his alma mater (now called the Municipal Boys' Home). There he donated radios, posed for pictures, and had a hearty meal of his old favorite, red beans and rice. Drowsy, he went over to the dormitory, found his old bunk, stretched out, and drifted off to sleep, much to the amusement of current inmates. And that cornet? On October 15, 2001, it was sold to an anonymous buyer at a Sotheby's auction for $115,000.

Columbia Records. Armstrong recorded a great deal of music for this well-known record company, beginning with the **King Oliver** band in 1923, Armstrong's

Armstrong and His Orchestra in the 1930s. (Louis Armstrong House and Archives at Queens College/CUNY)

first year in the studio. In January 1925 he made memorable Columbia recordings with **Bessie Smith** (e.g., the classic version of "St. Louis Blues"), and thirty years later, with the help of producer **George Avakian,** he did the landmark W.C. Handy and **Fats Waller** compilations. In between, he formed a friendship with Columbia producer **John Hammond,** a blue-blooded white man who once decked another white man **(Johnny Collins)** for insulting Armstrong. In the early 1960s, it was Columbia (albiet without much fanfare or publicity) who recorded ***The Real Ambassadors,*** an oratoriolike jazz work with music by **Dave Brubeck** and book/lyrics by Iola Brubeck. Columbia has been active in reissuing Armstrong on CD.

"Come Back, Sweet Papa." By **Paul Barbarin** and **Luis Russell;** rec. February 22, 1926, in Chicago by Louis Armstrong and His **Hot Five;** CD #10. Armstrong here gives the main solo work to alto saxophonist **Johnny Dodds,** who frankly doesn't do much with it. Nevertheless, the number became so popular that it was suggested for a mass performance by twenty-one bands simultaneously at a big **Okeh Records** ball in Chicago in June 1926. (Transcription by Castle, vol. 2, p. 20.)

"Come on, Coot, Do That Thing." By Leola B. "Coot" Grant; rec. October 1925 in New York City with vocalists "Coot" Grant and Wesley "Kid" Wilson and **Fletcher Henderson**'s Orchestra; CD #36. Here Armstrong is a sideman accompanying the popular duet act of Grant and Wilson. See additional comments on "Alabamy Bound."

composer. Armstrong has a whopping eighty music copyrights to his credit (see Chevan, 1997). Some of these he co-composed—for example, "I Hate to Leave You Now" with **Fats Waller** and "Throw It Out of Your Mind" with **Billy Kyle.** Some he generously allowed others to claim—for example "Muskrat Ramble" (his trombonist, **Kid Ory**) and "Struttin' with Some Barbecue" (his wife, **Lil Hardin Armstrong**). Interestingly, one song came to him in a dream. This happened in the winter of 1947 when Armstrong was on tour in North Dakota. As he himself tells the story: "It was so cold that I didn't even want to get up out of bed . . . and then this tune came to me. I couldn't get it out of my head. I said to myself well if you don't get up now you'll never remember it. I got up and wrote the thing out—'Someday You'll Be Sorry' " (Jones and Chilton, p. 243).

In a 1960 radio interview with British journalists in Kenya, Armstrong was complimented on the Noël Coward-like "Someday," and with characteristic modesty, he responded, "Can't you name somebody a little lesser than Noël?" (Giddins, 1988, p. 105). Frankly, though, one could instead take it up a notch and make a comparison with the great Viennese *Lieder* composer Franz Schubert, with whose songs of unrequited love, such as "Trockne Blumen" ("Withered Flowers"), Armstrong's "Someday" can favorably be compared.

Some of Armstrong's songs sound like those written by others, except that the other songs came much later. For example, his "Struttin' with Some Barbecue" (1927) sounds a lot like Bonfa's "Samba de Orpheus" (1960), and "Hotter Than That" (1927) is arrestingly similar to the

Ink Spots' version of Milton Drake's and Ben Oakland's "Java Jive" (1940). Imitation is a sincere form of admiration, though, and even Armstrong was capable of the practice. His "Someday," for example, bears a slight resemblance to a popular 1930s tune titled "Good Night, Angel," which, by the way, Armstrong recorded in the 1950s.

"Confessin'." See **"I'm Confessin' (That I Love You)."**

Congo. In 1956 on a forty-five-concert tour of Australia, the Far East, and Africa, Armstrong played three concerts at a soccer stadium in the Congo, recently declared the Republic of Zaire, where rival forces of Joseph Mobutu and of the recently assassinated Patrice Lumumba were at war. The combatants called a truce in honor of Armstrong's visit, and according to witnesses, both armies came to the concert and sat side by side.

Congo Square. In the eighteenth and nineteenth centuries, long before it became **Louis Armstrong Park** (1980), this area of New Orleans was also known as Place Congo and served as a gathering place for African Americans. Here they performed and danced to the musics of their homeland. From 1898 to 1917 **Storyville** was located a few blocks away. Many consider Congo Square one of the cradles of jazz. Armstrong remembered it as an area associated with "slavery, lynchings and all of that stuff" (Berrett, 1999, p. 6).

Connie's Hot Chocolates. The nightclubs of Harlem in the 1920s and 1930s (**Cotton Club, Smalls' Paradise, Connie's Inn,** and others) attracted an after-Broadway theater crowd. Soon the migration went both ways, as black musicals traveled the five miles down to Broadway. The revue *Hot Chocolates* (lyrics by Andy Razaf, music by **Fats Waller** and Harry Brooks), which began in 1929 as a Connie's Inn floor show, was one of the most successful. After a tryout at the Windsor Theatre in the Bronx in early June, it opened on Broadway at the Hudson Theatre on June 20 and ran to the very end of the year. *Chocolates* was a collection of skits, songs, and production numbers mostly about Harlem street life. The chorus girls were called "Hot Chocolate Drops," and the boys were "Bon Bon Buddies." Immediately after the final curtain every evening, the performers hustled back up to Connie's in Harlem and put on a less elaborate version of the same show. Armstrong joined the production shortly after the premiere and was assigned the inter-act song "Ain't Misbehavin'." "From the first time I heard it, that song used to 'send' me. I wood-shedded it until I could play all around it," he later wrote in ***Swing That Music.*** "I was all ready with it and it would bring down the house, believe me!" (p. 91). He was right. Initially, Armstrong sang in the pit, but before long he was right up there on the stage. His subsequent recording of "Ain't Misbehavin'" became his first big hit, and he backed it with another song from the show—"(What Did I Do to Be So) Black and Blue?"—that also became a hit. The *Connie's Hot Chocolates* experience certainly gave Armstrong's career a considerable boost. He proved he could be both an artistic and a commercial success. After *Chocolates* he turned from jazz to popular and theater works and began performing and recording exclusively with big band backing, which he continued until the early 1940s.

Connie's Inn. The famous New York nightclub was opened during June 1923 in Harlem (Seventh Avenue at West 131st Street) by brothers Connie and George Immerman, and it rivaled the **Cotton Club** in presenting colorful revues and outstanding jazz musicians. There were two nightly radio broadcasts from Connie's over WHN. Returning to New York after an absence of nearly four years, Armstrong led a band at Connie's for four months beginning June 24, 1929. He also joined Connie's spin-off floor show, ***Connie's Hot Chocolates,*** at the Hudson Theater on Broadway. The show (both versions) ran for over 200 performances each, right up to the end of the year. Armstrong's rendition of "Ain't Misbehavin' " was the highlight, and his recording of this number was his first big hit. When Connie's Inn moved downtown to 200 West 48th Street in 1933, Armstrong led a band there for four months beginning October 29, 1935. Connie's was eventually taken over by the Cotton Club in September 1936.

"Cool Yule." By Steve Allen; rec. October 22, 1953, in New York City with Louis Armstrong and the Commanders; CDs #7 and #33. Like most songwriters, Allen was surprised at the liberties that arrangers and performers take in their work. However, said the genial composer of arranger Tutti Camarata's and Armstrong's collaboration here, "[I]t's such an honor to have Louis Armstrong record your music that I didn't complain" (Liner notes, CD #33). See additional comments on "Christmas in New Orleans."

"Copenhagen." By Charlie Davis and Walter Melrose; rec. October 30, 1924, in New York City by **Fletcher Henderson** and His Orchestra; CD #61. In this popular tune, named after the smokeless tobacco, one can hear Armstrong ionizing the Henderson ensemble with his solo. Before he comes in, they are relatively inert; afterward, they **swing,** especially trombonist **Charlie Green** and clarinetist **Buster Bailey.** See additional comments on "Alabamy Bound."

"Coquette." By **Irving Berlin;** rec. April 17, 1942, in Chicago by Louis Armstrong and His Orchestra; CD #49.

cornet. A cornet has a more conical bore than a trumpet, and its sound is more mellow. Armstrong acquired his first cornet with the help of his employers and friends, the **Karnofsky family,** who lent him five dollars, which he paid back at fifty cents a week. When he was placed in the **Colored Waif's Home** on January 1, 1913, he was given cornet lessons as a reward for good behavior. (This instrument was sold to an anonymous buyer at Sotheby's on October 15, 2001, for $115,000.) He continued to play the cornet for a decade until October 1924, when he switched to the trumpet in order to match his two fellow trumpet players in the **Fletcher Henderson** Orchestra. He later recalled that once he began to listen critically to cornet players, he thought the trumpet prettier (Hodes and Hansen, p. 85). Armstrong's decision exemplifies a 1920s trend in which cornets were by and large replaced by the trumpet in popular music.

"Cornet Chop Suey." By Louis Armstrong; rec. February 26, 1926, in Chicago by Louis Armstrong and His **Hot Five;** CDs #3, #8, #10, #13, #48, and #52. One of the all-time great recordings, this is a showpiece for Armstrong. (The title alludes to Armstrong's enthusiasm for Chinese food.) He opens with four bars of a bugle call figure that musicologist Brian Harker traces back to the early influence of clarinet players (2003, p. 144). After the ensemble plays the tune and the pianist (Armstrong's wife **Lil**) takes a mediocre solo, Armstrong plays a now-famous sixteen-bar **stop-time** chorus. Inventive and virtuosic, it quickly became the talk of musicians and still remains a model for aspiring trumpet players. For those who would like to see the music, there is fortunately in the Library of Congress a copy of the lead sheet that Armstrong had submitted to the copyright office in Washington, D.C., in March 1924, and it is reprinted both in Miller (p. 105) and Gushee (1998, p. 299).

Corona. After Armstrong married **Lucille Wilson** in 1942, she insisted that they have a real home, and she herself saw to the purchase of one in Corona, Queens, outside Manhattan. Knowing the area well (since she grew up there and her family still lived there), Lucille settled on a clapboard house built in 1910 by architect Robert Johnson at 34-56 107th Street. Coincidentally, it turned out that she had gone to school with several members of the family who were selling the house. Taking possession in March 1943, she readied the place for her husband, who arrived by taxi in the early hours of the morning from a tour. Armstrong was overwhelmed. "The more Lucille showed me around the house, the more thrilled I got," he later wrote (Berrett, 1999, p. 98). Armstrong quickly adapted to home and neighborhood life, and quiet Corona became a refuge for him. He did a great deal of letter and memoir writing in his large den, and among these documents is one titled "Our Neighborhood," which he wrote around 1970. The pages express fondness for the Corona community and appreciation for the comforts of a home: the king-sized bed, the automatic garage door, a mirror-lined bathroom, his two schnauzers (**"Trumpet"** and **"Trinket"**), getting to know the neighborhood families, the several generations of children, and a local Chinese restaurant, the Dragon Seed. Visiting in 1949, jazz writer **Leonard Feather** was touched to see Armstrong "sitting out on the stoop of his neat, cozy home . . . playing with a happy group of neighborhood children" (Brothers, p. 164). The Armstrongs made many changes to the house and neighborhood. For example, they put a brick façade over the clapboard, and Louis, not wanting to "put on airs," offered to put brick on everyone's home. The Armstrong house was a source of great comfort in Louis's later years. He was able to gather a considerable amount of memorabilia, make and store tape recordings, decorate the storage boxes with collages made from clippings and photographs, and have his large library (biographies, books on diet, history, poetry, race relations, and numerous presentation copies) at his fingertips. The Corona house became a National Historic Landmark in 1977 and a City of New York Landmark in 1983. On September 7, 1995, to celebrate the new Armstrong postage **stamp,** a ceremony was held at the house. Since then it has been opened as a popular museum and study center. So attached in life was Armstrong to Corona that his **funeral** (July 9, 1971) took place at the Corona Congregational Church, and he is buried in Corona's Flushing Cemetery.

Two public schools in Corona have since been named in honor of Armstrong. **Louis Armstrong Middle School** (IS 227) is located at 30-02 Junction Boulevard in East Elmhurst, and **Louis Armstrong School,** located at 34-74 113th Street, is within a short walking distance of the **Louis Armstrong House and Archives.** Lucille Armstrong used to go to the latter school's graduation exercises every year to award the top prize, the Louis Armstrong Achievement Award. The Corona, Queens area has also been the home of other jazz greats such as **Dizzy Gillespie, Bobby Hackett, Clark Terry,** and **Clarence Williams.**

Cotton Club. Armstrong, like most prominent jazz entertainers of the 1920s and 1930s (**Duke Ellington, Cab Calloway,** Jimmie Lunceford, Ethel Waters, **Bill "Bojangles" Robinson,** and the Nicholas Brothers, to name but a few), appeared frequently at both the uptown (West 142nd Street) and the downtown (West 48th Street) locations of this famous New York institution. It opened at Lenox Avenue and West 142nd Street in 1922 and, when the race riots of 1935 threatened its exclusively white clientele, moved in 1936 to 200 West 48th Street. Armstrong mentor **King Oliver** and His Dixie Syncopators unwisely turned down a low-paying offer to work there in 1927, and the job went to the young Duke Ellington, who used the venue to establish a national reputation over the next five years. Armstrong met **Lucille Wilson** (stage name "Brown Sugar" and later his fourth and final wife) at the Cotton Club in 1939 when she was working as a chorus girl. "When I first saw her the glow of her deep-brown skin got me deep down," Louis affectionately recalled in the August 1954 issue of ***Ebony*** magazine. It also thrilled Armstrong to be on the same bill with his idol Bill Robinson. The Cotton Club closed in 1940. There were also "Cotton Clubs" (with different owners) in Chicago, Cicero (a suburb of Chicago), Culver City (just west of Los Angeles), Minneapolis, and elsewhere. Francis Ford Coppola's 1984 movie *The Cotton Club* gives those who weren't there a taste of what it might have been.

Cotton Club (Culver City). See **Sebastian's New Cotton Club.**

"Cottontail." By **Duke Ellington;** rec. April 4, 1961, in New York City by **Louis Armstrong and the All Stars** with Duke Ellington; CD #11. Armstrong's fresh approach to songs that Ellington had played for decades and recorded dozens of times delighted the composer. For example, Armstrong's rambunctious solo, extra lyrics, and improvised **scat**ting on "Cottontail" almost make it a new creation. See additional comments on "Azalea."

"Countin' the Blues." By **Gertrude "Ma" Rainey;** rec. October 16, 1924, in New York City with vocalist "Ma" Rainey and the Georgia Jazz Band; CD #36. Rainey's ensemble is drawn from the **Fletcher Henderson** band. Armstrong loosens up her big, somber voice with his bright rhythmic playing and uses a mute in **Joe Oliver** style on this number.

"Court House Blues." By **Clara Smith;** rec. April 2, 1925, in New York City with vocalist Clara Smith and pianist **Fletcher Henderson;** CDs #8, #36, and #52. Armstrong did some memorable work with "The Queen of the Moaners," and here is a good example. He returned to "Court House Blues" for *Satchmo: A Musical Autobiography* (CD #52), rerecording it on January 28, 1957, with **Velma Middleton** and the **All Stars.**

Covarrubias, Miguel (1902–1957). The Mexican-born illustrator frequently turned his attention to jazz subjects, and the results can be seen in a wide variety of publications, such as Marc Miller's *Louis Armstrong: A Cultural Legacy.* His interest paralleled that of many artists and intellectuals in the 1920s and 1930s, when popular culture began to gain respectability. See **Kreisler, Fritz.**

"Crab Man." By George Gershwin, DuBose Heyward, and Ira Gershwin; rec. October 14, 1957, in Los Angeles with a studio orchestra and choir conducted by Russell Garcia; CD #9. This Armstrong solo comes from Act II of *Porgy and Bess.* See additional comments on "Bess, You Is My Woman Now."

"Crazy Arms." Rec. August 1970 in New York City with the Nashville Group. See comments on "Almost Persuaded."

"Creator Has a Master Plan, The." By Pharaoh Sanders and Leon Thomas; rec. May 27, 1970, in New York City with a studio orchestra conducted by Oliver Nelson; CD #31. On his next-to-last album, Armstrong sings this song as a duet with Leon Thomas.

critics. Armstrong had his detractors. For example, many of his fans were disappointed when in 1929 he turned from the traditional New Orleans style to music that was more popular and commercially successful. Conversely, in 1947 he was again criticized for abandoning the big band style and going back to traditional New Orleans jazz. Then there were those who thought he could do more for his race, those who thought his repertory unvaried, and those who thought his jokes off-color (see **Agee, James; Baldwin, James; Baraka, Amiri; Blesh, Rudi; Davis, Miles Dewey, III; Finkelstein, Sidney**). Relatively little of this kind of criticism bothered Armstrong, though. "As long as they spell my name right," he would respond, "and keep it before the public," he was pleased (Berrett, 1999, p. 178).

Cronk, Billy. A bass player, Cronk was a member of the **All Stars** from 1962 to May 1963. He can be seen as well as heard in the 1962 film ***Louis and the Duke.***

Crosby, Harry Lillis "Bing" (1904–1977). Armstrong and Crosby first met in 1930 at Frank **Sebastian's New Cotton Club** in Los Angeles, and they began a musical friendship that lasted until Armstrong died in 1971. Their mutual influence emerged right away and can be heard in Armstrong's "ba-ba-ba-boo"-ing in "Star Dust" (1931) and Crosby's melodic embellishments in "Sweet Georgia Brown" (1932). The two worked together in the movies ***Pennies from Heaven*** (1936), ***Going Places*** and ***Doctor Rhythm*** (both 1938), ***Here Comes the Groom*** (1951), and ***High Society*** (1956). The color barrier initially kept them from singing together until on his own radio show in 1949 Crosby joined his guest in a performance of Armstrong's current hit "Blueberry Hill." The two went on to record such novelty songs as "Gone Fishin' " and

"Lazy Bones." Together they can be said to have created the American popular song style, as Will Friedwald amply demonstrates in his 1990 book *Jazz Singing.* On February 10, 1971, Armstrong and Crosby met for the last time on the **David Frost** show (Armstrong's last **television** appearance) to sing "Blueberry Hill." During the previous year, Cosby and other Hollywood entertainers financed a statue of Armstrong to be placed in **Louis Armstrong Park.** On July 9, 1971, Crosby was an honorary pallbearer at Armstrong's **funeral.** On the following day he wrote to **Lucille Armstrong** (in a letter of condolence that can be found in **Louis Armstrong House and Archives** Scrapbook #72): "I know of no man for whom I had more admiration and respect."

crossover. Armstrong pioneered the recording of music that appealed to more than one type of audience. With country music star **Jimmie Rodgers** in 1930 he recorded the still popular "Blue Yodel No. 9." Later that same year, Armstrong also did a Hawaiian crossover, recording "Song of the Islands" with the **Luis Russell** band (supplemented by violins). At about the same time, he did the Cuban rumba "The Peanut Vendor," with which some say he initiated Latin jazz. (**Dizzy Gillespie,** whom many credit with founding the Latin jazz movement, was thirteen years old at the time and had been playing the trumpet for only a few months.) Later, in 1938, Armstrong recorded the first jazz version of a spiritual, "When the Saints Go Marching In." Finally, at a 1940 session with drummer **Sid Catlett,** Armstrong anticipated rap music with three numbers, including the memorable "You've Got Me Voodoo'd."

"Crystal Chandeliers." Rec. August 1970 in New York City with the Nashville Group. See comments on "Almost Persuaded."

"Cuban Pete." By Jose Norman; rec. July 7, 1937, in New York City by Louis Armstrong and His Orchestra. Armstrong was always quick to pick up a hit and record it in his own inimitable way. Here he does so with the 1936 Desi Arnaz hit from the movie of the same name.

"Cucaracha, La." By Dominico Savion and Ned Washington; rec. October 3, 1935, in New York City by Louis Armstrong and His Orchestra; CD #51. When **Joe Glaser** took over as Armstrong's manager in 1935, he negotiated an exclusive record deal with **Decca,** then an ambitious new company. "La Cucaracha" was among the first batch of recordings, and although seemingly an unpromising choice, it inspired a memorable version from Armstrong.

"Cultural Exchange." By **Dave** and Iola **Brubeck;** rec. September 19, 1961, in New York City by **Louis Armstrong and the All Stars** with pianist Dave Brubeck and guests; CD #50. In the late 1950s, both Armstrong and Dave Brubeck were at the height of their fame. Nevertheless, Armstrong, frequently an official jazz ambassador to the world, could still be refused service in his own country. In 1960 both Brubeck and Armstrong had their southern U.S. tours canceled once the promoters discovered that their bands were racially mixed. This and other events like it, along with a general climate of racism, inspired Brubeck and his lyricist wife Iola to write ***The Real Ambassadors,*** a kind of jazz oratorio that focuses on Armstrong himself. The work was intended as lighthearted satire, but the result was pretty serious. "Cultural Exchange" (an Armstrong-**Trummy Young** duet which comes immediately after the opening "Everybody's Comin' ") states the theme of the entire work: jazz with its nearly universal appeal can unite diverse people.

cutting contest. This is the name for a competition between soloists or sometimes bands to decide which is better, as defined by either artistry or endurance. Armstrong grew up with the practice in New Orleans, when two bands would meet by chance on the streets. In the soloists' version, competing musicians typically alternate choruses of the same piece, and in this Armstrong excelled. In 1922 when he arrived in Chicago, he decisively won memorable cutting contests with **Freddie Keppard** and **Natty Dominique.** It is in the nature of such contests, however, that one day you'll loose. When the new **bop** style first showed up in the 1940s, Armstrong was drawn into what in retrospect can be seen as a hypothetical cutting contest with **Dizzy Gillespie,** Charlie Parker, Thelonious Monk, and others. At issue was the redefining of jazz, and Armstrong lost. Bop, too, eventually lost ground to new styles—free jazz, Latin jazz, and jazz fusions—although it, like New Orleans jazz and **swing** music, has taken a place in the pantheon of genres.

D

"Dallas Blues." By Lloyd Garrett and Hart A. Wand; rec. December 10, 1929, in New York City by Louis Armstrong and His Orchestra. In this recording of the first blues ever published (March 1912), Armstrong delivers the song with restraint, then lets trombonist **J.C. Higginbotham** have a solo. On the periphery is the young trumpeter **Red Allen,** whom some thought would be Armstrong's successor. It is said that this is the recording that led Gypsy guitarist **Django Reinhardt** to jazz (Morgenstern, *Cultural Legacy,* 1994, p. 125).

"Dardanella." By Fred Fisher, Felix Bernard, and Johnny S. Black; rec. July 5, 1960, in New York City with vocalist **Bing Crosby** and a studio band and choir conducted by Billy May. Armstrong and Crosby were magic together, and among their many duets is this popular 1919 song recorded for the *Bing and Satchmo* LP. Unfortunately, it did not get onto a CD. However, an earlier recording—made with **Louis Armstrong and the All Stars** on October 29, 1955, in Amsterdam—is on the *Ambassador Satch* CD reissue (CD #1).

Darensbourg, Joseph Wilmer "Joe" (1906–1985). This Baton Rouge-born clarinetist grew up musically in New Orleans, then toured extensively before settling in Seattle where from 1929 to 1944 he worked on cruise liners and played in local clubs. Deciding to specialize in New Orleans-style music, he was a member of **Kid Ory**'s band from 1947 to 1953, then formed the Dixie Flyers, with which he made the 1957 hit recording "Yellow Dog Blues." From June 1961 to February 1965 he worked with the **All Stars,** who toured the globe during these years. Afterward he worked with his own and other traditional jazz groups, such as the Legends of Jazz. Darensbourg appears in the 1962 film ***Goodyear Jazz Concert: Louis Armstrong,*** where his versatile technique and warm tone can be heard on "When the Saints Go Marching In" and other numbers. He was also a composer, example, "Lou-easy-an-ia." With the help of Peter Vacher, Darensbourg wrote an autobiography titled *Jazz Odyssey* (1988).

"Darling Nellie Gray." By B.R. Hamby; rec. April 7, 1937, in New York City with the **Mills Brothers.** Armstrong had good chemistry with the popular Mills Brothers, and here he creates some quietly marvelous figures (at first on open horn and then with a straight mute) behind their vocal lines. See additional comments on "Carry Me Back to Old Virginny."

Davis, Miles Dewey, III (1926–1991). The innovative jazz trumpeter had ambivalent feelings about Armstrong. In his 1989 autobiography Davis placed a photograph of Armstrong among photographs of the actors who played the fictional characters Beulah, Buckwheat, and Rochester with the caption: "Some of the images of black people that I would fight against throughout my career. I loved Satchmo, but I couldn't stand all that grinning he did" (following p. 96). However, Davis, like every other budding trumpeter in the 1940s, grew up with Armstrong's sound in his ears. After high school graduation, he headed to Juilliard but dropped out to play with Charlie Parker, his idol, as well as the big bands of Benny Carter, Billy Eckstine, and others. Davis struck out on his own in 1948. With the help of arranger Gil Evans, the Davis nonet made a series of recordings that were later reissued in 1950 as *The Birth of the Cool.* He went on to form various quintets and sextets, which included such players as Cannonball Adderley, John Coltrane, Herbie Hancock, and Keith Jarrett. Davis's performances and recordings from the 1950s to the 1970s received critical acclaim and earned the trumpeter financial rewards far beyond that of most contemporary musicians. **Drugs,** alcohol, an automobile accident, and in 1982, a stroke limited Davis's recording and touring.

Davis first came to Armstrong's attention as part of the mid-1940s development of the be**bop** style of jazz. It wasn't the trumpeter in particular but rather that "them cats [Kenny Clarke, **Dizzy Gillespie,** Thelonious Monk, Charlie Parker, Bud Powell, Max Roach, and others] play too much—a whole lot of notes, weird notes. . . . That stuff means nothing. You've got to carry the melody" (Brothers, pp. 216–217). Frankly, the controversy was overblown and exploited by Armstrong's management for the sake of publicity. There was always some grudging mutual respect. Davis and others (e.g., Dizzy Gillespie) perked up when Armstrong took a public stand over the school desegregation in **Little Rock** in 1957. Armstrong in turn paid attention and gave compliments when Davis's *Porgy and Bess* album came out the following year. Finally, in May 1970 Davis was one of the many admirers to show up for the making of the album *Louis Armstrong and His Friends,* Armstrong's next to last (CD #31). "You know you can't play anything on the horn that Louis hasn't played—I mean even modern," admitted Davis (Garner, p. 90).

Davis, Peter. Armstrong's first formal music teacher taught at the **Colored Waif's Home** where Armstrong was placed for shooting a pistol into the air on New Year's Eve 1912. Davis first gave Armstrong a tambourine, then a snare drum, alto horn, bass drum, bugle, and finally (to reward good behavior) the cornet. Eventually Davis made him the leader of the ensemble. "Then I was in seventh heaven," Armstrong recalled in ***Satchmo: My Life in New Orleans.*** "Unless I was dreaming, my ambition had been realized" (p. 46). When he was released on June 16, 1914, Armstrong felt ambivalent about leaving Davis and the Waif's.

Davis, Sammy, Jr. (1925–1990). The popular singer, actor, and dancer worked with Armstrong on the movie ***A Man***

Called Adam (1966), in which Armstrong at last had an opportunity to display his considerable dramatic range. In fact, Davis later observed that the film really became Armstrong's. A decade earlier, however, Davis had not been so generous with his praise. He and others (such as African American statesman Adam Clayton Powell) initially criticized Armstrong's speaking out against **segregation** in **Little Rock** public schools.

De Paris, Wilbur (1900–1973). Before he settled on the trombone and became a bandleader, Wilbur De Paris (older brother of trumpeter and tuba player Sidney De Paris [1905–1967]) played the alto horn with his father's circus band. In New Orleans in 1922, he played the C-melody saxophone with Armstrong, but the two did not work together again until 1937–1940. De Paris can be heard prominently on "I Double Dare You" (1938). He later worked with **Duke Ellington, Ella Fitzgerald, Roy Eldridge,** and others, and he led a band at Jimmy Ryan's in New York (1951–1962). Following in Armstrong's path, De Paris made a U.S. State Department tour of Africa in 1957 (see **African tours**). He continued as a bandleader until 1972.

"Dead Drunk Blues." By Hersal Thomas; rec. May 6, 1927, in Chicago with vocalist **Sippie Wallace** and clarinetist Artie Starks; CD #36. See additional comments on "Baby, I Can't Use You No More."

"Dear Old Southland." By Harry Creamer and Turner Leyton; rec. April 5, 1930, in New York City by Louis Armstrong and pianist **Buck Washington;** CDs #8, #13, #25, #49, #52, #60, and #61. In order to issue the Armstrong–**Hines** duet "Weather Bird" (1928), **Okeh Records** had to put something on the flip side and eventually decided on this nostalgic Armstrong–Washington instrumental duet. Armstrong plays the song (a.k.a. "Deep River" and well known by all African American musicians born in the South) mostly without strict tempo, except for a brief double-time passage. He kept "Southland" in his repertory as a change of pace. A January 28, 1957, recording with **Billy Kyle** at the keyboard shows how expressive Armstrong had become after more than a quarter of a century. In addition to quoting liberally from "Summertime" (perhaps getting ready for his upcoming *Porgy and Bess* recording date with **Ella Fitzgerald**), he and Kyle also get the traditional song to **swing.**

death. See **funeral.**

Decca Records. Established in England in 1929, this very successful record company in 1934 spun off an American branch due to the efforts of **Jack Kapp,** who signed Armstrong. It was a felicitous decision all around. During the next seven years (until the **American Federation of Musicians** [AFM] recording ban of 1942) Armstrong recorded more than 120 sides. It was also a controversial decision, since Kapp's philosophy was to have Armstrong record not only mainstream popular standards (e.g., "Ain't Misbehavin' "), but anything and everything. Jazz purists were upset when Armstrong cut novelty tunes (e.g., "The Music Goes 'round and Around"), Hawaiian songs ("To You, Sweetheart, Aloha"), sacred music ("Nobody Knows the Trouble I've Seen"), "hillbilly" music (i.e., country and western), duets with other singers (e.g., **Bing Crosby**) and vocal groups (e.g., the **Mills Brothers**), and covers of other artists' hits and made guest appearances with popular name bands (e.g., the **Jimmy Dorsey** Orchestra). The effect of all this vinyl was to (1) make Armstrong a household name and (2) show that Armstrong could make art out of unpromising material. Kapp also allowed Armstrong to give equal time to singing, which made his voice immediately recognizable throughout the United States. After the AFM record ban was lifted in 1944, Armstrong's manager **Joe Glaser** found it advantageous not to sign his client to exclusive contracts, although he did return to Decca from 1949 to 1954. During this second period, Armstrong had the good fortune to work with producer **Milt Gabler,** who, among other achievements, was responsible for the landmark four-LP set *Satchmo: A Musical Autobiography* (CD #52). In 1959 American Decca was bought by Music Corporation of America, which continued to use the Decca name for its backlist but issued subsequent recordings under the name MCA.

Deems, Barrett (1914–1998). Deems's reputation as "the world's fastest drummer" makes him sound more like a high-strung soloist than the steady, reliable sideman he really was in a great many bands (Joe Venuti's, **Muggsy Spanier**'s, the **Dukes of Dixieland,** and others), including **Louis Armstrong and the All Stars** from mid-1954 to early 1958. During this period, the band took U.S. State Department tours to Europe, Africa, and the Far East (as documented in the 1957 film ***Satchmo the Great***). (See **"Ambassador Satch."**) As a white man Deems must have been a plus in an ensemble that represented the United States, but he came in for criticism from those who thought jazz the sole province of African American musicians. Nevertheless, Armstrong liked his firm beat (e.g., "Now You Has Jazz" in the 1956 film ***High Society***) as well as his delicate brushwork (e.g., "Perdido," which featured pianist **Billy Kyle**). After the All Stars, Deems centered his activities in Chicago, although in 1976 he toured Eastern Europe with **Benny Goodman.** In the early 1980s he toured South America with Wild Bill Davison and Europe with Keith Smith.

"Deep Water Blues." By **Hociel Thomas;** rec. on February 24, 1926, in Chicago with vocalist Hociel Thomas and pianist Hersal Thomas; CD #36. See comments on "Adam and Eve Had the Blues."

Denmark. Armstrong was given large, enthusiastic receptions throughout his career, but the first was in Copenhagen, where he arrived on October 19, 1933, to begin a tour of Denmark, Norway, Sweden, and Holland. He was unaware that he had developed a big following in Scandinavia, where long before his arrival jazz fans had formed "Hot Clubs" to listen to and discuss jazz in general and his records in particular. Some 10,000 fans were waiting when he got off the train. Armstrong at first thought the lily white crowd was waiting for someone else until, presented with a huge bouquet of flowers arranged in the form of a trumpet, he was placed in an open car at the head of a parade. His subsequent performances were so popular that he was asked to be in the movie ***København, Kalundborg Og?***—which serves as a valuable historical document of his early performance style.

Armstrong returned to friendly Denmark frequently throughout his career—October 1949, February 1952, October 1955, January 1959 (when he made another film, ***Kaerlighedens Melodi***), February 1961, May 1962, and June 1965.

Depression. See **Great Depression.**

Dickerson, Carroll (1895–1957). Bandleader and violinist Dickerson had a polished ensemble when Armstrong joined it at the **Sunset Cafe** on April 10, 1926. "Dickerson's band was the best cabaret band on the South Side of Chicago at that time," Armstrong remembered (Brothers, p. 72). Early in 1927 Dickerson was fired for drunkenness, and Armstrong took over the band, now renamed Louis Armstrong and His Stompers (although pianist **Earl Hines** was the functional leader). In March 1928, Dickerson was back leading an orchestra at the newly opened **Savoy Ballroom,** and Armstrong joined him there. Armstrong took a few musicians from this ensemble (banjoist **Mancy Carr,** Earl Hines, trombonist **Fred Robinson,** drummer **Zutty Singleton,** and clarinetist **Jimmy Strong**) to make a batch of **Hot Five** recordings beginning in June 1928 (e.g., "West End Blues"). In May 1929 Armstrong took the ensemble, with Dickerson as conductor, to New York, where for a year they worked at **Connie's Inn.** They also made some enduring recordings, including three from ***Connie's Hot Chocolates:*** "Ain't Misbehavin'" (where Dickerson plays a brief, undistinguished violin solo); "(What Did I Do to Be So) Black and Blue?"; and "That Rhythm Man." When Armstrong's career began to move in different channels, Dickerson eventually returned to Chicago.

"Didn't It Rain." Traditional; rec. February 6, 1958, in New York City by **Louis Armstrong and the All Stars** with the **Sy Oliver** Choir; CD #27. Armstrong leaves his trumpet in its case on this call-and-response favorite. See additional comments on "Down by the Riverside."

Diet Does It. See **Hauser, Gayelord.**

"Dimi dimi dimi." Rec. December 11, 1967, in New York City by **Louis Armstrong and the All Stars,** trumpeter **Clark Terry,** and others.

"Dinah." By Sam M. Lewis, Joe Young, and Harry Akst; rec. May 4, 1930, in New York City by Louis Armstrong and His Orchestra; CDs #12, #21, #24, and #44. This was an old standard in 1930, and Armstrong freshens it with a quick tempo, which he makes seem faster than it is by playing just a few long notes. He plays it in the 1933 Danish film ***København, Kalundborg Og?*** offering a fascinating insight into the way he performed early in his career. After announcing the song, he zooms around the stage in a crouching position, perspiring and flourishing his handkerchief.

"Dippermouth." This is one of the earliest of Armstrong's many **nicknames.** It was used in the title of the 1923 song "Dippermouth Blues," which he co-wrote with his mentor **King Oliver.** Many of his nicknames affectionately refer to his mouth size, example, "Gatemouth" and "Satchelmouth" (= **Satchmo**).

"Dippermouth Blues." By **Joe Oliver** and Louis Armstrong; rec. April 6, 1923, in Richmond, Indiana, by King Oliver's Creole Jazz Band; CDs #8, #34, #35, #44, #52, and #61. Here is one of Oliver's best solos, boldly standing out from the general texture of the piece, and Armstrong directly imitated it the following year in a recording with **Fletcher Henderson.** The biggest differences between the two renditions are the addition of a secondary theme by arranger **Don Redman** and the change in title to "Sugar Foot Stomp." (The original title "Dippermouth" comes from one of Armstrong's early nicknames and refers to the size of his mouth.) Armstrong was the first of many cornet or trumpet players who, out of respect for both the originator and the solo itself, preserved Oliver's notes. Another performance tradition in "Dippermouth/Sugar Foot" is for someone to shout, "Oh, play that thing," which was originated by Oliver's banjo player Bill Johnson in an effort to coax the shy drummer, **Baby Dodds.** Armstrong returned to this number throughout his life, for example, at the pivotal **Carnegie Hall concert** on February 8, 1947. So influential is this piece that, like a Bach cantata, a Beethoven symphony, or a Brahms lied, it regularly appears in music appreciation textbooks.

discography. See Appendix 1.

Disney, Walter Elias "Walt" (1901–1966). At about the same time that the animation pioneer and movie producer was beginning to win fame for Mickey Mouse, the 1938 *Snow White,* and the 1939 *Pinocchio,* he had a tangential relationship with Armstrong. Disney made the sets for the 1939 Rockefeller Center production of a jazz version of Shakespeare's *A Midsummer Night's Dream* (see ***Swingin' the Dream***). His designs evoked Louisiana in the 1890s, and in the show Armstrong played **Bottom** the Weaver, in a bright red fireman's suit. Unfortunately, the production lasted only thirteen performances. In 1962 Armstrong performed at **Disneyland** on the *Mark Twain,* a recreated Mississippi riverboat. In 1968, an ailing Armstrong recorded the playful *Disney Songs the Satchmo Way* (CD #15), one of his last albums and the very last recording on which he played the trumpet.

Disneyland. Numerous prominent musicians have performed at the Anaheim, California, amusement park (brainchild of **Walt Disney**) since it opened in 1955, for example, Count Basie, **Benny Goodman,** and **Earl Hines.** Armstrong was there, too. In fact, there was somewhat of a reunion in 1962 when he appeared along with his longtime friends trombonist **Kid Ory** and banjoist **Johnny St. Cyr** on the *Mark Twain,* a recreated Mississippi riverboat. (A charming group portrait can be seen in Miller, p. 138.) Two years later, Armstrong further demonstrated the broad appeal of New Orleans-style jazz with a hit recording of "Hello Dolly!"

Disneyland after Dark. This Disney short subject film was released in April 1962. Armstrong appears prominently, along with Mouseketeers Annette Funicello, Bobby Rydell, Bobby Burgess, trombonist **Kid Ory,** the Osmond Brothers, and others. Disney, 1962; color; 16 mins.; Dir. H.S. Luske and William Beaudine.

"Dixie." By Daniel Decatur Emmett; rec. May 24 or 25, 1960, in New York City with the **Dukes of Dixieland;** CD #53. Armstrong and the Dukes give this famous Civil War song a rousing, straightforward performance. See additional comments on "Avalon."

Dixieland. This term has been used very loosely for everything from early New Orleans jazz played by white musicians to the post-1940 revival of traditional jazz. The term "Dixieland" itself came from a group of white New Orleans musicians who from 1917 became internationally famous as the Original Dixieland Jazz Band. Later, as the **Great Depression** wore on and World War II began, a wave of nostalgia made New Orleans jazz appealing to a people feeling the pressures of an increasingly complex world. **Louis Armstrong and the All Stars** (1947–1971) was one of many bands that was formed at this time. While not exactly a Dixieland band, it incorporated some traditional New Orleans jazz characteristics (e.g., the instrumentation and the polyphonic texture) and repertory ("Indiana" and "Muskrat Ramble"). See also **Dukes of Dixieland.**

"Do Nothin' Till You Hear from Me." By **Duke Ellington** and Bob Russell; rec. August 14, 1957, in Los Angeles with a studio orchestra conducted by arranger Russell Garcia; CD #11. Ellington wrote this in 1943 for his trumpet player Cootie Williams. He later adapted it with Bob Russell's lyrics, and it was picked up by Woody Herman, Stan Kenton, and others. It is interesting to compare Armstrong's dramatic performance here with the more intimate one recorded April 3, 1961, in New York City by **Louis Armstrong and the All Stars** with Ellington himself at the keyboard. See additional comments on "Azalea."

"Do You Know What It Means to Miss New Orleans?" By Lou Alter and Eddy DeLange; rec. October 17, 1946, in Los Angeles by Louis Armstrong and His Dixieland Seven; CDs #12, #13, #16, #17, #19, #21, #25, #28, #47, #57, and #60. During the previous month, Armstrong and his men, plus **Billie Holiday** and a choir, had recorded this nostalgic song for the **movie *New Orleans,*** and eventually it became one of his staples.

"Doctor Jazz." By **Joe Oliver** and Walter Melrose; rec. between September 30 and October 2, 1959, in Los Angeles by **Louis Armstrong and the All Stars.**

Doctor Rhythm. **Bing Crosby** stars in this comedy about a physician who fills in for a friend who is a policeman. Armstrong's only contribution, "The Trumpet Player's Lament," was cut from the final version and apparently lost. British Armstrong fans Jones and Chilton propose, but then dispose of, racist reasons for so doing: "Bing's brother, Larry, issued a statement denying discrimination and stressing that such scissor work was common practice in Hollywood, which indeed it was" (p. 196). Paramount, 1938; B&W; 81 mins.; Dir. Frank Tuttle.

Dodds, Johnny (1892–1940). When the young Armstrong left his New Orleans home in August 1922 to join his mentor **King Oliver** in Chicago, it was a great relief to find so many childhood friends, such as clarinetist Johnny Dodds (and his younger brother, the drummer **Baby Dodds**) on the bandstand. "I was tickled to death to see them all," he frankly admitted in ***Swing That Music*** (p. 69). Dodds's early career in many ways resembled Armstrong's. From 1912 to 1919 he worked on and off with the **Kid Ory** band, in 1917 he toured with **Fate Mar-**

able's riverboat band, and then around 1920 he joined King Oliver's Creole Jazz Band in Chicago. Dodds was there with Armstrong and the Oliver band for the now-famous 1923 recordings. He can be heard weaving elegantly in and out of the ensemble texture, for example, in "Chimes Blues." Like any good New Orleans-style clarinetist, Dodds knew how to filigree a chord change, as in "Dippermouth Blues." Later, when Armstrong led his **Hot Five** and **Hot Seven** in 1925–1927, he had Dodds by his side (or more precisely in front, since Armstrong's powerful sound required that he stand far away from the ensemble). Dodds played expressively and just slightly below pitch, which made for an effective blues sound. He also seemed occasionally to slide between notes and, like Armstrong, to use a terminal vibrato. Both characteristics can be heard on "Potato Head Blues" (1927). On "Weary Blues" (1927) and other numbers, Dodds demonstrates his excellent command of the low register. A savvy band leader, Dodds enticed Armstrong, under exclusive contract with **Okeh Records,** to quietly pick up a little extra cash by recording with his Black Bottom Stompers on **Vocalion Records.** In April 1927, they did three sides—"Weary Blues," "New Orleans Stomp," and "Melancholy." (Armstrong seems carefully to be disguising his style so as not to get caught moonlighting. For example, he plays with comparatively little invention, stays away from high notes, and never sings at all.) Dodds performed and recorded with others but mostly led his own band. Declining to tour, he remained in and around Chicago, frequently working with his brother.

Dodds, Warren "Baby" (1898–1959). The drummer and younger brother of clarinetist **Johnny Dodds** was one of the many musicians with whom Armstrong grew up in New Orleans. They both played, for example, with **Papa Celestin**'s snappy **Tuxedo Brass Band.** When Armstrong joined the **Fate Marable** band on the riverboat **S.S. *Sidney*** in 1919, Dodds had been there for a year, and he was already in Chicago with **King Oliver** when Armstrong arrived in 1922. (A drinking problem got Dodds fired by Marable, but he responded well to Oliver's tough love.) In both instances, Armstrong was happy to see Dodds's among other faces from his childhood. Dodds, however, recalls smiling more at the shabby clothes that Armstrong wore to his first day in the Marable orchestra. Armstrong reported for work in a jumper "faded so bad that it wasn't blue anymore.... He just sat there looking like the end man in a minstrel show" (Russell, p. 20). Along with his brother, Dodds worked with Armstrong in 1923 on those first King Oliver Creole Jazz Band recordings, but he is absent from the early **Hot Five** recordings (beginning November 1925) for the simple reason that drums could not be recorded well at the time. In 1927 the new electric technology permitted his part to be added, beginning with the **Hot Seven** recordings (cymbals, snare, and wood blocks mostly, and rarely bass drum, although Dodds plays effectively on the bass drum's rim). Dodds's performance on "Wild Man Blues" is a good example of his precise style. Baby Dodds shared his brother's aversion to touring (although he did go to Europe with **Mezz Mezzrow** in 1948), and he too remained in and around Chicago. In the 1930s, he often had to supplement his income by driving a taxi, but his fortunes took a positive turn with the New Orleans jazz revival in the 1940s. Dodds was much valued as a traditional performer, and his advice was often sought by the upcoming generation (e.g., Gene Krupa). In addition to a series of demonstration recordings for students, he left a fascinating account of his life in *The Baby Dodds Story* (as told to Larry Gara), published by the Louisiana State University Press in 1992.

dogs. Armstrong loved dogs and had several during his life. See **"General"; "Trinket"; "Trumpet."**

Dominique, Natty (1896–1982). Born in New Orleans, trumpeter Dominique grew up playing in parade brass bands, then, like so many musicians of the day, took his skill on the road, eventually settling in Chicago. When Armstrong caught up with him, Dominique represented somewhat of a challenge. They were both members of the **Carroll Dickerson** orchestra at the **Sunset Cafe** in 1926, where Dominique attempted to copy Armstrong's style. Although no recording was made, traces of this likeness still appear in Dominique's 1954 recording of "Big Butter and Egg Man," one of Armstrong's signature pieces. The story goes that Armstrong drew Dominique aside and strongly advised him to develop his own style. To underscore the point, Armstrong took Dominique to the Sunset bandstand for a "cutting contest" playing "Poor Little Rich Girl." After twenty-five choruses, Armstrong was still going strong, but Dominique had to sit down, put his trumpet in his lap, and listen. "I was angry at Louis once," he later recalled, but "I'm proud today that I'm not playing like Louis Armstrong" (Russell, pp. 150–152). When Armstrong left Chicago to follow his star, Dominique remained to work with **Johnny Dodds** and others. He wrote and recorded "Brush Stomp" in 1928. In the 1940s, though, he tapered off because of a heart condition and worked at the Chicago airport as a porter. However, he led a part-time group during the 1950s. Dominique was the uncle of trumpeter Don Albert (1908–1980) and cousin of clarinetist **Barney Bigard.**

"Don't Be That Way." By Edgar Sampson, **Benny Goodman,** and Mitchell Parish; rec. August 13, 1957, in Los Angeles with vocalist **Ella Fitzgerald** and the **Oscar Peterson** Quartet; CD #9. See comments on "April in Paris."

"Don't Fence Me In." By **Cole Porter** and Robert Fletcher; rec. January 21, 1955, live at the Crescendo Club in Los Angeles by **Louis Armstrong and the All Stars;** CD #6. Armstrong liked to cover hits, and this one, written in 1944 and introduced by Roy Rogers in the film *Hollywood Canteen,* was a natural choice. Here he is joined by All Star vocalist **Velma Middleton.**

"Don't Forget to Mess Around." By **Paul Barbarin** and Louis Armstrong; rec. June 16, 1926, in Chicago by Louis Armstrong and His **Hot Five;** CD #10. Clarinetist **Johnny Dodds** plays alto sax on this number, which Armstrong cowrote with an old New Orleans friend.

"Don't Get Around Much Anymore." By **Duke Ellington** and Bob Russell; rec. August 14, 1957, in Los Angeles with a studio orchestra conducted by arranger Russell Garcia; CDs #11 and #29. Armstrong could always breathe new life into an old classic (as this then fifteen-year-old song could already be called). He does so here, as well as four years later (April 3, 1961, in New York City) with the **All Stars** and Ellington himself at the keyboard. See additional comments on "Azalea."

"Don't Jive Me." By **Lil Hardin Armstrong;** rec. June 28, 1928, in Chicago by Louis Armstrong and His **Hot Five;** CD #10. Not released until 1940 probably because it was deemed inferior (e.g., lots of "wrong" notes by trombonist **Fred Robinson** and out-of-tune playing by clarinetist **Jimmy Strong**), this recording is distinguished by pianist **Earl Hines**'s **trumpet style**—clean single-note passages, a vibrato evoked by tremolo, and melodic lines within the trumpet range. Hines shows clearly that trumpet players were not the only ones influenced by Armstrong.

"Don't Play Me Cheap." By **Zilner Randolph** and Harry Dial; rec. April 26, 1933, in Chicago by Louis Armstrong and His Orchestra; CDs #12 and #24. Armstrong is not at his best on this song by trumpeter Randolph and drummer Dial. Perhaps it's just his interpretation, but he seems deeply tired, and the band is soggy. Gunther Schuller points out that Armstrong even forgets the words. You can hear the sheet music rustle as he turns the page quickly, and he fails to substitute **scat** for the missing text, which was his usual practice (Schuller, 1989, p. 184). Nevertheless, the show must go on and on and on. However, in January 1934 Armstrong rests in **England,** and in April he moves to Paris for an extended and much needed vacation.

Dorsey, Jimmy (1904–1957). Long before he became a popular bandleader, reed man Jimmy Dorsey and his trombonist brother Tommy (along with **Benny Goodman, Muggsy Spanier, Bix Beiderbecke,** and others) used to defy their parents and sneak down to the South Side of Chicago to hear Armstrong. Later Jimmy worked with Armstrong, memorably in ***Pennies from Heaven*** (1938), a cheerful movie about a wandering troubadour (**Bing Crosby**) recently released from prison. The plot involves a haunted house that is converted into a nightclub, and Armstrong is featured in the novelty tune "The Skeleton in the Closet," in which Dorsey band members wear ghostly masks.

Dorsey, Tommy (1905–1956). See **Dorsey, Jimmy.**

Douze années de jazz. See **Panassié, Hugues.**

Down Beat. One of the most widely respected jazz periodicals in the United States or anywhere, *Down Beat* has been published regularly (although the frequency has varied) since July 1934. The publication had an ambivalent relationship with Armstrong and still does. In the early annual reader polls, Armstrong's commercial success made him seem fairly insignificant. For example, the 1937 poll ranked him in third place as a trumpeter, and by 1944 his band did not get enough votes even to make the list. Throughout the year 1948 *Down Beat* had fun with Armstrong's speaking out against the new Be**bop** style (frequently quoting his " 'jujitsu' music" appraisal). "You get all them weird chords which don't mean nothing . . . and you got no melody to remember and no beat to dance to," he was quoted, Archie Bunker-like, in the April 7 issue (p. 2). When Armstrong reigned as **King of the Zulus** in the 1949 Mardi Gras Parade in New Orleans, *Down Beat*'s July 1 issue quoted the feisty young **Dizzy Gillespie**: "Louis is the plantation character that so many of us . . . resent" (p. 13). (However, in July 1950, they celebrated Armstrong's unofficial fiftieth birthday by devoting most of an issue to him.) *Down Beat* readers have sometimes been open-minded, however and in December 1952 not only elected him to the *Down Beat* Hall of Fame but also called him "the most important musical figure of all time" (p. 1). Armstrong beat out **Duke Ellington** (second place), Glenn Miller (fourth), and J.S. Bach (sixth).

Much of this publicity, especially the flap over bebop, was the work of Armstrong's manager, **Joe Glaser,** who worked hard to get articles about his client in *Down Beat* as well as ***Esquire*** and ***Vanity Fair.*** As the 1950s and 1960s wore on, though, not even Glaser could rally the interest of *Down Beat,* which tended to consider Armstrong more show business than jazz. Its writers and readers mostly ignored his concerts and records, even though no one else did. *Down Beat* shook itself awake long enough to dedicate the July 9, 1970, issue to Armstrong. (Nearly everyone was still under the mistaken notion that Armstrong's birthday was July 4, 1900.) Dan Morgenstern's reverential editorial read in part: "For more than half a century, this dedicated and beautiful man has been spreading joy on earth. Steadfastly, he has affirmed the eternal verities of love, beauty and goodness—as an artist and as a man" (p. 14).

When Armstrong died in 1971, the September 16 *Down Beat* began its story: "One of the greatest men of the twentieth century is dead . . ." (p. 12). Most recently, *Down Beat,* in flat-earth style, celebrated what they took to be Armstrong's one hundredth birthday with an all-Armstrong issue in July 2000. In addition to some good articles, including reprints of Armstrong's ever-fresh writing, they couldn't resist reviving the bebop subject.

Incidentally, the name *Down Beat* has also been used for nightclubs in Chicago, Los Angeles, New York, San Francisco, and elsewhere. The term "downbeat" itself refers to the first and strongest beat of the measure.

"Down by the Riverside." Traditional; rec. February 4, 1958, in New York City by **Louis Armstrong and the All Stars** with the **Sy Oliver** Choir; CD #27. Recorded for an album titled *Louis and the Good Book,* this number (which dates back at least as far as 1865) contrasts strongly with the typical All Stars music. Not surprisingly, though, Armstrong performs spirituals with the same verve as he does popular hits. Also not surprisingly, he gets them to **swing.**

"Down in Honky Tonk Town." By Chris Smith and Charles McCarron; rec. May 27, 1940, in New York City by Louis Armstrong and His Orchestra; CD #44. Everybody gets a chance to play on this lively number, and clarinetist **Sidney Bechet** once again tries to outshine Armstrong.

"Dream a Little Dream of Me." By Wilbur Schwant, Fabian Andre, and Gus Kahn; rec. July 23, 1968, in Las Vegas by **Louis Armstrong and the All Stars;** CDs #4, #28, #40, #61, and #62. This is a late recording of a 1931 song that Armstrong started singing with **Ella Fitzger-**

ald in the 1940s. He kept it in his repertory and here sings it solo with poignant nostalgia.

Dreamland Ballroom. This popular Chicago nightclub (at 35th and State Street) opened in 1912, and in 1920 it was renovated and reopened as the **Dreamland Café.**

Dreamland Café. After renovations in 1920 the **Dreamland Ballroom** was renamed the Dreamland Café. It was a luxurious nightclub where both white and black couples danced. Patrons would seat themselves at small tables to watch a floor show, and afterward jazz musicians would continue to play for general dancing. In the winter of 1923, Armstrong's mentor **King Oliver** took him there to meet a pianist by the name of **Lil Hardin,** who soon joined Oliver's Creole Jazz Band. Armstrong later wrote that Oliver "didn't know, or maybe he *did* have an idea, that he was introducing me to my second wife" (***Swing That Music,*** pp. 70–71). Armstrong and Hardin were married the following year on February 5. The ambitious Lil encouraged her husband to develop his career, which soon meant leaving Oliver. For a short time in 1924 Armstrong worked with **Ollie Powers** and his Harmony Syncopators at Dreamland. When he next stayed too long in New York with the **Fletcher Henderson** Orchestra on what was to have been a temporary gig, Lil issued an ultimatum, and he returned to Chicago to join Lil's Hot Shots at the Dreamland Café. He earned $75 per week. (A whopping sum, although **Bix Beiderbecke** was making $100 per week with the Goldkette band at about the same time.) Trumpeter Doc Cheatham had vivid memories of Armstrong's return to Dreamland: "They had trucks with banners with Louis' name on them going all around Chicago: 'Louis Armstrong Coming Back to Chicago!' They had a record playing all of his things. You could hear it all over the South Side" (Deffaa, 1992, p. 18). The Dreamland Café was closed down in 1928 for violating liquor laws, but it reopened in 1933 at another Chicago location.

"Drop Me Off in Harlem." By **Duke Ellington** and Nick Kenny; rec. April 4, 1961, in New York City by **Louis Armstrong and the All Stars** with Duke Ellington; CD #11. Ellington liked the way Armstrong treated his old songs, and to this one from 1931 he even brought fresh lyrics. See additional comments on "Azalea."

"Drop That Sack." By Louis Armstrong; rec. May 28, 1926, in Chicago with **Lil**'s Hot Shots; CDs #10 and #61. Although under exclusive contract with **Okeh Records,** Armstrong made this and "Georgia Bo Bo" for **Vocalion Records** with his wife Lil's band, the Hot Shots. Called on the carpet, so the story goes, he said: "I don't know who made those records, but I won't do it again" (Jones and Chilton, p. 226). He did, though, eight more times. Here he seems a little tired, or is he just trying to disguise his sound from the Okeh executives?

"Droppin' Shucks." By **Lil Hardin Armstrong;** rec. June 16, 1926, in Chicago by Louis Armstrong and His **Hot Five;** CD #10. Armstrong and Hardin were married on February 5, 1924, and his eye had begun to wander long before this song of romantic revenge.

drugs. Jazz has been associated with just about every kind of controlled and uncontrolled substance, and Louis was involved with one in particular. While he viewed trendy drugs such as heroin with disdain, he was a confirmed **marijuana** smoker. He praised it openly and actively advocated its use. However, while marijuana was important to him, he used it sparingly and basically to unwind after a gig. He was in most respects a very health-conscious person, who drank moderately (and never before a job), watched his diet (albeit in his own quirky way), and never used hard drugs. His grand addiction was his work, for which he tried to keep in shape. (He also smoked Camel cigarettes and had a fondness for **laxatives,** such as **Swiss Kriss,** which he urged on virtually everyone he met.)

DuConge, Peter (c. 1903–1965). The New Orleans-born saxophonist and clarinetist came from a musical family, played on riverboats, and settled for a time in New York. In 1928 he toured Europe, and like many other African American entertainers (such as **Josephine Baker, Arthur Briggs, Alberta Hunter,** and Bobby Jones), DuConge found life so amenable that he remained there. He was thus available when, in 1932 and 1934, Armstrong needed to put together tour bands. DuConge also worked with **Coleman Hawkins,** Benny Peyton, and others. His skill in accommodating New Orleans jazz and **swing** style, for example, on "Foxy and Grapesy" (1933), was much admired. DuConge was married to **Ada Smith,** a.k.a. "Bricktop," the singer and nightclub owner, and Armstrong was a frequent guest at their home.

Dukes of Dixieland. Organized in 1949 by New Orleans brothers Freddie and Frank Assunto from a group founded by them in 1946, the Dukes rocketed to fame in the 1950s and stayed there. They toured widely and, after settling in Las Vegas in 1956, issued a series of internationally popular recordings, including some with Armstrong. "They . . . were sensational from the first day that they left New Orleans," Armstrong wrote in 1969. "You can see how happy I am to know that I finally had a chance to *blow* with White Boys *at last* in my home town New Orleans (about time—*huh*?)" (Brothers, p. 35). Like **Louis Armstrong and the All Stars,** the Dukes of Dixieland were part and parcel of the wave of nostalgia that swept the country after World War II. Americans wanted to have the good old days back again, and traditional music seemed to help simplify an increasingly complex world. The Dukes' straightforward renditions of "Avalon," "Sweet Georgia Brown," "Dixie," "When It's Sleepy Time Down South," and other favorites met that need. Also like Armstrong's All Stars, the Dukes took **Dixieland** on tour—to Japan in 1964, Southeast Asia in 1967, and elsewhere. After the deaths of their founders (trombonist Freddie in 1966 and trumpeter Frank in 1974), the group was based in New Orleans, where for several years they had their own club at the Monteleone Hotel.

"Duke's Place." By Ruth Roberts, Bill Katz, Bob Thiele, and **Duke Ellington;** rec. April 3, 1961, in New York City by **Louis Armstrong and the All Stars** with Duke Ellington; CD #11. This sprightly 1958 number opens the 1961 Armstrong–Ellington album. Without lyrics, this number is called " 'C' Jam Blues." See additional comments on "Azalea."

"Dummy Song, The." By Lew Brown, Billy Rose, and Ray Henderson; rec. July 16, 1953, in New York City with the Jack Pleiss Orchestra; CDs #22 and #39.

"Dusky Stevedore." By Andy Razaf and J.C. Johnson; rec. April 24, 1933, in Chicago by Louis Armstrong and His Orchestra; CDs #12 and #24. With this and several other songs of the day, **Victor Records** was aiming for commercial success, and neither Armstrong nor the ensemble respond well to the Uncle Tom lyrics. Frankly, the piece had worked better for the white trumpeter (and Armstrong admirer) **Bix Beiderbecke,** who recorded it with the Frankie Trumbauer Orchestra in 1928. "Dusky Stevedore" eventually became the theme song of Nat Shilkret and His Orchestra.

Dutrey, Honoré (1894–1935). This trombonist and his clarinetist brother Sam, Sr. (c. 1888–1941) were among the many "good old-timers like **Joe Oliver,** Roy Palmer, **Oscar Celestin,** Oak Gasper, **Buddy Petit, Kid Ory** and **Mutt Carey** and his brother Jack" whom Armstrong affectionately remembered playing with as a teen in New Orleans funeral **brass bands** (***Satchmo,*** 1954, p. 92). With the outbreak of World War I, Dutrey went off to serve in the navy, where he suffered lung damage but, with medication, was still able to work with Oliver in Chicago from 1920 to 1924. Dutrey's face was one of several (**Baby Dodds**'s, **Johnny Dodds**'s, and Bill Johnson's) that Armstrong was happy to see on the bandstand when he arrived in Chicago in August 1922. Armstrong worked with Dutrey and the others until 1924, when both left—Dutrey to lead his own band and Armstrong to the **Fletcher Henderson** band in New York. Later in the 1920s and back in Chicago, the two worked together several more times, until Dutrey's poor health forced him into retirement in 1930. Before then, however, his sweet tone and elegant, cello-like lines left a distinctive mark on numerous recordings, such as "Chimes Blues," "Snake Rag," and "Tears"—all from 1923. Armstrong had the highest respect for Dutrey. "To me he was one of the *finest* Trombone players who left New Orleans and went to Chicago," he wrote nearly fifty years later (Brothers, p. 26). Dutrey was the uncle of clarinetist and saxophonist Sam Dutrey, Jr. (1909–1971).

E

"Early Every Morn." By Billy Higgins and W. Benton Overstreet; rec. December 22, 1924, in New York City with vocalist **Josephine Beatty** and the Red Onion Jazz Babies; CDs #35 and #36. In order to get around an exclusive **Gennett Records** contract, **Alberta Hunter** also recorded under the name of her half sister Josephine Beatty. She, Armstrong, and the Red Onion Jazz Babies did serviceable versions of this song and a few others, such as "Everybody Loves My Baby," "Of All the Wrongs You Done to Me," and "Texas Moaner Blues."

"Early in the Morning." By Billy Higgins and W. Benton Overstreet; rec. October 17, 1924, in New York City with vocalist Virginia Liston and **Clarence Williams' Blue Five;** CD #36. Liston was one of many minor blues singers (such as **Chippie Hill, Clara Smith,** and **Trixie Smith**) whom Armstrong accompanied while he was coming up in the 1920s. Typically here he supplies an inventive commentary.

"East of the Sun." By Brooks Bowman; rec. August 14, 1957, in Los Angeles with a studio orchestra conducted by arranger Russell Garcia. Armstrong seems comfortable with this large ensemble, and the sound engineers with their ever improving technology have been unusually careful to make his solo clearly audible.

"Easy Come, Easy Go Blues." By Roy Bergere; rec. April 21, 1927, in Chicago with **Jimmy Bertrand**'s Washboard Wizards. See comments on "The Blues Stampede."

"Easy Part's Over Now, The." Rec. August 1970 in New York City with the Nashville Group. See comments on "Almost Persuaded."

"Easy Street." By **Harold Arlen** and **Johnny Mercer;** rec. September 9, 1955, in Los Angeles by **Louis Armstrong and the All Stars** with vocalist Gary Crosby; CD #8. Like father like son, and here **Bing**'s boy gets along famously with Bing's friend, while trombonist **Trummy Young** noodles around leisurely in the background.

Ebony. Armstrong was a frequent contributor to and subject in the pages of this popular African American magazine, and whether the focus was personal or political, he always made good copy. To the August 1954 issue, for example, he contributed "Why I Like Dark Women," in which he affectionately recalls meeting

Lucille Wilson, eventually his fourth and last wife, at the **Cotton Club** in 1939. She was working as a chorus girl, and "when I first saw her the glow of her deep-brown skin got me deep down," he admitted (p. 61). Such sentiments exhibit more than a trace of black-is-beautiful pride, and it should therefore not have been a surprise when in September 1957 he spoke directly to the issue of racial prejudice as Arkansas Governor **Orval Faubus** tried with the help of the National Guard to keep **Little Rock** schools segregated. Reflecting later in "Daddy, How the Country Has Changed!" (May 1961, p. 81), Armstrong expressed disappointment that fellow African Americans had accused him of being an Uncle Tom. "How can they say that?" he asked. "I've pioneered in breaking the color line in many Southern states." (Indeed, as early as the 1930s he began stipulating in his contracts that he wouldn't perform where he couldn't stay.) Privately, Armstrong frequently used *Ebony* photos (e.g., baseball player **Jackie Robinson,** singer-pianist Nat "King" Cole) and headlines ("Negroes Who Work on Broadway") to make collages with which he decorated his scrapbook covers and reel-to-reel tape boxes. He did over seven dozen of the former and 650 of the latter, and he even spilled over onto the walls and ceiling of his study. *Ebony* was begun in Chicago in November 1945 and has continued monthly to the present.

education. In 1907 Armstrong began attending New Orleans' **Fisk School for Boys,** which was at 507 South Franklin, within a block of his home. There he learned to read and write. He also must have learned some music, since the school had choirs, put on operettas, and employed prominent Creole music teachers. However, his informal education took place at **Funky Butt Hall,** right across the street from the Fisk School (e.g., he first heard **Buddy Bolden** play there), and also in the company of his employers, the **Karnofskys.** Because he was often tired from going to work for the Karnofskys at dawn and returning to work in the evening, Armstrong frequently skipped school. He dropped out in 1912, when he was eleven years old and in the fifth grade. Shortly thereafter, his frequent delinquent behavior, capped by firing a gun on New Year's Eve, got him sent to the **Colored Waif's Home,** where he spent a year and a half and reached what would be the end of his schooling. Never again in a classroom after the age of thirteen, Armstrong was the most prolific musician-**writer** in the jazz world, having produced two **autobiographies,** dozens of articles, hundreds of often rather-lengthy letters, and hundreds more pages of miscellaneous memoirs.

Edwards, Jody (1895–1967), **and Susie Hawthorne** (c. 1896–1963). Known as "Butterbeans and Susie," this popular vaudeville couple (married on stage in 1917) flourished from 1914 to 1963. In 1942 they worked with Armstrong in ***Cabin in the Sky,*** then went on to establish their own production company.

Eisenhower, Dwight David (1890–1969). U.S. president from 1953 to 1961, and a distinguished general before that, Eisenhower was in office when, despite a 1957 U.S. Supreme Court order to integrate public schools in **Little Rock,** Arkansas governor **Orval Faubus** vowed to keep the schools segregated. When Faubus called out the National Guard to assist him, the story received worldwide media coverage. Armstrong's reaction to the event received wide coverage as well. On tour in the small town of Grand Forks, North Dakota, on September 18, he watched the Arkansas scene on the television in his dressing room. Armstrong told a reporter that President Eisenhower was "two-faced" and had allowed an "uneducated plowboy," Governor Faubus, to run the federal government (*New York Herald Tribune,* Sept. 19, 1957, p. A3). Eisenhower sent federal troops to Arkansas to enforce integration, and while it is unrealistic to say that Armstrong's statement prompted the president's decision, it surely must have had an influence. Armstrong then remarked that things were looking up and on September 24 sent a telegram to the Eisenhower, saying in part: "[I]f and when you decide to take those little negro children personally into Central High School along with your marvelous troops, please take me along." Eisenhower seems to have retained a strong admiration for Armstrong, as evidenced by a warm birthday telegram sent eight years after the Little Rock incident (now part of the **Louis Armstrong House and Archives** at Queens College, this document is reprinted in Giddins, 1988, p. 204).

All Stars' bassist and Armstrong friend **Arvell Shaw** summed up the Eisenhower-Armstrong relationship succinctly when in 1997 he told scholar Joshua Berrett: "Most people when they have a flap with the president, man, you're finished, especially a president that was as popular as Dwight Eisenhower. But Mr. Eisenhower and the State Department realized this man . . . made more friends for this country than all of us put together" (1999, p. 169). A provocative fictional account of the Armstrong-Eisenhower Little Rock showdown is presented in playwright Ishmael Reed's 1997 ***C above C above High C.*** (In the same play, two of Armstrong's wives, **Lil Hardin** and **Lucille Wilson,** are sharply contrasted with Mamie Eisenhower.) In one area, though, Armstrong was unable to influence Eisenhower whatsoever: He wrote to urge the president to legalize **marijuana,** but nothing ever came of that.

"Elder Eatmore's Sermons." Rec. August 11, 1938, in New York City with organist Harry Mills and a studio choir probably conducted by Lyn Murray; CD #27. Armstrong the actor comes to the fore here in his recreation of two old comedy monologues, "Throwing Stones" and "Generosity." "Elder Eatmore," the con-man preacher, is a creation of African American vaudevillian Bert Williams. Previously known mostly to collectors, the "sermons" were included in the 2001 CD reissue of his 1958 bestselling album *Louis and the Good Book.*

Eldridge, David Roy "Little Jazz" (1911–1989). If an onion could serve to illustrate the development of jazz trumpet playing, at the center would be **Buddy Bolden,** who lived from 1877 to 1931, flourished from 1895 to 1905, and left no known recordings. In the first layer would be **King Oliver** (1885–1938), who as a soloist can be heard only on a few blues numbers and whose best years were not recorded. The next layer would be Louis Armstrong and then Roy Eldridge, who, although five feet five inches, stood out above his contemporaries **Buck Clayton,** Red Nichols, **Oran "Hot Lips"**

Page, Charlie Shavers, Jabbo Smith, **Rex Stewart,** and others.

After several false starts, Eldridge landed in New York in 1930 and played with various Harlem dance bands. He won national fame as a soloist with the **Fletcher Henderson** band in 1936 and 1937, then formed his own band in Chicago, but the **Great Depression** temporarily forced him to work for a time as a radio engineer. Not for long, though. Widely regarded as the most prominent jazz trumpet soloist of the day, he began to receive lucrative offers from white **swing** bands, and finally in 1941 he joined Gene Krupa, with whom he made hit recordings of "Rockin' Chair" and, with the singer Anita O'Day, "Let Me Off Uptown" (both in 1941). He was also on staff at CBS and in 1944 joined Artie Shaw's band.

Like Armstrong, Eldridge was disheartened by the many racial incidents he had to put up with on tours with Krupa and Shaw, and he discussed the subject in a frank article in *Negro Digest* (1950) and later expanded on it for the "Jazz and Race" chapter of **Leonard Feather**'s *The Book of Jazz* (1965, pp. 47–49). (See **civil rights.**) Again like Armstrong, Eldridge fell out of favor with the advent of be**bop**, and when a 1950 tour with **Benny Goodman** ended, he took a year's sabbatical in Paris. Eldridge here found the same respect for music and lack of racial prejudice that Armstrong enjoyed in 1934, and he returned to the United States with renewed confidence. For the rest of his career he maintained a busy schedule, and from 1969 to 1980 he led a traditional group at Jimmy Ryan's in New York.

Eldridge's style was deeply influenced by Armstrong, but not in every way. Unlike Armstrong who carefully built up to climactic high notes, Eldridge gave them away randomly and generously, for example, in "Heckler's Hop" and "After You've Gone" (both from 1937). The latter piece features high-register flourishes and moves easily and quickly over nearly three octaves. But it was Armstrong, though, who polished off Eldridge's rough edges. "I had this thing about playing as fast as I could all the time," Eldridge once told an interviewer (Balliett, 1989, p. 106). Armstrong taught him how to tell a story complete with introduction and conclusion. One can hear the difference in "Rockin' Chair," Eldridge's most famous solo, as well as in "Body and Soul," "I Surrender, Dear," "Star Dust," "Twilight Time," and many others from around 1938. On these pieces his improvisations are undergirded with careful construction, and he is not in such a great hurry to wow his audience. Many listeners prefer this later Eldridge, who, in the opinion of one critic, "had a cathedral quality that no other jazz trumpeter—even the 1932 Armstrong—has surpassed" (Balliett, 1989, p. 107).

Taking another page from Armstrong's book, Eldridge also sang. His "Let Me Off Uptown" duet with Anita O'Day was one of the novelty hits of 1941, and he went on to sing "Knock Me a Kiss," "Saturday Night Fish Fry," "School Days," and others. However, Eldridge by no means took everything from his elder. Armstrong once lent him his lip salve concoction (which contained spirits of nitrate). "I put that shit on my lip, and I couldn't play for a week! It was good for him, but it didn't work for me *no* kind of way!" (Crow, p. 211). Like Armstrong, though, Eldridge had no formal students and gave little practical advice, but he enriched and expanded the trumpet's expressive capabilities and helped establish it as the premier solo instrument of the swing era.

Ellington, Edward Kennedy "Duke" (1899–1974). The careers of Duke Ellington and Louis Armstrong paralleled each other both in length and extent of influence. Born at the turn of the century, they began making names for themselves in the 1920s. In 1927, while Armstrong was finishing off his revolutionary **Hot Five** and **Hot Seven** recordings, Ellington and his orchestra were taking a leadership position in the development of jazz during a five-year residency at the **Cotton Club** in Harlem. Armstrong came to Harlem in 1929 and played at **Connie's Inn.** Both appeared on Broadway in 1929: Ellington in George Gershwin's *Show Girl* and Armstrong in **Fats Waller**'s ***Hot Chocolates.*** Ellington's first popular hits, such as "Mood Indigo" in 1930 and "It Don't Mean a Thing" (1932), came at about the same time as Armstrong's—"Body and Soul" (1930), "Star Dust" (1931), and "I've Got the World on a String" (1933). Following Armstrong's 1932 and 1933 trips to England and Europe, Ellington and his band set out in 1934.

The two worked together only occasionally—for example, in 1935 in Chicago, in 1943 on a national NBC broadcast, and in 1946 at the ***Esquire*** All-American Jazz Concert. However, it wasn't until the 1960s that they got together in a big way. Armstrong had spent December 1960 in Paris where he played Ellington's music in the film ***Paris Blues.*** In April 1961, after Armstrong returned to New York, he and Ellington collaborated on an album. Producer Bob Thiele helped the two jazz giants decide on content and personnel by persuading Armstrong to do Ellington songs with the **All Stars** and with Ellington at the piano. Even though the Ellington songs were not in Armstrong's repertory, he gave them the Satchmo treatment, and the result was a memorable album (CD #11). Armstrong's fresh approach to songs that Ellington had played for decades (and recorded dozens of times) delighted the composer. A good example is Armstrong's rambunctious solo, extra lyrics, and **scat singing** on "Cottontail," which make it almost a new creation. On Ellington's part, the small combo allowed his lean, suave piano style to be heard more clearly, example, on "Duke's Place." A sideman for these sessions, **Barney Bigard** (who had played extensively in both men's bands), told an interviewer he preferred working with Armstrong because of the unstructured solo opportunities. "It was just beautiful. Duke, on the other hand," he continued, "would write arrangements. . . . There would be about eight bars or sixteen bars, and that's it" (Berrett, 1999, p. 169).

Both artists received considerable attention in ***Down Beat*** after it began publication in 1934, although they didn't vie in the same popularity poll categories. In 1946, for example, the critics have Ellington in both the "sweet" and **"swing"** categories, while in December 1952 the readers elected Armstrong to the first *Down Beat* Hall of Fame. The same readers went on to call Armstrong "the most important musical figure of all time," beating out Ellington (second place), Glenn Miller (fourth), and J.S. Bach (sixth) (p. 1). There's no doubt that Ellington had at least one skill that Armstrong lacked, though—the handling of people and finances, which are essential in running a band. Armstrong could and did front a band, but he left the running of it to others, for example, **Joe Glaser.**

Perhaps the differences in their music as well as their personalities can best be seen in their respective cinema appearances. Ellington is the suave sophisticate (in *Belle of the Nineties* and *Murder at the Vanities,* both from 1934), while Armstrong is the gleeful jester (in ***Going Places*** and ***Every Day's a Holiday,*** both from 1938). The two can be seen in ***Cabin in the Sky*** (1943), although in different scenes. Ellington plays elegantly at the piano, while Armstrong blows a brief trumpet flourish and then jokes around as one of the helpers of Lucifer, Jr. The two also appear in ***L'Aventure du jazz*** and in the video ***Louis and the Duke,*** which features definitive versions of nearly a dozen jazz classics. However, the insistent presence of an unblinking camera makes these performances more than a little stiff.

In the eyes of white, intellectual jazz fans, Ellington has been given a higher place than Armstrong, perhaps because of the tendency in Western music to give primus inter pares status to the composer. However in general, African Americans, musicians, and the public have thought more highly of Armstrong. Jazz scholar James Lincoln Collier feels that if Armstrong hadn't been so active around 1927 when Ellington's "Black and Tan Fantasy" came out, jazz would have become a composers' rather than a melorhythmic improvisers' art (1983, p. 348). In any case, Ellington (along with **Ella Fitzgerald, Benny Goodman, Lionel Hampton, Dizzy Gillespie, Earl Hines, Bing Crosby, Frank Sinatra,** Gene Krupa, **Guy Lombardo,** and many others) went to Armstrong's **funeral.** Later in 1971 he wrote a "Portrait of Louis Armstrong" as part of his *New Orleans Suite.* Slyly dismissive, Ellington's much quoted but simplistic sound byte about his peer in his 1973 memoir *Music Is My Mistress* is true but nonetheless slights the genius: "I loved and respected Louis Armstrong. He was born poor, died rich and never hurt anyone on the way" (p. 236).

Ellison, Ralph (1914–1994). Before making his mark as a writer, Ellison studied jazz trumpet, so it was natural that his ear would be attuned to Armstrong. Ellison's landmark 1952 novel *Invisible Man* was inspired by Armstrong's "(What Did I Do to Be So) Black and Blue?"; and his fascination with Armstrong's persona features prominently in *Trading Twelves,* a selection of his letters published in 2000. In *Shadow and Act* (1964), a book of essays, Ellison compares Armstrong with the witty jester of Elizabethan drama (e.g., Touchstone in *As You Like It*). Armstrong "takes liberties with kings, queens and presidents," "emphasizes the physicality of his music with sweat, spittle and facial contortions," and "performs the magical feat of making romantic melody issue from a throat of gravel" (p. 67). Armstrong inspired many writers, including **James Baldwin, Amiri Baraka** (a.k.a. LeRoi Jones), and Ishmael Reed.

embouchure. Adapted from the French, this word refers to the position of the lips and surrounding muscles in playing wind instruments. Like hand and finger position in piano playing, it is important to learn good embouchure habits at an early stage. Unfortunately, Armstrong did not do so. He placed the **mouthpiece** too low, so that it rested on the soft part of the upper lip, crushing it back against the teeth. In addition, he used too much mouthpiece pressure in order to reach high notes. While at first this method results in powerful high notes, it will inevitably cause problems later on. Such was the case with Armstrong, whose upper lip was eventually scarred and his style limited. On the plus side, Armstrong's **lip problems** caused him to turn increasingly to singing, with memorable results.

"Endie." By Eddie DeLange and Louis Alter; rec. October 17, 1946, in Los Angeles by Louis Armstrong and His Orchestra; CD #12. Armstrong performs this amusing song in the 1947 **movie *New Orleans.***

England. Armstrong and the English had a long-term mutual love affair. It was on first arriving in England (July 1932) that Armstrong received his most enduring pet name: **Satchmo.** He was so dubbed by Percy Brooks of ***Melody Maker*** magazine, who, nervously contracting "Satchelmouth," said "Hello, Satchmo!" (Armstrong liked the **nickname** so much that he used it as the title of the second volume of his **autobiography,** had it inscribed on at least two of his **trumpets,** and put it on his stationery.) He and the adoring English were instantly off to a good start. Armstrong opened a two-week run at the London Palladium on July 18 and mesmerized audiences. Not everyone was entranced, however. Armstrong scholar Joshua Berrett cites a repulsively racist article in *The Daily Herald,* which reads in part: "[Armstrong] looks, and behaves, like an untrained gorilla. He might have come straight from some African jungle and then . . . put straight on the stage and told to sing" (1999, p. 50). However, after he toured England, crossed to the Continent, and left for home, the English missed him so much that they thought he was dead. On March 31, 1933, rumors of Armstrong's death were greatly exaggerated on the front page of the London *Daily Express.* Understandably the English were overjoyed to see him when he returned in July. When Armstrong was forced to fire his abusive manager **Johnny Collins,** he replaced him with English bandleader and impresario **Jack Hylton.** Armstrong opened this second **European tour** at the Holborn Empire and also played again at the Palladium in London (broadcasting from there for the BBC on July 28) before touring the United Kingdom. He returned to England frequently throughout his life. During a 1956 trip, he unwittingly violated protocol by acknowledging the presence of a member of the royal family at Empress Hall. "We've got one of our special fans in the house," he said to the astonished audience, "and we're really going to lay this one on for the Princess" (Berrett, 1999, p. 182). Princess Margaret smoothed things over, though, by applauding heartily as the **All Stars** began "Clarinet Marmalade."

Armstrong's 1932 trip to England was a first for a jazz artist as a soloist, and he scored another first when he appeared leading a band of Britain's white jazz musicians. His last trip abroad was in October 1970, when he flew to England for a charity concert.

Esquire. Begun in 1933, this magazine has carried many writings about contemporary developments in jazz. Their early coverage of Armstrong now seems laughable as well as racially insulting. For example, the October 1935 issue carried

Armstrong's biography in pseudo-black dialect. "**King Oliver** listen at Louis Armstrong and say, sho' you can play in my band, is you got a cornet hawn?" it read in part (p. 70). (***Vanity Fair*** did something similarly foolish at about the same time.) Later when jazz became more popular, *Esquire* ran a critics' poll regularly, to one-up ***Down Beat*** magazine's readers' polls. Armstrong was a frequent winner, but more often for his singing (four times) than for his trumpet playing (twice). The initial poll in 1943 led to a splashy series of yearly *Esquire* concerts. The first on January 18, 1944, at the Metropolitan Opera House featured Armstrong. He was also prominent at the January 1945 and 1946 concerts, so much so that critic-promoter **Leonard Feather** persuaded him to put on a **Carnegie Hall concert,** similar to that which another critic-promoter, **John Hammond,** had arranged for **Benny Goodman** in 1938. The Armstrong event, like Goodman's, was immensely successful and proved to be pivotal. The **All Stars** idea was born there, and Armstrong's career entered a new superstar phase.

It was in a letter to the editor in the June 1945 *Esquire* that the term **"moldy fig"** was coined to tag a jazz traditionalist, as opposed to the up-and-coming be**bop**pers. Poor Armstrong was caught in the middle, having inspired the energetic young artists (e.g., **Dizzy Gillespie**) but not particularly fond of what he at one point called their "jujitsu-style" music. The controversy was more hype than substance, having been fueled as a promotional tactic by Armstrong's manager **Joe Glaser.**

Eventually the editors wisely let Armstrong speak for himself. He wrote "Jazz on a High Note" for the December 1951 issue, and "Good-bye to All of You" in December 1969. The former piece provides valuable insights into the 1920s record-making process, and the latter is a poignant reflection on aging. In posthumous tribute, *Esquire*'s December 1971 issue reprinted Armstrong's affectionate "Scanning the History of Jazz," which first ran in the July 1960 issue of *The Jazz Review.* (All three articles are reprinted in Brothers' *Louis Armstrong, in His Own Words.*)

Esquire is also the name of a jazz record company that was founded in England in 1947 and, in spite of some ups and downs, continued into the 1990s.

"Esquire Bounce" (a.k.a. "Esquire Blues"). By **Leonard Feather;** rec. January 18, 1944, in New York City with the ***Esquire*** All Star Jazz Band. Armstrong had a long relationship with the British-born writer, composer, promoter, pianist, and broadcaster, who wrote this number for a splashy concert featuring Armstrong at the Metropolitan Opera House. It was Feather who, three years later, instigated the **Carnegie Hall concert** that launched **Louis Armstrong and the All Stars** and thereby a golden era of Armstrong's career.

estate. At the time of his death, Armstrong left an estate valued at a little over half a million dollars. Most of his assets went to his wife, **Lucille Armstrong,** but he gave $5,000 each to his sister **Beatrice Armstrong** and to **Clarence Hatfield Armstrong,** his cousin's son whom he had adopted. Mrs. Armstrong died on October 5, 1983, after attending a fund-raiser in honor of her husband. Armstrong's estate has since been administered by the private, not-for-profit

Louis Armstrong Educational Foundation, which works closely with the **Louis Armstrong House and Archives.**

European tours. On July 9, 1932, Armstrong, accompanied by his manager **Johnny Collins** and his girlfriend **Alpha Smith,** took the first of his many European tours when he set sail for **England** on the S.S. *Majestic.* His most famous and enduring nickname was acquired upon arrival, when he is met by Percy Brooks of ***Melody Maker*** magazine, who fumbled over "Satchelmouth" and said "Hello, **Satchmo!**" On July 18 Armstrong opened a two-week run at the London Palladium, where he mesmerized audiences. He toured the United Kingdom, visited Paris in October, and returned to New York in November. So successful was this first European tour that Armstrong went back in July 1933 for a longer stay and a wider itinerary. He returned many times and often during the rest of his life. For example, hardly were the **All Stars** formed when in 1948 they took off for Europe, participating memorably at the Nice Jazz Festival from February 22 to the 28. In March they appeared at the venerable **Salle Pleyel** and then later in the month broadcast from Switzerland. During October and November of the following year, the All Stars played to sold-out houses in Scandinavia, Switzerland, France, and Italy, where in Rome Mr. and Mrs. Armstrong had an audience with **Pope Pius XII.** Similar tours continued in the 1950s and 1960s, frequently under the auspices of the U.S. State Department. From September through December 1955, Armstrong and the All Stars were in Europe playing in Scandinavia, Germany, Holland, Belgium, Switzerland, and Italy. When they played in West Berlin, fans from the East Zone sneaked over to hear them. "Hardly any of them could speak any English, but that didn't bother them or us. The music did all the talking for both sides" (Jones and Chilton, p. 31). The All Stars cut some records while on this tour, and an LP appropriately titled ***Ambassador Satch*** (see CD #1) was issued the following year.

Every Day's a Holiday. In this high-spirited Mae West comedy, Armstrong, as a trumpet-playing street cleaner, performs **Hoagy Carmichael**'s "Jubilee" while leading a parade that is part of a political rally. He also plays the title song with Eddie Barefield's orchestra, a group probably composed of musicians from the **Luis Russell** orchestra. As always, Armstrong contributes considerable energy. Paramount, 1938; 79 mins.; B&W; Dir. A. Edward Sutherland.

"Everybody Loves My Baby." By Jack Palmer and **Clarence Williams;** rec. November 24, 1924, in New York City by **Fletcher Henderson** and His Orchestra; CDs #8, #48, and #52. Modest though it is, this is Armstrong's first recorded vocal. Henderson, who refused to recognize Armstrong as a vocalist, unfortunately confines him to just a few rhythmic words at the end of the number, but the genie is out of the bottle. Armstrong left the thick and stodgy Henderson Orchestra a year later. His best recording of this song is with vocalist **Eva Taylor** and **Clarence Williams' Blue Five** (November 6, 1924), when he has the freedom to play an inventive solo and even use a plunger mute (in the style of his mentor **King Oliver**). See CD #36.

"Everybody's Comin'." By **Dave Brubeck** and Iola Brubeck; rec. September 12, 1961, in New York City by **Louis Armstrong and the All Stars** with pianist Dave Brubeck and guests; CD #50. Armstrong does this up-tempo curtain raiser from ***The Real Ambassadors*** with singers Dave Lambert, Jon Hendricks, and Annie Ross. See additional comments on "Cultural Exchange."

"Everybody's Talkin'." By Fred Neil; rec. May 27, 1970, in New York City with a studio orchestra conducted by Oliver Nelson; CD #31. On his next-to-last album, Armstrong sings this poignant song, which was introduced a year earlier in the movie *Midnight Cowboy.*

"Ev'ntide." By **Hoagy Carmichael;** rec. May 18, 1936, in New York City by Louis Armstrong and His Orchestra; CDs #34 and #61. Carmichael was already a fairly accomplished songwriter, singer, and pianist when he met Armstrong in the 1920s. In 1929 they shared vocals on the first recording of Carmichael's "Rockin' Chair." During 1931, Armstrong made inspired recordings of Carmichael's "Star Dust," "Georgia on My Mind," and "Lazy River." Later, he did the same with both "Jubilee" (1938) and "Ev'ntide." Carmichael wrote this last song for his friend, who, with his rich voice and full, meditative **trumpet style,** gives it a definitive performance.

"Exactly Like You." By Jimmy McHugh and Dorothy Fields; rec. May 4, 1930, in New York City by Louis Armstrong and His Orchestra; CDs #8, #40, and #52. Armstrong made this new song into a jazz standard and kept it in his own repertory as well. For example, he recorded it, albeit at a quicker tempo, with the **All Stars** in 1956.

Ex-Flame. Armstrong's 1930–1931 residency at Frank **Sebastian's New Cotton Club** in Culver City put him in the right place at the right time with the right style to get into the movies. His first film appearance was in *Ex-Flame,* which seems to have been lost, although not before it was reviewed in the *New York Times* (Jan. 24, 1931: "mediocre direction and an embarrassingly old-fashioned psychology"). Armstrong's name is on the cast list in the 1931 *Film Daily* yearbook, but nothing is known about the manner and extent of his participation in what David Meeker describes in *Jazz and the Movies* as "a domestic drama based loosely on the 1861 play *East Lynne* and padded out with a few incidental songs" (Entry #1022). Tiffany Studios, 1930; B&W; 73 mins.; Dir. Victor Halperin.

"Ezekiel Saw De Wheel." Traditional; rec. February 7, 1958, in New York City by **Louis Armstrong and the All Stars** with the **Sy Oliver** Choir; CD #27. Armstrong leaves his trumpet in the case on this engaging spiritual. See additional comments on "Down by the Riverside."

F

"Faithful Hussar, The." By Heinrich Frantzen; rec. December 19, 1955, in Milan, Italy, by **Louis Armstrong and the All Stars;** CDs #1, #19, #46, and #59. Armstrong recorded this song frequently (e.g., June 1, 1956, live at the Medina Temple in Chicago) and took it on his tours abroad.

"Falling in Love with You." By Victor Young, Charles Newman, and Gus Kahn; rec. November 22, 1935, in New York City by Louis Armstrong and His Orchestra; CD #51. This Tin Pan Alley song brought out the sentimental side of Armstrong.

"Fantastic, That's You." By Bob Cates, Bob Thiele, and Mort Green; rec. July 24, 1968, in Las Vegas by **Louis Armstrong and the All Stars** with a studio orchestra conducted by Art Butler; CD #62. This turned out to be Armstrong's last recording before a lengthy struggle with acute heart failure (September 1968 to April 1969).

"Farewell to Storyville/Good Time Flat Blues." By **Clarence Williams;** rec. October 17, 1946, in Los Angeles by Armstrong and His **Hot Seven,** vocalist **Billie Holiday,** and a studio choir; CDs #36 and #48. The title "Good Time Flat Blues" (which Armstrong had recorded in 1924) was changed to "Farewell to Storyville" for the 1947 **movie *New Orleans.***

"Farfalina." Rec. December 12, 1967, in New York City by **Louis Armstrong and the All Stars,** trumpeter Jimmy Nothingham, and others.

"Fatha's Time." By **Earl Hines;** rec. December 26, 1950, by **Louis Armstrong and the All Stars;** CD #45. This number is from the 1951 **movie *The Strip.***

Faubus, Orval (1910–1994). As governor of Arkansas, Faubus called out the National Guard on September 18, 1957, to prevent court-ordered integration of Central High School in **Little Rock.** Rioting broke out, and the event was reported internationally. On tour in the small town of Grand Forks, North Dakota, Armstrong watched the Arkansas scene on the television in his dressing room. He was deeply moved and gave a local reporter quite an earful. "The way they are treating my people in the South, the government can go to hell," he said. He called Governor Faubus an "uneducated plowboy" and went so far as to accuse President **Dwight Eisenhower** of letting him take over the government. Eisenhower sent in U.S. troops to ensure integration of the school, and the crisis passed. Faubus remained governor until 1967. In 1974 he ran again but lost in the primaries.

FBI. Armstrong attracted the attention of the Federal Bureau of Investigation (FBI) because of his relationships with underworld figures, his occasional statements on **civil rights,** and his several State Department-sponsored tours to politically sensitive countries in Africa and Eastern Europe. According to documents obtained under the Freedom of Information Act, the Bureau's interest in Armstrong began in 1948 and continued to the end of his life. The twenty-four-page Armstrong file opens with Armstrong's name turning up in the address book of someone under investigation. It contains other documents concerning his association with people considered suspect, his involvement with alleged communist organizations, press clippings from his numerous foreign tours, and a 1963 message concerning Jack Ruby's relationship with **Joe Glaser.** There are also a name check request in 1965 from the Nixon White House; a note from J. Edgar Hoover himself stating that "Armstrong's life is a good argument against the theory that Negroes are inferior"; and a final item, dated January 28, 1971 (the last year of Armstrong's life), reporting that on November 5, 1970, some $30,000 worth of **Lucille Armstrong**'s jewelry had been stolen from the Los Angeles Century Plaza Hotel room where the Armstrongs had been staying during an engagement. A copy of Armstrong's FBI file is available at the **Louis Armstrong House and Archives.**

Feather, Leonard (1914–1994). The British-born writer, composer, promoter, pianist, and broadcaster had a lifelong relationship with Armstrong, who valued his friendship greatly. Their mutual admiration can be seen in many letters now housed in both the **Louis Armstrong House and Archives** at Queens College and the **Institute of Jazz Studies** at Rutgers University. Two of these (one of which runs to fourteen single-spaced, typewritten pages) can be found in the Berrett anthology. It was Feather who clearly foresaw Armstrong's potential as the leader of a small, New Orleans-style ensemble and proved it by setting up the pivotal February 8, 1947, **Carnegie Hall concert.** Here **Louis Armstrong and the All Stars** was born, and the final superstar stage of Armstrong's career was begun.

Feather was born and bred in London where he studied piano and clarinet at St. Paul's School. He moved to the United States both to be nearer to the music he loved and because of the onset of World War II, becoming an American citizen in 1948. Feather produced recordings for a wide range of emerging artists (e.g., Dinah Washington, Sarah Vaughan, **Dizzy Gillespie**), wrote hit songs (e.g., "Evil Gal Blues," "Signing Off," "I Remember Bird," and many others), and contributed numerous articles to many publications (***Metronome, Esquire, Down Beat,*** *Playboy, Jazz Times,* and from 1960 to the 1990s, the *Los Angeles Times*). Feather is probably best remembered as a writer since he wrote well and knew his subject from a practitioner's standpoint. Particularly memorable are his *Down Beat* articles from 1951 to 1986, especially the regular "Blindfold Test" interviews, in which prominent jazz musicians responded to hearing unidentified recordings. Much of his writing has been gathered into encyclopedias (such as the authoritative *Encyclopedia of Jazz,* 1955, rev. 1960, and supplemented in 1966 and 1976) and other monographs, including *From Satchmo to Miles* (1972), two books of humor, and an autobiography.

"Well Leonard Ol Boy—I hate like hell to stop this letter to you," Armstrong once ended a long letter to Feather from the road (Brothers, p. 149). Armstrong's tone indicates the nature of their relationship, as does a request that he makes earlier in the letter. He asks Feather to help him get written arrangements of his recent recordings in order to meet audience demands to hear live what they had been hearing on records. Artists tend to resent this common request, but Armstrong was happy to grant it and in general to please his audience in any way possible.

Federal Bureau of Investigation. See **FBI.**

50 Hot Choruses for Cornet. It did not take Armstrong long to acquire a name for himself after moving to Chicago in 1922 to join **King Oliver.** Underscoring his widening fame among both record collectors and musicians, the Melrose Bros. Music Company made available two volumes of transcriptions. *50 Hot Choruses* along with ***125 Jazz Breaks for Cornet*** were published in 1927. "Many of the greatest hot men we have today . . . will tell you they conceived many of their tricks and ideas from the Armstrong style of playing," read the advertisement. Two errors got started at Melrose, however, when the publisher attributed "Wild Man Blues" to Armstrong and **Jelly Roll Morton** as co-composers. Not only did they not write this piece (either together or separately), but they never even played together.

"Fifty-Fifty Blues." By Billy Moore, Jr.; rec. June 10, 1947, in New York City by **Louis Armstrong and the All Stars;** CDs #12, #17 and #47. This is a meditative number featuring Armstrong and trombonist **Jack Teagarden** in duet.

films. See **movies.**

Finale. In this film the **Bobby Hackett** Quintet, the Eureka Brass Band, and **Mahalia Jackson** join Armstrong on opening night of the **Newport Jazz Festival** (designated as a tribute to Louis Armstrong this year) on July 10, 1970. Armstrong sings "When the Saints Go Marching In" and "Just a Closer Walk with Thee." Three other films (***Anatomy of a Performance, The Antiquarians,*** and ***Trumpet Players' Tribute***) were also made in connection with this, Armstrong's last, Newport Festival. Festifilm, Inc., 1970; color; 45 mins.; Dir. Sidney J. Stiber; Prod. George Wein.

"Find Me at the Greasy Spoon, (If You Miss Me Here)." By Wesley Wilson; rec. October 1925 in New York City with vocalists Leola B. "Coot" Grant and Wesley "Kid" Wilson and **Fletcher Henderson**'s Orchestra; CD #36. Here Armstrong is merely a sideman accompanying Grant and Wilson, a popular duet act.

"Fine and Dandy." By Paul James and Kay Swift; rec. April 26 or 27, 1950, in New York City by **Louis Armstrong and the All Stars;** CD #8. On this feature number for pianist **Earl Hines,** Armstrong seems to be accompanying himself, so to speak, as trombonist **Jack Teagarden** cleverly imitates him beneath the ensemble's sustained final chord.

"Fine Romance, A." By Jerome Kern and Dorothy Fields; rec. August 13, 1957, in Los Angeles with vocalist **Ella Fitzgerald** and the **Oscar Peterson** Quartet; CDs #9 and #14. See comments on "April in Paris."

Finkelstein, Sidney (1909–1974). Armstrong came in for considerable criticism now and then, particularly from writers who felt he had abandoned traditional New Orleans jazz for commercial pop music. **James Agee, James Baldwin, Rudi Blesh,** and Sidney Finkelstein were among those who developed briefs against Armstrong's change in 1929 from hot jazz to **swing.** Finkelstein, a jazz-loving Marxist, found a symbol of utopian government in leaderless New Orleans ensembles. He eventually forgave Armstrong for moving on to a more commercially acceptable music, however. In his *Jazz: A People's Music,* first published in 1948 and reprinted several times since, he blamed the lack of a strong music culture in America and the "continual pressure to produce novelties, to plug new songs, or the same songs under new names. That Armstrong had the powers to produce a much greater music than he actually did is true" (1988, p. 106). Finkelstein also wrote about art, media, and literature. His books were widely translated.

"Fireworks." By Spencer Williams; rec. June 27, 1928, in Chicago by Louis Armstrong and His **Hot Five;** CD #10. As the title implies, this number (a variation on the chords of "Tiger Rag") moves along at a quick tempo. Armstrong's off-the-beat playing further extends the image.

firsts. During his nearly sixty-year-career Armstrong, like all geniuses, was a tremendous innovator. He can be credited with a great many "firsts" both as a musician and as an African American. He was:

- the first jazz player whom others widely imitated. "I went mad with the rest," remembered **Rex Stewart** of Armstrong's arrival in New York in 1924. "I tried to walk like him, talk like him, eat like him, sleep like him" (Shapiro and Hentoff, 1955, p. 206).
- the first to extend his instrument's upper range. High "C" was a glass ceiling that generally no one tried to shatter, but Armstrong gradually even went up to "D" and beyond. On "Tiger Rag" and "My Sweet," both recorded in the spring of 1930, he nailed the "E-flat" solidly, and in the fall of the same year he went on to a then-incredible "F" in the Eubie Blake/Andy Razaf hit "You're Lucky to Me." Armstrong thereby started a trend that led to regular double high "Cs" by the end of the big band era and, as Maynard Ferguson fans well know, still continues.
- the first bandleader to introduce his musicians ("Gut Bucket Blues," 1925). This stage band device always seems to have existed, but Armstrong was the first to employ it at a recording session.
- the first to record a medley of hits, combining "(I'll Be Glad When You're Dead) You Rascal, You," "When It's Sleepy Time Down South," and "Nobody's Sweetheart" in 1932.
- the first to crack racial barriers. In the 1930s he began putting it into his con-

tracts that he wouldn't perform where he couldn't stay. On his first **European tour** in 1932 he was the first black to front a white European band and the first jazz artist of any color to appear individually as a star. Back in the United States, in 1937 he was the first African American performer with a sponsored national network radio program, **The Fleischmann's Yeast Hour.** Twenty years later in **Little Rock,** Arkansas, he helped integrate public schools.

- the first to record **scat** successfully ("Heebie Jeebies" in 1926).
- the first to use pop songs as standard source material for improvisation ("Ain't Misbehavin,'" 1929), thereby setting the stage for the greatly expanded popularity of jazz at the end of the 1930s. In fact, **Benny Goodman**'s triumphal 1935 tour could not have taken place without Armstrong's recordings of "Lazy River" (1930), "Star Dust" (1931), "Between the Devil and the Deep Blue Sea" (1932), "I've Got the World on a String" (1933), "On the Sunny Side of the Street" (1934), and many others.
- the first to record a jazz version of a spiritual, "When the Saints Go Marching In" (1938).
- the first to make an interracial recording. Although **Jelly Roll Morton** had recorded in 1923 as a soloist accompanied by a mixed band, Armstrong's March 5, 1929, recording of "Knockin' a Jug" (with white trombonist **Jack Teagarden,** black tenor saxophonist **Happy Caldwell,** white pianist **Joe Sullivan,** white guitarist **Eddie Lang,** and black drummer **Kaiser Marshall**) was the first interracial jazz recording in which black and white musicians shared musical material equally.
- the first jazz musician to be the subject of a ***Time*** magazine cover story (Feb. 21, 1949).
- the first jazz artist to publish an **autobiography, *Swing That Music*** in 1936. He went on to write a second volume, ***Satchmo: My Life in New Orleans*** in 1954. In fact, Armstrong remains the most prolific musician-writer in the jazz world, having written dozens of articles, hundreds of often rather lengthy letters, and hundreds more pages of miscellaneous memoirs.
- the first African American featured in a major movie—***Pennies from Heaven,*** 1936—after which came a long film career of eventually over sixty credits.
- the first jazz artist to top the charts during the **Beatle** era (with "Hello Dolly!" in 1964).
- the first and only major figure in Western culture who has influenced the music of his time equally as an instrumentalist *and* a singer.
- the first musician to have an airport named after him. On July 13, 2001, the **Louis Armstrong New Orleans International Airport** became the first major airport to be named after a musician, jazz or otherwise, black or white, American or not.

Fisk School for Boys. In 1907 Armstrong began attending the Fisk School for Boys, which was at 507 South Franklin, within a block of his home in New Orleans. The school was run by Arthur P. Williams, whose wife ran the Fisk School for Girls next door. They were strict disciplinarians, and although Louis learned to read and write (he remembered reading the newspaper to illiterate senior citizens as a community service), he preferred the company of a **Mrs. Martin,** who seems to have been the school housekeeper. "She always had some kind of consolation for the underdog who would rap at her door and she could always find a bite to eat for him somewhere," he later wrote in ***Satchmo: My Life in New Orleans*** (1954, p. 31). Young Armstrong must have engaged in music making at Fisk, since the school had choirs, put on operettas, and employed prominent Creole music teachers. However, his informal **education** took place at **Funky Butt Hall,** right across the street from the Fisk School (e.g., he first heard **Buddy Bolden** play there), and also in the company of his employers, the **Karnofsky Family.** Because he was tired from going to work for the Karnofskys at dawn and returning to work in the evening, Armstrong frequently skipped school. He dropped out altogether in 1912, when he was eleven years old and in the fifth grade. Shortly thereafter, his frequent delinquent behavior capped off by shooting a gun on New Year's Eve got him put into the **Colored Waif's Home,** where he spent a year and a half and reached what would be the end of his schooling.

Fisk University. Pianist, singer, and composer **Lil Hardin Armstrong** (Louis's second wife from 1924 to 1938) encouraged the story that she was valedictorian of her Fisk University class. She even displayed a Fisk diploma on the wall above her piano. This intimidated Armstrong, who, having just arrived in Chicago in 1922 to work with **King Oliver,** remembered humbly hiding his feelings for her. "Who was I to think that a Big High-powered 'Chick like 'Lillian Hardin.... Who Me?—I thought to myself. I just couldn't conceive the Idea" (Brothers, p. 86). Fisk University records reveal, however, that Lil was not even a graduate, having dropped out after no more than a year. Fisk (in Nashville, Tennessee) is indeed a prestigious institution, having been founded in 1867 and winning fame at the time from the country-wide tours of its choir, the Fisk Jubilee Singers. Sociologist and **civil rights** leader W.E.B. Du Bois was an 1888 graduate of Fisk. It's little wonder that Lil wanted to have the University's stamp of approval.

Fitzgerald, Ella (1918–1996). Fitzgerald's voice, like Armstrong's, is one of that small handful that is immediately recognizable. In specific, her renditions of "A-tisket, A-tasket" and "Undecided" have remained in our popular music bloodstream since she recorded them in the late 1930s. Within a few years of these and many other recordings, she struck out on a solo career and won a large international audience.

Fitzgerald and Armstrong finally caught up with each other in the 1940s, when they performed occasionally. The pair collaborated so well that their mutual manager, **Joe Glaser** (who also had **Billie Holiday,** Sarah Vaughan, **Barbra Streisand,** and **Pearl Bailey** on his client list), got them together in a major way during the 1950s. The resulting albums *Ella and Louis* (1956) and *Ella and Louis Again* (1957) contain masterfully performed love songs at contemplative tempos. While some critics have thought these perhaps a little too autumnal, others have frankly called them models for aspiring jazz singers. In any case, one can hardly fail to be moved by the pair's mu-

Louis and Lucille Armstrong in the early 1940s. (Louis Armstrong House and Archives at Queens College/CUNY)

sicianship. The contrast between Fitzgerald's polished and Armstrong's rugged voices is especially piquant in "They All Laughed." Another gem is the energetic "I'm Putting All My Eggs in One Basket." However, there is one day's recording work that particularly stands out. On August 18, 1957, the two did their version of *Porgy and Bess,* and some consider it their best work together. Even the fussiest critic has to call these performances virtuosic. Gershwin's opera has been popular with African American artists since its premiere in 1935, but no one has surpassed this poignant interpretation.

Fitzgerald, of course, had an agile, girlish, and cheerfully **swing**ing style all her own, although, as many have pointed out (e.g., Leslie Gourse in her 1984 book *Louis' Children: American Jazz Singers*), that style was influenced by Armstrong. For one thing, she liked to imitate both his voice and his trumpet sound, and for another, she liked to improvise **scat** solos. Concerning this latter technique, Fitzgerald was one of many future singing stars (Billie Holiday and **Bing Crosby** also come to mind) who were youngsters in 1926 when Armstrong cut "Heebie Jeebies," the first successful recording of scat singing for a general audience. She (like the others) took up the technique and made it her own, often imitating jazz instruments. Fitzgerald's ability to improvise long, complex scat passages seemed inexhaustible and effortless. An excellent example is her "Flying Home" (1945).

Perhaps because they thought there would be plenty of time later, Fitzgerald and Armstrong met only sporadically or coincidentally after their three big albums. Along with **Duke Ellington,** the two had firmly established the **Newport Jazz Festival** by the end of the 1950s. Festival goers found such established, traditional, and show business-oriented artists more amenable than the younger, aggressively experimental performers. Fitzgerald appeared on the same bill with Armstrong at his July 4, 1957, **birthday** party in Newport. Then suddenly, in the blink of an eye, it was July 1971. On July 6, Armstrong died in his sleep at around 5 A.M., and on July 9, Fitzgerald, along with Bing Crosby, Pearl Bailey, **Frank Sinatra, Johnny Carson, David Frost,** and **Dizzy Gillespie,** served as an honorary pallbearer at the **Corona** Congregational Church in New York. Fitzgerald lived another quarter century, going on to make such albums as *Fine and Mellow* (1974), *Lady Time* (1978), and two albums of marvelous duets—*Take Love Easy* (1973) and *Speak Love* (1983)—with guitarist Joe Pass.

Five Pennies, The. **Danny Kaye** stars in this film biography of Red Nichols (1905–1965), and his great affection for Armstrong shines through in their every scene. As in ***The Glenn Miller Story,*** a budding white bandleader goes to Harlem to learn music from the black master. Later, after Nichols is established, the two sing a playful version of "When the Saints Go Marching In," in which Kaye imitates Armstrong, and Armstrong mimics Kaye's imitation. Many consider this to be Armstrong's strongest movie performance. Paramount, 1959; color; 117 mins.; Dir. Melville Shavelson.

"Flat Foot Floogie, The." By Bulee "Slim" Gaillard, Leroy "Slam" Stewart, and Bud Green; rec. June 10, 1938, in New York City with the **Mills Brothers** and guitarist Norman Brown. Guitarist "Slim" and bassist "Slam," a popular novelty duo, owned this number, but many covered it. See additional comments on "Carry Me Back to Old Virginny."

"Flee as a Bird (to Your Mountain)." By Mary Dana Shindler; rec. April 26 or 27, 1950, in New York City by **Louis Armstrong and the All Stars;** CDs #8, #19, #45, #52, #55, and #61. A religious song inspired by Psalms 11:1 and composed around 1857, "Flee as a Bird" (along with a few other slow numbers and hymns) was frequently used by New Orleans **brass band**s at the beginning of a funeral procession. Armstrong knew it well from his **childhood** and later included it in **All Stars** concerts. A medley called "New Orleans Function" would begin with the stately, mournful song, followed by the upbeat and rambunctious "Oh, Didn't He Ramble?" (Incidentally, Armstrong was the first to record a medley of hits, combining "You Rascal, You," "When It's Sleepy Time Down South," and "Nobody's Sweetheart" in 1932.)

Fleischmann's Yeast Hour, The. Armstrong did a great deal during his career to improve the lives of his fellow African Americans, and his radio work played a vital role in this several times. For example, in 1931 he returned to his native New Orleans to play at the **Suburban Gardens,** and the show was to be broadcast. When the regular announcer refused to introduce a black man, Armstrong took the microphone and introduced himself, thereby becoming the first African American to speak on the radio in that region. Armstrong then went on in 1937 to be the first African American performer to host a sponsored national network radio program for two month when he took over for Rudy Vallee on CBS's *The Fleischmann's Yeast Hour,* radio's first variety show.

"Flood Blues, The." By Porter Grainger; rec. May 6, 1927, in Chicago with vocalist **Sippie Wallace** and clarinetist Artie Starks; CD #36. See comments on "Baby, I Can't Use You No More."

"Flying Home." By **Benny Goodman, Lionel Hampton,** and Sydney Robin; rec. January 18, 1944, in New York City with the ***Esquire*** All Star Jazz Band. This **swing** anthem was written in 1941, introduced by Benny Goodman, and became the Lionel Hampton Orchestra theme song. Armstrong recorded it with an all-star band (including **Roy Eldridge,** Lionel Hampton, **Coleman Hawkins,** Oscar Pettiford, Art Tatum, and others) in an *Esquire* magazine special concert at the Metropolitan Opera House. It's sometimes called "Flying on a V-Disc" because this first recording of the piece was issued by the U.S. government on one of the special World War II–era records made for military personnel and bases and for broadcast by the Armed Forces Radio Service.

"Flying on a V-Disc." See **"Flying Home."**

"Foggy Day, A." By George Gershwin and Ira Gershwin; rec. August 16, 1956, in Los Angeles with vocalist **Ella Fitzgerald** and the **Oscar Peterson** Quartet; CD #9. This 1937 song was introduced by Fred Astaire in the movie *A Damsel in Distress.* See comments on "April in Paris."

"Fools Rush In." By Rube Bloom and **Johnny Mercer;** rec. January 29, 1957, in New York City with the **Sy Oliver** Orchestra; CD #26. Armstrong gives a memorable performance of this 1940 song, which Glenn Miller took to No. 1 in that year and which Ricky Nelson revived in 1963. See additional comments on "And the Angels Sing."

Formula for Love. See ***Kaerlighedens Melodi.***

Foster, George Murphy "Pops" (1892–1969). Born on a plantation in McCall, Louisiana, double bass player Pops Foster came up a little before Armstrong. He worked with **Fate Marable** a year before Armstrong arrived, and in 1921 he went with **Kid Ory**'s band to California. Foster had been in the **Luis Russell** band since 1929 when Armstrong took it over from 1935 to 1940. This was a highly productive time, which included the making of dozens of records with **Decca.** Although there are many gems, Foster's steady pizzicato nicely propels "Swing That Music" (1936), "Heart Full of Rhythm" (1937), and "What Is This Thing Called Swing?" (1939). Later, as befits a native Louisianian, Foster participated in the revival of traditional jazz and in 1947 was regularly featured on the *This Is Jazz* radio series. He can be seen as well as heard in the 1954 film *Jazz Dance.* Foster lived out his days in San Francisco, where, with Tom Stoddard's help, he wrote an autobiography full of both lively anecdotes and tales of travail from his life as a musician in New Orleans and elsewhere during the early twentieth century. "It was tough travelling through the South in those days [late 1930s]. . . . If you had a colored bus driver back there, they'd lock him up in every little country town for 'speeding.' It was very rough finding a place to sleep. You couldn't get into the hotels for whites and the colored didn't have any hotels. . . . The food was awful" (Foster, pp. 159–160).

Frank Sebastian's New Cotton Club. See **Sebastian's New Cotton Club.**

"Frankie and Johnny." Traditional; rec. between September 30 and October 2, 1959, in Los Angeles by **Louis Armstrong and the All Stars;** CD #19. Armstrong liked dark numbers like this enduring folk song, which dates at least as far back as 1870, and he joined a long list of luminaries (Johnny Cash, Elvis Presley, **Lena Horne**) who recorded it with success. In performance, he would group it in a medley with "Memphis Blues" and/or "Tiger Rag."

Freeman, Lawrence "Bud" (1906–1991). Growing up in Chicago, tenor saxophonist Freeman was one of the self-conscious, white, teenaged jazz apprentices who used to try to get by the bouncer to hear Armstrong at **Lincoln Gardens** in the early 1920s. Freeman went on to a distinguished career with his own band as well as those of Tommy Dorsey, **Benny Goodman,** and Eddie Condon. In his 1974 memoir, he reflected: "In the last forty-five years there has *not* been a soloist in jazz music who was not influenced by Louis Armstrong" (p. 14). An interview with Freeman can be seen in ***Satchmo: Louis Armstrong,*** the affectionate video based on the 1988 book by Gary Giddins.

Friendly, Fred. See ***Satchmo the Great.***

"Frim Fram Sauce, The." By Redd Evans and Joe Ricardel; rec. January 18, 1946, in New York City with vocalist **Ella Fitzgerald** and the **Bob Haggart** Orchestra.

Armstrong and Fitzgerald were magic together, and this collaboration charted at No. 4 on the ***Billboard*** rhythm and blues singles in 1946. Nat "King" Cole later covered it with great success. See additional comments on "April in Paris."

"Froggie Moore Rag." By **Jelly Roll Morton;** rec. April 6, 1923, in Richmond, Indiana, with **King Oliver**'s Creole Jazz Band; CDs #8, #35, and #52. In this Armstrong's second trip to the recording studio (his first was the day before), we hear the beginnings of **swing** style in his brief solo: an artful displacement of the accent, a wide variety of articulation, and a sensual vibrato added to longer notes. The number dates from 1908, and the title refers to the comedian "Frog-Eye" Moore.

Frost, David (b. 1939). Armstrong was a frequent guest on the syndicated *David Frost Show,* and in fact his last **television** appearance was with Frost on May 11, 1971, when he sang with **Bing Crosby.** Less than two months later, on July 9, 1971, Frost was an honorary pallbearer (as was Crosby) for Armstrong's **funeral** at the **Corona** Congregational Church in New York.

funeral. At around 5 A.M. on Tuesday, July 6, 1971, Armstrong died in his sleep at home from kidney and heart failure. The news made international headlines and op-ed pages. President Richard Nixon gave permission for his body to lie in state at the New York Seventh Regiment Armory (Park Avenue and 66th Street), where an estimated 25,000 mourners came by to pay their respects.

On Friday, July 9, from 1 to 2 P.M., a funeral service was held at the **Corona** Congregational Church in Queens (according to Armstrong's request), and it was broadcast to sixteen countries. CBS-TV presented an hour of taped highlights from Armstrong's career and his funeral at 7:30 P.M. Honorary pallbearers included **Pearl Bailey, Johnny Carson, Dick Cavett, Bing Crosby, Ella Fitzgerald, David Frost, Dizzy Gillespie,** and **Frank Sinatra.** Also in attendance were **Duke Ellington, Benny Goodman, Lionel Hampton, Earl Hines,** Gene Krupa, **Guy Lombardo,** and many others. Flowers were sent by Jimmy Stewart, Princess Grace of Monaco, B.B. King, President and Mrs. Richard M. Nixon, Governor Nelson Rockefeller, and other American royalty. Dr. **Billy Taylor** spoke, and New York disc jockey **Fred Robbins** delivered the eulogy. In addition to **Peggy Lee**'s singing of "The Lord's Prayer," Al Hibbler sang "Nobody Knows the Trouble I've Seen" and, concluding the service, "When the Saints Go Marching In." An unofficial hint of horn playing was heard when a Ghanaian musician, who later identified himself as Little Joe Ayesu, stood up near the pulpit and echoed "When the Saints" on a kazoo, but he was quickly told by an usher to stop. Another unscheduled musical offering was given by a gospel singer named Hugh Porter, who knelt near the coffin and, to everyone's surprise, sang "Just a Closer Walk with Thee." Some controversy was created by the presence of those who were not all that up close and personal with Armstrong (e.g., New York Mayor John Lindsay and gossip columnist Earl Wilson), but on the whole it was a dignified occasion. Afterward, Armstrong was buried in Flushing Cemetery.

Two days later in New Orleans, Armstrong got the New Orleans funeral that would have been more to his taste, with a big parade, a crowd of around 15,000, and music by the **Onward Brass Band,** which he used to follow as a little boy. Trumpeter Teddy Riley played taps on a cornet that once belonged to Armstrong, and the instrument was put on display at the New Orleans Jazz Museum, not to be played again. In all Mrs. Armstrong received some 20,000 letters of condolence from professional colleagues, entertainers, politicians, and ordinary fans. Among those in Scrapbook No. 72 at the **Louis Armstrong House and Archives** is the following note, dated July 10th, 1971, from Bing Crosby: "I know of no man for whom I had more admiration and respect."

Funky Butt Hall. Armstrong went to the **Fisk School for Boys** for his formal **education,** but much of his informal education took place across the street at Funky Butt Hall, 1319 Perdido Street. Established in 1866 as Union Son's Hall, the popular name came about to describe the kind of overtly sexual dancing—"funkybuttin'"—that women did there. In ***Satchmo: My Life in New Orleans*** Armstrong describes, as a five-year-old, hearing **Buddy Bolden** "blowing up a storm" and also **King Oliver** and others (1954, p. 23). Of course, children of his age were not allowed inside, but they could hear quite clearly from outside. Besides, it was customary then for a band to play outside a honky-tonk for a half hour or so to draw people in. Funky Butt provided an important locale for the development of jazz in New Orleans from the 1890s to roughly 1910. Armstrong himself eventually played there, as did **Sidney Bechet,** and many others. On Sunday mornings Baptist services were held in Funky Butt, and after the banning of prostitution in 1917 and the general decline of the honky-tonk business in the area, it became exclusively a church. In the 1950s the building was demolished and new civic buildings erected on the site.

"Funny Feathers." By **Victoria Spivey** and Reuben Floyd; rec. July 10, 1929, in New York City with vocalist Victoria Spivey and ensemble; CD #36. Following her big 1926 hit "Black Snake Blues" and her appearance in the 1929 movie *Hallelujah!* Spivey recorded extensively until 1937, singing mostly her own music. Here she works amicably with Armstrong, who always seemed to inspire blues singers. In 1932 Spivey worked with Armstrong again in the short film ***A Rhapsody in Black and Blue.***

G

Gabbard, Krin. Gabbard is the author of an influential book titled *Jammin' at the Margins: Jazz and the American Cinema* (1996), which has a chapter ("Actor and Musician") devoted to Armstrong's feature films. Gabbard employs semiotics (the study of signs and symbols) with remarkable skill to show the significance of Armstrong's gestures, his clothing, his relationships to other characters, and other aspects of his screen image. Example, "[In ***Artists and Models***] the phallicism of Armstrong's trumpet is uniquely emphasized through its association with a gangster's gun." (A revised version of the chapter appears in Berrett, 1999, pp. 201–233.)

Gabe, Mr. Young Louis referred to his mother's various boyfriends as "stepfathers," and while these men treated him with varying degrees of indifference, a certain Mr. Gabe was the one he liked the best. Gabe helped him get a job driving a coal wagon. As Armstrong later recalled, "[H]e taught me the knack of loading up a cart so I would not hurt my back so much" (***Satchmo,*** 1954, p. 60).

Gabler, Milt (1911–2001). Gabler was the **Decca Records** producer who worked so amicably with Armstrong and, more important, with **Joe Glaser,** Armstrong's manager. Before joining Decca, Gabler ran the Commodore Record Shop on 42nd Street in New York City, a favorite hangout for jazz enthusiasts, and in 1938 he founded the Commodore label, one of many independent jazz record companies. During World War II he supervised a popular jam session on Sunday afternoons at Jimmy Ryan's on 52nd Street in New York. Gabler promoted Armstrong's recording of pop tunes with big bands. His major achievement was the recording in December 1956 and January 1957 of the four-LP *Satchmo: A Musical Autobiography* (CD #52).

gage. Armstrong felt so strongly about the beneficial effects of smoking **marijuana** that he proposed this common nickname for it as the title for the third volume of his **autobiography.** He evidently got pretty far along in the writing before his manager, **Joe Glaser,** became alarmed at the prospect of his star attraction's advocating the use of a controlled substance. Glaser probably destroyed the manuscript, or thought he did, since Armstrong's introduction survives and can be seen at the **Louis Armstrong House and Archives.** Armstrong did express his views on the legalization of marijuana in a letter to President **Dwight Eisenhower,** which may account for the reference to the drug in Armstrong's **FBI** file.

Galli-Curci, Amelita. See **"Louis Armstrong and Opera."**

"Gambler's Dream." By **Hociel Thomas;** rec. November 11, 1925, in Chicago by vocalist Hociel Thomas and Louis Armstrong's Jazz Four; CDs #10 and #36. For comments, see "Adam and Eve Had the Blues."

Garland, Joseph Copeland "Joe" (1903–1977). The versatile Joe Garland brought considerable experience as a saxophonist, clarinetist, composer, arranger, and bandleader when in 1939 he joined Armstrong's big band. When Garland eventually took over from **Luis Russell** as leader, the ensemble developed more precision, and an appreciative Armstrong kept him on until the band gave way to the **All Stars** in 1947. Garland can be heard on "Leap Frog" (1941), which, along with "In the Mood" and others, is his own composition.

Gautier, Madeleine. The first volume of Armstrong's **autobiography,** ***Swing That Music*** (1936), was heavily edited and at times unreliable. It also skipped lightly over his youth. So after a failed experiment in supplying **Robert Goffin** with notes for an official **biography,** Armstrong decided to write another volume on his own. Besides, during the intervening years he had successfully published numerous articles in a wide variety of periodicals. The resulting manuscript, with its lurid stories of knife fights and whores, did not appeal to an American publisher. However, in France, where Armstrong was very popular, he found an eager publisher in Editions René Julliard and a skilled translator in Madeleine Gautier. The success of *Ma Nouvelle Orléans,* as it was entitled, encouraged Prentice-Hall to publish ***Satchmo: My Life in New Orleans*** in 1954, two years later.

"Gee, Baby, Ain't I Good to You?" By **Don Redman** and Andy Razaf; rec. July 23, 1957, in Los Angeles with vocalist **Ella Fitzgerald** and the **Oscar Peterson** Quartet; CDs #9 and #28. See comments on "April in Paris."

"General." Armstrong loved **dogs** and, despite the rigors of 300 nights per year on the road, had several. "General" (a gift from **Joe Glaser,** as the schnauzer **"Trinket"** was later) was a Boston terrier who, during the 1940s, often accompanied Armstrong on tour. "General eats more red beans and rice than I can," wrote Louis to a friend (Berrett, 1999, p. 130). See also **"Trumpet."**

Gennett Records. Armstrong made his first recordings after moving from New Orleans to Chicago in 1922 and playing with the **King Oliver**'s Creole Jazz Band for eight months. Oliver took the band to Richmond, Indiana, about 200 miles southeast of Chicago, and there on April 5 and 6, 1923, they made jazz history by recording nine tunes for the Gennett Record Company: "Just Gone," "Canal St. Blues," "Mandy Lee Blues," "I'm Going Away to Wear You Off My Mind," "Chimes Blues" (featuring Armstrong's first recorded solo), "Weather Bird Rag," "Dippermouth Blues," "Froggie Moore

Rag," and "Snake Rag." These were some of the first recordings of New Orleans jazz.

Gennett began making records in 1917 and had issued thousands by the time the better part of its catalog was absorbed by **Decca** in the mid-1930s. Ironically, for a company located in a city with a large and active Ku Klux Klan population, Gennett specialized in making **race records.** It was, however, the only record company to use the term on its label. Along with the King Oliver, Gennett recorded **Jelly Roll Morton** and an assortment of blues singers.

Compared to contemporaneous record companies, Gennett was poor technologically. In addition, the studio was near railroad tracks, so recording had to cease when a train came by. Furthermore, Armstrong's playing was so strong that he had to stand behind the group at a considerable distance so as not to overwhelm them and the primitive recording equipment. "He thought it was bad for him to be away from the band," **Lil Hardin** (who ten months later would be Mrs. Armstrong) remembered. "He was looking so sad and I'd look back at him, smile, you know.... Louis was at least 12–15 feet from us the whole session" (Berrett, 1999, p. 38). As the year 1923 moved along, Oliver gave his ensemble over to the more sophisticated **Okeh, Columbia,** and Paramount recording companies. The result was a musical monument more lasting than bronze.

"Georgia Bo Bo." By Jo Trent and **Thomas "Fats" Waller;** rec. May 28, 1926, in Chicago with **Lil**'s Hot Shots; CD #10. Under exclusive contract to **Okeh Records,** Armstrong got caught making this recording for **Vocalion** because he sang. His trumpet playing might have been confused with that of others, but there's no mistaking that voice, simultaneously rough and sophisticated even then. See additional comments on "Drop That Sack."

"Georgia Grind." By **Clarence Williams;** rec. February 26, 1926, in Chicago by Louis Armstrong and His **Hot Five;** CDs #10 and #52. Mr. and Mrs. Armstrong trade singing choruses here, but it's not all that red hot. **Lil** sounds both amateurish and inhibited on the sexually suggestive lyrics (Compare **Velma Middleton**'s saucy January 25, 1957, rendition with **Louis Armstrong and the All Stars.** See CD #8.) This was the first number recorded on a big day that included the more influential "Heebie Jeebies" and "Cornet Chop Suey."

"Georgia Man, A." By Richard M. Jones; rec. February 23, 1926, in Chicago with vocalist **Bertha "Chippie" Hill** and the composer on piano; CD #36. Always a sensitive accompanist for blues singers, Armstrong recorded frequently with Hill, whose hard life began as one of sixteen children in Charleston, South Carolina. Her big voice recalls **Bessie Smith**'s but without the subtlety. Nevertheless, her gritty singing style is complemented by the contrapuntal web that Armstrong and pianist Jones weave.

"Georgia on My Mind." By **Hoagy Carmichael** and Stuart Gorrell; rec. November 5, 1931, in Chicago by Louis Armstrong and His Orchestra; CDs #8, #28, #40, #52, and #58. Almost thirty years before Ray Charles made this a No. 1 hit and won a Grammy, Armstrong recorded the definitive "Georgia." Dan Morgenstern reports that this recording so moved British trumpeter Nat Gonella that he made it his theme song and named his band the Georgians (Morgenstern, 1993, p. 13).

Gerlach, Horace (1909–1984). The pianist, composer, and arranger was a contributor to Armstrong's first **autobiography,** ***Swing That Music*** (1936), and the coauthor with Armstrong of the song by the same name. Some speculate that Gerlach was *Swing That Music*'s ghost writer or editor and in that capacity extracted much of the book's spice. At any rate, he certainly did contribute a brief appendix on Armstrong's **swing** style, which is interesting mostly for its colorful but idiosyncratic wordplay, example, "contrapointal inventions" and "melodic obbligatos." Gerlach's brief glossary of swing terms is more corny than informative (at least in retrospect), but he made some elementary transcriptions of how various artists, such as **Benny Goodman,** Tommy Dorsey, **Bud Freeman,** and others, treated the song "Swing That Music." As Dan Morgenstern observes in his introduction to the 1993 Da Capo reprint: "It's safe to say that no other popular song ever got such a sendoff" (p. xiii). Gerlach and Armstrong also cowrote the songs "If We Never Meet Again" (1936), "Heart Full of Rhythm" (1937), and "What Is This Thing Called Swing?" (1939). Gerlach later collaborated with others, including Bobby Burke (with whom he wrote the **Mills Brothers'** hit "Daddy's Little Girl" in 1949). In the 1940s Gerlach worked as an intermission pianist at Jimmy Ryan's Club on West 52nd Street in New York.

Gersh (Girsback), William "Squire" (b. 1913). The agile double bass and tuba player was with **Louis Armstrong and the All Stars** from late 1956 to 1958, during which time he made numerous recordings (e.g., the landmark *Satchmo: A Musical Autobiography,* CD #52) and toured Latin America. Prior to that he played traditional jazz in his native San Francisco, and afterward he worked in Europe with **Red Allen** and **Kid Ory.**

Gershwin, George (1898–1937). See CDs #9 and #29.

"Get Together." Rec. August 1970 in New York City with the Nashville Group. See comments on "Almost Persuaded."

Ghana. In the spring of 1956 **Louis Armstrong and the All Stars** went on a three-month tour sponsored by the U.S. State Department (see **"Ambassador Satch"**). The itinerary included Australia, the Far East, and then **England,** Scotland, and Ireland, before heading to Africa where some 10,000 fans turned out to greet him on May 24 at Accra Airport in recently independent Ghana. Armstrong was struck by the resemblance between himself and the Ghanaians. His first performance there (May 25) drew a crowd conservatively estimated at 100,000 (***Life*** magazine put the number at 500,000). Another highlight of the tour was his performance of "Black and Blue," which brought tears to the eyes of Prime Minister Kwame Nkrumah. A news crew from CBS **television** followed the All Stars, and their footage later became part of the 1957 documentary ***Satchmo the Great.*** (Some of the same Ghana sequences were also used in the 1971 documentary *Black Music in America: From Then Till Now.*) In

1960 Armstrong returned to Ghana as part of an extensive tour of Nigeria, central Africa, and Kenya. See **African tours.**

Ghost Cafe. In this musical by James P. Mirrione, actors portraying Armstrong and **Bessie Smith** tell and sing about their triumphs and tragedies. The New York premiere was on March 22, 1996, at Queens Theatre in the Park.

Gillespie, John Birks "Dizzy" (1917–1993). While there was some rivalry between Armstrong and Dizzy Gillespie, they were really quite fond of each other. One can see this plainly on the videos ***Trumpet Kings*** (1985) and ***Satchmo: Louis Armstrong*** (1989), which contain excerpts of the two on televised broadcasts, such as the *Timex All Star Show.* Their rendition of "Umbrella Man" is a warm-hearted, hilarious treat. The Gillespies lived within a short walking distance of the Armstrongs in **Corona,** Queens, and **Clark Terry** remembers going with Dizzy to visit Armstrong, saying to him: "Pops, we came to get our batteries charged" (Bergreen, p. 486). Going in the other direction, the **Louis Armstrong House and Archives** has a breezy, affectionate letter from Armstrong to Gillespie and his wife Lorraine, whom Armstrong wrote from Italy in 1959 while recovering from a heart attack (see Berrett, 1999, p. 156). Furthermore, Gillespie came to see Armstrong in the hospital, for example, in June 1969 (and stayed to give blood for Armstrong's manager **Joe Glaser**). Black men in a white man's world, the lives of Armstrong and Gillespie had many striking parallels.

Both were children of the South (Gillespie was born in Cheraw, South Carolina), both had disappointing fathers, and both came through nearly crushing poverty with the help of natural talent and the kindness of others. Gillespie showed up in 1935 at the musicians' union in Philadelphia with his trumpet in a paper bag, and he moved up quickly, even though his style was largely an imitation of **Roy Eldridge**'s (who was deeply influenced by Armstrong). Before the decade was over, Gillespie began to find his own voice as a member of **Cab Calloway**'s big band. In extracurricular jam sessions, Gillespie, along with Charlie Parker, Thelonious Monk, and others, experimented with the style that was to develop into be**bop** and change the course of jazz. If Armstrong didn't care for what he called this "jujitsu" music, Gillespie also had trouble with the next trend, Cool Jazz, as espoused by **Miles Davis** (ten years Gillespie's junior), Chet Baker, and others.

Soon, though, taking a path that Armstrong had just blazed, Gillespie's career picked up when the U.S. State Department asked him to undertake a cultural mission to Africa, the Near East, Asia, and Eastern Europe. The tour was so successful that a few months later he was asked to do the same in South America. Although, like Armstrong, Gillespie basically let the Free Jazz movement pass him by, he participated in Third Stream experiments. However, again like Armstrong, he was most at home playing with his own small groups, serving in all-star ensembles such as the Giants of Jazz, and appearing as a featured artist.

They did have some differences, however. "Louis is the plantation character that so many of us . . . resent," Gillespie said in the July 1 issue of ***Down Beat*** shortly after Armstrong's reign as **King of the Zulus** in the 1949 New Orleans Mardi Gras parade (p. 13). Later, though, Gillespie realized that, coming from a younger generation, he had misjudged Armstrong. He wrote in his autobiography: "I began to recognize that what I had considered Pops's grinning in the face of racism was his absolute refusal to let anything, even anger about racism, steal the joy from his life and erase his fantastic smile" (p. 296). The difference between the two quotes is the passage of time during which Armstrong, who had been a **civil rights** pioneer all along, had spoken out about school desegregation in **Little Rock** in 1957, for example, and during the 1962 march on Selma. What young black militant wouldn't have been proud of Armstrong's justifiably calling President **Dwight Eisenhower** "two faced"?

Then there was the bebop controversy. Armstrong clearly did not like the new music of Gillespie and Co. and even called it a "modern malice." In the *Down Beat* issue of April 7, 1948, he said that "bop will kill business unless it kills itself first" (p. 2). While some of this acrimony can again be attributed to generational differences (after all, Armstrong was at heart a **Guy Lombardo** fan), the disagreement was exaggerated by Joe Glaser for publicity purposes. Elsewhere, example, in a 1949 ***Time*** magazine cover story, Armstrong was more conciliatory, saying that "bop is nice to listen to for a while, but not all night" (p. 56). Armstrong and the boppers eventually came to terms and even performed together. To celebrate in 1950 what was then thought to be his fiftieth **birthday,** Armstrong performed at Bop City, a trendy New York nightclub, and *Down Beat* devoted most of an issue to him.

Two revealing symbols of the difference between Armstrong and Gillespie are the latter's upturned bell and spinnaker cheeks. Combine with these Gillespie's goatee, sunglasses, and beret, his cohorts' drug preference for the dangerous heroin instead of the relatively benign **marijuana,** and their slang ("cool," "gone," and "crazy"), and one can see some of the differences between traditional and modern jazz artists. Armstrong slyly derided these and other bebopper behaviors in a satirical version of "The Whiffenpoof Song," which he dedicated to Gillespie. To his credit, Gillespie took it as the kind of puckish prank he himself might have played. The two gradually grew to like as well as respect each other. "If it weren't for him, there wouldn't be any of us," Gillespie eventually concluded (Miller, p. 63). On July 9, 1971, he was an honorary pallbearer at Armstrong's **funeral.**

Highlights of the rest of Gillespie's career include a mock bid for the U.S. presidency in 1964; a 1977 visit to then forbidden Cuba; singing "Salt Peanuts" with President Jimmy Carter during a 1978 performance at the White House; publication to wide critical acclaim of his memoirs, *To Be or Not to Bop* (1979); playing trumpet for Oscar the Grouch on a 1982 *Sesame Street* episode (something that one can easily picture Armstrong doing); more trips to still forbidden Havana in 1985 and 1986; numerous euphoric special festivals on the occasion of his seventieth birthday in 1987; the release in 1989 of his documentary *A Night in Havana;* dozens of appearances on NBC's *Tonight Show;* and of course the various doctorates and Grammies. As reissues of his old recordings alternated with the releases of new recordings, Gillespie became an elder statesman of jazz. Like Armstrong, Gillespie was one of those rare individuals who, according to close friends, was as great a man in his life as he was in his art.

"Girl from Ipanema, The." By Antonio Carlos Jobim with English lyrics by Norman Gimbel; rec. July 2, 1968, in London by **Louis Armstrong and the All Stars.**

"Girl of My Dreams." By Sunny Clapp; rec. July 1, 1960, live at the **Newport Jazz Festival** by **Louis Armstrong and the All Stars;** CD #20. This 1927 song was a feature for pianist **Billy Kyle.**

"Give Me Your Kisses." By Leonard Whitcup and Bob Thiele; rec. July 23, 1968, in Las Vegas by **Louis Armstrong and the All Stars;** CD #62.

"Give Peace a Chance." By John Lennon and Paul McCartney; rec. May 29, 1970, in New York City with a studio orchestra and chorus conducted by Oliver Nelson; CD #31. On his next-to-last album, Armstrong sings this **Beatles** favorite with a mixed chorus.

Glaser, Joe (1897–1969). Before Armstrong at age twenty-one left his native New Orleans for Chicago and the world beyond, one of the older neighborhood toughs, **"Black Benny" Williams,** drew him aside and gave him the following advice: "As long as you live, no matter where you may be—always have a *White Man* (who like you) and can + will put his Hand on your shoulder and say—*'This is "My" Nigger'* and, Can't Nobody Harm Ya." This statement appears in an August 2, 1955, letter to Joe Glaser, who, as Armstrong's manager from 1935 on, functioned in just this protective capacity. (The letter, in which Glaser is addressed as "Boss Man" and signed "From Your Boy," is reproduced in Brothers, pp. 158–163.) Black Benny's advice did not always serve Armstrong well. Before hooking up with Glaser, he suffered through two white managers, **Tommy Rockwell** (1929–1930) and **Johnny Collins** (1930–1933), who watched out for themselves first and foremost and in fact nearly got Armstrong killed. Things came to such a pitch with Collins that Armstrong had no choice but to fire him in 1933 on board the S.S. *Homeric* en route to his second **European tour.** (While abroad, Armstrong had two temporary managers, the English bandleader and impresario **Jack Hylton** and the French promoter Jacques Canetti.)

Glaser was no stranger to Armstrong in 1935. The two first met in Chicago in 1926. Early in 1927, Glaser, then manager of the **Sunset Cafe,** hired Louis Armstrong and His Stompers (featuring **Earl Hines** on piano) to take the place of the **Carroll Dickerson** orchestra. After a year in and around Chicago, Armstrong went to New York and Los Angeles and made two trips to Europe before the two began a professional relationship in Chicago with a simple handshake in May 1935.

Glaser came from a privileged Jewish family (which must have further increased Armstrong's comfort level, having been nurtured by the Jewish **Karnofsky family** as a youth). He was supposed to have studied medicine and become a doctor like his father (and other family members), but instead he majored in bootlegging and racketeering, with a double minor in pedophilia and rape. He frequented the racetrack and nightclubs, was named in several paternity suits, and developed mob connections. Eventually he helped run the Sunset Cafe, a popular South Side "black and tan" nightclub (i.e., the audience was racially mixed) that was owned by relatives. However, with the repeal of Prohibition in 1933 and the waning of business at the Sunset (it closed altogether in 1937), he was not doing much when Armstrong returned from Europe in 1935.

Wonderful to say, Glaser went right to work for his client. He paid Collins a $5,000 buyout fee, settled **Lil Hardin Armstrong**'s suit for $6,000 in "maintenance," put his client's name up in lights as "The World's Greatest Trumpet Player," hired the **Luis Russell** Orchestra for him to front, negotiated a lucrative record contract with **Decca,** made movie deals (***Pennies from Heaven*** in 1936, ***Artists and Models*** in 1937, and ***Going Places*** in 1938), and got Armstrong a coast-to-coast radio series, **The Fleischmann's Yeast Hour,** on the CBS Network. Armstrong biographer Laurence Bergreen, who also wrote a book about **Al Capone,** puts it this way: "To the extent that [Joe Glaser] could ever redeem his own sins, he would do so through the vehicle of Louis Armstrong" (p. 376).

At first, Armstrong was his only client, but by 1940 Glaser had established **Associated Booking Corporation,** with dozens of artists. ABC eventually booked more black musicians than any other agency. **Pearl Bailey, Duke Ellington, Billie Holiday,** Josh White, and others were on their roster, along with white artists **Dave Brubeck, Benny Goodman,** Stan Kenton, the Kingston Trio, and **Barbra Streisand.** In the early days, though, Glaser had so little other business that he traveled with Armstrong, learning the managerial ropes from the ground up and no doubt preventing white club managers from cheating his client. Glaser found food for Armstrong and fellow band members when they were refused service, and he even slept with them on the bus when they were turned away from hotels. As years wore on and Glaser had more clients, he sent a road manager in his place.

Armstrong craved an audience, and Glaser kept him happily busy. For the rest of his life (until the last few months), Armstrong spent most of every year either on stage or getting to and from one. While Armstrong worked, Glaser aggressively hustled to make him the subject of articles in ***Down Beat, Esquire,*** and ***Vanity Fair.*** In 1936 he even got Armstrong himself to help with publicity by writing a book, ***Swing That Music,*** the first **autobiography** by a jazz artist. (The book was heavily edited for a general white audience, as were future writings, especially when Armstrong tried to express his advocacy of **marijuana.**) In the 1940s, Glaser turned Armstrong's distaste for the new be**bop** style into a publicity bonanza, and he cagily turned Armstrong's potentially harmful 1957 political stand on school desegregation in **Little Rock** into valuable press exposure. On Armstrong's occasional day off, Glaser booked him in the Decca studios, where he made commercial recordings, sometimes as many as six in one session. By 1954 Glaser found it more lucrative to free Armstrong from an exclusive recording contract and move him from label to label.

Glaser had questionable musical taste, but he knew what would sell. He nixed many promising projects (e.g., a series of single composer-based recordings proposed by **George Avakian** in the 1950s) and nearly passed on the pivotal opportunity to form the **All Stars** in 1947. On the other hand, for example, his sharply tuned antennae picked up the pending **American Federation of Musicians** strike against the recording industry in 1942. Glaser cleverly had Armstrong make four **soundies** (short films intended for use in coin-operated viewing machines). This exposure led to an offer to appear in ***Cabin in the Sky*** for $7,500 a week, providing a handy war chest for enduring the strike.

According to Dave Gold and Joe Sully, longtime ABC employees, Glaser could tell Armstrong where and what but never *how* to play (Collier, 1983, p. 201). Armstrong's letters to Glaser also indicate that the performer and not the manager was in the driver's seat. Although happy to give up some control for nearly unlimited access to ready cash, Armstrong knew how to make his will known and when necessary subtly show who was boss. For example, although Armstrong preferred not to make personnel decisions, he did so occasionally, such as hiring tenor saxophonist **Dexter Gordon** in 1944 and offering him a raise when he threatened to quit. Also over Glaser's objections, Armstrong insisted on accepting the invitation to be **King of the Zulus** at the 1949 Mardi Gras.

Glaser continued to manage Armstrong's finances even after the marriage to **Lucille,** giving her a stipend too, and taking care of the monthly mortgage payments on the house in **Corona.** For example, he allowed Lucille $350 per month on her Saks charge account. Louis preferred cash, typically a $1,000 roll plus occasional bonuses. He liked to peel off bills for needy friends and followers and once gave television sets to five elderly acquaintances. Occasionally he bestowed a Cadillac or a Chrysler New Yorker, and he would direct Glaser to make the monthly payments.

Did Glaser cheat Armstrong? When Glaser died, he left an estate valued at over $3 million, while (as writer Laurence Bergreen discovered by inspecting documents at the Surrogate Court, Queens County, New York) Armstrong's total worth was $530,775 (Bergreen, p. 494). Those who worked at ABC claimed that Glaser only took the standard 15 percent. However, Lucille maintained that Glaser took 50 percent, which she thought fair since he did much more than merely book the band. Armstrong biographer James Lincoln Collier, who interviewed numerous industry sources, gathered that Glaser did take 50 percent and also 15 percent of the remaining 50 percent (Collier, 1983, p. 330). In the early days, though, when record keeping was sketchy and taxes not paid at all, Glaser probably took as much as he could and still keep Armstrong happy.

There was genuine affection between Armstrong and Glaser, although the evidence comes almost entirely from the former. For example, during the last fifteen or so years of his life, Armstrong made collages, usually decorating reel-to-reel tape boxes but also covering scrapbooks, thereby revealing a great deal about his feelings. Along with his mentors (e.g., **Joe Oliver**), colleagues (**Bix Beiderbecke**), and fellow African American pioneers (**Jackie Robinson**) were affectionate depictions of Lucille and Glaser. Finally, Armstrong began a memoir on March 31, 1969, while recuperating in **Beth Israel Hospital.** Clearly intended to be a book, the dedication reads: "... to my manager and pal/Mr. Joe Glaser/The best Friend/ That I've ever had..." (Brothers, p. 6). Glaser died nine weeks later of complications following a massive stroke.

Glenn, (Evans) Tyree (1912–1974). Before he played trombone with **Louis Armstrong and the All Stars** from 1965 to 1971, Glenn worked with local bands in his native Texas, then moved to the West Coast, eventually settling down with **Cab Calloway** (1939–1946). He later toured Europe, worked with **Duke Ellington,** and served as a studio player. He can be heard on "Tyree's Blues," which he co-wrote with Armstrong, and he contributes a vocal on "Cheesecake" (both 1966). Armstrong always liked to do a duet routine with his trombone players, and with Glenn (as with **Jack Teagarden** and **Trummy Young** earlier) he did "Rockin' Chair," "That's My Desire," or "Back o' Town Blues." The versatile Glenn also played the vibraphone, which he can be seen playing on the 1965 film ***Solo.***

Glenn Miller Story, The. In this romanticized biography of the famous bandleader whose airplane was lost during World War II, Armstrong performs "Basin Street Blues" in a jam session with Gene Krupa. The scene takes place right after Mr. and Mrs. Miller (James Stewart and June Allyson) get married, and the Armstrong–Krupa musical style helps Miller find his own sound. In ***Time*** magazine the unnamed critic (Mar. 1, 1954) said that Armstrong's contribution made "the audience wish for a few wild minutes that this were Armstrong's story and not Miller's." Universal, 1954; color; 116 mins.; Dir. Anthony Mann.

"Glory Alley." By Mack David and Jerry Livingston; rec. November 17, 1951, in Los Angeles with pianist Milt Raskin and bass player Artie Shapiro; CD #45. Armstrong plays and sings this number in the 1952 **movie** of the same title.

Glory Alley. Set in New Orleans and starring Leslie Caron and Ralph Meeker, this film features Armstrong as a boxing trainer, Shadow Johnson, who supplies some laughs and music. Among the latter are "Glory Alley" (with piano and bass), forty-nine seconds of "South Rampart Street Parade" (with **Jack Teagarden** and the M-G-M studio orchestra), and all of "That's What the Man Said" (again with Teagarden and the M-G-M ensemble). The film is basically pretty dull except, as Bosley Crowther wrote in *The New York Times* on July 30, 1952: "Every now and then, Louis Armstrong sticks his broad, beaming face into the frame and sings or blasts a bit on his trumpet. That makes the only sense in the whole film." The film's title refers to New Orleans' Bourbon Street. M-G-M, 1952; B&W; 79 mins.; Dir. Raoul Walsh.

"Go Down, Moses." Traditional; rec. February 7, 1958, in New York City by **Louis Armstrong and the All Stars** with the **Sy Oliver** Choir; CD #27. In addition to singing the text with conviction, Armstrong takes a heartfelt solo and inspires the ensemble to get an unlikely song to

swing. See additional comments on "Down by the Riverside."

"Go 'long Mule." By Henry Creamer and Robert King; rec. October 7, 1924, in New York City by **Fletcher Henderson** and His Orchestra. Here is an example of early **swing** style. Armstrong sprinkles his improvised solo with a recurring three-note pattern, placing the first two short notes slightly against the beat and applying a touch of vibrato to the end of the longer third note. The result is a relaxing of the rhythm that eventually became an important part of the new popular music. Transcription by Schuller (1968, p. 95); see additional comments on "Alabamy Bound."

"God Bless America." By Irving Berlin. Armstrong was deeply affected by the assassination of President John Kennedy and made his feelings known at a Smith College concert on December 1, 1963, nine days after the event. As Gary Giddins tells the story, Armstrong set aside his usual show closer, "When It's Sleepytime Down South," and substituted a dirgelike solo performance of "God Bless America." "That was for President Kennedy. Good night," he told the stunned audience and left the stage (Giddins, 1988, p. 184).

Goffin, Robert (1898–1984). As a black man in a white man's world, Armstrong sought out white managers (**Tommy Rockwell, Johnny Collins,** and **Joe Glaser**) and white writers (**Hugues Panassié, Leonard Feather,** and Robert Goffin) to help him smooth his way. The relationships in this latter group grew out of genuine friendship at some level, but Armstrong, a **writer** himself, was aware of the power of the written word to bring him closer to his audience. Belgian jazz critic Robert Goffin (a lawyer by profession, poet by avocation, and the author of books on finance and other subjects) caught Armstrong's attention by dedicating his 1932 book ***Aux frontières du jazz*** "To Louis Armstrong, the Real King of Jazz in testimony of my high admiration." When Armstrong first arrived in Paris, Goffin ceremoniously gave him a copy of this just published book and hung out with him while he worked. The result was Goffin's wide-ranging if naive "Hot Jazz" essay (translated by playwright Samuel Beckett and reprinted in Berrett, 1999, pp. 56–60).

Later, when Goffin fled to the United States from World War II–torn Belgium, Armstrong thought he had found just the right person to write his official **biography.** The fact that Goffin came from Europe, where Armstrong was treated with far more respect than in his native land, was also attractive. Between 1943 and 1944, Armstrong sent him what came to be known as **"The Goffin Notebooks,"** colorful remembrances of his life during the period 1918–1931, along with some payment to help with living expenses. "I have four books of stories to send to you the first chance I can get to a Post Office," Armstrong wrote Goffin on May 7, 1944, from Tucson, Arizona. "There may be several spots that you might want to straighten out—or change around.... What ever you do about it is alright with me." Then from Bremerton, Washington, on July 19, 1944: "Here's another hundred dollars toward the five hundred.... That makes a balance of one hundred dollars more" (Brothers, pp. 78, 80). Actually, Armstrong had more than just a book in mind, since, having been in half a dozen feature films already, he had dreams of a movie about himself. Goffin would write the book, which was to be filmed by **Orson Welles.** Unfortunately, Goffin's *Horn of Plenty* (1947) was a disaster. The book mostly revealed his ignorance of the United States, flimsy grasp of English, and eccentric political views. Worse, he tended to ignore Armstrong's colorful language and made up dialogue that he tried to write in dialect. (" 'Tain't no two ways 'bout it—we's gwine leave dis head mizzable dump!") Goffin eventually moved back to Belgium and resumed his day job, while Armstrong added his own memoir ***Satchmo: My Life in New Orleans*** (1954) to his previous ***Swing That Music*** (1936). The "stories" that he wrote for Goffin were acquired by the **Institute of Jazz Studies** at Rutgers University and published in 1999 (see Brothers, pp. 82–110).

"Goffin Notebooks, The." Between 1943 and 1944, Armstrong wrote what he called "four books of stories" for the Belgian jazz critic **Robert Goffin** to use in writing his **biography.** These lively notebooks cover 1918 to 1931, beginning in New Orleans with Armstrong separating from his first wife, **Daisy,** and ending in Chicago with mobster Frankie Foster's gun in his ribs. Unfortunately, Goffin's eventual *Horn of Plenty* (1947) mostly ignored Armstrong's colorful language. Instead, he made up his own dialogue, which he tried to write in a dialect beyond his ability. ("Yo' makin' nuf money now, an' ah kin wohk.") Overall, the book mostly revealed Goffin's ignorance of the United States, his flimsy grasp of English, and his eccentric political views. "The Goffin Notebooks" were finally published in 1999 in a book of Armstrong writings edited by Thomas Brothers (pp. 82–110).

Going Places. In this race horse film, starring Dick Powell and Anita Louise (with the young Ronald Reagan as her son), Armstrong, now a popular Hollywood actor, does more than simply jump in for a number or two. He plays the role of stable hand Gabriel ("Gabe," and also, most unfortunately, "Uncle Tom"), who is in charge of the high-spirited horse Jeepers Creepers. The horse is uncontrollable except when he hears the song that bears his name (and was composed for this movie). This Armstrong plays and sings in a corny but curiously touching way. It's little wonder that the performance earned him an Oscar nomination. The film's big musical number, less integral to the plot, is the exuberant "Mutiny in the Nursery," which Armstrong performs with **Maxine Sullivan,** the Dandridge Sisters, and some extras. Armstrong did *Going Places* on loan to close out a contract with Paramount, and even though his acting talent was recognized for the first time, he would not make another screen appearance for five years until ***Cabin in the Sky.*** Warner Brothers, 1938; B&W; 84 mins.; Dir. Ray Enright.

"Going to Shout All Over God's Heaven." Traditional; rec. June 14, 1938, in New York City with the **Decca** Mixed Choir conducted by Lyn Murray; CD #27. Armstrong's recording of "When the Saints Go Marching In" made a month earlier was so successful that he recorded a batch of spirituals. Here when the white choir quaintly sings "gwine" and "hebbin," Armstrong responds distinctly with "going" and "heaven."

"Gone Fishin'." By Nick Kenny and Charles Kenny; rec. April 27, 1951, in Los Angeles with vocalist **Bing Crosby** and a studio orchestra conducted by John Scott Trotter; CDs #4, #7, #28, #39, and #40. Although they met in 1930, influenced each other's singing, and appeared in several of the same **movies,** the color barrier kept Armstrong and Crosby from singing together. Their radio broadcast duet of Armstrong's 1949 hit "Blueberry Hill" on Crosby's radio show changed all that, however. Armstrong thereafter appeared frequently with Crosby on the radio (1949–1951), and the two made popular records with this and many other numbers. Together the two can be said to have created the American popular song style, as Will Friedwald amply demonstrates in his 1990 book *Jazz Singing.*

Good Morning, Vietnam. Armstrong has made aural appearances in countless **movies,** but this one deserves special comment. In it Robin Williams stars as a popular Armed Forces Radio disc jockey in Vietnam, and among the many records he plays, Armstrong's 1967 "What a Wonderful World" is the most memorable. Heard about halfway through the film, the song's affectionate, mystical quality contrasts starkly with scenes of the war-ravaged country and people. Armstrong is not even mentioned, nor is his trumpet heard, but the voice evokes everything good about America, even in the midst of the temporary lapse depicted on the screen. The song, originally more popular abroad (especially in **England**), was subsequently reissued and spent six weeks among the ***Billboard*** Top 100. As Dan Morgenstern observed, the event amounted to a posthumous encore and a measure of immortality (Miller, p. 145). Touchstone, 1987; color; 120 mins.; Dir. Barry Levinson.

"Good Night, Angel." By Allie Wrubel and Herb Magidson; rec. January 30, 1957, with the **Sy Oliver** Orchestra; CD #26. See comments on "And the Angels Sing."

"Good Reviews." By **Dave Brubeck** and Iola Brubeck; rec. September 19, 1961, in New York City by **Louis Armstrong and the All Stars,** pianist Dave Brubeck, and vocalist Carmen McRae; CD #50. With her smoky voice and pristine diction, McRae blends nicely with Armstrong on this song. See additional comments on "Cultural Exchange."

"Good Time Flat Blues." By Spencer Williams; rec. December 17, 1924, in New York City with vocalist **Maggie Jones** and pianist **Fletcher Henderson;** CDs #36 and #48. This number was later retitled "Farewell to Storyville" and performed by Armstrong and **Billie Holiday** in the 1947 **movie *New Orleans*.** See additional comments on "Anybody Here Want to Try My Cabbage?"

Goodman, Benny (1906–1986). Born in Chicago, Goodman's formative years were spent soaking up the New Orleans sound from **Joe "King" Oliver,** Armstrong, and especially the clarinetists associated with them, example, **Barney Bigard, Johnny Dodds,** and **Jimmie Noone.** Goodman and other early teenage musicians (**Bix Beiderbecke,** Tommy and **Jimmy Dorsey, Muggsy Spanier,** and others) used to defy parents and sneak down to the South Side of Chicago to hear Armstrong. By the time Goodman reached New York in 1928, his career was well on its way. In the 1930s, Goodman, like Armstrong, was a pioneer crossing racial lines, recording with both **Lionel Hampton** and **Teddy Wilson.**

Following an October 1939 appearance at the **Waldorf Astoria** in New York, Goodman and Armstrong both worked in the ill-fated ***Swingin' the Dream,*** a jazz version of Shakespeare's *A Midsummer Night's Dream,* which opened at the then-new Rockefeller Center Theater on November 29, 1939. The Goodman sextet played Jimmy Van Heusen's music, and Armstrong portrayed **Bottom** the Weaver in a bright red fireman's suit. Despite the abundance of talent (**Maxine Sullivan,** Butterfly McQueen, and others), there were only thirteen performances.

A year and a half earlier, though, Goodman had brought big band **swing** music to Carnegie Hall on January 16, 1938. Later, Armstrong did something similar on February 8, 1947, with small band traditional jazz, which gave rise to the idea of the **All Stars.** When this venerable group was launched on the following August 13 at **Billy Berg's Swing Club** on Vine Street in Hollywood, Goodman—along with other celebs such as **Hoagy Carmichael,** Woody Herman, and **Johnny Mercer**—was on hand.

Unfortunately, Armstrong and Goodman did not get along well, and this quickly became apparent when **Joe Glaser,** who managed both, sent them on a six-week tour in April 1953. Advance sales for the **Big Band All Stars** were excellent, over a million dollars, but the principals quickly revealed their differences when Goodman called mandatory rehearsals. Armstrong was not in the habit of rehearsing and not about to start. On opening night, Goodman insisted that Armstrong go on first, a time-tested show business technique to get the audience warmed up for the more important act to follow. In a 1976 interview, All Stars trombonist **Trummy Young** remembers the way things went. "When he put Louis on first he could hardly get on afterwards," Young remembered. Also, Armstrong's sets were an hour or more, while Goodman stuck to his usual forty-minute limit. After about a week, Goodman decided to put himself on first. However, "When Benny went on, people would be out in the lobby smoking," Young continued. Goodman at one point got so frustrated with Armstrong's extra-musical antics on stage that he hurled a glass of scotch against the wall and declared, "Hey, that guy ain't doing nothing but clowning out there.... That's not music, you know." (This wide-ranging interview is transcribed in Berrett, 1999, pp. 172–176.) The clash of egos and personal styles came to such a pitch that Goodman refused to continue, and in Boston he was admitted to a hospital for possible heart troubles. Further engagements were canceled, much to everyone's relief. Years later Goodman tried to patch things up and invited the Armstrongs to dinner. "Are you crazy?" Louis said to his wife. "I don't want to have dinner with that motherfucker" (Jones, 1988, p. 120).

Goodman continued to tour and record in the 1950s, 1960s, and 1970s, although he had no regular band such as Armstrong's All Stars. His life was made into a movie, *The Benny Goodman Story* (in 1956, starring Steve Allen and Donna Reed), and in 1982 he received a Kennedy

Center Honor. Goodman was one of the many musicians and celebrities to attend Armstrong's **funeral.**

Goodyear Jazz Concert: Louis Armstrong. Produced by the Goodyear Tire and Rubber Company for foreign distribution (to be coupled with United Artists feature films), this short film is a miniversion of a typical Armstrong concert or nightclub performance. After a studio orchestra opens with a bit of **Duke Ellington**'s "The Good Years of Jazz," Armstrong does his "Sleepy Time Down South" theme, a currently popular favorite (here "C'est si bon"), and then one of his own compositions, "Someday You'll Be Sorry." In the featured sideman slot, there is only vocalist **Jewel Brown** doing "Jerry," followed by Armstrong performing the contemplative "Nobody Knows the Trouble I've Seen." A rousing "When the Saints Go Marching In" closes out the set, which is bookended by another excerpt from "The Good Years of Jazz." Television Graphics, 1962; color; 29 mins.; Dir. Bernard Rubin. (A video version was released in 1989 by Storyville Publications. In 1986 K-Twin Communications released a video, ***Louis and the Duke,*** combining the Louis Armstrong material with a similar miniconcert by the Duke Ellington Orchestra.)

Gordon, Dexter (1923–1990). Although he rarely made personnel decisions, Armstrong thought so highly of this trend-setting tenor saxophonist that he personally hired him in 1944 to play in his big band, and he even overruled **Joe Glaser** in offering Gordon a raise when he threatened to quit. They worked together for only six months, but the experience was still memorable for Gordon who, more than forty years later, spoke in high praise of Armstrong on the ***Satchmo: Louis Armstrong*** video. When Dexter left the band in 1944 he joined Billy Eckstine's group and went on to record with **Dizzy Gillespie** and others. He became a major **bop** artist, lived in Europe for fifteen years, and was active into the late 1980s.

"Got a Bran' New Suit." By Howard Dietz and Arthur Schwartz; rec. October 3, 1935, in New York City by Louis Armstrong and His Orchestra; CD #51. Armstrong made this recording at the beginning of his long and fruitful association both with manager **Joe Glaser** and with **Decca Records.** His relaxed confidence more than makes up for the weak accompaniment.

"Got No Blues." By **Lil Hardin Armstrong;** rec. December 9, 1927, in Chicago by Louis Armstrong and His **Hot Five;** CD #10. The authorship of this and other numbers is in dispute, although Lil, uncontested, won the rights in court. Armstrong indicated that "Got No Blues" was "one of those quickies that was made up on the spur of the moment right there in the studio" (Brothers, p. 135). In any case, the improvisation is all Armstrong's. In a procedure similar to that which Beethoven or Bartók might have followed, he uses a recurring triplet motif both to unify his improvised solo and to move the band to a new key.

Granz, Norman (1918–2001). The impresario and record producer had a limited but significant relationship with Armstrong, whom he paired with **Ella Fitz-**

gerald for three landmark LPs. *Ella and Louis* was recorded in 1956, *Ella and Louis Again* the following year, and in one day (August 18, 1957) *Porgy and Bess* (CD #9).

"Grassa e bella." Rec. December 12, 1967, in New York City with **Louis Armstrong and the All Stars,** trumpeter Jimmy Nothingham, and others.

Great Day. In May 1929 Armstrong's manager **Tommy Rockwell** directed his new client to leave Chicago and come to New York to make some recordings and be part of a musical called *Great Day.* Armstrong arrived with most of the **Carroll Dickerson** band in tow, but that's another story. *Great Day* was rehearsing in Philadelphia, which was Armstrong's next stop. He found a messy situation. Composer Vincent Youmans (1898–1946) was trying to produce the show, with little success. Despite several attractive numbers (the title song, "More Than You Know," and "Without a Song"), *Great Day* could not bear the weight of a complex *Show Boat*-like plot involving gamblers, African Americans, and a plantation. Also, in life-imitates-art fashion, the story involved numerous personnel squabbles over white musicians replacing blacks. Armstrong was let go before *Great Day* made it to Broadway for a mere thirty-six performances. Meanwhile, he had joined the very successful Broadway production of ***Connie's Hot Chocolates,*** which lasted from June to December 1929, as scheduled. Youmans, who previously had been successful with such musicals as *No, No, Nanette* ("Tea for Two," "I Want to Be Happy"), went on to write *Smiles* (1930), *Through the Years* (1932), and *Take a Chance* (1932).

Great Depression. Precipitated by the stock market crash of 1929, the economic depression of the 1930s had a pervasive effect on all aspects of American life, including the entertainment industry. Nightclubs closed for lack of patrons (see **Connie's Inn; Cotton Club; Sunset Cafe**), and eventually musicians had to turn to other sources of employment. **Kid Ory** worked on a chicken farm and in a railroad office from 1930 to 1933, and he did not fully resume his music career until 1942. Drummer **Baby Dodds** drove a taxi; **Sidney Bechet** worked as a tailor; **Roy Eldridge** went into radio engineering; and **Johnny St. Cyr** had to make ends meet as a plasterer. Down in New Orleans musicians were already handicapped by the closing of **Storyville** in 1917. **Alphonse Picou** had to focus on his day job, which in his case was tinsmithing, but by 1940 he was musically active again, recording with **Kid Rena** and later working with **Oscar "Papa" Celestin.** Celestin, too, had to take other employment but revived his **Tuxedo Brass Band** at the end of World War II. (In fact, the postwar revival of interest in traditional jazz, which evoked simpler and happier times, fueled these performance opportunities.)

Armstrong, however, worked all during the 1930s, happily meeting the nation's need to laugh and sing despite hard times. He hit 250 high "Cs" in a row on "Shine"; sponsored a baseball team, **Armstrong's Secret Nine,** in New Orleans; made uplifting **movies** (e.g., ***Pennies from Heaven***); published an **autobiography** (***Swing That Music***); and went coast to coast on a national radio show, **The Fleischmann's Yeast Hour.** Having grown up poor, however, he always had empathy with those who suffered hardships. On one occasion in January 1932, while on tour in Baltimore, he learned that people in the neighborhood surrounding his concert venue were suffering from very cold weather. He thereupon ordered a ton of coal, had it delivered to the theater lobby, and invited everyone to help themselves.

Green, Charles "Charlie" "Big" "Long Boy" (c. 1900–1936). When Armstrong went to New York in September 1924 to play with the **Fletcher Henderson** band, he immediately admired trombonist Green both for his musicianship and for his regular-guy behavior. "I *know* I'm going to like this band," Armstrong said to Henderson after being boisterously welcomed by Green and others (***The Record Changer***, July–Aug. 1950, p. 15). Green was born in Omaha, Nebraska, and learned his trade in brass bands there. He worked with Henderson (1924–1926 and occasionally thereafter) and also with both Benny Carter and Chick Webb. Green became famous for accompanying **Bessie Smith** (e.g., "Work House Blues" from 1924 and "Empty Bed Blues" from 1928), Ida Cox ("Misery Blues," 1925), **Ma Rainey** ("Chain Gang Blues," 1926), and others. His rough yet songlike style combined well with trumpet players, too, and Armstrong enjoyed working with him. Green "could hit a Bell tone so solid and distinct," Armstrong still remembered more than thirty years later (Brothers, p. 126).

"Groovin'." By Teddy McRae, Brown, and O'Nan; rec. August 9, 1944, in New York City by Louis Armstrong and His Orchestra; CD #61. On his first trip to the studio after the **American Federation of Musicians** recording ban, which began in 1942, Armstrong seems to want to move more lightly and quickly than this big band is able to.

"Gully Low Blues." By Louis Armstrong; rec. May 14, 1927, in Chicago by Louis Armstrong and His **Hot Seven;** CDs #5, #8, #10, #48, and #52. Following an arresting "Listen up, now!" flourish by Armstrong, this blues soon gets down and dirty. **Johnny Dodds** plays a mournful clarinet solo, and Armstrong sings a plaintive, "Mama, mama, mama, why do you treat me so?" The outstanding feature here, however, is Armstrong's masterful solo with its repeated descending arpeggio pattern that was subsequently much imitated. Armstrong himself was to play a similar pattern, as well as a similar but more elaborate opening cadenza a year later in "West End Blues." Jazz scholar Charles H. Garrett's article "Louis Armstrong and the Sound of Migration" sheds considerable light on the musical style as well as the cultural context of "Gully Low Blues" and its companion "S.O.L. Blues" (Walser, forthcoming). Transcriptions by Castle, vol. 1, p. 16; and Garrett in Walser, forthcoming.

"Gut Bucket Blues." By Louis Armstrong; rec. November 12, 1925, in Chicago by Louis Armstrong and His **Hot Five;** CDs #8, #10, #48, and #52. Along with many other innovations, Armstrong was the first to introduce band members during a recording session. He does so on this recording from the first of nearly two dozen sessions that would profoundly influence the development of jazz. In turn, he himself is introduced by his former

New Orleans bandleader **Kid Ory.** Armstrong then contributes a playful solo that skips nimbly around the melody (a transcription appears in Castle, vol. 2, p. 2). Banjo player **Johnny St. Cyr** tells an interesting story about the origin of the song and its title. After the Hot Five had recorded three numbers, the producer asked if they had anything else. Armstrong thought about it for a moment, then held a short rehearsal and they cut the number. Asked for a name, Armstrong said "The Gut Bucket." However, "Louis could not explain the meaning," St. Cyr remembered. "He said it just came to him. But I will explain it. In the fish markets in New Orleans the fish cleaners keep a large bucket under the table where they clean the fish, and as they do this they rake the guts in this bucket. Thence 'The Gut Bucket,' which makes it a low down blues" (St. Cyr, p. 2).

"G'wan I Told You." By Blair and Lethwick; rec. February 24, 1926, in Chicago with vocalist **Hociel Thomas** and pianist Hersal Thomas; CD #36. See comments on "Adam and Eve Had the Blues."

"Gypsy, The." By Billy Reid; rec. October 22, 1953, in New York City by Louis Armstrong and the Commanders; CDs #6, #19, #28, and #40. Both Armstrong and Dinah Shore covered this 1945 song after the Ink Spots took it to No. 1 the next year. Jazz musician Charlie Parker also liked this number.

H

Hackett, Robert Leo "Bobby" (1915–1976). Like many budding cornetists and trumpeters in his day, Bobby Hackett's idol was Louis Armstrong. "I first heard him when I was about fourteen," he reflected in 1973. "I've never been the same. . . . Louis simply outplayed anybody outside, inside, any way. To me he was just the greatest man who ever lived" (Napoleon, p. 3). For his part, Armstrong admired Hackett's sweet tone and graceful technique. When Armstrong was having a stomach ulcer flair-up, Hackett was called on to organize and rehearse the band for what later became known as the landmark **Town Hall concert** on May 17, 1947 (CD #13). The event underscored what the earlier **Carnegie Hall concert** (February 8, 1947) had demonstrated, namely, that the future of jazz belonged to small combos. Before this, however, Hackett with his cornet had achieved more than a little success on his own with the now-classic "String of Pearls" solo that he recorded in 1941 with the Glenn Miller Orchestra and, even before that, a still much admired "Embraceable You," which he recorded in 1939 with his own ensemble. Like Armstrong, Hackett was an especially sympathetic accompanist for singers. In the late 1930s he worked memorably with Red McKenzie and with the Andrews Sisters, on whose hit "Bei mir bist du schön" (1937) he added the sparkling obbligato. Thirty years later he was the first choice of Tony Bennett. Hackett's model was Louis Armstrong. He (along with Bennett and many others) joined his idol on May 29, 1970, in New York City to record the album *Louis Armstrong and His Friends* (CD #31), and he subsequently joined many of the same people in contributing testimonials to the July 9, 1970, issue of ***Down Beat*** (for what was then thought to be Armstrong's seventieth **birthday**). "Louis Armstrong could only happen once—for ever and ever," wrote Hackett. "I, for one, appreciate the ride" (p. 18).

Haggart, Bob (Robert Sherwood) (1914–1998). This excellent string bass player (and composer-arranger) was part of the dream team that was put together for the historic May 17, 1947, **Town Hall concert.** Unfortunately, he couldn't stay long, only until September 1947. Previously, Haggart had had a long association with the Bob Crosby band, for which he wrote extensively (e.g., "The Big Noise from Winnetka," 1938). Later, Haggart led a band with Yank Lawson, and eventually the two formed the modestly tagged World's Greatest Jazz Band. That and the numerous Crosby band reunions kept Haggart too busy to work with Armstrong.

Hall, Alfred "Tubby" (1895–1946). The New Orleans drummer, brother of **Minor "Ram" Hall** (also a drummer), learned his trade in much that same way that other budding musicians, including Armstrong, did in New Orleans, that is, by playing in local ensembles. In Hall's case, these included the Crescent Orchestra and the Eagle Band. In 1918 he moved to Chicago (as did so many African American musicians when the U.S. Navy had the **Storyville** district cleaned up). After a stint in the military, he returned in 1920 to work with **Joe Oliver.** A gentleman, he saw to it that Dempsey Hardin's daughter Lil, the group's pianist (and eventually **Lil Hardin Armstrong**), got safely home at night. Hall moved over to the **Carroll Dickerson** orchestra and was there to record with Armstrong in 1927. Although drums were severely muted because of the primitive recording apparatus, Hall's sure touch is discernable on "Chicago Breakdown." When Armstrong returned to Chicago from Hollywood in April 1931, he and trumpeter **Zilner Randolph** put together a band that included Tubby Hall to play briefly at the **Regal Theater** and then at the **Showboat Cabaret.** This group was together for about a year and recorded about two dozen numbers (including "Them There Eyes," "When Your Lover Has Gone," "Little Joe," "You Can Depend on Me," and "When It's Sleepy Time Down South," which eventually became Armstrong's theme song) for **Okeh Records.** Hall's fine playing can be heard on the novelty number "(I'll Be Glad When You're Dead) You Rascal, You," recorded in 1931, which was rerecorded in 1932 for the sound track to a **Betty Boop** cartoon of the same name and for the brief Walter Mitty-like film ***A Rhapsody in Black and Blue.***

In **"The Goffin Notebooks,"** Armstrong remembers his and Hall's consternation over gaining weight, so much so that, not being able to find appropriate sports outfits, they had to wear their bathing suits to play basketball on the dance floor at the **Savoy Ballroom** against the Clarence Black band in a 1929 publicity stunt (Brothers, p. 102). Armstrong also relates that earlier at the **Sunset Cafe** he and Hall with Little Joe Walker and lanky pianist **Earl Hines** would do a Charleston, which, as a foil to the formal show, was hilarious (Shapiro and Hentoff, 1955, p. 111). Hall later moved on to lead his own groups in the 1930s and 1940s.

Hall, Edmond (1901–1967). Five of Edward Hall's eight children became professional musicians, and three of those five, like their father, played the clarinet. Edmond was born a few months earlier on May 15 in the same year as Louis, and he played in some of the same bands around New Orleans. Armstrong left his native town in 1922, but Hall remained there until 1928. Nearly twenty years later, Hall led the sextet (i.e., the embryonic **All Stars**) with which Armstrong blew everyone away at the **Carnegie Hall concert** on February 8, 1947, but Hall did not join the All Stars until 1955. Instead, he distinguished himself with the Eddie Condon and the **Teddy Wilson** ensembles. When he finally joined the Armstrong team, he stayed for two memorable years, during which it toured extensively (Australia, the Far East, the British Isles, and Africa) for the U.S. State Department. See **African tours; European tours.**

One can easily concur with both James Lincoln Collier's and Dan Morgenstern's assessment of Hall. The former wrote in the *New Grove Dictionary of Jazz* that "as a member of the All Stars, Hall supplied energy and drive to a band that was becoming increasingly a commercial backdrop for Armstrong's singing" (1988, p. 471), while the latter stated in *Louis Armstrong: A Cultural Legacy* that Hall "was the best clarinet in All Star history" (Miller, p. 139). (The All Stars had eight clarinetists in its twenty-four-year span.) A good place to see Hall in action is the 1956 film ***High Society,*** especially during the All Stars ensemble number "Now You Has Jazz." After leaving the All Stars, Hall worked as a freelance musician to the end of his life.

Hall, Minor "Ram" (1897–1959). The New Orleans drummer sometimes filled in for his brother, **Alfred "Tubby" Hall,** in groups led by **Kid Ory** and **Sidney Bechet.** When business suffered from the U.S. Navy's 1917 **Storyville** district cleanup, both went to Chicago, along with countless other African American musicians. Tubby was called to military service in 1918, and Ram filled in for him in Lawrence Duhé's band, which soon became **King Oliver**'s Creole Jazz Band. Ram also worked with **Jimmie Noone**'s band, then moved to Southern California, where he caught up with Kid Ory and also played in the movies (e.g., *Tailgate Man from New Orleans,* 1956). Hall did not make any recordings until 1945. His mixture of **swing** and traditional techniques can be heard on the "Mahogany Hall Stomp," which he recorded in 1946 with Louis Armstrong and His Dixieland Seven.

Halsman, Phillipe (1906–1979). For its April 15, 1966, cover portrait of Armstrong, ***Life*** magazine chose an innovative photo by celebrated photographer Phillipe Halsman. A special pull-out cover was necessary to accommodate the now-familiar shot, which was taken from above with a wide-angle lens. Halsman also took the almost-as-familiar closeup of Armstrong's perspiring, eye-popping face while playing the trumpet. Both pictures can be seen in Marc Miller's widely available *Louis Armstrong: A Cultural Legacy* (pp. 1, 11).

"Hammock Face." See **nicknames.**

Hammond, John Henry, Jr. (1910–1987). Well born and well educated (Hotchkiss School, Yale University), Hammond was attracted to African American music as a teenager and frequented the musical venues of New York. His family gardener, with a relative who was manager there, helped sneak him into the **Roseland Ballroom.** In his early twenties he began producing records, and he helped **Benny Goodman** start his band in 1934. He also promoted the careers of **Fletcher Henderson,** Benny Carter, **Teddy Wilson, Billie Holiday,** and especially Count Basie. In 1938 and 1939 he produced the now-historic "Spirituals to Swing" concerts in Carnegie Hall.

Hammond was present for several of the important events in Armstrong's career, sometimes as an observer and sometimes as a participant, and he wrote about these and other matters in his memoir *John Hammond on Record* (1977). For example, when in November 1932 Armstrong returned from his first tour of Europe, Hammond was at **Connie's Inn** for the triumphal homecoming. For Armstrong's next **European tour**—July 1933—he was on board the S.S. *Homeric* with the entourage. On this trip Armstrong's manager, **Johnny Collins,** became drunk and abusive (as he frequently did), and Hammond (a civil rights idealist) objected to his use of the word "nigger." Collins thereupon took a sloppy swing in Hammond's direction. As Hammond continues the story, "Somehow . . . I managed to counter his punch and knock him on his behind. I think Louis never forgot that fight. It was probably the first time a white man had thought enough of him to fight someone who abused him" (Hammond, p. 105). Armstrong later fired Collins and completed the tour with local managers.

Hammond was not exactly an uncritical Armstrong fan, however. He (along with many) expressed disappointment when in 1928 Armstrong changed from the New Orleans band style to the big dance band style. He also worried that Armstrong had made a mistake in thinking of himself as a star instead of as a member of an ensemble. Toward the end of that second European tour, Hammond was in Armstrong's audience at the venerable **Salle Pleyel** on November 9, 1934, to look for signs of deterioration (unsuccessfully). Much later he was pleased when Armstrong returned to the traditional format in 1947. Finally, Hammond was with the ill-fated tour with Benny Goodman in 1953 and, like everyone else, was relieved when it was canceled prematurely.

Armstrong evidently found Hammond easy to talk to, since the two spoke often, for example, about his advocacy of **marijuana.** "It makes you feel good, man. It relaxes you, makes you forget all the bad things that happen to a Negro. It makes you feel wanted, and when you're with another tea smoker it makes you feel a special kinship" (Hammond, p. 105).

An idealist as well as a talent scout, Hammond went on to champion the careers of a wide range of artists: Charlie Christian, George Benson, Aretha Franklin, Bob Dylan, and Bruce Springsteen. Hammond was mainly associated with **Columbia Records,** and in addition to his autobiography, he wrote numerous articles on jazz and popular music. When contributing to the leftist *New Masses,* he used the pseudonym Henry Johnson.

Hampton, Lionel (1909–2002). The careers of Armstrong and vibraphonist-drummer-bandleader Lionel Hampton were more parallel than intertwined. When they first met (in July 1930 at Frank **Sebastian's New Cotton Club** in Culver City near Los Angeles), the established Armstrong gave the aspiring Hampton, then a drummer, some wise advice: Take up the vibraphone. The rest is history. Hampton quickly became the leading exponent of the vibraphone (at first with **Les Hite**'s band and then **Benny Goodman**'s) and eventually established a place for the instrument in jazz. In 1940 Hampton formed his own big band, which proved to be one of the most enduring and successful in the business. Like Armstrong, Hampton also took numerous U.S. State Department tours to Europe beginning in the 1950s. Other highlights of a career that continued to the end of the millennium include founding his own record label (Who's Who in Jazz), playing at the White House for President Jimmy Carter in 1978 and for President Bill Clinton in 1998, and being named 1983 alumnus of the year by the University of Southern California. His "vivacious" (as Armstrong called it) style can be heard on "Flying Home" (1942), "Hey Ba-ba-rebop" (1945), and "Midnight Sun" (1947). However, Hampton's first memorable vibraphone playing can be heard on the Eubie Blake/Andy Razaf "Memories of You" recording, which he made with Armstrong in 1930, shortly after they met.

Handy, William Christopher "W.C." (1873–1958). See CD #38.

"Happy Birthday." By Mildred Hill and Patty Hill; rec. April 25, 1939, in New York City by Louis Armstrong and His Orchestra. Armstrong did this perennial for a special private **Decca** recording to mark his friend **Bing Crosby**'s thirty-fifth birthday. A version of this classic sung to Armstrong on his supposed sixtieth **birthday** at the **Newport Jazz Festival** can be heard on CD #20.

Hardin, Lil. See **Armstrong, Lillian Hardin "Lil."**

Hatfield, Clarence. See **Armstrong, Clarence Myles Hatfield.**

Hauser, Gayelord (c. 1895–1984). When **Lucille Armstrong** introduced her husband to **Swiss Kriss,** a **laxative** advocated by the German natural foods advocate Gayelord Hauser, she found a receptive audience. Armstrong had from **childhood** followed his mother's advice to "take a physic at least once a week as long as you live" (***Satchmo,*** 1954, p. 16), and Swiss Kriss quickly became his laxative of choice. He became such an advocate that he carried around little sample packages to give to friends and acquaintances. He even gave it to puzzled government officials when he toured foreign countries and to amused nurses when he spent a good deal of time toward the end of his life in New York City's **Beth Israel Hospital.** Hauser's book *Diet Does It* (1943) was in the Armstrong library. Hauser also wrote other popular books on nutrition and physical fitness—*Eat and Grow Beautiful* (1936), *Look Younger, Live Longer* (1950), *Be Happier, Be Healthier* (1952), and others—which were widely translated and reprinted even into the 1970s and 1980s.

"Have You Ever Been Down?" By Hersal Thomas; rec. May 6, 1927, in Chicago with vocalist **Sippie Wallace** and clarinetist Artie Starks; CD #36. This blues number is by Wallace's brother. See additional comments on "Baby, I Can't Use You No More."

"Have You Met Miss Jones?" By Richard Rodgers and Lorenz Hart; rec. August 14, 1957, in Los Angeles with a studio orchestra conducted by arranger Russell Garcia; CD #29. Armstrong puts his own stamp on this 1937 number from the musical *I'd Rather Be Right.*

"Have Your Chill, I'll Be Here When Your Fever Rises." By Wesley Wilson; rec. October 1925 in New York City with vocalists Leola B. "Coot" Grant and Wesley "Kid" Wilson and **Fletcher Henderson**'s Orchestra; CD #36. Here Armstrong is a sideman accompanying Grant and Wilson, a popular duet act.

"Hawaiian Hospitality." By Ray Kinney and Harry Owens; rec. March 24, 1937, in New York City with Andy Iona and His Islanders. This is one of a little batch of numbers that Armstrong did with the popular Hawaiian group (a.k.a. The Polynesians), and although jazz purists were embarrassed if not irked, the result is really pretty good. The ensemble plays the melody strongly, which gives Armstrong plenty of room to improvise. Sam Koki is the able singer here.

Hawkins, Coleman Randolph (1904–1969). The remarkable tenor sax player started out in Kansas City and soon wound up in New York, where he worked with the **Fletcher Henderson** Orchestra (1924–1934). From September 1924 to November 1925 Armstrong was in the same ensemble, which made several dozen recordings. On one of the earliest, "Naughty Man" (November 14, 1924), Hawkins can be heard playing both the C-melody saxophone and the tenor. "T.N.T," recorded near the end of Armstrong's stay (October 21, 1925), reveals a more confident and sensitive Hawkins. On both, Armstrong's glittering solos seem hamstrung by the stodgy ensemble and the limited amount of solo time.

By 1934 Hawkins was Henderson's star, and when the band's tour of Great Britain fell through, he made the trip alone. The musical result was so successful and the personal treatment he received so welcome (many other African American entertainers—**Josephine Baker, Cab Calloway, Duke Ellington**—had and would receive abroad the respect they lacked at home) that he remained in Europe until war clouds gathered in 1939. While in **England,** Hawkins and Armstrong had a brief encounter that left a bad taste in many mouths. The two American jazz giants were to appear together, but suddenly the concert was canceled. Some say that Armstrong refused to participate, fearing that Hawkins would overshadow him. Others say that Hawkins would not show up for rehearsals, and that troubled Armstrong. The latter explanation does not fit well, though, since Armstrong had a lifelong aversion to rehearsing. He also had a lifelong insecurity about losing his audience, and he was having **lip problems** at the time. Armstrong's solution was to cross the channel for an extended vacation in Paris.

The two giants did eventually appear on the same program, though. In January 1944, he, Hawkins, and others played in a jam session with fellow ***Esquire*** jazz poll winners at the Metropolitan Opera House in New York City. Before then Hawkins had achieved immortality with his 1939 recording of "Body and Soul," which has since become a classic. He inspired the new generation of jazz musicians (**Miles Davis,** Fats Navarro, J.J. Johnson, and others) and continued to expand the boundaries of musical expression, for example, his 1948 "Picasso," an unaccompanied improvisation. During the 1950s and 1960s, Hawkins toured widely and appeared on television and in films. He also recorded prolifically, much to the delight of his many fans and tenor saxophone players, for example, President Bill Clinton.

"He Likes It Slow." By W. Benton Overstreet; rec. June 18, 1926, in Chicago with **Jody** "Butterbeans" **Edwards** and **Susie Hawthorne Edwards;** CDs #10 and #36. Armstrong recorded only once with this popular vaudeville couple ("Butterbeans and Susie"), although they did meet up again in 1942 on the **movie** set of ***Cabin in the Sky.***

"Hear Me Talkin' to Ya." By Louis Armstrong; rec. December 12, 1928, in Chicago, by Louis Armstrong and His **Savoy Ballroom Five;** CDs #5, #10, #30, and #61. Armstrong takes only one solo chorus here, leaving one each for pianist **Earl Hines** and alto saxophonist/arranger **Don Redman.** Armstrong rerecorded the number in April 1939 to meet a rising demand for small band jazz.

"Heebie Jeebies." By **Boyd Atkins** (who borrowed a portion of "Heliotrope Bouquet" by Scott Joplin and Louis Chauvin); rec. February 26, 1926, in Chicago by Louis Armstrong and His **Hot Five;** CDs #3, #8, #10, #14, #44, #48, #52, and #60. It makes a good story that in recording this number Armstrong invented **scat singing** to cover for having dropped the sheet music. However, scatting had been around long before 1926, and moreover Armstrong seamlessly moves through the entire song, singing lyrics at both the beginning and the end. Besides, how could he forget the words to his own song? It seems more likely that, given the nature of his musical mind, he did not want merely to sing the same words twice. Certainly, however, this is the first successful scat recording, it began a **scat-singing** trend (**Billie Holiday, Ella Fitzgerald, Bing Crosby,** and the future be**bop**pers were out there listening), and it was the Hot Five's first big hit. "Heebie Jeebies" sold 40,000 copies in a few weeks, at a time when selling 5,000 copies of a record was excellent and 10,000 was astounding. Transcription by Castle, vol. 2, p. 13.

"Heigh-Ho." By Larry Morey and Frank Churchill; rec. March 17, 1968, in Hollywood by **Louis Armstrong and the All Stars** with a studio orchestra and mixed choir; CD #15. Yes, this is the tiny miners' marching song from *Snow White and the Seven Dwarfs,* and Armstrong manages to make something out of it despite the corny arrangement. He also contributes one of his very last trumpet solos on record.

"Hello Brother." By George David Weiss and Bob Thiele; rec. July 24, 1968, in Las Vegas by **Louis Armstrong and the All Stars** with a studio orchestra conducted by Art Butler; CD #62. This was one of three numbers done on what turned out to be Armstrong's last recording session before a lengthy struggle with acute heart failure (September 1968 to April 1969).

"Hello Dolly!" By Jerry Herman; rec. December 3, 1963, in New York City by **Louis Armstrong and the All Stars;** CDs #2, #4, #14, #28, #39, #40, #59, and #61. First and foremost, this is an excellent recording, one in which Armstrong and the All Stars (plus a whiff of strings and the introductory banjo) make no concessions to mainstream popular music and play outstanding traditional jazz. Armstrong's accomplished singing and trumpet playing are backed by a solid rhythm section, trombone, and clarinet. However, a variety of external factors (American nostalgia must be high on the list) turned it in May 1964 into the most widely listened to song in the nation. It bumped **The Beatles'** "Can't Buy Me Love" off the No. 1 spot on the ***Billboard*** Top 40 list, and the *New York Post* estimated that the song was played 10,000 times a day on the North American continent. Armstrong recorded it to introduce a new Broadway musical, and it became a central feature at All Stars concerts. He was written into the 1969 **movie** version to reproduce his definitive performance, and it was common for the audience to applaud spontaneously when the camera moved in on Armstrong. It is not too farfetched to say that the song is about him, looking swell, going strong, back on top where he belonged.

Hello Dolly! This album reached the No. 1 spot in the 1964 ***Billboard*** Top 40 list and, **The Beatles** notwithstanding, held that position for six weeks. It was Armstrong's only No. 1 album, although *Satch Plays Fats* (CD #56) was No. 10 in 1955 and *Louis and Ella* was No. 12 in 1956.

Hello Dolly! Armstrong was written into this film because of his megahit recording of the title song, which he sings toward the end with **Barbra Streisand.** While opinions on the movie's merits are widely diverse, everyone agrees that Armstrong adds a special magic, if not the only magic. "The moment, brief as it is," writes critic Donald Bogle, "remains moving and incandescent, a glimpse of a mighty old warrior, who after almost fifty years in films, is still giving his best" (Miller, pp. 177–178). Indeed, it was common in movie theaters for audiences to burst into spontaneous applause when the camera moved to Armstrong. 20th-Century Fox, 1969; color; 118 mins.; Dir. Gene Kelly.

"Hellzapoppin'." By Marion Grudeff and Raymond Jessel; rec. August 16, 1967, in New York City by **Louis Armstrong and the All Stars;** CD #62. Armstrong has a great deal of fun with the rowdy lyrics of this boisterous novelty song.

Henderson, Fletcher Hamilton, Jr., "Smack" (1897–1952). Armstrong was working in the **Kid Ory** band when in 1921 Fletcher Henderson came through New Orleans leading a band for a revue featuring Ethel Waters. Henderson was so impressed with Armstrong that he immediately tried to hire him, but without success. Three years later, Henderson made a much better offer, having landed a job at the **Roseland Ballroom** in New York City. Henderson needed a jazz soloist, and he again asked Armstrong, who this time agreed and spent fourteen memorable months. "It was the first big band that was ever heard of on these United Shores and about the biggest that Fletcher had done up until that time," Armstrong remembered (Brothers, p. 125). The run ended only because **Lil Hardin Armstrong,** who originally had encouraged Armstrong to take the job, now gave her husband an ultimatum to return to Chicago or forget about the marriage. She also guaranteed him a $75-per-week job, $20 higher than his Henderson salary. The band gave Armstrong a rollicking farewell party at **Smalls' Paradise** in Harlem, and poor Armstrong got so drunk that he threw up on Henderson while trying to thank him.

As their several dozen recordings show, Armstrong was handicapped by Henderson's procrustean style. Far more inventive is the batch of extracurricular recordings that he made during this period with the more nimble **Clarence Williams' Blue Five** or with blues singers such as **Bessie Smith** (often with Henderson at the piano). Armstrong was also frustrated at not being allowed to sing with Henderson's group. He had been singing all his life, in fact longer than he had been playing the trumpet, but Henderson, like **King Oliver** before him, kept brushing Armstrong's wishes aside. "I wondered what he could possibly do with the big fish horn voice of his" was the way he put it later in ***The Record Changer*** (July–Aug. 1950, p. 15). On rare occasions Henderson allowed Armstrong to sing on stage and in the studio once let him sing at the end of the 1924 "Everybody Loves My Baby," Armstrong's first vocal recording. Armstrong's theory was that bandleaders just didn't let instrumentalists sing in those days. "I gathered that those two Big shot Boys, Joe + Fletcher, just was afraid to let me sing, thinking maybe, I'd sort of ruin their reputations," he later wrote (Brothers, pp. 63–64). When it came to judging singers, Henderson must also have had a large blind spot, since ten years later he declined a chance to hire **Ella Fitzgerald.**

Henderson was one of a new breed of African American musicians who came on the scene immediately after World War I. **Duke Ellington,** Claude Hopkins, Jimmy Lunceford, and **Don Redman** were all middle-class born and well-educated, and their parents generally considered jazz to be at least vulgar if not immoral. Henderson went to New York with his Atlanta University degree in chemistry but found neither work in his field nor admission to a graduate degree program at Columbia University. Instead, he got a job as a song demonstrator, which quickly turned into leading bands at dances and in cabarets. The ensemble that he led for ten years at Roseland in many ways set the pattern for the big band era. With his arranger, Don Redman, Henderson developed the formula of alternating woodwinds with brass and throwing jazz solos into the mix. It was Armstrong who made the artistic case for these solos, contributing fifteen in all on their recordings. His choruses on "Bye and Bye," "Copenhagen," "Go 'long Mule," "Money Blues," "Shanghai Shuffle," and especially "Sugar Foot Stomp" can be said to have created the jazz soloist, a role that cannot be underestimated in its impact not only on jazz but on all popular music. Also, with early help from Armstrong, Henderson was able to get a large ensemble to **swing.**

Armstrong next worked with Henderson in May 1929 on Vincent Youmans's ill-fated ***Great Day.*** Henderson (never a strong leader) capitulated to the white producers in musical matters and thus earned the enmity of most of his players. Before the show opened on Broadway (to fold after just thirty-six performances), Armstrong dropped out, and shortly thereafter Henderson's band broke up. Suffering from financial problems, Henderson sold arrangements to **Benny Goodman,** who liked the work and in 1939 hired him as a full-time staff arranger. Henderson thereby continued to have a strong influence on swing bands. Never quite the same after a collarbone was broken in an automobile accident in 1928, he was forced into retirement by a stroke in 1950.

"Hep Cats' Ball." By Jack Palmer, Louis Armstrong, and J.R. Robinson; rec. March 14, 1940, in New York City by Louis Armstrong and His Orchestra; CD #18.

Herbert, Mort (Morton Herbert Pelovitz) (1925–1983). The self-taught bassist was a steadfast member of **Louis Armstrong and the All Stars** from 1958 to 1961, leaving a few weeks after participating in the landmark LP recording with **Duke Ellington** (CD #11). Before joining the All Stars, he made an album, *Night People* (1956) with his own ensemble, and also recorded with Gene Krupa. Herbert can be seen in the 1959 films ***The Beat Generation*** and ***Die Nacht vor der Premiere.*** Later, Herbert had a law career, although he continued to work as a musician on a freelance basis.

"Here Come de Honey Man." By George Gershwin, DuBose Heyward, and Ira Gershwin; rec. October 14, 1957, in Los Angeles with vocalist **Ella Fitzgerald** and a studio orchestra and choir conducted by Russell Garcia; CD #9. See comments on "Bess, You Is My Woman Now."

Here Comes the Groom. In this entertaining film, an American (played by **Bing Crosby**) has a chance to adopt two Parisian orphans on the condition that he get married within a week. He quickly returns to the States but finds that his fiancée (played by Jane Wyman) is about to marry someone else. He manages to win her back, though, just inside the time limit. The big production number, "Misto Christofo Columbo," is performed on the plane taking Crosby and the children from Paris to New York. Armstrong is among the passengers, along with Cass Dailey, Phil Harris, and Dorothy Lamour. The big hit from this film was the **Johnny Mercer/Hoagy Carmichael** song "In the Cool, Cool, Cool of the Evening," which recurs throughout and won the Oscar for best song of 1951. Paramount, 1951; B&W; 113 mins.; Dir. Frank Capra.

"Here Is My Heart for Christmas." Rec. May 26, 1970, in New York City with a studio orchestra conducted by Oliver Nelson; CD #31. See comments on "Boy from New Orleans."

"He's a Son of the South." By Andy Razaf, Joe Davis, and Reginald Forsythe; rec. January 26, 1933, in Chicago by Louis Armstrong and His Orchestra; CDs #12, #17, #21, and #24. Here, as so often, Armstrong makes a great deal of music out of not much material, even when tired. "Son of the South" was his sixth and final recording of the day, and his many silences indicate a tired lip. At the end, however, he somehow plays a marvelously dramatic cadenza over sustained saxophones.

"Hesitating Blues." By W.C. Handy; rec. July 12, 1954, in Chicago by **Louis Armstrong and the All Stars;** CD #28. This is a duet number for Armstrong and his vocalist **Velma Middleton.** Both the recording and the rehearsal sequence can be heard on the reissue (CD #38) of *Louis Armstrong Plays W.C. Handy.* See additional comments on "Atlanta Blues."

"Hey, Lawdy Mama." By S. Easton; rec. April 11, 1941, in New York City by Louis Armstrong and His **Hot Seven.** Armstrong gives new life to this old blues number.

"Hey, Look Me Over." By Cy Coleman and Carolyn Leigh; rec. April 18, 1964, in New York City by **Louis Armstrong and**

Armstrong and Jack Teagarden in 1948. (Louis Armstrong House and Archives at Queens College/CUNY)

the All Stars. This was a popular number introduced by Lucille Ball and Paula Stewart in the 1960 musical *Wildcat.*

Higginbotham, Jay C. "J.C." (1906–1973). Armstrong and this Georgia-born trombonist considerably enhanced the **Luis Russell** band during the years when they coincided there (1929–1930 and 1937–1940). Nearly a third of a century later, Armstrong would write in his "Open Letter to Fans" that Higginbotham was "the best *trombonist* of them *all* at that time," and one can hear proof of this on his solos in "I Can't Give You Anything But Love" and "Mahogany Hall Stomp," both recorded in 1929 (Brothers, p. 185). Although Armstrong is a tough act to follow, Higginbotham nicely mixes the traditionally rough gutbucket sound with the new legato **swing** style. Higginbotham's playing is even more vivid on the nonvocal, tangolike version of "St. Louis Blues" (recorded in 1930 but not issued until the 1990s), and he shows the controlled inventiveness that modern players such as Urbie Green idolized on "Save It, Pretty Mama" (1939).

Between stints with Armstrong and Russell, Higginbotham worked with the bands of Benny Carter, **Fletcher Henderson,** and Chick Webb. He also worked in small groups, such as that of **Red Allen,** his good friend. From the late 1940s, he worked on a freelance basis in the New York area.

"High Society." By **Clarence Williams** and A.J. Piron; rec. January 26, 1933, in Chicago by Louis Armstrong and His Orchestra; CDs #8, #12, #21, #22, #24, #25, #46, #52, and #54. Armstrong gives a genial introduction to this old northern march, which was adopted by New Orleans **brass band**s.

High Society. In this musical adaptation of the play *The Philadelphia Story* (starring **Bing Crosby,** Grace Kelly, **Frank Sinatra,** and Celeste Holm), Armstrong makes an extensive contribution. He and the **All Stars** serve as a kind of narrator/chorus. At the very beginning, Armstrong sets the stage with "High Society Calypso," then he reappears at regular intervals to comment on the action, and finally he closes the film with a trumpet flourish and the words "End of story!" Armstrong's "Now You Has Jazz" duet with Bing Crosby, during which the All Stars are individually introduced, is one of the most memorable musical moments in all of cinema. Armstrong also adds some trumpet fill-ins as Crosby sings "Little One" and "I Love You, Samantha." In addition, Armstrong and the All Stars knock out an abbreviated swing version of the "Wedding March" from *Lohengrin* to wrap things up. As in ***New Orleans*** (1947), ***Paris Blues*** (1961), and ***A Man Called Adam*** (1966), Armstrong contributes to a subtext about the value of jazz. Except for a few measures from Richard Wagner, **Cole Porter** wrote the music for what should have been Armstrong's greatest film achievement. Unfortunately, times had changed by the mid-1950s. In comparison to confident black actors of the same time such as Dorothy Dandridge and Sidney Poitier, and sophisticated musicians such as Billy Eckstine and Nat "King" Cole, Armstrong was perceived by many to be the outdated Negro clown. Good art survives the test of time, however, and today Armstrong can be seen more clearly as a puckish genius who oversees the rather silly lives of wealthy white folk. M-G-M, 1956; color; 107 mins.; Dir. Charles Walters.

"High Society Calypso." By **Cole Porter;** rec. between January 10 and 18, 1956, in Los Angeles by **Louis Armstrong and the All Stars;** CDs #20, #23, #43, #45, and #63. The 1956 **movie *High Society*** opens with Armstrong and his band in a bus en route to Newport, Rhode Island, playing rhythm instruments in this clever song.

"High Society Rag." By Walter Melrose and Porter Steele; rec. between June 22 and 29, 1923, in Chicago by **King Oliver**'s Jazz Band. This popular **Dixieland** number, written in 1901, was also revived in 1938 by Bob Crosby and His Orchestra. See additional comments on "Alligator Hop."

Hill, Bertha "Chippie" (1905–1950). Armstrong was always a sensitive accompanist for blues singers, and he recorded with many (**Alberta Hunter, Margaret Johnson, Ma Rainey,** and **Bessie Smith**) while coming up in the 1920s. With Chippie Hill in 1925–1926 he did worthwhile versions of "Lonesome Weary Blues," "Low Land Blues," "Mess, Katie, Mess," and "Pleadin' for the Blues." On this last number, Armstrong does some colorful word painting with his trumpet. The **Great Depression** was hard on Hill, although she did manage to work part-time in Chicago. However, she quit music altogether for several years to raise children, returning after World War II to participate on the New York radio series *This Is Jazz.* Thereafter, she seemed to be everywhere, even at Carnegie Hall with **Kid Ory** (1948) and in Paris (1948). Unfortunately, her career renewal was abruptly ended by a fatal car crash.

Hines, Earl Kenneth "Fatha" (1903–1983). In the first volume of his **autobiography, *Swing That Music*** (1936), Armstrong wrote: "It was at the **Vendome** that I got to know that great **swing** piano player, Earl Hines. Earl could swing a gang of keys. He and I liked each other from the first and were to see a lot of each other afterwards" (p. 84). Hines was born in Duquesne, Pennsylvania, into a middle-class household, and after learning piano from his mother and local teachers, he eventually moved to Chicago in 1923. In 1926 he and Armstrong worked together in the **Carroll Dickerson** band at the **Sunset Cafe.** Hines took over as leader and Armstrong as front liner, and thus began one of the most fruitful partnerships in American music. They also had a lot of fun together. Armstrong relates that at the Sunset he and the corpulent drummer **Tubby Hall** with Little Joe Walker and the lanky Hines would do a Charleston, which, as a foil to the formal show, was hilarious (Shapiro and Hentoff, 1955, p. 111). They suffered through the bad times as well. For example, late in 1927 and early in 1928 they (and mutual friend **Zutty Singleton**) tried unsuccessfully to establish their own dance hall. All three soon found themselves broke and scrounging around for work.

In 1927–1928, Hines and Armstrong made around three dozen recordings together. Armstrong had at that time put together a new, more modern version of the **Hot Five,** and the felicitous results were soon noticeable in "West End Blues" and "Basin Street Blues." Although Hines contributes some sparkling passage work to the former and an evocative celeste solo to open the latter, his artistry can best be heard on "Fireworks," "Skip the Gutter," "A Monday Date," "Two Deuces," "Save It, Pretty Mama," and a few others. In "Skip the Gutter" he plays a famous break, trading fours with Armstrong, showing he is both an ensemble player and a soloist with a style all his own. "Weather Bird," recorded a few months later, is their most famous collaboration and some say the most famous recorded jazz duet. A salient feature of Hines's technique is his "trumpet style," which, in the words of pianist and scholar James Dapogny, means: "clearly articulated melody without ragtime figuration, often played in octaves, and tremolo approximating wind vibrato" (p. 526).

In the 1930s Hines struck out on his own as a bandleader based in Chicago. Early in 1948 he and Armstrong linked up again when Hines joined the **All Stars** for three seasons, but he had been a leader for too long to be comfortable taking orders. Nevertheless, his appearance in the movie ***The Strip*** (1950) is worthwhile, and in it he performs both "Hines' Retreat" and "Fatha's Time." In later years, Hines worked as both a leader and a freelance soloist. In 1966 his group took a U.S. State Department–sponsored tour of the Soviet Union. Five years later he was one of the many musicians and celebrities who were in attendance at Armstrong's **funeral** (July 9, 1971) at the **Corona** Congregational Church. Hines himself remained active until the weekend before his death, following a heart attack, on April 22, 1983, in Oakland, California.

Hinton, Milton John "Milt" "The Judge" (1910–2000). Double bassist Hinton was briefly associated with **Louis Armstrong and the All Stars** in the early 1950s (e.g., he went on the 1954 tour of Japan), and in addition to his fine feeling for rhythm and harmony, he made a valuable contribution by taking many candid pictures of the band and life on the road. This practice he began while a member of **Cab Calloway**'s band (1936–1951). Many of these photos can be seen in various **books** about Armstrong, as well as in Hinton's own *Bass Lines* (1988).

"His Father Wore Long Hair." By George David Weiss, Bob Thiele, and P. Rivelli; rec. May 27, 1970, in New York City with an ensemble conducted by Oliver Nelson; CD #31. This triple-meter song about Jesus' father was recorded for Armstrong's next-to-last album, *Louis Armstrong and His Friends.*

Hite, Les (1903–1962). In July 1930, Armstrong was troubled in his marriage to **Lil Hardin Armstrong** and had other problems, so he took a transcontinental train trip from Chicago to greener pastures in Los Angeles. He eventually landed at **Sebastian's New Cotton Club** in Culver City as a soloist with a band at first led by Leon Elkins but later by saxophonist Les Hite. Although born in Illinois, Hite had learned the New Orleans style from **Mutt Carey** and others and was an excellent musician. With Armstrong as soloist, they made outstanding recordings of "Body and Soul," "Just a Gigolo," "Memories of You," "The Peanut Vendor," "Shine," "Sweethearts on Parade," and others. Hite takes a short solo on this last one, but his main musical contribution is to lead the band in supporting Armstrong. April 1931 found Armstrong back in Chicago, but Hite's band stayed together until 1945, when he retired to become a booking agent.

"Hobo, You Can't Ride This Train." By Louis Armstrong; rec. December 8, 1932, in Camden, New Jersey, with the Chick Webb Orchestra (although the label reads "Louis Armstrong and His Orchestra"); CDs #3, #5, #8, #12, #21, #24, #44, and #52. Armstrong was said to have been suffering from **lip problems** at this recording session (during which he cut three other sides), but one can hardly tell. He takes "Hobo," a novelty number, at a quick pace, does some cute jive talking, sings, and ends with a short solo. Tenor saxophonist Elmer Williams and trombonist **Charlie Green** also take short but confident solos.

Holiday, Billie "Lady Day" (Eleanora Fagan) (1915–1959). Like many singers in her day, Holiday was influenced by Armstrong, a debt that she openly acknowledged. It therefore must have been a treat to work with him in 1946 on the film ***New Orleans,*** where she gives moving performances of "Do You Know What It Means to Miss New Orleans?"; "Farewell to Storyville" (a.k.a. "Good Time Flat Blues"); and "The Blues Are Brewing." On the other hand, Holiday was furious at her manager (and Armstrong's) **Joe Glaser** for getting her a role as a maid. "I'd fought my whole life to keep from being somebody's damn maid," she wrote in her autobiography *Lady Sings the Blues.* "After making more than a million bucks and establishing myself as a singer who had some taste and self-respect, it was a real drag to go to Hollywood and end up as a make-believe maid" (p. 119). Armstrong must also have noticed that the movie was demeaning to him and his music, but he took it in stride. He even wrote happily to **Madeleine Berard** that Holiday is "my sweetheart in the picture. . . . Ump Ump Ump. Now isn't that something? The great Billy [*sic*] Holiday, my sweetheart?" (Berrett, 1999, p. 130). By this time, Holiday was suffering from the effects of a deteriorating private life, and in fact she was jailed in 1947 on drug charges. The singer of "Strange Fruit," "Lover Man," and "God Bless the Child" thereafter went downhill. However, for many she remains the quintessential female jazz singer.

"Home (When Shadows Fall)." By Harry Clarkson, Jeff Clarkson, and Peter Van Steeden; rec. January 27, 1932, in Chicago by Louis Armstrong and His Orchestra; CD #58. This song, new the previous year, became the Peter Van Steeden Orchestra's theme song. It was revived in 1950 by Nat "King" Cole.

"Home Fire, The." By George David Weiss and George Douglass; rec. July 24, 1968, in Las Vegas by **Louis Armstrong and the All Stars** with a studio orchestra conducted by Art Butler; CD #62. This was the second of three numbers done on what turned out to be Armstrong's last recording session before a lengthy struggle with acute heart failure (September 1968 to April 1969).

Home for Colored Waifs. See **Colored Waif's Home for Boys.**

"Home! Sweet Home!" By Henry R. Bishop and John Howard Payne. Written in 1823, this was one of Armstrong's favorite songs. Piecing together several accounts (his two published **autobiographies** and a 1969 memoir manuscript), "Home! Sweet Home!" was one of the first tunes he learned at age six, when his employers, the **Karnofsky family,** lent him $5 for a pawn shop **cornet.** He also mentions playing the song at the **Colored Waif's Home** roughly six years later where he was given a cornet for good behavior by the music teacher, **Peter Davis.** "Then I was in seventh heaven," he wrote. "Unless I was dreaming, my ambition had been realized" (***Satchmo,*** 1954, p. 46).

"Honey, Do!" By Andy Razaf and J.C. Johnson; rec. January 27, 1933, in Chicago by Louis Armstrong and His Orchestra; CDs #12, #21, and #24. Armstrong's lip was giving him trouble (see **lip problems**) at this session, so the opening is played by trumpeter Elmer Whitlock.

"Honey, Don't You Love Me Anymore?" By Fred Meadows and Terry Shand; rec. April 24, 1933, in Chicago by Louis Armstrong and His Orchestra; CD #12. Here is a rare instance of Armstrong singing out of tune, but the lapse may be at least partially attributed to mediocre musical material.

"Honeysuckle Rose." By Andy Razaf and **Thomas "Fats" Waller;** rec. April 26, 1955, in New York City by **Louis Armstrong and the All Stars;** CDs #6, #42, #56, and #57. Vocalist **Velma Middleton** joins Armstrong on this Fats Waller favorite. See additional comments on "Ain't Misbehavin'."

Hoover, John Edgar (1895–1972). See **FBI.**

horn. See **cornet; trumpet.**

Horn of Plenty. See **"The Goffin Notebooks."**

Horne, Lena Calhoun (b. 1917). Already an accomplished singer (a fact underscored by performing in Carnegie Hall in 1941), Horne added "actress" to her job description when in 1942 she went to Hollywood to play in ***Cabin in the Sky,*** *Stormy Weather,* and other movies. For *Cabin,* she and Armstrong did a big production number, "Ain't It the Truth?," which unfortunately was cut from the final version. However, Horne's very convincing portrayal of the temptress Georgia Brown survived the cutting room floor, as did her earthy rendition of "Honey in the Honeycomb." Horne went on to a stellar career in nightclubs and on television. Her expressive voice is most commonly recognizable on "Stormy Weather."

Hot Chocolates. See ***Connie's Hot Chocolates.***

Hot Club de France. Founded by French author and jazz enthusiast **Hugues Panassié** in 1932, this organization was dedicated to the promotion of traditional jazz and remains active to the present. Not merely a music appreciation society, the Hot Club formed the Quintette du Hot Club de France (1934–1949), produced recording sessions (e.g., **Coleman Hawkins** in 1937), organized jazz festivals (e.g., **Nice** in 1948 and Montauban annually since 1982), sponsored tours (e.g., **Earl Hines** in the 1960s), and published journals (e.g., the *Bulletin du Hot Club de France* since 1950). The idealistic, fastidious, and partisan Hot Club members have had some stormy battles over the years, for example, over the emergence of be**bop** in the later 1940s.

Armstrong was delighted to discover the Hot Club's existence (as well as other such clubs in Britain and elsewhere) on his trips abroad in the early 1930s. The Hot Club members idolized Armstrong and elected him their Honorary President in 1936, a position that he held until his death in 1971. At present there are over two dozen local chapters in France, with headquarters thirty miles outside Paris in St.-Vrain (near Corbeil-Essonnes). The Hot Club's library, expanded from Panassié's core collection of 6,000 78 rpm records and 9,000 LPs, is housed at the Discothèque Municipale in Villefranche-de-Rouergue in southern France.

Hot Five. On November 12, 1925, Armstrong took his new wife **Lil** and a few old friends into the studios of **Okeh Records** to record the first of over five dozen sides that profoundly influenced the course of jazz. The Hot Five went through various name and personnel changes over the next three years, but at first it consisted of Armstrong playing the trumpet and singing, Lil Armstrong on the piano, and his longtime New Orleans friends **Kid Ory** on trombone, **Johnny Dodds** on clarinet, and **Johnny St. Cyr** on banjo. (Guitarist **Lonnie Johnson** made it the "Hot Six" for a session on December 13, 1927.) This initial group made such now-classic recordings as "Cornet Chop Suey," "Gut Bucket Blues," and "Struttin' with Some Barbecue." When recording for the **Vocalion** label ("Georgia Bo Bo" and "Drop That Sack" on May 28, 1926), the same ensemble was known as Lil's Hot Shots. Likewise, for eleven recordings in May 1927 ("Potato Head Blues," "S.O.L Blues," and others), the group was known as the **Hot Seven,** adding **Baby Dodds** on drums and **Pete Briggs** on tuba. (Again, guitarist Lonnie Johnson sometimes made it the "Hot Eight.") In 1928 Armstrong reconstituted the Hot Five personnel, replacing Lil with **Earl Hines,** Dodds with **Jimmy Strong** (on both clarinet and tenor sax), Ory with **Fred Robinson,** St. Cyr with **Mancy Carr,** and since recording technology now permitted drums, adding **Zutty Singleton.** This second Hot Five's recordings are regarded by many the zenith of Armstrong's career, with such masterpieces as "West End Blues," "Fireworks," "Basin Street Blues," and "St. James Infirmary."

For all its weighty influence on the development of music, the Hot Five made only one public appearance and that rather early on in their career. On February 27, 1926, after cutting six sides the previous day (four was considered a busy session), the group performed at the Chicago Coliseum in a promotional concert organized by Okeh. The Five appeared along with Okeh's other "race" ensembles: **King Oliver**'s and **Erskine Tate**'s. Although the advertised performance of "Cornet Chop Suey" by twenty-one jazz orchestras simultaneously did not take place, some 10,000 people attended and at long last heard the mysterious Hot Five, which they'd previously heard only on records.

The Hot Five and Hot Seven emphasized solos over the standard polyphony of the day, thereby changing the performance histories first of jazz and eventually of popular music in general.

Hot Four. Between 1925 and 1928, Armstrong's ensembles seemed to be called the **Hot Five** or **Hot Seven,** according to whatever musicians were on hand. Had someone been doing the numbers seriously, there would have been on occasion a "Hot Six" or a "Hot Eight." However, there was briefly an official Hot Four when in three sessions during 1928 (i.e., the interim between the "old" and the "new" Hot Five), **Lillie Delk Christian** recorded eight songs with the Hot Five minus a trombone player (CD #36). "Too Busy" is, unfortunately, the best of a pretty bad lot, since Christian had so little talent. What saves the song, in addition to instrumental solos by Armstrong and **Earl Hines,** is the last verse when Armstrong jumps in and **scat** sings around Christian's stiff, old-fashioned delivery. Dan Morgenstern comments: "If anyone needs a definition of **swing** and the lack thereof, this is made to order" (*Portrait,* 1994, p. 16).

Hot Seven. This studio ensemble had a recording career consisting of eleven sides—"Keyhole Blues," "Potato Head Blues," "S.O.L. Blues," "Wild Man Blues," and others—made in five sessions for **Okeh Records** in May 1927. The Hot Seven is Armstrong's original **Hot Five** plus drummer **Baby Dodds** and tuba player **Pete Briggs.**

"Hot Time in the Old Town Tonight." By Theodore M. Metz, Joe Hayden, and C.L. Mays; rec. between September 30 and October 2, 1959, in Los Angeles by **Louis Armstrong and the All Stars.** Armstrong and the All Stars give a rousing performance of this 1896 minstrel song, first introduced by Dan Quinn.

"Hotter Than That" By **Lil Hardin Armstrong** (see authorship note on "Got No Blues"); rec. December 13, 1927, in Chicago by Louis Armstrong and His **Hot Five;** CDs #8, #10, #48, and #52. This is a musical masterpiece, not only because of Armstrong's trumpetlike **scat** vocal (which he shares briefly with guitarist **Lonnie Johnson**) but also because of his admirable trumpet solos. Toward the end, the ensemble mostly stands back in silence as he executes a series of acrobatic breaks, preceded by twelve electrifying high "Cs". Some credit here must go to arranger **Don Redman,** who provided the framework within which Armstrong works his magic. So well thought of is this performance that it is examined right along with Mozart **opera** arias and Beethoven piano sonatas in music appreciation books. Furthermore, it has been lovingly and painstakingly transcribed by William W. Austin (pp. 282–283) and others. Other performers have also paid their respects; for example, the Ink Spots adapted a passage of "Hotter Than That" in their 1940 "Java Jive."

"How Come You Do Me Like You Do?" By Gene Austin and Roy Bergere; rec. between November 17 and 22, 1924, in New York City by **Fletcher Henderson** and His Orchestra. Gunther Schuller has pointed out two Armstrong trademarks that show up in this early recording: a simple short-short-long rhythm and a half-valve glissando or "rip" to a high note. Both occur in dozens of subsequent solos, and they influenced not just trumpeters but other musicians as well. Transcription by Schuller (1968, p. 95).

"How Do You Do It That Way?" By **Victoria Spivey** and Reuben Floyd; rec. July 10, 1929, in New York City with vocalist Victoria Spivey and ensemble; CD #36. See comments on "Funny Feathers."

"How High the Moon." By Morgan Lewis and Nancy Hamilton; rec. January 30, 1951, live at the Pasadena Civic Auditorium in California by **Louis Armstrong and the All Stars;** CD #6. This 1940 tune was a regular All Stars feature number for bassist **Arvell Shaw.**

"How Long Has This Been Going On?" By George Gershwin and Ira Gershwin; rec. October 14, 1957, in Los Angeles with the **Oscar Peterson** Quartet; CD #37. Armstrong does this 1928 Broadway number (from the show *Rosalie*) in one of his exquisitely slow tempos, with Peterson's sparkling ad lib backing. See additional comments on "Blues in the Night."

Howard University. Armstrong had mixed feelings about invitations to the White House and offers of honorary doctorates and other awards that came during the latter part of his life. In the 1960s Howard University, the prestigious and prominently black institution, wanted to give him an honorary doctorate, but he declined, saying: "Where were they forty years ago when I needed them?" (Giddins, 1988, p. 168).

"Hucklebuck, The." By Roy Alfred and Andy Gibson; rec. January 30, 1951, live at the Pasadena Civic Auditorium in California by **Louis Armstrong and the All Stars;** CD #6. Armstrong turns in a solid performance of this 1948 song, which Tommy Dorsey introduced.

Hucko, Michael Andrew "Peanuts" (1918–2003). Born in Syracuse, New York, this fine clarinetist and tenor saxophonist had a colorful career with numerous bands, including Glenn Miller's, **Benny Goodman**'s, and Eddie Condon's. He was tapped for the history-making **Town Hall concert** (May 17, 1947) and later succeeded **Edmond Hall** in the **All Stars** (July 1958 to mid-1960). After that he worked in various bands (including the modestly titled World's Greatest Jazz Band) and in 1981 toured with his own Pied Piper Quintet.

Hughes, Langston (1902–1967). In his **Corona** home, where he lived from 1942 to 1971, Armstrong had a library with a wide range of books (biography, diet, history, poetry, etc.). Many of these were presentation copies from admirers such as Richard Avedon, Truman Capote, and poet Langston Hughes, who gave Armstrong his *Famous American Negroes* (1954).

Hunter, Alberta (a.k.a. Josephine Beatty) (1895–1984). Armstrong accompanied many blues singers, and he recorded with **Chippie Hill, Margaret Johnson, Ma Rainey, Bessie Smith,** and others while coming up in the 1920s. With Alberta Hunter and the Red Onion Jazz Babies he did memorable versions of "Everybody Loves My Baby," "Of All the Wrongs You Done to Me," "Texas Moaner Blues," and others. In order to get around an exclusive **Gennett** contract, Hunter also recorded under the name of her half sister Josephine Beatty. She became famous for her rendition of "Down Hearted Blues" (1923). In 1926 she replaced Bessie Smith in the musical *How Come?* From 1927 to 1937 she (like many other black entertainers, such as **Josephine Baker, Arthur Briggs, Peter DuConge,** and Bobby Jones), found life more amenable in Europe, and during World War II and the Korean War she did United Service Organizations (USO) tours. From 1954 she worked as a nurse and performed less frequently. In 1977 she returned to music full-time and was still active in the 1980s.

"Hurdy Gurdy Man." By Saul Chaplin and Sammy Cahn; rec. August 7, 1936, in Los Angeles with **Jimmy Dorsey** and His Orchestra. This is one of a handful of recordings that Armstrong made with Dorsey before they worked together in the 1936 **movie *Pennies from Heaven.*** During the previous decade, Jimmy (along with his brother Tommy, **Benny Goodman, Muggsy Spanier, Bix Beiderbecke,** and others) used to sneak down to the South Side of Chicago to hear Armstrong.

"Hustlin' and Bustlin' for Baby." By Harry Woods; rec. January 26, 1933, in Chicago by Louis Armstrong and His Orchestra; CDs #12, #21, and #24. Here is Armstrong again making something special out of something ordinary, beginning with a straight-mute statement of the melody in which he pushes and pulls the beat artfully. Having established the tune, he feels free to sing much of it all on one note, then float around dreamily on the trumpet.

Hylton, Jack (1892–1965). When in July 1933 Armstrong went to Europe for his second tour, he was forced to fire his abusive manager, **Johnny Collins,** en route. Luckily, the outstanding English bandleader and impresario Jack Hylton was available to shepherd Armstrong, and he did so in such a way that his client better met the expectations of English and continental audiences. He also scheduled Armstrong so that he could rest adequately between engagements. So well did things go with Hylton at the helm that Armstrong briefly fantasized about basing himself in London. Hylton also worked similar wonders for **Duke Ellington** and **Coleman Hawkins.** Hylton's own orchestra broke up in 1940, and he helped produce London stage shows, for example, *Camelot* in 1964.

I

"I Ain't Gonna Give Nobody None of My Jelly Roll." By **Clarence Williams** and Spencer Williams; rec. between September 30 and October 2, 1959, in Los Angeles by **Louis Armstrong and the All Stars.**

"I Ain't Gonna Play No Second Fiddle (If I Can Play the Lead)." By Perry Bradford; rec. May 27, 1925, in New York City with vocalist **Bessie Smith,** trombonist **Charlie Green,** and pianist Fred Longshaw; CD #36. As good as it is, this recording was eclipsed by another made a few months later (November 2) with the composer's own group, the Jazz Phools (also CD #36). On this later recording Bradford's singing is undistinguished, but Armstrong's swaggering cornet solo is a knockout. The tempo is fast to begin with, but Armstrong increases it by playing three notes in the place of two. He also can be heard tentatively testing out the vibrato that will eventually add so much to his (and others') **swing** style. Transcription by Schuller (1968, p. 96). See additional comments on "Careless Love Blues."

"I Ain't Gonna Tell Nobody." By Richard M. Jones; rec. between October 5 and 15, 1923, in Chicago with **King Oliver**'s Jazz Band. See comments on "Alligator Hop."

"I Ain't Got Nobody." By Roger Graham and Spencer Williams; rec. December 10, 1929, in New York City by Louis Armstrong and His Orchestra; CD #44. As Armstrong began singing more and more, he developed a sweet and smooth style for popular ballads such as this 1916 song (which was also in the repertories of **Bessie Smith** and Sophie Tucker). Here he trades trumpet licks with **Red Allen.**

"I Believe." By Sammy Cahn and Jule Styne; rec. March 12, 1947, in New York City by Louis Armstrong and His Orchestra; CD #12. This number (brand new in 1947, from the movie *It Happened in Brooklyn* with **Frank Sinatra**) comes from Armstrong's last big band session before the **All Stars** era began. The ensemble plays marvelously, though, and Armstrong sings in his best crooner style. His spirited trumpet playing between verses and especially at the end defies superlatives.

"I Can't Believe That You're in Love with Me." By Jimmy McHugh and Clarence

Gaskill; rec. April 5, 1930, in New York City by Louis Armstrong and His Orchestra; CDs #8, #40, #48, and #52. Backed by a solid band (e.g., Theodore McCord on tenor saxophone), Armstrong pumps up this otherwise flat 1927 number from the review *Gay Paree.*

"I Can't Give You Anything But Love." By Jimmy McHugh and Dorothy Fields; rec. March 5, 1929, in New York City by Louis Armstrong and His **Savoy Ballroom Five;** CDs #8, #10, #13, #17, #18, #23, #28, #36, #40, #41, #42, #48, #52, and #61. Armstrong had recorded this song a few months earlier with vocalist **Lillie Delk Christian** and his **Hot Four,** but here he is both the singer and the trumpet soloist. The result was a No. 1 hit as well as a landmark event. Hereafter, he regularly covered popular songs and reached huge audiences. Here too he established what might be called his lyric sandwich pattern, in which he sings after opening with a trumpet solo (often muted) and closes with a hot trumpet solo ending dramatically on a high note. With the confident instrumental backing of his group, he takes a lot of liberties with the material on the vocal solo, and not only did the record-buying public respond, but, as Gary Giddins points out, professionals such as Ethel Waters and **Bing Crosby** imitated him (Giddins, 1988, p. 110; 2001, passim). Armstrong kept the number in his repertory, and he performed it in the 1944 **movie *Jam Session.*** The vocal solo can be found transcribed in Kernfeld and Feather (vol. 3, p. 590), and the instrumental solo in Schuller (1989, p. 163).

"I Come from a Musical Family." By Dave Franklin; rec. April 28, 1936, in New York City by Louis Armstrong and His Orchestra; CD #34. Like its companion piece "Somebody Stole My Break," this number is not exactly an immortal masterwork, but Armstrong makes it both live and swing.

"I Cover the Waterfront." By Johnny Green and Ed Heyman; rec. March 10, 1941, in New York City by Louis Armstrong and His **Hot Seven;** CD #41. Armstrong performs this melodramatic song in the 1933 Danish **movie *København, Kalundborg Og?*** The song itself is from a 1933 movie of the same name, starring Ben Lyon and Claudette Colbert.

"I Cried for You." By Arthur Freed, Abe Lyman, and Gus Arnheim; rec. November 30, 1947, live at Symphony Hall, Boston, by **Louis Armstrong and the All Stars.** This feature number for vocalist **Velma Middleton** is unaccountably left out of the CD reissue.

"I Didn't Know Until You Told Me." By **Dave Brubeck** and Iola Brubeck; rec. September 13, 1961, in New York City by **Louis Armstrong and the All Stars,** pianist Dave Brubeck, and guests; CDs #42 and #50. Armstrong's rough and Carmen McRae's sophisticated voices blend nicely in this tender love song. See additional comments on "Cultural Exchange."

"I Double Dare You." By Terry Shand and Jimmy Eaton; rec. January 13, 1938, in Los Angeles by Louis Armstrong and His Orchestra; CDs #14, #18, and #41. Armstrong's voice is smoothly sweet on this popular number, and he plays a brilliant trumpet solo full of arresting contrasts.

"I Feel Good." By Hersal Thomas; rec. March 3, 1926, in Chicago, with vocalist **Sippie Wallace** and pianist Hersal Thomas; CD #36. See comments on "Baby, I Can't Use You No More."

"I Get a Kick Out of You." By **Cole Porter;** rec. July 31, 1957, in Los Angeles with the **Oscar Peterson** Quartet; CDs #9, #28, #29, and #37. After a leisurely introduction, Armstrong and the Quartet take this 1932 classic (which Ethel Merman introduced in *Anything Goes*) at a nice clip. See additional comments on "Blues in the Night."

"I Get Ideas." By Julio Sanders and Dorcas Cochran; rec. July 24, 1951, in New York City with the **Sy Oliver** Orchestra; CDs #28, #32, and #39. This is one of numerous popular love songs that Armstrong recorded in the early 1950s. Latin Americans know it as the tango "Adios, Muchachos," a farewell song by a bridegroom to his buddies. Armstrong takes a slow tempo, savoring the words, and playing a fiery trumpet solo. "Ideas," first popularized by Tony Martin, was also covered by **Peggy Lee.**

"I Got It Bad and That Ain't Good." By Paul Francis Webster and **Duke Ellington;** rec. April 3, 1961, in New York City by **Louis Armstrong and the All Stars** with Duke Ellington; CDs #11 and #28. Here in a number from the 1941 musical *Jump for Joy* are Armstrong and Ellington at their meditative best. It's easy to agree with Ellington scholar Stanley Dance, who feels that this performance of the song outclasses all others before or since (2000, p. 6). See additional comments on "Azalea."

"I Got Plenty of Nuttin'." By George Gershwin, DuBose Heyward, and Ira Gershwin; rec. August 18, 1957, in Los Angeles with vocalist **Ella Fitzgerald** and a studio orchestra and choir conducted by Russell Garcia; CD #9. An Armstrong–Fitzgerald duet from Act II of *Porgy and Bess.* See additional comments on "Bess, You Is My Woman Now" and "April in Paris."

"I Got Rhythm." By George Gershwin and Ira Gershwin; rec. November 6, 1931, in Chicago by Louis Armstrong and His Orchestra; CDs #45 and #58. Shortly after this song from the 1930 Broadway musical *Girl Crazy* was popularized by Ethel Merman, Armstrong covered it and thereafter kept it in his repertory. It was still fresh when he played it with the **All Stars** in the 1965 **movie *When the Boys Meet the Girls*** (a remake of the 1943 film version of *Girl Crazy*). "I Got Rhythm" has the kind of active melody and confident lyrics that Armstrong liked. This plus an engaging chord structure has made it a perennial favorite among jazz musicians.

"I Gotta Right to Sing the Blues." By Ted Koehler and **Harold Arlen;** rec. January 26, 1933, in Chicago by Louis Armstrong and His Orchestra; CDs #3, #12, #21, #24, #25, #29, #32, #44, and #61. Armstrong sings this 1932 popular ballad with remarkable tenderness, but it's his final trumpet solo that blew everyone away. It still does. After reconstituting the melody into a simpler shape, he takes it to a parallel universe where rhythmic laws don't apply. "I Gotta Right" eventually became the **Jack Teagarden** Orchestra theme song.

"I Guess I'll Get the Papers and Go Home." By Hughie Prince, Dick Rogers, and Hal Kanner; rec. July 23, 1968, in Las Vegas by **Louis Armstrong and the All Stars;** CDs #28 and #62. The **Mills Brothers** made this song popular in 1946, and Armstrong brings much of their smooth style to it.

"I Hate to Leave You Now." By Dorothy Dick, Harry Link, and **Thomas "Fats" Waller;** rec. December 8, 1932, in Camden, New Jersey, with the Chick Webb Orchestra (although the label reads "Louis Armstrong and His Orchestra"); CD #12. Here Armstrong opens with a cup mute, which is unusual since he preferred the livelier straight mute. After singing, he untypically focuses in his trumpet solo on pieces of the melody rather than paraphrasing it as a whole, perhaps because the band came with three other trumpet players who could and did firmly carry the tune.

"I Hope Gabriel Likes My Music." By Dave Franklin; rec. December 19, 1935, in New York City by Louis Armstrong and His Orchestra; CDs #44 and #51. This number was introduced into the big band repertory by Armstrong, who at this point in his career was much more relaxed and popular music–oriented than he had been as an early jazz trailblazer in the 1920s.

"I Left My Heart in San Francisco." By George Cory and Douglas Cross; rec. March 22, 1965, live at Friedrichsstadt Palast, East Berlin, by **Louis Armstrong and the All Stars;** CD #2. This 1954 song was one of vocalist **Jewel Brown**'s specialties at All Star concerts, and here she sings it to a huge and very appreciative audience.

"I Like This Kind of Party." Rec. August 1965 in Hollywood by **Louis Armstrong and the All Stars.** This recording was released only in Europe.

"I Love Jazz." By Sydney Shaw; rec. October 8, 1958, in Los Angeles by **Louis Armstrong and the All Stars** with a studio vocal group; CD #8. Armstrong and company cut this number to lead off a **Decca** LP anthology, and although it's pretty light fare, there are solid solos by Armstrong and tenor saxophonist Eddie Miller.

"I Love You, Samantha." By **Cole Porter;** rec. between January 6 and 18, 1956, in Los Angeles by **Louis Armstrong and the All Stars** with vocalist **Bing Crosby** and the MGM Studio Orchestra conducted by Johnny Green; CD #45. Bing Crosby is featured on this love song, which is heard twice in the 1956 **movie *High Society*.** The first is a fast version done with the band mostly offscreen. The second time, Armstrong supplies a solo and some trumpet fill-in but again remains mostly unseen.

"I Married an Angel." By Richard Rodgers and Lorenz Hart; rec. January 29, 1957, in New York City with the **Sy Oliver** Orchestra; CD #26. See comments on "And the Angels Sing."

"I Miss My Swiss." By Abel Baer and L. Wolfe Gilbert; rec. August 7, 1925, in New York City with Billy Jones and the Southern Serenaders; CD #36. Working with members of the **Fletcher Hender-**

son Band, perhaps sprinkled with members of Sam Lanin's white band, Armstrong plays an energetic sixteen-bar solo that includes some intriguing syncopation with drummer **Kaiser Marshall.** As in the case of "Alone at Last," recorded at the same session, one can hear Armstrong getting the ensemble to **swing.**

"I Must Have That Man." By Jimmy McHugh and Dorothy Fields; rec. December 12, 1928, in Chicago by vocalist **Lillie Delk Christian** with Louis Armstrong and His **Hot Four;** CDs #36 and #48. Christian is clearly out of her league with this stellar ensemble (which includes guitarist **Mancy Carr,** pianist **Earl Hines,** and clarinet **Jimmie Noone**), but at least she delivers the text on pitch. The song itself is from *Lew Leslie's Blackbirds of 1928,* and as Dan Morgenstern points out, it marks Armstrong's first recording of a McHugh–Fields song and of one from Tin Pan Alley (*Portrait,* 1994, p. 18).

"I Never Knew." By Ted Fiorito and Gus Kahn; rec. April 17, 1942, in Chicago by Louis Armstrong and His Orchestra; CD #41.

"I Never Saw a Better Day." See "Never Saw a Better Day."

"I Only Have Eyes for You." By Al Dubin and Harry Warren; rec. August 14, 1957, in Los Angeles with a studio orchestra conducted by arranger Russell Garcia. Written for the 1934 movie *Dames* (starring Dick Powell and Ruby Keeler), this song has a sweetness that appealed to Armstrong and many others as diverse as Eddy Duchin, Jane Froman, The Flamingos, The Lettermen, Jerry Butler, and Art Garfunkel. Armstrong recorded it during a marathon day's work along with sixteen other numbers, including many complete alternate takes.

"I Still Get Jealous." By Jule Styne and Sammy Cahn; rec. April 18, 1964, in New York City by **Louis Armstrong and the All Stars;** CDs #4 and #39. Both Armstrong and his admirer Harry James covered this 1947 song from the musical *High Button Shoes.*

"I Surrender, Dear." By Gordon Clifford and Harry Barris; rec. April 20, 1931, in Chicago by Louis Armstrong and His Orchestra; CDs #8, #23, #28, #40, and #52. Rudy Vallee wrote that this recording illustrated Armstrong's "perfect command" of musical expression, and any argument to the contrary seems futile (Armstrong, 1936, p. xvi). The song nevertheless is most often associated with **Bing Crosby.** During the **All Stars** years, "Surrender" became a feature number for clarinetist **Barney Bigard,** but Armstrong continued to leaven it with at least a vocal chorus. Incidentally, Vallee was only one of this recording's many fans. **Louis Prima** was another. As Gary Giddins suggests, one "can project Louis Prima's whole career from this performance" (1988, p. 127).

"I Used to Love You." By Albert von Tilzer and Lew Brown; rec. November 16, 1941, in Chicago by Louis Armstrong and His Orchestra. Armstrong takes this popular 1920 song slowly and sweetly, staying close to the melody. In fact, his cautious performance has come in for some criticism by such otherwise ardent fans as Gunther Schuller, who expresses disappointment over Armstrong's giving in to a commercial style and his effort to create a sound "indistinguishable from a hundred other sweet or dance bands of the period" (Schuller 1989, p. 194).

"I Want a Little Girl." By Billy Moll and Murray Mencher; rec. September 6, 1946, in Los Angeles by Louis Armstrong and His **Hot Seven;** CDs #12, #21, #28, and #47. Armstrong seems particularly at ease on this number recorded with a small group similar to the one with which he was working on the **movie** ***New Orleans*** at the time. See additional comments on "Blues for Yesterday."

"I Was Doing All Right." By George Gershwin and Ira Gershwin; rec. October 14, 1957, in Los Angeles with the **Oscar Peterson** Quartet; CD #37. What particularly distinguishes this recording of a 1938 song (from the movie *The Goldwyn Follies*) is the beautiful simplicity of Armstrong's opening trumpet solo. See additional comments on "Blues in the Night."

"I Will Wait for You." By Michel Legrand and Jacques Demy, with English lyrics by Norman Gimbel; rec. March 26, 1968, in New York City by **Louis Armstrong and the All Stars.** This recording of a sentimental favorite (from *The Umbrellas of Cherbourg*, 1964) seems like a stretch for Armstrong, but he approaches it like a pro. Besides, he knew very well what's in the mind of a man who waits longingly for a woman.

"I Wish I Could Shimmy Like My Sister Kate." By Louis Armstrong (and/or **Clarence Williams?**). "I wrote that tune, 'Sister Kate,'" Armstrong once said, "and someone said that's fine, let me publish it for you" (Shapiro and Hentoff, 1955, p. 57). He further remembered that he received $50. The year was 1918, and the young Armstrong seems to have sold the piece to Armand Piron, the bandleader. Piron also had a music publishing business with Clarence Williams, and that is probably how Williams's name came to be on the piece. Williams (a pianist, composer, and promoter as well) was frequently accused (by **Barney Bigard, Pops Foster,** and others) of adding his name to bylines or sometimes claiming a piece outright. In any case, "Sister Kate" was a big hit for Armstrong, although he apparently never recorded it. He did perform it, though, for example, on NBC TV's *Flip Wilson Show* (Hollywood, October 22, 1970) in duet with the host and backed by the NBC studio orchestra conducted by George Wyle.

"I Wonder." By Cecil Gant and Raymond Leveen; rec. January 14, 1945, in New York City by Louis Armstrong and His Orchestra; CDs #40 and #49. Armstrong's cover of this hit reached the No. 3 spot on the ***Billboard*** **chart** (R & B Singles). Unfortunately, it caused a rift among his fans, many of whom did not like to see him cross categories.

"I Wonder, I Wonder, I Wonder." By Daryl Hutchinson; rec. March 12, 1947, in New York City by Louis Armstrong and His Orchestra; CD #12. See comments on "I Believe" and "It Takes Time."

"I Wonder Who." By Sid Barbarin; rec. April 26, 1933, in Chicago by Louis Armstrong and His Orchestra; CD #12. This number is sometimes mistakenly credited to Armstrong. His singing and the excellent work of the saxophone section here distinguish the recording.

"I Won't Dance." By Jerome Kern, Jimmy McHugh, Oscar Hammerstein II, Otto Harbach, and Dorothy Fields; rec. August 13, 1957, in Los Angeles with vocalist **Ella Fitzgerald** and the **Oscar Peterson** Quartet; CD #9. Many associate this eminently danceable tune with Fred Astaire and Ginger Rogers (who introduced it in the 1934 film *Roberta*), but Armstrong and Fitzgerald do it at least equally as well. Their hot flirtation and Peterson's rhythmic drive turn the foxtrot into a **swing.** See additional comments on "April in Paris."

"If." By Tolchard Evans, Robert Hargreaves, and Stanley J. Damerell; rec. February 6, 1951, in Los Angeles with Gordon Jenkins and His Orchestra; CD #28. Perry Como took this song to No. 1 in 1950, and it was also covered by Jo Stafford, Dean Martin, and Billy Eckstine.

"If I Could Be with You (One Hour Tonight)." By James P. Johnson and Harry Creamer; rec. August 19, 1930, in Los Angeles by Louis Armstrong and His **Sebastian New Cotton Club** Orchestra; CDs #8, #28, #40, #42, and #52. Armstrong liked to cover popular songs, such as this 1926 gem, which was the theme song of McKinney's Cotton Pickers. On his trumpet solo he both stays close to the melody and takes it through seemingly every possible rhythmic pattern. Assisting him is the young **Lionel Hampton** playing drums (which later in his career at Armstrong's urging he exchanged for the vibraphone). Transcription by Schuller (1989, p. 168).

"If I Had the Wings of an Angel." See "The Prisoner's Song."

"If I Lose, Let Me Lose." By Tom Delaney; rec. December 17, 1924, in New York City with vocalist **Maggie Jones** and pianist **Fletcher Henderson;** CD #36. See comments on "Anybody Here Want to Try My Cabbage?"

"If We Never Meet Again." By **Horace Gerlach** and Louis Armstrong; rec. April 29, 1936, in New York City by Louis Armstrong and His Orchestra; CDs #34 and #41. In addition to contributing to Armstrong's first volume of **autobiography,** ***Swing That Music,*** Gerlach also collaborated with him on several songs, such as this engaging ballad.

"If You Wanna Be My Sugar Papa (You Gotta Be Sweet to Me)." By A. Wayne, Irving Mills, and Bob Schaffer; rec. April 21, 1927, in Chicago with **Jimmy Bertrand**'s Washboard Wizards. See comments on "The Blues Stampede."

"I'll Be Glad When You're Dead, You Rascal, You." See "You Rascal, You (I'll be Glad When You're Dead)."

I'll Be Glad When You're Dead, You Rascal, You. In this 1932 **Betty Boop** cartoon, Armstrong first appears "live" with his band, then as a cartoon cannibal, next as a disembodied head in the upper corner of the screen singing the title song, and lastly with the band performing "Chinatown, My Chinatown" and the finale. (Paramount, 1932; B&W; 7 mins.; Dir. Dave Fleischer.) On April 20–24, 1942, Armstrong also filmed a concert performance of the title song as a **soundie,** of which there are two versions. One briefly shows **Luis Russell** reading a newspaper with a picture of Adolf Hitler; the second merely shows members of the band. (RCM Productions, 1942; B&W; 3 mins.; Dir. Josef Berne.)

"I'll Never Be the Same." By Matty Malneck, Frank Signorelli, and Gus Kahn; rec. October 14, 1957, in Los Angeles with the **Oscar Peterson** Quartet; CDs #28 and #37. Perhaps because it was written by a jazz pianist, Peterson warms to this 1931 number. Armstrong is in his best low, lonesome voice. He mistakenly mixes up the lyrics, going from the end of the first chorus to the second eight measures of the next. It matters little, however, and in any case the words were a later addition to this number. See additional comments on "Blues in the Night."

"I'll See You in My Dreams." By Isham Jones and Gus Kahn; rec. mid-January 1925 in New York City by **Fletcher Henderson** and His Orchestra. This sweet song was brand new and a No. 1 hit when Henderson recorded it. (The Doris Day movie of the same title was not made until 1951.) As usual, Henderson keeps a lid on Armstrong, who nevertheless can be detected getting the ensemble to **swing.** See additional comments on "Alabamy Bound."

"I'll String Along with You." By Harry Warren and Al Dubin; rec. January 30, 1957, in New York City with the **Sy Oliver** Orchestra; CD #26. See comments on "And the Angels Sing."

"I'll Take Her Back If She Wants to Come Back." By James V. Monaco and Edgar Leslie; rec. May 19, 1925, in New York City by **Fletcher Henderson** and His Orchestra. See comments on "Alabamy Bound."

"I'll Walk Alone." By Jule Styne and Sammy Cahn; rec. April 19, 1952, in Denver, Colorado, by Louis Armstrong and His Orchestra; CD #8. This was a No. 1 song for Dinah Shore, who introduced it in the 1944 movie *Follow the Boys.* Armstrong's version features the vocal equivalent of a soft shoe with muted trombonist Russ Phillips.

"I'm a Ding Dong Daddy (from Dumas)." By Phil Baxter; rec. July 21, 1930, in Los Angeles by Louis Armstrong and His **Sebastian New Cotton Club** Orchestra; CDs #44 and #48. Not long after arriving in Southern California, Armstrong landed a highly visible job at Frank Sebastian's New Cotton Club, and shortly thereafter he took the house band into the recording studio. Here he and the group unleashed a bounty of musical ideas, as evidenced by this 1928 cowboy song. For example, trombonist **Lawrence Brown**'s quirky octave-jumping melody (a displacement paired with a rhythmic syncopation) was taken up fifteen years later by **Dizzy Gillespie** for the be**bop** classic "Salt Peanuts." In "Ding Dong Daddy" Armstrong also does some clever **scat singing,** confessing in the song's middle, "I done forgot the words." Transcription in Gushee (1998, pp. 318–319).

"I'm a Little Blackbird (Looking for a Little Bluebird)." By George W. Meyer, Arthur Johnston, Grant Clarke, and Roy Turk; rec. December 17, 1924, in New York City with vocalist **Eva Taylor** and **Clarence Williams' Blue Five;** CD #36. This **Okeh "race record"** song's clever lyrics boldly deal with miscegenation. See additional comments on "Cast Away."

"I'm Beginning to See the Light." By Harry James, Johnny Hodges, Don George, and **Duke Ellington;** rec. April 3, 1961, in New York City by **Louis Armstrong and the All Stars** with Duke Ellington; CDs #11 and #20. Armstrong puts his own stamp on this 1944 song that Armstrong admirer Harry James and vocalist Kitty Kallen had taken to No. 1 in 1945. See additional comments on "Azalea."

"I'm Coming, Virginia." By Will Marion Cook and Donald Heywood; rec. December 26, 1950, in Los Angeles by **Louis Armstrong and the All Stars;** CD #45. Armstrong recorded this 1927 song (introduced by Ethel Waters) for the 1951 **movie *The Strip*.** Unfortunately, it wasn't used.

"I'm Confessin' (That I Love You)." By Al J. Neiburg, Doc Daugherty, and Ellis Reynolds; rec. August 19, 1930, in Los Angeles by Louis Armstrong and His **Sebastian New Cotton Club** Orchestra; CDs #3, #18, #40, #41, #42, #44, #48, and #61. Armstrong here both sings sweetly and accompanies himself with **scat**like asides that mimic his instrumental playing, a technique that eventually became a trait of his style. One can hear the vocal influence on Armstrong of such crooners and megaphone users as Rudy Vallee (who introduced the song), **Bing Crosby,** and even Al Jolson. However, Armstrong also influences others, for example, the self-accompanying figures and double-time passages in **Lawrence Brown**'s fine trombone solo. Later, **Dizzy Gillespie** (an early teenager in 1930) would in an edgy, backhanded form of flattery record an exaggerated imitation called "Pops Confessin'," which Armstrong rather liked. However, we don't know how Armstrong felt on his own recording about the weird introduction by Ceele Burke playing his steel guitar Hawaiian-style, which, to many ears, is yet another marvel.

"I'm Crazy 'bout My Baby and My Baby's Crazy 'bout Me." By **Thomas "Fats" Waller** and Alex Hill; rec. April 27, 1955, in New York City by **Louis Armstrong and the All Stars;** CDs #42 and #56. See comments on "Ain't Misbehavin'."

"I'm Goin' Huntin'." By J.C. Johnson and **Thomas "Fats" Waller;** rec. April 21, 1927, in Chicago with **Jimmy Bertrand**'s Washboard Wizards; CD #61. See comments on "The Blues Stampede."

"I'm Going Away to Wear You Off My Mind." By Lloyd Smith, Warren Smith, and Clarence Johnson; rec. April 5, 1923, in Richmond, Indiana, with **King Oliver**'s Creole Jazz Band; CD #35. One of five songs recorded on Armstrong's very first day in the studio, this is historically rather than musically important. Only the two brothers, clarinetist **Johnny Dodds** and drummer **Baby Dodds,** stand out in a musical texture that itself is obscured by poor recording techniques. See additional comments on "Alligator Hop."

"I'm Gonna Gitcha." By **Lil Hardin Armstrong;** rec. June 16, 1926, in Chicago by Louis Armstrong and His **Hot Five;** CD #10. Although not a particularly winning song, it's at least done in a key in which Armstrong can both use a full sound and play high notes.

"I'm in the Market for You." By James F. Hanley and Joseph McCarthy; rec. July 21, 1930, in Los Angeles by Louis Armstrong and His Orchestra; CDs #42 and #44. Soon after arriving in Southern California, Armstrong became the featured soloist at Frank **Sebastian's New Cotton Club** and took the house band into the recording studio. This love song is from the first of six sessions.

"I'm in the Mood for Love." By Dorothy Fields and Jimmy McHugh; rec. October 3, 1935, in New York City by Louis Armstrong and His Orchestra; CDs #41, #44, #51, and #61. This recording dates from the beginning of Armstrong's long association with manager **Joe Glaser,** who landed him a contract with newly formed **Decca Records.** "I'm in the Mood" is the first of some 120 sides recorded during the next seven years with them. Armstrong approaches this No. 1 hit (from the 1935 movie *Every Night at Eight*) in a relaxed and subdued manner, serving the song more than his need to wow listeners with his virtuosity.

"I'm Just a Lucky So and So." By **Duke Ellington** and Mack David; rec. April 4, 1961, in New York City by **Louis Armstrong and the All Stars** with Duke Ellington; CD #11. Armstrong and Ellington treat this song in a duetlike fashion. See additional comments on "Azalea."

"I'm Not Rough." By Louis Armstrong and **Lil Hardin Armstrong** (see authorship note on "Got No Blues"); rec. December 10, 1927, in Chicago by Louis Armstrong and His **Hot Five;** CD #10. Although Armstrong usually inspired his sidemen, here he receives inspiration from guitarist **Lonnie Johnson,** who temporarily joined the Hot Five for this number (as well as "Hotter Than That" and "Savoy Blues" three days later). The song's title is deceptive, as Armstrong plays edgy blue notes and sings harshly ("The woman that gets me got to treat me right . . ."). Armstrong also pushes and pulls the beat, artfully doling out the lyrics in defiance of meter and phrase length. (This rubato lyric style became one of his salient performance characteristics.) All this plus particularly outstanding work by trombonist **Kid Ory** and clarinetist **Johnny Dodds** add up to one of the most powerful recordings of the day. Transcription by Castle (vol. 1, p. 20).

"I'm Putting All My Eggs in One Basket." By **Irving Berlin;** rec. August 13, 1957, in Los Angeles with vocalist **Ella Fitzgerald** and the **Oscar Peterson** Quartet; CDs #9 and #51. Armstrong first recorded this No. 1 hit song (from the movie *Follow the Fleet* with Fred Astaire and Ginger Rogers) when it was new in 1936, and the upwardly bound **Bunny Berigan** was in the trumpet section of his orchestra (see CD #41). (It was Berigan who supposedly observed that all a musician needs on tour is "a toothbrush and a picture of Louis Armstrong.") Although a fine recording, the one made twenty years later with Ella Fitzgerald and Oscar Peterson is in a category of its own. Armstrong leaves his horn in the case, and his rough voice blends thrillingly with Fitzgerald's smooth one. See additional comments on "April in Paris."

"I'm Shooting High." By Ted Koehler and Jimmy McHugh; rec. November 22, 1935, in New York City by Louis Armstrong and His Orchestra; CDs #41 and #51. Jan Garber and His Orchestra first popularized this song from the 1935 movie *King of Burlesque,* and Armstrong recorded it in the same year. **Lip problems** result in Armstrong's playing more conservatively than he did during 1933–1934, but he still can't resist a high "F" at the end.

Immerman, Connie. See **Connie's Inn.**

"In a Mellow Tone." By **Duke Ellington;** rec. April 3, 1961, in New York City by **Louis Armstrong and the All Stars** with Duke Ellington; CD #11. This number features drummer **Danny Barcelona** and bassist **Mort Herbert.** See additional comments on "Azalea."

"In Pursuit of Happiness." By Carolyn Leigh and Cy Coleman; rec. December 14, 1956, in New York City by Louis Armstrong and His Orchestra; CD #8. Armstrong takes this reflective tune at a leisurely tempo, singing dreamily and playing a short but sweet solo.

"In the Gloaming." By Annie Fortescue Harrison and Meta Orred; rec. October 3, 1941, in New York City by Louis Armstrong and His **Hot Seven;** CD #18.

"In the Shade of the Old Apple Tree." By Harry H. Williams and Egbert Van Alstyne; rec. June 29, 1937, in New York City with the **Mills Brothers;** CD #61. This recording was made during a period when the hot new bands were trying to get some of the old songs to **swing.** "Apple Tree" maybe didn't turn out as well as other Armstrong-Mills collaborations, but it's engaging nonetheless. See additional comments on "Carry Me Back to Old Virginny."

"Indian Cradle Song." By Mabel Wayne and Gus Kahn; rec. May 4, 1930, in New York City by Louis Armstrong and His Orchestra.

"Indiana, (Back Home Again in)." By James F. Hanley and Ballard MacDonald; rec. January 30, 1951, live at Pasadena Civic Auditorium in California by **Louis Armstrong and the All Stars;** CDs #2, #6, #19, #20, #22, #43, #46, #55, #57, and #59. This recording is one of nearly four dozen that Armstrong made of the **Dixieland** standard. The upbeat 1917 number frequently opened All Stars concerts.

innovations. See **firsts.**

Institute of Jazz Studies. Housed in the Dana Library at Rutgers University in Newark, New Jersey, the IJS has a huge collection of sound recordings, books, periodicals, research files on individual performers, oral histories, photographs, sheet music, instruments, and memorabilia. Because of Director Dan Morgenstern's lifelong interest in Armstrong, the IJS has accumulated numerous documents—letters, photos, memoirs—related to him. For example, the IJS has a copy of the typescript of the second volume of Armstrong's 1954 **autobiography** ***Satchmo: My Life in New Orleans.*** Studies of this document and other Armstrong writings by William Kenney (1991, pp. 48–51) and Thomas Brothers (pp. 47–48, 200–204) indicate that Armstrong's public writing was heavily edited (e.g., racial slurs and impolite language removed), probably at the behest of Armstrong's manager, **Joe Glaser,** who didn't want controversy to get in the way of moneymaking. The IJS also has a fascinating **Associated Booking Corporation** "Publicity Manual" from the late 1940s, which shows how Glaser exploited the be**bop** controversy. For example, he provides such fill-in-the-blanks copy as the following: "The national jazz controversy, which began in ***Time*** magazine will be centered in ____ when Louis Armstrong arrives for his ____ [Date Here] concert at ____ [Name of Hall Here]" (Brothers, x–xi, 216).

Another valuable IJS resource is its collection of oral histories, many of which have been transcribed. Several interviewees were Armstrong associates. Excerpts from interviews with members of the **All Stars** (trombonists **Russell "Big Chief" Moore** and **Trummy Young,** bassist **Arvell Shaw,** and clarinetist **Barney Bigard**) can be found in Berrett's *The Louis Armstrong Companion* (pp. 161–176).

integration. See **civil rights.**

"Intermezzo" from *Cavalleria Rusticana.* Armstrong loved all sorts and conditions of music, including **opera,** which was a significant ingredient in his **childhood** cultural milieu. Before taking up the cornet, he and his friends sang operatic excerpts on New Orleans street corners, and his first record acquisitions in 1917–1918 included such singers as Enrico Caruso, John McCormack, and Luisa Tetrazzini (see **"Louis Armstrong and Opera"**). Armstrong was therefore right at home from 1925 to 1926 in Chicago's **Vendome Theater Symphony Orchestra,** which typically played an operatic overture (e.g., Rossini's *William Tell*) before accompanying a movie. Afterward Erskine Tate's smaller group, the Jazz Syncopators (including Armstrong), would take over. Armstrong played jazz solos as well as operatic selections, such as the famous 1890 "Intermezzo" by Pietro Mascagni (1863–1945). He kept this beautiful melody in his repertory, sometimes using it as a preconcert warm up. "One day," he told Max Jones and John Chilton, "a guy knocked at the dressing-room door and said he'd heard me playing it as he was walking by. He was a flute player from the Philadelphia Symphony Orchestra and he complimented me on my interpretation and phrasing—after all those years—I felt good about that and we talked for hours about music" (p. 237).

Invisible Man. See **Ellison, Ralph.**

Irene. Armstrong's 1954 **autobiography** tenderly records how at age sixteen he met a twenty-one-year-old woman temporarily down on her luck, helped her financially, fell deeply in love, and finally learned a bitter lesson about the bond between prostitutes and pimps. "I had not had any experience with women, and she taught me all I know" (***Satchmo,*** pp. 101–102). Naturally, Armstrong did not at first tell his mother, who wisely tried to keep calm when she eventually caught on to the situation. Armstrong and Irene lived together for a time until she became ill. He nursed her and even went to the expense of taking her to a doctor. Trumpeter **Joe Oliver** let him substitute at a popular honky-tonk to make some extra money. Irene's illness remains unclear, and it may very well be that Armstrong's money went toward an abortion. She eventually made up with her pimp-boyfriend (a tough fellow called Cheeky Black), and Armstrong went his own way, a little wiser in the ways of love. He also came out of the affair with a little more confidence about the value of his music making.

"Irish Black Bottom." By Percy Venable and Louis Armstrong; rec. November 27, 1926, in Chicago by Louis Armstrong and His **Hot Five;** CD #10. In spite of Armstrong's having to sing the questionable line "I was born in Ireland," this collaboration with the **Sunset Cafe**'s floorshow producer gets a fine performance. Henry Clark subs for trombonist **Kid Ory** on this number, and perhaps it's the absence of his old New Orleans friend that accounts for the lack of exuberance in Armstrong's trumpet solo. Transcription by Castle (vol. 2, p. 14).

"Is You Is or Is You Ain't My Baby?" By Louis Jordan and Billy Austin; rec. September 12, 1944, live at Camp Reynolds, Pennsylvania (an Armed Forces Radio Service broadcast), by Louis Armstrong and His Orchestra. Armstrong first teamed up with singer **Velma Middleton** in 1942, and this tune from the 1944 movie *Follow the Boys* was their first recorded duet. It was a hit, the first of many, and the two had an admirable working relationship right up to Middleton's untimely death in 1961 while on tour with **Louis Armstrong and the All Stars** in Africa.

"Isn't This a Lovely Day?" By **Irving Berlin** and I. Balin; rec. August 16, 1956, in Los Angeles with vocalist **Ella Fitzgerald** and the **Oscar Peterson** Quartet; CD #9. Fred Astaire may own this 1935 song from *Top Hat,* but Armstrong and Fitzgerald, at their flirtatious best, borrow it with considerable interest. See additional comments on "April in Paris."

"It Ain't Necessarily So." By George Gershwin, DuBose Heyward, and Ira Gershwin; rec. August 18, 1957, in Los Angeles with vocalist **Ella Fitzgerald** and a studio orchestra and choir conducted by Russell Garcia; CD #9. This Armstrong-Fitzgerald duet comes from Act II of *Porgy and Bess.* See additional comments on "Bess, You Is My Woman Now" and "April in Paris."

"It Don't Mean a Thing (If It Ain't Got That Swing)." By Irving Mills and **Duke Ellington;** rec. April 3, 1961, in New York City by **Louis Armstrong and the All Stars** with Duke Ellington; CD #11. One can't imagine better teachers than these to give a lesson in **swing.** See additional comments on "Azalea."

"It Takes Time." By Arthur Korb; rec. March 12, 1947, in New York City by Louis Armstrong and His Orchestra; CD #12. Made between the landmark **Carnegie Hall** and **Town Hall concerts** (February 8, 1947, and May 12, 1947), this recording amply demonstrates the appeal of the big band, which nevertheless was on its way out. The spirited ensemble backs Armstrong's heartfelt singing in what Dan Morgenstern notes is a lesson in how to communicate a lyric, specifically "how he stresses the repeated title phrase, really hitting those 't's' " (Morgenstern, *The Complete RCA Victor Recordings,* 1997, p. 31).

"It Takes Two to Tango." By Al Hoffman and Dick Manning; rec. August 25, 1952, in New York City with the **Sy Oliver** Orchestra; CD #39. Sy Oliver's arrangement of this clever song showcases Armstrong as both singer and trumpeter, keeping the band mainly to a rhythm section.

Armstrong's friend **Pearl Bailey** had a huge hit with this number in the same year.

"It's a Most Unusual Day." By Jimmy McHugh and Harold Adamson; rec. November 17, 1951, in Los Angeles with guest artists (including **Jack Teagarden**), backed by the MGM Studio Orchestra and Choir and directed by George Stoll; CD #45. This 1948 song was unfortunately cut from the 1952 **movie** ***Glory Alley.***

"It's Been a Long, Long Time." By Jule Styne and Sammy Cahn; rec. April 18, 1964, in New York City by **Louis Armstrong and the All Stars.** Armstrong brought this popular 1945 song to a new generation with this nostalgic yet uptempo performance.

"It's Easy to Remember." By Richard Rodgers and Lorenz Hart; rec. June 4, 1965, live at the Palais des Sports in Paris by **Louis Armstrong and the All Stars.** This 1935 song from the movie *Mississippi* was a feature number for pianist **Billy Kyle.**

"It's Wonderful." Cameron S. Wells, Stuff Smith, and Mitchell Parish; rec. May 18, 1938, in New York City by Louis Armstrong and His Orchestra; CD #41.

"I've Got a Feeling I'm Falling." By Billy Rose, Harry Link, and **Thomas "Fats" Waller;** rec. April 26, 1955, in New York City by **Louis Armstrong and the All Stars;** CDs #42 and #56. Armstrong had an endearing maudlin streak, and it really comes out in the 1929 song. See additional comments on "Ain't Misbehavin'."

"I've Got a Gal in Kalamazoo." By Harry Warren and Mack Gordon; rec. early 1943 in Los Angeles by Louis Armstrong and His Orchestra; CD #49. Armstrong responds warmly to this wartime favorite (from the 1942 movie *Orchestra Wives*), which Glenn Miller took to No. 1.

"I've Got a Heart Full of Rhythm." By Louis Armstrong and **Horace Gerlach** in 1937; rec. July 7, 1937, in New York City by Louis Armstrong and His Orchestra; CD #34. In this appealing song, clarinetist **Albert Nicholas** and alto saxophonist Charlie Holmes follow Armstrong's vocal with some very fine solo work. Armstrong then changes both the key and the voltage when he returns for a final chorus.

"I've Got a Pocketful of Dreams." By Johnny Burke and James V. Monaco; rec. June 24, 1938, in New York City by Louis Armstrong and His Orchestra; CD #41. Although a No. 1 hit (from the 1938 movie *Sing, You Sinners,* starring **Bing Crosby**), this tune is rather dull. Nevertheless, as he did so often with unpromising material, Armstrong's **swing** style makes it bright.

"I've Got a Right to Sing the Blues." See **"I Gotta Right to Sing the Blues."**

"I've Got My Fingers Crossed." By Ted Koehler and Jimmy McHugh; rec. November 21, 1935, in New York City by Louis Armstrong and His Orchestra; CDs #41 and #51. Supported by bass player **Pops Foster** and drummer **Paul Barbarin,** Armstrong's liberties with the rhythm further the development of the emerging **swing** style in this popular song from the 1935 film *King of Burlesque.* There is also an intriguing solo passage in which he noodles around with the whole-tone scale. Transcription by Schuller (1989, p. 185).

"I've Got My Love to Keep Me Warm." By **Irving Berlin;** rec. August 13, 1957, in Los Angeles with vocalist **Ella Fitzgerald** and the **Oscar Peterson** Quartet; CD #9. Nearly everyone seems to have recorded this No. 1 song from the 1937 film *On the Avenue.* See additional comments on "April in Paris."

"I've Got the World on a String." By Ted Koehler and **Harold Arlen;** rec. January 26, 1933, in Chicago by Louis Armstrong and His Orchestra; CDs #12, #21, #24, and #48. Armstrong made memorable recordings of many Arlen-Koehler songs (e.g., "I Gotta Right to Sing the Blues"), and both the easy syncopation and the disjunct melody of this one suited him perfectly. Following a breezy introduction by the young pianist **Teddy Wilson,** Armstrong's trumpet solo closely follows the melody for about four measures. He then starts improvising artfully, switches to **scat singing,** and wraps it all up with some thrilling high notes.

"I've Stopped My Man." By **Hociel Thomas;** rec. November 11, 1925, in Chicago with vocalist Hociel Thomas and Louis Armstrong's Jazz Four; CDs #10 and #36. See comments on "Adam and Eve Had the Blues."

J

"Jack Armstrong Blues." By Louis Armstrong and **Jack Teagarden;** rec. June 10, 1947, by **Louis Armstrong and the All Stars;** CDs #12, #13, #21, and #47. Armstrong and Jack Teagarden first collaborated on this piece in 1944 for a V-disc, calling it "Play Me the Blues." The retitled version became an All Stars staple. The two good friends here trade fours, inspiring each other to ever greater heights of vocal and instrumental virtuosity. For comments on V-discs, see "Flying Home."

"Jack o'Diamond Blues." By **Sippie Wallace;** rec. March 1, 1926, in Chicago with vocalist Sippie Wallace and pianist Hersal Thomas; CD #36. See comments on "Baby, I Can't Use You No More."

Jackson, Eddie (c. 1867–1938). This tuba and string bass player must have made a deep impression on the young Armstrong, who wrote in his 1954 **autobiography:** "A bad tuba player in a brass band can make work hard for the other musicians, but Eddy [*sic*] Jackson knew how to play that tuba and he was the ideal man for the **Onward Brass Band**" (***Satchmo,*** p. 90). A seasoned performer on advertising wagons and in dance halls, Jackson played with the OBB from 1910 to 1912. During the 1920s he led a dance band and played with **Oscar "Papa" Celestin**'s snappy **Tuxedo Brass Band** and Orchestra. In the 1930s he played in the reorganized Tuxedo Brass Band. Armstrong still remembered Jackson in 1969, when he wrote: "Jackson used to really Swing the Tuba when the band played Marches. They sounded like a forty piece brass **swing** band" (Brothers, p. 27). The actual number of musicians in such bands was probably twelve.

Jackson, Mahalia (1911–1972). The Gospel Queen, whose 1947 rendition of "Move on Up a Little Higher" sold more than a million copies, once said, "If you don't like Louis, you're not human" (Berrett, 1999, p. 199). The two sang "Just a Closer Walk with Thee" and "When the Saints Go Marching In" together at the 1970 **Newport Jazz Festival.** A film called ***Finale*** (1970) includes their performance.

Jackson, Preston (1902–1983). Like so many other New Orleans musicians, trombonist Jackson left town after the 1917 closing of the **Storyville** district and found work in the Chicago area. He became a valuable sideman with both **Erskine Tate** and **Carroll Dickerson,** and he then formed his own band. When

Armstrong returned to Chicago from Los Angeles in April 1931, he fronted a band consisting mostly of old New Orleans friends such as Jackson. Led by trumpeter **Zilner Randolph,** this group was together for about a year, toured widely, and recorded about two dozen numbers under the name "Louis Armstrong and His Orchestra."

Jackson was an occasional writer and shed a little light on the still-murky picture of Armstrong's problems with gangland figures, on the related conflict between **Tommy Rockwell** and **Johnny Collins** over who was Armstrong's manager, and on some of the racial incidents that took place on the road. For example, he wrote about how on October 10, 1931, Armstrong and the whole band were arrested in Memphis, apparently for simply arriving as a group of well-dressed black men with a white woman, Mrs. Johnny Collins, in their bus. "It looked like half the Memphis police force met us there," Jackson recalled (Jones and Chilton, p. 239). Jackson also got to know **Lil Armstrong** and came to feel strongly that she deserved a lot of credit for the success of her husband (Hentoff and McCarthy, p. 115). Jackson went on to work with **Jimmie Noone, Roy Eldridge, Johnny Dodds,** and Lil (with whom he recorded in 1961). In the 1970s he was a member of the New Orleans Joymakers. Later he was associated with the Preservation Hall Jazz Band, both at the New Orleans home base and with its touring bands. His autobiography was published in the July and October 1974 issues of *The Mississippi Rag.* On July 4, 1976, he was a special guest at the unveiling of **Elizebeth Catlett**'s statue of Armstrong in New Orleans's Jackson Square.

Jam Session. Short on plot but long on **swing,** this musical stars Ann Miller and Jess Barker and features the orchestras of Charlie Barnet, Jan Garber, Glen Grey, Teddy Powell, and Alvino Rey. Armstrong, a musical bartender, plays and sings a suggestive "I Can't Give You Anything But Love" to a row of lovely young black women. There's a magical moment at the end of his trumpet solo, as he floats up to the B-flat above high "C" before the boisterous band brings the song back to earth. According to Klaus Stratemann (1977, p. 30), Armstrong also recorded something called "Go South, Young Man" for this film, but it didn't survive the editing room. Columbia, 1944; B&W; 77 mins.; Dir. Charles Barton.

James, George (1906–1995). The Oklahoma-born reed player moved to Chicago in his early twenties, where he worked in several bands (e.g., **Jimmy Noone**'s) before joining Louis Armstrong's 1931–1932 tour through the Midwest and South. "Now there's a Band that really 'deserved a *whole lot* of '*credit* that they *didn't* get," wrote Armstrong over a decade later (Brothers, p. 108). Despite the **Great Depression,** they drew huge crowds, although they also faced much racial prejudice. The group recorded some classics, such as "All of Me," "Between the Devil and the Deep Blue Sea," "I Got Rhythm," "I've Got the World on a String," "Star Dust," and the first of many "When It's Sleepy Time Down South" (Armstrong's most recorded song, which he did nearly a hundred times).

James went on to work with **Fats Waller, Teddy Wilson,** and others. He also led bands in New York (residing for long periods at the Famous Door and at the Café Society) and elsewhere. In the 1970s and 1980s, he toured internationally with Clyde Bernhardt and the Harlem Blues and Jazz Band. James was interviewed by James Lincoln Collier for his 1983 book on Armstrong, and he expounded on **Johnny Collins**'s status in the underworld. Apparently Collins had ambitions to become a big-time gangster but was simply not clever enough. Collier, however, according to James, was able on one particular occasion, when two mobsters threatened Armstrong at gunpoint, to move quickly and decisively, putting Armstrong and his band on the next train for an extended tour of the Midwest (p. 224, et passim).

"Jammin' the Vibes." By **Lionel Hampton** and Red Norvo; rec. January 18, 1944, in New York City with the ***Esquire*** All Star Jazz Band. This number from a special concert at the Metropolitan Opera House features vibraphonist Lionel Hampton and drummer **Sid Catlett,** two of Armstrong's favorite people. See additional comments on "Flying Home."

Jane Alley. Armstrong was born on this street in the **Back o' Town** section of New Orleans, between Perdido and Poydras Streets. See **birthplace.**

Jazz. This set of ten videocassettes (roughly nineteen hours long) was first broadcast on PBS beginning on January 8, 2001. In it producer-director **Ken Burns** documents the history of jazz from its roots in the African American community of New Orleans to the present. It was written by Geoffrey C. Ward (who also wrote the companion volume) and narrated by Keith David. Burns reflected in an on-air PBS interview before the broadcast of the series: "I think the person who became our talisman, the sort of pole star for the series . . . was Louis Armstrong."

Jazz Legends (Parts One and Two), The. In these videos, Armstrong performs "Sleepy Time Down South," "Hello Dolly!" and "C'est si bon." There are other jazz performances from the 1930s and 1940s as well, including Tex Beneke, Tommy and **Jimmy Dorsey, Benny Goodman,** Nat King Cole, Andy Kirk, **Cab Calloway,** Sonny Dunham, Mike Bryan, **Bobby Hackett,** Eddie Condon, and Jimmy Rushing. The intelligent narration by Jack Moore is read by Don Cavitt and Hugh Cardenas. K-TWIN/De Flores Productions, 1986; B&W with color sequences; 91 mins. on two cassettes; Prod. Tom Pelissero.

"Jazz Lips." By **Lil Hardin Armstrong,** Louis Armstrong, and S. Robbin; rec. November 16, 1926, in Chicago by Louis Armstrong and His **Hot Five;** CDs #10 and #44. Armstrong stays very close to the melody of this simple number, making it very snappy with some **stop-time** playing. The hocketlike texture must have been worked out in advance, which, despite the myth of constant improvisation, was not unusual in the New Orleans style. Transcription by Castle (vol. 1, p. 14).

Jazz on a Summer's Day. To this intimate record of the 1958 **Newport Jazz Festival,** Armstrong and the **All Stars** contribute "Lazy River," "Tiger Rag," "Rockin' Chair" (in duet with **Jack Teagarden**), and (with the addition of cornetist **Bobby Hackett**) "When the Saints Go Marching In." **Critic Pauline Kael** calls this "one of the most pleasurable of all concert films" (p. 379). Union Films,

1960; Technicolor; 86 mins.; Dir. Bert Stern. Reissued in 2000 as a New Yorker Video.

"Jazzin' Babies Blues." By Richard M. Jones; rec. between June 22 and 29, 1923, in Chicago with **King Oliver**'s Jazz Band. See comments on "Alligator Hop."

"J.C. Holmes Blues." By G. Horsley; rec. May 27, 1925, in New York City with vocalist **Bessie Smith,** trombonist **Charlie Green,** and pianist Fred Longshaw; CD #36. See comments on "Careless Love Blues."

"Jealous Woman Like Me, A." By Hersal Thomas; rec. March 1, 1926, in Chicago with vocalist **Sippie Wallace** and the composer at the piano; CD #36. See comments on "Baby, I Can't Use You No More."

"Jeepers Creepers." By Harry Warren and **Johnny Mercer;** rec. September 1938 in Los Angeles with a studio orchestra; CDs #6, #40, #41, #44, #60, and #61. Armstrong introduced this catchy song in the 1938 **movie** ***Going Places,*** and he kept it in his repertory. Silly yet oddly appealing, in the film the song serves to calm a high-spirited racehorse, and only Armstrong's inimitable singing and trumpet playing can do the job.

"Jelly Bean Blues." By **Gertrude "Ma" Rainey** and Lena Arant; rec. October 16, 1924, in New York City with vocalist Ma Rainey and Her Georgia Jazz Band; CD #36. See comments on "Countin' the Blues."

"Jelly Roll Blues." By **Jelly Roll Morton;** rec. between September 30 and October 2, 1959, in Los Angeles by **Louis Armstrong and the All Stars.**

"Jerry." By Scott Turner; rec. April 2, 1962, in New York City by **Louis Armstrong and the All Stars.** This is a feature number for vocalist **Jewel Brown,** who joined the All Stars in 1961 after the sudden death of **Velma Middleton.** Brown can be both seen and heard singing "Jerry" on the 1962 film ***Goodyear Jazz Concert: Louis Armstrong.***

"Jodie Man." By Alan Roberts and Doris Fisher; rec. January 14, 1945, in New York City by Louis Armstrong and His Orchestra. Although Armstrong expressed some negative criticism of the new **bop** style, his opposition was exaggerated by jazz journalists to make hot copy. Proof of his sympathy can be found in this his first recording after the lifting of the **American Federation of Musicians** recording ban (1942–1944). "Jodie Man" is a dark bebopish piece, both harmonically and melodically complex.

Johnson, Albert J. "Budd" (1910–1984). See **Johnson, Keg.**

Johnson, Alonzo "Lonnie" (1889–1970). The New Orleans guitarist and singer was born into a large musical family and got his first professional experiences playing in **Storyville** cabarets. After performing on riverboats, he worked in vaudeville and went with Will Marion Cook's Southern Syncopators' 1919 tour to Europe. He then settled in Chicago, where he participated in several **Hot Five** and **Hot Seven** sessions. It is Johnson whom one hears supporting Armstrong's **scat singing** in the middle of "Hotter Than That" (1927), playing an evocative guitar duet with **Johnny St. Cyr** in "I'm Not Rough" (1927), and coming to the surface now and then in both "I Can't Give You Anything But Love" and "Mahogany Hall Stomp" (both 1929). Asked in 1951 to comment in ***Esquire*** magazine on some of his 1920s recordings, Armstrong wrote that he took great "delight in blowin' with [Lonnie Johnson] that fine boy and a wonderful musician" (Brothers, p. 136). Johnson also recorded frequently as a blues singer, at first accompanying himself on the violin, and he also recorded guitar duets with **Eddie Lang.** Over a forty-year career he made some 500 recordings. He never returned to New Orleans.

Johnson, Frederick H. "Keg" (1908–1967). Along with his little brother, tenor saxophonist Budd, trombonist Keg Johnson grew up in Dallas and settled in Chicago. There from 1932 to 1933 both brothers worked in the band that Armstrong formed with trumpeter **Zilner Randolph.** With this fine ensemble, Armstrong made numerous recordings, including "I've Got the World on a String," "I've Gotta Right to Sing the Blues," and "Basin Street Blues." On this last piece, probably arranged by Budd, Keg Johnson can be heard playing the melody in the beginning, just after the celesta opening. The Johnsons then went separate ways: Keg to long associations with **Cab Calloway** and Ray Charles, and Budd to become one of the most important **bop** arrangers.

Johnson, Henry. Pseudonym for **John Hammond.**

Johnson, Margaret. During the 1920s Armstrong recorded with a great many blues singers (**Alberta Hunter, Chippie Hill, Ma Rainey, Bessie Smith,** and others), including Margaret Johnson (CD #36). Their "Papa, Mama's All Alone" and "Changeable Daddy of Mine" (both 1924) are noteworthy, particularly the latter where Armstrong foreshadows his famous opening cadenza on "West End Blues" (1928). Johnson also wrote blues lyrics, for example, "Dead Drunk Blues."

Johnson, William Geary "Bunk" (1889–1949). By the time jazz was well established in the late 1930s and 1940s, there was a surge in interest to discover and document its origins. Researchers such as Fred Ramsey, Bill Russell, and Charles Edward Smith were advised by Armstrong, **Clarence Williams,** and others to look up Bunk Johnson as one of the few living performers of early jazz. "You really heard music when Bunk Johnson played the cornet with the Eagle Band [roughly 1910–1914]," Armstrong said in ***Satchmo: My Life in New Orleans*** (p. 23).

Johnson, however, had a way of making things up and telling interviewers what they wanted to hear. He claimed to have been taught by **Buddy Bolden** and to have passed his skill on to Louis Armstrong. "[Louis] would fool with my cornet every chance he could get until he could get a sound out of it. Then I showed him just how to hold it and place it to his mouth and he did so and it wasn't long before he began getting a good tone out of my horn" (Ramsey and Smith, p. 23 f). Johnson in fact made a great many unverifiable and plainly untrue statements, and Russell and others, blinded by the romance of their projects, took his pronouncements uncritically.

Johnson, however, did play a role, albeit a very minor one, in the development of jazz. Although subsequent researchers have cast doubt on his claim to have performed with Buddy Bolden during the 1890s, he did work in New Orleans with the Eagle Band, and later he toured in the region. In the early 1930s dental problems prevented him from playing the cornet, and he found work in New Iberia, Louisiana, as a field laborer. In return for his help with their project, Russell and his friends raised the money to buy dentures for Johnson and found him a secondhand trumpet. While he got his lip back in shape, publicity began to circulate (e.g., the 1939 publication of Russell and Smith's *Jazzmen*), creating keen anticipation. There was quite a Bunk Johnson craze in the mid-1940s when he appeared at the Stuyvesant Casino in New York. Even the normally sagacious music critic **Virgil Thomson** fell for Johnson, saying that "he was the greatest master of the blue or off-pitch note I have ever heard" (*The Musical Scene,* 1925, p. 28). The performances turned out to be of poor quality, though, and Johnson, a notorious drinker, sometimes did not even show up.

Armstrong waited to set the record straight until after Johnson's death in 1949. "Bunk didn't show me nothing. He didn't even know me," he stated unequivocally in the July-August 1950 issue of ***The Record Changer*** (excerpts reprinted in Brothers, p. 40 f). Ever the gentleman and diplomat, though, Armstrong continued to give mixed signals. He would mention Johnson along with **Jimmie Noone, Joe Oliver, Kid Ory,** and others of much greater stature, for example, in his 1951 ***Esquire*** article on selected recordings from the middle 1920s. Armstrong also wrote about Johnson enthusiastically in letters to jazz writers, such as **Leonard Feather.** One thing seems certain: Johnson did have a sweet tone, and that made an impression on the adolescent Armstrong. Listening closely to Johnson's records, though—for example, "Tiger Rag" and "See See Rider" from 1944—one can hear a style that Armstrong himself evolved during the 1920s and by the end of the decade had made all his own.

Musicologist Thomas Brothers does a good job of sorting out the supposed Armstrong-Johnson student-teacher relationship in his 1999 *Louis Armstrong: In His Own Words* (pp. 197–198).

"Jonah and the Whale." By Robert MacGimsey; rec. June 14, 1938, in New York City with the **Decca** Mixed Choir conducted by Lyn Murray and on February 4, 1958, in New York City by **Louis Armstrong and the All Stars** and the **Sy Oliver** Choir; CD #27. Armstrong has considerable fun with this mock-serious number. See additional comments on "Going to Shout All Over God's Heaven."

Jones, Dale (b. 1902). Born in Nebraska and early associated with **Jack Teagarden,** bassist Dale Jones filled in for **Arvell Shaw** in early 1952, when Shaw took some time off to study music theory and composition in Geneva, Switzerland. Jones also played with the **All Stars** in the summer of 1956. A steady, reliable performer, Jones could have worked more with Armstrong and others, but life on the road did not appeal to him. Instead, he worked near his home in California and in Las Vegas.

Jones, David "Davey" (c. 1888–1956). When in 1919 Armstrong joined **Fate Marable**'s band on the Mississippi riverboat **S.S. *Sidney,*** he immediately had to improve his music reading ability since the band used written arrangements. His instructor was **Davey Jones,** the band's mellophonist and a friend of Armstrong's from New Orleans. "You'll never be able to **swing** any better than you already know how until you learn to read," Jones told Armstrong. "Then you will swing in ways you never thought of before" (Armstrong, 1936, p. 48).

Jones taught Armstrong for half an hour every afternoon through the six months they were on the river, and Armstrong was always grateful. The experience would also be valuable to Jones who, after losing his cotton farm to boll weevils, ran a music school in New Orleans. Before that, though, he switched instruments to the more popular saxophone, worked with **King Oliver** and others in the 1920s, and was cofounder of the Jones-Collins Astoria Hot Eight. Jones also spent some time on the West Coast and played his last notes in Los Angeles.

Jones, LeRoi. See **Baraka, Amiri.**

Jones, Maggie. Armstrong memorably accompanied blues singers (**Alberta Hunter, Margaret Johnson, Ma Rainey, Bessie Smith,** and others) in the 1920s and made six recordings with Maqgie Jones in December 1924 (CD #36). The ensemble was bare-bones (just Jones, Armstrong, and **Fletcher Henderson** on piano), but therefore all the better for portraying the desolation of the blues. Particularly outstanding are "Anybody Here Want to Try My Cabbage?" and "Good Time Flat Blues." In "Cabbage" Armstrong growls arrestingly, and in "Good Time" we hear a Spencer Williams melody that came back as "Farewell to Storyville" in the 1947 movie ***New Orleans.*** Dan Morgenstern reports that decades later Armstrong heard these collaborations with Jones and was pleasantly surprised to find that he liked them just as much as his recordings with Bessie Smith (1994, p. 10).

Jones Home. See **Colored Waif's Home for Boys.**

"Joseph 'n' His Brudders." By Louis Armstrong, Barbara Belle, and Bobby Kroll; rec. April 27, 1946, in New York City by Louis Armstrong and His Orchestra; CDs #7 and #12. Armstrong matches a clever text with some sophisticated trumpet playing here. A dozen years later he recorded an entire album of snappy musical versions of biblical stories, along with some traditional spirituals (*Louis and the Good Book,* CD #27).

"Jubilee." By Stanley Adams and **Hoagy Carmichael;** rec. January 12, 1938, in Los Angeles by Louis Armstrong and His Orchestra; CDs #34 and #61. Armstrong introduced this song as a trumpet-playing street cleaner in the 1938 Mae West comedy ***Every Day's a Holiday.*** Hardly reworking the melody at all, he gradually builds toward a joyous, uplifting ending on a spectacular high "F." See additional comments on "Ev'ntide."

"Just a Closer Walk with Thee." Traditional. Although Armstrong never recorded it, this spiritual was in his repertory, and he sang it movingly with **Mahalia Jackson** at the **Newport Jazz Festival** on July 10, 1970. Their performance was included on a film titled ***Finale.***

"Just a Gigolo." By Irving Caesar and Leonello Casucci; rec. March 9, 1931, in Los Angeles by Louis Armstrong and His **Sebastian New Cotton Club** Orchestra. Armstrong and many others (such as his fellow New Orleanian and admirer **Louis Prima**) covered this popular song. Armstrong's interpretation is both nostalgic and surprisingly intricate musically, as he artfully modifies the rather simple repeated descending phrase. Unfortunately, the band plays out of tune, but there is some nice mallet work by **Lionel Hampton.**

"Just Gone." By **Joe Oliver** and Bill Johnson; rec. April 5, 1923, in Richmond, Indiana, by King Oliver's Creole Jazz Band; CD #35. This is Armstrong's very first recording (see **firsts**). **Lil Hardin Armstrong** later recalled that they had to play into one big horn, all except for her husband-to-be. He played so much stronger than Oliver and the rest that "they put Louis about fifteen feet over in the corner" (Jones and Chilton, p. 80). See additional comments on "Alligator Hop."

"Just One of Those Things." By **Cole Porter;** rec. October 14, 1957, in Los Angeles with the **Oscar Peterson** Quartet; CD #37. Armstrong's was one of many recordings of this song from the 1935 **movie** *Jubilee* (also used in the 1960 movie *Can-Can*). With the energetic support of the Peterson ensemble, he gives it an upbeat interpretation, his voice floating smoothly above any undercurrent of regret. See additional comments on "Blues in the Night."

"Just Squeeze Me." By Lee Gaines and **Duke Ellington;** rec. April 3, 1961, in New York City by **Louis Armstrong and the All Stars** with Duke Ellington; CD #11. Armstrong does more singing than trumpet playing on this number, which the Ellington Orchestra and vocalist Ray Nance introduced in 1946. Now fifteen years later, Ellington sets a leisurely tempo but with a strong beat, and Armstrong stays close to the rather simple melody. Clarinetist **Barney Bigard** and trombonist **Trummy Young** each take roomy, sentimental solos. See additional comments on "Azalea."

"Just Wait 'Til You See My Baby Do the Charleston." By Clarence Todd, R. Simmons, and **Clarence Williams;** rec. October 6, 1925, in New York City with vocalist **Eva Taylor** and **Clarence Williams' Blue Five;** CD #36. This recording was made to feature Williams's wife, Eva Taylor, but Armstrong gets at least a little exposure. See additional comments on "Cast Away."

"Just You, Just Me." By Raymond Klages and Jesse Greer; rec. January 30, 1951, live at the Pasadena Civic Auditorium, California, by **Louis Armstrong and the All Stars;** CD #6. This popular 1929 song from the movie *Marianne,* was taken up by **Benny Goodman** in 1935, and clarinetist **Barney Bigard** turned it into a flashy feature number with the All Stars.

juvenile literature. The Armstrong story has been a popular topic for all ages, and over two dozen books about him have been written for a younger audience. Jeanette Eaton's *Trumpeter's Tale: The Story of Young Louis Armstrong* (1955) was one of the first and remains one of the best.

Roxane Orgill's *If I Only Had a Horn* (1997) is also excellent. (Orgill is also the author of a perceptive article on the fourteen-year effort, 1981–1995, to get a postage **stamp** issued in Armstrong's honor.) See the selected bibliography for other examples of juvenile literature about Armstrong.

K

Kael, Pauline (1919–2001). The author of a dozen books on the movies and film critic for *The New Yorker* was an Armstrong admirer. In the October 3, 1970, issue she wrote: "The greatest moviemakers—men like Griffith and Renoir—were the men who not only wanted to give the audience of their best but had the most to give. This is also, perhaps, the element that, combined with originality of temperament, makes the greatest stars and enables them to last—what links a Louis Armstrong and an Olivier and a **Streisand**" (p. 76). In addition to admiring Armstrong's contribution to such films as ***Cabin in the Sky, High Society,*** and ***The Five Pennies,*** Kael felt that Armstrong helped make ***Jazz on a Summer's Day*** "one of the most pleasurable of all concert films" (1985, p. 379).

Kaerlighedens Melodi (Formula for Love). Armstrong always received a warm welcome in **Denmark,** which he visited eight times during his career. As part of the 1959 tour, he paused to make a movie with the popular actors Nina and Frederik van Pallandt. In *Kaerlighedens Melodi*—as in his other European films, such as ***La botta e risposta*** and ***La route du bonheur***—Armstrong plays the role of a famous visiting entertainer whose performance is the musical high point and begins the denouement. Here **Louis Armstrong and the All Stars** open a young couple's new nightclub with an eight-and-a-half-minute sequence of "Struttin' with Some Barbecue" (including lyrics specifically added for **Velma Middleton**) and "Formula for Love," assuring the success of both the business and the owners' romance and closing the film. ASA Films, 1959; color; 87 mins.; Dir. Bent Christenson.

Kaminsky, Max (1908–1994). Many soon-to-be-great jazz trumpeters like Kaminsky openly expressed their debt to Armstrong during the 1920s and 1930s. **Rex Stewart, Red Allen, Roy Eldridge,** and scores of others were greatly influenced. **Bunny Berigan** once said that every traveling jazz musician should pack a toothbrush and a photograph of Armstrong. According to Armstrong biographers Jones and Chilton, **Bix Beiderbecke** said that Armstrong was a god, and Max Kaminsky echoed him: "I'm very religious, I worship Louis" (Jones and Chilton, p. 248).

Kaminsky grew up in the Boston area and gravitated to Chicago, where, still a teenager, he heard Armstrong with **Earl Hines** in the **Carroll Dickerson** orchestra at the **Sunset Cafe.** It was so dazzling that "I felt as if I had stared into the sun's eye. All I could think of doing was run away and hide till the blindness left me" (Firestone, p. 44). The experience stayed with Kaminsky throughout a full career, which included tenures with Tommy Dorsey, Artie Shaw, and **Jack Teagarden,** loads of television work, and seemingly countless festivals. Like his colleagues, Kaminsky succeeded in finding his own full-toned voice, but in *Tea for Two,* an album he made as a leader in the mid-1970s, one can still detect traces of the Armstrong **swing** style (a constant displacement of accent, the terminal vibrato, and the playing of notes just in front of or behind the beat) in "Do You Know What It Means to Miss New Orleans?" and "I Wish I Could Shimmy Like My Sister Kate."

Kapp, Jack (1901–1949). Kapp was a record producer who in 1934 founded the **Decca** label with the idea of making commercial recordings cheaply and selling them cheaply (thirty-five cents each at first). Kapp successfully attracted some big names, including **Bing Crosby,** the **Mills Brothers,** and in October 1935, Armstrong. For the next seven years Kapp infuriated a great many jazz fans by having Armstrong record not only mainstream popular standards but also anything and everything else. In his wisdom, Kapp allowed Armstrong to give equal time to singing, which made his voice immediately recognizable throughout the United States. The exposure Armstrong received from this avalanche of varied recordings made his name a household word.

After the **American Federation of Musicians** strike against the record industry (August 1942 to August 1944), Armstrong's manager **Joe Glaser** found it advantageous not to sign his client to exclusive contracts. He continued to record occasionally with Decca, though. In 1963 Kapp had his own label, Kapp Records, and on December 3 **Louis Armstrong and the All Stars,** plus a string section and a banjo, recorded "Hello Dolly!" for it. Early in May 1964, "Hello Dolly!" reached the No. 1 spot (bumping **The Beatles**) on ***Billboard***'s Top 40 list, where it stayed for six weeks. The *New York Post* estimated that the song was played 10,000 times a day on the American continent.

Karnofsky family. A Russian Jewish family in New Orleans, the Karnofskys employed the young Louis Armstrong in their junk and coal businesses. They became a second family for him, and he often ate and socialized with them at the end of the working day. Exactly how old he was when this all took place is confused because his several accounts—two **autobiographies** (1936 and 1954) and a 1969 memoir—differ. (Musicologist Thomas Brothers has done a careful job of trying to sort out the chronology on pages 3 and 192–193 of his 1999 book.) It must be true that Armstrong played a tin horn from the seat of their wagon in order to attract customers, since that was a common practice of the day. It is also not unlikely that the Karnofskys helped him buy his first instrument, a pawn shop cornet. Armstrong says they lent him the five dollars that it cost, and he paid them back at fifty cents a week. He then worked out how to play "Home! Sweet Home!" (unless this song was later taught to him by **Peter Davis** at the **Colored Waif's Home**), and on his own he learned to play the blues.

In any case, the Karnofskys had a big influence on his life. Their satisfaction with his work, their good food (always a sure way to Armstrong's heart), their teaching him some Russian songs, and their advice on the value of singing from the heart stayed with him throughout his life. One of these songs would return to him over sixty years later, when his heart and lung specialist **Dr. Gary Zucker** chanced to sing it. The incident catalyzed the writing of a memoir titled **"Louis Armstrong + the Jewish Family** [i.e. the Karnofskys] **in New Orleans, La., the Year of 1907."** Armstrong writes out the lyrics of this song four times in the seventy-seven pages of this document (which was published in its entirety for the first time in Brothers, pp. 5–36). "Everyday when I went to do my Days work for this Fine Jewish Family I felt great," Armstrong wrote. "I felt just like a young man trying to accomplish something in life."

The Karnofskys immigrated from Lithuania some time before the turn of the century. They lived frugally and eventually prospered. In a 1941 letter to **Leonard Feather,** Armstrong mentioned having just visited his "old boss of years ago, Mr. Morris Karnofsky and his wife" in New Orleans, and they did some wonderful reminiscing (Berrett, 1999, p. 121). A photo of the Karnofsky family can be found in Marc Miller's 1994 book (p. 19).

Kaye, Danny (1913–1987). The great actor and comedian thoroughly admired Armstrong, and it shows in their 1959 collaboration in ***The Five Pennies.*** In one memorable scene, the two sing a playful version of "When the Saints Go Marching In," in which Kaye imitates Armstrong, and Armstrong mimics Kaye's imitation. The two worked together earlier but less extensively in the 1948 ***A Song Is Born,*** where Kaye plays musicology Professor Hobart Frisbee, the leader of seven professors who have been laboring in total isolation for nine years to write a complete history of music. When the scholars come to jazz, Professor Frisbee goes out one night to gather data, and Armstrong is one of the musicians who helps him.

"Keepin' Out of Mischief Now." By **Thomas "Fats" Waller** and Andy Razaf; rec. March 11, 1932, in Chicago by Louis Armstrong and His Orchestra; CDs #42, #56, #57, and #58. See comments on "Ain't Misbehavin'."

Kelly, Grace (1929–1982). See ***High Society;*** **Nice Jazz Festival.**

Keppard, Freddie (1890–1933). Along with **Buddy Bolden, Bunk Johnson, King Oliver,** and **Buddy Petit,** Freddie Keppard was a leading cornetist on the New Orleans scene in the early part of the twentieth century. In 1914 he went to the West Coast and then toured some, eventually settling in Chicago. However, either hard living took its toll or maybe Keppard was not all that great to begin with, because by the middle 1920s (when he finally got around to making records) he was not playing well at all. Nevertheless, he did have a following in Chicago, where he worked with the top bands (including **Erskine Tate**'s), and even founded his own recording group, the

Jazz Cardinals, whose "Stock Yards Strut," "Salty Dog," and other numbers are considered to be excellent examples of early New Orleans brass style.

Lil Armstrong, admittedly proud of her talented ex-husband, remembered a **cutting contest** between Keppard and Armstrong. "Boy, he blew and people started standing up on top of tables and chairs, screaming," she recalled. "And Freddie eased out real slow" (Berrett, 1999, p. 42). When Armstrong later reflected on Keppard and his career, he stated frankly that he "sure did not play the cornet seriously at any time. Just Clowned all the way. Good for those Idiots' fans' who did not care whether he played correct, or they did not know good music, or cared less" (Brothers, p. 25).

"Keyhole Blues." By N. Wilson; rec. May 13, 1927, in Chicago by Louis Armstrong and His **Hot Seven;** CDs #10, #36, and #44. Except for one clarinet chorus by **Johnny Dodds,** Armstrong dominates this recording, contributing a wonderful **scat** solo and some forward-looking trumpet riffs.

"Kickin' the Gong Around." By Ted Koehler and **Harold Arlen,** 1931; rec. January 25, 1932, in Chicago by Louis Armstrong and His Orchestra; CD #58. Written in 1931 and introduced by **Cab Calloway** in the revue *Rhythmania,* this popular song was covered by Armstrong, whose trumpet solo builds to a thrilling climax.

"Kid Man Blues." By Richard M. Jones; rec. November 9, 1925, in Chicago with vocalist **Bertha "Chippie" Hill** and the composer at the piano; CD #36. See comments on "A Georgia Man."

King, Coretta Scott (b. 1927). The **civil rights** leader and widow of Martin Luther King, Jr., wrote to **Lucille Armstrong** on July 8, 1971, that she remembered how the "eloquence of [Louis Armstrong's] horn" helped "bridge generation, racial, political, and national gaps." This letter of condolence (and many, many others from the likes of Richard Nixon, Nelson Rockefeller, professional colleagues such as **Dizzy Gillespie** and the Nicholas Brothers, and ordinary fans) can be found at the **Louis Armstrong House and Archives,** Queens College, New York.

"King for a Day." By **Dave Brubeck** and Iola Brubeck; rec. July 2, 1961, in New York City by **Louis Armstrong and the All Stars,** pianist Dave Brubeck, and guests; CD #50. Armstrong and his trombonist **Trummy Young,** already very accomplished as a duet team from countless All Stars concerts, here both speak and sing politically idealistic lyrics (which now seem sadly dated and sophomoric). See additional comments on "Cultural Exchange."

"King of the Zulus." By **Lil Hardin Armstrong;** rec. June 23, 1926, in Chicago by Louis Armstrong and His **Hot Five;** CDs #8, #10, #48, and #52. Armstrong always loved a novelty number, such as this one about a Jamaican who crashes a barbecue. While his 1926 performance, with its stirring minor-key cornet solo, was widely admired, his rerecording in 1957 for the four-disc *Satchmo: A Musical Autobiography* (CD #52) represents a peak in his career.

This second version, with its authoritative trumpet playing, even thrilled such hard-to-please critics as Whitney Balliett ("majestic"), James Lincoln Collier ("wonderful"), Gary Giddins ("inspired"), Dan Morgenstern ("outstanding"), and Martin Williams ("astonishing"). In between the two recordings, Armstrong really was crowned **King of the Zulus.** During the 1949 Mardi Gras parade, he presided over the Zulu Social Aid and Pleasure Club's float, dressed in an elaborate tribal costume (a red velvet gown plus a grass skirt), drinking champagne, and tossing coconuts to the crowd. "It was the dream of every kid in my neighborhood," Armstrong later recalled (***Satchmo,*** 1954, p. 126).

King of the Zulus. Armstrong was thrilled to accept (over the strenuous objections of his manager **Joe Glaser**) an invitation from the **Zulu Social Aid and Pleasure Club** to be the 1949 King of the Zulus. "It was the dream of every kid in my neighborhood," Armstrong wrote in his **autobiography** (1954, p. 126). He got to wear heavy makeup (blackface with loads of white grease paint around the eyes and lips), an elaborate tribal costume (a red velvet gown plus a grass skirt), and ride in a float on a throne, drinking champagne and tossing coconuts to the crowd. The event prompted a great deal of publicity, and newspapers around the country carried a picture of the outlandish "Zulu King Louis." ***Time*** magazine even devoted its February 21, 1949, cover story to the event—incidentally the first such honor for a jazz musician. According to some, the occasion underscored Armstrong's status as a first-rank show business figure. Others criticized Armstrong for promoting an unsuitable racial image. "Louis is the plantation character that so many of us . . . resent," **Dizzy Gillespie** said in the July 1 issue of ***Down Beat*** (p. 13). Armstrong had a blast, though, and it was one of the many high points in his life.

"Kiss of Fire." By Angel G. Villodo; English lyrics by Lester Allen and Robert B. Hill; rec. April 19, 1952, in Denver, Colorado, by Louis Armstrong and His Orchestra; CDs #8, #28, and #39. With his fondness for minor key numbers, Armstrong has a high time with this 1911 tango (originally titled "El Choclo"). He bends both the lyrics and the trumpet notes, ending with an interjected, "Ah, boin me!" that is inspired corn.

"Kiss to Build a Dream On, A." By Bert Kalmar, Harry Ruby, Oscar Hammerstein II; rec. April 23, 1951, in Los Angeles by **Louis Armstrong and the All Stars** and on July 24, 1951, in New York City with the **Sy Oliver** Orchestra; CDs #28, #39, #40, #45, #46, and #61. This song was written for the Marx Brothers' 1935 movie *A Night at the Opera,* but it took Armstrong to make it a hit with his performance in the 1951 **movie *The Strip.*** It was to become a regular item on All Stars programs. The earlier recording can best be heard as a rehearsal for the later one, when Armstrong does more singing and is altogether more sure of himself.

"Kisses in the Night." By Lothar Ollas and Hans Bradtke; rec. February 23, 1959, in Hamburg, Germany, by **Louis Armstrong and the All Stars.** Armstrong recorded this number for the 1959 film ***Die Nacht vor der Premiere.***

Klonisch, Gabriele. See ***La paloma.***

"Knee Drops." By **Lil Hardin Armstrong;** rec. July 5, 1928, in Chicago by Louis Armstrong and His **Hot Five;** CDs #10 and #30. Like "Fireworks," "Hotter Than That," and "Symphonic Touches," "Knee Drops" was inspired by the chords of "Tiger Rag." In this performance, everyone gets a chance to shine. Pianist **Earl Hines** is in especially fine form, at one point nimbly skipping scale-wise up from the bass with his left hand while accenting the melody in his right hand. Armstrong's bright, agile solo has been transcribed by Castle (vol. 2, p. 11).

"Knockin' a Jug." By Louis Armstrong and Eddie Condon; rec. March 5, 1929, in New York City; CDs #8, #10, #48, and #52. This is considered by many to be the first interracial recording (see **firsts**). Although there had been previous incidents (such as **Jelly Roll Morton**'s 1923 recording with the New Orleans Rhythm Kings), the one here with **Jack Teagarden** (white trombonist), **Happy Caldwell** (black tenor saxophonist), **Joe Sullivan** (white pianist), **Eddie Lang** (white guitarist), and **Kaiser Marshall** (black drummer) is the first jazz recording where black and white musicians exchange musical ideas equally. The story of the recording session itself is right out of a novel or movie: Musicians gather to jam after their last set, someone (Eddie Condon, in this case) suggests the music is too good not to record, and they grab their jug of whiskey and go into the studio. As for the title, Kaiser Marshall later recalled that a studio man came around to get composer, title, and so on, and Armstrong looked around and saw the empty jug. "Man, we sure knocked that jug—you can call it 'Knockin' a Jug' " (Shapiro and Hentoff, 1955, p. 281). This session also marks the first of many times that Armstrong and Teagarden would record together.

"Ko Ko Mo (I Love You So)." By Eunice H. Levy, Jake Porter, and Forest Wilson; rec. January 18, 1955, in Los Angeles with vocalist Gary Crosby, the Sonny Burke Orchestra, and the Jud Conlon Rhythmaires; CDs #19, #20, and #42. This 1955 song was done by everyone from Perry Como to the Crew Cuts. Here Armstrong performs it with Gary Crosby, son of his friend **Bing.** Armstrong most often did it as a duet with **Velma Middleton.**

København, Kalundborg Og? ("Copenhagen, Kalundborg, and ?"). This Danish film, which Armstrong made during his first visit to **Denmark** in October–November 1933, consists of a series of vaudevillelike acts. Armstrong performs "I Cover the Waterfront," "Dinah," and "Tiger Rag." He announces the songs, too, and during the performances he zooms around the stage in a crouching position, perspiring and flourishing his handkerchief. It's a fascinating insight into the way he performed early in his career. The film isn't widely available, but luckily these excerpts are included on two videos: ***Trumpet Kings*** (1985) and ***Satchmo: Louis Armstrong*** (1989). In 1959 Armstrong contributed to another Danish film, ***Kaerlighedens Melodi (Formula for Love).*** He returned to Denmark eight times and was always given a warm welcome. Palladium Pictures, 1933; B&W; 70 mins.; Dir. Holger Madsen.

Kreisler, Fritz (1875–1962). The famous classical violinist was also a jazz fan, as were many artists and intellectuals in the 1920s and 1930s when popular culture began to gain respectability. Underscoring both Kreisler's interest and this new sensibility was the appearance in ***Vanity Fair***'s February 1936 issue of an "Impossible Interview" (a regular fictional feature in this trendy magazine), in which Armstrong and Kreisler exchange a few clever words. Kreisler opens by declaring: "With your talent, you, the most famous trumpeter in America, should be in a symphony orchestra" and ends with Kreisler joining Armstrong's band. The approximately 200-word text is accompanied by an illustration worth at least another thousand words. Artist **Miguel Covarrubias** depicts Kreisler happily thumping a piano, and Armstrong, horn in hand, beaming out a song. A color version of this priceless caricature can be found in Marc Miller's *Louis Armstrong: A Cultural Legacy* (p. 210).

"Krooked Blues." By Benjamin F. Spikes, John C. Spikes, and Dink Johnson; rec. October 5, 1923, in Richmond, Indiana, with **King Oliver** and His Creole Jazz Band; CD #35. Despite Armstrong's subordinate status, this number comes off well because virtually everyone plays well. Oliver plays a strong lead, and his young protégé fills in around him. See additional comments on "Alligator Hop."

Kyle, William Osborne "Billy" (1914–1966). The Philadelphia-born pianist was firmly established by the time he joined **Louis Armstrong and the All Stars.** He was also well known to Armstrong since he worked in the **Sy Oliver** orchestra (1946–1952), which frequently accompanied Armstrong. Previously, Kyle had recorded with **Lionel Hampton** and O'Neill Spencer (1938), **Rex Stewart** (1940 and 1946), **Billie Holiday** (1946 and 1949), and many others. The 1942–1945 gap in his résumé is accounted for by military service.

Kyle joined the All Stars in late 1953. In addition to playing the piano, he also did some arranging and served as an advance man. When the All Stars would arrive in town for an event, according to longtime All Star trombonist **Trummy Young,** "Bill would go and tell them what songs Louis was doing . . . what key Louis did this or that in, and how many choruses" (Berrett, 1999, p. 173). Armstrong would usually just go to the hotel and relax. Kyle stayed with the All Stars until he died while on tour early in 1966. (Armstrong kept up a grueling tour schedule—300 days a year—and All Star clarinetist **Buster Bailey** and singer **Velma Middleton** also died on the road.) However, Kyle can still be seen in action performing with the All Stars in the 1956 movie ***High Society.*** His distinctive single-note style can be heard mostly in the background, providing brief introductions (e.g., "A Kiss to Build a Dream On," 1951), beguiling obbligatos ("Mack the Knife," 1955), and smooth transitions ("I Get Ideas," 1951). However, he did have a feature number: "When I Grow Too Old to Dream," recorded in 1965.

L

La Scala. See **Teatro alla Scala.**

"La vie en rose." See **"Vie en rose, La."**

Lafayette Theatre. Armstrong was a frequent performer in 1929 and the early 1930s at this Harlem variety theater, 2227 Seventh Avenue at West 131st Street in New York City. For a week in late June 1929, he would rush there to front the **Carroll Dickerson** band, right after finishing the ***Connie's Hot Chocolates*** show at the Hudson Theatre on Broadway (about a five-mile trip), and afterward wind up the evening playing at **Connie's Inn** (2221 Seventh Avenue). As he wrote to **Leonard Feather** a decade later, "That's what one might call 'slinging a whole lots of 'Chops into one Trumpet" (Brothers, p. 148). In January 1932, after a very successful tour through the South (where despite the **Great Depression** he drew huge crowds), he again found himself at the Lafayette. Toward the end of 1932, after returning from his first trip to Europe, he was featured in a new version of *Hot Chocolates* at the Lafayette Theatre with drummer Chick Webb and his band. Irving Kolodin (*Saturday Review* classical music critic, New York Philharmonic program annotator, and Juilliard School faculty member) caught Armstrong's Lafayette show in 1933 and left a vivid account. "He announces 'When You're Smiling,' and . . . backs off, downstage left, leans halfway over like a quarter miler, begins to count, (swaying as he does) 'one, two, three.' . . . He has already started racing toward the rear where the orchestra is ranged, and he hits four, executes a slide and a pirouette; winds up facing the audience and blowing the first note as the orchestra swings into tune." Kolodin continues, "It's mad, it's meaningless, it's hokum of the first order, but the effect is electrifying" (Giddins, 1988, p. 116; Collier, 1983 p. 260).

By 1935, the effects of the Depression forced the Lafayette, like other Harlem institutions (e.g., the Harlem Opera House), to reinvent itself as a movie theater. Gone were the days when it was a jazz venue for such greats as **Duke Ellington** and the Washingtonians (1927), **Fletcher Henderson** (irregularly 1928–1934), Bennie Moten (1931–1934), and Chick Webb (1933).

Lala, Pete. From 1906 to the closing of **Storyville** by the U.S. Navy in 1917, Lala (whose real name was Pete Ciacocio) ran a cabaret at 1300 Customhouse Street, at Marais Street. There was a bar in front and a dance hall in back, and the club catered to a racially mixed clientele. "What I appreciated most about being able to go into Storyville without being bothered by the cops, was Pete Lala's cabaret where **Joe Oliver** had his band and where he was blowing up a storm on his cornet." So Armstrong later wrote about this place where he had gained valuable professional experience (***Satchmo,*** 1954, p. 95). When in 1917 his girlfriend **Irene** needed medical attention, Oliver generously let Armstrong substitute for him in **Kid Ory**'s band at Lala's. In June 1918, when Oliver left for Chicago, Armstrong took his place. He held his own very well, and his song "I Wish I Could Shimmy Like My Sister Kate" was a great hit. When Armstrong registered for the draft in September of that year (either erroneously thinking he was eighteen or hoping to prove a maturity that, at age seventeen and one month, a draft card would certify), he gave his occupation as musician and his employer as Pete Lala. Armstrong was performing at Lala's in November 1919 when **Fate Marable** heard him and hired him to play on a Mississippi riverboat.

In addition to Armstrong, Oliver, and Ory, **Freddie Keppard, Sidney Bechet,** and many others gained valuable experience at Pete Lala's.

Lang, Eddie (1902–1933). Guitarist Lang had a busy and influential if brief professional life. He was born in Philadelphia to a musical family and formed an enduring musical partnership with violinist Joe Venuti, his former schoolmate. In 1925 they moved to New York and played with a long list of leading musicians, including **Benny Goodman** and **Jack Teagarden.** Their many recorded duos (e.g., "Stringing the Blues" from 1926) inspired the upcoming **Django Reinhardt** and Stephane Grappelli in Paris. Before becoming **Bing Crosby**'s accompanist, Lang worked with Paul Whiteman (1929–1930). Overall, he did more than anyone to establish the guitar (and thereby to replace the banjo) as a jazz instrument with his attractive middle register single-string solos and ensemble-building chordal textures.

Lang was in a small pickup group that recorded "Knockin' a Jug" on March 5, 1929, in New York. It was one of those storybooklike sessions, where the musicians had finished their evening's work, stayed on to jam, and then went into the studio before calling it a night. The result was a recording that is considered by many jazz critics to be on a par with the best of the **Hot Five.** Also distinctive about this recording are the facts that it was Armstrong's first with trombonist Jack Teagarden, and it was the first interracial recording. So highly did Armstrong think of Lang that he dedicated the first volume of his autobiography, ***Swing That Music,*** to him (in addition to **King Oliver** and **Bix Beiderbecke**).

"Last Night I Dreamed You Kissed Me." By Gus Kahn and Carmen Lombardo; rec. June 26, 1928, in Chicago by vocalist **Lillie Delk Christian** with Louis Armstrong and His **Hot Four;** CDs #10 and #36. Armstrong seems effortlessly to glide around Christian's stiff singing, even doing a little double-time passage behind her at the beginning. Elsewhere, he blends harmoniously with clarinetist **Jimmy Noone** and pianist **Earl Hines.** See additional comments on "Baby" and "I Must Have That Man."

"Last Time, The." By Billy V. Ewing and Sara Martin; rec. September 6, 1927, in Chicago by Louis Armstrong and His **Hot Five;** CD #10. Because of trombonist **Kid Ory**'s poor performance, this recording was not issued until **George Avakian** dug it out of the **Okeh** vaults in the early 1940s. Ory can and did play better, but Armstrong is in his usual fine form.

"Laughin' Louie." By Clarence Gaskill; rec. April 24, 1933, in Chicago by Louis Armstrong and His Orchestra; CDs #12, #17, #21, and #24. Although some jazz fans are embarrassed by this hilarious recording, it shows us what an energetic performer Armstrong was and also that he was part of the comic tradition. Here he opens with a theme so stale that the entire band quickly breaks up in laughter. After some joking around, Armstrong launches into a poignant unaccompanied melody that remained unidentified until 1995 when Vince Giordano discovered it to be Minnie T. Wright's 1920 "Love Scene." Armstrong's operatic climb into the upper register still causes trumpeters to shake their heads in awe. Clarinetist-tenor saxophonist **Budd Johnson** testifies that Armstrong and the band were very high on **marijuana** for the recording session. "We were floating when we made that 'Laughin' Louis' and Louis played that trumpet like a bird," he recalled in a 1975 oral history interview available at the **Institute of Jazz Studies** at Rutgers University.

"Lawd, You Made the Night Too Long." By Victor Young and Sam M. Lewis; rec. March 11, 1932, in Chicago by Louis Armstrong and His Orchestra; CDs #44 and #58. Armstrong's last recording for **Okeh** is a masterpiece from its three introductory "alleluias" to the majestic coda. In between he gives one of his now-famous low-register trumpet solos, a moving vocal, and a break so full of intricate grace note scoops that even Gunther Schuller declared it "virtually unnotatable" (1989, p. 180).

laxatives. Armstrong developed his lifelong preoccupation with laxatives from his mother. As he later wrote, she taught him to "remember when you're sick nobody ain't going to give you nothing," urged him to try to stay healthy, and made him promise he would "take a physic at least once a week" (***Satchmo,*** 1954, p. 16). He kept the promise. His laxative of choice came to be **Swiss Kriss,** which he urged on virtually everyone he met, from fellow musicians to puzzled heads of state to amused nurses at **Beth Israel Hospital.** He was also fond of Abalena Water and Pluto Water. In his curious view of anatomy and physiology, Armstrong viewed laxatives as cleansers for the body in much the same way as he considered **marijuana** a cleanser for the mind. He wrote in his unpublished memoir **"The Satchmo Story"** about how his mother "and her church sisters used to go out by the railroad track and pick baskets full of pepper grass, dandelions, and lots of weeds similar to gage [a marijuana synonym], and they would bring it to their homes, get a big fat slice of salt meat—and make one most 'deelicious pot of greens anyone would want to smack their lips on . . . *physics you too*" (Brothers, p. 112).

"Lazy Bones." By **Hoagy Carmichael** and **Johnny Mercer;** rec. September 9, 1955, in Los Angeles by **Louis Armstrong and the All Stars** with Gary Crosby; CD #8.

This performance would probably not be tolerated in a politically correct climate, but the two singers have good chemistry and blend well. See additional comments on "Ev'ntide."

"Lazy Man Blues." By Hersal Thomas; rec. May 6, 1927, in Chicago with vocalist **Sippie Wallace** and clarinetist Artie Starks; CD #36. See comments on "Baby, I Can't Use You No More."

"Lazy River." By **Hoagy Carmichael** and Sidney Arodin; rec. November 3, 1931, in Chicago by Louis Armstrong and His Orchestra; CDs #6, #8, #14, #28, #40, #43, #48, #49, #52, and #59. This song seems tailor-made for Armstrong, who on February 8, 1947, included it in the landmark **Carnegie Hall concert** and kept it in his repertory well into the **All Stars** era. Here he plays and sings it so well that he even compliments himself ("Boy, am I riffin' this evening!"). His spectacular glissandos were regularly misperceived as having been played on a slide trumpet. Not so, however, as one can both hear and see in the 1960 **movie *Jazz on a Summer's Day.*** See additional comments on "Ev'ntide."

"Lazy 'sippi Steamer." By Louis Armstrong, Victor Selsman, and **Luis Russell;** rec. March 14, 1940, in New York City by Louis Armstrong and His Orchestra; CDs #5 and #18. Here we find Armstrong performing one of the many works that he co-composed, in this case a big band–style number that he croons smoothly. His trumpet solo stays close to the melody, in the manner he learned from **King Oliver.** Unfortunately, Armstrong did not keep this appealing number in his repertory during the **All Stars** era.

"Lazy Woman Blues." By Richard M. Jones; rec. November 9, 1925, in Chicago with vocalist Blanche Calloway (1902–1978) and the composer at the piano; CD #36. Armstrong made two recordings with **Cab Calloway**'s sister, whose singing was outshone by her work as a bandleader and later as a radio executive in Florida.

"Leap Frog." By **Joe Garland;** rec. November 16, 1941, in Chicago by Louis Armstrong and His Orchestra. The composer of this popular instrumental number (who also wrote "In the Mood") here plays bass saxophone and does some clever antiphonal work with the muted brass. Armstrong stays out until the last eight bars, then considerably peps up an already pretty lively ensemble. "Leap Frog" was adopted by Les Brown as his theme song.

"Learnin' the Blues." By Dolores Vicki Silvers; rec. July 23, 1957, in Los Angeles with vocalist **Ella Fitzgerald** and the **Oscar Peterson** Quartet; CD #9. Armstrong and Fitzgerald winningly cover this 1955 song that **Frank Sinatra** took to No. 1 in the same year. See additional comments on "April in Paris."

Lee, Peggy (1920–2002). This popular jazz singer ("Why Don't You Do Right?" and "Fever"), lyricist (over 500 songs), actress (*The Jazz Singer* from 1953), and wife of **Dave Barbour** sang the Lord's Prayer at Armstrong's **funeral** on July 9, 1971, at the **Corona** Congregational Church.

"Let That Be a Lesson." By **Johnny Mercer** and Richard A. Whiting; rec. January 13, 1938, in Los Angeles by Louis Armstrong and His Orchestra; CD #18.

"Let's Call the Whole Thing Off." By George Gershwin and Ira Gershwin; rec. July 23, 1957, in Los Angeles with vocalist **Ella Fitzgerald** and the **Oscar Peterson** Quartet; CD #9. Armstrong sets his horn aside for this playful duet with Fitzgerald. Not even Fred Astaire and Ginger Rogers did it better in the 1937 film *Shall We Dance?* See additional comments on "April in Paris."

"Let's Do It (Let's Fall in Love)." By **Cole Porter;** rec. October 14, 1957, in Los Angeles with the **Oscar Peterson** Quartet; CDs #9, #29, and #37. Although **Frank Sinatra**'s is the more widely known recording, Armstrong's has its charm. The leisurely tempo gives word-loving Armstrong a chance to savor Porter's delicious lyrics. Peterson weaves wonderful accompanying lines, and his sidemen carry their hero along on a comfortable cushion of sound. See additional comments on "Blues in the Night."

"Let's Sing Like a Dixieland Band." By Bergman; rec. July 5, 1960, in New York City by Louis Armstrong, vocalist **Bing Crosby,** and a studio band and choir conducted by Billy May. See comments on "At the Jazz Band Ball."

Life. While ***Time*** magazine put Armstrong on its cover in 1949, it took *Life* until 1966 to do so. As with *Time,* Armstrong was the first jazz musician to get cover story treatment (unless one counts **Frank Sinatra,** who was featured on both the August 23, 1963, and April 23, 1965 covers). Before 1966, *Life* had of course published both articles about and photos of Armstrong. For example, on his 1956 U.S. State Department **African tour,** Armstrong was captured mingling with scantily clad though dignified African chiefs and playing his trumpet while exotically dressed locals danced in the street (June 11, pp. 38–39). However, for the April 15, 1966, cover story they pulled out all the stops. **Phillipe Halsman** took his now-familiar but then-innovative pullout cover portrait from above his subject with a wide-angle lens. The photo is reprinted widely (e.g., in Miller, p. 11). The article by Richard Meryman, "An Interview with Louis Armstrong," wisely lets the colorful Armstrong mostly speak for himself. The text was slightly edited for publication as a book, *Louis Armstrong—a Self-Portrait,* in 1971. Such attention from a publication that both reflected and affected American life amounted to Armstrong's and jazz's acceptance into popular culture. (As a footnote, it is interesting that before Armstrong only two other covers featured African Americans, **Jackie Robinson** in 1950 and the trio of Harry Belafonte, **Sammy Davis, Jr.,** and Sidney Poitier, also in 1966.)

"Life Is So Peculiar." By Johnny Burke and James Van Heusen; rec. August 23, 1950, in New York City by Louis Armstrong with Louis Jordan and His Tympany Five. Shortly after **Bing Crosby** introduced this song in the 1950 film *Mr. Music,* Armstrong teamed up with his admirer Louis Jordan and made this energetic recording.

"Limehouse Blues." By Philip Braham and Douglas Furber; rec. May 24 or 25, 1960, in New York City with the **Dukes of Dixieland;** CD #53. Popularized in the mid-1920s by Paul Whiteman and His Orchestra, this number became a regular in the Dukes' repertory. On this occasion the Dukes let their hero go on for five delicious choruses. For additional comments, see "Avalon."

Lincoln Gardens. When the twenty-one-year-old Armstrong left his native New Orleans and arrived in Chicago in 1922 to join **King Oliver**'s Creole Jazz Band at the Lincoln Gardens, he was nearly overwhelmed. "It was a big place, with a big balcony all around, and I felt a little frightened, and wondered how I was going to make out," he later wrote (1936, p. 69). The Gardens was indeed a grand venue, with room for around a thousand dancers and, above the dance floor, the traditional big rotating ball studded with reflecting glass. Spotlights shone on the ball, creating enchantment as it threw bits of light all about. Armstrong found his way to the bandstand and there the familiar, welcoming faces of Oliver, drummer **Baby Dodds,** trombonist **Honoré Dutrey,** clarinetist **Johnny Dodds,** and bass player Bill Johnson. Later, Armstrong seems to have had mixed feelings about the Lincoln Gardens. In his 1954 **autobiography** he mentions with pride that his workplace "had a beautiful front with a canopy that ran from the doorway to the street." However, he ridiculed the management for turning down the heat three nights a week. "Johnny Dodds would actually play his horn with gloves [and] practically all the fellows wore their overcoats" (Brothers, p. 54).

Opened just after the turn of the twentieth century, Lincoln Gardens (459 East 31st Street, at South Cottage Grove Avenue) was known as the Royal Gardens until 1921. In 1918 it was established as a jazz place and became a magnet for New Orleans musicians, such as King Oliver, who was in residence from 1922 to 1924. After a fire late in 1924, Lincoln Gardens was lavishly renovated, its name changed to the New Charleston Café, and Oliver returned for another residency. It later had another name change to the Café de Paris. Unfortunately, a bomb in June 1927 (probably the result of mob activity) closed the hall down for good.

Perhaps only the Harlem **Cotton Club** could claim to have been a more celebrated venue for the development of jazz. Lincoln Gardens at first catered to a mostly African American clientele, along with the occasional self-conscious white or teenage jazz apprentice (e.g., saxophonist **Bud Freeman**) who could get by the bouncer. Eventually the Gardens became more integrated, with the white management setting aside just one night a week for whites only when the audience consisted of a goodly number of white musicians who had finished work and wanted to hear the Oliver band, Armstrong in particular. As pianist Tom Thibeau told Armstrong biographer James Lincoln Collier, trumpeter Louis Panico and the brass sections from both the Don Bestor and the Ted Fiorito bands would always be there. "We'd fill that place and just sit and listen to these guys—white musicians, mainly, just sitting around listening to these Negroes play" (Collier, 1983, p. 94).

Lindsay, Johnny (1894–1950). Armstrong was very fond of the New Orleans bassist and trombone player Johnny Lindsay, who was in a 1931–1932 touring and recording band that Armstrong formed in Chicago with the trumpeter **Zilner Randolph.** "Now there's a Band that really 'deserved a *whole lot* of '*Credit* that they *didn't* get," Armstrong later wrote in **"The Goffin Notebooks"** (Brothers,

Armstrong with manager Joe Glazer in 1949. (Louis Armstrong House and Archives at Queens College/CUNY)

p. 108). Among their numerous recordings ("Between the Devil and the Deep Blue Sea," "Blue Again," "Chinatown, My Chinatown," "Lazy River," "Star Dust," and others), Lindsay's contributions stand out on "The Lonesome Road" and "When It's Sleepy Time Down South." The latter is the first of what would eventually total ninety-eight recordings of "Sleepy Time." Lindsay's flexible approach to the beat may make it the best. His speaking voice can be heard on "The Lonesome Road" in a bit of vaudeville when he plays the role of "the little Creole member" to "Reverend Satchelmouth Armstrong." When Lindsay says he wants "to pick up a good collection here tonight for Brother Armstrong," Armstrong jumps in with, "And if you ever get it, Brother Lindsay, *please* don't put it in your pocket, will you?"

Lindsay's first musical employment was as a trombonist, but by the time he and Armstrong caught up with each other in Chicago, he was almost exclusively a bassist. In addition to touring and recording, Lindsay also worked with Armstrong in ***A Rhapsody in Black and Blue,*** a nine-and-a-half-minute film made at Paramount Studios in 1932. In later years, Lindsay worked with the Harlem Hamfats, **Jimmie Noone,** and **Johnny Dodds.**

"Linger in My Arms a Little Longer." By Herb Magidson; rec. April 27, 1946, in New York City by Louis Armstrong and His Orchestra; CDs #12, #21, and #28. The landmark February 8, 1947, **Carnegie Hall concert** will soon mark the end of the big band era, but here a few months before then Armstrong coaxes his group into playing some very sweet music.

lip problems. Most trumpet players, especially professionals, have lip problems from time to time since it's easy to overtax such a small, delicate area of the anatomy. Armstrong had considerable lip troubles, and they contributed both to a change in his **trumpet style** and to the increased frequency of his singing. His problems began at the very beginning, when he learned poor **embouchure** habits. Unsupervised, he placed the **mouthpiece** too low, so that it rested on the soft part of the upper lip, crushing it back against the teeth. In addition, he used too much pressure in order to reach high notes. A good teacher would have noticed this and corrected it, but Armstrong picked up his technique largely on his own. While at first his method resulted in powerful high notes, it inevitably caused problems later on. Complicating matters was Armstrong's overwhelming desire to please audiences with high-register pyrotechnics—he once played more than 200 high "Cs' in a row on "Swing That Music"—and years of too many concerts without sufficient rest. By the 1930s his lip problems were chronic. **Mezz Mezzrow** recalled that in December and January 1932–1933 Armstrong's lip was raw and swollen. "To make things worse, he kept picking at the great sore with a needle. I couldn't stand to see it, every prick went all through me, I was so afraid he might infect himself and have to stop playing altogether" (Mezzrow, p. 222). Later, in **England** in March 1934, Armstrong without explanation refused to participate in a concert with **Coleman Hawkins.** One likely theory is that he was having lip problems, since shortly thereafter he crossed the channel for an extended vacation in Paris. Finally, in May 1935 he came under the management of **Joe Glaser,** who helped straighten out his life in many ways, including seeing to it that he rested between jobs. The damage had been done by then, however. Armstrong's upper lip was scarred and his range of expression somewhat limited. However, he developed a leaner, more spare style, which can be heard by comparing two versions of "Struttin' with Some Barbecue," one recorded in 1927 and the other in 1938. In the latter, one finds many pauses and not so many fast notes but still the originality of invention, emotional depth, and irresistible **swing** style for which Armstrong was famous. Also on the plus side, Armstrong's lip problems caused him to turn increasingly to singing with memorable results.

"Listen to Ma." By **Hociel Thomas;** recorded on February 24, 1926, in Chicago with vocalist Hociel Thomas and pianist Hersal Thomas; CDs #36 and #48. This performance with a popular blues singer of the day exemplifies a relatively overlooked aspect of Armstrong's trumpet style, namely, that he was one of the first to exploit the lower register (see **firsts**).

"Listen to the Mockingbird." By Richard Milburn and Septimus Winner; rec. September 22, 1952, in Los Angeles with the Gordon Jenkins Orchestra and Choir. Copyrighted in 1855, this song was a favorite of President Abraham Lincoln, who likened it to the laughter of a little girl at play. The sentimental Armstrong is backed up by an instrumental ensemble consisting mainly of his **All Stars.**

"Little Girl Blue." By Richard Rodgers and Lorenz Hart; rec. August 14, 1957, in Los Angeles with a studio orchestra conducted by arranger Russell Garcia; CD #29. Between its introduction in the 1935 musical *Billy Rose's Jumbo* and its revival in the 1962 Doris Day film *Jumbo,* Armstrong recorded this in a session that included a whopping seventeen numbers (two full LPs), many of which, like "Little Girl Blue," were done multiple times.

"Little Joe." By Jules K. Stein and Ned Miller; rec. April 28, 1931, in Chicago by Louis Armstrong and His Orchestra. While Armstrong was criticized by some for singing a mammy song that is far beyond politically incorrect, he was praised by others for bringing a much-needed sense of humor to the jazz stage. Moreover, as Joshua Berrett and Dan Morgenstern point out, lines such as "although your color isn't white, you're more than mighty like a rose to me" were later welcomed in the "Black Is Beautiful" movement (Berrett, 1999, p. 196).

"Little Louis." One of Armstrong's many **nicknames,** "Little Louis" referred to his height, just as "Gatemouth," **"Dippermouth,"** and "Satchelmouth" affectionately referred to his large mouth. It is interesting that first-rate jazz trumpeters tend to be diminutive. **Bix Beiderbecke,** Ruby Braff, **Billy Butterfield, Miles Davis, Roy Eldridge, Bobby Hackett,** Ray Nance, Charlie Shavers, and a few others certainly fit the description. Armstrong at five feet six inches and usually on the hefty side was taller than some, for example, Bobby Hackett at five feet four and a quarter inches and 125 pounds (see Meckna, 1994, p. 123).

"Little Ol' Tune." By **Johnny Mercer;** rec. July 5, 1960, in New York City by Louis

Armstrong, vocalist **Bing Crosby,** and a studio band and choir conducted by Billy May. For comments see "At the Jazz Band Ball."

"Little One." By **Cole Porter;** rec. January 6, 1956, in Los Angeles with vocalist **Bing Crosby** and the MGM Studio Orchestra conducted by Johnny Green; CD #45. Crosby sings this sweet number in the 1956 **movie *High Society.*** Armstrong takes a one-chorus trumpet solo and fills in here and there, but he mostly remains offscreen.

Little Rock. On September 18, 1957, Arkansas Governor **Orval Faubus** called out the National Guard to prevent court-ordered integration of Central High School in Little Rock. Rioting broke out, and the event was reported internationally. Armstrong was on tour in the small North Dakota town of Grand Forks and watched the coverage on television in his dressing room. Long accustomed to holding his tongue, Armstrong could keep quiet no more. He told a reporter that "the way they are treating my people in the South, the government can go to hell." He said that President **Dwight Eisenhower** was "two-faced" and had allowed an "uneducated plowboy," Governor Faubus, to run the federal government (*New York Herald Tribune,* Sept. 19, 1957, p. A3). The incident was a turning point in the musician's career. Without becoming a vociferous **civil rights** advocate, he did speak out on occasion and, in his State Department-sponsored tours to Africa, Russia, and South America, literally took on ambassadorial status (see **"Ambassador Satch"**).

"Livin' High (Sometimes)." By Maceo Pinkard and Alex Belledna; rec. October 6, 1925, in New York City with vocalist **Eva Taylor** and **Clarence Williams' Blue Five;** CD #36. Although Taylor sings well, Armstrong the accompanist nearly obliterates her with final chorus high notes. Perhaps feeling that he is outplaying the ensemble, he moves an octave down for the second half of the chorus. See additional comments on "Cast Away."

Lombardo, Gaetano Alberto "Guy" (1902–1977). Many Armstrong fans are surprised to learn of his steadfast admiration for the music of Canadian bandleader Guy Lombardo. "You know, this is the band that inspired me," he said to readers of the September 1949 issue of ***Metronome*** (p. 18). Armstrong's attraction for Lombardo's sentimental style began in Chicago in 1927–1928 and was shared by other African American musicians as well. The feeling was mutual since (as Armstrong biographer James Lincoln Collier points out) Lombardo invited Armstrong and drummer **Zutty Singleton** to be his guests at Chicago's all-white Grenada Café on September 21, 1928 (1983, p. 219). Armstrong liked Lombardo's "sweet music"—the way he enriched rather than obscured a melody, adding little more than a tremulous vibrato, fleshing out the implied chords, and providing a clear, danceable beat. Lombardo, like Armstrong, aimed for and reached the widest possible audience. There is a direct lineage from the Lombardo sound to Armstrong's performances of "Among My Souvenirs" (1942), "Just a Gigolo" (1931), "Sweethearts on Parade" (1930), and "When You're Smiling" (1929), all of which in fact Armstrong said Lombardo had inspired him to record.

After two years at the Grenada, Lombardo went to New York in 1929 where he spent the next thirty-three years at the Roosevelt Grill. During this time, Lombardo and His Royal Canadians were frequently heard on radio and appeared on television and in film. They also toured seemingly everywhere and for many years ushered in the New Year on the nationwide CBS broadcast. In addition to its broad appeal, Lombardo's band had the advantage of stable membership, partly due to the presence of so many Lombardos—Lebert on trumpet, Victor on reeds, and singer Rose Marie. Carmen Lombardo not only served as musical director but also composed for the band (e.g., "Sweethearts on Parade"), sang, and played the saxophone.

In May 1966, shortly after he performed for Prince Philip in Los Angeles, Armstrong did a brief, valedictorylike stint with the Lombardo orchestra. All too soon after that, Lombardo was one of the many musicians and celebrities who were in attendance at Armstrong's **funeral** on July 9, 1971, at the **Corona** Congregational Church in New York.

"London (Café) Blues." By **Jelly Roll Morton;** rec. October 16, 1923, in Chicago with **King Oliver**'s Jazz Band. Armstrong had been in the recording studio nearly a dozen times before the Oliver Band recorded this Morton tune. See additional comments on "Alligator Hop."

"Lonesome." By **Dave Brubeck** and Iola Brubeck; rec. September 19, 1961, in New York City by **Louis Armstrong and the All Stars,** pianist Dave Brubeck, and guests; CD #50. Thanks to the wonders of technology, this tender song appears on the CD reissue of ***The Real Ambassadors,*** although there was not room for it (and indeed about half of this jazz oratorio) on the 1961 LP. Armstrong sings from the heart to the heart on the lines "All of my life I've been lonely" and about the young boy who "grew up far too fast." See additional comments on "Cultural Exchange."

"Lonesome, All Alone and Blue." By Richard M. Jones; rec. February 23, 1926, in Chicago with vocalist **Bertha "Chippie" Hill** and the composer at the piano; CD #36. Armstrong manages to make something of this relatively uninspired tune, which is sometimes listed as "Lonesome, All Alone Blues." See additional comments on "A Georgia Man."

"Lonesome Blues." By **Lil Hardin Armstrong;** rec. June 23, 1926, in Chicago by Louis Armstrong and His **Hot Five;** CD #10.

"Lonesome Hours." By **Hociel Thomas;** rec. February 24, 1926, in Chicago with vocalist Hociel Thomas and pianist Hersal Thomas; CD #36. See comments on "Adam and Eve Had the Blues."

"Lonesome Lovesick Blues." By Richard M. Jones; rec. November 9, 1925, in Chicago with vocalist Blanche Calloway and the composer at the piano; CD #36. See comments on "Lazy Woman Blues."

"Lonesome Road, The." By Gene Austin and Nathaniel Shilkret; rec. November 6, 1931, in Chicago by Louis Armstrong and His Orchestra; CD #58. Armstrong had vaudeville and church music in his blood, and he combined both in this number from the 1927 Ziegfeld musical *Show Boat.* As Reverend Satchelmouth in his hilarious banter with bass player **John Lindsay,** he satirizes deacons ("I thank you for your little offering. Of course, it could have been better. Two dollars more would have gotten my shoes out of pawn."), introduces the band (which has taken on the role of a choir), and points out that someone in the congregation is smoking a Louis Armstrong Special cigar.

"Lonesome Weary Blues." By Richard M. Jones; rec. November 26, 1926, in Chicago with vocalist **Bertha "Chippie" Hill** and the composer at the piano; CD #36. See comments on "A Georgia Man."

"Long Gone (from Bowlin' Green)." By W.C. Handy and C. Smith; rec. July 12, 1954, in Chicago by **Louis Armstrong and the All Stars;** CD #38. See comments on "Atlanta Blues."

"Long, Long Ago." By Thomas Haynes Bayly; rec. March 10, 1941, in New York City by Louis Armstrong and His **Hot Seven.** With the solid support of bassist John Williams and drummer **Sid Catlett** in his rhythm section, Armstrong plays an especially wonderful trumpet chorus in this 1835 song. During the following year, the melody got a new set of lyrics and became a hit called "Don't Sit Under the Apple Tree with Anyone Else But Me."

"Long, Long Journey." By **Leonard Feather;** rec. January 10, 1946, in New York City with the ***Esquire*** All-American 1946 Award Winners; CD #12. **Duke Ellington** provides a spoken introduction and takes a nice solo in this number written by Armstrong's English-born friend and champion. Also featured are the great alto saxophonist Johnny Hodges (in his only recording session with Armstrong) and trumpeter Charlie Shavers, who fills in around Armstrong's final vocal chorus.

"Lord Don't Play Favorites, The." Armstrong found the medium of **television** very congenial, and he was an active participant beginning as early as 1948. On this NBC-TV *Producer's Showcase,* he had an acting role as the leader of a circus band, and he performs "Never Saw a Better Day" and (with Kay Starr and Dick Haymes) "Rain, Rain." The ninety-minute show was aired at 8 P.M. on September 17, 1956.

"Lot of Livin' to Do, A." By Lee Adams and Charles Strouse; rec. December 3, 1963, in New York City by **Louis Armstrong and the All Stars.** This number was introduced in the 1960 musical *Bye Bye Birdie,* and Armstrong's handlers had him record it as the "B" side to what surprisingly turned out to be the megahit "Hello Dolly!" According to clarinetist **Joe Darensbourg,** a lot of people thought " 'A Lot of Livin' was a better number than 'Hello Dolly!' " (Darensbourg, p. 183).

Louis and the Duke. This video features definitive performances of nearly a dozen jazz classics. On his half of the tape, **Armstrong and the All Stars** perform "When It's Sleepy Time Down South," "C'est si bon," "Someday," "Jerry," "Nobody Knows the Trouble I've Seen," and a politely rousing "When the Saints Go Marching In." Then **Ellington** and his band do "Take the 'A' Train," "Satin Doll," "Blow by Blow," "Things Ain't

What They Used to Be," and "Kinda Dukish." One can easily agree with the publicity blurb, which reads: "Wonderful performances by the two unparalleled greats of jazz with rare footage of their most famous tunes." But the conspicuous absence of an audience and the insistent presence of an unblinking camera make these performances more than a little stiff. The All Star incarnation here consists of **Joe Darensbourg** (clarinet), **Danny Barcelona** (drums), **Billy Kyle** (piano), **Billy Cronk** (bass), **Trummy Young** (trombone), and the effervescent **Jewel Brown** (vocalist). The Armstrong material was recorded in New York City on April 2, 1962. K-TWIN Communications, 1986; B&W; VHS format; 50 mins.; Dir. Bob DeFlores.

Louis Armstrong. Armstrong's name is sometimes used as a collective title for the four **soundies** that he made with the **Luis Russell** orchestra in 1942. Produced by the Soundies Distributing Corporation of America, the songs included *"Swingin' on Nothing," "When It's Sleepy Time Down South," "I'll Be Glad When You're Dead, You Rascal, You,"* and *"Shine."* Usually two soundies were spliced together for a running time of around six minutes. The viewer used a coin-operated viewing machine, an ancestor of today's music video.

Louis Armstrong and His Hot Five/Hot Seven. See **Hot Five; Hot Seven.**

Louis Armstrong and His Savoy Ballroom Five. See **Savoy Ballroom Five.**

"Louis Armstrong and Opera." This is the title of a fascinating article by Joshua Berrett, who examines the influence of **opera** on Armstrong's musical style. Opera was a surprisingly significant ingredient in Armstrong's cultural milieu. Before taking up the cornet, he sang operatic excerpts on New Orleans street corners, and his first record acquisitions in 1917–1918 included such singers as Henry Burr, Enrico Caruso, Amelita Galli-Curci, John McCormack, and Luisa Tetrazzini. Berrett convincingly demonstrates that Armstrong's mature musical style drew complete melodic phrases, breaks, and gestures from such renowned operas as Gounod's *Faust,* Leoncavallo's *Pagliacci,* and Verdi's *Rigoletto.*

Louis Armstrong and the All Stars. With the fading of the big band movement after World War II, Armstrong formed the New Orleans–style All Stars, an elite sextet that lasted, with relatively few personnel changes, from a historic May 17, 1947, **Town Hall** debut all the way to 1971. Armstrong last appeared with the All Stars in March 1971, when he spent two weeks at the **Waldorf Astoria**'s Empire Room. On July 5, 1971, the day before Armstrong died, he asked that the All Stars get ready to rehearse for some big jobs coming up.

The ensemble attracted the very best players, such as **Jack Teagarden,** who stayed on board from the beginning to the end of 1951. He was followed by trombonists Russell Philips (early 1952), **Trummy Young** (summer 1952 to 1963), **Russell "Big Chief" Moore** (1964 to early 1965), and **Tyree Glenn** (who also played vibraphone, from 1965 to 1971).

On clarinet were **Peanuts Hucko** (from the beginning to September 1947, and July 1958 to mid-1960), **Barney Bigard** (September 1947 to late 1952, 1953 to September 1955, and mid-1960 to mid-1961), Bob McCracken (late 1952), **Edmond Hall** (September 1955 to 1957), **Joe Darensbourg** (June 1961 to February 1965), **Eddie Shu** (February 1965 to June 1965), **Buster Bailey** (June 1965 to mid-1967), and **Joe Muranyi** (mid-1967 to 1971).

The pianists were **Dick Cary** (from the beginning to early 1948), **Earl Hines** (early 1948 to 1951), **Joe Sullivan** (early 1952), **Marty Napoleon** (early 1952 to early 1953 and 1966 to 1971), **Joe Bushkin** (mid-1953), and **Billy Kyle** (late 1953 to 1964).

The All Star bassists included **Bob Haggart** (from the beginning to September 1947), **Arvell Shaw** (September 1947 to 1951, 1952 to June 1956, and mid-1963 to June 1965), **Dale Jones** (early 1952 and July-August 1956), **William "Squire" Gersh** (late 1956 to 1958), **Mort Herbert** (1958 to 1961), Irving Manning (June to December 1961), **Billy Cronk** (1962 to May 1963), and **George "Buddy" Catlett** (June 1965 to 1971).

The All Stars five drummers were **Sid Catlett** (from the beginning to mid-1949), **Cozy Cole** (July 1949 to late 1953), Kenny John (late 1953 to mid-1954), **Barrett Deems** (mid-1954 to early 1958), and **Danny Barcelona** (April 1958 to 1971).

There were only two All Star vocalists—**Velma Middleton** (1947 to 1961) and **Jewel Brown** (1961 to 1968).

This stellar ensemble's recordings of "Basin Street Blues" (1954), "Hello Dolly!" (1963), and other pieces rank among the finest achievements of American culture. All in all, Louis Armstrong and the All Stars made, in addition to alternate takes, nearly 450 formal recordings.

"Louis Armstrong + the Jewish Family in New Orleans, La., the Year of 1907." Begun on March 31, 1969, during an extended stay at **Beth Israel Hospital** in New York, and ended sometime in 1971, the year of his death, this seventy-seven-page manuscript celebrates the many Jews who helped Armstrong throughout his life. It also criticizes with unusual candor the attitudes of many fellow African Americans. "Negroes *never* did stick together and they *never* will," he here writes. "They hold too much *malice—Jealousy* deep down in their hearts for the *few* Negroes who *tries*" (Brothers, p. 9). Armstrong praises Jewish values enthusiastically and fondly recalls the **Karnofsky family,** his manager **Joe Glaser,** and his physician **Gary Zucker.** He goes on to exhort African Americans to be more honest, loyal, and hardworking. There's every indication that Armstrong wanted this frank document to be published, but it had to wait until 1999, when it was included in a book of Armstrong writings edited by Thomas Brothers.

Louis Armstrong–Chicago Style. Ben Vereen and Red Buttons star in this movie based on Armstrong's efforts in the early 1930s to stay out of the Mafia's way. A good deal of the action takes place in a Mob-run Chicago nightclub where Vereen (as Armstrong) does a pretty good job of evoking Armstrong's singing style. He is more successful in the dramatic scenes, and Buttons is wonderfully odious as **Johnny Collins,** Armstrong's exploitative manager. Despite many faults, this movie strongly makes the point that Armstrong had to deal not only with racial prejudice but also with unscrupulous underworld characters on his way to success. MTV, 1976; color; 72 mins.; Dir. Lee Phillips.

Louis Armstrong Educational Foundation, Inc. In 1969 Armstrong himself created this Foundation, which is dedicated to promoting a wide range of educational programs in music. At the time he said, "I wanna give back to the world some of the goodness the world gave me." From supporting jazz concerts for young people at Lincoln Center in New York to helping maintain the **Louis Armstrong House and Archives,** from fostering music history programs in schools to music therapy at **Beth Israel Hospital,** the Foundation (325 East 79th Street, New York, New York, 20021) fulfills Armstrong's generous wish.

Louis Armstrong House and Archives. Located at 34-56 107th Street in **Corona,** Queens, New York, this invaluable collection consists of approximately 5,000 photographs of Armstrong performing or posing with other celebrities, 650 reel-to-reel tapes, 1,600 phonograph records, 400 books and journals, 270 sets of band parts, 120 awards and plaques, eighty-six scrapbooks lovingly decorated with collages, twelve linear feet of personal papers, correspondence, and autobiographical manuscripts, eight **trumpet**s and fourteen **mouthpieces,** his well-stamped passports, his 1957 gold record for "Mack the Knife," some unreleased recordings, and a set of Louis Armstrong Russian matruska dolls. The reel-to-reel tapes, inside boxes carefully adorned with Armstrong's collages, contain monologues, conversations, and bits of music recorded at home and abroad (hotel rooms, dressing rooms, and backstage) from the late 1940s until his death in 1971. Armstrong would sometimes just turn the tape recorder on and leave it running to catch whatever it would. These tapes give interesting glimpses into the home life of the Armstrongs. There's also a veritable mountain of materials that have been donated (e.g., his **FBI** file) or acquired since 1971. The Archives are easily accessible to the general public as well as students and professional researchers.

In 1977 the Armstrong house was officially declared a national historic landmark and in 1983, after the death of Mrs. Armstrong, a city landmark. The house became a museum and study center, under the aegis of Queens College, in 2003. In that same year, curator Michael Cogswell published *Louis Armstrong: The Offstage Story of Satchmo,* which contains a generous selection of photographs, facsimile collages, transcribed tape recordings, and other materials.

Louis Armstrong Middle School. One of two Louis Armstrong schools in Queens, New York, IS 227 is located at 30-02 Junction Boulevard in East Elmhurst. See also **Louis Armstrong School.**

Louis Armstrong New Orleans International Airport. In celebration of the August 4, 2001, centennial of Armstrong's birth, the city of New Orleans renamed its airport in honor of its most famous native son. First called Moisant Field in the 1940s (after the French Canadian aviator John B. Moisant, who died in 1910 when his plane crashed there), the airport became the New Orleans International Airport in 1962. The official name change to Louis Armstrong New Orleans International Airport took place on July 13, 2001. A public celebration unveiling the new logo took place at an August 2 event during which around 500 guests (many who just happened to be on hand because of flight delays and/or cancellations) ate red beans and rice, shared a cake adorned with Armstrong's face, and listened to jazz.

It is common practice to name airports after famous individuals, even popular entertainers (Oklahoma City's Will Rogers and Orange County's John Wayne). A regional airport in Liverpool opened in 2002 and pays tribute to musician and native son John Lennon. The Louis Armstrong New Orleans International Airport, however, is the first major airport to be named after a musician, jazz or otherwise, black or white, American or whatever.

Louis Armstrong Park. Dedicated in 1980 and located less than a mile from Armstrong's **birthplace,** this thirty-one-acre park with a concert hall is on the historic site of **Congo Square.** The centerpiece is a statue of Armstrong by **Elizabeth Catlett.**

Louis Armstrong School. In May 1977 the Meadow School (a.k.a. PS 143) became one of two schools in Queens, New York, named after Louis Armstrong. Located at 34-74 113th Street, it is within a short walking distance of Armstrong's house. **Lucille Armstrong** used to go to graduation every year to award the top prize, the Louis Armstrong Achievement Award. See also **Louis Armstrong Middle School.**

Louis Armstrong Special. See **trumpet.**

Louis "Country and Western" Armstrong. Armstrong's last album (his final recording was Clement Moore's classic **Christmas** poem **"The Night before Christmas"**) was a set of country and western songs, which he recorded with a Nashville group in New York in August 1970. His sidemen were guitarists Jack Eubanks, Stu Basore, and Billie Grammer, pianist Larry Butler, bass player Henry Strzelecki, and drummer Willie Ackerman. The songs were "Miller's Cave," "Almost Persuaded," "Running Bear," "Get Together," "Crystal Chandeliers," "You Can Have Her," "The Easy Part's Over," "Black Cloud," "Why Did Mrs. Murphy Leave Town?", "Wolverton Mountain," "Ramblin' Rose," and "Crazy Arms." Not exactly Armstrong's typical repertory, although his first **crossover** recording was "Blue Yodel No. 9" (1930) with country music star **Jimmie Rodgers,** and he went on to record Hawaiian music, Latin jazz, and spirituals. Armstrong even anticipated rap music with "You've got Me Voodoo'd" and other numbers recorded with drummer **Sid Catlett** in 1940. *"Country and Western" Armstrong* (Avco Embassy AVE-33022) was never reissued and is not available on CD.

"Louis" or "Louie." Despite the title of his 1933 hit "Laughin' Louie," and the persistence of many broadcasters and fans, Armstrong seems to have preferred his first name to be pronounced with the final "s." On his 1964 megahit, he sings, "Hello Dolly!, this is Louisssss, Dolly!" Furthermore, according to Michael Cogswell (director of the **Louis Armstrong House and Archives** at Queens College, who has listened to countless hours of Armstrong's home-recorded tapes), Armstrong consistently pronounced his own name with that final "s." **Lucille,** his last wife (to whom he was married the longest, 1942–1971), and musicians close to him tended to call him "Pops." Complicating matters, however, is Lucille's calling him "Louie" on tape in 1983, the last year of her life. Go figure.

Louise, Anita. See ***Going Places.***

L'Ouverture, Toussaint (1743–1803). In his home library in **Corona,** Armstrong had numerous books (poetry, history, diet, biography, race relations, etc.), including *World's Great Men of Color: 3000* B.C. *to 1940* by J.A. Rogers. In the table of contents one finds a check beside the name of Toussaint L'Ouverture indicating that Armstrong had studied the entry on the well-known black revolutionary who helped Haiti gain its independence from France. (The book is available for inspection at the **Louis Armstrong House and Archives,** Queens College.)

"Love Is Here to Stay." By George Gershwin and Ira Gershwin; rec. July 23, 1957, in Los Angeles with vocalist **Ella Fitzgerald** and the **Oscar Peterson** Quartet; CDs #9 and #28. This last song George Gershwin wrote before his death in 1937 gets a tender yet spirited performance. See additional comments on "April in Paris."

"Love Walked In." By George Gershwin and Ira Gershwin; rec. May 18, 1938, in New York City by Louis Armstrong and His Orchestra; CD #41. Armstrong was one of many performers (e.g., Sammy Kaye and His Orchestra) to cover this hit song from the film *The Goldwyn Follies* of the same year.

"Love, You Funny Thing." By Fred Ahlert and Roy Turk; rec. March 2, 1932, in Chicago by Louis Armstrong and His Orchestra; CD #58. Seemingly in frustration over the torpid ensemble, Armstrong shouts, "Play out!" after which the temperature rises a few degrees. In spite of weak backing, however, Armstrong turns out a solo with a bridge so remarkable that Gunther Schuller considered it worthy of transcription (1989, p. 180).

"Loveless Love." By W.C. Handy; rec. July 12, 1954, in Chicago by **Louis Armstrong and the All Stars;** CD #38. See comments on "Atlanta Blues."

"Lovely Weather We're Havin'." By John Devries and **Joe Bushkin;** rec. October 16, 1947, in Chicago by **Louis Armstrong and the All Stars;** CDs #12 and #47. Armstrong still had to play out his **Victor** recording contract even though he had disbanded his big orchestra, and in this his last number on his last session he uses the new All Stars ensemble. An Armstrong solo opens this enjoyable song by two admirers, and trombonist **Jack Teagarden,** muted, backs his singing elegantly.

"Lover." By Richard Rodgers and Lorenz Hart; rec. November 30, 1947, live at Symphony Hall, Boston, by **Louis Armstrong and the All Stars;** CD #54. This triple-meter song was first introduced by Jeanette MacDonald in the 1932 film musical *Love Me Tonight.*

"Lover, Come Back to Me." By Sigmund Romberg and Oscar Hammerstein II; rec. June 4, 1965, live at the Palais des Sports in Paris by **Louis Armstrong and the**

All Stars; CDs #2 and #6. This was a feature number for vocalist **Jewel Brown.**

"Lover's Leap." Rec. December 7, 1951, live at the Pasadena Civic Auditorium, California, with the Les Brown Big Band; CD #32. This was a feature number for alto saxophonist Pud Brown.

"Lovesick Blues." By Irving Mills and Cliff Friend; rec. November 26, 1926, in Chicago with vocalist **Bertha "Chippie" Hill** and pianist Richard M. Jones; CD #36. See comments on "A Georgia Man."

"Low Land Blues." By Richard M. Jones; rec. November 9, 1925, in Chicago with vocalist **Bertha "Chippie" Hill;** CDs #36 and #48. See comments on "A Georgia Man."

Lucie, Lawrence (b. 1907). Armstrong's guitarist from 1940 to 1944 studied at the Brooklyn Conservatory, then performed with Benny Carter (1932–34), the **Mills Blue Rhythm Band** (1934–1946), **Fletcher Henderson** (1934 and 1936–1939), and others. To Armstrong's ensemble he brought a solid knowledge of harmony and sense of rhythm, which can be heard on dozens of recordings, for example, "I Cover the Waterfront" (1941). Equally competent with both **swing** and New Orleans styles, Lucie went on to form a band with his wife (the singer and guitarist Nora Lee King), work as a freelance and studio musician, and teach.

"Lucy Long." By Perry Bradford; rec. November 2, 1925, in New York City with Perry Bradford's Jazz Phools; CD #36. Before Armstrong returned to Chicago in November 1925, he made one last recording with an ensemble consisting mostly of **Fletcher Henderson** band members. Bradford here sings his own tune, but the distinguishing features of the recording are Armstrong's brief solos and strong leadership.

Lumumba, Patrice (1925–1961). See **Congo.**

"Lyin' to Myself." By **Hoagy Carmichael** and Stanley Adams; rec. May 18, 1936, in New York City by Louis Armstrong and His Orchestra; CD #34. Armstrong follows a ruminative trumpet solo with an inventive vocal, but it's his dramatic final trumpet cadenza that astounds the listener. See additional comments on "Ev'ntide."

M

Ma Nouvelle Orléans. See **Gautier, Madeleine; *Satchmo: My Life in New Orleans.***

"Mabel's Dream." By Ike Smith; rec. early September 1923 in Chicago with **King Oliver**'s Jazz Band; CD #35. See comments on "Alligator Hop."

"Mack the Knife." By Kurt Weill and Bertold Brecht, with English lyrics by Marc Blitzstein; rec. September 28, 1955, in Los Angeles by **Louis Armstrong and the All Stars;** CDs #2, #14, #16, #19, #20, #23, #28, #39, #43, #46, #55, #57, and #59. Armstrong helped fuel the Kurt Weill revival with this recording from *The Three Penny Opera* (1928). Although it was subsequently taken up by many singers (e.g., Bobby Darin), no one quite has Armstrong's authority, since he brought to it an extensive firsthand knowledge of shady, Mack-like characters. At any rate, it was a big hit, eventually going gold in 1957. Armstrong went on to record "Mack" forty-two times in all, and he kept it in the All Stars repertory.

Mahogany Hall. Jazz developed not only in the cabarets and honky-tonks of New Orleans but also in the brothels, especially the most famous of them all, Mahogany Hall. Located at 325 Basin Street in the **Storyville** district of New Orleans, Mahogany Hall was run by the colorful madam Lulu White, a.k.a. the "Octoroon Queen" ("octoroon" means one-eighth African American ancestry). "It was a pleasure house, where those rich ofay (white) business men and planters would come from all over the South and spend some awful large amounts of loot," Armstrong later wrote in his **autobiography** (1954, p. 147). According to a souvenir booklet, Mahogany Hall was "built of marble and is four story; containing five parlors, all handsomely furnished, and fifteen bedrooms.... [Miss Lulu has] none but the fairest of girls—those gifted with nature's best charms" (Shapiro and Hentoff, 1955, pp. 8–9). Musicians did very well there, since the tips were big, and they also got paid at the end of every evening (because such places were liable to be closed down at a moment's notice). **Jelly Roll Morton** played ragtime, French quadrilles, popular songs and dances, and even light classics there in the early part of the century. Spenser Williams's "Mahogany Hall Stomp" was well known to Armstrong before he finally got around to recording it on March 5, 1929. "Basin Street Blues" (which Armstrong recorded fifty times during his career) is also associated with Mahogany Hall and its locale. Like so many similar establishments, Mahogany Hall was closed by the U.S. Navy in 1917.

"Mahogany Hall Stomp." By Spencer Williams; rec. March 5, 1929, in New York City by Louis Armstrong and His **Savoy Ballroom Five;** CDs #3, #8, #10, #12, #14, #21, #24, #34, #43, #47, #48, #52, #54, #55, and #61. Armstrong and his sidemen knew the New Orleans club that inspired this instrumental, and they turn in a superlative performance, though one slightly faster than the composer originally intended. That's a minor innovation compared to Armstrong's three muted solos, which have influenced trumpet players ever since. Especially remarkable is the second of these, in which he dramatically holds a high note for twelve thrilling measures. This technique, which he had experimented with for some time, became an Armstrong hallmark with this recording. The chorus just previous consists of a series of short, excited, arrhythmic phrases, and the chorus just after features six repetitions of a five-note pattern. Simultaneously simple and complex, improvised and organized, Armstrong's creations still have the capacity to thrill. Transcriptions by Schuller (1989, pp. 164, 182–183) and Gushee (1998, pp. 314–315).

mail. Armstrong received thousands of letters and cards throughout his career, and some 20,000 letters of condolence were sent to **Lucille Armstrong.** Many of these are preserved at the **Louis Armstrong House and Archives** at Queens College, and they make fascinating reading, since they range widely from Richard Nixon, **Coretta Scott King,** and Armstrong's professional colleagues to outpourings of admiration from fans. A measure of Armstrong's fame is indicated by the fact that mail could reach him without an address and sometimes without even his name. One letter from abroad is addressed to "LOIS AMSTRONG/Rex jazz/U.S.A./NEW YORK," another "For the King of jazz/Louis Armstrong/*U.S.A.,"* and one simply " 'Ole **Satchmo**' Himself/Where ever he is." After his death, people expressed their grief to Lucille in envelopes with such addresses as "Mrs. Satchmo/Queens, N.Y./America" and "Lady Louis Armstrong/New York."

"Mail Train Blues." By Blair and Lethwick; rec. March 3, 1926, in Chicago with vocalist **Sippie Wallace** and pianist Hersal Thomas; CD #36. See comments on "Baby, I Can't Use You No More."

"Make Me One Pallet on Your Floor." See "Atlanta Blues."

"Makin' Whoopie." By Walter Donaldson and Gus Kahn; rec. July 31, 1957, in Los Angeles with the **Oscar Peterson** Quartet; CDs #9 and #37. Eddie Cantor's 1928 signature song is taken at a relaxed tempo by Armstrong, who chuckles knowingly when the judge orders that the hapless husband pay in alimony more than he earns. See additional comments on "Blues in the Night."

Mama Lucy. See **Armstrong, Beatrice "Mama Lucy."**

"Mame." By Jerry Herman; rec. May 1966 in New York City by **Louis Armstrong and the All Stars;** CD #28. Patrick Dennis's 1955 bestseller *Auntie Mame,* about his uninhibited and wealthy relative, saw many incarnations: a Broadway play, a Broadway musical, and two movie productions. Armstrong's is the definitive rendition of this mock-Southern song, but composer Herman was undoubtedly disappointed in his hopes for a popular and commercial success comparable to that of his 1964 "Hello Dolly!"

Man Called Adam, A. **Sammy Davis, Jr.,** stars in this film as world-class jazz musician Adam Johnson (trumpet playing dubbed by Nat Adderley), who is guilt-ridden over his role in the accidental death of his wife and child. Armstrong plays Sweet Daddy, a sad and burned-out older musician whom Johnson treats callously. Subconsciously, Johnson is worried that he may one day end up like Sweet Daddy. Armstrong here has a chance to show his dramatic talents, and his success is attested to by Davis himself, who later observed that the film really became Armstrong's. The music is by Benny Carter; Armstrong performs "Someday Sweetheart" and his own "Back o' Town Blues." The cast includes Peter Lawford, Mel Tormé, **Frank Sinatra,** Lola Falana, Ossie Davis, and Cicely Tyson. Embassy Films, 1966; B&W; 103 min.; Dir. Leo Penn.

"Man for Every Day of the Week, A." By Hersal Thomas; rec. March 3, 1926, in Chicago with vocalist **Sippie Wallace** and the composer at the keyboard; CD #36. See comments on "Baby, I Can't Use You No More."

"Man I Love, The." By George Gershwin and Ira Gershwin; rec. January 21, 1955, live at the Crescendo Club in Los Angeles by **Louis Armstrong and the All Stars;** CD #6. This popular 1924 song was a feature number for bassist **Arvell Shaw.**

manager. See **Collins, Johnny; Glaser, Joe; Hylton, Jack; Rockwell, Tommy.**

"Manda." By Eubie Blake and Noble Sissle; rec. October 7, 1924, in New York City by **Fletcher Henderson** and His Orchestra. See comments on "Alabamy Bound."

"Mandy Lee Blues." By Marty Bloom and Walter Melrose; rec. April 5, 1923, in Richmond, Indiana, by **King Oliver**'s Creole Jazz Band; CD #35. Not a true blues, this number, which comes from Armstrong's very first studio recording session, is more historically than musically important. There are no Armstrong solos, but he duets gracefully with Oliver. See additional comments on "Alligator Hop."

"Mandy, Make Up Your Mind." By George W. Meyer, Arthur Johnston, Grant Clarke, and Roy Turk; rec. early December 1924 in New York City by **Fletcher Henderson** and His Orchestra, and December 17, 1924, in New York City with vocalist **Eva Taylor** and **Clarence Williams' Blue Five;** CDs #8, #36, and #52. These recordings show why Armstrong was already at this very early point in his career a much-admired player. He teases the beat, spices up the melody, and extends his instrument's range. His only rival as a jazz soloist is **Sidney Bechet,** who can be heard playing the cumbersome sarrusophone (a saxophonelike instrument with a double reed, common in military bands) on the Blue Five date.

"Manhattan." By Richard Rodgers and Lorenz Hart; rec. June 1, 1956, live at the Medina Temple in Chicago by **Louis Armstrong and the All Stars;** CD #19. One would like to hear more of what Armstrong could do with this 1925 evergreen, but the All Stars dwell on it only briefly as part of a medley done for a Multiple Sclerosis Society benefit concert.

Manhattan. In this 1979 **Woody Allen** film, protagonist Isaac Davis (played by Allen) puts Armstrong's "Potato Head Blues" on a list of the best things in life. "Why is life worth living? That's a very good question. There are certain things that make it worthwhile. For me? . . . I would say Groucho Marx, to name one thing, and Willie Mays, and the second movement of the Jupiter Symphony, and Louis Armstrong . . . his recording of 'Potato Head Blues.' "

Manhattan Transfer. To the Armstrong Centennial in 2001 this thirty-year-old, multiple Grammy Award-winning ensemble contributed a CD titled *The Spirit of St. Louis* (Atlantic 83394-2). Producer Craig Street put the venerable singers with modern sidemen in arrangements that nicely exploit both Transfer's polished jazz style and the playfulness of vintage Armstrong. Beyond excellent performances of "A Kiss to Build a Dream On," "Old Man Mose," "Do You Know What It Means to Miss New Orleans?", and "Nothing Could Be Hotter Than That," each singer was allowed to pick his or her own Armstrong favorites. Tim Hauser's "Blue Again," Cheryl Bentyne's "Sugar," Janis Siegel's "The Blues Are Brewin'," and Alan Paul's "Gone Fishin' " are all memorable. The CD closes with a soulful "When You Wish Upon a Star."

"Maple Leaf Rag." By Scott Joplin; rec. in Chicago in 1927. Armstrong was such a proven commercial success in the mid-1920s that the publisher Melrose had him come into the studio and improvise onto wax cylinders. Pianist Elmer Schoebel would then transcribe his solos (such as this one, which comes from a popular 1899 piece) for publication. See ***50 Hot Choruses for Cornet; 125 Jazz Breaks for Cornet.***

Marable, Fate (1890–1947). When Armstrong was a little boy in New Orleans selling newspapers and doing other odd jobs, he used to go down to the end of Canal Street and hear Fate Marable playing the calliope on a **Streckfus** line riverboat. Marable must have created an enchanting atmosphere as he tried to attract customers on Fridays, Saturdays, and Sundays. In later years, Armstrong would marvel over what a "*small* and beautiful world" it was that he would one day be a featured trumpet player in Marable's famous band (Brothers, p. 70).

Marable—a lanky, redheaded, light-skinned African American—grew up in Peducah, Kentucky, learned piano from his mother, and later studied at Straight University in New Orleans. In 1907 the Streckfus family hired him and a violinist to play dance music aboard their riverboat. Marable would also play the calliope as the riverboat approached a town and just before it left for a three- or four-hour excursion on the Mississippi. By 1917 he had formed a riverboat band, for which he liked to hire New Orleans musicians. He recruited Armstrong in 1919, and Armstrong worked for three seasons. It was a big step up. Unlike **Kid Ory**'s band, Marable's players had to read music fluently so that they could play all the latest hits. Armstrong immediately had to improve his reading ability, which the band's mellophonist **Davey Jones,** and sometimes Marable himself, helped him do. Also, daily performances gave him the kind of professional experience he so far lacked.

"Fate Marable was a good Band Leader. . . . He is Absolutely responsible for a lot of 'youngsters Successes. Any whom ever worked under Fate's Directions can gladly verify this. And will Admit he's one of the Grandest and Finest Musicians in the Biz," Armstrong states in **"The Goffin Notebooks"** (Brothers, p. 83). In fact, Marable's band eventually became known as "the floating conservatory," since not only Armstrong but also **Red Allen,** Jimmy Blanton, **Baby Dodds, Pops Foster, Johnny St. Cyr, Zutty Singleton,** and many other sidemen went on to fame after developing their professional chops on the **S.S. *Sidney*.** As the 1930s began to unfold, Marable shared leadership duties with Charlie Creath. Illness eventually forced Marable to limit his activities. He left only two recordings—"Frankie and Johnny" and "Pianoflage," both from 1924—as souvenirs of the sound and style that so many musicians enthusiastically praised.

"Mardi Gras March, The." By P.F. Webster and S. Fain; rec. October 8, 1958, in Los Angeles by **Louis Armstrong and the All Stars** and a studio vocal group; CD #8. Discounting the corny anonymous vocal ensemble, this **Dixieland** number has some appeal. There is a stirring moment at the end when Armstrong whales on this Charleston number in unison with trombonist **Trummy Young** and clarinetist **Peanuts Hucko.**

Margaret, Princess. See **England.**

"Margie." By J. Russel Robinson, Benny Davis, and Con Conrad; rec. March 19, 1954, in New York City by **Louis Armstrong and the All Stars;** CDs #6, #8, #19, and #23. This 1920 favorite, first introduced by the Original Dixieland Jazz Band (see **Dixieland**), became a feature number for All Star trombonist **Trummy Young.**

"Marie." By **Irving Berlin;** rec. April 11, 1940, in New York City with the **Mills Brothers;** CD #14. The Armstrong-Mills Brothers treatment of this 1928 hit owes something to the familiar Tommy Dorsey arrangement, but they make it their own by trading lead and vocal fill-in duties. See additional comments on "Carry Me Back to Old Virginny."

marijuana. Armstrong liked marijuana and smoked it regularly from around 1925 to the end of his life. He talked and wrote about it often, for example, to his friend **John Hammond**: "It makes you feel good, man. It relaxes you, makes you forget all the bad things that happen to a Negro. It makes you feel wanted, and when you're with another tea smoker it makes you feel a special kinship" (Hammond, p. 105). In **"The Satchmo Story,"** which was to be a continuation of his 1936 and 1954 **autobiographies,** he advocated the legalization of marijuana, which is probably why the manuscript remained unpublished since Armstrong's manager, **Joe Glaser,** knew this would be asking for trouble. In March 1931, Armstrong had been arrested and jailed in Los Angeles for nine days for smoking marijuana with drummer **Vic Berton** in the **Sebastian's New Cotton Club** parking lot. Moreover, the **FBI** was well aware of Armstrong's practice. His file contains an entry dated November 30, 1950, suggesting that the FBI could take care of his dissatisfaction over something that happened at the Flamingo Hotel in Las Vegas "by calling him on the telephone and by sending him a bottle of Scotch or a couple of reefers."

"Reefers," "tea," "muggles," "weed," and other names were slang terms for marijuana among jazz musicians and friends. Those who used the drug were known as "**viper**s," a term that appears in several song titles: "Send in the Vipers" (**Mezz Mezzrow**), "If You're a Viper" (Stuff Smith), and "Viper's Drag" (**Fats Waller**). Other related titles were "Golden Leaf Strut," "Texas Tea Party," "Chant of the Weed," and "Smoking Reefers"—all recordings made in the 1920s and 1930s. Armstrong himself celebrated marijuana in such songs as "Muggles" (1928) and "Song of the Vipers" (1934). He was not a heavy user, though, and he viewed trendy drugs such as heroin with disdain. He used marijuana sparingly and basically to unwind after a gig. He was in most respects a very health-conscious person, who drank moderately (and not before a job), watched his diet, and never used hard drugs. His grand addiction was his work, for which he scrupulously kept in shape. He also smoked Camel cigarettes and had a fondness for **laxatives,** which, in his curious view of anatomy and physiology, he seemed to equate with marijuana: The one was a cleanser for the mind and the other a cleanser for the body.

Marsalis, Wynton (b. 1961). The New Orleans-born trumpeter is another in a long line of musicians who has been deeply influenced by Armstrong, and he openly, frequently, and eloquently acknowledges the debt. By performing Armstrong's music and honoring traditional jazz, Marsalis has done more than any other single musician to change the contemporary perception of Armstrong. Moreover, through various educational outreach programs, Marsalis has turned even younger musicians on to the old master. He provides respectful commentary on the 1989 video ***Satchmo: Louis Armstrong*** and does a pretty fair rendition of the impossible "West End Blues" opening cadenza as part of his hosting duties on the 1985 ***Trumpet Kings.***

Marsalis has his own voice, too. He studied both jazz and classical music and has recorded frequently in both styles. He has won several Grammies, appeared on *Sesame Street,* been on the cover of ***Time*** magazine, and won a Pulitzer Prize for his oratorio *Blood on the Fields* (1994). As the head of the Jazz Division at Lincoln Center, New York, he has been an energetic if controversial figure, championing causes such as the big band music of **Duke Ellington** but, according to some, neglecting avant-garde and jazz-fusion styles. However, Armstrong has steadfastly remained his favorite musician. As he says on the **Ken Burns *Jazz*** series, the sound of Armstrong's horn "was a pure spiritual essence, the sound of America and of freedom."

Marshall, Kaiser (1899–1948). Born in Savannah, Georgia, Marshall was raised in Boston, where he learned the drums. He moved to New York in the early 1920s and in 1924 was chosen to play in the newly formed **Fletcher Henderson** band. The band had moved from the Club Alabam to the **Roseland Ballroom** by the time Armstrong joined them in September later that year. "He was a real sharp 'Cat indeed," Armstrong later recalled when he first heard Marshall. "I'd never seen or heard of anything that was anywheres near the ever sharp Kaiser Marshall" (Brothers, p. 126). As for Marshall's impressions of Armstrong, he admired the younger man's work habits and thrift, and he joined other band members in making fun of his thick-soled shoes and long underwear. (Band members tended to spend lavishly and even wear spats, while Armstrong sent most of his money back to **Lil** in Chicago.) Marshall tells an interesting story about Armstrong's singing, which Henderson kept the lid on (and thereby contributed to Armstrong's departure in 1925). Evidently, there was an amateur show every Thursday at Roseland, and on one occasion they were short an act. "We got Louis out on the stage and he did 'Everybody Loves My Baby,'" Marshall said. "He sang it and he played it on the trumpet; the crowd surely went for it . . . from then on they used to cry for Louis every Thursday night" (Hodes and Hansen, pp. 83–85).

Although Marshall can be heard on the many recordings that Armstrong made with Henderson in 1924–1925 ("Everybody Loves My Baby," "Sugar Foot Stomp," "T.N.T.," and many others), his playing is much freer and more improvised on later recordings such as the 1929 "Knockin' a Jug." Marshall left Henderson in 1930 and for the rest of his life moved around between the bands of **Sidney Bechet, Cab Calloway, Duke Ellington, Lionel Hampton, Mezz Mezzrow,** and others.

Martin, Mrs. When Armstrong attended the **Fisk School for Boys** from 1907 to 1912, he befriended the caretaker/housekeeper, Mrs. Martin, and her large family. There were four boys and three girls, nearly all of whom were musical. One of the boys, Henry, became an accomplished New Orleans drummer, performing with the dance bands of **Kid Ory** and **Joe Oliver** and also with the **Onward Brass Band.** Evidently, the father was no longer present. Armstrong had a big crush on one of Mrs. Martin's daughters, Wilhelmina, about whom he wrote touchingly in his **autobiography:** "I was in love with Wilhelmina, but the poor child died before I got up the nerve to tell her. . . . I had an inferiority complex and felt that I was not good enough for her." He continued about her Mother: "[Mrs. Martin] always had some kind of consolation for the underdog who would rap at her door and she could always find a bite to eat for him somewhere" (1954, p. 31). Many New Orleans musicians spoke of Mrs. Martin with similar reverence.

"Maryland, My Maryland." Traditional melody with lyrics by James Ryder Randall; rec. on or shortly after September 11, 1946, in Los Angeles with a small ensemble. Armstrong and friends play this favorite early in the **movie *New Orleans.*** The musicians are in a wagon that advertises the Orpheum Cabaret, the **Storyville** club where much of the story takes place.

Matranga's. There were numerous honkytonks in the area of Liberty, Perdido, Franklin, and Poydras Streets, near where the young Armstrong lived. Matranga's was one of these, and owner Henry Matranga presented jazz there as early as 1915. It was here in 1917 that Armstrong made his professional debut. According to Jones and Chilton, he eventually earned $1.25 a night, but in those days his mother could make a good meal for $.15, and one could get a tailor-made suit for $10 (p. 233). Fifty years later, Armstrong reflected in ***Life*** magazine: "When I got my first job in New Orleans playing in a honky-tonk—Matranga's at Franklin and Perdido—I was 17, and it was the same as Carnegie Hall to me. Yeah. Night I made my debut, I thought I was somebody" (Meryman, 1966, p. 104).

Mayann. See **Armstrong, Mary Albert "Mayann."**

McCarthyism. See ***New Orleans.***

McQueen, Butterfly. See ***Swingin' the Dream.***

McRae, Carmen (b. 1922). See CD #50.

McRae, Theodore "Teddy" "Mr. Bear" (1908–1999). This tenor saxophonist, arranger, and composer was Armstrong's music director from 1944 to 1945, just as he was for **Ella Fitzgerald** earlier in the 1940s. To Armstrong's band he contributed excellent arrangements, which for the most part unfortunately went unrecorded. Instead, the band did a good many Armed Forces Radio Service and other broadcasts, in addition to a brief appearance in the 1945 movie ***Pillow to Post.*** After working for Armstrong, McRae went out on his own. However, musical style was changing at this time from big **swing** bands to both **bop** and smaller ensembles. As Armstrong found in his **Carnegie Hall** and **Town Hall** triumphs (1947), McRae too learned that smaller bands were the wave of the future. He went on to form several and also continued to write arrangements. With pianist-arranger Eddie Wilcox, he founded the record company Raecox. Among his enduring compositions is "Back Bay Shuffle," which Artie Shaw recorded in 1938.

"Me and Brother Bill." See **"Brother Bill."**

"Meanest Kind of Blues, The." By Louis Katzman; rec. November 14, 1924, in New York City by **Fletcher Henderson** and His Orchestra. Henderson generally gave Armstrong very little solo time, except for this recording where he is in the spotlight, either as a soloist or blending with the reeds, for nearly half the time. See additional comments on "Alabamy Bound."

Meeker, Ralph. See ***Glory Alley.***

"Melancholy." By Marty Bloom and Walter Melrose; rec. April 22, 1927, in Chicago by **Johnny Dodds**'s Black Bottom Stompers; CDs #10 and #61. Armstrong's music is predominantly upbeat—in major keys, with a strong beat, and an irresistible rhythmic propulsion. However, there is the occasional pensive piece, such as "Skid-Dat-De-Dat," "St. James Infirmary Blues," "Tight Like This," and "Melancholy." This last number is Armstrong's first experience with the commercially sentimental world of Tin Pan Alley, which in a few years would become his main source of material. It is an altogether restrained performance, as one would expect from the title. Even pianist **Earl Hines** holds his usual technical displays to a minimum.

Melody Maker. The English were entranced in the 1920s and 1930s by America's exotic blues and **swing,** as well as the new music's star performer, whose recordings circulated widely. As former colonial masters, they also perhaps felt a kind of parental pride. The Armstrong phenomenon had its British headquarters at the offices of the periodical *Melody Maker* (*MM;* founded in 1926 and still going strong), which was to a large extent responsible for bringing Armstrong to the attention of the English public. *MM* writers thoroughly covered his 1932 tour. "Well, he's here! And has been for a fortnight by the time this appears," began Dan S. Ingman breathlessly in the August 1932 issue. "After [London], probably the Continent, as big offers have already been received from Berlin, Paris and Monte Carlo" (Berrett, 1999, p. 50). Another *MM* writer, Percy Brooks, met Armstrong when he first arrived and gave him his most famous and enduring **nickname.** Nervously contracting "Satchelmouth," Brooks said "Hello, **Satchmo**!" Armstrong liked the new twist on an old moniker, and eventually all the world came to know him by it. Not only did he use it as the first word in the title of his 1954 **autobiography,** but he also had it printed on his stationery and inscribed on two of his **trumpet**s.

Although Armstrong was by no means universally acclaimed at his first few Palladium shows, *MM* was sufficiently impressed to broker agreements with provincial theaters. These engagements they also enthusiastically reported on in their pages. Armstrong himself wrote nearly a dozen articles for *MM,* ranging from a paean to red beans and rice and an appreciation of his mentor **Joe Oliver** to a miniseries titled "My Kicks in Europe."

"Memories of You." By Andy Razaf and Eubie Blake; rec. October 16, 1930, in Los Angeles by Louis Armstrong and His **Sebastian New Cotton Club** Orchestra; CDs #8, #28, #40, #44, #48, and #52. This is the recording that put both **Lionel Hampton** and the vibraphone on the jazz map, and to it Armstrong contributes some memorable singing and trumpet playing, especially the dramatic climb to a concert E-flat at the end. During the **All Stars** years, this became clarinetist **Eddie Shu**'s feature number.

"Memphis Blues, The." By George A. Norton and W.C. Handy; rec. July 13, 1954, in Chicago by **Louis Armstrong and the All Stars;** CDs #19 and #38. See comments on "Atlanta Blues" and "Flee as a Bird."

"Memphis Bound." By Frank Banta and Peter DeRose; rec. April 18, 1925, in New York City by **Fletcher Henderson** and His Orchestra. See comments on "Alabamy Bound."

mentor. See **Oliver, Joe "King."**

Mercer, John Herndon "Johnny" (1909–1976). Armstrong frequently performed and recorded many Mercer songs, including "And the Angels Sing," "Blues in the Night," "Fools Rush In," "Jeepers Creepers," "Moon River," and "Why Doubt My Love?"

Merrill, Robert (b. 1917). Armstrong's path occasionally crossed those of legit artists, such as conductor **Leonard Bernstein,**

pianist **Van Cliburn,** and the **opera** singer Robert Merrill. Armstrong and Merrill worked together at the Sands Hotel in Las Vegas in 1955, and during that same year they appeared together on the nationally televised *Ed Sullivan Show,* where they switched roles, Merrill singing "Honeysuckle Rose" and Armstrong singing (odd as this may seem) the famous "Vesti la giubba" aria from *Pagliacci.* Armstrong had a lifelong attraction to opera. Among the first records he bought were those of Enrico Caruso and Amelita Galli-Curci, and they influenced the development of his style. See **"Louis Armstrong and Opera."**

"Mess, Katie, Mess." By Kapp and Eller; rec. November 23, 1926, in Chicago with vocalist **Bertha "Chippie" Hill;** CD #36. See comments on "A Georgia Man."

Metronome. The venerable American periodical was published from 1885 to 1961, usually monthly. It covered Armstrong's negative reaction to the new be**bop,** which he expressed in several 1948–1949 issues. In September 1949, Armstrong got reverential treatment by critic (and Armstrong friend) **Leonard Feather,** who, in mountain-goes-to-Mohammed style, traveled to Armstrong's cozy home in **Corona** and administered a "blindfold test." This was a regular *Metronome* feature, in which an outstanding artist was asked to identify and comment on a batch of unnamed recordings. Feather was supposed to have brought back a tirade on bop. In the first of two articles, "Lombardo Grooves Louis!" (reprinted in Brothers, pp. 165–66), Armstrong doesn't have as much to say about the new musical style as he does about blues and **swing,** especially the "sweet music" of **Guy Lombardo,** which he gives "eight stars." A month later, however, Feather finished his report in an article tellingly named "Pops Pops Top on Sloppy Bop." Another *Metronome* article in the same vein, George T. Simon's "Bebop's the Easy Way Out, Claims Louis" (March 1948) is reprinted in Berrett (1999, pp. 141–144). These and other writings of the day can now be seen as period pieces in which facts and feelings were exaggerated. Moreover, the controversy was in no small degree exploited by Armstrong's manager, **Joe Glaser,** as an opportunity to draw a seat- and record-buying public to his client.

Metronome also lent its name to some ephemeral recording ensembles, all called the Metronome All Stars. After its annual readers' polls between the years 1939 and 1956, the winners were rounded up and put in a studio and set to vinyl. Naturally, some years were better than others, but the overall result is an interesting survey of the development of jazz.

Mezzrow, Mezz (Milton, Mesirow) (1899–1972). Born in Chicago this white clarinetist is best remembered for the recording sessions he organized in the 1930s and 1940s, his championship of African American music, his devotion to Armstrong, and his role as a drug pusher. He wrote a memoir, *Really the Blues* (1946), that creates a vivid picture of his and Armstrong's milieu. About Armstrong's effect on the young Harlem blacks he wrote: "All the raggedy kids . . . were so inspired with self-respect after digging how neat and natty Louis was, they started to dress up real good, and took pride in it too, because if Louis did it it must be right" (p. 183). The book is often self-serving, though, as in it Mezzrow describes a closer relationship with Armstrong than he probably had, claims to have written arrangements for him, and says that he even served as Armstrong's manager. When in January 1935 he returned to New York from Europe, Armstrong may have considered the idea of Mezzrow's managing him, but unfortunately Mezzrow was then in the throes of heroin addiction.

Mezzrow was in fact more of a drug pusher than a musician. He is said to have introduced numerous performers, including Armstrong, to **marijuana** in the mid-1920s. The term "Mezzroll" referred in his day to a fat, well-packed marijuana cigarette. In *Celebrating the Duke and Louis,* Ralph Gleason wrote: "Mezz sold his grass by the shoebox coast to coast, mail order, as well as standing on 125th Street underneath the tree of life [a.k.a. "Tree of Hope" in New York City, whose bark aspiring entertainers would come to rub], dealing with all who came by" (1975, p. 56). As Thomas Brothers points out, there is evidence in an Armstrong letter to Mezzrow from Europe dated September 18, 1932, that Mezzrow kept Armstrong supplied with marijuana (Brothers, p. 208). In any case, Armstrong had a high regard for Mezzrow, called him "some kind of a god," and compared him favorably with his mentor **Joe Oliver.**

Mezzrow was indeed in Armstrong's company frequently, and his accounts give an intimate, backstage picture of his idol's life. Citing only instances where others have also given similar accounts, Mezzrow was in the studio when "Hobo, You Can't Ride This Train" was recorded (December 8, 1932), although his only role was to ring the train bell at the beginning of the number. Later, he was present at a be**bop** discussion (with Armstrong, **Barney Bigard,** and Ernest Borneman), which was written up in the April 7, 1948, issue of ***Down Beat.*** While mixed feelings are expressed by Bigard and Borneman, Mezzrow clearly lines up on the side of Armstrong. Reading between the lines in this and other writings, one gets the picture that Mezzrow is an amiable amateur, a kind of "groupie" before the term was coined.

After moving to Paris in the 1950s, Mezzrow organized and promoted touring bands and became something of a cult figure. Never an accomplished clarinet player, he nonetheless recorded frequently (bolstered by abler musicians) and kept active into the 1960s.

"Mi va di cantare." Rec. December 11, 1967, in New York City by **Louis Armstrong and the All Stars,** trumpeter **Clark Terry,** and others.

Middleton, Velma (1917–1961). During the nearly quarter century–long life of **Louis Armstrong and the All Stars,** Armstrong had only two vocalists: Middleton and **Jewel Brown** (1961–1968). (Contrast this to five drummers, five trombonists, six pianists, eight bass players, and eight clarinetists during the same period.) Middleton was associated with Armstrong even before the All Stars days. After singing in clubs during the 1930s, she first teamed up with him in 1942, and by 1944 the two had a hit in "Is You Is or Is You Ain't My Baby?" Although Middleton did not have a particularly pretty voice, it was reliable and matched Armstrong's perfectly. They developed a comedic-romantic style that some **"moldy**

Armstrong with Velma Middleton in the 1940s. (Louis Armstrong House and Archives at Queens College/CUNY)

figs" thought distasteful but everyone else found delicious. They can be heard together in many songs, such as the 1947 "That's My Desire." By the time "Yeh!", "Mm-mm," and "Baby, Your Sleep Is Showing" were recorded in 1955, the two had developed a wonderfully relaxed and intimate parlando style. Their "Baby, It's Cold Outside," used to bring down the house.

A familial loyalty to one another evolved between Armstrong and Middleton over the years. In 1942 she helped facilitate his marriage to **Lucille,** and in 1946 he had her as his guest on the New Orleans Mardi Gras **King of the Zulus** float. Although he took a great deal of criticism for her less-than-perfect vocal style as well as her on-stage antics (Middleton weighed 250 to 300 pounds yet liked to amaze and delight audiences by doing the splits), he stubbornly insisted on her presence. Once, at the 1957 **Newport Jazz Festival,** he refused to perform at his own **birthday** concert until promoters had restored Middleton to the lineup. She was, as Leslie Gourse aptly puts it in *Louis' Children: American Jazz Singers,* Armstrong's "professional soul sister" (p. 29).

Middleton seemed to have had a blast working with Armstrong, but it was work indeed. Armstrong kept up a grueling tour schedule—300 days a year. In fact, as did All Star clarinetist **Buster Bailey** and pianist **Billy Kyle,** she died on the road. While on tour in Africa, she suffered a stroke and breathed her last in Freetown, Sierra Leone (see **African tours**).

Midsummer Night's Dream, A. See ***Swingin' the Dream.***

"Mighty River." By Billy Baskette; rec. April 26, 1933, in Chicago by Louis Armstrong and His Orchestra; CD #12. Armstrong here takes this sprightly 1902 march and at the end transforms it into something operatic.

"Milenberg Joys." By **Jelly Roll Morton;** rec. on or shortly after September 11, 1946, in Los Angeles with a small ensemble. Armstrong and friends play a portion of this 1925 number early in the **movie *New Orleans.*** The musicians are in a wagon advertising the Orpheum Cabaret and heading down Basin Street.

"Miller's Cave." By Jack Clement; rec. August 1970 in New York City with the Nashville Group. See comments on "Almost Persuaded."

Mills, Irving (1884–1985). See **Mills Blue Rhythm Band.**

Mills Blue Rhythm Band. This New York group was at first known as the Blue Rhythm Band when it was founded in 1930 by drummer Willie Lynch. In February of that year Armstrong began fronting it at the Coconut Grove in New York. He also cut a few recordings with the group—for example, "My Sweet," "I Can't Believe That You're in Love with Me," "Indian Cradle Song," "Exactly Like You," and "Dinah"—and also played with them (throughout the first half of the year) in Detroit, Baltimore, Philadelphia, Pittsburgh, and Chicago. The band's name changed in 1931 when Irving Mills took over as manager, and later dancer-entertainer Lucky Millinder led the group from 1934 to its breakup in 1938. The Mills Blue Rhythm Band used to sub for both the **Cab Calloway** and the **Duke Ellington** ensembles. The group was famous for high musical standards and its repertory of amusing pop and novelty numbers, such as "Futuristic Jungleism" (1931), "Rhythm Spasm" (1932), and "Balloonacy" (1936).

Mills Brothers. This popular vocal quartet was composed of four brothers (Herbert, Harry, Donald, and John, Jr.) until the eldest (John, Jr.) died in 1935 and was replaced by their father John, Sr. They worked with Armstrong on several occasions with memorable success. Their "Darling Nellie Gray" (1937) is a good example. Made at a time when the hot new bands were trying to get some of the old nineteenth-century songs to **swing** (e.g., **Bunny Berigan**'s "Wearing o' the Green" and **Benny Goodman**'s "Loch Lomond"), the recording features Armstrong playing some engaging straight mute obbligato figures behind the Brothers' singing. "Carry Me Back to Old Virginny" and "In the Shade of the Old Apple Tree" did not turn out as well, but "The Old Folks at Home" took nicely to swing treatment. (These three were also recorded in 1937.) "Old Folks" can also be heard as a sign of the times. To the Mills Brothers singing of "All the world is sad and lonely/Everywhere I go./Oh darkies, how my heart grows weary/Far from the old folks at home," Armstrong responds: "Well, lookie here—we *are* far away from home. . . . Yeah man!" Throughout the song, Armstrong delivers his lines with a broad wink. Those good old days were sad indeed and frankly good riddance to them.

The Mills Brothers were well established by the time they worked with Armstrong. After traveling at first on the small-town vaudeville circuit, they got their break on radio station WLW in Cincinnati in the late 1920s. Within a few years they seemed to be singing everywhere and also appearing in films. The Mills Brothers were managed by Armstrong's manager **Joe Glaser,** and both recorded for **Decca,** so their teaming up seemed natural. After making the old chestnut recordings, they turned back to the current century with a sweet recording of "The Song Is Ended" (1938) and others. "Old Folks" was not their only foray into social commentary, either. On April 10, 1940, they waxed "W.P.A. Blues," a searing if swinging indictment of the popular **Great Depression**-era Work Projects Administration (WPA). In contrast to "Old Folks," both the words and the delivery leave no doubt as to how they and many others felt about the efficacy of the WPA. (The agency had been the subject of a sharply critical Senate report in 1939, with the result that the WPA appropriation was severely cut and many projects either curtailed or abolished.)

Purists have tended to consider the Mills Brothers' smooth, close harmony style closer to the white popular tradition than to jazz. However, on "W.P.A.," as well as previous recordings such as "Tiger Rag" and "Nobody's Sweetheart" (both 1931), the group made inventive use of jazz techniques such as **scat singing.** After "W.P.A." and the **American Federation of Musicians** strike, the Mills Brothers 1943 hit "Paper Doll" sold some 6 million records. Father Mills retired in 1957, but the three brothers continued into the 1970s.

"Mining Camp Blues." By **Trixie Smith;** rec. mid-February 1925 in New York City with vocalist Trixie Smith and her Down Home Syncopators; CD #36. Armstrong accompanied numerous blues singers during the 1920s, and three were named Smith (**Bessie Smith, Clara Smith,** and Trixie Smith—none related). Trixie Smith's light, high, wobbly voice can best be compared to **Ma Rainey**'s, as jazz writer Mait Edey has pointed out. "She has Ma Rainey's faults without Ma's depth" (Williams, 1962, p. 110). Nevertheless, Smith did some memorable work with Armstrong, mostly on her own compositions.

Minnelli, Vincente (1910–1986). See ***Cabin in the Sky.***

"Minnetonka." See **"By the Waters of Minnetonka."**

Minnie the Moocher. See ***Swing Wedding/ Minnie the Moocher's Wedding Day.***

"Mississippi Basin." By Andy Razaf and Reginald Foresythe; rec. April 24, 1933, in Chicago by Louis Armstrong and His Orchestra; CDs #12 and #18. This and other numbers such as "Dusky Stevedore" date from a period when **Victor Records** tried to reach white audiences with songs about happy black folk. Here Armstrong sings: "Even though the work was heavy/I was happy on da levee./Goin' to take my rightful place on that Mississippi Basin." Before and after singing these regrettable lyrics, however, Armstrong does some mighty trumpet playing.

"Misto Cristofo Columbo." By Jay Livingston and Ray Evans; rec. between December 1 and 13, 1950, in Los Angeles with a studio orchestra. This attractive song becomes a big production number in the 1951 **movie *Here Comes the Groom,*** when Armstrong and friends perform it on a Paris-to-New York airplane.

"Mm-mm." By M. Napoleon, G. Sitto, and J. Roy; rec. April 25, 1955, in New York City by **Louis Armstrong and the All Stars;** CD #8. This is one of several flirtatious duets that Armstrong sang with **Velma Middleton.** He also does a sparkling trumpet solo.

Mobutu, Joseph (1930–1997). See **Congo.**

"moldy fig." This derogatory term was coined in a letter to the editor in the June 1945 ***Esquire*** to tag jazz traditionalists, as opposed to the growing number of **bop** fans. The hapless Armstrong was caught in the middle, having inspired the energetic young artists (e.g., **Dizzy Gillespie**) but not particularly liking what he repeatedly called their "jujitsu music." The controversy was more hype than real, having been fueled as a promotional tactic by Armstrong's manager **Joe Glaser. All Star** bassist **Arvell Shaw** put it well when he said that the controversy was basically fabricated. Jazz writers "created that thing for publicity just to have something to write about" (Berrett, 1999, pp. 167–168).

"Moments to Remember." By Al Stillman and Robert Allen; rec. September 8, 1955, in Los Angeles with the Benny Carter Orchestra. Armstrong and the ensemble turn out an excellent recording of this brand-new song, but it was The Four Lads who made it a hit.

"Monday Date, A." By **Earl Hines** and Sid Robin; rec. June 27, 1928, in Chicago by Louis Armstrong and His **Hot Five,** and on April 25, 1939, in New York City by Louis Armstrong and His Orchestra; CDs #6, #10, #13, #48, #52, and #61. This song received its title, so the story goes, when Armstrong and Hines were discussing upcoming engagements, and the latter reminded the former about their next one, which was on a Monday. In the original version, we hear Hines on solo piano, then Armstrong interrupting with a chiding request to let the rest of the band join in, and he makes a reference to Mrs. Searcy, Hines's Chicago bootlegger. Armstrong's vocal chorus with Hines and his clarion trumpet sound make up for an otherwise ragged ensemble.

"Money Blues." By Dave Leader, G.M. Coleman, and Harry Eller; rec. May 19, 1925, in New York City by **Fletcher Henderson** and His Orchestra. See additional comments on "Alabamy Bound."

"Mooche, The." By Irving Mills and **Duke Ellington;** rec. April 4, 1961, in New York City by **Louis Armstrong and the All Stars** with Duke Ellington; CD #11. The ensemble gives this 1925 song a pensive performance. Armstrong takes an inventive if subdued low-register solo, as do trombonist **Trummy Young** and former Ellington clarinetist **Barney Bigard.** Ellington scholar Stanley Dance (who was at the session) reports that Young remarked of Armstrong's playing: "Even when he's blowing softly, that's a big tone!" (2000, p. 5). See additional comments on "Azalea."

"Mood Indigo." By **Duke Ellington,** Irving Mills, and **Barney Bigard;** rec. April 4, 1961, in New York City by **Louis Armstrong and the All Stars** with Duke Ellington, and May 26, 1970, in New York City with a studio ensemble conducted by Oliver Nelson; CDs #11, #17, #28, and #31. There is so much to like in this interpretation of the 1931 masterpiece—the meditative tempo, Armstrong's bemused delivery of the text, his **scat** accompaniment to **Trummy Young**'s trombone solo, and Ellington's elfin light piano. It's especially attractive when placed next to the noisy, cluttered, and extroverted recording made with a studio orchestra nearly a decade later.

"Moon River." By **Johnny Mercer** and Henry Mancini; rec. April 18, 1964, in New York City by **Louis Armstrong and the All Stars;** CD #40. It took Armstrong a little longer than usual to cover one of the big hits of the day, but it was worth the wait for this 1961 Oscar and Grammy Award winner from the movie *Breakfast at Tiffany's.*

"Moon Song." By Arthur Johnston and Sam Coslow; rec. October 14, 1957, in Los Angeles with the **Oscar Peterson** Quartet; CD #37. Armstrong was so pleased with this old Kate Smith song (1932) and with the Peterson rhythm section that, according to **Leonard Feather,** he extended his trumpet solo to two choruses (Feather, 1997, p. 5). See additional comments on "Blues in the Night."

"Moonlight in Vermont." By Karl Suessdorf and John Blackburn; rec. August 16, 1956, in Los Angeles with vocalist **Ella Fitzgerald** and the **Oscar Peterson** Quartet; CD #9. See comments on "April in Paris."

Moore, Russell "Big Chief" (1912–1983). This Native American, born in Arizona of the Pima tribe, was taught trombone by his uncle in Chicago beginning in 1924, and it was there that he heard Armstrong perform at the **Sunset Cafe.** Moore eventually went to California for additional study and some professional experience (1935–1939), then went to New Orleans. Here he found soul mates in **Papa Celestin, Kid Rena, John Robichaux,** and others who played traditional New Orleans jazz. Moore finally landed in Armstrong's band (1944–1947), during which time he appeared in the film ***New Orleans.*** After an interval of touring and recording with others, he landed in the **All Stars** from 1964 to early 1965, where his Armstrong-influenced style can be heard on numerous recordings, for example, "I Still Get Jealous." "Louis, he's so congenial and so great.... It was beautiful just to be with him," Moore told Ron Welburn in a 1980 interview for the **Institute of Jazz Studies** archive (see transcribed excerpts in Berrett, 1999, pp. 161–163, and in Collier, 1983, p. 160). Evidently, we have Moore to thank for suggesting **Arvell Shaw** to replace a bass player in 1945, and conversely in late 1963, Shaw suggested Moore to replace **Trummy Young.**

"Mop Mop." By **Coleman Hawkins;** rec. January 18, 1944, in New York City with the ***Esquire*** All Star Jazz Band; CDs #2 and #6. This recording was made during the first *Esquire* critics' awards concert at the Metropolitan Opera House, and frankly it's not clear whether or not Armstrong is playing on this particular number. In any case, he kept "Mop Mop" in his repertory, where it was a feature number for his drummer **Sid Catlett.**

Morton, Ferdinand Joseph Le Menthe "Jelly Roll" (1890–1941). The lives of Morton and Armstrong are closely linked. Both were born in New Orleans, albeit eleven years apart; both arrived in Chicago in 1922; and both started recording in 1923 for the same record company, **Gennett.** Morton was the first important jazz composer, just as Armstrong was the first important jazz soloist, and Armstrong played much of Morton's music—such as "Froggie Moore Rag" (1908), "Wolverine Blues" (1915–1916), and "Milenberg Joys" (1923). Armstrong was also the first player to fully develop the **swing** style of playing, and it seems appropriate that he initially reveals this monumental musical development on "Froggie Moore Rag" (1923). Here Armstrong takes Morton's work and applies to it the basic elements of swing style: the placing of notes just behind or before the beat (usually before), the uneven distribution of notes of equal value, the quiver at the end of longer-held notes, and the continual crescendo and diminuendo. Armstrong's swing style rapidly became a regular feature not only of trumpet playing but of jazz in general, and he thus became the first jazz player whom other players widely imitated.

However, none of this would have happened without Morton, whose achievement was to synthesize ragtime and African American musical styles. In such pieces as "King Porter Stomp" (composed in 1906 but not recorded until 1924), he evolved an ensemble style that provided a context for the three basic ingredients of jazz: solo improvisation, polyphonic improvisation, and variety of texture. Although the recordings of Jelly Roll Morton and his Red Hot Peppers sound stiff in comparison to those made simultaneously by **King Oliver**'s Creole Jazz Band (featuring Armstrong), Morton earned a prominent place in the pantheon of jazz.

Morton is sometimes credited with

having made the first interracial recording (with the New Orleans Rhythm Kings in 1923), although it wasn't a true collaboration but rather soloist Morton accompanied by a mixed band. On Armstrong's 1929 recording of "Knockin' a Jug," however, there is a free and equal exchange of musical ideas among black and white musicians. Morton also claimed to have been using **scat** in 1906 and 1907, predating Armstrong's 1926 "Heebie Jeebies," but Armstrong had never been credited with inventing scat, just having made the first *successful* scat recording. ("Heebie Jeebies" became the **Hot Five**'s first big hit, selling 40,000 copies in a few weeks, at a time when selling 5,000 copies of a record was excellent and 10,000 was astounding.) Morton and Armstrong are listed as co-composers of "Wild Man Blues" (1927), though Armstrong said he did not write it by himself, and he never could figure out how they could have written it together, since, as he remembered: "I never had a conversation with him until 1936; guess he was working for the publisher at the time" (Albertson, 1978, p. 36). This statement sounds like the two did not get along well, but, according to **Zutty Singleton,** in the 1920s Morton used to drop by the Armstrong house in Chicago, where **Lil** had a brand new baby grand piano. "Jelly sat down at that piano and really gave us a serenade. He played and played, and after each number he'd turn around on that stool and tell us how he wrote each number and where it came from. It was a real lecture, just for the benefit of me and Lil and Louis" (Shapiro and Hentoff, 1955, p. 95).

Morton suffered from not having white management in a white man's show business world. He was eclipsed by more exciting new performers in the 1930s, until ethnomusicologist Alan Lomax recorded a series of interviews in 1938 that revived public interest. Morton revealed himself to be an articulate historian and critic, and soon he was back in the recording studio for several sessions in 1939–1940. Unfortunately, the revival of his career was curtailed by failing health. Lomax published a biography of Morton in 1950, which Armstrong favorably reviewed in the *New York Times Book Review* (June 18, 1950, sec. 7, pp. 3, 19). "It is one of the finest stories ever written," wrote Armstrong.

mouthpiece. There are fourteen mostly custom-made mouthpieces in the **Louis Armstrong House and Archives** collection. Most are by Robert Giardinelli of New York. There are also a Parduba Harry James model, a Schilke, a Holton 28, a LeBlanc stock 7C, and two by Al Cass. Several are gold-plated, and several have Louis's name engraved on the outside of the rim. Those that show evidence of greatest use—that is, the metal is well worn at the point where it's inserted into the trumpet—have thick rims, shallow cups, and a large backbore. These specifications accommodated the serious **lip problems** that Armstrong had developed from years of strenuous playing with a faulty **embouchure.**

movies. From the late 1930s on, Armstrong was one of very few African Americans to appear regularly in Hollywood films. He could always be counted on to enliven a movie, and he saved some (such as ***Atlantic City,*** 1944, and ***The Beat Generation,*** 1959) from oblivion. He appeared in twenty-eight full-length films, plus several short features, from 1931 to 1969, and the various roles he played—from Gabe in ***Going Places*** (1938) to himself in ***Hello Dolly!*** (1969)—contribute to the history of the African American in cinema. The Armstrong movies also stand as a history of the struggle to win respect for jazz, along with the corollary themes of classical music versus jazz, and new jazz versus old jazz. ***New Orleans*** (1947), ***High Society*** (1956), ***Paris Blues*** (1961), and ***A Man Called Adam*** (1966) document the acceptance of jazz as legitimate musical expression. The money was good, too: $7,500 for ***Cabin in the Sky*** (1943), $20,000 for **Louis Armstrong and the All Stars** for seven days' work on ***The Strip*** (1951), $25,000 all to himself for ***Glory Alley*** (1952), and a whopping $50,000 for eleven days' work on ***The Five Pennies*** (1959). See Appendix 3.

mugging. The making of exaggerated comic faces was a show business practice with which Armstrong grew up and which became integral to his performance style. It can readily be seen in his **movies.** From ***København, Kalundborg Og?*** (1933) to ***Hello Dolly!*** (1969), he engagingly widens and rolls his eyes, raises and lowers his eyebrows, makes his lips tremble, and crinkles his nose—all in the service of expressing a song's lyric. In retrospect, Armstrong can be seen as having perfected a comic art that Gary Giddins aptly compares to Jack Benny's deadpan, Oliver Hardy's slow burn, or Cary Grant's second take (1988, p. 111). However, in his day a younger generation of performers (**Dizzy Gillespie,** Charlie Parker, Thelonious Monk, and others) found mugging objectionable at best. In comparison to sophisticated African American actors (such as Dorothy Dandridge and Sidney Poitier) and musicians such as (Billy Eckstine and Nat "King" Cole), Armstrong was perceived by many to be playing the outdated Negro clown. Today, however, Armstrong's signature mugging can be appreciated as another aspect of his eagerness to entertain.

"Muggles." By Louis Armstrong; rec. December 7, 1928, in Chicago by Louis Armstrong and His Orchestra; CDs #10, #30, and #48. Here is another masterpiece from the amazing year in which he also made "West End Blues," "Fireworks," "Basin Street Blues," "St. James Infirmary," "No One Else But You," and "Tight Like This." "Muggles" (a nickname for **marijuana**) progresses in an unusual way as a succession of slow blues solos. When it's Armstrong's turn, he doubles the speed and reduces the melody to basically one note ("C"). If a partial definition of art is doing a lot with a little, here is a prime example. As the piece unfolds, Armstrong plays a series of intricate rhythmic inventions, then descends into the original blues tempo and closes with a series of passionate blue notes. "Muggles" is a favorite among many Armstrong fans, such as Gunther Schuller, who calls it "one of his greatest flights of imagination" (1968, p. 127). Armstrong's solo has been a strong influence on trumpet players and transcribed numerous times (e.g., Castle, vol. 1, p. 2, and Feather, 1965, p. 217).

Muranyi, Joseph Paul "Joe" (b. 1928). Having worked with many prominent **Dixieland** groups (including one of his own) after being discharged from a U.S. Air Force band, Joe Muranyi was a natural choice to replace **Buster Bailey** as a member of **Louis Armstrong and the All Stars** from mid-1967 to the end in

1971. His amiable clarinet obbligatos can be heard on numerous recordings, example, the 1968 *Disney Songs the Satchmo Way* (CD #15). After it was all over, Muranyi continued playing and singing with many groups (e.g., the World's Greatest Jazz Band in 1975). He also worked as a producer for several record companies. On the 1989 video ***Satchmo: Louis Armstrong,*** Muranyi, seated in the Armstrong living room in **Corona,** gives an affectionate on-camera interview.

Murrow, Edward R. See ***Satchmo the Great.***

"Music Goes 'round and Around, The." By Red Hodgson, Ed Farley, and Mike Riley; rec. January 18, 1936, in New York City by Louis Armstrong and His Orchestra; CD #51. This No. 1 novelty song of 1935 was introduced by the Farley-Riley band and quickly covered by Tommy Dorsey, Hal Kemp, and many others. It was also featured in numerous **movies,** for example, *Holiday in Mexico* (1946) and ***Pennies from Heaven*** (1936). Armstrong takes it at a relaxed **swing** tempo, offering two cheerful choruses and some clever metrical play.

"Muskrat Ramble." By Louis Armstrong but claimed by **Edward "Kid" Ory;** rec. February 26, 1926, in Chicago by Louis Armstrong and His **Hot Five;** CDs #1, #2, #6, #8, #10, #13, #25, #44, #52, #54, #59, and #60. The "B" side of "Heebie Jeebies," this was also a hit and has since become a traditional jazz standard. Armstrong is more an ensemble member than a soloist here. He misses a chord change in his solo, and some commentators have chalked such clinkers up to the Hot Five's growing pains. The piece is really a showcase for trombonist Ory, who does some virtuosic scale work and energetic glissandos. "Muskrat Ramble" is one of the many pieces that Armstrong wrote and allowed others to claim. As he told Dan Morgenstern in 1965: "Ory named it, he gets the royalties. I don't talk about it" (Morgenstern, 1965, p. 15). Nevertheless, Armstrong adopted "Muskrat Ramble" and went on to record it over forty times.

"Mutiny in the Nursery." By Harry Warren and **Johnny Mercer;** rec. September 1938 in Los Angeles with a studio orchestra. This big production number from the 1938 **movie *Going Places*** is set in a mansion garden and is introduced by Maxine Sullivan, who sings from a balcony. Armstrong and his band join in, as gradually do the Dandridge Sisters, Etta Jones, and some extras. The high-spirited song features some delightful wordplay on nursery rhymes (e.g., "Little Bo Peep"). Armstrong and Sullivan built a routine out of this sequence as the opening number for the fall 1939 **Cotton Club** revue. Every night for six months the film sequence was projected on a paper screen through which Armstrong and Sullivan burst.

"My Bucket's Got a Hole in It." By **Clarence Williams;** rec. April 26 or 27, 1950, in New York City by **Louis Armstrong and the All Stars;** CDs #6, #8, #19, #20, #22, #23, #28, #46, #55, #61, and #63. Armstrong probably first heard this soulful number as a little boy while standing outside **Funky Butt Hall,** the famous New Orleans honky-tonk. It was one of his lifelong favorites, and he regularly featured it on All Stars programs. As evidenced by this recording, he liked to take it at the slow, grinding tempo at which Funky Butt patrons did their overtly sexual dancing. Here trombonist **Jack Teagarden** takes an appealing vocal and instrumental solo, he and Armstrong do a little verbal bantering, and Armstrong leads the ensemble out with some of his most memorable trumpet work. In addition to playing up there in the stratosphere, he defies tempo and meter by pushing and pulling the beat with complete authority.

"My Darling Nellie Gray." By B.R. Hanby; rec. April 7, 1937, in New York City with the **Mills Brothers.** This poignant song about a female slave sold from her Kentucky plantation home is one of the best collaborations between Armstrong and the Mills Brothers. Jazz scholar James Lincoln Collier was so moved by Armstrong's performance in one brief passage (specifically an ascending and descending figure in measures four to six) that he called it "a gem, modest and unassuming as wild flowers in a milk bottle on a country kitchen table" (1983, p. 292). See additional comments on "Carry Me Back to Old Virginny."

"My Dream Man." By F. Dale; rec. November 10 or 11, 1924, in New York City by **Fletcher Henderson** and His Orchestra. See comments on "Alabamy Bound."

"My Heart." By **Lil Hardin Armstrong;** rec. November 12, 1925, in Chicago by Louis Armstrong and His **Hot Five;** CD #10. This is the very first of over five dozen Hot Five/**Hot Seven** recordings that would profoundly influence the development of jazz. Although one of the most pervasive of these influences has been Armstrong's gradual creation of the soloist, the basic texture here is that of the ensemble. Armstrong takes several breaks, however, and generally provides a strong lead.

"My John Blues." By Edgar Dowell; rec. April 2, 1925, in New York City with vocalist **Clara Smith,** trombonist **Charlie Green,** and pianist **Fletcher Henderson;** CD #36. An earlier recording of this blues number (January 17, 1925) was rejected and never released, but the remake survives, perhaps because Green was added to the ensemble. Armstrong generally stays in the background, where he does some deft plunger work. See additional comments on "Broken Busted Blues."

"My Man." By Channing Pollock and Maurice Yvain; rec. July 1965 in Hollywood by **Louis Armstrong and the All Stars;** CD #2. This up-tempo rhythm and blues number featured vocalist **Jewel Brown,** who can be seen and heard performing it in the 1965 TV concert film ***Solo.***

"My Old Kentucky Home." By Stephen Foster; rec. between September 30 and October 2, 1959, in Los Angeles by **Louis Armstrong and the All Stars.** This evergreen dates from 1853. See additional comments on "Carry Me Back to Old Virginny."

"My One and Only Love." By Guy Wood and Robert Mellin; rec. May 26, 1970, in New York City with a studio orchestra conducted by Oliver Nelson; CD #31. Although more than a little on the cornball side (the strings are too heavy and the solo flute annoying), this performance is nevertheless touching. **Frank Sinatra** introduced the song in 1953.

"My Rose Marie." By Ray Henderson, Bud DeSylva, and R. King; rec. between October 10 and 13, 1924, in New York City by **Fletcher Henderson** and His Orchestra. See comments on "Alabamy Bound."

"My Sweet." By **Hoagy Carmichael** and Stuart Gorrell; rec. April 5, 1930, in New York City by Louis Armstrong and His Orchestra; CDs #42 and #48. Several commentators have pointed out the influence of Al Jolson on Armstrong's singing style here (e.g., Jones and Chilton, p. 268), but the magnificent trumpet playing and dramatic high "E-flat" he plays at the end ("F" above high "C" on his "B-flat" trumpet) are all his own. Armstrong seems to be working hard to carry along the lagging band, but he gets some assistance from not one but two excellent pianists, Joe Turner and **Buck Washington.** See additional comments on "Ev'ntide."

"My Sweet Hunk o' Trash." By James Johnson and Flourney Miller; rec. September 30, 1949, in New York City with vocalist **Billie Holiday** and the **Sy Oliver** Orchestra. Holiday openly acknowledged her debt to Armstrong, and the admiration was mutual. Three years before this recording, Armstrong wrote to a friend about their work together in the **movie** ***New Orleans.*** Holiday is "my sweetheart in the picture," he brags. "Ump Ump Ump. Now isn't that something? The great Billy [*sic*] Holiday, my sweetheart? (Berrett, 1999, p. 130). By the time of this recording, Holiday was suffering from the effects of a deteriorating private life, and in 1947 she was jailed briefly on drug charges.

"My Walking Stick." By **Irving Berlin;** rec. June 13, 1938, in New York City with the **Mills Brothers** and guitarist Norman Brown. This song was one of twenty in the 1938 movie *Alexander's Ragtime Band.* See additional comments on "Carry Me Back to Old Virginny."

Myles, Clarence. See **Armstrong, Clarence Myles Hatfield.**

Myles, Flora. Flora was Armstrong's mother's second cousin, one of the seven children of "Uncle" **Isaac Myles.** When Myles's wife died, Armstrong admired how he took charge of the children. "They were about as worthless as any kids I have ever seen, but we grew up together just the same," he later wrote in his **autobiography** (1954, p. 19). Flora, the youngest, became involved with an older white man and had an illegitimate child (**Clarence Myles Hatfield Armstrong**) on August 8, 1915. She died shortly after childbirth, and Armstrong used to help with babysitting. On one occasion he was distracted, playing records with his girlfriend **Daisy Parker,** and Clarence slipped from the porch and landed one story down on his head. The terrified Armstrong rushed him to a doctor who said that Clarence would never be quite the same. Later, when Armstrong was established in Chicago, he sent for Clarence, whom he adopted and provided for all his life.

Myles, Isaac "Ike." Armstrong's extended family included his Uncle Ike, a cousin of his mother's, who as a widower was spread pretty thin with seven children of his own, one of whom was **Flora.** This large family apparently lived with **Mayann,** Louis, and **Mama Lucy,** keeping to one side of the house. Armstrong remembered Uncle Ike as a good father whose stevedore job was irregular but who still "managed to keep the kids eating and put clean shirts on their backs. . . . God bless Uncle Ike." He further explained that "when Mayann got the urge to go out on the town we might not see her for days and days. When this happened she always dumped us into Uncle Ike's lap" (***Satchmo,*** 1954, p. 19).

N

Nacht vor der Premiere, Die. In his European films (***La botta e risposta, Kaerlighedens Melodi, La route du bonheur,*** and others), Armstrong frequently plays the role of a famous visiting entertainer whose presence insures the success of a musical endeavor. In this German production, a vehicle for the singer-dancer Marika Rökk, he and the **All Stars** appear three times, performing the Lothar Ollas/Hans Bradtke song "Kisses in the Night." Real Film GmbH, 1959; color; 96 mins.; Dir. Georg Jacoby.

Napoleon, Marty. (Matthew Napoli) (b. 1921). Marty Napoleon at first wanted to play trumpet like his Uncle Phil, but heart problems caused him to follow his older brother, Teddy, on the piano. Before he turned to small-group traditional jazz in 1945, he briefly replaced his brother in the Gene Krupa band. Napoleon played with **Louis Armstrong and the All Stars** from early 1952 to early 1953, returning in 1966 to stay until the end in 1971. During his first tour of duty, he left his mark on such fine recordings as "Kiss of Fire." Later, he is featured in "Mame" and "Tin Roof Blues" (both 1966). Napoleon reminisces warmly about Armstrong in the 1989 video ***Satchmo: Louis Armstrong***.

"Nashville Woman's Blues." By Fred Longshaw; rec. May 26, 1925, in New York City with vocalist **Bessie Smith,** trombonist **Charlie Green,** and the composer at the piano; CD #36. See comment on "Careless Love Blues."

"Naturally." By Harry Barris and Joe McCarthy; rec. June 24, 1938, in New York City by Louis Armstrong and His Orchestra. Armstrong always stuck close to the melody, even when it wasn't a very good one, in which case he would supply liberal amounts of accent displacement, vibrato, and other techniques. "Naturally" gets this treatment, and it's especially effective in the second half of the last chorus, where the written rhythmic pattern is repeated several times. Armstrong plays each one slightly differently, taking them off the page and getting them to **swing.**

"Naughty Man." By **Don Redman** and Cliff Dixon; rec. November 7, 1924, in New York City by **Fletcher Henderson** and His Orchestra; CD #48. Armstrong gets a brief moment of solo time here, but it sparkles compared to the performances of the other two soloists (trombonist **Charlie Green** and the young **Cole-**

man Hawkins). See additional comments on "Alabamy Bound."

"Nearness of You, The." By **Hoagy Carmichael** and Ned Washington; rec. August 16, 1956, in Los Angeles with vocalist **Ella Fitzgerald** and the **Oscar Peterson** Quartet; CD #9. See comments on "April in Paris" and "Ev'ntide."

"Never Saw a Better Day." By Hal Stanley and Irving Taylor; rec. August 1, 1956, in Los Angeles with Hall Mooney's Orchestra; CD #12. This recording was made for the NBC **television** musical ***"The Lord Don't Play Favorites,"*** in which Armstrong had an acting role as the leader of a circus band. Although not exactly the light, agile **All Stars,** the Mooney band (with trumpeter Manny Klein, drummer Irv Cottler, and pianist Gerry Wiggins) provides a marvelous big band sound. The ninety-minute show was aired on NBC on September 17, 1956. See also "Rain, Rain."

New Cotton Club. See **Sebastian's New Cotton Club.**

New Orleans. **Billie Holiday** plays a maid to Dorothy Patrick, an aspiring opera singer, in this movie that opens in the title city in 1917. Patrick is entranced by the new rhythmic music called jazz and gets Holiday to take her to a **Storyville** club, where she finds her opera coach listening to none other than Armstrong. The film is loaded with other first-rate musicians, including **Kid Ory, Barney Bigard, Charlie Beal, Red Callender,** and **Zutty Singleton.** Although Armstrong holds a cornet in the film, a trumpet is heard on "Where the Blues Were Born," "Mahogany Hall Stomp," "Endie," and "Do You Know What It Means to Miss New Orleans?"—a song that became an Armstrong staple. McCarthyism came to Hollywood during the making of this film, and as a result the studio shifted the focus from the talented African American musicians who had created jazz to the white actors who treated it as an ornament to their rather silly lives. Life imitated art in one respect, though. Armstrong's magnetic success with the small band attracted the attention of promoters, and within months of the film's release, the fantastically successful **Carnegie Hall** and **Town Hall concerts** took place. **Louis Armstrong and the All Stars** was thus born, and Armstrong's career received a much-needed boost. As the later ***High Society*** (1956), ***Paris Blues*** (1961), and ***A Man Called Adam*** (1966), this film contributed to the legitimacy of jazz. United Artists, 1947; B&W; 90 mins.; Dir. Arthur Lubin.

"New Orleans Function." By W.C. Handy; rec. April 26 or 27, 1950, in New York City by **Louis Armstrong and the All Stars;** CDs #8, #52, and #61. Here Armstrong plays a traditional medley ("Flee as a Bird" and "Oh, Didn't He Ramble?"), which he often both heard and performed at funerals in New Orleans.

"New Orleans Stomp." By Louis Armstrong and **Lil Hardin Armstrong;** rec. April 22, 1927, with **Johnny Dodds**'s Black Bottom Stompers; CD #10. See comments on "The Blues Stampede."

"New Tiger Rag, The." By Nick La Rocca; rec. March 11, 1932, in Chicago by Louis Armstrong and His Orchestra. Armstrong thrived on competition, and this recording of a revised version of "Tiger

Rag" (1917) provides a good example. He takes the number at a dizzying tempo, which he jokes is necessary in order to catch the tiger. As in "Dinah" and other numbers, he makes it seem even faster than it is by gracefully playing just a few long notes very slowly. Chorus after chorus fly by, and at the climax he plays a series of high "Cs" (on occasion he would play as many as 200), topping it off by climbing to high "F."

Newman, Paul. (b. 1925). See ***Paris Blues.***

Newport Jazz Festival. Begun in 1954, the Newport Jazz Festival in Rhode Island was the oldest annual jazz event in the United States. (The **Nice Jazz Festival** began in 1948.) Founded by the wealthy Lorillard family, it represented the acceptance of jazz by an affluent white audience. The summertime Festival became a showcase for Armstrong, perhaps because its run usually included what was thought to be his July 4 **birthday.** It was given a boost in 1956 by the movie ***High Society,*** in which Armstrong figures prominently. Also in 1956 Armstrong did a **Voice of America** broadcast from the Festival. During the 1957 Festival, he uncharacteristically put his foot down and refused to perform at a concert in his honor unless his singer, **Velma Middleton,** was restored to the lineup. However, things went smoother the following year, and the good vibes are palpable in a documentary titled ***Jazz on a Summer's Day,*** which critic **Pauline Kael** calls "one of the most pleasurable of all concert films" (p. 379). Four films, ***Anatomy of a Performance, Trumpet Players' Tribute, The Antiquarians,*** and ***Finale,*** were made in connection with the 1970 Festival, which was billed "A Tribute to Louis Armstrong." It turned out to be Armstrong's last Festival. In any case, because of a riot at the Festival in 1971, it was moved to New York the following year, and as the 1970s unfolded, "Newport Jazz Festival" events took place in other cities as well. The name was changed to the Kool Jazz Festival in the early 1980s to reflect its tobacco company sponsor and, when an electronics corporation jumped in, to the JVC Jazz Festival/New York in 1986.

Nice Jazz Festival. The Nice Jazz Festival, founded in 1948 by **Hugues Panassié** and the **Hot Club de France,** has the distinction of being the first international jazz festival. Armstrong, the Club's honorary president from 1936 to 1971, began the festivities. Armstrong returned often to Nice, where, as all across France, he felt very welcome. In 1974, in the presence of **Lucille Armstrong** and Princess Grace of Monaco (Grace Kelly), a bust of Armstrong was dedicated in Nice's Jardins de Cimiez.

Nicholas, Albert (1900–1973). One of the great New Orleans clarinetists (such as **Sidney Bechet, Barney Bigard, Johnny Dodds,** Sam Dutrey, **Jimmy Noone,** and **Alphonse Picou),** Nicholas did not leave with the diaspora of African American musicians following the **Storyville** closure by the U.S. Navy in 1917. Instead, he tended the jazz flame at **Tom Anderson**'s cabaret and elsewhere, before finally joining his friends in Chicago in 1924. He worked with **King Oliver** for two years; then in 1927 he toured the East Indies, Java, and the Middle East, spending a year in Cairo. Back in Chicago, he joined the **Luis Russell** band, which frequently backed Armstrong. (The presence of so many New Orleans–

born and-bred musicians in this ensemble must have made Armstrong feel comfortable.) Nicholas was there for the 1929 recording of "I Can't Give You Anything But Love," with which Armstrong first reached a mass audience. Nicholas here plays alto saxophone and unobtrusively blends in with the other two section players, as he does in "Mahogany Hall Stomp" from the same session. However, he can be heard loudly and clearly on clarinet in "St. Louis Blues" (1929, but not discovered until the 1990s), when he takes a beguiling, nimble-tipsy chorus in the high range. Nicholas was again in the Luis Russell band backing Armstrong in 1937–1939 for recordings of "Public Melody Number One," "The Skeleton in the Closet," "Jeepers Creepers," and many others.

Nicholas also worked with Chick Webb and **Rex Stewart** (with whom he recorded a classic solo on "Basin Street Blues" in 1953) and led his own groups. From the 1950s on he lived in Europe but returned for occasional engagements.

Nichols, Ernest Loring "Red" (1905–1965). See ***The Five Pennies.***

nicknames. At the beginning of his life Armstrong acquired the moniker **"Little Louis,"** in the middle he was known as "Pops" (which he turned around and used on countless others, young and old), and in later years **"Ambassador Satch."** Writing some informal memoirs in a hospital bed in 1969, Armstrong remembered "some Nick Names that very few fans, I doubt ever heard of. Such as—*Boat Nose*—Hammock Face—*Rhythm Jaws*" (Brothers, p. 21). Many of his nicknames affectionately referred to his mouth size—"Gatemouth," **"Dippermouth,"** and "Satchelmouth." His most famous and enduring nickname was acquired on arriving in **England** for his first tour abroad in 1932. He was met by Percy Brooks of ***Melody Maker*** magazine, who, nervously contracting "Satchelmouth," said "Hello, **Satchmo!**" Armstrong liked the name so much that he used it in the title of the second volume of his **autobiography.** He also had it inscribed on at least two of his **trumpets** and printed on his stationery.

"Night before Christmas, The." Armstrong made his last recording at home in **Corona** on February 26, 1971. He neither sang nor played the trumpet, but did a poignant reading of Clement Moore's classic Christmas poem (CD #7).

Night before the Premiere, The. See ***Nacht vor der Premiere, Die.***

Nkrumah, Kwame (1909–1972). See **Ghana.**

"No (Papa, No)." By **Victoria Spivey;** rec. December 4, 1928, in Chicago by Louis Armstrong and His Orchestra; CDs #10 and #30. This number marks a technical landmark in that recording engineers were finally able to include full percussion. On this blues number, Armstrong's fellow soloists are undistinguished, but he is in excellent form.

"No One Else But You." By **Don Redman;** rec. on December 5, 1928, in Chicago by Louis Armstrong and **His Savoy Ballroom Five;** CDs #10 and #30. This is another masterpiece from 1928, that incredible year during which Armstrong recorded "Basin Street Blues," "Save It, Pretty Mama," "St. James Infirmary," "West End Blues," and other gems. Don

Redman must take a good deal of the credit for "No One Else," not only for creating an excellent tune but also for skillfully arranging it so that both Armstrong and pianist **Earl Hines** get the spotlight.

"No Time." Rec. December 18, 1967, in New York City by **Louis Armstrong and the All Stars,** trumpeter **Clark Terry,** and others.

"No Variety Blues." By Louis Armstrong and Herman Fairbanks; rec. April 27, 1946, in New York City by Louis Armstrong and His Orchestra; CD #12. This number is distinguished by the great chemistry between Armstrong and his singer **Velma Middleton.**

"Nobody Knows the Trouble I've Seen." Traditional; rec. June 14, 1938, in New York City with the **Decca** Mixed Choir conducted by Lyn Murray, and on February 4, 1958, in New York City by **Louis Armstrong and the All Stars** and the **Sy Oliver** Choir; CDs #27, #46, and #59. Armstrong wisely doesn't try to make this spiritual **swing** (as he did so successfully the previous month with "When the Saints Go Marching In"). In the second recording his approach is more friendly than preachy.

"Nobody Knows the Way I Feel This Morning." By Tom Delaney and Pearl Delaney; rec. December 22, 1924, in New York City with vocalist **Josephine Beatty** and the Red Onion Jazz Babies; CDs #35 and #36. See comments on "Early Every Morn."

"Nobody's Sweetheart." By Elmer Schoebel, Ernie Erdman, Gus Kahn, and Billy Meyers; rec. December 21, 1932, in Camden, New Jersey, by Louis Armstrong and His Orchestra; CDs #12, #21, and #24. Armstrong does a one-chorus version of this number, along with "You Rascal, You" and "Sleepy Time Down South," as part of a medley of hits.

"Nomad." By **Dave Brubeck** and Iola Brubeck; rec. September 19, 1961, in New York City by **Louis Armstrong and the All Stars,** pianist Dave Brubeck, and guests; CD #50. This is one of many songs from the jazz oratorio ***The Real Ambassadors*** for which there was no room on the 1961 LP but which happily was included on the 1994 CD reissue. Armstrong confidently sings a piece that he must have just learned, and he takes a fine middle-range trumpet solo. See additional comments on "Cultural Exchange."

Noone, Jimmie (or Jimmy) (1895–1944). The outstanding New Orleans clarinetist was similar to many other musicians of his time and place in that he, too, migrated from New Orleans to Chicago after the closing of **Storyville** in 1917. Before leaving, though, he, along with the rest of **Joe Oliver**'s band, made a deep impression on Armstrong, who wrote more than forty years later that the members of that band "have become legendary in music. The world will never be able to replace them, and I say that from the bottom of my heart" (***Satchmo,*** 1954, p. 96).

Although they grew up together musically, Armstrong and Noone collaborated very little in the recording studio. There was the one occasion in October 1923 when Oliver had to replace **Johnny Dodds** with Noone, and the only other time was in June 1928, when Armstrong used Noone for a set of four accompaniments for singer **Lillie Delk Christian.** Because of Christian's singing style, the result sounds campy by today's standards, although the band is engagingly nimble. Noone was at the time leading his own group at the Apex Club and made some now-classic recordings.

Except for brief trips to New York, Noone stayed in Chicago. He participated in the New Orleans revival movement in the 1940s, working with **Kid Ory, Zutty Singleton, Jack Teagarden,** and others on the West Coast. His legacy can be found in clarinetist/bandleaders, such as **Benny Goodman,** who literally used to sit at his feet.

"Now Do You Call That a Buddy?" By Wesley Wilson; rec. April 11, 1941, in New York City by Louis Armstrong and His **Hot Seven;** CD #18. Armstrong had a fondness for minor key numbers ("The Beautiful American," "Chim Chim Cheree," "Kiss of Fire," and "Remember Who You Are," for example), and here he ratchets up the intensity with a low-register trumpet solo. His singing is similarly dramatic, but unfortunately the recording quality is inferior.

"Now You Has Jazz." By **Cole Porter;** rec. between January 10 and 18, 1956, in Los Angeles by **Louis Armstrong and the All Stars** with vocalist **Bing Crosby;** CDs #20, #43, #45, #46, and #63. Armstrong performs this clever number as a duet with Bing Crosby in the 1956 **movie *High Society,*** and it's one of the most memorable musical moments in all of cinema. Each of the All Stars is introduced during the course of the performance.

O

"Of All the Wrongs You've Done to Me." By Len Payton, Chris Smith, and Edgar Dowell; rec. November 6, 1924, in New York City with vocalist **Eva Taylor** and **Clarence Williams' Blue Five;** CDs #8, #35, #36, and #52. Although Armstrong mostly supports the singer here, he does play a marvelously inventive syncopated solo with a plunger mute against a **stop-time** background. Armstrong revisited this number in 1957 with the **All Stars,** retaining some of the stop-time rhythm and ending with a graceful cadenza. See additional comments on "Cast Away."

"Oh, Bess, Oh Where's My Bess?" By George Gershwin, DuBose Heyward, and Ira Gershwin; rec. August 18, 1957, but rejected and rerecorded October 14, 1957, in Los Angeles with a studio orchestra conducted by arranger Russell Garcia; CD #9. Armstrong plays a moving solo on this number from Act III of *Porgy and Bess.* See additional comments on "Bess, You Is My Woman Now."

"Oh, Didn't He Ramble?" By W.C. Handy; rec. April 26 or 27, 1950, in New York City by **Louis Armstrong and the All Stars;** CDs #8, #19, #45, #52, #55, and #61. This 1902 song forms part of the funeral medley "New Orleans Function," which begins with the stately, mournful song "Flee as a Bird."

"Oh, Lawd, I'm on My Way." By George Gershwin, DuBose Heyward, and Ira Gershwin; rec. August 18, 1957, in Los Angeles with a studio orchestra and choir conducted by Russell Garcia; CD #9. Armstrong's singing of this last number from *Porgy and Bess* is accompanied by a choir. See additional comments on "Bess, You Is My Woman Now."

Okeh Records. This important record company and label was established in 1918 in New York and three years later set up a **race record** series (called the "Colored Catalog") as separate and distinct from their general popular series (for which **Bix Beiderbecke, Eddie Lang,** and others were recorded). The race series was overseen by Richard M. Jones (a pianist, composer, and arranger) in Chicago and **Clarence Williams** (an accomplished pianist and composer) in New York. In addition to Williams's own **Blue Five,** Okeh also recorded **King Oliver**'s Creole Jazz Band in 1923, Armstrong's **Hot Five** and **Hot Seven** from 1925 to 1929, and many others. Before the race series was discontinued in 1934, nearly a thousand recordings had been issued. The name

Okeh was dropped entirely between 1934 and 1938 while ARC-BRC (a joint venture between American Record Company and Brunswick Record Company) owned the label. CBS revived the name in 1938, however, when they acquired the company, and they used "Okeh" for rhythm and blues recordings.

"Old Folks at Home." By Stephen Foster; rec. June 29, 1937, in New York City with the **Mills Brothers.** This popular 1851 song takes nicely to a **swing** treatment. While the Brothers sing it straight and sweet, Armstrong delivers his lines with a sophisticated wink. For example, after they sing nostalgically about life on the old plantation home, Armstrong conversationally ad-libs: "Well, lookie here—we *are* far away from home.... Yeah man!" Frankly, good riddance to those good old days. See additional comments on "Carry Me Back to Old Virginny."

"Old Man Mose." By Louis Armstrong and **Zilner Randolph;** rec. November 21, 1935, in New York City by Louis Armstrong and His Orchestra; CDs #5, #6, and #51. Along with his "Brother Bill," this lively hit about a dead man was one of Armstrong's most requested songs. It may not be one of his best compositions, but it was one of his personal favorites. He admitted his prejudice about it in a letter to **Leonard Feather:** "Every Old Crow thinks her children are White as Snow" (Brothers, p. 148). In 1936 the French magazine *Jazz-Hot* awarded "Old Man Mose" its Grand Prix for best recording.

"Ole Miss Blues." By W.C. Handy and W. Hirsch; rec. July 12, 1954, in Chicago by **Louis Armstrong and the All Stars;** CDs #38 and #45. This lively instrumental became an All Stars staple. See additional comments on "Atlanta Blues."

Oliver, Joe "King" (1885–1938). After leaving the **Colored Waif's Home** in June 1914, Armstrong came under the influence of Joe Oliver, then considered the best jazz cornetist in New Orleans. Oliver took Armstrong under his wing, offering lessons in exchange for miscellaneous errands. Eventually, he trusted both Armstrong's playing and reliability enough to send him as a substitute. When Oliver left for Chicago in 1918, Armstrong replaced him in **Kid Ory**'s band. Four years later Oliver (now having acquired his royal nickname) summoned Armstrong to play second cornet in his popular Creole Jazz Band.

By all accounts, Oliver was one of the most important New Orleans musicians. He performed regularly with the best of the city's dance and brass bands from around 1907 until his move to Chicago. Unfortunately, this was before the recording era. By 1923 when he finally went into the studio, he was past his prime. What his cornet playing lacked, he made up for in leadership skills, running a tightly disciplined band and developing the distinctive ensemble-style polyphony that is one of the essential ingredients of jazz. He could also take a good solo as well, for example, on "Dippermouth Blues" (1923). As Laurence Gushee points out in his *New Grove Dictionary of Jazz* entry on Oliver, this solo (especially its wa-wa effects) was memorized by many trumpet players who came up in the 1920s and 1930s.

The addition of Armstrong to Oliver's Creole Jazz Band was magic, according to witnesses. The two cornet players together developed a way of playing short, intricate, harmonized solos that sounded improvised. On listening closely, however, one could hear Oliver giving signals in the preceding ensemble chorus. This technique can be heard in "Snake Rag" (1923), one of their first recordings together, in which there are seven such duets. Armstrong's early solos were hardly less exciting, as one can hear in "Chimes Blues" (1923) and especially six months later in "Tears." Both "Snake Rag" and "Chimes Blues" are Oliver tunes, which reveals another facet of his musicianship. (Oliver eventually took credit for forty-nine songs.)

In 1924 Armstrong's new bride, **Lil Hardin,** felt that Oliver was holding her husband back, and she encouraged him to strike out on his own. After Armstrong left Oliver's Creole Jazz Band that year, the two still saw each other occasionally. Oliver reorganized his group as the Dixie Syncopators and moved to New York in 1927. He unwisely declined an offer to work at the **Cotton Club,** thinking the pay too low. (**Duke Ellington** thought otherwise, though, and during the next five years used the venue to establish a national reputation.) Oliver did have a successful if brief run at the **Savoy Ballroom,** after which his band broke up, and he stayed in New York as a freelance player. From 1930 to 1936 he toured as a bandleader in the Midwest and South, but he seldom performed because of tooth and gum problems. He also avoided big cities, fearing to disappoint those who had heard him in better days. He eventually retired from playing and lived out his final days in Savannah, Georgia. Armstrong met up with him there on a 1937 tour through the South. (This was a year after Armstrong dedicated the first volume of his **autobiography,** ***Swing That Music,*** to Oliver.) Seeing Oliver in dire straits, he took up a collection from his band members and, characteristically, contributed most generously himself. This provided only temporary relief, however, and Oliver soon had to give up selling vegetables from a pushcart and take a job, his last, working as a pool hall attendant. Armstrong later worried that Oliver had died of a broken heart.

Looking upon Oliver as a father-figure, Armstrong called him "Papa Joe" in his 1936 autobiography and elsewhere. Armstrong still felt the same way years later, writing from his hospital bed in 1970: "No one has replaced him as yet in my heart" (Brothers, p. 29). In between, Armstrong never tired of expressing his debt to Oliver, for example, in an article titled "Joe Oliver Is Still King" for the July–August 1950 issue of ***The Record Changer*** (Brothers, pp. 37–39). Oliver obviously filled a vacuum created by Armstrong's absentee father. Armstrong once wrote: "I had made up my mind that I would not leave New Orleans unless the King sent for me" (***Satchmo,*** 1954, p. 226). On first arriving in Chicago, Armstrong lived with Oliver and his wife (whom Armstrong called "Mama Stella"). Shortly thereafter, Oliver introduced his protegé to Lil Hardin, who soon became the second Mrs. Armstrong.

Musically the styles of Oliver and Armstrong differ quite a bit. Armstrong played higher, faster, and more inventively. He had little attraction to Oliver's considerable mute technique—for example, using a plunger to get vocal effects (in which Oliver had a successor in Ellington sideman Bubber Miley). Armstrong also played more strongly. On their few recordings together, Oliver aimed directly into the recording horn, while Armstrong had to stand as far back as the room would allow. However, Armstrong incorporated Oliver's policy of, as he later told Dan Morgenstern, "always playing that lead. I used to run all over the horn.... But King Oliver taught me to play that lead" (Miller, p. 97).

While Oliver influenced other trumpet players as well (Johnny Dunn and Bubber Miley, for sure, and probably also **Natty Dominique,** Tommy Ladnier, and **Muggsy Spanier**), his effect on Armstrong went beyond music. During the latter part of his life, Armstrong made collages to decorate reel-to-reel tape boxes and the covers of scrapbooks, revealing a great deal about his personality in the process. These fascinating artworks are housed at the **Louis Armstrong House and Archives,** Queens College. On the first page of one of the larger and more formal scrapbooks (#20, dated 1952) is a photo of Armstrong, surrounded by photos of the faces of jazz players that he admired (**Bix Beiderbecke, Jack Teagarden, Bing Crosby, Bunny Berigan,** Duke Ellington, and others). In the very center of Armstrong's forehead is King Oliver.

It is natural, however, to have mixed feelings even about those whom we admire. The reel-to-reel tapes inside the lovingly decorated boxes contain monologues, conversations, and bits of music recorded in his home in **Corona** from the late 1940s until his death in 1971, and on them Armstrong expresses some criticism of Oliver, whom he came to feel had held him back in the early part of his career. On one tape Armstrong discusses how Lil urged him to leave Oliver. " 'As much as you idolize him, Daddy,' " Armstrong remembers his wife saying, " 'you must leave him immediately, because King Oliver and his ego and wounded vanity may hurt you.' I didn't say or mumble a word," comments Armstrong, astounded that "a thought like that [would be] in King Oliver's mind." Elsewhere on these tapes Armstrong talks about "all that... crap" that Oliver put him through.

Oliver's decline must also have influenced Armstrong's decision to become more of an entertainer than strictly a musician. He saw how sole dependence on trumpet playing would make increasingly difficult physical demands, and he began to sing more in order to give his lip a rest. Beginning in 1928–1929, he became more of a showman who would sing, dance, joke, and perform the latest music. **Joe Glaser** pushed him firmly along this path beginning in the late 1930s, but it was Oliver's demise, his dying in resentful poverty, that must have influenced him as well.

"It is really too bad that the world did not have a chance to dig the real Joe King Oliver and his greatness. His conceptions of things—life, music, people in general were really wonderful," Armstrong later wrote (Miller, p. 13). Oliver has achieved a kind of immortality, however. Most of his recordings are still available, and jazz scholars study them with care. A good book on Oliver is Allen and Rust's 1987 *"King" Oliver.*

Oliver, Melvin James "Sy" (1910–1988). Sy Oliver was a well-seasoned musician by the time he conducted his studio orchestra for Armstrong in the early 1950s. In 1933 he had joined up with Jimmie Lunceford, for whom he wrote arrangements and compositions, played trumpet, and sometimes sang. Good examples of his work are "My Blue Heaven" (1934) and

"Margie" (1938). During this time he also wrote arrangements for **Benny Goodman.** In 1939 he set aside his trumpet and joined the Tommy Dorsey Orchestra as an arranger and singer (e.g., "On the Sunny Side of the Street," 1944). Then after World War II service, he did freelance arranging and in 1946 led his own band and worked as a music director for various record companies. It was in this capacity that Armstrong's manager, **Joe Glaser,** got Oliver and his client together to make some memorable recordings.

While Armstrong made almost all of his public appearances with the **All Stars** from 1947 to 1971, he also recorded with big studio orchestras, such as Oliver's. "La vie en rose" (1950), "I Get Ideas" (1951), "A Kiss to Build a Dream On" (1951), "It Takes Two to Tango" (1952), "Skokiaan" (1954), and "When You're Smiling" (1956) were among their many collaborations, all arranged and conducted by Oliver. If these aim for the widest possible audience, they are nonetheless supremely well executed. Oliver is a master of the brief introduction, smooth transition, uncluttered accompaniment, and glitzy show business ending. He also used some of the very best musicians available, often one of the All Stars, such as pianist **Billy Kyle.**

Oliver continued as a record company music director, and he toured frequently during the 1960s and 1970s. In the 1970s he again took up his trumpet and led a popular New York City nonet, which was still active into the 1980s.

"On a Coconut Island." By R. Alex Anderson; rec. August 18, 1936, in Los Angeles with The Polynesians (a.k.a. Andy Iona and His Islanders). See comments on "Hawaiian Hospitality."

"On a Little Bamboo Bridge." By Al Sherman and Archie Fletcher; rec. March 24, 1937, in New York City with Andy Iona and His Islanders. See comments on "Hawaiian Hospitality."

"On Her Majesty's Secret Service." See **"We Have All the Time in the World."**

On Her Majesty's Secret Service. Armstrong can be heard singing "We Have All the Time in the World" at the beginning and end of this 1969 James Bond movie (starring George Lazenby as 007). He had recently been ill and hospitalized, but in October 1969 he was back in the studio. He sang only, trumpet playing having been strictly forbidden by his doctors. United Artists, 1969; Technicolor; 140 mins.; Dir. Peter Hunt.

"On My Way (Got on My Travelin' Shoes)." By Columbus Chapman and Roy Carroll; rec. February 6, 1958, in New York City by **Louis Armstrong and the All Stars** with the **Sy Oliver** Choir; CDs #9 and #27. Armstrong gives this song an appropriate blues treatment. See additional comments on "Down by the Riverside."

"On the Alamo." By Isham Jones, Gilbert Keyes, and Joe Lyons; rec. June 4, 1965, live at the Palais des Sports in Paris by **Louis Armstrong and the All Stars;** CD #2. This popular 1922 song was a feature number for clarinetist **Eddie Shu.**

On the Frontiers of Jazz. See ***Aux frontières du jazz.***

"On the Sentimental Side." By Johnny Burke and James V. Monaco; rec. May 18, 1938, in New York City by Louis Armstrong and His Orchestra; CD #41. Introduced by vocalist **Bing Crosby** in the 1938 film ***Doctor Rhythm,*** this song, with its sequential eighth notes, is a good example of Armstrong's ability to get unlikely material to **swing.**

"On the Sunny Side of the Street." By Jimmy McHugh and Dorothy Fields; rec. November 7, 1934, in Paris by Louis Armstrong and His Orchestra; CDs #8, #13, #16, #18, #19, #28, #34, #40, #41, #48, #49, #52, #54, #55, #57, and #61. Armstrong featured this popular 1930 number in his repertory long before he finally recorded it, probably because of contract difficulties with **Victor Records.** Fortunately, he finally did on the French Brunswick label, both a vocal and an instrumental version, taking both sides of a ten-inch 78 rpm disc. His singing is sweet and direct, while his trumpet playing is full of clever inventions and builds dramatically to a final high "C."

"On Treasure Island." By Joseph A. Burke and Edgar Leslie; rec. December 13, 1935, in New York City by Louis Armstrong and His Orchestra; CDs #41, #51, and #61. The Tommy Dorsey Orchestra took this song to No. 1, but Armstrong's version has more musical merit, for example, the way he alternates legato and staccato phrases.

"Once in a While." By Michael Edwards and Bud Green; rec. November 15, 1937, in Los Angeles by Louis Armstrong and His Orchestra; CDs #34, #41, and #61. Not to be confused with an instrumental number of the same title that Armstrong had recorded ten years earlier, this "Once in a While" was initially popularized by the Tommy Dorsey Orchestra (Jack Leonard, vocal) and later covered by Patti Page.

"Once in a While." By W. Butler; rec. December 10, 1927, in Chicago by Louis Armstrong and His **Hot Five;** CD #10. The Hot Five/**Hot Seven** had been together for nearly two years and over a dozen recording sessions by this date. Nevertheless, they seem a little uncomfortable with the Charleston-like rhythm and even with each other. There are numerous bobbled notes and abrupt transitions. Armstrong manages to take a creative **stop-time** solo, but even he sounds forced. After one more session together, Armstrong did not take the Hot Five back into the studio for six months, by which time he had replaced everyone (his wife included).

"One Hour." See **"If I Could Be with You (One Hour Tonight)."**

125 Jazz Breaks for Cornet. It did not take Armstrong long to acquire a name for himself after moving to Chicago in 1922 to join **King Oliver.** Underscoring his widening fame among both record collectors and musicians, the Melrose Bros. Music Company made available two volumes of transcriptions. *125 Jazz Breaks for Cornet* and ***50 Hot Choruses*** were published in 1927. "Many of the greatest hot men we have today . . . will tell you they conceived many of their tricks and ideas from the Armstrong style of playing," read the advertisement. Two errors got started at Melrose, however, when the publisher attributed "Wild Man Blues" to both Armstrong and **Jelly Roll Morton.** Neither wrote the song, and in addition they never played together.

"One I Love Belongs to Somebody Else, The." By Isham Jones and Gus Kahn. Unfortunately, Armstrong never recorded this song, but it brought him together with **Earl Hines** and initiated one of the twentieth century's most important musical relationships. Hines, the story goes, was playing it on the local musicians' union hall piano in Chicago in 1923 when Armstrong walked in, took out his horn, and began to play along. "I knew right away he was a giant," Hines later recalled (Dance, 1977, p. 45).

"One Moment Worth Years." By **Dave Brubeck** and Iola Brubeck; rec. September 13, 1961, in New York City by **Louis Armstrong and the All Stars,** pianist Dave Brubeck, and guests; CDs #42 and #50. Armstrong and Carmen McRae sing this sweet love duet from the jazz oratorio ***The Real Ambassadors*** in one of those exquisitely slow Armstrong tempos. Brubeck noodles genially on the keyboard. See additional comments on "Cultural Exchange."

"One o'Clock Jump." By William "Count" Basie; rec. December 28 or 29, 1950, in Los Angeles by **Louis Armstrong and the All Stars;** CD #45. This 1938 number was the Count Basie Orchestra theme song. Armstrong recorded it for the 1951 **movie** ***The Strip,*** in which Mickey Rooney plays a drummer who joins Armstrong's band.

"One of these Days." By D.A. Hoffman; rec. November 10 or 11, 1924, in New York City by **Fletcher Henderson** and His Orchestra. Armstrong's thirty-two-measure solo here is like gold surrounded by granite. See additional comments on "Alabamy Bound."

"Only You." Rec. September 8, 1955, in Los Angeles with Benny Carter's Orchestra. This ensemble is really an augmented **All Stars,** with which Armstrong recorded some **Christmas** music ("Christmas in New Orleans" and "Christmas Night in Harlem").

Onward Brass Band. Armstrong grew up hearing the Onward Brass Band on the streets of New Orleans. "I was so crazy about **Perez'** brass band I would follow them on the streets when they paraded with the Elks and Moose and other societies," he wrote in his **autobiography.** Manuel Perez was among those early great players who, as Armstrong continued, "lived jazz, slept jazz, ate jazz and brought jazz into being" (1936, p. 15). The OBB—along with others such as the Eureka Brass Band, Excelsior Brass Band, Reliance Brass Band, and **Tuxedo Brass Band**—played at dances, parades, picnics, and especially funeral processions (see **brass band**). In this last category, they played somber music on the way to a burial and lively music on the way back.

Many considered the OBB to be consistently the best of the brass bands. One of its longtime members was **Joe Oliver,** Armstrong's mentor. It was founded in 1885 and broke up in 1930. However, Armstrong still had their sound in his ears in 1969, when he wrote that "they sounded like a forty-piece brass **swing** band" (Brothers, p. 27). The OBB had a revival when drummer **Paul Barbarin,** son of the prominent early OBB member **Isidore Barbarin,** reestablished the ensemble in 1960. It toured widely, gave historically informed concerts, and recorded until 1978. In 1971 the OBB played in Armstrong's raucous New Orleans **funeral.**

opera. Armstrong had a lifelong attraction to opera. Among the first records he bought were those of Enrico Caruso and Amelita Galli-Curci, and they influenced the development of his style. See **"Louis Armstrong and Opera."**

"Oriental Strut." By **Johnny St. Cyr;** rec. February 26, 1926, in Chicago by Louis Armstrong and His **Hot Five;** CD #10. Armstrong loved an exotic minor key number, and in this one he takes a fine **stop-time** solo. There are occasional fluffs and momentary losses of direction, however, which may be attributed to the fact that the ensemble's personnel had been completely replaced recently. Transcription of Armstrong's solo by Castle (vol. 2, p. 22).

Original Dixieland Jazz Band. See **Dixieland.**

Ory, Edward "Kid" (c. 1890–1973). Although Creole trombonist Kid Ory was born at least a decade before and died a few years after Armstrong, their careers wove in and out of each other's frequently. Ory's trombone was one of the earliest musical sounds that Armstrong paid attention to, and when the thirteen-year-old came out of the **Colored Waif's Home,** Ory was more than encouraging. "Louis came up and played 'Ole' Miss' and the blues, and everyone in the park went wild over this boy in knee trousers who could play so great," recalled Ory. "I liked Louis's playing so much that I asked him to come and sit in with my band any time he could" (Shapiro and Hentoff, 1955, p. 48). Armstrong did so, eventually substituting for cornetist **Joe Oliver.** When Oliver left for Chicago in 1918, Armstrong took his place. (It was while Armstrong was playing with the Ory band that **Fate Marable** heard him and hired him to play on the **Streckfus** riverboat.)

The 1917 closing of **Storyville** had left little work for musicians, so Ory formed a band and took it to California in 1919. His first choice for cornet was Armstrong, who declined, fearing to be stranded far from home as had been the fate of many of his friends. (Armstrong's decision to join Joe Oliver three years later was different, since he felt more confident by then and would be under the wing of a father-figure.) In 1925 Ory turned up in Chicago, where he recorded with Joe Oliver and with **Jelly Roll Morton.** Between November 1925 and December 1927 he went often into the studio with Armstrong's **Hot Five** to make a series of now-classic recordings, including "Cornet Chop Suey," "Struttin' with Some Barbecue," and "Gut Bucket Blues." On this last number from November 12, 1925, Armstrong introduces all the players (a first in the history of recording) and shouts at Ory an encouraging, "You can really blow that thing!"

Ory did just that for the next two years. His bouncy, sometimes swaggering style and long glissandos can be heard, for example, on "Muskrat Ramble" (1926), and he plays a memorable sixteen-bar solo on "Hotter Than That" (1927). **Lil Hardin Armstrong** wrote the latter piece, and for many years Ory was credited with the former, which has become a traditional jazz anthem. However, "Muskrat Ramble" turns out to be one of the many pieces that Armstrong wrote and allowed others to claim. He told Dan Morgenstern in 1965 that it was his. "Ory named it, he gets the royalties. I don't talk about it" (Morgenstern, 1965). Ory did write "Savoy Blues," though, and on the Hot Fives' December 1927 recording, he plays his characteristic glissandos, as he also does on "I'm Not Rough," made a few days earlier.

The Hot Five also recorded "Ory's Creole Trombone" a few months earlier. It is an old tune that fascinated Armstrong as a child back in New Orleans. Ory's band used to play it for the St. Katherine Hall dancers at 1509 Tulane Avenue. As Armstrong wrote in 1951: "The more choruses they played, the softer they would get. . . . And they would get so soft until you could hear the feet of the dancers, 'justa shufflin.' . . . My, my, they sure used to knock me out" (Brothers, p. 134).

Ory returned to Southern California in 1930, but the **Great Depression** forced him, as it did so many other musicians, to find a day job, which he did on a chicken farm and later in a railroad office. By 1942, though, he was back on the stage and remained a popular performer. He was an honored guest during the July 1957 appearance of **Louis Armstrong and the All Stars** at the **Newport Jazz Festival.** In 1962 he and Armstrong (along with banjo player **Johnny St. Cyr,** a longtime associate of both) had a reunion when they performed at **Disneyland** on the recreated paddlewheel riverboat *Mark Twain.* Four years later, Ory retired to Hawaii, where he lived out his days.

A good place to see as well as hear Ory is in the 1947 film ***New Orleans,*** where Armstrong heads a band that includes the trombonist. Ory also appears prominently playing "Muskrat Ramble" in the hard-to-find short film ***Disneyland after Dark*** (1962).

"Ory's Creole Trombone." By **Edward "Kid" Ory;** rec. September 2, 1927, in Chicago by Louis Armstrong and His **Hot Five;** CD #10. Here is an old tune that used to fascinate Armstrong as a child back in New Orleans. Ory's band would play it for the St. Katherine Hall dancers at 1509 Tulane Avenue. As Armstrong relates: "The more choruses they played, the softer they would get. . . . And they would get so soft until you could hear the feet of the dancers, 'justa shufflin.' . . . My, my, they sure used to knock me out" (Brothers, p. 134). Ory had previously recorded this showpiece with his own group in 1922, but the Hot Five version is the one that made history. Perhaps because he is not in tip-top form and Armstrong himself has a few lapses, this recording went unreleased. Finally, in 1941 record producer **George Avakian** discovered it in **Columbia**'s dusty vaults and included it with some Armstrong reissues.

"Otchi-tchor-ni-ya." Traditional; rec. October 8, 1958, in Los Angeles by **Louis Armstrong and the All Stars;** CD #8. This song, "Dark Eyes" in English, was a favorite of Armstrong, who liked minor keys. He recorded this number several times, usually at a lingering tempo, and he gave his sidemen a chance to improvise.

"Our Love Is Here to Stay." See **"Love Is Here to Stay."**

"Our Monday Date." See **"Monday Date, A."**

P

Paddio, Villard (1895–1947). Paddio was one of two African American photographers (the other was **Arthur P. Bedou,** his teacher) in early-twentieth-century New Orleans who did portraits and commercial work for the city's black clientele. Paddio took the only surviving picture of Armstrong's family, and some of his other photos captured high points in Armstrong's career. While the originals are in **archives** such as that at Queens College, they have been widely reproduced in such publications as Marc Miller's *Louis Armstrong: A Cultural Legacy.*

Page, Oran Thaddeus "Hot Lips" (1908–1954). Page, a singer as well as a trumpeter, was one of so many musicians influenced by Armstrong. He accompanied **Ma Rainey, Bessie Smith,** and others before joining Count Basie in 1936. Page's similarity to Armstrong brought him to the attention of **Joe Glaser,** who urged him to become a soloist. When that didn't work out, Page led his own bands and later concentrated on small groups. Although inspired by Armstrong, Page had his own style that was best expressed in impromptu jam sessions and improvised blues lyrics. He made many recordings from 1938 to 1954, among them two versions of "St. James Infirmary Blues," one with Artie Shaw in 1941 and the other with his own band in 1947.

paloma, La. Armstrong appears twice in this German musical revue, first arriving at the airport and then on stage at the very end. Klaus Stratemann reports that he was also filmed with the famous Kessler Twins, a song and dance duo, but the footage was not used (1996, p. 436). A great many popular German entertainers are featured, singing everything from the title song to "Tom Dooley." Armstrong plays and sings "Uncle Satchmo's Lullaby," written by Erwin Halletz and Olaf Bradtke, which he later recorded in Vienna with the child vocalist Gabriele Klonisch. The record reached the No. 9 spot on German record charts in July 1959. Alta Films, 1959; color; 84 mins.; Dir. Paul Martin.

"Panama." By William H. Tyers and Carl Sigman; rec. April 26 or 27, 1950, in New York City by **Louis Armstrong and the All Stars;** CDs #8 and #61. This 1911 song became one of the standard numbers of the New Orleans **brass band** repertory, and Armstrong often recalled both hearing and playing it as a youngster (e.g., Armstrong, ***Satchmo,*** 1954, p. 143).

Panassié, Hugues (1912–1974). Armstrong was very fond of this French jazz enthusiast and writer, who (along with the Belgian **Robert Goffin**) left a vivid record of Armstrong's effect on Europe in the early 1930s. Panassié founded the **Hot Club de France** in 1932, edited its journal *Jazz hot* (1935–1946), wrote several books (including *Le jazz hot,* 1934, and *Douze années de jazz,* 1946), and contributed seemingly hundreds of articles on jazz to a wide variety of publications. In 1934 he met and made a fast friend in Armstrong, who responded warmly to the Frenchman's adoration. Panassié's attitude was shared by many Frenchmen, who tended to romanticize African American entertainers—that is, consider them "noble savages" à la Jean-Jacques Rousseau. Such treatment was not unappreciated, and African Americans (such as **Josephine Baker** and **Duke Ellington**) found a level of hospitality to which they were not accustomed.

Also, as a black man in a white man's world, Armstrong welcomed the help of white writers in smoothing his way. His relationship with Panassié (and Robert Goffin and **Leonard Feather**) grew out of genuine friendship, but Armstrong, a **writer** himself, was also aware of the power of the written word to bring him closer to his audience. What performer would not be grateful for an essay such as the one Panassié wrote about Armstrong's two memorable concerts at the **Salle Pleyel** on November 9 and 10, 1934? "The entrance of Louis on stage was something unforgettable... like a brilliant meteor" (Berrett, 1999, p. 65). Earlier, in *Le jazz hot,* Panassié had written: "I do not think I am making too strong a statement when I say that Louis Armstrong is not only a genius in his own art, but is one of the most extraordinary creative geniuses that all music has ever known" (p. 64). Panassié went on to write an entire book on Armstrong in 1947, and in the meantime he saw to it in 1936 that Armstrong was named Honorary President of the Hot Club.

After founding (with Jack Auxenfans) the Hot Club, Panassié was not content merely to have created a music appreciation society. He also helped form the Quintette du Hot Club de France (a showcase for Stephane Grappelli and **Django Reinhardt,** 1934–1949), produce recording sessions (e.g., **Coleman Hawkins** in 1937), organize jazz festivals (e.g., **Nice** in 1948 and Montauban since 1982), and sponsor tours (e.g., **Earl Hines** in the 1960s). In his spare time, he published the *Bulletin du Hot Club de France,* beginning in 1950. The idealistic, fastidious, and partisan Hot Club members had some stormy battles over the years, for example, over the emergence of be**bop** in the 1940s. Here Panassié took an extremely conservative position, vociferously expressing the opinion that bebop was not jazz. In general, he looked askance at any variation from traditional New Orleans jazz. Panassié also had other blind spots as well, for example, his advocacy of the self-serving musician-cum-drug-pusher **Mezz Mezzrow.**

Panassié's collection of 6,000 78 rpm records and 9,000 LPs became the core of The Hot Club's library, which is housed at the Discothèque Municipale in Villefranche-de-Rouergue in southern France. One of the items in this collection is called "Panassié Stomp," written and recorded by Count Basie in 1938.

"Papa De Da Da." By Spencer Williams, **Clarence Williams,** and Clarence Todd;

rec. March 4, 1925, in New York City with vocalist **Eva Taylor** and **Clarence Williams' Blue Five;** CDs #36 and #48. An homage to a prominent New Orleans dandy, this tune was very popular in its day. Armstrong neatly decorates Taylor's lively singing, bending notes expressively and trading licks with the reeds. See additional comments on "Cast Away."

"Papa, Mama's All Alone." By **Clarence Williams** and W. Higgins; rec. November 25, 1924, in New York City with vocalist **Margaret Johnson** and **Clarence Williams' Blue Five;** CD #36. Armstrong recorded twice with Johnson, who also wrote blues lyrics. See additional comments on "Changeable Daddy of Mine."

Paris Blues. Paul Newman and Sidney Poitier play American expatriate jazz musicians who fall for two lovely tourists, Joanne Woodward and Diahann Carroll. The movie is graced by **Duke Ellington**'s score and Armstrong's portrayal of fictional jazz legend Wild Man Moore. In fact, the movie gets off the ground with Moore's arrival in Paris and ends when he leaves. In the interim, Armstrong helps Newman get recognition for his music and performs "Battle Royal" and "Wild Man Moore." As in ***New Orleans*** (1947), ***High Society*** (1956), and ***A Man Called Adam*** (1966), Armstrong also contributes positively to a subtext about the value of jazz. United Artists, 1961; B&W; 98 mins.; Dir. Martin Ritt.

Parker, Daisy. See **Armstrong, Daisy Parker.**

Paul VI (1897–1978). See **pope.**

"Peanut Vendor." By Moises Simons; rec. December 23, 1930, in Los Angeles by Louis Armstrong and His **Sebastian New Cotton Club** Orchestra. **Dizzy Gillespie** (whom many credit with starting the Latin jazz trend) was thirteen years old and had been playing trumpet for only a few months when Armstrong recorded this Cuban rumba. Armstrong performs well, despite the imprecise and out-of-tune band.

"Pennies from Heaven." By John Burke and Arthur Johnston; rec. August 17, 1936, in New York City with vocalists **Bing Crosby** and Frances Langford and the **Jimmy Dorsey** Orchestra; CDs #12, #13, #28, #41, and #61. Armstrong and Crosby introduced this evergreen in the 1936 **movie** of the same name (see ***Pennies from Heaven***), and in this recording they perform it with fellow **Decca** star Frances Langford. Armstrong kept the song in his repertory and programmed it on the pivotal May 17, 1947, **Town Hall concert** in New York City.

Pennies from Heaven. **Bing Crosby,** a wandering troubadour recently released from prison, inherits a haunted house, which he converts into a nightclub in this cheerful film. Armstrong is featured in "The Skeleton in the Closet" with the **Jimmy Dorsey** band (wearing white masks and with **Lionel Hampton** on drums). *Variety* felt that the "best individual impression is by Louis Armstrong" (Dec. 16, 1936, p. 14), and indeed this is the film that firmly launched his career in the **movies. Critics** have pointed out that he was given demeaning material (his character can't do simple math, his song evokes familiar racial stereotypes, and folksy fears and superstitions abound), but Armstrong handles it all with consummate artistry and charm. Columbia, 1936; B&W; 81 mins.; Dir. Norman Z. McLeod.

"Perdido." By Juan Tizol, Hans Lengsfelder, and Ervin Drake; rec. September 12, 1944, live at Camp Reynolds, Pennsylvania, by Louis Armstrong and His Orchestra; CDs #2, #6, #19, #23, and #63. This enduringly popular 1942 song by **Duke Ellington**'s famous valve trombone player, Juan Tizol, became an **All Stars** staple. Armstrong's first recording of it here featured a young tenor saxophonist by the name of **Dexter Gordon.**

"Perdido Street Blues." By **Lil Hardin Armstrong;** rec. May 27, 1940, in New York City by Louis Armstrong and His Orchestra; CD #61. Armstrong here plays up a storm and so does clarinetist **Sidney Bechet.** They make the rest of the ensemble seem pale by comparison, and this troubled Bechet, who later recalled in his autobiography that he would have preferred "working together for that real feeling that would let the music come new and strong" (p. 176).

Perez, Manuel (or Emanuel) (1871–1946). A cigar maker by day, Perez was a New Orleans cornet player and bandleader. The young Armstrong remembered him as one of those early great players who "lived jazz, slept jazz, ate jazz and brought jazz into being" (Armstrong, 1936, p. 15). Perez did this with various ensembles, especially the **Onward Brass Band,** which he joined in 1900 and, with a few little breaks, led from 1903 to its dissolution in 1930. Along with other groups such as the Excelsior Brass Band and the **Tuxedo Brass Band,** the OBB played dances, parades, picnics, and especially funeral processions. In this last category, they played somber music on the way to a burial and lively music on the way back.

Many considered the OBB to be consistently the best of the **brass band**s. This may have been due to Perez's insistence that its members be technically accomplished and able to sight-read new arrangements. Eventually, he wisely allowed improvisation. One of his star players was **Joe Oliver,** Armstrong's mentor. Perez himself is said to have had a wide range, a clean attack, and a remarkably beautiful tone. Unfortunately, he made no recordings. However, Armstrong still had the OBB sound in his ear in 1969 when he wrote that "they sounded like a forty-piece brass swing band" (Brothers, p. 27).

Pete Lala's Cabaret. See **Lala, Pete.**

Peterson, Oscar Emmanuel (b. 1925). Armstrong first worked with the talented Canadian pianist in 1956 while making an album with **Ella Fitzgerald** (CD #9), and it was such a comfortable fit that the two men (with Peterson's rhythm section) soon got together on an album of their own (CD #37). Since the early 1970s Peterson has focused on solo performances and has become one of the greatest pianists in the history of jazz.

Petit, Buddy (Joseph Crawford) (c. 1897–1931). The stepson of trombonist Joe Petit (c. 1880–1946), Buddy was one of the many talented black Creole jazz musicians with whom Armstrong grew up in New Orleans. "He had a style all his own," recalled Armstrong more than fifty years later. "He blew from the side + his jaw poked on one side" (Brothers, p. 31).

Evidently this unorthodox method did not negatively affect his playing, since by all accounts it was very expressive. During his relatively brief career, Petit played in the New Orleans region with various dance bands and also worked with **Jimmie Noone.** In 1917 Petit went to California with **Jelly Roll Morton,** and in 1922 he went again with Frankie Dusen. Neither of these trips seems to have been successful, though, so he returned home to lead his own regional band. In the late 1920s he worked on the riverboat S.S. *Madison.*

Petit influenced several New Orleans cornetists (e.g., Wingy Manone, Punch Miller, and Herb Morland). Armstrong himself may have taken a few pages from Petit's book, since the two played many funerals together. "He kind of what you call set a pace around New Orleans," said clarinetist **Edmond Hall,** who later played with **Louis Armstrong and the All Stars.** "I mean these other bands would hear Buddy play something and they would all want to play it" (Shapiro and Hentoff, 1955, p. 22). Unfortunately, we will never know exactly what that influence was since Petit (who seems to have had a drinking problem) died young and never recorded. Armstrong was a pallbearer at the funeral and noted that Petit's death, which seems to have been from the effects of overeating at a July 4 picnic, "broke everybody's heart" (Brothers, p. 31).

Peyton, Dave (c. 1885–1956). African American bandleader, pianist, and music journalist, Dave Peyton was an influential figure on the Chicago musical scene. As a bandleader in the 1920s, his sidemen included many of the upcoming New Orleans musicians, such as **Baby Dodds, Kid Ory,** and **Zutty Singleton.** As a contractor, he supplied bands for a wide variety of occasions. Finally, as a journalist, he wrote a weekly column from 1925 to 1929 for the *Chicago Defender,* in which he chronicled the developing jazz scene and became a spokesman among black musicians. Here he happily reported on the breakdown of color restrictions in nightclubs, for example, Armstrong at the Black Hawk nightclub in July 1927. He even boldly reported how white musicians, not liking the competition, tried to fight back by lying to white club owners about the unsavory habits of black musicians.

Naturally, Peyton wrote frequently about Armstrong, who was the talk of the town. Although this coverage often had a society page tone (Mr. and Mrs. Armstrong going on vacation, Mr. Armstrong ill, etc.), Peyton gives us articulate eyewitness accounts of Armstrong's success in New York in the fall of 1925, his triumphant return to Chicago in November 1925, his one and only appearance with the **Hot Five** (February 27, 1926), the time **Guy Lombardo** gave Armstrong and Zutty Singleton royal treatment at the Granada Café, and other key events. However, Peyton was not shy about criticizing or even moralizing. In the May 19, 1926 issue, he got after Armstrong and his orchestra for being "noisy, corrupt, contemptible, and displeasing to the ear." Peyton was preoccupied not so much with musical style as he was with personal behavior and racial advancement. He wanted fellow African American musicians to capitalize on their progress by dressing correctly, behaving properly, and playing good music. As Armstrong biographer James Lincoln Collier observes, Peyton's attitude represented that of upwardly mobile African Americans who were unhappy to have the race associated strictly with jazz and the blues (Collier, 1983, pp. 163–164).

Peyton's musical career continued in the 1930s, when so many musicians had to seek other sources of income. His orchestra had a long-term engagement at Chicago's posh **Regal Theater,** and he worked as a soloist into the late 1940s. Perhaps because he was too busy organizing sessions for others, Peyton made only one recording, "Baby o' Mine," for **Decca** in 1935.

physical attributes. While Armstrong had a fine musical mind, he was also a natural trumpet player in every physical way. He had an ideal lip size, relaxed and open throat muscles, a large and powerful diaphragm, good strong teeth, and robust health. He used these gifts generously, although perhaps not always wisely. An overwhelming desire to please audiences with high-register pyrotechnics—he once played more than 200 high "Cs" in a row—and years of too many concerts without sufficient rest resulted in chronic **lip problems.** Armstrong's response, however, was to develop a leaner, sparer style, which can be heard, for example, by comparing a 1927 recording of "Struttin' with Some Barbecue" with one made in 1938. Here one finds many pauses and not so many fast notes but still the originality of invention, emotional depth, and irresistible **swing** style for which Armstrong was famous.

"Pickin' on Your Baby." By Billy James and Paul V. Reynolds; rec. January 8, 1925, in New York City with vocalist **Eva Taylor** and **Clarence Williams' Blue Five;** CDs #36 and #48. Armstrong waits until this sweet song is nearly two-thirds over before he comes in, and his entrance dovetails smoothly with the singer. He also stays up in her stratospheric range, where very few players dared go. See additional comments on "Cast Away."

Picou, Alphonse Floristan (1878–1961). Armstrong was in seventh heaven when in 1918 he was accepted into the musically and sartorially splendid **Tuxedo Brass Band.** "The fact that I belonged to the best brass band in town put me in touch with all the top musicians," he later wrote in his **autobiography.** "One of them was Picou" (1954, p. 220). In this ensemble, Picou was famous for having adapted the piccolo part on "High Society" to his clarinet, and it quickly became a regular part of the piece's performance. A reference to this solo can be heard in Armstrong's introduction to "Cornet Chop Suey" (1926).

Picou could improvise as well as read music, and this gave him entree into smaller jazz groups. However, during the **Great Depression,** he, like so many other musicians, had to focus on his day job, which in his case was tinsmithing. By 1940 he was musically active again, recording with **Kid Rena** and later working with **Oscar "Papa" Celestin.** The revival of interest in traditional jazz fueled these performance opportunities, so much so that Picou was eventually able to lead his own group in the early 1950s at the Paddock Lounge on Bourbon Street. The Paddock Jazz Band made an LP in 1953 on which Picou can be heard playing admirably on "Eh la bas." His 1961 Mardi

Armstrong with Bing Crosby on the set of *High Society* in 1956. (Louis Armstrong House and Archives at Queens College/CUNY)

Gras funeral is said to have been one of the biggest in New Orleans history.

Pillow to Post. This comedy, starring Ida Lupino and Sydney Greenstreet, is about a young saleswoman who needs to find a temporary husband in order to stay in a married-only motel. Armstrong is featured with Dorothy Dandridge in a sexually charged version of the Ted Koehler–Burton Lane song "Whatcha Say?" The sequence was often omitted in southern theaters. Warner Bros., 1945; B&W; 96 mins.; Dir. Vincent Sherman.

Pius XII (1876–1958). See **pope.**

Place Congo. See **Congo Square.**

Plantation Café. Located at 338 East 35th Street at Grand Boulevard in Chicago, this popular nightclub opened in October 1924. The Plantation was a "black-and-tan" establishment, meaning that black entertainers performed for both black and white patrons, who, although often seated separately, could dance together. Such an environment was very advanced socially, and the atmosphere was charged with excitement. Like many clubs, the Plantation was under the control of the **Capone** syndicate. **Dave Peyton**'s dance orchestra opened the Plantation, with **King Oliver** as his featured soloist. Oliver then formed his Dixie Syncopators, which was the house band from February 1925 to spring 1927. Armstrong would have been a member had he not gone in September 1924 to join **Fletcher Henderson** in New York, and he might have also joined up on his return to Chicago in November 1925. History is full of might-have-beens, however, and Armstrong's career had begun to go in a different direction. Besides, **Lil Armstrong** did not want her husband to go back under what she considered the stifling wing of Oliver. The Plantation Café closed in the 1930s.

"Planter from Havana." See **"She's the Daughter of a Planter from Havana."**

"Play Me Slow." By Milt Hagen and Charles O'Flynn; rec. January 23, 1925, in New York City by **Fletcher Henderson** and His Orchestra. See comments on "Alabamy Bound."

"Play Me the Blues." See **"Jack Armstrong Blues."**

"Pleadin' for the Blues." By **Bertha "Chippie" Hill** and Richard M. Jones; rec. November 23, 1926, in Chicago with vocalist Chippie Hill and pianist Richard M. Jones; CDs #36 and #48. Armstrong here does some marvelous antiphonal work with Hill and in his solo some colorful word painting. See additional comments on "A Georgia Man."

"Please Don't Talk About Me When I'm Gone." By Sidney Clare and Sam H. Stept; rec. July 26, 1967, live in Juan-Les-Pins, France, by **Louis Armstrong and the All Stars.**

"Please Stop Playin' Those Blues, Boy." By Claude Demetrius and Fleecie Moore; rec. October 16, 1947, in Chicago by **Louis Armstrong and the All Stars;** CDs #12 and #47. Here is another example of the marvelous chemistry between Armstrong and trombonist **Jack Teagarden.**

Plessy v. Ferguson. See ***Brown v. Board of Education.***

Poitier, Sidney (b. 1927). See ***Paris Blues.***

"Poor House Blues." By Spencer Williams; rec. December 9, 1924, in New York City with vocalist **Maggie Jones** and pianist **Fletcher Henderson;** CD #36. See comments on "Anybody Here Want to Try My Cabbage?"

"Poor Little Rich Girl." By Noel Coward. Evidently Armstrong never recorded this popular 1926 song, but it was his specialty with the **Erskine Tate** Orchestra at the **Vendome Theater** in Chicago (December 1925 through April 1927). According to Doc Cheatham, the band would play a dramatic introduction, "and then Louis would stand up in the pit and the spotlight would hit him . . . and the people started *screaming.*" Cheatham (who would occasionally substitute for Armstrong at the Vendome and suffer the audience's uninhibited disappointment) recalled that "you couldn't get in that theater the whole time Louis was there, it was standing room only because of him. He was the biggest thing in the world. I mean, nobody had ever heard anything like this guy" (Deffaa, 1992, p. 20).

"Poor Old Joe." By **Hoagy Carmichael;** rec. December 18, 1939, in New York City by Louis Armstrong and His Orchestra. See comments on "Ev'ntide."

pope. Armstrong met two popes in his long career. While in Rome in 1949, Armstrong and wife **Lucille** (who was a Catholic) had an audience with Pope Pius XII. The event seems also to have been attended by numerous diplomats and members of the press. Evidently it was the pope's idea, since from his days as a young priest he had been a jazz fan in general and an Armstrong fan in particular. Years later **All Stars** bass player **Arvell Shaw** gave an account to Joshua Berrett. "The Pope was telling Louis how he loved his records and how he had his records from when he was a young priest and everything." According to Shaw, the pope asked the Armstrongs if they had any children. Louis responded, "No, but we're having a hell of a lot of fun trying." The air suddenly went out of the room, but the pope laughed amiably and eventually so did the momentarily shocked bystanders (Berrett, 1999, pp. 166–167). On a 1968 tour of Italy, Armstrong also met Pope Paul VI.

"Poplar Street Blues." By Al Short and Will Mont; rec. February 4, 1925, in New York City by **Fletcher Henderson** and His Orchestra. See additional comments on "Alabamy Bound."

"Pops." See **nicknames.**

Porter, Cole Albert (1891–1964). Armstrong had a special affinity for Cole Porter's elegant, sophisticated music. He made memorable recordings of "Don't Fence Me In," "I Get a Kick Out of You," "I Love Paris," "Just One of Those Things," and "You're the Top." To Porter's music in the movie ***High Society,*** Armstrong brought an insider's knowledge to "Now You Has Jazz" and a puckish sense of humor to "High Society Calypso." He also contributed extra magic to **Bing Crosby**'s singing of "I

Love You, Samantha" and "Little One" (CD #45).

Postal Service, U.S. See **mail; stamp.**

"Potato Head Blues." By Louis Armstrong; rec. May 10, 1927, in Chicago by Louis Armstrong and His **Hot Seven;** CDs #5, #8, #10, #14, #44, #48, and #52. For this recording Armstrong turned his **Hot Five** into the Hot Seven by adding tuba player **Pete Briggs** and drummer **Baby Dodds.** As the piece unfolds, one can hear the richness of Armstrong's musical imagination as well as many of his innovations. For example, he plays numerous concert "As" and even a high "C," while predecessors such as **King Oliver** did not venture beyond a "G." He also varies his timbre by such means as alternate fingerings for the same note, and his solos imply minor and diminished chords. Most important, he improvises a solo against **stop-time** accompaniment (i.e., the rest of the band plays only on the first note of every other measure), thus creating the model of the featured soloist. The result has entranced listeners ever since. **Woody Allen,** playing protagonist Isaac Davis in the 1979 movie *Manhattan,* enumerates this song as one of "the things that make life worth living." Actress **Tallulah Bankhead** also loved the piece. "It is one of the greatest things in life," she said, and she played the record every night "to alleviate the tedium of playing the same part for so long" during the three-year Broadway run of *Private Lives* in the late 1940s (Giddins, 1988, p. 92). So admired and influential is Armstrong's unique solo that it has been transcribed by many, including Peter Eklund (Kernfeld, 2002, vol. 1, p. 70), Lee Castle (vol. 1, p. 22), and Gunther Schuller (1968, p. 108). A facsimile of Armstrong's original manuscript can be found in the work of Lawrence Gushee (1998, p. 306).

Powers, Ollie. Shortly after Armstrong arrived in Chicago in August 1922, his mentor **Joe "King" Oliver** took him to hear Ollie Powers and His Harmony Syncopators at the **Dreamland Café** (and also to meet the band's pianist, **Lil Hardin,** who a year and a half later became the second Mrs. Armstrong). Armstrong was greatly impressed, not only with Powers's singing and drum playing but also with his duo partner, **May Alix** (with whom he would record "Big Butter and Egg Man" and "Sunset Cafe Stomp" in 1926). When at the urging of his wife Armstrong gave notice to Joe Oliver in June 1924, it was Powers who gave him a job and the opportunity to expand musically as a soloist.

Before the advent of Armstrong, Powers led bands in the Chicago area at the Pompeii Buffet, Elmwood Café, Deluxe Café, and other venues beginning in the mid-1910s. He was a polished and cultivated man who, as William Howland Kenney notes in *Chicago Jazz,* was able to help poorer, recently arrived southern musicians find work (1993, p. 38). Powers had a fine tenor voice, and one of his specialties was **Irving Berlin**'s "What'll I do?," which he would sing going from table to table. "No matter how much noise the people made you could still hear, very clearly, the golden voice of Ollie Powers," Armstrong later wrote (Brothers, p. 55).

"Pratt City Blues." By **Bertha "Chippie" Hill** and Richard M. Jones; rec. November 23, 1926, in Chicago with vocalist Chippie Hill and pianist Richard M. Jones; CD #36. See comments on "A Georgia Man."

"Preacher, The." By Horace Silver; rec. July 5, 1960, in New York City with vocalist **Bing Crosby** and a studio band and choir conducted by Billy May. This duet is from the popular album that Crosby and Armstrong made together. See comments on "At the Jazz Band Ball."

"Pretty Little Missy." By Louis Armstrong and **Billy Kyle;** rec. April 25, 1955, in New York City by **Louis Armstrong and the All Stars;** CD #8. In this agreeable number, one can hear an echo of "Honeysuckle Rose" and some excellent ensemble work. Armstrong recorded it several times, for example, on October 28, 1969, in London for the **movie *On Her Majesty's Secret Service*** (though it was not used).

Prima, Louis (1911–1978). While Armstrong and Prima may have played together, there's no record of it. Both were born in New Orleans, though, and Prima eventually—after a distinguished career in Chicago, Los Angeles, Las Vegas, and leading his own big and small bands—returned there for his final days. Prima was one of a large group of trumpet-playing vocalists (**Henry "Red" Allen, Roy Eldridge,** and Wingy Manone, Cootie Williams, **Hot Lips Page,** and others) who were inspired by both Armstrong's trumpet playing and his vocal style. Not that Prima was a mere imitator, though. His voice was hoarse in a distinctly different way and his trumpet playing more flashy. Many jazz critics feel that Prima's recordings don't do justice to his magnetism as a performer.

"Prisoner's Song, The" ("If I Had the Wings of an Angel"). By Guy Massey; rec. January 30, 1957, in New York City with the **Sy Oliver** Orchestra; CD #26. Of the dozen selections that Armstrong recorded for the album *Louis and the Angels,* this one is the closest to real jazz, and despite the square string section, he gets it to **swing** nicely. See additional comments on "And the Angels Sing."

PS 143. See **Louis Armstrong School.**

"Pseudo-Folk." See **Agee, James.**

"Public Melody Number One." By Ted Koehler and **Harold Arlen;** rec. July 2, 1937, in New York City by Louis Armstrong and His Orchestra; CDs #18 and #34. This catchy number, which was used in the 1937 **movie *Artists and Models,*** is about the power of music and the artists who make it. Armstrong sings that the new music is "gonna sneak right up upon you/and kind of put the finger on you./So look out for Public Melody Number One." In the film version, an **FBI** man says, "Let's start raiding every rhythm den," as if jazz is a threat to the American way of life. But Armstrong responds, "Ain't no use hidin'/I'm going to take you ridin'./Look out for Public Melody Number 1." Armstrong performs this number on screen with Martha Raye, who dresses in a sexy outfit, with her skin darkened. On the screen it seemed to many that Louis was trying to use jazz to seduce Ms. Raye, and the scene was cut in many southern states.

Pugh, Doc. Armstrong was more often than not on the road, yet he also liked to feel at home. In order to accomplish this have-your-cake-and-eat-it-too feat, Armstrong's faithful valet, Doc Pugh, would arrange the contents of Armstrong's twenty-four suitcases in the same order and position everywhere they went. Medicine chest, transistor radio, typewriter, two tape recorders (in case one broke down), and other objects would always be readily at hand. The medicine chest was especially important to Armstrong. After many years on the road, he had discovered effective treatments for sore throats, eye strain, toothaches, constipation, **lip problems,** and the like, and he liked to have them all readily available, both for himself and friends. For example, he was famous for dispensing a **laxative** called **Swiss Kriss** to all he met. He also liked to brew up a gargle concoction, the use of which **Hugues Panassié** amusingly described: "He begins in the usual way, then starts to pluck the skin under his chin and on his neck, so that the liquid can reach the remotest parts of his throat." Finally, "he spits out the liquid and to demonstrate success releases a superb 'Oh, yes!' with arms outstretched exactly as if on stage" (1971, p. 32).

Doc Pugh is mentioned in correspondence as early as 1946. Although he was prone to lapses in his service (he lost music on more than one occasion), Armstrong was fond of him. On June 23, 1959, Pugh played a crucial role in getting Armstrong to a doctor following his heart attack in Spoleto, Italy.

"Put 'em Down Blues." By Eloise J. Bennett; rec. September 2, 1927, in Chicago by Louis Armstrong and the **Hot Five;** CDs #10 and #48. This number marks the beginning for Armstrong of a new and mellower singing style, which would be fully developed by 1929 in such popular ballads as "I Can't Give You Anything But Love." This upbeat song (which is decidedly not a blues despite the title) also features some hearty trombone playing by **Kid Ory** and, led by Armstrong, a nimbly swinging ensemble.

"Put It Where I Can Get It." By **Hociel Thomas;** rec. November 11, 1925, in Chicago by vocalist Hociel Thomas and Louis Armstrong's Jazz Four; CDs #10 and #36. See comments on "Adam and Eve Had the Blues."

Q

Queens College. See **Louis Armstrong House and Archives.**

Queens neighborhood, New York. See **Corona.**

Quintette du Hot Club de France. See **Hot Club de France.**

R

race records. Between the early 1920s and World War II, the term "race record" was used for phonograph recordings made especially for African American listeners. The term strikes modern ears as demeaning if not insulting, but it was widely used in its day, for example, by African American newspapers, which also referred to "race musicians." Race records were not, however, segregated into separate catalogs, as James Lincoln Collier points out, citing archival evidence (1983, pp. 96–97). Understandably, Armstrong made numerous race records, especially during the early part of his career. His first recordings (in 1922) were for **Gennett,** which specialized in race records and in fact was the only record company to use the term on its labels. In May 1926, Armstrong made two race records for **Vocalion** ("Georgia Bo Bo" and "Drop That Sack") with his wife's **Lil**'s Hot Shots. Unfortunately, he was at the time under exclusive contract with the **Okeh** record company, which was the first to have a race series. Asked to explain, so the story goes, he said: "I don't know who made those records, but I won't do it again" (Collier, 1983, p. 177). He did though, eight more times. Other companies to have a race series included **Columbia,** Paramount, and **Victor.**

racism. See **civil rights; Little Rock; segregation.**

"Railroad Blues." By **Trixie Smith;** rec. between March 16 and 22, 1925, in New York City with vocalist Trixie Smith and her Down Home Syncopators; CD #36. Armstrong is still finding his own trumpet style at this date, and his playing here (except for the unique vibrato) resembles that of his mentor, **Joe Oliver.** See additional comments on "Mining Camp Blues."

"Rain, Rain." By Hal Stanley and Irving Taylor; rec. August 1, 1956, in Los Angeles with vocalists Kay Starr and Dick Haymes, Hall Mooney's Orchestra, and a studio choir; CD #12. This recording was made for the NBC **television** musical ***"The Lord Don't Play Favorites."*** See additional comments on "Never Saw a Better Day."

Rainey, Ma (Gertrude Pridgett) (1886–1939). Among Armstrong's earliest recordings were accompaniments for blues singers, such as **Alberta Hunter, Margaret Johnson, Chippie Hill,** and **Bessie Smith** (CD #36). With the dynamic Ma Rainey, he recorded "Countin' the Blues" (in which he effectively uses the plunger), "Jelly Bean Blues," and a very moving "See See Rider" (all from 1924). Rainey was very popular and had a big following before she worked with Armstrong. She toured throughout the South and Mexico. However, her popularity faded, and in 1935 she retired to her birthplace, Columbus Georgia, to devote her remaining years to the Baptist church.

"Ramblin' Rose." By Noel Sherman and Joel Sherman; rec. August 1970 in New York City with the Nashville Group. See comments on "Almost Persuaded."

"Ramona." By Mabel Wayne and L. Wolfe Gilbert; rec. April 21, 1953, in New York City by Louis Armstrong and His Orchestra; CD #8. From the film of the same name, this popular 1927 waltz (first introduced by Dolores Del Rio) gets a warm performance by Armstrong and company (the **All Stars** supplemented by a saxophone section).

Randolph, Zilner (1899–1994). In April 1931, Armstrong returned to Chicago from Los Angeles and formed a band with trumpeter/arranger Zilner Randolph to perform at the **Regal Theater** and then at the **Showboat Cabaret.** "Now there's a Band that really 'deserved a *whole lot* of '*Credit* that they *didn't* get," he later wrote in **"The Goffin Notebooks"** (Brothers, p. 108). This group was together for about a year and recorded about two dozen numbers (including "Them There Eyes," "When Your Lover Has Gone," "Little Joe," "You Can Depend on Me," and "When It's Sleepy Time Down South," which eventually became Armstrong's theme song).

Randolph led this band. Throughout his life, Armstrong preferred to be a soloist and leave the details of band directing to others. Randolph was a good choice for the job, since he came with considerable musical experience in St. Louis, Milwaukee, and elsewhere. He had also studied music theory and arranging and was therefore able to polish the band's arrangements. His work (as well as his trumpet playing) can be heard prominently on "Swing, You Cats" (1933). Together with Armstrong he wrote the novelty tune "Old Man Mose," which in 1935 was one of Armstrong's most requested numbers.

Randolph's leadership style sometimes attracted unwanted attention. Once on a tour stop at the **Suburban Gardens** in New Orleans, his conducting hand attracted an intoxicated white woman, who took it and, much to everyone's alarm, danced with him, in flagrant violation of southern racial barriers. "My teeth began to chatter," said New Orleans–born and –bred trombonist **Preston Jackson** (Jones, 1988, p. 136). Luckily, the incident passed quickly as an occasion for amusement. Later, on October 10, 1931, Armstrong and the whole band were arrested in Memphis, apparently for simply arriving as a group of well-dressed black men with a white woman (Armstrong manager **Johnny Collins**'s wife) in their bus. Randolph's jaunty French beret and outrage singled him out as the leader, which nearly made him the target for extra punishment. Luckily, one of the band members made a quick phone call to Collins, who straightened things out.

Randolph went on to form two more short-lived bands in the next four years for Armstrong. Between these temporary gigs, Randolph was content to be a sideman with **Carroll Dickerson.** In 1936 he put together his own big band. He also continued working as an arranger, doing charts for Woody Herman, **Earl Hines, Duke Ellington, Fletcher Henderson,** and others. In the 1940s he had his own quartet and with his children worked up a musical act. He also began a nearly thirty-year teaching career at this time.

Raye, Martha. See ***Artists and Models.***

Reagan, Ronald. See ***Going Places.***

"Real Ambassadors, The." By **Dave Brubeck** and Iola Brubeck; rec. September 13, 1961, in New York City by **Louis Armstrong and the All Stars,** pianist Dave Brubeck, and guests; CD #50. The title song from the Brubecks' jazz oratorio features Armstrong backed by a three-voice chorus (Dave Lambert, Jon Hendricks, and Annie Ross), which, in combination with the Brubeck instrumentalists, manages to sound like a choir. As throughout the work, the lyrics are busy but clever, for example, "In our nation, segregation isn't a legality./Soon our only differences will be in personality." See additional comments on "Cultural Exchange."

Real Ambassadors, The. Originally conceived as a Broadway show, this oratoriolike jazz work with music by **Dave Brubeck** and book/lyrics by Iola Brubeck was recorded in July and September 1961, but it was not performed until the summer of 1962. The Brubecks had become incensed at how Armstrong, frequently an official jazz ambassador to the world, could still be refused service in his own country. Also, in 1960 both Brubeck and Armstrong had their southern U.S. tours canceled once the promoters discovered that their bands were racially mixed. Such discrimination was the inspiration for this piece. Brubeck, who like Armstrong was represented by **Joe Glaser,** tells the full story of the work in the album liner notes (with Chip Stern; CD #50) and in *Jazz Spoken Here* (by Wayne Enstice and Paul Rubin). The score was published by Derry Music Co., San Francisco, in 1963.

Really the Blues. See **Mezzrow, Mezz.**

"Reckless Blues." By Fred Longshaw and Jack Gee; rec. January 14, 1925, in New York City with vocalist **Bessie Smith** and Fred Longshaw on the harmonium; CDs #8, #36, and #52. Smith dominates this recording, but Armstrong is still a powerful presence. He uses a harmon or wa-wa mute, which is unusual for him. (See also "Careless Love Blues"; "Cold in Hand Blues"; "You've Been a Good Ole Wagon.") Nearly three decades later (January 28, 1957, in New York City), Armstrong takes center stage in a rerecording of "Reckless Blues" with **Velma Middleton** and the **All Stars** for his *Satchmo: A Musical Autobiography* project (CD #52).

Record Changer, The. Armstrong wrote for and frequently was a subject in this American jazz periodical, published in Fairfax, Virginia, from 1942 to 1957. During the be**bop** controversy in the late 1940s, *The Record Changer,* under the editorship of Bill Grauer and with the help of writers such as Orrin Keepnews, argued for tolerance and open-mindedness, trying to give equal attention to both sides. In all, *The Record Changer* published fifteen volumes containing 152 issues.

"Red Beans and Ricely Yours." Armstrong was an avid and vivid letter-writer from the moment he left home for Chicago in 1922 to the very end of his days. He always carried a typewriter with him while on tour and often wrote letters from his dressing room. His prose is full of delightfully idiosyncratic usage, punctuation, puns, salutations, and sign-offs (such as the frequent "Red Beans and Ricely Yours," in reference to his favorite dish). The majority of his letters are in the collection of the **Louis Armstrong House and Archives.** Selections from his correspondence are reprinted in Brothers's and Berrett's 1999 books. See **writer.**

"Red Cap." By Ben Hecht and Louis Armstrong; recorded on July 2, 1937, in New York City by Louis Armstrong and His Orchestra. Jazz writer Will Friedwald coined the term "Satchmoification" to describe the way that Armstrong made a modest song sound immortal, and "Red Cap" is a good example (Friedwald, excerpted in Berrett, 1999, p. 196). The title refers to members of the then powerful Sleeping Car and Pullman Porters' Union.

"Red Nose." By Marion Lake and Bonnie Lake; rec. May 18, 1936, in New York City by Louis Armstrong and His Orchestra.

Red Onion Jazz Babies. See **Christian, Narcisse J. "Buddy"; Clarence Williams' Blue Five; Hunter, Alberta.**

"Red Sails in the Sunset." By Wilhelm Grosz, James B. Kennedy, and Hugh Williams; rec. December 13, 1935, in New York City by Louis Armstrong and His Orchestra; CDs #41 and #51. Although some critics feel that this is the worst band Armstrong ever fronted and that his years with it represent a low point in his career, he stayed with it (but not exclusively) until well into the 1940s. "Red Sails" is a good example of Armstrong playing his heart out (especially on his twenty-four-measure muted solo) while the band lumbers along.

Redhead, Happy. See **Bolton, "Redhead" "Happy."**

Redman, Donald Matthew "Don" (1900–1964). Although a fine alto saxophone and clarinet player, Redman is best remembered as a jazz arranger and composer. He came from a musical family, learned to play many different instruments, and was graduated from Storer College (Harper's Ferry, West Virginia) in 1920 with a degree in music. His skill in playing reed instruments and in making arrangements brought him to the attention of **Fletcher Henderson,** who in January 1924 was forming a band in New York. Together with Armstrong (who arrived the following September) and **Coleman Hawkins,** Redman evolved the big band arranging style that eventually became standard jazz procedure. It was Redman who first integrated solo improvisations with written ensemble passages and notated such previously improvised devices as breaks (brief solos during interruptions in the accompaniment), chases (traded solos), and call-response patterns (e.g., brasses echoing saxes).

The influence of Armstrong on Redman's arrangements (and on the Henderson band) can be easily heard on "Sugar

Foot Stomp" (1925), recorded seven months after Armstrong's arrival. Armstrong had come to the Henderson band with some of the **King Oliver** band material, and Redman picked out "Dippermouth Blues" (which Armstrong had co-composed), changing far more than the country mouse title. He starts with a dramatic scoring of the diminished seventh, makes a smooth transition to a clarinet trio, gives Armstrong plenty of solo space (both accompanied and unaccompanied), gives another solo to trombonist **Charlie Green,** and provides an evocative blues ending. Many (even Henderson himself) consider "Sugar Foot" Henderson's best recording. Redman was of the opinion that "that recording was the record that made Fletcher Henderson nationally known" (Allen, p. 134).

Redman was a performer, too. Among the nearly four dozen tunes that Armstrong recorded with Henderson, Redman's clarinet or alto saxophone can be heard especially well on his arrangements of "Go 'long Mule," "Shanghai Shuffle," and "Copenhagen" (all from 1924). Redman later added luster to Armstrong's **Hot Five,** when in 1928 he contributed to such gems as "No One Else But You" and "Tight Like This." His high-pitched speaking voice can be heard on the latter recording. Redman also sang, and in fact he anticipated Armstrong's scatting on the 1926 "Heebie Jeebies" with his own **scat** performance on "My Papa Doesn't Two-Time No Time" (1924). (Although Armstrong never claimed to have invented or perfected scat singing—as did, for example, **Jelly Roll Morton**—it can be said with certainty that Armstrong was the first to bring it to a wide audience.)

Composition frequently goes hand in hand with jazz arranging, and Redman wrote quite a few popular tunes. When in the early 1930s he formed his own band, he wrote "Chant of the Weed," which many consider his masterpiece. He worked for most of the 1940s in radio and with the big bands of Count Basie, **Jimmy Dorsey,** and others. After World War II he toured Europe with his own big band. In the 1950s he served as music director for **Pearl Bailey** and composed more music, some of which has never been publicly performed.

Reed, Ishmael. See ***C above C above High C.***

Regal Theater. Located at 4719 South Parkway Boulevard in Chicago, this variety theater opened the doors to its 1,500-person capacity foyer and 3,500-seat auditorium on February 4, 1928. Inspired by the Moorish architecture so popular at the time, it had silk and velvet draperies, rhinestone-studded stage curtains, and elaborate chandeliers. The Regal booked the best acts of the day, which in the jazz category included Louis Armstrong, **Duke Ellington,** Count Basie, and others. In supplying material in 1944 for his designated biographer **Robert Goffin,** Armstrong wrote with pride that when he returned to Chicago from California in 1931 and played an engagement at the Regal, "You couldn't get 'Standing Room the whole week" (Brothers, p. 107). This account is entirely believable, since the previous year it was reported in the February 15 issue of the *Chicago Defender* that "the capacity crowd started a reception that lasted several minutes. . . . Such an ovation as was given him [Armstrong] has not been seen in these parts for a long time" (Collier, 1983, p. 218). As time marched on, the Regal was also a popular venue for cool jazz players, such as **Miles Davis,** and **bop**pers such as **Dizzy Gillespie.**

Reinhardt, Jean Baptiste "Django" (1910–1953). Much speculation surrounds Armstrong's relationship with the Belgian-born Gypsy guitarist Django Reinhardt. The two met in Paris in 1934, while Armstrong was taking some much-needed time off. Reinhardt was then well on his way to becoming both an incomparable guitarist and the first European to become a celebrated jazz artist. Since Armstrong was Reinhardt's idol, the guitarist wanted to see what they might do in tandem. However, according to various independent accounts, Armstrong ignored Reinhardt's overtures. It has been commonly speculated that Armstrong might have been afraid of the competition, but that seems unlikely, given his frequent collaboration with **Earl Hines, Duke Ellington,** and others. More likely is that there was simply some personal or musical chemistry that Armstrong found uncomfortable. It is said that Reinhardt was hurt by the rejection, but he nevertheless went on to achieve international fame. He led both big and small bands, made records, wrote music, and toured the United States as a soloist with Ellington's band. See **Briggs, Arthur; Lang, Eddie; Panassié, Hugues.**

religion. "As far as religion, I'm a Baptist *and* a good friend of the Pope, and I always wear a Jewish Star for luck" (Jones and Chilton, p. 244). Although he probably didn't know it, Armstrong was baptized a Catholic on August 25, 1901, at the Sacred Heart of Jesus Church on Lopez Street in New Orleans. Basically, however, Armstrong was not religious in the traditional sense of being a church member and attending services. Nevertheless, he had deep spiritual feelings, such as the inclusiveness expressed in his respect for all religions, as well as his legendary generosity toward those whom he considered in need. He also frequently revealed this spirituality in music, for example, in the recordings collected in the album ***Louis and the Good Book*** (CD #27).

"Remember Who You Are." By **Dave Brubeck** and Iola Brubeck; rec. September 19, 1961, in New York City by **Louis Armstrong and the All Stars,** pianist Dave Brubeck, and guests; CD #50. Armstrong and trombonist **Trummy Young,** that unbeatable duet team, have fun with this sardonic, minor key song. It's based on a government briefing given to Brubeck at the airport before one of his State Department tours. See additional comments on "Cultural Exchange."

Rena, Henry René "Kid" (1898–1949). Rena was another **Colored Waif's Home** alumnus, and in fact his time there (around 1912) overlapped Armstrong's. Music instructor **Peter Davis** taught them both, and Rena picked up additional pointers from **Manuel Perez,** leader of the famed **Onward Brass Band.** "We kids [Rena, **Buddy Petit,** Joe Johnson, and Armstrong] were very fast on our cornets," Armstrong later fondly recalled for readers of ***Esquire*** magazine (1951, p. 85). Rena eventually took Armstrong's place in the **Kid Ory** band, then in 1921 put together the Dixie Jazz Band, which worked in New Orleans during the 1920s. He also played with the **Tuxedo Brass Band,** and his own group was featured at the Brown Derby, a dime-a-dance establishment.

Unlike Armstrong, Rena never really left New Orleans (although the Dixie Jazz Band made several successful trips to Chicago). He went into the recording studio only once, in 1940, unfortunately well after his prime. However, he left memories of a warm tone, a graceful technique, and a remarkable high range. Like Armstrong, his style was influenced considerably by the clarinet, as musicologist Brian Harker has convincingly shown (2003, p. 137). His high obbligato on the last strain of "High Society" has become a traditional part of the piece's performance.

Rhapsody in Black and Blue, A. In this Walter Mitty-like short film, a hen-pecked man (Sidney Easton) is knocked unconscious by a wife **(Victoria Spivey)** fed up with his laziness, and he dreams of a land called Jazzmania where he is emperor. All powerful, he delights in having Armstrong perform "You Rascal, You" and "Shine." Armstrong wears a leopard skin robe and a three-foot-high headpiece and wades through soap bubbles intended to evoke clouds. Nevertheless, he manages to remain dignified by means of his comportment and the high artistic quality of his music. This is the kind of performance that made Armstrong a hero to black audiences in the 1930s but then object of derision in the 1960s. Since it is an excellent and rare example of his early **singing** and **trumpet style**s, and acting, excerpts from *A Rhapsody in Black and Blue* are found on nearly every Armstrong documentary. Paramount, 1932; B&W; 9½ mins.; Dir. Aubrey Scotto.

"Rhythm Jaws." See **nicknames.**

"Rhythm Saved the World." By Sammy Cahn and Saul Chaplin; rec. January 18, 1936, in New York City by Louis Armstrong and His Orchestra; CD #51. Here is a good example of the middle-era, big band Armstrong, now more relaxed and popular music-oriented than the earlier jazz trailblazer of the 1920s.

"Riff Blues." Traditional; rec. July 4, 1957, live at the **Newport Jazz Festival** by **Louis Armstrong and the All Stars;** CD #43. Just before this concert, there had been a major argument backstage. It seems that the promoters wanted Armstrong to appear with an assortment of previous associates rather than his regular All Stars and vocalist **Velma Middleton.** Always protective of his sidemen, Armstrong put his foot down. However, consummate professional that he was, Armstrong does not admit a trace of storm and stress in his performance.

riverboat music. See **Marable, Fate; Streckfus.**

"Riverside Blues." By Thomas A. Dorsey and Richard M. Jones; rec. early September 1923 in Chicago with **King Oliver**'s Jazz Band; CD #35. Although still subservient to his mentor (cornetist Oliver), Armstrong here breaks away for a chorus and a coda. See additional comments on "Alligator Hop."

Robbins, Fred (1918–1992). Robbins was a widely known celebrity interviewer, radio personality, and television host who served as master of ceremonies at Armstrong's pivotal New York **Town Hall concert** on May 17, 1947. He also seems to have organized the hour-long concert that was broadcast from the Winter Garden Theatre, as part of the June 9, 1947, premiere of ***New Orleans.*** Twenty-four years later—on July 9, 1971—Robbins delivered the eulogy at Armstrong's **funeral** at the **Corona** Congregational Church.

Robeson, Paul (1898–1976). Armstrong had no professional relationship with the great African American singer and actor, but they were well aware of each other's careers. For example, Armstrong had a biography of Robeson in his **Corona** home library, and Robeson, along with his wife Eslanda, went to Armstrong concerts. Eslanda later wrote how her husband and "most of black America rejoiced" when Armstrong spoke out on school desegregation at **Little Rock** (Duberman, p. 716). Robeson was much more politically active than Armstrong, having joined the Communist Party in the 1940s. This and other **civil rights** activities hampered his American career, which before World War II included appearances in such plays as *The Emperor Jones* in 1925, *Show Boat* in 1928, and *Othello* in 1930. In the 1950s he appeared frequently in Europe.

Robichaux, John (1886–1939). Among the many talented New Orleans musicians who filled the young Armstrong's ears were cornetists **Buddy Bolden** and **Joe "King" Oliver,** clarinetist **Sidney Bechet,** pianist **Jelly Roll Morton,** and John Robichaux, a violinist best known for leading the area's most successful orchestra. This ensemble, formed in 1913, varied in size from seven or eight to thirty-six, depending on the occasion, and it played for white audiences at restaurants such as La Louisiane or at private parties. The orchestra also gave Sunday afternoon public concerts and played for dancing in the evening. Robichaux employed the best musicians, who had to be able to read music, since he made written arrangements. Armstrong (in a manuscript supplement to his 1954 **autobiography**) remembered it as "the best Orchestra in town because they could read music fluently on sight.... Yea, they could read even a fly speck if it got on to their music sheet" (Brothers, p. 125).

A savvy and versatile musician, Robichaux began his career in the 1890s playing the bass drum in the Excelsior Brass Band. In addition to arranging music, he was also the composer of over 350 songs. His manuscripts can be seen at the **William Ransom Hogan Jazz Archive** at Tulane University.

Robinson, Bill "Bojangles" (1878–1949). Just as Armstrong admired **Joe Oliver**'s trumpet playing and **Guy Lombardo**'s band sound, his ideal entertainer was Bill Robinson, whose dancing, miming, and comedy captivated an entire generation (and continues to reach an audience on film). Armstrong first saw Robinson in 1922 at the Erlanger Theater in Chicago, after hearing about him for years. The experience blew him away. "Every move was a beautiful picture," he wrote nearly fifty years later. "I [was] sitting in my seat in thrilled ecstasy' and delight, even in a trance.... I was sold on him ever since" (Brothers, p. 184).

Like Armstrong, Robinson was a very different stage performer from the one we see playing submissive, agreeable roles in the movies. His range was much wider than the loyal servant/buddy he played to Shirley Temple in *The Littlest Rebel* and *The Little Colonel* (both 1935). On the stage he was a sophisticated, urbane performer who could hold an audience completely on his own. He was also an innovator who explored tap dancing on the toes. As for his clothes, according to Armstrong, "that man was so sharp he was bleeding" (Brothers, p. 184). Robinson's sartorial splendor had an influence on Armstrong, who early on developed into quite a natty dresser himself.

It must have been a dream come true for Armstrong when in 1939 **Joe Glaser** put him with Robinson on the same bill at the **Cotton Club.** The two complemented each other wonderfully, and there followed nearly a year of working together, beginning with a New Year's party at the Strand Theater in New York. Although there were songs and skits by other entertainers, the highlights were Armstrong's trumpet playing and Robinson's tap dancing. They literally stopped the show. An insight into Armstrong's performance ideal can be seen in what he admired about Robinson. "Audiences *loved* him very much. He was *funny* from the first time he *opened* his *mouth* til he finished. So to *me* that's what *counted.* His *material* is what *counted*" (Brothers, p. 28). This is a revealing statement, since it explains Armstrong's approach to his work as well as his need for approval.

A good place to see Robinson at his best is the 1978 documentary film *No Maps on My Taps.* He also has major parts in *Stormy Weather* (1943) and *Hooray for Love!* (1935).

Robinson, Frederick L. "Fred" (1901–1984). Armstrong was fond of this Memphis-born trombonist whom he met in Chicago in 1927 when they both worked in **Carroll Dickerson**'s band at the **Savoy Ballroom.** When in June 1928 Armstrong had to shuffle several **Hot Five** personnel, he replaced **Kid Ory** with Robinson. Many regard this second Hot Five incarnation as the zenith of Armstrong's recording career, and Robinson can be heard sliding supportively on such masterpieces as "Basin Street Blues" and "St. James Infirmary." On these and others he generally stays in the background, but his inspired solo on "West End Blues" is one of the many facets of this enduring gem.

When in May 1929 Armstrong's new manager, **Tommy Rockwell,** called him to New York, Armstrong took the ensemble and some additional Dickerson men, and for a year they worked at **Connie's Inn.** They also made some enduring recordings, including three from ***Connie's Hot Chocolates:*** "Ain't Misbehavin'," "(What Did I Do to Be So) Black and Blue?" and "That Rhythm Man," all recorded in July 1929. Except for a brief hot solo in "That Rhythm Man," Robinson again doesn't emerge from the general texture in these tunes, but the following September he took a few sweet bars in a recording of "When You're Smiling." Smiles became less frequent the following month, however, when the **Great Depression** began. Armstrong's career then moved in different channels, and Robinson, a reliable sideman, went on to work with **Fletcher Henderson, Cab Calloway, Sy Oliver,** and many others. In addition to his work with the Hot Five, Robinson is also remembered for his 1939 recordings with **Jelly Roll Morton.**

Robinson, Jackie (1919–1972). As the first African American to play major league baseball, Robinson inspired many, Armstrong included. Armstrong was a baseball fan and liked to use Robinson's photos (clipped from ***Ebony*** magazine and other publications) prominently in the collages with which he decorated his scrapbooks, reel-to-reel tape boxes, and even the ceiling of the den in his home in **Corona,** New York (see **art by Armstrong**). Robinson and Armstrong were two of the most influential African Americans in their era, which documentary filmmaker **Ken Burns** brought out in an on-air interview from January 8, 2001, just before the PBS broadcast of his ***Jazz*** series: "I think the person who became our talisman, the sort of pole star for the series (just as Abraham Lincoln was in *The Civil War* [1989] series and Jackie Robinson was in *Baseball* [1994]) was Louis Armstrong."

"Rock My Soul." By Richard Huey; rec. February 6, 1958, in New York City by **Louis Armstrong and the All Stars** and the **Sy Oliver** Choir; CD #27. It took Armstrong with his considerable blues experience to show the possibilities in this spiritual. See additional comments on "Down by the Riverside."

"Rockin' Chair." By **Hoagy Carmichael;** rec. December 13, 1929, in New York City by Louis Armstrong and His Orchestra with vocalist Hoagy Carmichael; CDs #6, #12, #13, #14, #17, #19, #21, #23, #28, #32, #44, #47, #57, #60, and #61. First recorded in 1929 as a duet with the composer, this cozy song remained in Armstrong's repertory all his life, especially after the landmark May 17, 1947, **Town Hall concert.** There he and trombonist **Jack Teagarden** created the definitive version, including both instrumental and vocal dueting plus a comic routine. After Teagarden left the **All Stars** in 1951, Armstrong did a similar version of "Rockin' Chair" with **Trummy Young, Tyree Glenn,** or other All Star trombonists. Armstrong and Teagarden can be both heard and seen doing "Rockin' Chair" in the 1960 **movie *Jazz on a Summer's Day.*** See additional comments on "Ev'ntide."

Rockwell, Tommy. Armstrong's first manager has been frequently maligned, but he really did a great deal to promote his client. Although not a musical person, Rockwell changed Armstrong's musical style, marketing him as a star. He promoted Armstrong as an entertainer and soft-sold his talent as a jazz musician. For example, in 1929 Rockwell got Armstrong his first Broadway job in Vincent Youmans' ***Great Day.*** When that didn't work out, he placed Armstrong in the very successful ***Connie's Hot Chocolates,*** which lasted as scheduled from June to December 1929. Armstrong's career received a considerable boost when his singing of the inter-act song "Ain't Misbehavin' " became a sensation. His subsequent recording of it became his first big hit, and he backed it with another song from the show (although he didn't sing it there), "(What Did I Do to Be So) Black and Blue?" An executive for **Okeh,** Rockwell also got Armstrong to record popular commercial numbers, such as "Body and Soul" and "Sweethearts on Parade" (both 1930), thereby attracting a large and diverse audience.

In July 1930 Rockwell booked Armstrong into Frank **Sebastian's New Cotton Club** in Culver City (near the MGM movie studios). When in March 1931 Armstrong was arrested for smoking **marijuana,** Rockwell sent his associate **Johnny Collins** to deal with the situation. Back in Chicago, there arose a misunderstanding as to whether Rockwell or Collins was now in charge. The Mafia became involved, and to prevent violence, Collins quickly sent Armstrong and his band on a tour through the upper Midwest and South. Rockwell tried to regain control by proxy and then through the courts, but by then he had other concerns, such as managing the **Mills Brothers, Bing Crosby,** and others. Armstrong's contract eventually went in 1935 to a third, tough, persuasive white man, **Joe Glaser,** who placated Rockwell with a cash settlement and, to underscore the deal, rented office space in Rockwell's booking agency.

"Rocky Mountain Moon." By **Johnny Mercer;** rec. July 5, 1960, in New York City with vocalist **Bing Crosby** and a studio band and choir conducted by Billy May. See comments on "At the Jazz Band Ball."

Rodgers, James Charles "Jimmie" (1897–1933). The great country music singer, songwriter, and guitarist made one of his 111 recordings with Armstrong in 1930, when they did "Blue Yodel No. 9." This was the first of Armstrong's **crossover** recordings, a practice that he pioneered and a term that had not been invented yet. It was also the last of his blues accompaniments, begun in 1924 with **Ma Rainey.** Rodgers—considered by many to be the father of country music—was deeply influenced by the blues and had been recording blue yodels since 1927. He was the first performer to be elected to the Country Music Hall of Fame (1961).

"Room Rent Blues." By Irving Newton; rec. between October 5 and 15, 1923, in Chicago with **King Oliver**'s Jazz Band. See comments on "Alligator Hop."

Rooney, Mickey. See ***The Strip.***

"Rose Room." By Harry H. Williams and Art Hickman; rec. January 21, 1955, live at the Crescendo Club in Los Angeles by **Louis Armstrong and the All Stars;** CD #6. This was a feature number for All Stars clarinetist **Barney Bigard.**

Roseland Ballroom. Roseland, at Broadway and West 51st Street, opened on New Year's Day 1919 and quickly became a downtown center for hot music and dancing on its large floor. There were plenty of "dime-a-dance" taxi dancers available for those without partners. Many people, however, including professional musicians, came simply to listen. Although the clientele was white, black bands played there in the early 1920s because they were less expensive and because of the growing popularity of African American entertainers. The 1919 admission price of $.85 had only gone up to between $1.10 and $1.50 by 1953, according to Walter Allen, author of the fascinating 1973 book *Hendersonia.* Allen also notes that black musicians were allowed in to listen but had to stand in a special area, out of sight of the white patrons (pp. 113–114). In its day, Roseland was the best ballroom in New York, which had the best ballrooms in the country.

Fletcher Henderson began his long association with Roseland in 1924, and before the end of the year, Armstrong came from Chicago to join him as soloist. According to various accounts, people tended to stop dancing and crowd around the stage to listen to him. The Henderson ensemble set the standard and style for the big band era, and these were followed by all the major **swing** bands. Live broadcasts from Roseland went all across the United States. In 1956 when the ballroom was closed, a new and larger Roseland opened nearby at 239 West 52nd Street. Count Basie played there frequently in the 1970s, and the music and dancing have continued into the twenty-first century.

route du bonheur, La. **Louis Armstrong and the All Stars** play "Struttin' with Some Barbecue" in this French-Italian film. Here—as in other European films, such as ***La botta e risposta*** and ***Kaerlighedens Melodi***—Armstrong plays the role of a famous visiting entertainer whose performance comes as the musical high point and begins the denouement. In this case, a radio station employee overcomes obstacles to assemble music hall, ballet, opera, and jazz stars for a benefit performance. Among the talent are **Sidney Bechet** and **Django Reinhardt.** The All Stars play their number in the street, where Armstrong at first waits for his band, which eventually arrives by truck. Italian title: *Saluti e baci.* CLM-Athena, 1952; 92 mins.; Dir. Maurice Labro and Giorgio Simonelli.

"Royal Garden Blues." By **Clarence Williams** and Spencer Williams; rec. November 30, 1947, live at Symphony Hall in Boston by **Louis Armstrong and the All Stars;** CDs #1, #13, #25, #32, #54, #55, #59, and #61. This 1919 piece (named after the Chicago club that in 1921 became the famous **Lincoln Gardens**) was a staple of Armstrong's repertory throughout his life, and here it gets a rollicking performance. A generation earlier the number received some extravagant publicity when (according to the *Chicago Defender* of February 20, 1926, p. 6) it was performed in the 1,500-seat **Vendome Theater** by an orchestra hidden in different parts of the theater. On cue, the performers played it while marching toward the stage. (See also Kenney, 1999, pp. 49–50, and Brothers, p. 127.) It seems very likely that the orchestra was **Erskine Tate**'s, fronted by Armstrong.

Royal Gardens. See **Lincoln Gardens.**

"Running Bear." By J.P. Richardson; rec. August 1970 in New York City with the Nashville Group. See comments on "Almost Persuaded."

Russell, Luis Carl (1902–1963). After working together briefly but successfully on a few records in New York in 1929 (e.g., "I Can't Give You Anything But Love" and "Mahogany Hall Stomp"), Armstrong opened with the Luis Russell band on October 29, 1935, at **Connie's Inn** in New York. The engagement lasted four months during which time Louis Armstrong and His Orchestra, led by Russell, was frequently heard over CBS radio. Everyone was so pleased that the arrangement basically continued for nearly a decade. Some critics feel Russell's was the worst band Armstrong ever fronted and that his years with it represent a low point in his career. However, Armstrong was the first to stand up for his friends. "I am sure this is one of the finest aggregations of colored **swing** players, all in one band, that you will find in the world today," wrote Armstrong in his **autobiography** (1936, p. 94).

Russell and Armstrong were well acquainted before beginning their professional association. Although born in

Panama, Russell had early New Orleans experience and worked with **King Oliver** in Chicago (1925–1927). In his own band he tried to carry on the New Orleans ensemble tradition, with the help of New Orleans musicians such as drummer **Paul Barbarin,** bassist **Pops Foster,** and clarinetist **Albert Nicholas.** Nevertheless, the band was best known for its improvising soloists. Armstrong was first and foremost, of course, but also featured were **Henry "Red" Allen** on trumpet, **J.C. Higginbotham** on trombone, and Albert Nicholas on clarinet.

Russell's was not so much a jazz band as it was a commercial swing band, and during his years with the group, Armstrong became more of a general entertainer than exclusively a jazz musician. Performances and recordings of tunes such as "The Music Goes 'round and Around" (1936), "Cuban Pete" (1937), and " 'S Wonderful" (1938) went hand in hand with recyclings of "Mahogany Hall Stomp" (1936), "Dinah" (1937), and "Struttin' with Some Barbecue" (1938). Armstrong reached out to the widest possible audience, and in the end, his name became a household word. Unfortunately, Russell's fate was less glamorous. Not much of a disciplinarian, he gradually relinquished control and in 1943 retired to the piano bench when saxophonist **Joe Garland** took over. Russell eventually started another band, which worked in New York until 1948, when he retired from music and worked as a chauffeur and businessman.

"Russian Lullaby." Traditional Russian-Jewish folk song, adapted by **Irving Berlin;** rec. April 26 or 27, 1950, in New York City by **Louis Armstrong and the All Stars;** CD #8. Armstrong learned this song during his childhood, around 1907, from the **Karnofsky family,** his employers. "I was real relaxed singing the song called 'Russian Lullaby' with the Karnofsky family, when mother Karnofsky would have her little baby boy in her arms, rocking him to sleep," he wrote in March 1969 during an extended stay at **Beth Israel Hospital** in New York City. "We all sang together until the little baby would doze off... then bid each other good night" (Berrett, 1999, pp. 7–9). The version here features All Star bassist **Arvell Shaw,** firmly supported by drummer **Cozy Cole** and pianist **Earl Hines.**

S

" 'S Wonderful." By George Gershwin and Ira Gershwin; rec. January 21, 1955, live at the Crescendo Club in Los Angeles by **Louis Armstrong and the All Stars;** CDs #6 and #41. This jazz standard from the 1927 musical *Funny Face* is a feature number for All Star clarinetist **Barney Bigard.**

Salle Pleyel. The venerable Parisian concert hall, so important for cultivated chamber music in the nineteenth century, became a popular twentieth-century venue for jazz performances, and Armstrong was one of the first to make it so. He gave two memorable concerts there–November 9 and 10, 1934. French jazz enthusiast **Hugues Panassié** devoted a chapter to these events in his 1946 *Douze années de jazz*: "The entrance of Louis on stage was something unforgettable . . . like a brilliant meteor" (Berrett, 1999, p. 65). Although on the first evening there were problems with the microphone and composer Darius Milhaud demurred, the show was well received, and it went even better the following night. Armstrong remembers in ***Swing That Music*** that the French manager told him to sing in French or risk being a "flop." Armstrong declined. "Anyway," he recalled, "I got such a big hand I had to come out of my dressing room in my bathrobe for the curtain calls" (p. 114). After World War II, Armstrong was followed in the Salle Pleyel by **Dizzy Gillespie, Duke Ellington,** Gerry Mulligan, and a parade of other jazz greats.

Salute to Louis Armstrong. This short film is a compilation of scenes from the four documentaries (***Anatomy of a Performance, The Antiquarians, Finale,*** and ***Trumpet Players' Tribute***) made in connection with the July 10, 1970, opening concert of the **Newport Jazz Festival,** which was billed as a tribute to Louis Armstrong. Festifilm, Inc., 1970; 26 mins.; color; Dir. Sidney J. Stiber; Prod. George Wein.

Saluti e baci. See ***route du bonheur, La.***

"Santa Claus Blues." By Charley Straight and Gus Kahn; rec. November 26, 1924, in New York City with the Red Onion Jazz Babies; CDs #7, #35, and #36. This agile performance seems like a harbinger of the **Hot Five,** which was formed a year later. Before then Armstrong recorded "Santa Claus Blues" twice (October 8 and 16, 1925) with vocalist **Eva Taylor** and also with **King Oliver.** See additional comments on "Christmas in New Orleans."

"Satchel Mouth Swing." By Louis Armstrong, **Lil Hardin Armstrong,** and **Clarence Williams;** rec. January 12, 1938, in Los Angeles by Louis Armstrong and His Orchestra; CD #34. Armstrong here turns one of his **nicknames** (many of which affectionately referred to his mouth size—"Gatemouth" **"Dippermouth,"** etc.) into an attractive **swing** number. After a smooth crooner-style vocal, he improvises a memorable trumpet solo that builds dramatically to a "D" above high "C."

"Satchelmouth." See **nicknames.**

Satchmo. Armstrong's most famous and enduring nickname was acquired in July 1932 on arriving in **England** for his first tour abroad. He was met by Percy Brooks of ***Melody Maker*** magazine, who, nervously contracting "Satchelmouth" (an earlier nickname), said, "Hello Satchmo!" Armstrong liked the new name so much that he used it in the title of the second volume of his **autobiography.** He also had it inscribed on two of his **trumpets** and printed at the top of his stationery.

Satchmo: Louis Armstrong. This affectionate video is based on the 1988 book *Satchmo* by Gary Giddins. It includes over a dozen excerpts from Armstrong's film performances ranging from 1932 to the late 1960s: ***Pennies from Heaven,*** a **Betty Boop** cartoon, ***Going Places, Jam Session, New Orleans*** with **Billie Holiday,** ***High Society*** with **Bing Crosby,** and ***Hello Dolly!*** with **Barbra Streisand.** Also included are portions of televised live concerts with **Dizzy Gillespie** as well as **Jack Teagarden** and **Louis Armstrong and the All Stars.** Among the songs are: "West End Blues," "Potato Head Blues," "Heebie Jeebies," "Weather Bird," "Struttin' with Some Barbecue," "Blue Turning Grey," "On the Sunny Side of the Street," "When You're Smiling," "Mack the Knife," and "What a Wonderful World." As if that weren't enough, the film also generously presents interviews with **Arvell Shaw,** Tony Bennett, **Wynton Marsalis, Dexter Gordon, Dave Brubeck,** Iola Brubeck, Lester Bowie, **Milt Gabler, George Avakian,** Milt Hinton, **Bud Freeman, Marty Napoleon, Joe Muranyi,** Doc Cheatham, **Barrett Deems,** and **Zilner Randolph.** Snippets from Armstrong's **autobiographies** and letters are read by Melvin Van Peebles. Originally issued by Sony in VHS format in 1989, a DVD version came out in 2000 for the Armstrong Centennial. CBS, 1989; B&W and color; 86 mins.; Dir. Gary Giddins and Kendrick Simmons.

Satchmo: My Life in New Orleans. This 1954 publication (first published in 1952 in France as *Ma Nouvelle Orléans)* and the 1936 ***Swing That Music*** are the two volumes of **autobiography** that Armstrong published during his lifetime. It is a genial and vivid document, which covers his life up to joining **King Oliver** in Chicago in 1922. Armstrong describes his rough and tumble **childhood** milieu in a matter-of-fact way. He says his mother told him "that the night I was born there was a great big shooting scrape in the Alley and the two guys killed each other" (p. 8). Armstrong affectionately recalls the kindness shown to him by a wide variety of people, especially the Jewish **Karnofsky family** in New Orleans, and he describes numerous incidents of racial discrimination with virtually no indignation. "We were not much good the rest of that day," he says after a drunken white man mock-threatened one of Armstrong's playmates with a rifle, "but we weren't so scared that we could not eat all the spaghetti and beer they gave us when they were through eating. It was good" (pp. 48–49). Although no doubt heavily edited, as we can now see in the light of subsequent writings not meant for the public (e.g., the letters and unpublished memoirs in the **Louis Armstrong House and Archives** at Queens College), it's a fascinating and engrossing book about growing up black in the South and getting out alive. See **Gautier, Madeleine.**

"Satchmo Story, The." Like **"The Armstrong Story," "The Goffin Notebooks,"** and **"Louis Armstrong + the Jewish Family . . . ,"** "The Satchmo Story" is an autobiographical manuscript that remained unpublished until 1999 (when Thomas Brothers edited a selection of Armstrong's writings). However, Armstrong intended all these documents for publication. "The Satchmo Story," written in 1959, was to have been the sequel to his 1954 ***Satchmo: My Life in New Orleans*** (or so it was announced at the time of publication). However, since "The Satchmo Story" focuses so much on **marijuana,** jazz writer Gary Giddins plausibly speculates that it and other writings were suppressed by Armstrong's manager, **Joe Glaser,** who wanted to avoid problems. Armstrong's original document can be seen at the **Louis Armstrong House and Archives,** Queens College.

Satchmo the Great. CBS television cameras followed **Louis Armstrong and the All Stars** on U.S. State Department tours of Europe and Africa in 1955 and 1956. With the resulting footage, Edward R. Murrow and Fred Friendly made a half-hour profile of Armstrong for their popular *See It Now* program (which aired on December 13, 1955, and included only the **European tour** of 1955). With the 1956 tour there was so much more good material that they expanded it into an hour-long documentary *Satchmo the Great.* The grave Murrow comments on the various scenes, while Armstrong has fun reminiscing about old New Orleans, discussing jazz, and defining certain terms, such as "cat" and "gutbucket." The film has a number of memorable moments. In one scene some 100,000 natives celebrate Armstrong's arrival on May 24, 1956, in the Gold Coast (which had recently become the new and independent nation of **Ghana**), and in another Armstrong's singing of "(What Did I Do to Be So) Black and Blue?" visibly moves the new prime minister Kwame Nkrumah. At the end, Armstrong performs on July 14, 1956, before a sold-out house of 20,000 in New York's Lewisohn Stadium, along with the **Dave Brubeck** Quartet and the Stadium Symphony Orchestra conducted by **Leonard Bernstein.** The event symbolized to some that jazz had now become an accepted part of musical tradition and to others the lamentable homogenization of culture. Although the concert lasted until shortly before midnight, the "still quivering" audience (so described by the *New York Times* reporter on the following day, p. A64) willingly remained to be filmed en masse for the documentary. Especially with its scenes in partitioned Berlin, the film underscored Armstrong's identity as a goodwill ambassador, dispensing jazz as a curative tonic around the world. A *Satchmo the Great* album was also made (and reissued on CD #55). United Artists, 1957; B&W; 63 mins.; Dir. Edward R. Murrow, Fred W. Friendly, and Mill Lerner. (The Ghana sequence from the film was also used in the 1971 documentary *Black Music in America: From Then Till Now.*)

"Save It, Pretty Mama." By **Don Redman,** Joe Davis, and Paul Dennicker; rec. December 5, 1928, in Chicago by Louis Armstrong and His **Savoy Ballroom Five;** CDs #3, #10, #12, #13, #30, and #47. Redman was a sterling influence on everyone he worked with (**Fletcher Henderson,** Count Basie, **Jimmy Dorsey, Pearl Bailey,** and others), and here he adds luster to what is essentially Armstrong's **Hot Five.** The influence went both ways, too, as demonstrated by Redman's Armstrong-like sax solo, before and after which he plays the clarinet. **Earl Hines** does some flashy piano work, and the final chorus is an outstanding example of jazz ensemble improvisation at its best. See also the comments on "No One Else But You."

Savoy Ballroom. Opened in Chicago in 1927 (its New York cousin had opened a year and a half earlier), the Savoy astonishingly had music and dancing all seven nights of the week. The **Carroll Dickerson** Orchestra, led by Armstrong, appeared there early in the Ballroom's twenty-year life. There were in fact usually two bands, which alternated sets, and Armstrong enjoyed the rivalry. Outside the ballroom Armstrong made recordings with small studio groups, variously called the **Hot Five** or **Hot Seven** or **Savoy Ballroom Five.** With this last ensemble he recorded "St. James Infirmary," "I Can't Give You Anything But Love," and "Mahogany Hall Stomp," among other pieces, between December 1928 and March 1929. The Savoy Ballroom did not have a particularly prosperous life, especially after the stock market crash in 1929. By 1938 the number of dance nights was down to four per week, and eventually it was Sundays only. Such activities as boxing and skating were tried but without much success. Nevertheless, it served as a major jazz venue and engaged virtually all the major bands. Beginning in 1938, live broadcasts dramatically increased its audience. Like the **Cotton Club,** there were many Savoy Ballrooms throughout the country, and there were also at least two Savoy record labels.

Savoy Ballroom Five. "Louis Armstrong and His Savoy Ballroom Five" was one of the various studio band names that "Louis Armstrong and His **Hot Five**" went by during its November 1925 to March 1929 life. (Another was "Louis Armstrong and His **Hot Seven**.") In personnel, the Savoy Ballroom Five resembled the second incarnation of the Hot Five (i.e., after December 1927), and it had at least six performers (including Armstrong) and sometimes as many as ten. The name "Savoy" was taken from Chicago's **Savoy Ballroom,** where many of the band members worked in **Carroll Dickerson**'s orchestra. The Savoy Ballroom Five had only three studio sessions between December 1928 and March 1929 but waxed such immortal numbers as

"St. James Infirmary," "I Can't Give You Anything But Love," and "Mahogany Hall Stomp."

"Savoy Blues." By **Edward "Kid" Ory;** rec. December 13, 1927, in Chicago by Louis Armstrong and His **Hot Five;** CDs #10, #44, #48, and #61. With the help of hindsight, it's easy to see here that Armstrong was outgrowing the original Hot Five (which had been together for two years) and why he was about to replace everyone. Pianist **Lil Armstrong** plays heavy-handed piano chords, but they must have been okay by composer Ory, who was there, sounding similarly brutish, although one can admire his delicious glissandos (which influenced Tommy Dorsey's 1937 recording of "The Dipsy Doodle"). Only guest guitarist **Lonnie Johnson** gives Armstrong something to work with, but Armstrong sounds like a soloist even when he's part of the ensemble. Anyone who wonders what constitutes genius in jazz might find an insight in the way Armstrong takes the simple three-note opening figure and artfully varies it for sixteen immortal measures.

"Savoyagers' Stomp." By Louis Armstrong and **Earl Hines;** rec. July 5, 1928, in Chicago by **Carroll Dickerson**'s Savoyagers; CD #30. This recording anticipates the big band style that would make Armstrong famous during the 1930s and early 1940s. His sweet, languid solo seems to float over the ensemble. Of special interest is co-composer Hines's piano solo, which is so intricate rhythmically that Gunther Schuller transcribed it in *Early Jazz* (p. 123).

scat singing. The practice of singing nonsense syllables had been around long before Armstrong, but he was the first to popularize it with a successful recording—"Heebie Jeebies" in 1926. It makes a good story that Armstrong sang scat on this recording to cover for having dropped the music, but he seamlessly moves through the entire song, singing lyrics at both the beginning and the end. Besides, why would he forget his own lyrics? It seems more likely that, given the creative nature of his mind, he did not want merely to sing the same words twice. The technique was very quickly picked up by **Cab Calloway** (whose nickname the "Hi-de-ho-Man" has a scat origin) and others, such as **Ella Fitzgerald,** who stretched it to imitate a variety of instruments and even individual soloists. Be**bop** singers (e.g., Betty Carter and **Dizzy Gillespie**) next increased the velocity, and in the 1960s, the Swingle Singers applied scat syllables to the classical repertory. Also in the 1960s scat's palette was expanded by non-Western sources (e.g., Flora Purim from Brazil) and even sounds previously considered nonmusical (cries, whispers, and screams). In more recent times, Al Jarreau has created vocal versions of very complex rhythms, and Bobby McFerrin has used his amazing range to create entire songs by consecutively recording percussive pops, inner voices, bass grunts, and the solo line. All these many other artists can be considered, as the title of Leslie Gourse's 1984 book puts it, *Louis' Children.* See also **"Ba-Ba-Bo-ZET!"** and *Disney Songs the Satchmo Way* (CD #15).

Schiff, Dr. Alexander. As Armstrong got into his late fifties, his wife **Lucille** became concerned over the possibility of his becoming ill while touring in a foreign country. Armstrong's manager **Joe Glaser** responded by retaining his personal physician, Alexander Schiff, who was for many years the physician for the New York State Boxing Commission. Lucille's instincts turned out to be correct. On June 23, 1959, while on tour in Spoleto, Italy, Armstrong suffered a heart attack and had to be hospitalized. Schiff not only quickly got him proper medical attention but he also prevented him from getting penicillin, as Armstrong was allergic to the drug. In September 1968, Schiff persuaded Armstrong to see a specialist about his shortness of breath caused by a chronic heart condition, and he even accompanied him to the appointment. He attended Armstrong right to the very end, and Armstrong mentions in his "Open Letter to Fans" (June 1, 1970) that Schiff as well as Joe Glaser visited him every day at **Beth Israel Hospital,** when he was suffering with heart and kidney ailments (Brothers, p. 182). Armstrong was "a kind man, he was a humble man, he was a charitable man," Schiff recalled. "I mean you had to irritate him until he was sinking. He was going down for the third time before he would blow his top" (Collier, 1983, p. 202).

school integration. See **Little Rock.**

Scott, Arthur, Jr. "Bud" (1890–1949). It is fitting that before the end of his life banjoist, guitarist, and singer Bud Scott would appear with Louis Armstrong in the 1947 film ***New Orleans,*** since he helped create the music that the film is about. Born in New Orleans, he learned his craft in various ensembles led by **John Robichaux** and others. He then traveled the vaudeville circuit, picked up some formal schooling, and wound up in Chicago with **King Oliver**'s Creole Jazz Band about the same time as Armstrong (1922–1923). It is Scott's banjo that one hears on the very first recordings that Armstrong made on April 5 and 6, 1923, and it's his voice that shouts, "Oh, play that thing!" on "Dippermouth Blues." Scott went on to perform and record with **Jelly Roll Morton** and others. After 1929 he was based in California, where he worked with **Mutt Carey** and **Kid Ory.** Scott was with Ory when he died.

"Screamin' the Blues." By **Maggie Jones** and **Fletcher Henderson;** rec. December 17, 1924, in New York City with vocalist Maggie Jones and pianist Fletcher Henderson; CD #36. See comments on "Anybody Here Want to Try My Cabbage?"

Sebastian's New Cotton Club. From the 1920s to 1939, Frank Sebastian owned and operated the lively New Cotton Club in Culver City (just west of Los Angeles), where one could not only hear jazz but see big floor shows. In July 1930 Armstrong began an extended engagement there as soloist and was favorably impressed with the house band (especially drummer **Lionel Hampton** and trombonist **Lawrence Brown**). Unfortunately, in early November Armstrong and drummer **Vic Berton** were arrested in the Cotton Club parking lot for smoking **marijuana** (a habit that Armstrong had acquired early in his career in Chicago). The two spent nine days in jail. In February 1932 Armstrong returned to Sebastian's club, this time staying for three months. The Club's proximity to movie studios put Armstrong in the right place at the right time with the right attitude to get into films, and he appeared in ***Ex-Flame*** (1931), in ***A Rhapsody in Black and Blue*** (1932), and in the **Betty Boop** cartoon ***I'll Be Glad When You're Dead, You***

Rascal, You (1930). Louis Armstrong and His Sebastian New Cotton Club Orchestra also made some excellent records, such as "I'm Confessin' (That I Love You)," "Memories of You," and "Sweethearts on Parade." Frank Sebastian's was one of many "Cotton Clubs" (i.e., named after the New York original) in Chicago, Cicero, Minneapolis, and elsewhere.

second lining. See **brass band.**

See It Now. See ***Satchmo the Great.***

"See See Rider Blues." Adapted from a traditional blues song by **Gertrude "Ma" Rainey** and Lena Arant; rec. October 16, 1924, in New York City with vocalist Ma Rainey and Her Georgia Jazz Band; CDs #8 and #36. See comments on "Countin' the Blues." Armstrong memorably rerecorded "See See Rider" on January 28, 1957, in New York City with **Velma Middleton** and the **All Stars** for his *Satchmo: A Musical Autobiography* project (CD #52).

segregation. Born at the turn of the twentieth century, Armstrong lived most of his life in a de facto if not a de jure segregated society. Two U.S. Supreme Court school segregation cases can serve to illustrate. The 1954 decision in ***Brown v. Board of Education*** declared that an earlier ruling—*Plessy v. Ferguson,* 1896—that permitted "separate but equal" educational facilities was unconstitutional. Although the decision was limited to public schools, it implied that segregation was not permissible in other public facilities as well. The ruling gave impetus to the growing **civil rights** movement, which Armstrong publicly joined during the 1957 **Little Rock** school desegregation crisis.

A child of the South, Armstrong early on learned how to live in a segregated society. His 1954 **autobiography** matter-of-factly records numerous examples of white oppression and overt cruelty. Later, he recalled in a May 1961 ***Ebony*** article titled "Daddy, How the Country Has Changed!" incidences while on tour: "We couldn't get into hotels. Our money wasn't even good. We'd play night clubs and spots which didn't have a little boy's room for Negroes. We'd have to go outside, often in the freezing cold, and in the dark" (p. 81). By the 1930s, however, he began quietly stipulating in his contracts that he would not perform where he could not stay. Without any fanfare, in 1932 he led the first African American band ever to play the Roof Garden of the Kentucky Hotel in Louisville. Later that same year he returned to his native New Orleans to play at the white-only **Suburban Gardens,** where he became the first African American to speak on the radio in that region. Armstrong then went on in 1937 to become the first African American performer to host a sponsored national network radio program, when he took over for Rudy Vallee on **The Fleischmann's Yeast Hour.** On his first **European tour** in 1932 he was the first black man to head a white European band and the first jazz artist of any color to appear as an individual star. Back in the United States, he was the first African American actor to be featured in full-length, mainstream **movies,** beginning in 1936 with ***Pennies from Heaven.***

Nevertheless, he regularly endured racial prejudice and even hate crimes. For example, in February 1957, Armstrong was playing a concert in Knoxville, Tennessee, before an audience of approximately 8,000 whites and 1,000 African

Americans. A stick of dynamite went off outside the auditorium. Armstrong, who knew how to avoid trouble by flashing a bright smile and saying, "Yes, sir," kept everyone calm by joking: "That's all right, folks, it's just the phone" (Giddins, 1988, p. 160). He'd often dealt with similar situations before.

Armstrong was among the large number of people who worked to make integration a reality. Before he came along, many Americans never saw a black person in any other capacity than that of a servant. As with so many other facets of life, Armstrong brought a sense of humor to this most volatile of subjects. According to Gary Giddins, "Erroll Garner [jazz pianist] liked to tell about the time he stuck his head in Louis's dressing room after a show and said, 'What's new?' 'Nothin' new,' came back at him. 'White folks still ahead' " (1988, p. 184).

Selmer. Armstrong began his long association with Selmer, a European musical instrument company, on his first trip to Europe in 1932. His preference seems to have been influenced by Selmer's paying him for endorsing their **trumpet.** An advertisement in the October 1932 issue of *Rhythm,* timed for Armstrong's first tour of **England,** enthusiastically touted both the Selmer "Challenger" model trumpet and the new "Louis Armstrong Special," based on it. Nearly forty years later, Armstrong had mostly Selmer horns on hand, and these can be seen at the Queens College **Louis Armstrong House and Archives.** There's a particularly beautiful Selmer, a "K-modified" model, which bears the inscription "Louis 'Satchmo' Armstrong" on the bell pipe.

"Shadrack." By Robert MacGimsey; rec. June 14, 1938, in New York City with the **Decca** Mixed Choir conducted by Lyn Murray, and on February 6, 1958, in New York City by **Louis Armstrong and the All Stars** and the **Sy Oliver** Choir; CDs #6, #14, #22, #27, #45, and #61. Armstrong first recorded this modern spiritual following the success of his "When the Saints Go Marching In." In the 1951 **movie** ***The Strip,*** he sings it as a segue to "When the Saints." So busy is he with the text that he leaves his trumpet in the case.

Shakespeare. See ***Swingin' the Dream.***

"Shanghai Shuffle." By Gene Rodemich and Larry Conley; rec. between October 10 and 13, 1924, in New York City by **Fletcher Henderson** and His Orchestra; CD #61. Although Armstrong doesn't seem entirely at home with either the arrangement or the plunger mute here, his performance left a deep impression on the young tenor saxophone player **Coleman Hawkins.** In an interview with ***Esquire*** magazine some twenty years later, he still remembered that "the musicians were like demons" who created "an orgy of music" at the **Roseland Ballroom.** Hawkins continued: "The high spot came when Louis Armstrong began 'Shanghai Shuffle.'... After that piece a dancer lifted Armstrong up onto his shoulders... and I stood silent, feeling almost bashful, asking myself if I would ever be able to attain a small part of Louis Armstrong's greatness" (August 1944, p. 142). See additional comments on "Alabamy Bound."

"Shanty Boat on the Mississippi." By Terry Shand and Jimmy Eaton; rec. June 15, 1939, in New York City by Louis Armstrong and His Orchestra; CD #18.

Shaw, Arvell (1923–2002). When the teenaged Shaw heard Armstrong play at the Comet Theater in St. Louis, he resolved to join his band one day, and his wish came true. First, though, he gained valuable experience playing with **Fate Marable** on Mississippi riverboats (as did the young Armstrong from 1919 to 1921) and then with navy bands. As Shaw told Joshua Berrett in a 1997 interview (Berrett, 1999, pp. 163–168), fifty years earlier he had just been discharged from the navy and returned home to St. Louis to decide what to do with his life, when by chance Armstrong was in town with his big band. Armstrong needed a bass player, the musician's union called Shaw, and the rest is history.

Shaw remained with Armstrong for many years, and the two became great friends. Shaw did take some time away, first to study music theory and composition in Geneva, Switzerland (1951) and in 1958 to tour Europe with **Benny Goodman.** Much in demand, he also performed and recorded with the elite **Teddy Wilson** Trio, and many others. However, from September 1947 to the late 1960s, Shaw was the **All Stars**' principal bassist. Like the other sidemen, he had a feature number, which was "How High the Moon."

In that same 1997 Berrett interview, Shaw describes the electrifying effect that the All Stars had on audiences all over the world. "Traveling with Louis was like traveling with the President of the United States," he said. "No matter what language or culture, the people reacted the same way. . . . All he had to do was walk on stage and flip that handkerchief and smile" (p. 168).

After the Armstrong days, Shaw recorded in France, did freelance work in New York, served in Broadway pit bands, and toured with English trumpeter Keith Smith's "The Wonderful World of Louis Armstrong." There is some excellent footage of Shaw performing with the All Stars in the 1956 movie ***High Society.***

Shaw, Sam (1912–1999). One of many photojournalists who liked Armstrong for a subject, Shaw was the producer of the 1961 feature film ***Paris Blues.*** He collaborated with artist **Romare Bearden** on a book project to be called "Paris Blues Suite," but it was never realized. A similar project about the history of jazz met the same fate. However, many of Shaw's photos were used by Bearden in collages that can be seen in Marc Miller's exhibition catalog.

"Sheik of Araby." By Ted Snyder, Harry B. Smith, and Francis Wheeler; rec. May 24 or 25, 1960, in New York City with the **Dukes of Dixieland;** CD #53. This 1921 song was revived in 1939 by **Jack Teagarden,** who made it his own. For additional comments, See "Avalon."

"She's the Daughter of a Planter from Havana." By Saul Chaplin and Gus Kahn; rec. July 7, 1937, in New York City by Louis Armstrong and His Orchestra.

Shindig. See ***Solo;* television.**

"Shine." By Lew Brown, Ford Dabney, Cecil Mack, and R.E. McPherson; rec. March 9, 1931, in Los Angeles by Louis Armstrong and His **Sebastian New Cotton Club** Orchestra. Despite this 1924 song's baggage of racial condescension, Armstrong performs with unabashed vigor, ending with some thrilling high "Cs." He thoroughly delighted in the response of the audience to the high notes and eventually chewed up his lip (see **lip problems**) by trying to please them with too many. Sidemen recall dozens of high "Cs," "as many as 350," according to drummer Harry Dial, who accompanied him on tour (Pinfold, p. 58). Outstanding among the sidemen on this recording is **Lionel Hampton,** playing both the vibraphone (Armstrong's suggestion) and drums. Armstrong also performs "Shine" in a 1932 short film titled ***A Rhapsody in Black and Blue,*** where he is dressed in a leopard-skin outfit. He recorded it again in 1942 for a **soundie,** a short film for use in a coin-operated, personal viewing machine.

Shine. One of four **soundies** that Armstrong made in 1942 for use in a coin-operated viewing machine. The brief film not only features Armstrong but also the comic "Nicodemus" Stewart dancing, three female extras, and several shoeshine boys. RCM, 1942; B&W; 3 mins.; Dir. Josef Berne.

"Shipwrecked Blues." By Spencer Williams; rec. January 17, 1925, in New York City with vocalist **Clara Smith** and pianist **Fletcher Henderson.** This recording was rejected and unreleased, but a remake on April 2, 1925, survives (CD #36). In it, Armstrong adds some inventive minor key touches. See additional comments on "Broken Busted Blues."

"Shoe Shine Boy." By Sammy Cahn and Saul Chaplin; rec. December 19, 1935, in New York City by Louis Armstrong and His Orchestra; CDs #41 and #51. Armstrong had a marvelous way of dignifying racially offensive songs, and here is a good example. (See also "Shine"; "Snowball.") Written by a pair of youngsters who would eventually make it big, "Shoe Shine Boy" evokes the subservient African American trying to ingratiate himself in a white world. Armstrong sings with sincere admiration for the hard-working child laborer who more than possibly may remind him of his own **childhood.** He introduced the song at **Connie's Inn,** a Harlem nightclub that, like the **Cotton Club,** featured black entertainers but was owned and patronized by whites.

"Short But Sweet." By S. Rosen, T. Puglisi, and Louis Armstrong; rec. July 1965 in Hollywood by **Louis Armstrong and the All Stars.**

"Shout All Over God's Heaven." See "Going to Shout All Over God's Heaven."

Showboat Cabaret. Located on North Clark Street on the Chicago Loop, the Showboat was a speakeasy controlled by the **Capone** syndicate. Armstrong performed there in 1931, but his residency suddenly ended one night because of a dispute between two managers, **Tommy Rockwell** and **Johnny Collins,** both of whom claimed to represent Armstrong. Called back to his dressing room, Armstrong found a bearded man pointing a gun at him and ordering him to leave for New York in the morning to work at **Connie's Inn**—or else. The threat appeared to have come from New York–based Rockwell, and Collins's response was to send Armstrong immediately on an extended tour throughout Illinois, Michigan, Ohio, West Virginia, and Kentucky until he, Collins, could establish firm control.

Shu, Eddie (Edward Shulman) (1918–1986). This versatile clarinetist (he could also play the trumpet, violin, guitar, and harmonica and sing) was a member of the **All Stars** from February to June 1965, during which time the ensemble toured extensively. In February, they went to Nova Scotia, Iceland, the West Indies, and Miami, and March found them in Eastern Europe. In April, back in the States, Armstrong took six weeks off for dental surgery, but late in May the band was off again for stops in London, Manchester, Paris, the Antibes Festival on the French Riviera, Stockholm, Malmö, Copenhagen, Helsinki, and Budapest. While in Paris at the Palais des Sports on June 4, 1965, the All Stars made a live recording that is aptly named *The Best Live Concert* (CD #2). Here Shu's lively clarinet playing can be heard on "Tiger Rag," "Back Home Again in Indiana," and other favorites. Armstrong always let his sidemen have a feature number, and Shu's was "Memories of You." Before the All Stars, Shu had a colorful career as a vaudeville performer and as a sideman with Gene Krupa and others. He worked in Cuba until Castro took over in 1959, then moved to Miami. After Armstrong, Shu worked in the Virgin Islands a while before living out his days in Tampa, Florida, where he died on the Fourth of July.

***Sidney*, S.S.** The *Sidney* was one of several riverboats in the **Streckfus** Line and the only one with a colored band. (Other Streckfus riverboat bands had white leaders such as Ralph Williams and Isham Jones.) **Fate Marable** was in charge of the *Sidney*'s music, and so many of his sidemen went on to fame that it was dubbed "the floating conservatory." Armstrong signed on for the summer of 1919 and reenlisted the next two summers. While on board he both perfected his music reading skills and gained the valuable professional experience of daily performance. Standing on the dock in New Orleans one day in 1919, **Jack Teagarden** first heard Armstrong play as the steamboat pulled in. As he later recalled, it was "one of the most beautiful notes I've ever heard.... [I]t was Louis Armstrong coming down from the skies like a god" (Boujut, p. 22). In 1920 when the boat stopped in Davenport, Iowa, Armstrong met the young **Bix Beiderbecke.**

Sinatra, Francis Albert "Frank" (1915–1998). Sinatra is one of Armstrong's few rivals for the twentieth century's most identifiable voice, and the latter's relaxed **swing** style greatly influenced the former. The two giants were also fond of each other and frequently improvised duets on **television,** for example, the January 1, 1952, CBS-TV *Edsel Show*. In 1964 as a salute to Armstrong's return to the ***Billboard* charts,** Sinatra recorded a "Hello Louis!" version of "Hello Dolly!" On July 9, 1971, Sinatra was an honorary pallbearer for Armstrong's **funeral** at the **Corona** Congregational Church.

"Since I Fell for You." By Buddy Johnson; rec. November 30, 1947, live at Symphony Hall, Boston, by **Louis Armstrong and the All Stars;** CDs #6 and #54. This then new song featured vocalist **Velma Middleton.**

"Since Love Had Its Way." By **Dave Brubeck** and Iola Brubeck; rec. between September 12 and 19, 1961, in New York

City by **Louis Armstrong and the All Stars,** pianist **Dave Brubeck,** and guests; CD #50. This number is in the second half of the jazz oratorio ***The Real Ambassadors.*** See additional comments on "Cultural Exchange."

"Sincerely." By Harvey Fuqua and Alan Freed; rec. January 18, 1955, in Los Angeles with Sonny Burke's Orchestra. The McGuire Sisters owned this song from the starting gate, but Armstrong also recorded it when it was new in 1955. During the following decade, it was revived by The Four Seasons, Paul Anka, and others.

singing style. Armstrong was and remains the only artist in Western culture to influence the music of his time equally as an instrumentalist and as a singer. His gravelly baritone is the most immediately recognizable voice of the twentieth century, but it is his style that set him apart from the other vocalists of his era. "Most of you have heard his records," Rudy Vallee wrote in his deferential introduction to Armstrong's 1936 **autobiography,** "and are familiar with that utterly mad, hoarse, inchoate mumble-jumble that is Louis' 'singing.' And yet when you study it, you will come to see that it is beautifully timed and executed, and to perceive that a subtle musical understanding and keen mind are being manifest through this seemingly incoherent expression" (p. xvi).

Vallee's assessment of Armstrong's style is both vague and overwritten (though charming), but he has the root of the matter in him. First, Armstrong was an early exponent of the "inchoate mumble-jumble" otherwise known as **scat singing.** He did not invent it, but he did make the first popular scat recording with "Heebie Jeebies" in 1926. (This became the **Hot Five**'s first big hit, selling 40,000 copies in a few weeks, at a time when selling 5,000 copies of a record was excellent and 10,000 was astounding.) By 1930 (e.g., on "I'm Confessin' ") he had gone a step further and was both singing and accompanying himself with scatlike asides that mimicked his instrumental technique. He was both inside and outside of a song simultaneously.

Second, Armstrong's "subtle musical understanding" enabled him to bring lyrics to life with sensitive, actorlike expression and realism of delivery and to sell almost any song: down-and-out blues, novelty tunes filled with humor and sometimes nonsense, pop songs, and ballads. He early developed a mellow style that one can hear beginning with "Put 'em Down Blues" in 1927 and that blossomed fully in his pleading rough breathlessness on "love" and "baby" in "I Can't Give You Anything But Love" (1929). This same song reveals not only a maturation in his art but also the strong influence of his friend **Bing Crosby** (e.g., the scat "babala, babala," a Crosby mantra, and the much smoother-toned voice of the crooning tradition). Indeed, a "manifestation" of his "keen mind," this style well suited not only popular ballads but much of his repertory.

Third, on "Star Dust" (1931), "Lazy River" (1931), "Basin Street Blues" (1933) and others, Armstrong liked to recompose a song's melody, often delivering large portions of text on repeat pitches. Finally, and most important for the emerging **swing** style, Armstrong usually sang either ahead of or behind the beat, rarely right on it. An example of this is his 1927 "I'm Not Rough," on which he pushes and pulls the beat, artfully doling out the lyrics in defiance of meter and phrase length.

"Style is, perhaps, the most important factor in the success of a musician," Armstrong wrote in an article titled "Greetings to Britain!" in the August 1932 issue of *Rhythm.* "I determined from the start to cultivate an original style, and while I tried hard not to force it, I tried out all sorts of ideas, discarding some, practicing others, until I reached, not perfection, since that is unattainable for the true musician, but the best that was in me" (Berrett, 1999, p. 47). Although this article appears to have been heavily edited, it does reveal Armstrong's belief in finding one's own style. His can be heard as a vocal counterpart to his **trumpet style,** and with these he inspired numerous imitators. Simultaneously unpolished and sophisticated, earthy and artful, Armstrong's singing style as an extension of his personality brought a fresh sincerity and individualism to performance.

Singleton, Arthur "Zutty" (1898–1975). "We went everywhere together and had some real righteous kicks," said Armstrong about drummer Zutty Singleton, with whom he developed side-by-side in New Orleans (Berrett, 1999, p. 108). The two often played in the same groups, such as the **Tuxedo Brass Band** and **Fate Marable**'s riverboat band. When in 1921 Armstrong attracted the attention of **Fletcher Henderson** and was asked to come to New York, he answered that he would only if Singleton could come along, too. (The offer evaporated but was successfully repeated later.) In the mid-1920s, Singleton and Armstrong both found themselves in Chicago. In November 1927 the two opened the Warwick, an ill-fated club, with their friend **Earl Hines.** The business venture lasted only a few weeks. Singleton and Armstrong continued to work and record together (e.g., the **Hot Five**'s 1928 "Basin Street Blues" and "Muggles"). The two went to New York in 1929 but worked separately, not without some hard feelings on Singleton's part when Armstrong's career as a soloist began to take off. An excellent musician, Singleton adapted to **swing** music in the 1930s, and he either led or played as a sideman in both traditional and mainstream bands. He retired after a long residency (1963 to 1970) at Jimmy Ryan's Club in New York, where he was admired as an elder statesman of jazz. Singleton can be seen playing drums in the 1947 film ***New Orleans.***

"Sinner Kissed an Angel, A." By Ray Joseph and Mack David; rec. January 29, 1957, in New York City with the **Sy Oliver** Orchestra; CD #26. See comments on "And the Angels Sing."

"Sit Down, You're Rockin' the Boat." By Frank Loesser; rec. August 31, 1950, in New York City with the **Sy Oliver** Chorus and a rhythm section led by pianist **Billy Kyle;** CD #27. Armstrong loved to cover new hits, and he obviously has fun with this witty song from the 1950 musical *Guys and Dolls.* It was an inspired choice for inclusion on the 1958 album *Louis and the Good Book.*

"Sittin' in the Dark." By Harold Adamson and Jesse Greer; rec. January 26, 1933, in Chicago by Louis Armstrong and His Orchestra; CDs #12 and #21. Working here with a lugubrious ensemble, Armstrong nevertheless succeeds in making this song **swing,** first with some warm vocal glissandos, then some cool trumpet syncopation, and finally a dramatic operatic ending on an impossibly high "F." This ending—with its progression of ascending and descending glissandos, repeated high "Cs", and will-he-make-it? climb to the final note—has troubled many otherwise ardent Armstrong fans (e.g., Schuller, 1989, p. 181, and Collier, 1983, p. 260), who see in it an unfortunate tendency toward grandstanding.

"Sittin' in the Sun." By **Irving Berlin;** rec. July 16, 1953, in New York City with the Jack Pleiss Orchestra; CD #39. Armstrong leaves his trumpet in its case on this genial song, which is backed by an augmented **All Stars** ensemble.

"Six Foot Four." By B. Morrow and Louis Armstrong; rec. January 24, 1956, in Los Angeles by **Louis Armstrong and the All Stars;** CD #16.

"Skeleton in the Closet, The." By Johnny Burke and Arthur Johnson; rec. August 7, 1936, in Los Angeles with **Jimmy Dorsey** and His Orchestra; CD #34. Armstrong worked well with the highly disciplined Dorsey Orchestra. This novelty number from the 1936 **movie *Pennies from Heaven*** featured Armstrong the actor as well as Armstrong the musician, as he performed with a dancing skeleton at the Haunted House Café. This was the big production number that firmly launched his movie career.

"Skid-Dat-De-Dat." By Louis Armstrong and **Lil Hardin Armstrong;** rec. November 16, 1926, in Chicago by Louis Armstrong and His **Hot Five;** CDs #10 and #48. Armstrong thrilled listeners with high notes, but he was also one of the first to explore his instrument's lower register, and no jazz player (except possibly **Bunny Berigan**) has ever surpassed him there. Before his 1931 "Star Dust" or even the 1928 "Basin Street Blues," he was playing warm low notes in "Skid-Dat-De-Dat," which, despite its zany title, is a dark piece. It's based on a simple theme consisting of four long notes, which Armstrong places around but never on the beat. The musical spotlight moves through the band in a series of four-bar solos and ensemble interludes. Clarinetist **Johnny Dodds**'s and trombonist **Kid Ory**'s breaks are noteworthy, yet no comparison to Armstrong's. Armstrong's solo has been transcribed by Lee Castle (vol. 2, p. 4).

"Skip the Gutter." By Spencer Williams; rec. June 27, 1928, in Chicago by Louis Armstrong and His **Hot Five;** CDs #10 and #48. Despite several trumpet fluffs, many wrong trombone notes, an out-of-tune clarinet, and a harmonically wayward banjo, this performance is memorable because of the collaboration between Armstrong and pianist **Earl Hines.** They challenge each other frequently and good-naturedly, foreshadowing both "A Monday Date" and "Weather Bird," two masterpieces that they would record before the year was out.

"Skokiaan." By August Machon Msarurgwa and Tom Glazer; rec. August 13, 1954, in New York City with the **Sy Oliver** Orchestra; CD #39. This novelty song originated in Zimbabwe, supposedly based on the name of a Zulu soft drink. It then acquired the whimsical English lyric and was subsequently recorded by such non-African groups as Sammy Kaye,

The Four Lads, and Spike Jones. Armstrong's hit recording preserves the song's playfulness, even though his articulation barely keeps up with the tongue-twisting lyrics.

slang. Much of Armstrong's colorful language entered the national vocabulary. According to Wentworth and Flexner's definitive *Dictionary of American Slang*, terms credited to Armstrong include "jive," "solid," "**scat**," "chops," "mellow," and forms of address such as "pops," "cat," and "daddy." Always colorful and poetic, slang greatly appealed to his interest in words and wit, and Armstrong frequently used other expressions that were widely popular, for example, "dig," "drag," and "sharp." Joshua Berrett lists these and dozens more in his 1999 edition of Louis Armstrong commentary (pp. 20–23). One term that Armstrong didn't use, though, is "armstrong," which is either a high note or series of them played, of course, on the trumpet.

"Sleepy Time Down South." See "When It's Sleepy Time Down South."

Sleepy Time Down South. One of four **soundies** that Armstrong made between April 20 and 24, 1942, for use in a coin-operated viewing machine. The film features Armstrong singing his signature tune "When It's Sleepy Time Down South," surrounded by children, and comedian "Nicodemus" Stewart dancing. RCM, 1942; B&W; 3 mins.; Dir. Josef Berne.

"Slender, Tender, and Tall." Rec. early 1943 in Los Angeles by Louis Armstrong and His Orchestra with vocalist Ann Baker; CD #49.

Smalls' Paradise. Located on Seventh Avenue at West 135th Street, Ed Smalls' was, along with **Connie's Inn** and the **Cotton Club,** one of the most famous Harlem nightclubs in the 1920s and 1930s. Patrons would come after the Broadway shows were over and not infrequently stay until morning. "In the audience, any old night," wrote Armstrong in ***Swing That Music,*** "would be famous actresses and critics and authors and publishers and rich Wall Street men and big people of all kinds, being gay and enjoying the hot **swing** music and the fast-stepping floor shows" (p. 90). Smalls', however, featured more music than spectacle, and it was the only major Harlem nightclub that admitted African Americans as patrons. When Armstrong decided to return to Chicago after fourteen months in New York with the **Fletcher Henderson** Orchestra (September 1924 to November 1925), Henderson gave him a big farewell party at Smalls'. Unlike the other two clubs, Smalls' survived the **Great Depression,** the post–World War II years, and even the racial strife of the 1960s and 1970s, only to close in 1986.

Smith, Ada "Bricktop" (1894–1984). In the spring of 1934 when Armstrong spent a few months in Paris licking wounds inflicted by the music business, he got to know the African American expatriate community, including **Josephine Baker,** Bobby Jones, **Arthur Briggs,** and Ada Smith, a.k.a. "Bricktop" (for her reddish hair). At this time, Smith, a singer, was the successful proprietor of Chez Bricktop, a Rue Pigalle club frequented by celebrities such as Ernest Hemingway and the future King Edward VIII. Armstrong and Smith stayed in contact through the years, as one can see from letters in the Louis Armstrong **archives** at Queens College, for example, one to **Dizzy Gillespie** and his wife written in Rome on July 1, 1959, in which Armstrong expresses great pleasure in visiting again with his old friend. (This letter is reproduced in Berrett, 1999, p. 156.) Armstrong met Smith through her husband, the New Orleans reed man **Peter DuConge** (1903–1965), who had also settled in Europe. Smith established eponymous nightclubs in Biarritz, Rome (on the Via Veneto, naturally), and Mexico City. In 1934 **Cole Porter** wrote the song "Miss Otis Regrets, She's Unable to Lunch Today" for her, and in 1983 New York Mayor Edward Koch presented her with a certificate of appreciation for her "extraordinary talent and indomitable spirit." Smith is the subject of the 1973 documentary *Honeybaby, Honeybaby!* and the author (with James Haskins) of *Bricktop* (1983).

Smith, Alpha. See **Armstrong, Alpha Smith.**

Smith, Bessie (1894–1937). Smith, the most successful African American singer in her day, made almost 200 recordings, the best of them with Armstrong (CD #36). It is said that she preferred cornetist **Joe Smith** (no relation) as an accompanist, but perhaps only because he followed her lead, while Armstrong gave her challenges and split the spotlight. Their "St. Louis Blues" (1925) is perhaps the best known of all early blues songs. Here Smith sings with a visceral passion, and Armstrong nimbly fills in around her. Fred Longshaw's harmonium, with its evocation of a church organ, adds a subtext about the sanctity of suffering. Their rendition of the lines "Feeling tomorrow like I feel today./I'll pack my grip and make my getaway" seems simultaneously both personal and universal. "Everything I did with her, I *like,*" Armstrong later told ***Life*** magazine's Richard Meryman (1971, p. 32). A sensitive accompanist, as the 1920s wore on Armstrong recorded with other blues singers, such as **Chippie Hill, Alberta Hunter,** and **Ma Rainey.**

Smith, Clara (1894–1935). Although Clara Smith spent most of her life in the shadow of **Bessie Smith** (who was no relation), she was a worthy exponent of the blues. On their "Shipwrecked Blues" (1925), Armstrong adds some inventive minor key touches, and on "My John Blues" (also 1925), he does some deft plunger work. Smith also recorded with **Fletcher Henderson** and **Don Redman.** Later she toured widely with her own show, in which she was billed as "the Queen of Moaners" (CD #36).

Smith, Joseph C. "Joe" (1902–1937). Smith played trumpet in the **Fletcher Henderson** orchestra from 1925 to 1928 (as did his brother Russell from 1925 to 1941), and for a time he was considered Armstrong's chief rival. However, the two represented very different styles of playing. "I've seen a drunken noisy cabaret crowd get quiet as a mouse when Joe started off on a sweet sentimental tune," recalled pianist Tiny Parham (Shapiro and Hentoff, 1955, p. 210). Smith's mellow, lyrical style combined with a plunger (he also liked to use a coconut shell) won him many admirers and made him a favorite collaborator with such singers as Ethel Waters (e.g., "I'm Coming, Virginia") and especially **Bessie Smith** (e.g., "Money Blues" and "Baby Doll"). Health problems prevented Smith from performing regularly, and after attempting to rejoin Henderson's band in the 1930s, he retired to a sanatorium in New York. While Armstrong's more virtuosic and inventive style makes Smith seem pale by comparison, there is evidence of Smith's influence on Armstrong. Gunther Schuller points out the second solo on the Henderson Orchestra recording of "T.N.T.," where Armstrong "does a flawless imitation of Joe Smith's smoother playing" (1968, p. 263). The recording was made in New York on October 21, 1925. On February 26, 1926, back in Chicago and recording with his own **Hot Five,** one can hear the same phrase in the coda of "Cornet Chop Suey." Furthermore, it was a backhanded compliment when, in April 1927, Armstrong disguised his style to moonlight (he was under contract with **Okeh**) in recordings with **Jimmy Bertrand**'s Washboard Wizards and **Johnny Dodds**'s Black Bottom Stompers, adopting Smith's thinner toned, middle-register, and altogether less exciting style.

Smith, Trixie (1895–1943). Armstrong was a busy blues accompanist during the 1920s, and in the first five months of 1925 he recorded with three singers named Smith, none related: **Bessie Smith, Clara Smith,** and Trixie Smith (CD #36). With the last, he did some memorable work on "Railroad Blues" and "The World's Jazz Crazy (and So Am I)." During the period 1920–1933, Smith performed frequently both as a singer and as an actor in New York's African American theaters. Her career got a boost when she won the 1922 Manhattan Blues Contest. From 1923 to 1939 she recorded nearly fifty sides (see Harrison, 1988).

"Snafu." By **Leonard Feather;** rec. January 10, 1946, in New York City with ***Esquire*** All-American 1946 Award Winners; CD #12. Pianist Billy Strayhorn, alto saxophonist Johnny Hodges, tenor saxophonist Don Byas, and others back Armstrong on this easygoing number written by his English-born friend and champion.

"Snag It." By **Joe Oliver;** rec. January 25, 1957, in New York City by **Louis Armstrong and the All Stars;** CD #8. Armstrong did not record this 1926 number earlier but nevertheless included it on his *Satchmo: A Musical Autobiography* project. (CD #52). Yank Lawson here takes Oliver's place, and Armstrong ends the number with a splendid cadenza.

"Snake Rag." By **Joe Oliver;** rec. April 6, 1923, in Richmond, Indiana, by King Oliver's Creole Jazz Band; CDs #35 and #48. Armstrong and his mentor Oliver were famous for duet breaks, and there are seven of them on this recording, which also features excellent work by drummer **Baby Dodds** and his older brother **Johnny** on clarinet. See additional comments on "Alligator Hop."

"Snowball." By **Hoagy Carmichael;** rec. January 28, 1933, in Chicago by Louis Armstrong and His Orchestra; CD #12. Modern ears may very well stumble over what have become politically incorrect lyrics in this tender song sung by an African American father to his son, but Armstrong croons it from the heart to the heart. His trumpet playing is similarly tender. See additional comments on "Ev'ntide."

"So Long, Dearie." By Jerry Herman; rec. September 3, 1964, in New York City by **Louis Armstrong and the All Stars.**

"Sobbin' Blues." By Art Kassell and Vic Burton; rec. between June 22 and 29, 1923, in Chicago by **King Oliver**'s Jazz Band. See additional comments on "Alligator Hop."

"Sobbin' Hearted Blues." By Perry Bradford, R. Layer, and G. Davis; rec. January 14, 1925, in New York City with vocalist **Bessie Smith** and pianist Fred Longshaw; CDs #36 and #48. This number, one of five blues recorded that day, is introduced by Armstrong, who stays just slightly in the background with his vocal-like cornet commentary on Smith's singing. See additional comments on "Careless Love Blues."

"S.O.L. Blues." By Louis Armstrong; rec. May 13, 1927, in Chicago by Louis Armstrong and His **Hot Seven;** CD #10. This recording of a number (which with some variation in lyrics is called "Gully Low Blues") was rejected by **Okeh Records.** The reason has more to do with commercial than musical values, since the title (an acronym for "Shit-Out-of-Luck") and some similarly earthy lyrics were obviously unsuitable. Along with cleaner words, "Gully" (recorded the next day) has a cleaner, crisper ensemble ending. The "S.O.L." version was discovered in the **Columbia Records** vault in 1940. Jazz scholar Charles H. Garrett has a thorough comparison of the two songs in Walser's *Playing Changes* (forthcoming).

"Solitude." By Edgar DeLange, **Duke Ellington,** and Irving Mills; rec. December 19, 1935, in New York City by Louis Armstrong and His Orchestra; CD #51. After the high-loud-fast excesses of the early 1930s (see "Shine"), here is a more subdued and subtle Armstrong. He is even more relaxed fifteen years later when on April 3, 1961, he rerecorded "Solitude" (CDs #11 and #28) with Ellington himself playing majestic solitary chords at the keyboard. See additional comments on "Azalea."

Solo. Made for telecast on ABC's popular mid-1960s *Shindig* series, *Solo* is an abbreviated concert by **Louis Armstrong and the All Stars.** After the customary "Sleepy Time Down South," Armstrong kicks it up with "Struttin' with Some Barbecue," which provides solo opportunities. Next is "A Lot of Livin' to Do" from the musical *Bye, Bye, Birdie,* followed by feature numbers: **Tyree Glenn**'s "Avalon" (which he plays on his second instrument, the vibraphone) and **Jewel Brown**'s "My Man." Armstrong winds up the show with two "good old good ones": "Mack the Knife" and "Ole Miss." A video version is available on Jazz Classics JCVC 102. Selmur Productions, November 4, 1965; B&W; 25 mins.; Dir. Jørn Winther.

"Some of These Days." By Shelton Brooks; rec. September 10, 1929, in New York City by Louis Armstrong and His Orchestra, and December 12, 1956, in New York City by **Louis Armstrong and the All Stars;** CDs #8, #40, and #52. This 1910 song by the composer of "Darktown Strutters Ball" was a good place for Armstrong to show what he could do in the low register. His mesmerizing work in the depths here inspired many trumpeters. Rerecorded nearly thirty years later, the piece gets a spirited performance and Armstrong can be heard extending his upper range to "D" above high "C" in the exciting conclusion.

"Some Sweet Day." By Ed Rose, Tony Jackson, and Abe Olman; rec. January 27,

1933, in Chicago by Louis Armstrong and His Orchestra; CDs #12, #17, and #24. Armstrong had **lip problems** at this time, but he hides it well, singing a little more than usual. He also gets unusually excellent support from the band, particularly from trombonist **Keg Johnson** and the young pianist **Teddy Wilson.** At any rate, Armstrong's trumpet playing sounds strong throughout, and he ends with a flourish.

"Somebody Stole My Break." By Dave Franklin; rec. April 28, 1936, in New York City by Louis Armstrong and His Orchestra; CD #34. Ray "Dutch" Smith, the speaking voice, unsuccessfully tries to help Armstrong find his break (i.e., his short solo cadenza between ensemble passages) in this novelty number, a companion to the same composer's "I Come from a Musical Family."

"Someday, Sweetheart." By John C. Spikes and Benjamin Spikes; rec. November 1965 in New York City by **Louis Armstrong and the All Stars.** This song serves as background music for a discussion between **Sammy Davis, Jr.** (playing jazz trumpeter Adam Johnson) and Cicely Tyson (playing **civil rights** activist Claudia Ferguson, granddaughter of Armstrong's character) in the 1966 **movie *A Man Called Adam.***

"Someday You'll Be Sorry." By Louis Armstrong; rec. on June 10, 1947, in New York City by **Louis Armstrong and the All Stars;** CDs #5, #6, #12, #16, #17, #25, #28, #40, #47, #53, #60, and #61. This enduring song came to Armstrong in a dream during the winter of 1947 while on tour in North Dakota. As he himself tells the story: "It was so cold that I didn't even want to get up out of bed . . . and then this tune came to me. I couldn't get it out of my head. I said to myself well if you don't get up now you'll never remember it. I got up and wrote the thing out" (Jones and Chilton, p. 243).

"Sometimes I Feel Like a Motherless Child." Traditional; rec. February 7, 1958, in New York City by **Louis Armstrong and the All Stars** and the **Sy Oliver** Choir; CD #27. Armstrong plays an appropriately soulful trumpet solo on this number for the *Louis and the Good Book* album. See additional comments on "Down by the Riverside."

Song Is Born, A. In this musical film starring **Danny Kaye** and Virginia Mayo, the title song is performed by Armstrong, along with **Benny Goodman,** Tommy Dorsey, Charlie Barnet, **Lionel Hampton,** Mel Powell, the Golden Gate Quartet (a vocal ensemble), and Russo and the Samba Kings. Kaye plays musicology Professor Hobart Frisbee, the leader of seven professors who have been laboring in isolation for nine years to write a complete history of music. When the scholars come to jazz, Professor Frisbee goes out to gather data, and Armstrong is one of the musicians who helps him out. This film is a remake (with music) of the 1941 *Ball of Fire,* also by Hawkes. RKO, 1948; B&W; 113 mins.; Dir. Howard Hawkes.

"Song Is Ended But the Melody Lingers On, The." By **Irving Berlin;** rec. June 13, 1938, in New York City with the **Mills Brothers** and guitarist Norman Brown; CD #40. This is one of the Mills Brothers' signature songs, and Armstrong's contribution deepens its impact. It sounds like an entire big band is at work here, as one brother supplies a trumpetlike vocalise in back of Armstrong's singing, another does a convincing tuba part, and in one miraculous section, all come together in a convincing imitation of a multiple-trombone chorus. Armstrong responds to the Brothers' virtuosity with two outstanding trumpet solos. See additional comments on "Carry Me Back to Old Virginny."

"Song of the Islands" (Na Lei Hawaii). By Charles E. King; rec. January 24, 1930, in New York City by Louis Armstrong and His Orchestra; CDs #8, #48, and #52. Before the term was coined, Armstrong did many **crossover**s such as this popular 1915 Hawaiian song. He sings a subtly swinging **scat** chorus (to the band's tradewind humming) and plays a delicate, muted trumpet solo on this piece as relaxed as an island vacation. There are two innovations in this recording: Armstrong's first time with strings (three violins) and the first occurrence of a solo vibraphone introduction and coda (nine months before **Lionel Hampton**'s "Memories of You") (see **firsts**). The gooey strings, lugubriously bowed bass, and bleating saxophones keep "Song of the Islands" from masterpiece status, but Armstrong's contribution is masterful.

"Song of the Vipers." By Louis Armstrong; rec. October 1934 in Paris by Louis Armstrong and His Orchestra; CD #48. Armstrong was a firm advocate of **marijuana,** which he praised to whomever would listen. He wrote to President **Dwight Eisenhower** about legalizing it and celebrated it in both this number and his earlier "Muggles." Like "gage," "reefers," and "tea," "muggles" is a nickname for marijuana, and "**viper**s" refers to those who smoke it. Now dated, the term was once widely used and found its way into numerous song titles: **Mezz Mezzrow**'s "Sendin' the Vipers," Stuff Smith's "If You're a Viper," and **Fats Waller**'s "Viper's Drag." (Other related titles were "Golden Leaf Strut," "Texas Tea Party," "Chant of the Weed," and "Smoking Reefers"—all recordings made in the 1920s and 1930s.) "Song of the Vipers" has both a blues and a spiritual sound but a format all its own. Armstrong murmurs and moans along with the trombone solo, and his trumpet solo floats sans souci over the beat.

"Song Was Born, A." By Don Raye and Gene DePaul; rec. August 6, 1947, in Los Angeles with vocalists Jeri Sullivan and the Golden Gate Quartet, the Leaders Orchestra (Tommy Dorsey, Charlie Barnet, Louis Armstrong, **Benny Goodman, Lionel Hampton,** Mel Powell, and Louie Bellson), and Russo and The Samba Kings ("The Brazilians" in the **movie**); CD #47. This is the title song from the whimsical 1948 movie ***A Song Is Born,*** which is about seven professors (led by **Danny Kaye**/Professor Hobart Frisbee) who have been laboring in isolation for nine years to write a complete history of music. When the scholars come to jazz, Professor Frisbee ventures out from this academic cloister to gather data, and Armstrong is one of the musicians who helps him. The "A Song Was Born" sequence includes drummer Louie Bellson on a floor tom tom, the Samba Kings (to demonstrate primitive rhythms), the Golden Gate Quartet (to demonstrate spirituals), Jeri Sullivan (as the voice of Virginia Mayo), and the "Bandleaders" ensemble (to demonstrate contemporary styles). A version of this song was issued separately to benefit cancer research.

"Sonny's Blues." See **Baldwin, James.**

soundies. In 1942 Armstrong made four short films (ancestors of today's music videos) for use in coin-operated viewing machines. The Soundies Distributing Corporation of America produced ***Swingin' on Nothing; Sleepy Time Down South; I'll Be Glad When You're Dead, You Rascal, You;*** and ***Shine*** (for details, see Stratemann, 1996, pp. 101–115).

"South Rampart Street Parade." By Ray Bauduc and **Bob Haggart;** rec. November 14, 1951, in Los Angeles with trombonist **Jack Teagarden** and the MGM Studio Orchestra and Choir; CD #45. Armstrong performs this popular 1938 song in the 1952 **movie** ***Glory Alley,*** in which he plays a boxing trainer, Shadow Johnson. Although Armstrong only plays forty-nine seconds of this piece, his work here (and in the title song and in "That's What the Man Said") enlivens a pretty dull film. As a reviewer wrote in the *New York Times* (July 30, 1952, p. 20): "Every now and then, Louis Armstrong sticks his broad, beaming face into the frame and sings or blasts a bit on his trumpet. That makes the only sense in the whole film."

"Southern Stomp, The." By Richard M. Jones; rec. early September 1923, in Chicago by **King Oliver**'s Jazz Band; CD #35. See comments on "Alligator Hop."

Spanier, Francis Joseph "Muggsy" (1906–1967). Cornetist Spanier and other white teenagers (e.g., **Benny Goodman**) used to defy their parents and sneak down to the South Side of Chicago to hear Armstrong. Occasionally an indulgent bouncer would let in these ardent fans. "How can you help loving a guy that makes the world smile and a happy place like Louis does?" Spanier later recalled (Shapiro and Hentoff, 1955, p. 117). Spanier began his professional life with several Chicago-area bands. In 1939 he founded the Ragtime Band, an eight-piece, all-white **Dixieland** group that contributed to the New Orleans revival and whose recordings still stand as models of traditional jazz. Until he retired in 1964, Spanier worked in similar ensembles either as a leader or as a sideman.

"Spanish Shawl." By Billy Meyers, Walter Melrose, and Elmer Schoebel. Although unfortunately Armstrong never recorded this 1925 song, it was the first he played with the **Erskine Tate** Orchestra in December 1925 at the **Vendome Theater** in Chicago where he was a big hit. Within two weeks he was making records with Tate. Eventually some of the audience came specifically to hear Armstrong and left as soon as he finished.

"Speak Now or Hereafter Hold Your Peace." By Wesley "Kid" Wilson; rec. October 1925 in New York City with vocalist Leola B. "Coot" Grant, pianist **Fletcher Henderson,** and either Armstrong or **Joe Smith** playing cornet. This song was written by Coot's vaudeville partner. There is some dispute as to who the cornetist is both here and on "When Your Man Is Going to Put You Down, (You Can Never Tell)."

"Special Delivery Blues." By **Sippie Wallace;** rec. March 1, 1926, in Chicago with vocalist Sippie Wallace and pianist Hersal Thomas; CD #36. In the introduction to this minor masterpiece Armstrong nicely contrasts Thomas's rolling piano with crisp staccato. Later, Wallace's ascending lines combine with Hersal's tremolo and Armstrong's brief broken phrases to fully express each word. See additional comments on "Baby, I Can't Use You No More."

Spivey, Victoria Regina "Queen Vee" (1906–1976). Spivey grew up in a musical family in Texas and absorbed her singing and piano playing abilities seemingly by osmosis. In 1926 she combined both skills on her recording of "Black Snake Blues," which was a big hit. In 1929 she appeared in the movie *Hallelujah!*; and during the same year she recorded "Funny Feathers" and "How Do You Do It That Way?"—both her own songs. Spivey recorded extensively until 1937, writing most of her own music. In 1932 she worked with Armstrong in the short film ***A Rhapsody in Black and Blue,*** playing an angry wife who knocks out her husband with a broom for keeping time too loudly with Armstrong's recording of "(I'll Be Glad When You're Dead) You Rascal, You." In the 1940s Spivey worked in various New York jazz clubs, in the 1950s she devoted herself to church activities, and in the 1960s she was part of the blues revival, forming her own record company, appearing on radio and television, and touring college campuses.

"S'posin'." By Andy Razaf and Paul Denniker; rec. June 4, 1929, in New York City with vocalist Seger Ellis, trombonist Tommy Dorsey, clarinetist **Jimmy Dorsey,** violinist Harry Hoffman, piano-celeste player Justin Ring, and drummer Stan King; CD #36. Ellis has a sweet, smooth voice, but Armstrong and the Dorsey brothers are the real stars of this ensemble.

"Squeeze Me." By **Clarence Williams** and **Thomas "Fats" Waller;** rec. October 26, 1925, in New York City with vocalist **Eva Taylor** and **Clarence Williams' Blue Five;** CDs #10, #30, #36, #42, and #56. Despite Armstrong's remarkable **scat** vocal, this recording has both musical and technical flaws. It's a rare example of him not singing in tune, and there's an extra-musical crash in the finale. Schuller feels that everyone is trying too hard to be flashy and hip (1968, p. 119). See additional comments on "Cast Away."

St. Cyr, John Alexander "Johnny" (1890–1966). Growing up in New Orleans, Armstrong was well aware of the fine banjo and guitar player Johnny St. Cyr, eleven years his senior. In 1915, they both played in a band that included **Kid Ory** and **Joe Oliver.** Later, when Armstrong joined **Fate Marable**'s riverboat band in 1919, St. Cyr had already been there for a year. They next met up in Chicago in 1923, where they both played and recorded in Oliver's Creole Jazz Band. Finally on his own to record for **Okeh** beginning late in 1925, Armstrong quickly lined up St. Cyr for the **Hot Five.** St. Cyr's contribution can be heard on nearly all those early classics: "Potato Head Blues," "Muskrat Ramble," "Yes, I'm in the Barrel," and "Cornet Chop Suey," to name but a few. St. Cyr played an unusual six-string "guitar banjo," which he made from a guitar neck and a banjo head. Although he later played a standard guitar and even an electric guitar, the "guitar banjo" can be heard on "Gut Bucket Blues," in which he plays chords against a low, single-string solo. "I cherish the memories of my associations with Louis and the Hot Five," said St. Cyr of these record-making days. "He always did his best to feature each individual in his combo. It was not Louis Armstrong, it was the Hot Five, if you get what I mean" (St. Cyr, p. 2). For a time during the **Great Depression,** St. Cyr had to make ends meet as a plasterer, but by the 1950s he was playing music again full-time in Los Angeles. St. Cyr and Armstrong teamed up one last time (with their old friend the trombonist Kid Ory) in 1962 at **Disneyland,** where St. Cyr was leading a band on the riverboat *Mark Twain.*

"St. James Infirmary." By Joe Primrose; rec. December 12, 1928, in Chicago by Louis Armstrong and His **Savoy Ballroom Five;** CDs #10, #12, #13, #21, #24, #30, #44, and #47. Here is one of Armstrong's best recordings from one of his best years. The **Don Redman** arrangement sets a somber, minor key mood, and it culminates in a long vocal by Armstrong. Although **Earl Hines** does some marvelous piano work, the other band members' solos are undistinguished, perhaps because of the song's lack of harmonic variety.

"St. Louis Blues." By W.C. Handy; rec. January 14, 1925, in New York City with vocalist **Bessie Smith** and Fred Longshaw on the harmonium; CDs #3, #6, #12, #14, #17, #20, #21, #24, #25, #36, #38, #44, #48, #55, #57, and #63. Armstrong recorded W.C. Handy's most famous song (and perhaps the most famous of all blues) some forty times, but none better than the first with Bessie Smith. Her stately voice seems perfectly complemented by Armstrong's agile commentary and Longshaw's churchlike harmonium. (A 1956 recording of Armstrong playing "St. Louis Blues" with **Leonard Bernstein** conducting the Lewisohn Stadium Symphony Orchestra was used in the 1957 documentary ***Satchmo the Great*** [CD #55].) See additional comments on "Careless Love Blues."

"St. Peter Blues." By Nolan Welsh and Richard Jones; rec. June 16, 1926, with vocalist Nolan Welsh and pianist Richard Jones; CD #36. Armstrong rarely recorded with male singers, but this is one of two he did with Welsh. See also "Bridwell Blues."

stamp. Although Armstrong (like anyone else) became eligible for a commemorative postal stamp ten years after his death, it took over twice that long (until September 7, 1995) for the U.S. Postal Service to issue one. In doing so, they followed the lead of Burkina, Faso, Chad, Dominica, Gabon, Guyana, Madagascar, Mali, Niger, Rwanda, Senegal, St. Vincent, and Tanzania. Many have wondered if the delay was caused by Armstrong's speaking out during the **civil rights** movement, specifically the **Little Rock** school integration issue in 1957. By way of comparison, Elvis Presley, who died in 1977, appeared on a stamp in 1993.

"Standin' on the Corner." See "Blue Yodel No. 9."

"Star Dust." By **Hoagy Carmichael** and Mitchell Parish; rec. November 4, 1931, in Chicago by Louis Armstrong and His Orchestra; CDs #3, #6, #14, #44, #48, and #58. For a sterling example of Armstrong's genius, one could hardly do better than consider how he treats this song, one of the most popular of the twentieth century. For starters, he nearly rewrites it, stretching and compressing the phrases, almost ignoring Carmichael's melody (but not his chords) and Parish's lyrics. He sings long passages all on the same note, and with his trumpet he often recasts the song's rhythms. Armstrong thereby shows how to make jazz versions of popular songs, and with this and others (such as "Lazy River," "Between the Devil and the Deep Blue Sea," "I've Got the World on a String," and "On the Sunny Side of the Street") he also sets the stage for the greatly expanded popularity of jazz at the end of the 1930s. Did Carmichael mind the liberties taken with his creation? No, he haunted record stores for alternate takes and in fact preferred Armstrong's recording to all others (including his own). Transcription by Schuller (1989, pp. 173–176, 182). See additional comments on "Ev'ntide."

"Star Spangled Banner." By John Stafford Smith and Francis Scott Key; rec. January 18, 1944, in New York City with the ***Esquire*** All Star Jazz Band; CDs #19 and #20. Armstrong frequently concluded concerts with the national anthem, and there's a moving story about when African American activist and writer **James Baldwin** heard him do so at the 1958 **Newport Jazz Festival.** Jazz scholar Dan Morgenstern was sitting with Baldwin, and as the notes were dying away, Baldwin said: "You know, that's the first time I've liked that song" (Berrett, 1999, p. 185).

"Stars Fell on Alabama." By Frank Perkins and Mitchell Parish; rec. August 16, 1956, in Los Angeles with vocalist **Ella Fitzgerald** and the **Oscar Peterson** Quartet; CDs #9, #28, and #54. This 1934 song was first popularized by **Jack Teagarden.** See additional comments on "April in Paris."

State Department. See **African tours; "Ambassador Satch."**

"Static Strut." By Jack Yellen and Phil Wall; rec. May 28, 1926, in Chicago with **Erskine Tate**'s **Vendome Theater Symphony Orchestra.** This is a rare recording of the unfairly neglected pianist Teddy Weatherford, who helped his instrument make the transition from ragtime to jazz. Armstrong plays an outstanding solo with this big, fifteen-piece band, and it is interesting to compare his dazzling sound here to the more subtle style of contemporaneous recordings with his **Hot Five.**

statue. See **Catlett, Elizabeth; Nice Jazz Festival.**

"Steak Face." Traditional blues; rec. November 30, 1947, live at Symphony Hall, Boston, by **Louis Armstrong and the All Stars;** CDs #32 and #54. **Sid Catlett** was Armstrong's favorite drummer (despite his unfortunate tendency to get into fights with fellow band members, including Armstrong), and here is one of his feature numbers. Catlett can be seen and heard in Warner Brothers' 1944 documentary *Jammin' the Blues.*

Stepin Fetchit. See ***Swing Wedding/Minnie the Moocher's Wedding Day.***

Stewart, Jimmy. See ***Glenn Miller Story, The.***

Stewart, Rex (1907–1967). "I went mad with the rest," remembered Stewart of Armstrong's arrival in New York in 1924. "I tried to walk like him, talk like him, eat like him, sleep like him" (Shapiro and Hentoff, 1955, p. 206). It is little wonder, then, that Stewart felt self-conscious on trying to fill Armstrong's recently vacated place in the **Fletcher Henderson** band in 1926. Unsuccessful, he tried again two years later, and this time remained (with a little time off here and there) for five years. Stewart hit his stride and found his own voice with **Duke Ellington,** with whom he played from 1934 to 1945, developing a "talking" style, exploring half-valve effects, and co-composing such pieces as "Boy Meets Horn" and "Morning Glory." Later he joined Jazz at the Philharmonic and toured Europe from 1947 to 1951, lecturing on jazz at the Paris Conservatoire. Although semiretired in the 1950s, he led Henderson reunion bands and, like Armstrong, wrote about his life in jazz.

"Stomp Off, Let's Go." By Elmer Schoebel; rec. May 28, 1926, in Chicago with **Erskine Tate**'s **Vendome Theater Symphony Orchestra;** CDs #48 and #61. See comments on "Static Strut."

"Stompin' at the Savoy." By Andy Razaf, **Benny Goodman,** Edgar M. Sampson, and Chick Webb; rec. on July 23, 1957, in Los Angeles with vocalist **Ella Fitzgerald** and the **Oscar Peterson** Quartet; CDs #6, #9, #19, #20, #23, #43, #59, and #61. See comments on "April in Paris."

stop-time. This is a technique in which an accompanying ensemble plays in rhythmic unison a simple one- or two-measure pattern of short accents between long rests, thereby giving a soloist plenty of room to shine. Armstrong probably first heard stop-time used by clarinetist **Johnny Dodds** on the **King Oliver** "Dippermouth Blues" (1923). In any case, Armstrong uses it on "Cornet Chop Suey" and "Jazz Lips" (both recorded in 1926), "Potato Head Blues" (1927), and frequently thereafter. Many scholars feel that the stop-time technique eventually led to the phenomenon of the featured soloist, a hallmark of jazz performance style.

"Stormy Weather." By **Harold Arlen** and Ted Koehler; rec. August 14, 1957, in Los Angeles with a studio orchestra conducted by arranger Russell Garcia; CD #29. Although the most popular recording of this song is by **Lena Horne** (who introduced it in the 1943 film of the same name), it was also performed by Armstrong, Ethel Waters, and many others.

Story, Sidney. This is the New Orleans alderman who in 1898 created **Storyville** by successfully promoting legislation to confine prostitution to an area adjacent to the French Quarter.

Storyville. Named after New Orleans politician **Sidney Story,** Storyville was a twenty-block-square red-light district next to the French Quarter. Filled with brothels and honky-tonks, its boundaries were North Basin, Customhouse, North Robertson, and St. Louis Streets. Three blocks away was **Black Storyville,** bounded by Perdido, Gravier, Locust, and

Armstrong with Edward R. Murrow in 1956. (Louis Armstrong House and Archives at Queens College/CUNY)

Franklin Streets. The six-year-old Armstrong delivered coal to the women who worked in the area, and he loved hearing the music of **Bunk Johnson, Jelly Roll Morton, Joe Oliver,** and others in the many honky-tonks. The development of jazz made quantum leaps in Storyville until 1917 when the U.S. Navy had prostitution banned there. Many musicians were suddenly out of work, and this contributed to the diaspora of jazz. Even Armstrong went to Houma, Louisiana, where he played for a time with a funeral band before returning to New Orleans. Eventually he followed fellow musicians to Chicago, St. Louis, New York, Los Angeles, and all over the world. The name "Storyville" has been used for two record labels, numerous nightclubs, and a remarkable jazz journal, based in **England,** which began publication in 1965 and continues to the present.

Streckfus. The Streckfus brothers (John, Joseph, Roy, and Vern) owned a steamboat line, which began operation in 1884 and, with a subsequent decline of freight business, devoted itself from early in the twentieth century to the **Great Depression** to pleasure excursions. "Captain Joe" Streckfus hired pianist and bandleader **Fate Marable** to provide music, and Marable in turn hired so many young musicians from the New Orleans area that his ensemble was dubbed "the floating conservatory." Armstrong was recruited in 1919 for the summer season for the riverboat **S.S. *Sidney*,** which plied the waters between New Orleans and St. Louis. He later wrote of this period, "I wanted to get away from New Orleans for another reason and that was because I was not happy there just then. Ten months before . . . I got married. In the seven months to come, I was to follow the Mississippi for nearly two thousand miles and visit many places. It was a handful of travelling . . . for a kid who'd always been afraid to leave home before" (1936, pp. 36–40). The experience of playing several shows daily turned Armstrong into a professional. During intermissions he learned to read music better with help from mellophonist **Davey Jones** and from Marable himself. Armstrong spent the next two summers on the river. Standing on the dock in New Orleans one day in 1919, **Jack Teagarden** first heard Armstrong play as the steamboat pulled in. As he later recalled, it was "one of the most beautiful notes I've ever heard. . . . [I]t was Louis Armstrong coming down from the skies like a god" (Boujut, p. 22). In 1920 when the boat stopped in Davenport, Iowa, Armstrong met the young **Bix Beiderbecke.** In September 1921 Armstrong (along with clarinetist **Johnny Dodds**) resigned over artistic differences with Marable and took the train back to New Orleans, where he played with **Kid Ory**'s band and the **Tuxedo Brass Band,** until joining **King Oliver** in Chicago the following August. Armstrong was very fond of "Captain Joe" Streckfus, who years later took his family on vacation from St. Louis to hear Armstrong play in New York.

Streisand, Barbra (Joan) (b. 1942). Armstrong had great admiration and respect for the popular actress and singer with whom he worked charismatically in the 1969 movie ***Hello Dolly!*** "Sings her ass off," he used to say. Streisand's recordings were among the twenty or so, mostly his own, that he traveled with and listened to on a portable record player. (He also liked **The Beatles.**) Like Armstrong (and **Duke Ellington, Dave Brubeck, Benny Goodman,** and many other luminaries), Streisand was represented by **Joe Glaser**'s **Associated Booking Corporation.**

Strip, The. Mickey Rooney plays a drummer (and Korean War veteran, recently discharged from a mental hospital) who joins Armstrong's band in a Sunset Strip nightclub in order to court a young woman who works there as a dancer. It is a dark film, which ends with Rooney finding solace in music after his girlfriend is murdered. Armstrong has no lines, but he and the **All Stars** are heard in "Shadrack," "Basin Street Blues," and "A Kiss to Build a Dream On." M-G-M, 1951; 86 mins.; Dir. Leslie Kardos.

Strong, Jimmy (1906–1977). After playing with the Nighthawks band in Chicago, touring, and working in California with several groups, this clarinet and tenor sax player settled in Chicago and played with the **Carroll Dickerson** Orchestra from 1927 to 1929. Armstrong chose him for both the **Hot Five** and the **Savoy Ballroom Five.** Good examples of his playing can be heard on "Fireworks," "Basin Street Blues," and "West End Blues," all recorded in Chicago in June 1928. While not the equal of **Johnny Dodds,** Strong's hoarse tone is distinctive in a thick polyphonic texture. In the now-classic "West End Blues," he makes his mark after the trombone solo, gingerly alternating with Armstrong's **scat** vocal. Strong was among the Dickerson men who went to New York with Armstrong in May 1929, but he returned to Chicago when it became obvious that manager **Tommy Rockwell**'s invitation was for Armstrong only. Strong went on to lead his own groups in Chicago, then moved to New Jersey where he worked from the 1940s on.

"Struttin' with Some Barbecue." By Louis Armstrong and **Lil Hardin Armstrong** (see authorship note on "Got No Blues"); rec. December 9, 1927, in Chicago by Louis Armstrong and His **Hot Five;** CDs #5, #6, #8, #10, #13, #19, #23, #34, #46, #48, and #52. Here is a jazz masterpiece and one of Armstrong's favorites. The title was inspired by the barbecued meals that a cook called "Dad" made for Armstrong and fellow musicians at a café in Chicago at 48th and State Street. The melody intriguingly outlines a major seventh chord and the tempo is lively. Armstrong plays here a delicious solo to **stop-time** accompaniment, clarinetist **Johnny Dodds** contributes a meaty low-note chorus, and trombonist **Kid Ory** adds some sweet counterpoint. Armstrong recorded "Barbecue" forty-two more times during his career, and some prefer the one from January 12, 1938, made in Los Angeles with his orchestra. Although "Barbecue" is an instrumental, words were added for the January 18, 1955, Los Angeles recording with Gary Crosby and for the January 26, 1959, recording made in Copenhagen by **Louis Armstrong and the All Stars** for the **movie *Kaerlighedens Melodi (Formula of Love).*** Transcriptions have been done by Lee Castle (vol. 1, p. 4), James L. Collier (Kernfeld, 1988, p. 30), and Frank Tirro (p. 63).

Studio Visit. A short Pete Smith film released May 11, 1946. According to Klaus Stratemann, it once included Armstrong and **Lena Horne** performing "Ain't It the Truth?"–which was cut in 1943 from ***Cabin in the Sky*** (1996, p. 143). However, the footage appears to be lost.

style. See **singing style; trumpet style.**

Suburban Gardens. After nine years away from his hometown, Armstrong returned to New Orleans to play an extended engagement at the Suburban Gardens in nearby Jefferson Parish. His appearance there showed just how far he had come up in the world and also how far behind New Orleans had remained. Returning home a national celebrity, Armstrong was the object of both adulation and the kind of brutish racism that poisoned the American South. He was given a hero's welcome by a huge crowd of both whites and blacks, but at the Suburban Gardens the radio announcer nevertheless refused to introduce an African American. Armstrong smoothly and casually took the microphone and introduced himself, thereby becoming the first African American to speak on the radio in that region. During this same engagement at the Gardens, an intoxicated white woman took bandleader **Zilner Randolph**'s hand one night and, much to everyone's alarm, danced with him, in flagrant violation of southern racial barriers. "My teeth began to chatter," remembered New Orleans-born and -bred trombonist **Preston Jackson** (Jones, 1988, p. 136). Luckily, the incident passed quickly as an occasion for amusement. Finally, at the close of this engagement, Armstrong wanted to give a free concert for the city's African American citizens, who had been excluded by the Suburban Gardens's **segregation** policy. A venue was arranged at a local army base, and a big crowd gathered in eager anticipation. However, the gate was locked, and as the crowd began to express disappointment the National Guard was called in with drawn bayonets. Not even manager **Johnny Collins** could solve the problem, and Armstrong wept in frustration (Goffin, 1947, pp. 290–291).

"Sugar." By Maceo Pinkard, Edna Alexander, and Sidney Mitchell; rec. September 6, 1946, in Los Angeles by Louis Armstrong and His **Hot Seven;** CDs #12, #21, #28, and #47. Around the time of the filming of ***New Orleans,*** Armstrong and some of the small group players from the set recorded this and several other numbers ("Blues for Yesterday," "Blues in the South," and "I Want a Little Girl") at a session organized by his friend **Leonard Feather.** "Sugar," with its suave rhythm section and Armstrong's superb vocal interplay with trombonist Vic Dickenson, comes off particularly well. In a later (July 5, 1960) recording of "Sugar," Armstrong plays Dickenson to vocalist **Bing Crosby.**

"Sugar Foot Stomp." By **Joe Oliver** and Louis Armstrong; rec. May 29, 1925, in New York City by **Fletcher Henderson** and His Orchestra; CDs #10 and #48. Originally "Dippermouth Blues," this number got its more sophisticated name and arrangement from **Don Redman.** Armstrong had been with the Henderson ensemble for seven months by the time of this recording, and he's now entrusted with a three-chorus solo. Nevertheless, he basically preserves the solo as played by his mentor and co-composer, King Oliver, and thereby sets a tradition for future cornet and trumpet players to do the same out of respect.

"Sugar Foot Strut." By Billy Pierce, Henry Myers, and Charles M. Schwab; rec. June 28, 1928, in Chicago by Louis Armstrong and His **Hot Five;** CD #30. Here is another example of Armstrong's good musical chemistry with pianist **Earl Hines.** Armstrong's **stop-time** solo, however, is a little wobbly.

Sullivan, Joseph Michael "Joe" (1906–1971). Before he played for a short time in early 1952 with **Louis Armstrong and the All Stars,** pianist Joe Sullivan had had a long and varied career. He grew up in the Chicago area and was a member of the **Austin High Gang.** After a few years at the Chicago Conservatory and then touring on the vaudeville circuit, he resettled in Chicago for a time and in 1927 had a big hit with "China Boy." He developed tuberculosis in 1936 but fortunately recovered and in 1940 led one of the earliest racially integrated ensembles at New York's Café Society. Eleven years earlier, however, Sullivan had been involved in another integration milestone when he played on Armstrong's recording of "Knockin' a Jug" with white trombonist **Jack Teagarden,** black tenor saxophonist **Happy Caldwell,** white guitarist **Eddie Lang,** and black drummer **Kaiser Marshall.** This March 5, 1929, recording was the first in which black and white musicians shared musical material equally, although there were claims of integrated recording earlier (see **Jelly Roll Morton**). In his post–All Stars years, Sullivan worked in the San Francisco area.

Sullivan, Maxine (1911–1987). See ***Going Places; Swingin' the Dream.***

"Summer Song." By **Dave Brubeck** and Iola Brubeck; rec. September 13, 1961, in New York City by **Louis Armstrong and the All Stars,** pianist Dave Brubeck, and guests; CD #50. This gentle song provides momentary relief from the generally satirical tone of the jazz oratorio ***The Real Ambassadors.*** See additional comments on "Cultural Exchange."

"Summertime." By George Gershwin, DuBose Heyward, and Ira Gershwin; rec. August 18, 1957, in Los Angeles with vocalist **Ella Fitzgerald** and a studio orchestra and choir conducted by Russell Garcia; CDs #9 and #28. Armstrong and Fitzgerald sing this famous song from Act I of *Porgy and Bess* as a duet. See additional comments on "Bess, You Is My Woman Now" and "April in Paris."

"Sun Showers." By Nacio Herb Brown and Arthur Freed; rec. July 7, 1937, in New York City by Louis Armstrong and His Orchestra; CDs #18 and #34. Armstrong sings this standard ballad with more conviction than did **Billie Holiday,** and his trumpet solo, ending on the "D" above high "C," is amazing.

"Sunrise, Sunset." By Jerry Block and Sheldon Harnick; rec. March 26, 1968, in New York City by **Louis Armstrong and the All Stars** with a studio choir. This is one of the best covers of this popular song from the 1964 Broadway musical *Fiddler on the Roof.*

Sunset Cafe. Opened on August 3, 1921, at 35th and Calumet in Chicago and controlled by the **Al Capone** syndicate, this club was at the very center of South Side nightlife in the roaring 1920s. The Sunset was a "black-and-tan club" (i.e., the audience was racially mixed) and, with the residency of **Carroll Dickerson**'s orchestra, quickly became known as a jazz venue. Armstrong's presence in the orchestra from 1926 to 1927 was a great commercial success and drew fellow musicians from far and wide. Trumpeter **Max Kaminsky** later said of Armstrong's playing: "I felt as if I had stared into the sun's eye. All I could think of doing was run away and hide till the blindness left me" (Firestone, p. 44). When Dickerson left the Sunset in February 1927, manager **Joe Glaser** (who would become Armstrong's manager in 1935) hired Louis Armstrong and His Stompers (featuring **Earl Hines** on piano) as the house band, who were also known as the **Sunset Stompers.** Armstrong moved on that same year, but the Sunset continued to prosper until the **Great Depression** eventually closed it down in 1937.

"Sunset Cafe Stomp." By Percy Venable, Louis Armstrong and/or **Lil Hardin Armstrong;** rec. November 16, 1926, in Chicago by vocalist **May Alix** with Louis Armstrong and His **Hot Five;** CD #10. Chicago-born May Alix did only one other recording ("Big Butter and Egg Man") with Armstrong. Although reputedly a good-looking woman and a fine dancer, she was not much of a singer.

Sunset Stompers. When **Carroll Dickerson** left the **Sunset Cafe** in February 1927, Louis Armstrong and His Stompers (with **Earl Hines** as principal pianist and music director) was hired as the house band. Until April of that year, Armstrong typically began a long performance day with **Erskine Tate** at the **Vendome Theater** (often playing as many as four shows a night and finishing up at 11 P.M.), then rushed off to play with the Stompers at the Sunset. The Sunset Stompers made a single recording, "Chicago Breakdown," on May 9, 1927. In July when the Sunset Cafe was temporarily closed, probably because of a liquor violation, the Stompers moved to a white club called the **Blackhawk.** The engagement ended two weeks later, and with band morale low and discipline slack, the Stompers went their separate ways. Armstrong's career entered a relatively slack period until the next year, when he recorded such masterpieces as "West End Blues," "Basin Street Blues," "No One Else But You," and "Tight Like This" with the **Hot Five.**

"Sunshine Baby." By **Hociel Thomas;** recorded on November 11, 1925, in Chicago by vocalist Hociel Thomas and Louis Armstrong's Jazz Four; CDs #10 and #36. Like some other recordings with blues singers (e.g., **May Alix**), this is interesting mostly for Armstrong's inventive accompaniment. See additional comments on "Adam and Eve Had the Blues."

"Sunshine of Love, The." By Leonard Whitcup, C. Gierich, and George Douglass; rec. August 16, 1967, in New York City with studio orchestra and chorus; CD #62. This is the "B" side to "What a Wonderful World."

"Sweet as a Song." By Mack Gordon and Harry Revel; rec. January 13, 1938, in Los Angeles by Louis Armstrong and His Orchestra. Here is a fine example of both Armstrong's smooth and tender **singing style** and his ability to make something of relatively nothing.

"Sweet Baby Doll." By George W. Thomas and Wilbur LeRoy; rec. between October 5 and 15, 1923, in Chicago by **King Oliver**'s Jazz Band. See comments on "Alligator Hop."

"Sweet Georgia Brown." By Ben Bernie, Maceo Pinkard, and Kenneth Casey; rec. May 24 or 25, 1960, in New York City with the **Dukes of Dixieland;** CDs #43 and #53. Armstrong and the Dukes give this popular 1925 song a straightforward treatment. For additional comments see "Avalon."

"Sweet Little Papa." By **Edward "Kid" Ory;** rec. June 23, 1926, in Chicago by Louis Armstrong and His **Hot Five;** CD #10. On this recording we can hear Armstrong taking some of his previous experiments—long descending lines, double-time breaks, flutter tonguing, and shakes—and integrating them smoothly into his playing. Compared to his work a year earlier with the **Fletcher Henderson** Orchestra ("Sugar Foot Stomp" or "T.N.T."), one can plainly hear Armstrong forging his own style.

"Sweet Lorraine." By Cliff Burwell and Mitchell Parish; rec. October 14, 1957, in Los Angeles with the **Oscar Peterson** Quartet; CDs #28, #37, and #61. It's odd that Armstrong did not get to this 1928 song sooner, since it seems as much written for him as it does for Nat "King" Cole, who owns it. See additional comments on "Blues in the Night."

"Sweet Lovin' Man." By Walter Melrose and **Lil Hardin;** rec. between June 22 and

29, 1923, in Chicago with **King Oliver**'s Jazz Band. See additional comments on "Alligator Hop."

"Sweet Savannah Sue." By **Thomas "Fats" Waller,** Andy Razaf, and Harry Brooks; rec. July 22, 1929, in New York City by Louis Armstrong and His Orchestra; CD #56. See additional comments on "Ain't Misbehavin'."

"Sweet Sue, Just You." By Will J. Harris and Victor Young; rec. April 26, 1933, in Chicago by Louis Armstrong and His Orchestra; CDs #12, #21, and #24. This is a feature number for vocalist Budd Johnson (a reed man in the orchestra), but it brings out the comedian in Armstrong, who jumps in on Johnson's **scat** singing.

"Sweethearts on Parade." By Carmen Lombardo and Charles Newman; rec. December 23, 1930, in Los Angeles by Louis Armstrong and His **Sebastian New Cotton Club** Orchestra; CDs #13, #36, #48, #53, and #61. It often comes as a surprise that Armstrong had a profound admiration for the **Guy Lombardo** style, especially the way Lombardo stuck to the melody and provided a clear, danceable beat. (The admiration was mutual.) Here, however, in a song written by Lombardo's music director and brother, Armstrong takes great liberties with both the melody and rhythm. He dominates the number first with a muted trumpet solo, then a vocal solo, and finally another trumpet solo (open horn), with brief transitional interludes by the band. In the first solo, he plays a series of asymmetrical phrases that give us a glimpse of the melody. He similarly recomposes the vocal, adding expressive sighs and moans, and in his final solo he seems to be playing notes everywhere, sometimes in double time, and even quoting other tunes ("High Society" and the bugle call "Assembly"). The total effect is overwhelming, as Armstrong makes such stellar music with perfect ease.

"Sweets." Armstrong, who loved women with the same joyous intensity that he loved music, had many extramarital affairs. These were more or less tolerated by his four wives. **Lucille,** for example, learned to give him plenty of advance warning when she planned to join him on the road. In 1954 one of his girlfriends, nicknamed "Sweets," convinced him that she was pregnant with his child. This news thrilled Armstrong, who was so far without progeny (and seems never to have fathered any children). "Sweets," however, pregnant with another man's child, seems merely to have been exploiting Armstrong's generous and easygoing nature. As **All Stars** clarinetist **Barney Bigard** relates the incident, Armstrong, "walking around like a peacock," began putting his loose change (plus dollars, fives, and tens) in a bag, explaining this was for the child. Armstrong went a little too far, though, when he tried to talk Lucille into adopting the baby. She very quickly burst his bubble, saying, "You couldn't make a baby with a pencil," Bigard reports. "Now you're talking about your kid. She done fool you and she's got a boyfriend. He must have did it and he's telling her to tell you that you're the father. You sure are stupid." Bigard concluded in his own voice: "Well, that's how he was. He'd go for anything" (Berrett, 1999, pp. 169–172). Armstrong's boisterous affection for "Sweets" is also the main subject of a 1955 letter to **Joe Glaser** (reprinted in Brothers, pp. 158–163).

swing. One of Armstrong's major achievements was to develop a rhythmic style that subsequently became a distinctive feature of all of jazz. This style, "swing," tends to inspire more heated argument than accurate description, but most will agree that it is a type of musical momentum that a wide variety of devices can produce against a fixed pulse. For one thing, Armstrong liked to place notes either ahead of or behind the beat, rarely right on it. He would also divide the basic pulse into three smaller parts, accenting the third almost as often as the first and frequently not sounding the second at all (e.g., Jack, BE nim-BLE, Jack, BE quick). Finally, he would combine this displacement of accent with the alteration of individual notes, varying their beginning and ending, modifying their tone quality, and changing their intonation. These innovations can be heard in his earliest recordings, such as "Mandy, Make Up Your Mind" and "Texas Moaner Blues," both from 1924. By the time of "Potato Head Blues" in 1927 and "West End Blues" in the following year, the techniques are well developed. By the early 1930s they were part of the style of virtually every other jazz musician.

"Swing Bells." By **Dave Brubeck** and Iola Brubeck; rec. September 12 or 13, 1961, in New York City by **Louis Armstrong and the All Stars,** pianist Dave Brubeck, and guests; CD #50. Armstrong performs this number with singers Dave Lambert, Jon Hendricks, and Annie Ross in the finale of the jazz oratorio ***The Real Ambassadors.*** Unfortunately, it sounds strained, both in the singers' efforts to hit correct pitches and Armstrong's to get a wordy text to **swing.** See additional comments on "Cultural Exchange."

Swing High, Swing Low. Carol Lombard and Fred McMurray play entertainers stranded in Panama in this film based on the 1929 backstage drama *The Dance of Life.* McMurray plays a trumpeter but not the trumpet, which, according to the *New York Times* reviewer (April 15, 1937), was handled by Armstrong. Maybe. There were lots of good jazz musicians around, and most of them tried to imitate Armstrong. Paramount, 1937; B&W; 95 mins.; Dir. Mitchell Leisen.

"Swing Low, Sweet Chariot." Traditional; rec. February 7, 1958, in New York City by **Louis Armstrong and the All Stars** and the **Sy Oliver** Choir; CD #27. Armstrong takes this very slowly, giving it a gentle **swing** and playing one of those trumpet choruses that underscore the beauty of a melody. See additional comments on "Down by the Riverside."

"Swing That Music." By Louis Armstrong and **Horace Gerlach;** rec. May 18, 1936, in New York City by Louis Armstrong and His Orchestra; CDs #5, #6, #34, #44, #60, and #61. This song and the first volume of Armstrong's **autobiography** came out at the same time (November 1936), and both have since become jazz standards. Having been under the stable management of **Joe Glaser** for a year, Armstrong sounds refreshed and confident. He zips along at around 150 beats per minute (cf. the average fox trot, which ranges between 60 and 80 beats per minute), and ends strongly with a thrilling high "E-flat" after a long string (forty-two) of rhythmically varied high "Cs." The band is unusually strong, too, with a spirited yet steady rhythm section, busy yet disciplined saxophones, and precise gunshotlike figures from the brass.

Armstrong would record "Swing That Music" again but never with the concertolike drama of this original. Transcription in ***Swing That Music*** (p. 138f).

Swing That Music. Shortly after coming under the management of **Joe Glaser,** Armstrong published his **autobiography.** It was another of many **firsts** for him, since no other jazz musician had yet written one. Although heavily edited and sometimes unreliable, *Swing That Music* (1936) contains much essential information, including details not to be found later in his other volume of autobiography, ***Satchmo: My Life in New Orleans*** (1954), which covers some of the same ground. However, while *Satchmo* ends in 1922, *Swing That Music* continues to 1936. The book was published complete with an admiring introduction by Rudy Vallee. Another contributor was **Horace Gerlach,** the pianist, composer, arranger, and coauthor with Armstrong of the song of the same name as the book. Some speculate that Gerlach might have been *Swing That Music*'s ghostwriter or editor and that he may have extracted some of the book's spice. At any rate, he did in fact contribute an appendix on Armstrong's **swing** style and a glossary of swing terms. In retrospect, both are more corny than informative. Gerlach also made some elementary transcriptions of how various artists, such as **Benny Goodman,** Tommy Dorsey, **Bud Freeman,** and others treated the song "Swing That Music." As Dan Morgenstern observes in his introduction to the 1993 Da Capo reprint: "It's safe to say that no other popular song ever got such a sendoff" (p. xiii).

Swing Wedding/Minnie the Moocher's Wedding Day. This 1937 M-G-M cartoon features Armstrong, Stepin Fetchit, **Fats Waller, Bill "Bojangles" Robinson, Cab Calloway,** and members of the Calloway band, all wonderfully drawn as frogs singing and playing instruments. Based on Calloway's 1931 hit record "Minnie the Moocher's Wedding Day," it is about the marriage of Minnie the Moocher and Smokey Joe, who, however, is late in arriving. While waiting for the groom, Calloway wins Minnie over with his singing and dancing, eventually taking her to the altar himself. Nevertheless, Armstrong urges Smokey Joe to try to win Minnie back by dancing. In various surrealistic touches, Waller smashes his piano, the bass player uses his instrument as a pogo stick, and Armstrong takes in so much air for his trumpet that he floats out onto the pond.

"Swing, You Cats." By **Zilner Randolph;** rec. January 28, 1933, in Chicago by Louis Armstrong and His Orchestra; CDs #12, #17, #21, and #24. Not one of Armstrong's better recordings, this has numerous fluffs, false starts, and out-of-tune notes. He may have been tired, since this is the last of a dozen songs recorded over three days. (Two months later, rumors of his death were greatly exaggerated on the front page of the London *Daily Express.*) Also, bandleader Randolph's arrangement with its boisterous saxophone section tends more to obscure than to enhance the soloist.

"Swingin' on Nothing." By **Sy Oliver** and Billy Moore; rec. April 20, 1942, in Los Angeles by Louis Armstrong and His Orchestra. This number, which Tommy Dorsey had made popular during the previous year, was a feature for vocalists **Velma Middleton** and **George Wash-**

ington. Two or three days after this recording, it was made into a **soundie,** a short film for use in a coin-operated viewing machine, an ancestor of today's music video.

Swingin' on Nothing. One of four **soundies** that Armstrong made in 1942 for use in a coin-operated viewing machine. RCM, 1942; B&W; 3 mins.; Dir. Josef Berne.

Swingin' the Dream. This jazz version of Shakespeare's *A Midsummer Night's Dream,* set in Louisiana in 1890, opened at the new Rockefeller Center Theater in New York on November 29, 1939. A number of distinguished and accomplished people put the show together: Gilbert Seldes and Eric Charell adapted the text, **Walt Disney** designed the sets, Jimmy Van Heusen wrote the music, the **Benny Goodman** sextet played it, and Butterfly McQueen and "Moms" Mabley were cast, respectively, as Puck and Quince. Armstrong played Bottom the Weaver and wore a bright red fireman's suit. Despite the abundance of talent (Maxine Sullivan was also in the cast), there were only thirteen performances. Postmortem theorizing cited the proliferation of corny or poor lines (e.g., "go fly a kite," which is neither Shakespearean nor fin-de-siècle New Orleans), the difficulty of filling the huge Rockefeller theater, and the costly, overambitious production.

Swiss Kriss. Armstrong had a lifelong preoccupation with **laxatives.** When he was five years old, so he wrote in ***Satchmo: My Life in New Orleans,*** his mother told him to "remember when you're sick nobody ain't going to give you nothing," urged him to try to stay healthy, and made him promise he would "take a physic at least once a week" (1954, p. 16). He kept the promise, and his favorite remedy was Swiss Kriss, an herbal laxative recommended by health enthusiast **Gayelord Hauser.** Armstrong himself became an advocate and gave little packages of it to friends and acquaintances. He even gave it to puzzled government officials when he toured foreign countries and to amused nurses when he spent a good deal of time toward the end of his life in New York City's **Beth Israel Hospital.** Armstrong once went so far as to design a Christmas card with the words "Swiss Krissly" above a keyhole-view photograph of himself sitting on the toilet. Below is printed "Satchmo-Slogan/(Leave It All Behind Ya)," apparently as both advice and wishes for the new year. The product is still widely available in health food stores.

"Symphonic Raps" (a.k.a. "Symphonic Touches"). By Bert Steven and Irwin Abrams; rec. July 5, 1928, in Chicago with **Carroll Dickerson**'s Savoyagers; CDs #30 and #48. Dickerson's eleven-piece ensemble is excellent (except for a few bumps in the last chorus), but this recording is dominated by Armstrong and pianist **Earl Hines,** whose mutual influence can be heard. Transcription by Schuller (1968, p. 123).

"Symphonic Touches." See "Symphonic Raps."

T

" 'Tain't What You Do (It's the Way That Cha Do It)." By **Sy Oliver** and **Trummy Young;** rec. July 14, 1954, in Chicago by **Louis Armstrong and the All Stars;** CD #6. This 1939 song was a feature number for All Stars trombonist Trummy Young.

"Talk to the Animals." By Leslie Bricusse; rec. March 26, 1968, in New York City by **Louis Armstrong and the All Stars** with a studio choir. Armstrong has a good deal of fun with this number (e.g., at the mention of crocodiles he jumps in with, "Scared of me as I am of them"), which Rex Harrison introduced in the 1967 movie *Doctor Doolittle.*

tapes, reel-to-reel. Armstrong became entranced by the tape recorder in 1947 when he heard a bootleg recording of his **Carnegie Hall concert.** He bought not one but two machines (in case one broke down) and took them with him on tour. Since he frequently turned a recorder on while relaxing with friends, some of his tapes contain wonderfully spontaneous conversations, often earthy and humorous (especially when discussing racism). Besides these casual Louis-at-home recordings, Armstrong also had on tape his own records, interviews, and "every classical number that you can think of," as he reports on one tape. He decorated the tape boxes with collages (see **art by Armstrong**). "My hobby is to pick out the different things during what I read and piece them together and making a little story of my own," he wrote to a friend in 1953 (Miller, p. 212). A generous sample can be seen in Marc Miller's *Louis Armstrong: A Cultural Legacy* and Michael Cogswell's *Louis Armstrong: The Offstage Story of Satchmo.* Some 650 tapes with their boxes have been preserved unedited and are available for anyone to see and hear at the **Louis Armstrong House and Archives.**

Tate, Erskine (1895–1978). Born in Memphis to a musical family, Tate grew up in Chicago and studied formally at the American Conservatory, focusing on the violin. He led a popular orchestra at Chicago's **Vendome Theater** (1919–1928), where his most important sideman was Armstrong (1925–1926), and at the **Savoy Ballroom** (1931–1938). After World War II, Tate worked mainly as a teacher. He made three recordings in 1926 with Armstrong ("Static Strut" and "Stomp Off, Let's Go" twice) and offered numerous up-and-coming jazz musicians (including **Earl Hines, Milt Hinton,**

Freddie Keppard, and Jabbo Smith) valuable experience.

Taylor, Eva (Irene Gibbons) (1895–1977). Between September 1924 and November 1925, when Armstrong was not working in New York with the **Fletcher Henderson** band at **Roseland Ballroom** and elsewhere, he spent considerable time in the recording studio with such blues singers as **Ma Rainey, Alberta Hunter, Margaret Johnson, Bessie Smith,** and **Clara Smith.** Eva Taylor belongs to this distinguished group (CD #36). Married to pianist, composer, publisher, and promoter **Clarence Williams,** she often recorded her husband's songs, such as "Cake Walking Babies (from Home)." Here and elsewhere, despite excellent diction, Taylor is overshadowed by Armstrong's inventiveness. This is especially true on "Everybody Loves My Baby," where Armstrong uses a plunger mute in the vocal manner of his mentor **Joe Oliver.** Taylor continued to record until the early 1940s, when she gave up full-time performing. She revived her career in the mid-1960s and worked in New York, also touring England, Denmark, and Sweden.

Taylor, William "Billy" (b. 1921). Pianist, educator, bandleader, radio and television personality, and unofficial spokesperson for jazz, Dr. Taylor was one of the two speakers at Armstrong's **funeral** at the **Corona** Congregational Church on July 9, 1971.

"Tea for Two." By Vincent Youmans and Irving Caesar; rec. November 30, 1947, live at Symphony Hall in Boston by **Louis Armstrong and the All Stars;** CD #54. The newly formed All Stars had been enthusiastically received earlier in the year at **Town Hall** in New York City, and here they met with similar success in Boston. As befits one of the bishoprics of classical music, the venue must have influenced Armstrong to concentrate on the established repertory, such "Mahogany Hall Stomp," "Muskrat Ramble," and this 1925 song, which was introduced in the Broadway musical *No, No, Nanette.*

"Teach Me Tonight." By Gene DePaul and Sammy Cahn; rec. June 4, 1965, live at the Palais des Sports in Paris by **Louis Armstrong and the All Stars.** This 1953 song was a feature number for All Stars trombonist **Tyree Glenn.**

Teagarden, Weldon Leo "Jack" (1905–1964). Armstrong's favorite trombone player and close friend was born in Vernon, Texas, and began a life in music at age five with piano lessons from his mother. He then turned to the baritone horn until his father, an enthusiastic but mediocre amateur cornetist, gave him a trombone. On his own the boy, who had perfect pitch, worked out a way to play any note and still keep the slide between himself and the bell. This eccentric technique, which works best in the upper range and enables rapid passage work, confounded a local teacher, to whom Teagarden was taken at age nine. Observing that he was playing incorrectly but getting fine results, the teacher prudently declined to interfere. By the age of fifteen, Teagarden was playing professionally and soon gravitated to New York City, where he caused a sensation among jazzmen. He spent the years 1928 to 1933 in Ben Pollack's band, during which time he also made important recordings with Armstrong, such as "Knockin' a Jug" in 1929 and others. In 1933 he joined Paul Whiteman's band and remained as star soloist and singer until 1938, when he and the trumpeter Charlie Shavers formed a big band. Musically successful but financially disastrous, this group broke up in 1946, and in the following year, Teagarden joined **Louis Armstrong and the All Stars.**

In the wake of the All Stars' phenomenal worldwide success, Teagarden in August 1951 formed his own All Stars, and he continued to lead small groups until his death. Along with Jimmy Harrison, Miff Mole, and **Dicky Wells,** Teagarden brought the trombone from its early harmonic-percussive background to the melodic forefront of the jazz ensemble. In "Makin' Friends" from 1928, Teagarden's solo passages seem freed of rhythmic constraints, and one can even hear the delightful anticipatory grace notes that were to become his trademark. His expressive virtuosity opened eyes and ears to the solo capabilities of the trombone. Like Armstrong, Teagarden expanded the upper range of his instrument, and he had astonishing lip control. In fact, he sometimes gave the impression that the trombone slide was superfluous. In "Knockin' a Jug" he introduces an upward glissando using lip pressure only. His solos abound with quick triplet ornamentations, nimble gestures that suggest a soft-shoe step. "After You've Gone" (1931) shows off these expressive techniques, as well as the warm and woolly singing for which he was also justly famous. Despite extraordinary technical mastery, Teagarden was a restrained player, rarely calling attention to his virtuosity. In recordings like "The Sheik of Araby" (1944), "My Bucket's Got a Hole in It" (1950), and "Body and Soul" (1953), one hears a deceptively simple style that was also so personal that Teagarden had few followers. Hardly any trombone players even hold the slide the way he did—between the index and middle fingers. However, he did start trombonists using Pond's Cold Cream on the slide, later switching to the cooking lubricant Pam.

Like many jazz musicians, Teagarden did not take care of himself very well. He had no head for money. He drank too much. By the time he was forty, he had lost all his teeth, and he had had pneumonia several times. He was, however, universally liked by fellow musicians, and many are indebted to him for his innovations. As Armstrong was to his instrument, so was Jack Teagarden to the trombone.

"Tears." By Louis Armstrong and **Lil Hardin;** rec. between October 5 and 15, 1923, in Chicago by **King Oliver**'s Jazz Band; CD #48. With few exceptions, Armstrong's early recordings were made in the shadow of King Oliver, his mentor. This is one such exception, perhaps because it's Armstrong's own composition. In it he takes a series of solo breaks that reveal his developing artistry. In the third of these, for example, he plays a figure that will turn up later in "Potato Head Blues" (1927). It helps that Armstrong is surrounded by excellent players, for example, trombonist **Honoré Dutrey,** whose sweet tone and elegant, cellolike lines gave the Oliver band a distinctive texture.

Teatro alla Scala. While in Milan during his 1955–1956 world tour, Armstrong took the time and trouble to have his picture taken at La Scala, the most famous opera house (founded 1778) in the land where opera was invented. After finishing a concert, he wrote, "I had to rush over to La Scala and stand by those big cats like Verdi and Wagner . . . 'cause they figure our music is the same—we play 'em both from the heart." See **"Louis Armstrong and Opera";** also Berrett, 1999, p. 24f.

television. Armstrong was a frequent guest on such television programs as *The Ed Sullivan Show* (CBS, 1948–1971), *The Eddie Condon Floor Show* (NBC, 1949–1950), *The Perry Como Show* (NBC or CBS, 1948–1963), *The Hollywood Palace* (ABC, 1964–1974), *The **Danny Kaye** Show* (CBS, 1963–1967), *The Dean Martin Show* (NBC, 1965–1974), *The Jackie Gleason Show* (CBS, 1952–1970), *The **David Frost** Show* (Syndicated, 1969–1972), *The **Pearl Bailey** Show* (ABC, 1971), and *The Flip Wilson Show* (NBC, 1970–1974). Many viewers, especially African Americans, felt that his performances on these shows sometimes made him look like a docile clown. Notable exceptions were two appearances on ABC's *Shindig,* which aired on November 4 (see ***Solo***) and November 11, 1965. On the latter edition Armstrong spoke of his early days as a jazz musician before he metamorphosed into a popular entertainer.

The best place to see these television appearances is the Museum of Television and Radio in New York City or in Los Angeles.

"Tell Me, Dreamy Eyes." By Gus Kahn, Phil Spitalny, and Stubby Gordon; rec. between October 10 and 13, 1924, in New York City by **Fletcher Henderson** and His Orchestra. See additional comments on "Alabamy Bound."

"Ten Feet Off the Ground." By Richard M. Sherman and Robert B. Sherman; rec. February 27, 1968, in New York City by **Louis Armstrong and the All Stars;** CD #15. This so-so song about the power of music was introduced in **Disney**'s 1967 movie *The One and Only, Genuine, Original Family Band,* and Armstrong treats it kindly. In his trumpet solo (one of his last on record) he quotes "Way Down Yonder in New Orleans."

"Tenderly." By Walter Gross and Jack Lawrence; rec. August 16, 1956, in Los Angeles with vocalist **Ella Fitzgerald** and the **Oscar Peterson** Quartet; CDs #2, #8, #9, #19, and #28. Armstrong frequently programmed this 1946 song, often pairing it in a medley with "You'll Never Walk Alone." He and Fitzgerald brought out the best in each other in this collaboration. See additional comments on "April in Paris."

"Terrible Blues." By **Clarence Williams;** rec. November 26, 1924, in New York City by the Red Onion Jazz Babies; CD #35. Sandwiched in between recording dates with the relatively inert **Fletcher Henderson** Orchestra and with blues singers as a subservient accompanist, this cut is a breath of fresh air. Armstrong sounds liberated, taking breaks and solos full of imaginative melodic lines and fresh rhythmic inventions. This recording and "Santa Claus Blues" from the same session are a harbinger of the **Hot Five,** which he formed a year later.

Terry, Clark "Mumbles" (b. 1920). Like Armstrong, Terry grew up poor and learned to play the trumpet on a substitute instrument. Whereas in Armstrong's case this was a toy tin horn with which he attracted customers from the **Karnofsky**'s coal/junk wagon, for Terry it was a length of garden hose attached to a kerosene funnel. Eventually both acquired pawn shop instruments, although the 1908 price for Armstrong's was $5, while Terry's 1935 model cost $12.50. Finally, both musicians spent a valuable period in the **Fate Marable** riverboat orchestra, from which so many sidemen went on to fame that it was dubbed "the floating conservatory."

Although Terry never worked with Armstrong, he, like so many other musicians, trumpet players or otherwise, was deeply influenced by him. On his very first recordings (e.g., "Kidney Stew" and "Railroad Porter Blues" made with Eddie Vinson in the 1940s), one can hear echoes of Armstrong's **trumpet style,** modified by the be**bop** innovations of **Dizzy Gillespie.** However, Terry soon developed his own voice with Count Basie from 1948 to 1951 and especially with **Duke Ellington** from 1951 to 1959. In "Such Sweet Thunder" and "A Drum Is a Woman" (1956–1957), Terry created memorable solos, full of talking effects, debonair bent notes, and exquisite diminished chord passages. Beginning at about this time he revived the use of the fluegelhorn in "Juniflip." He also developed his own singing voice, again with the inspiration of Armstrong, who told him: "The people love trumpet playing, but you gotta sing more" (Voce, p. 17). Although Terry sings well in the traditional manner, he earned the nickname "Mumbles" for his amusing wordless blues patter.

Like Gillespie, Terry was a neighbor of Armstrong's in **Corona** and used to drop in occasionally "to get his batteries charged" (Bergreen, p. 486). He has since charged the batteries of many others. As a musician in New York, Terry's outstanding trumpet skills and infectious good humor, like Armstrong's, did much to break an invisible color barrier and pave the way for other African American musicians. From the 1960s on he played on the *Tonight Show,* in his own Big B-A-D Band, with **Oscar Peterson,** and elsewhere. He has also been an active educator and the recipient of numerous honorary doctorates.

Tetrazzini, Luisa (1862–1938). See **"Louis Armstrong and Opera."**

"Texas Moaner Blues." By **Clarence Williams** and F. Barnes; rec. October 17, 1924, in New York City by **Clarence Williams' Blue Five;** CDs #35, #36, and #48. This tempo is slow even for a blues, and that plus the absence of a singer gives the instrumentalists a chance to express themselves. Armstrong plays one of his first double-time breaks, for example. This is also Armstrong's first recording with clarinetist/soprano saxophonist **Sidney Bechet,** another jazz pioneer, and they inspire each other. In transcribing the solo, Gunther Schuller admits in awe that Armstrong's rhythmic freedom and *rubato* tempo defy exact notation (Schuller, 1968, p. 96).

"Thankful." By Saul Chaplin and Sammy Cahn; rec. May 18, 1936, in New York City by Louis Armstrong and His Orchestra. At the time of this recording, Armstrong had been under the stable management of **Joe Glaser** for a year, and his sound is full and relaxed.

"Thankful" comes from a fatiguing six-song session (which included "Swing That Music"), but Armstrong has plenty to give to it. His masterful solo has been transcribed by Gunther Schuller (1989, p. 190) and studied by up-and-coming trumpeters.

"Thanks a Million." By Sammy Cahn and Saul Chaplin; rec. December 19, 1935, in New York City by Louis Armstrong and His Orchestra; CDs #41, #51, and #61. Armstrong here does one of the day's popular songs, playing and singing agreeably.

"That Lucky Old Sun." By Beasley Smith and Haven Gillespie; rec. September 6, 1949, in New York City with Gordon Jenkins and His Orchestra; CDs #4, #28, #39, and #40. "Blueberry Hill," recorded as the flipside to this prayerlike song, turned out to be the hit, but "That Lucky Old Sun" has much to recommend it. Armstrong knows whereof he sings with this text about the work, sweat, and fuss that constitute the human condition.

"That Old Feeling." By Sammy Fain and Lew Brown; rec. October 14, 1957, in Los Angeles with the **Oscar Peterson** Quartet; CDs #28 and #37. This 1937 song is one of the best from the *Louis Armstrong Meets Oscar Peterson* album. Armstrong sings nostalgically yet with a devilish twinkle in his eye. See additional comments on "Blues in the Night."

"That Rhythm Man." By **Thomas "Fats" Waller,** Andy Razaf, and Harry Brooks; rec. July 22, 1929, in New York City by Louis Armstrong and His Orchestra; CDs #44, #48, and #56. One of three tunes from the 1929 revue ***Connie's Hot Chocolates*** on which he stamped his name ("Ain't Misbehavin'" and "Black and Blue" are the others), this quickstep features the ensemble more than soloists since it accompanied a dance number. Nevertheless, Armstrong takes a half-**scat** vocal chorus and two spirited high-note solos, the latter of which gently brings the music to a quiet close.

"That's a Plenty." By Lou Pollack and Ray Gilbert; rec. December 26, 1950, in Los Angeles by **Louis Armstrong and the All Stars;** CD #45. After Armstrong made this recording for the 1951 **movie** ***The Strip,*** he added this song to his repertory. He made another excellent recording (CD #53) with the **Dukes of Dixieland** on May 24 or 25, 1960, in New York City. See additional comments on "Avalon."

"That's for Me." By Richard Rodgers and Oscar Hammerstein II; rec. April 26 or 27, 1950, in New York City by **Louis Armstrong and the All Stars;** CDs #8 and #28. Here is Armstrong the crooner, singing a number introduced in the 1945 film *State Fair.* He's up in his infrequent tenor range but succeeds. Trombonist **Jack Teagarden,** clarinetist **Barney Bigard,** and especially pianist **Earl Hines** provide superb support.

"That's My Desire." By Carroll Loveday and Helmy Kresa; rec. November 1, 1967, in New York City by Louis Armstrong with the Dick Jacobs Orchestra; CDs #19, #23, #28, #40, and #57. This 1931 song was a **Velma Middleton** feature with the **All Stars** in 1948, which was around the same time that Frankie Laine made it popular. As the All Stars developed, it became one of the duets (like "Rockin'

Chair" or "Back o' Town Blues") that Armstrong liked to do with trombone players **Jack Teagarden, Trummy Young,** or, as here, **Tyree Glenn,** who was a member of the All Stars from 1965 to 1971.

"That's My Home." By Leon René, Otis René, and Ben Ellison; rec. December 8, 1932, in Camden, New Jersey, with the Chick Webb Orchestra (although the label reads "Louis Armstrong and His Orchestra"); CDs #8, #12, #17, #21, #23, #24, #28, #44, #52, and #59. This is the first of two takes of this nostalgic song, written by the René brothers of New Orleans for Armstrong when he returned from his first trip to Europe (see **European tours**) in November 1932. Both versions are in circulation, but this first one has the more inventive trumpet playing with thrilling glissandos and high notes.

"That's What the Man Said." By Willard Robison; rec. August 31, 1950, in New York City with the **Sy Oliver** Chorus and a rhythm section led by pianist **Billy Kyle;** CDs #27 and #45. Armstrong and **Jack Teagarden** sang this catchy number in the 1952 film ***Glory Alley.***

"That's When I'll Come Back to You." By F. Biggs or **Lil Hardin Armstrong;** rec. May 14, 1927, in Chicago by Louis Armstrong and His **Hot Seven;** CD #10. Writing for ***Esquire*** magazine in 1951, Armstrong recalls that his wife Lil wrote this song (Brothers, p. 134), but other sources name F. Biggs. Perhaps because he and Lil had such success with it, Armstrong may have felt she wrote the song, which did mirror the growing strain in their marriage. Their duet, replete with invective and threats, was all done in broad comedic style, though, and in performance evidently brought down the house.

"Them There Eyes." By Maceo Pinkard, William Tracey, and Doris Tauber; rec. April 29, 1931, in Chicago by Louis Armstrong and His Orchestra; CDs #8 and #52. Armstrong turned this Tin Pan Alley product into a jazz number, and later **Billie Holiday** took over. Armstrong must have been fond of the song because he chose it to open his first European concert (July 18, 1932, at the London Palladium) and on his second tour to open at the venerable **Salle Pleyel** in Paris (November 9, 1934). (See **European tours.**)

"There Must Be a Way." By Sammy Gallop and David Saxon; rec. July 23, 1968, in Las Vegas by **Louis Armstrong and the All Stars;** CD #62. Before Armstrong got around to it, this 1945 song was popularized by Charlie Spivak and His Orchestra.

"There's a Boat Dat's Leavin' Soon for New York." By George Gershwin, DuBose Heyward, and Ira Gershwin; rec. August 18 or 19, 1957, in Los Angeles with a studio orchestra and choir conducted by Russell Garcia; CDs #9 and #29. Armstrong sings solo on this number from Act III of *Porgy and Bess.* See additional comments on "Bess, You Is My Woman Now."

"There's a Cabin in the Pines." By Billy Hill; rec. April 26, 1933, in Chicago by Louis Armstrong and His Orchestra; CDs #12, #21, and #24. While some jazz critics and fans regret Armstrong's managers' foisting inferior material such as this song on him for commercial gain, there are some good moments on this recording, particularly toward the end when he does some terrific half-valve work.

"There's No You." By Hal Hopper and Tom Adair; rec. October 14, 1957, in Los Angeles with pianist Oscar Peterson and guitarist Herb Ellis; CD #37. Evidently this was a last-minute addition to the album *Louis Armstrong Meets* ***Oscar Peterson.*** Armstrong sings movingly to the smoky accompaniment of Herb Ellis's guitar. The result is a treasure, to be set alongside the 1944 original by Jo Stafford.

"They All Laughed." By George Gershwin and Ira Gershwin; rec. July 23, 1957, in Los Angeles with vocalist **Ella Fitzgerald** and the **Oscar Peterson** Quartet; CD #9. The Gershwins wrote this for the movie *Shall We Dance?* (1937, the year George died), and here Armstrong, Fitzgerald, and the Peterson ensemble perform it with finger-wagging insouciance. See additional comments on "April in Paris."

"They Can't Take That Away from Me." By George Gershwin and Ira Gershwin; rec. August 16, 1956, in Los Angeles with vocalist **Ella Fitzgerald** and the **Oscar Peterson** Quartet; CD #9. See comments on "April in Paris."

"They Say I Look Like God." By **Dave Brubeck** and Iola Brubeck; rec. September 12, 1961, in New York City by **Louis Armstrong and the All Stars,** pianist Dave Brubeck, and guests; CD #50. The most impressive number in ***The Real Ambassadors*** is this blues sung by Armstrong, against a Gregorian chantlike chorus. On this recording, you can hear him almost cry when he sings about being truly free. See additional comments on "Cultural Exchange."

"This Black Cat Has Nine Lives." By Lorenzo Pack; rec. May 29, 1970, in New York City with a studio orchestra and chorus conducted by Oliver Nelson; CD #31. On his next-to-last album, Armstrong is all but smothered by heavy arrangements, but he enjoyed the luxury of having so many musicians around him. The multilived black cat image resonates nicely with Armstrong's career.

"This Train." By Rosetta Tharpe; rec. February 4, 1958, in New York City with **Louis Armstrong and the All Stars** and the **Sy Oliver** Choir; CD #27. Armstrong does some quick call-and-response singing and some spirited trumpet playing on this religious standard. See additional comments on "Down by the Riverside."

"This Younger Generation." By B. Merrill and E. Merrill; rec. December 14, 1956, in New York City by Louis Armstrong and His Orchestra; CD #8. The flipside of "In Pursuit of Happiness" was a stretch, even for Armstrong, who nevertheless accommodated the rhythm and blues style, backbeat and all.

Thomas, Hociel. Thomas was one of the many African American blues singers (e.g., **Alberta Hunter, Ma Rainey,** and **Bessie Smith**) with whom Armstrong recorded in the 1920s. He accompanied Thomas on "Adam and Eve Had the Blues" (1925), "Deep Water Blues" and "Listen to Ma" (both 1926), and others, mostly her own compositions. Frankly, these recordings are interesting mostly for Armstrong's inventive playing. "Listen to Ma," for example, exemplifies a relatively ignored aspect of Armstrong's **trumpet style,** namely, that he was one of the first to exploit the lower register.

Thomson, Virgil (1896–1989). When popular culture began to gain respectability in the 1920s and 1930s, Armstrong became a popular topic among artists and intellectuals. **Fritz Kreisler,** the famous classical violinist, was a jazz and an Armstrong fan; **Pauline Kael,** author of a dozen books on film, was an admirer; and poet and playwright **Amiri Baraka** defended Armstrong as an "honored priest of his culture" (p. 154). Virgil Thomson can be added to this list. The venerable American composer-critic had a high opinion of Armstrong, about whom he wrote: "His style of improvisation would seem to have combined the highest reaches of instrumental virtuosity with the most tensely disciplined melodic structure and the most spontaneous emotional expression, all of which in one man you must admit to be pretty rare" (Thomson, p. 31). On the other hand, Armstrong also had his high-brow detractors, such as **James Agee, James Baldwin, Rudi Blesh,** and **Sidney Finkelstein.**

"Three of Us, The." Rec. August 1965 in Hollywood by **Louis Armstrong and the All Stars.**

"Throw It Out of Your Mind." By **Billy Kyle** and Louis Armstrong; rec. July 26, 1965, in Hollywood by **Louis Armstrong and the All Stars;** CD #45. This song is from the 1965 **movie *When the Boys Meet the Girls.***

"Thunderstorm Blues." By Spencer Williams and Arthur Ray; rec. December 10, 1924, in New York City with vocalist **Maggie Jones** and pianist **Fletcher Henderson;** CD #36. An enterprising sound engineer added thunderstorm effects to this recording. See additional comments on "Anybody Here Want to Try My Cabbage?"

"Tiger Rag." By D.J. "Nick" La Rocca; rec. May 4, 1930, in New York City by Louis Armstrong and His Orchestra; CDs #1, #2, #13, #19, #20, #23, #25, #46, #58, #60, and #63. The chord sequence of this **Dixieland** standard (first published and popularized in 1917 and revised and reprinted with lyrics in 1932 as "The New Tiger Rag") has been used in other numbers such as "Fireworks," "Hotter Than That," "Knee Drops," and "Symphonic Raps." Armstrong included the piece on the pivotal **Carnegie Hall concert** in 1947, and it became a staple in his repertory. He usually took it at a very quick pace, joking with the audience about how fast tigers run and how many choruses it might take to catch this one. On this particular recording early in his career, we can hear him extending the range of the trumpet, solidly nailing the "E-flat" above high "C." The high-loud-fast pyrotechnics are thrilling. One Armstrong fan, the Duke of Windsor, reputedly said, "I'd rather hear Louis Armstrong play 'Tiger Rag' than wander into Westminster Abbey and find the lost chord" (Giddins, 1988, p. 105). The piece is featured in the 1960 concert film ***Jazz on a Summer's Day.***

"Tight Like This." By Langston Curl; rec. December 12, 1928, in Chicago by Louis

Armstrong and His **Savoy Ballroom Five;** CDs #10, #14, #30, #44, and #48. Alto sax player and arranger **Don Redman** teamed up with Armstrong on numerous occasions, but this is generally considered their masterpiece, in that it richly combines so many opposites—suggestive and overstated, obscure and direct, lean and florid. Redman's high-pitched speaking voice can be heard in the beginning and here and there afterward. Pianist **Earl Hines** contributes an inspired solo (and then did not record again with Armstrong for twenty years). However, this is mostly Armstrong's show, as he constructs a four-chorus, sixty-four-measure solo out of only a few sequenced notes, with time out to noodle around a little on the risqué World War I song "Oh, the Girls in France." In his casual juxtaposition of art and entertainment, Armstrong here creates a monument more lasting than bronze. Transcription by Castle (vol. 1, p. 10).

Time. When the popular weekly newsmagazine devoted its cover story to Armstrong (February 21, 1949), it was the first such honor for a jazz musician. (The next honoree, **Dave Brubeck,** had to wait until November 8, 1954, unless one counts Rosemary Clooney on February 23, 1953.) The event also brought two bonuses: a marvelous and often reprinted portrait by artist **Boris Artzybasheff** and the gratuitous addition of "Daniel" to Armstrong's name (which he rather liked—see **Armstrong, "Daniel" Louis).** Thereafter, *Time* kept him regularly in its pages, favorably reviewing his parts in **movies** (e.g., ***The Glenn Miller Story***) and keeping track of his U.S. State Department-sponsored tours abroad. The respectful attention of a mainstream publication underscored Armstrong's status as a first-rank show business figure.

"Tin Roof Blues." By Walter Melrose, Paul Mares, George Brunies, Leon Roppolo, Melville Stitzel, and Ben Pollack; rec. April 25, 1955, in New York City by **Louis Armstrong and the All Stars;** CDs #1, #6, #8, #22, and #46. Writing in 1970, Armstrong fondly remembered first having heard this song in the early 1920s, which is about the time that it was written. He recorded it more than once with the All Stars, and he liked to take it very slowly. The arrangement here is probably by pianist **Billy Kyle,** who gives himself some nice interludes and an introductory duet with bassist **Arvell Shaw.** There's also some clever interplay between clarinetist **Barney Bigard** and trombonist **Trummy Young.** Armstrong stays mostly on the sidelines.

"T.N.T." By Elmer Schoebel; rec. October 21, 1925, in New York City by **Fletcher Henderson** and His Orchestra; CD #48. Armstrong both inspired and was at times inspired by Henderson's New York musicians, as one can hear on this recording from Armstrong's last session with the Henderson Orchestra before he returned to Chicago. The **Don Redman** arrangement gives him three solos—two of four measures and one of sixteen. He's distinctively himself on the short solos, but on the long one, as Gunther Schuller points out in *Early Jazz,* "he does a flawless imitation of [Henderson Orchestra trumpet player] **Joe Smith**'s smoother style" (1968, p. 263).

"To Be in Love." By Fred E. Ahlert and Roy Turk; rec. June 4, 1929, in New York City by Louis Armstrong with vocalist Seger Ellis, trombonist Tommy Dorsey, clarinetist **Jimmy Dorsey,** violinist Harry Hoffman, piano-celeste player Justin Ring, and drummer Stan King; CDs #36 and #48. See comments on "S'posin'."

"To You, Sweetheart, Aloha." By Harry Owens; rec. August 18, 1936, in Los Angeles with The Polynesians (a.k.a. Andy Iona and His Islanders). See comments on "Hawaiian Hospitality."

"Tomorrow Night (After Tonight)." By Ralph Mathews, **Lil Hardin Armstrong,** and **Clarence Williams;** rec. April 24, 1933, in Chicago by Louis Armstrong and His Orchestra; CD #12. Both Armstrong and the band seem a little soggy on this number. His singing voice sounds tired, and he just barely squeezes out the final high notes.

"Too Busy." By Ned Miller and Chester Cohn; rec. June 26, 1928, in Chicago by vocalist **Lillie Delk Christian** with Louis Armstrong and His **Hot Four;** CDs #10, #36, and #48. "Too Busy" is the best of an unfortunately bad batch of numbers on which Armstrong accompanied the pretty but not musically gifted Christian. What saves the song, in addition to instrumental solos by Armstrong and **Earl Hines,** is the last verse when Armstrong jumps in and scats around Christian's stiff, old-fashioned singing. See additional comments on "Baby" and "I Must Have That Man."

"Top Hat, White Tie, and Tails." By **Irving Berlin;** rec. August 14, 1957, in Los Angeles with a studio orchestra conducted by arranger Russell Garcia; CD #29. This superb song was first introduced by Fred Astaire in the 1935 movie *Top Hat.*

Town Hall concert. This May 17, 1947, event, which followed the **Carnegie Hall concert** by three months, emphasized Armstrong's success with a small ensemble and marked a new phase in his career (as well as a major turning point in the evolution of jazz). Gone was the hefty big band; back was the small and agile New Orleans-style group. **Dixieland** nostalgia (with its yearning for simpler pre-World War II days) had been building before the Town Hall concert, and the prodigal son now gave it a national voice. Since Armstrong was ailing from an ulcer around concert time, cornetist **Bobby Hackett** put together a dream team ensemble, the **All Stars: Peanuts Hucko** (tenor saxophone, clarinet), **Jack Teagarden** (trombone, vocals), **Dick Cary** (piano), **Bob Haggart** (bass), and **Sid Catlett** and George Wettling (drums). Promoter **Ernie Anderson** coordinated this pivotal event. Some of the magic of this landmark concert can still be heard on a two-CD, twenty-one-song RCA recording issued in 1992 (CD #13). *Footnote:* In fact there actually were two Town Hall concerts since, in response to the demand for tickets, a second show was added at midnight.

"Trinket." The Armstrong's female pet schnauzer was a gift in the late 1960s from **Joe Glazer,** who thought their male schnauzer, **"Trumpet,"** might like some company. "We just love those dogs," Armstrong wrote in 1970. "They're like Human Beings." Armstrong also got a kick out of what fine watch dogs they made. "When the two of them start Barking together—Oh Boy what a *Duet,*" he wrote (Brothers, pp. 178, 182). See also **"General,"** a Boston terrier that accompanied Armstrong on the road in the 1940s.

"Trouble Everywhere I Roam." By Hersal Thomas and **Sippie Wallace;** rec. November 28, 1924, in New York City with vocalist Sippie Wallace and **Clarence Williams' Blue Five;** CD #36. See comments on "Baby, I Can't Use You No More."

"Trouble in Mind." By Richard M. Jones; rec. February 23, 1926, in Chicago with vocalist **Bertha "Chippie" Hill** and pianist Richard M. Jones; CDs #8, #36, and #52. (See additional comments on "A Georgia Man.") On January 28, 1957, Armstrong rerecorded this unusual blues (in that it is an eight-bar and not a twelve-bar pattern) with **Velma Middleton** and the **All Stars** for his *Satchmo: A Musical Autobiography* project (CD #52).

"Trumpet." In the 1960s the Armstrongs had two dogs (both schnauzers), "Trumpet" and **"Trinket."** Armstrong gave "Trumpet" (a male) to **Lucille** as a gift, and later his manager **Joe Glaser** brought him a female, "Trinket," from California. "We just love those dogs," Armstrong wrote in June 1970. "They're like Human Beings." Armstrong also got a kick out of what fine watchdogs they made. "When the two of them start Barking together—Oh Boy what a *Duet,*" he wrote (Brothers, pp. 178, 182). See also "**General,**" a Boston terrier that accompanied Armstrong on the road in the 1940s.

trumpet. Armstrong switched from the cornet to the trumpet in October 1924 in order to match the two trumpet players in the **Fletcher Henderson** Orchestra with whom he was working at the time. It did not seem to be a big deal to him, and he liked the trumpet's mellower and richer sound. He later recalled that once he began to listen critically to the cornet sound, he found that "it just didn't come out as pretty as a trumpet" (***The Record Changer,*** July–Aug. 1950, p. 21). One of his first instruments was a Columbia "B-flat" trumpet, manufactured by Harry P. Jay of Chicago around 1920 (see photo in Miller, p. 2). The trumpet he played on his **Hot Five** and **Hot Seven** recordings (1925–1928) was a Buescher 10-22 model. In 1929 he switched to a Conn 56B with a rotary valve, which could change the horn from "B-flat" to "A" (see photo on cover of Collier, 1983). After that, Armstrong endorsed **Selmer** horns and maintained a relationship with the company for the rest of his life. This arrangement began with an advertisement in the October 1932 issue of *Rhythm,* timed for Armstrong's first tour of **England,** enthusiastically touted both the Selmer "Challenger" model and the new "Louis Armstrong Special" based on it. He preferred the "balanced action" model, which had the valves set closer to the bell. (Selmer may have created this model for the long-armed Harry James.) At the end of his life, Armstrong had mostly Selmer horns on hand, and these can be seen at the **Louis Armstrong House and Archives.** There is a particularly beautiful Selmer, a "K-modified" model, that bears the inscription "Louis **'Satchmo'** Armstrong" on the bell pipe. There is also a more ornate LeBlanc trumpet, which reads "Satchmo Louis Armstrong" in raised letters near the bell. One is struck by how heavy all these trumpets are and how hard Armstrong had to work just to hold them up, compared to modern horns of new, lighter alloy mixtures.

Trumpet Kings. On this video hosted by **Wynton Marsalis,** Armstrong is rightfully the first and foremost performer. He is shown in excerpts from the 1933 film ***København, Kalundborg Og?*** playing "Dinah" at breakneck speed, followed by the more subdued "I Cover the Waterfront." Armstrong announces these songs, too, and during the performances he zooms around the stage in a crouching position, perspiring, and flourishing his handkerchief. It gives a fascinating glimpse into the way he performed early in his career. The documentary continues with what might well be called Louis's Children: **Red Allen, Bunny Berigan, Miles Davis, Roy Eldridge,** Harry James, Cootie Williams, and the rest. At the end, Armstrong and **Dizzy Gillespie** affectionately trade fours in the spirit of a friendly competition, both as trumpeters and singers performing "Umbrella Man" in a 1959 clip from *The Jackie Gleason Show.* Video Artists International, 1985; B&W and color; 72 mins.; written, prod., and dir. Burrill Crohn.

"Trumpet Player's Lament, The." By Johnny Burke and James V. Monaco; rec. January 12, 1938, in Los Angeles by Louis Armstrong and His Orchestra. Armstrong had filmed this number on November 4, 1937, with a studio orchestra for the **movie *Doctor Rhythm,*** but unfortunately the sequence was cut. Some felt that there were racist reasons for this, but according to British Armstrong fans Jones and Chilton, this was not the case. They note that a statement was issued "denying discrimination and stressing that such scissor work was common practice in Hollywood, which indeed it was," and that the star of the film, **Bing Crosby,** in an interview said that "they always shot more film than they needed in musicals . . . and they sometimes had to make a deeper cut" (p. 196). More details can be found in Klaus Stratemann's book (1996, pp. 71–74). In any case, the number was rerecorded and issued by **Decca.**

Trumpet Players' Tribute. This documentary was filmed on July 10, 1970, at the opening concert of the **Newport Jazz Festival,** which was billed as a tribute to Armstrong. Trumpeters **Dizzy Gillespie, Bobby Hackett,** Joe Newman, Wild Bill Davidson, Jimmy Owens, and Ray Nance each played an Armstrong favorite from different points in his career. Armstrong sings a bit on two numbers. Three other films (***Anatomy of a Performance, The Antiquarians,*** and ***Finale***) were made in connection with this, Armstrong's last, Newport Festival. Festifilms Inc., 1970; color; 45 mins.; Dir. Sidney J. Stiber; Prod. George Wein.

trumpet style. Trumpet playing was never the same after Louis Armstrong came on the scene. Even before switching from the **cornet** to the more popular trumpet in 1924, he had begun to lead the way in extending the upper range of these instruments. He seems to have been influenced to do so, as well as to develop quick fingering, by the great clarinet players of his day (Harker, 2003). At any rate, high "C" was a glass ceiling that no one shattered (except perhaps some turn-of-the-century cornet soloists, most of whom unfortunately went unrecorded). Armstrong gradually worked his way up to "D" and "E-flat." On "Tiger Rag" and "My Sweet," both recorded in the spring of 1930, he nailed the "E-flat" solidly, and in the fall of the same year he went on to a then-incredible "F" in the Eubie Blake/Andy Razaf hit "You're Lucky to Me." (Asked by a radio interviewer about how high he could go, he once quipped: "Well, I can get up to 'P.' ") He thereby started a trend that led to regular double high "Cs" by the end of the big band era and, as Maynard Ferguson fans well know, still continues.

Armstrong also did something similar at the opposite end of the range. He was one of the first to improvise in the lowest register, and no jazz player (not even **Bunny Berigan**) has ever surpassed him there. Good examples of this can be heard on his 1928 version of "Basin Street Blues," the 1929 "Some of These Days," and the 1931 "Star Dust." In the last eight measures of "Basin Street," for example, one hears a full-toned, low register, eight-measure coda that, coming as it does on the heels of an impassioned high-range improvisation, still thrills today's listener.

Armstrong's trumpet style, however, affected far more than just trumpet performance: it contributed enormously to the development of **swing.** Although difficult to define, most will agree that swing is characterized by a type of musical momentum that a wide variety of devices can produce against a fixed pulse: placing notes either ahead of or behind the beat, dividing the basic pulse into smaller unequal parts, and displacing the accent with alterations in individual notes (varying their beginning and ending, modifying their tone quality, changing their intonation, and especially adding vibrato at the end of longer notes). These innovations can be heard here and there in Armstrong's earliest recordings, such as "Mandy, Make Up Your Mind" and "Texas Moaner Blues," both from 1924. By the time of "Potato Head Blues" in 1927 and "West End Blues" in the following year, the techniques are well developed. By the early 1930s they were part of the style of virtually every jazz musician.

"Potato Head Blues" also illustrates other Armstrong innovations. For one, he varies his tone quality by such means as alternate fingerings on repeated notes. For another, his improvisations sketch out minor and diminished seventh chords, playing the notes sequentially instead of simultaneously. Finally and most important, he solos to **stop-time** accompaniment, thereby creating the model of the featured instrumental soloist, a development that revolutionized popular music.

"West End Blues" underscores all these innovations. Here Armstrong plays consistently higher, more inventively, and with more confidence than any trumpeter before and, some say, since. Many jazz fans consider this to be the greatest of all recorded trumpet performances, and Gunther Schuller suggests that it be heard by anyone who does not understand the difference between jazz and other music (1968, p. 116). Particularly remarkable is the final chorus, which Armstrong begins with a high "B-flat," held for nearly four measures, followed by a dazzling repetitive descending phrase.

Armstrong's earliest repertory basically consisted of blues, rags, stomps, and novelty numbers, until he recorded "Ain't

Misbehavin' " in July 1929. This was a landmark event, which both boosted his already rising popularity and started the use of pop songs in the jazz repertory. Armstrong thus set the stage for the greatly expanded popularity of jazz at the end of the 1930s. **Benny Goodman**'s triumphal 1935 tour could not have taken place without Armstrong's first having recorded "Lazy River" (1930), "Star Dust" (1931), "Between the Devil and the Deep Blue Sea" (1932), "I've Got the World on a String" (1933), "On the Sunny Side of the Street" (1934), and many others.

Finally, in addition to his technical and stylistic innovations, Armstrong knew how to sell a song, simply and directly, from the heart to the heart. He had a stirring, beautiful tone, and he performed with admirable authority. **Dizzy Gillespie,** early on Armstrong's rival but later his friend, observed that "if it hadn't been for him there wouldn't have been none of us" (Hentoff, 1976, p. 60). Even **Miles Davis,** who found so much fault with his shadow mentor, admitted that "you can't play anything on the horn that Louis hasn't played" (Giddins, 1988, p. 65).

Tuxedo Brass Band. A.k.a. the Original Tuxedo Orchestra and the Tuxedo Jazz Orchestra, this ensemble was founded by cornet player **Oscar "Papa" Celestin** and trombone player William "Baba" Ridgley in 1917. In ***Satchmo: My Life in New Orleans,*** Armstrong praises the TBB and expresses great pleasure in playing second cornet in it (1954, pp. 143, 179–180). The TBB nurtured such players as **Isidore Barbarin, Mutt Carey,** Sam Dutrey, Sr., Louis Keppard, and **Alphonse Picou** and remained active until 1927, when the members argued and split up. Ridgley formed a new band with the old name, and Celestin formed the Tuxedo Jazz Orchestra. Celestin revived his by-then defunct ensemble at the end of World War II, and in 1953 he was invited to play for President **Dwight Eisenhower.**

"Twelfth Street Rag." By Euday L. Bowman and Andy Razaf; rec. May 11, 1927, in Chicago by Louis Armstrong and His **Hot Seven;** CDs #1, #6, #8, #10, and #22. Probably because of its unusually slow tempo and several cracked notes in the trumpet chorus, this recording was not released until **George Avakian** got **Columbia** to do so in 1941. Armstrong later rerecorded it with the **All Stars** (on April 26 or 27, 1950, in New York City), and it remained in their repertory. In contrast to the Hot Seven, the All Stars do what some would call a corny version, in which each member hams it up on his solo. It's at least entertaining and sometimes even artistic.

"Two Deuces." By **Lil Hardin Armstrong** (see authorship note on "Got No Blues"); rec. June 29, 1928, in Chicago by Louis Armstrong and His **Hot Five;** CDs #8, #10, #30, #48, and #52. Here is a good example of the influence of **opera** on Armstrong's musical style. Yes, opera. Before taking up the cornet, he sang operatic excerpts on New Orleans street corners, and his first record acquisitions in 1917–1918 included famous opera singers of the day. Musicologist Joshua Berrett has shown that Armstrong's mature musical style exhibits phrases, breaks, and gestures from such works as

Gounod's *Faust,* Leoncavallo's *Pagliacci,* and Verdi's *Rigoletto* (1992, p. 216–240). Armstrong's "Deuces" solo has been transcribed by Castle (vol. 2, p. 6).

"Two Nineteen Blues." See "2:19 Blues."

"2:19 Blues." By Mamie Desdume; rec. May 27, 1940, in New York City by Louis Armstrong and His Orchestra; CD #61. Armstrong's recording of this traditional New Orleans standard (one that **Buddy Bolden** used to play) came as a relief to those hard-core fans who feared that he was neglecting jazz for pop songs and novelties.

typewriter. See **writer.**

"Tyree's Blues." By **Tyree Glenn** and Louis Armstrong; rec. April 1966 in New York City by **Louis Armstrong and the All Stars.** This is a feature number for Glenn, who was the All Stars' trombonist from 1965 to 1971. A versatile musician, he also sang ("Cheesecake") and played the vibraphone ("Avalon").

Tyson, Cicely. See ***A Man Called Adam.***

U

"Umbrella Man." By Vincent Rose, James Cavanaugh, and Larry Stock; rec. January 7, 1959, live on CBS-TV for the *Timex All Star Show—The Golden Age of Jazz* in New York City with **Dizzy Gillespie** and a studio ensemble. Armstrong never cut a studio recording of "Umbrella Man," but he and Dizzy Gillespie did it together on this **television** broadcast. The warm-hearted, hilarious performance can be seen on the videos ***Trumpet Kings*** (1985) and ***Satchmo: Louis Armstrong*** (1989).

"Uncle Satchmo's Lullaby." By Erwin Halletz and Olaf Bradtke; rec. May 20, 1959, in Vienna with child vocalist Gabriele Klonisch and the Johannes Fehring Orchestra conducted by Erwin Halletz. This number was used in the 1959 musical review film ***La paloma*** (which featured a great many German song and dance acts of the day), and the recording reached the No. 9 spot on German record charts in July.

"Undecided." By Charlie Shavers and Sid Robin; rec. October 29, 1955, live at the Concertgebouw in Amsterdam by **Louis Armstrong and the All Stars;** CDs #1, #9, #20, and #23. With its clever lyrics and lively beat, this is just the kind of song Armstrong liked. He took it on the road to Holland, Italy, Africa, and elsewhere. Back home he recorded it again live on August 15, 1956, at the Hollywood Bowl with vocalist **Ella Fitzgerald.**

"Under a Blanket of Blue." By Jerry Livingston, Al J. Neiburg, and Marty Symes; rec. August 16, 1956, in Los Angeles with vocalist **Ella Fitzgerald** and the **Oscar Peterson** Quartet; CD #9. See comments on "April in Paris."

union, labor. See **American Federation of Musicians.**

"Unless." By Tolchard Evans, Robert Hargreaves, and Stanley J. Damerell; rec. April 23, 1951, in Los Angeles by **Louis Armstrong and the All Stars;** CD #8. Here, as often in his career, Armstrong does a great deal with very little. He adds **scat** to a stodgy vocal and both vibrato and grace notes to a short trumpet solo.

U.S. State Department. See **African tours; "Ambassador Satch."**

V

Vallee, Rudy. See ***Swing That Music.***

Vanity Fair. Founded in 1923, the fashionable monthly magazine both led and reflected the interest in popular culture that began during the 1920s and 1930s, and Armstrong was naturally one of their frequent subjects. For one thing, he loved the camera, and vice versa, as *Vanity Fair*'s **Anton Bruehl** discovered in photographing Armstrong for the November 1935 issue. Dimly lit and shot from below, Armstrong holds his trumpet in one hand and his handkerchief in the other. The friendly and dignified picture so pleased Armstrong that he commissioned painter **Calvin Bailey** to make an oil version, which hung in Armstrong's living room until his death. (Frequently reproduced, the photo was used on the cover of Laurence Bergreen's 1997 biography and its oil version on the cover Marc Miller's 1994 exhibition catalog.) Armstrong was also always quotable, and in February 1936 he was paired with **Fritz Kreisler,** the famous classical violinist (and jazz fan) in a fictional "Impossible Interview" (a regular *Vanity Fair* series). Kreisler declares: "With your talent, you, the most famous trumpeter in America, should be in a symphony orchestra," but the exchange ends with him joining Armstrong's band. The text is accompanied by artist **Miguel Covarrubias**'s caricature depicting Kreisler happily thumping a piano, and Armstrong, horn in hand, beaming out a song. The subtext here and elsewhere in the magazine's pages at the time was that jazz had been embraced by the upper classes and had a place alongside classical music.

Vendome Theater. Built in 1909 at 3145 South Street, the 1,500-seat Vendome was one of the busiest Chicago variety theaters. At first it had silent movies accompanied by live music and floorshows during intermissions. From 1919 to 1928, the Vendome became an important jazz venue, due to the influence of **Erskine Tate** and his **Vendome Theater Symphony Orchestra.** Armstrong was pleased when Tate asked him to join this ensemble in December 1925, and he remained until April 1927. It had grown from a quintet to a twenty-piece orchestra and was sometimes doing up to four shows a night. Typically they played an "overture" (e.g., Rossini's *William Tell*), then accompanied the movie, after which Tate's smaller Jazz Syncopators would take over. Armstrong played jazz solos as well as operatic arias, such as the **"Intermezzo" from *Cavalleria Rusticana*** (see

"Louis Armstrong and Opera"). He also did vaudeville routines, such as dressing as the Reverend Satchelmouth and giving mock sermons. Eventually many in the audience came solely to see Armstrong and left when he finished, skipping the movie entirely. A nineteen-year-old girl by the name of **Alpha Smith** sat in the front row, and Armstrong, although married to **Lil,** quickly noticed what he considered her "big pretty eyes" (Brothers, p. 95). They began seeing each other, but it was not until October 11, 1938, two weeks after his divorce from Lil, that they were married. As for the Vendome Theater, its popularity declined later in the 1920s. Armstrong and pianist Clarence Jones tried unsuccessfully to revive business there late in 1927. The Vendome was demolished in 1949.

Vendome Theater Symphony Orchestra. It is a good thing that Armstrong had learned to read music both at the **Colored Waif's Home** and with **Davey Jones** in the **Fate Marable** Orchestra since he had to play difficult trumpet parts without rehearsal with the Vendome Theater Symphony Orchestra in the late 1920s. Led by **Erskine Tate** from 1919 to 1928 and again in the 1930s, the Vendome orchestra nurtured the growing art of jazz, as well as several of its important practitioners. Armstrong developed his chops there in 1926, **Fats Waller** was the house organist in 1927, and others who stayed for more than a little while included Stump Evans, **Freddie Keppard, Buster Bailey,** and **Earl Hines.** The Vendome orchestra played rousing overtures, provided musical accompaniment during silent movies, and also gave hour-long floorshows. Armstrong developed a large following not only for his playing in this ensemble but also for his singing and comedic hijinks during these floorshows.

Victor Records. Although one of the earliest record companies (1901), Victor was late getting into jazz, despite their surprising success in recording the Original Dixieland Jazz Band in 1917. They were not noted for jazz records until later in the 1920s, and they were slow in responding to the market for **race records.** Victor was bought out by Radio Corporation of America (RCA) in 1929, and Armstrong recorded for them for six months in 1932–1933. The results were mixed, however, because his manager **Johnny Collins** put commercial success ahead of artistic quality. In 1946 and 1947, now more humanely managed by **Joe Glaser,** Armstrong made a few recordings for RCA Victor (as it was now called) before returning to **Decca.** By the 1940s, RCA Victor was one of the three big labels along with Decca and **Columbia.** In February 1949 it issued the first 45 rpm single, in the 1950s it became a pioneer in reissuing early jazz, and in one way or another (e.g., the creation of the Camden label for low-cost records), it has remained important for dispensing and preserving jazz.

"Vie en rose, La." By R.S. Louiguy and Edith Piaf, with English lyrics by Mack David; rec. June 26, 1950, in New York City with the **Sy Oliver** Orchestra; CDs #23, #28, #39, and #40. This is unusually tender and sentimental for an Armstrong–Oliver arrangement, but aided by **Earl Hines**'s rococo piano, it charted and frequently appears on "Best of Armstrong" compilations. Like "Mack the Knife" and "Blueberry Hill," "La Vie en rose" also became a staple of **Louis Armstrong and the All Stars** concerts. See additional comments on "C'est si bon."

viper. "Tea," "muggles," "reefers," and other names for **marijuana** were part of the vocabulary of "vipers," that is, those (including Armstrong) who used the drug. Now dated, the term was once common, especially among jazz folk, and found its way into numerous song titles: **Mezz Mezzrow**'s "Sendin' the Vipers," Stuff Smith's "If You're a Viper," **Fats Waller**'s "Viper's Drag," and Armstrong's own piece "Song of the Vipers."

Vocalion Records. Vocalion was founded in 1916 as a subdivision of the Aeolian piano company and, after being sold to the Brunswick Record Company in 1926, specialized in making **race records.** In May 1926, Armstrong made two recordings for Vocalion ("Georgia Bo Bo" and "Drop That Sack") with his wife **Lil**'s Hot Shots. However, here was a problem: He was under contract to the **Okeh** record company. Called on the carpet, so the story goes, he said: "I don't know who made those records, but I won't do it again" (Collier, 1983, p. 177). He did, though, eight more times—four each with **Jimmy Bertrand**'s Washboard Wizards and **Johnny Dodds**'s Black Bottom Stompers. However, Armstrong attempted to disguise himself by playing more simply, with a thinner tone and few high notes. Naturally, he didn't sing at all. Vocalion lasted until 1930, when it was taken over by Warner Brothers.

Voice of America. Begun in 1942 to promote the understanding of American culture abroad, the official radio program of the United States Information Agency broadcasts music, news, and information in over forty languages to an audience of over 200 million people in Europe, the Middle East, Asia, and Latin America. Armstrong's was a voice frequently heard. He represented American jazz, which, during the World War II era, became a symbol of freedom and liberation. Along with his international tours in the late 1940s and U.S. State Department–sponsored tours in the 1950s and 1960s, his VOA broadcasts gave his music a political subtext. During the Cold War, as **Felix Belair** observed on the front page of the November 6, 1955, *New York Times*: "America's secret weapon is a blue note in a minor key. Right now its most effective ambassador is Louis (**Satchmo**) Armstrong. American jazz has now become a universal language. It knows no national boundaries, but everyone knows where it comes from and where to look for more." **"Ambassador Satch"** and the **All Stars** broadcast not only from VOA headquarters in Washington, D.C., but also from such locales as the **Newport Jazz Festival** (July–August 1956) and the Monterey Jazz Festival (September 1965). The immense crowds that met him on his international tours (90,000 in Budapest, 100,000 in Accra) were in large part due to his VOA reputation. On an extended European tour from September to December 1955, Armstrong and the All Stars performed in West Berlin, and fans, including Russians, came over from the East Zone to hear them. "Hardly any of them could speak any English, but that didn't bother them or us," Armstrong told Jones and Chilton. "The music did all the talking for both sides" (p. 31). The All Stars cut some records during this trip, and the LP *Ambassador Satch* was issued the following year (CD #1).

"Volare." By Domenico Modugno; rec. June 4, 1965, live at the Palais des Sports in Paris by **Louis Armstrong and the All Stars;** CD #2. This very popular 1958 song was a feature number for All Star trombonist **Tyree Glenn.**

W

Waif's Home. See **Colored Waif's Home for Boys.**

Waldorf Astoria. Jazz has been performed in this landmark New York City hotel almost from its opening in November 1931, and Armstrong was a frequently featured artist. He performed there with **Benny Goodman** in 1939, and he played there for President Kennedy in 1963. On March 15, 1971, he finished a two-week engagement there that turned out to be his last anywhere.

"Walkin' My Baby Back Home." By Roy Turk and Fred E. Ahlert; rec. April 20, 1931, in Chicago by Louis Armstrong and His Orchestra. Armstrong's sensitive melodic paraphrasing established this 1930 tune, and trombonist **Preston Jackson** can be credited with an assist. Twenty years later, "Walkin' My Baby Back Home" was revived by pop vocalist Johnnie Ray and became a big hit. The song gave rise to a 1953 movie of the same title, starring Donald O'Connor.

Wallace, Sippie (Beulah Belle Thomas) (1898–1986). This fine blues singer came from a musical family and began to perform at an early age. Armstrong frequently accompanied her between 1924 and 1926, as he did so many other blues singers of the day (e.g., **Alberta Hunter, Ma Rainey, Bessie Smith),** and some of these sessions are distinguished by the piano playing of her brother Hersal Thomas. In the introduction to "Special Delivery Blues," for example, Armstrong nicely contrasts Thomas's rolling piano with crisp staccato lines. Later in the song, Wallace's ascending lines combine with Hersal's tremolo and Armstrong's brief broken phrases to fully express each word on "Mr. Mailman, did you bring me any news?/'Cause if you didn't it will give me those 'Special Delivery Blues.' " After 1933 Wallace focused on church music, and in the 1960s she was a part of the blues revival, appearing throughout the United States and Europe. In 1983 her album *Sippie* was nominated for a Grammy.

Waller, Thomas "Fats" (1904–1943). The short-lived Waller was multitalented (pianist, organist, singer, bandleader, and composer), and Armstrong considered him to be among the greatest musicians of his day. Fortunately their paths crossed numerous times. They first met in New York, where Armstrong had a small part in the Waller–Andy Razaf–Harry Brooks hit review ***Connie's Hot***

Chocolates (1929). Armstrong's performance of "Ain't Misbehavin'" became very popular, and this song, along with another from the show, "(What Did I Do to Be So) Black and Blue?", became part of his permanent repertory. On February 11, 1945, Armstrong participated in radio station WNEW's Fats Waller Memorial program in New York, and ten years later, Armstrong spent most of April and May in New York recording the album *Satch Plays Fats* (CD #56). This album—which included such Waller hits as "Honeysuckle Rose" and "Squeeze Me" in addition to "Black and Blue" and "Ain't Misbehavin'"—charted at No. 10 on the ***Billboard*** Top 40.

"Was It a Dream?" By Sam Coslow and Larry Spier; rec. June 26, 1928, in Chicago by vocalist **Lillie Delk Christian** with Louis Armstrong and His **Hot Four;** CDs #10 and #36. See comments on "Baby" and "I Must Have That Man."

Washington, Ford Lee "Buck" (1903–1955). The versatile pianist, singer, and trumpet player first worked (from the age of nine) with John Sublett in a comedy and dance duo called Buck and Bubbles, which performed on Broadway, toured Europe, and appeared in such films as ***Cabin in the Sky.*** With Armstrong in 1930 he recorded "Dear Old Southland" as a complement to "Weather Bird," which Armstrong and **Earl Hines** had recorded in 1928. ("Weather Bird" had remained unreleased because **Okeh** executives seemed to think that it needed something breezier on the flip side.) Washington went on to work with **Coleman Hawkins** and **Bessie Smith** (he worked her last recording session, 1933) and as a soloist. The Buck and Bubbles act also kept him busy until 1953.

Washington, George (b. 1907). Born in Brunswick, Georgia, Washington's early jobs were in New York, where he worked with such ensembles as **Fletcher Henderson**'s (1936–1937). He joined Louis Armstrong's orchestra in 1937 as the "first trombone man and the comedian in the band," and he stayed until 1943 (Berrett, 1999, p. 113). In addition to Washington's considerable performance skills, he was an arranger for the **Mills Blue Rhythm Band** and the publisher Irving Mills. This talent became important on the road with Armstrong. Audiences would come to concerts expecting to hear the same tunes that they had heard on records or the radio. However, the band did not always have all the arrangements. Armstrong had to write his manager, **Joe Glaser,** to have the records sent, and Washington would make arrangements from the recordings. After his time with Armstrong, Washington moved to the West Coast, where he worked with Horace Henderson and others, led his own band, played with the drummer Johnny Otis, and worked as a studio musician and arranger.

"Washington and Lee Swing." By Thornton Allen, M.W. Sheafe, and C.A. Robbins; rec. May 24 or 25, 1960, in New York City with the **Dukes of Dixieland;** CD #53. See comments on "Avalon."

"Washwoman Blues." By **Hociel Thomas** and Bollinger; rec. November 11, 1925, in Chicago by vocalist Hociel Thomas with Louis Armstrong's Jazz Four; CD #36. See comments on "Adam and Eve Had the Blues."

Waters, Ethel (1896–1977). See ***Cabin in the Sky.***

"Way Down Yonder in New Orleans." By Henry Creamer and Turner Layton; rec. July 5, 1960, in New York City with vocalist **Bing Crosby** and a studio band and choir conducted by Billy May; CDs #6, #16, #25, #32, and #60. This 1922 song was in Armstrong's bloodstream, so much so that he quotes it in one of his last recorded trumpet solos on "Ten Feet Off the Ground." For additional comments, see "At the Jazz Band Ball."

"We Have All the Time in the World." By John Barry and Hal Davis; rec. October 28, 1969, in London by Louis Armstrong and a studio orchestra. This is one of Armstrong's last recordings, and it both opens and closes the James Bond film (George Lazenby plays Bond) ***On Her Majesty's Secret Service.***

"We Shall Overcome." By Zilphia Horton, Frank Hamilton, Guy Carawan, and Pete Seeger; rec. May 29, 1970, in New York City with a studio orchestra and chorus conducted by Oliver Nelson; CD #31. On this number from his penultimate album (which was issued in July in conjunction with the **Newport Jazz Festival**'s putative seventieth **birthday** party for him), Armstrong was joined by horn players Ruby Braff, **Miles Davis,** and **Bobby Hackett,** vocalist Tony Bennett, and among many others singing as well, critic Stanley Dance and producer George Wein. It's a little corny and a little too long, but everyone means well and the result is heartwarming.

"Weary Blues." By Arty Matthews; rec. May 11, 1927, in Chicago by Louis Armstrong and His **Hot Seven;** CDs #8, #10, #36, #48, #52, and #61. Armstrong grew up with this piece. He had recorded it a month earlier with another ensemble (**Johnny Dodds**'s Black Bottom Stompers) and returned to it in the 1950s with his **All Stars.** However, he had a particular fondness for this Hot Seven version, which he discussed in a famous article for ***Esquire*** (December 1951, pp. 85–86ff; rpt. in Brothers, pp. 127–136). He doesn't mention Johnny Dodds's excellent low-register clarinet solo, but he fondly recalls both trombonist Johnny Thomas (who during the **Great Depression** found work as an embalmer) and tuba player **Pete Briggs** ("one of the finest musicians and has one of the finest big hearts of any man"). "This particular tune," Armstrong wrote, "every time I play it, I find something else to write and tell the world about." The modest Armstrong does not mention either his strong lead or his wonderful **stop-time** solo.

"Weather Bird." By Louis Armstrong (often inaccurately attributed to **Joe Oliver**); rec. December 5, 1928, in Chicago by Louis Armstrong and pianist **Earl Hines;** CDs #10, #30, and #48. This is the only Armstrong–Hines duet, although the two worked together frequently and played off each other memorably in portions of "Skip the Gutter," "A Monday Date," and other numbers. In "Weather Bird," however, it's just the two of them alone. Taking their initial inspiration from a 1923 recording of "Weather Bird Rag" by King Oliver's Creole Jazz Band (which included Armstrong), their work shows how far jazz improvisation had developed in just a few years. Armstrong and Hines follow the

Armstrong in the 1960s. (Louis Armstrong House and Archives at Queens College/CUNY)

form of the earlier recording by playing solo choruses and trading breaks at the end. Although the two accomplished artists echo each other to some extent, they also pretty much stick to their own individual styles and are at times fiercely and thrillingly independent. They have in common a marvelous inventiveness and a swinging rhythm. The final cadence is the unusual (for jazz) but familiar subdominant to tonic (i.e., the "Amen" pattern of countless hymns). Many jazz fans consider this recording to be the most outstanding of Armstrong's early years. The authorship of "Weather Bird" has been confused because of Oliver's name on the recording. However, research in the Library of Congress copyright files by David Chevan (1997) confirms that the composition (along with some seventy-nine others) is indeed by Armstrong. A handy summary of the "Weather Bird" authorship case can be found in the essay by Dan Morgenstern in Miller (p. 101). "Weather Bird" has been transcribed by Schuller (1968, pp. 124–127) and Gushee (1998, p. 297).

"Weather Bird Rag." By Louis Armstrong (see note on authorship above); rec. April 6, 1923, in Richmond, Indiana, by **King Oliver**'s Creole Jazz Band; CD #35. A progressive feature of this recording is the time given in the final choruses for instrumental breaks and especially the two cornetists, Armstrong and Oliver. See additional comments on "Alligator Hop" and "Weather Bird."

"We'll Be Together Again." By Carl Fischer and Frankie Laine; rec. August 14, 1957, in Los Angeles with a studio orchestra conducted by arranger Russell Garcia.

Welles, Orson (1916–1985). In the early 1940s, Armstrong became determined to write a more complete story of his life than he had done in ***Swing That Music*** (1936) and also to have his life story made into a movie. For the former project he enlisted the help of Belgian jazz writer **Robert Goffin** and for the latter Hollywood's Orson Welles. Armstrong actually went so far as to have a meeting with Welles to discuss casting possibilities. For example, Armstrong suggested **Louise Beavers**—of *Imitation of Life* (1934) pancake-making fame and later star of the TV series *Beulah* (1952–1953)—to play the part of his mother. The disaster of Goffin's contrived *Horn of Plenty* (1947) probably cooled Welles's enthusiasm, and he moved on to other projects.

Wells, Dicky (1907–1985). Born in Tennessee, Wells arrived with his trombone in New York in 1926 and worked with **Fletcher Henderson** and others. He spent the better part of his career (intermittently from 1938 to 1950) with Count Basie. Reminiscing about the 1930s and 1940s, he later wrote in his memoirs that "everybody was trying to play something like Louis Armstrong. . . . His records influenced all jazz musicians, not only trumpet players" (p. 33).

"We're a Home." Rec. December 18, 1967, in New York City by **Louis Armstrong and the All Stars,** trumpeter **Clark Terry,** and others.

West, Mae (1892/1893–1980). See ***Every Day's a Holiday.***

West Berlin. See **Voice of America; European tours.**

"West End Blues." By **Clarence Williams** and **Joe Oliver;** rec. June 29, 1928, in Chicago by Louis Armstrong and His **Hot Five;** CDs #1, #3, #10, #14, #22, #30, #39, #48, and #61. "West End Blues" is one of the masterpieces of twentieth-century music, if not of all time, and it underscores all of Armstrong's innovations—his **swing** style of playing, his extension of the upward range of the trumpet, his unique ways of varying the trumpet's timbre (e.g., by alternate fingerings for the same note), his minor and diminished chord improvisations, and most important, his soloing to **stop-time** accompaniment (a practice that created the model of the featured soloist). Here Armstrong plays consistently higher, more inventively, and with more authority than any trumpeter before and, some say, since. Many jazz fans consider this to be the greatest of all recorded trumpet performances, and Gunther Schuller suggests that it be heard by anyone who does not understand the difference between jazz and other music (1968, p. 116). Armstrong's opening cadenza has been widely imitated, but also remarkable is the final chorus, which he begins with a high "B-flat," held for nearly four measures, followed by a dazzling descending phrase. It comes as no surprise that "West End Blues" has been used alongside Beethoven symphonies and Wagner operas in music appreciation textbooks (e.g., Sadie, p. 512), and it has been both widely transcribed (e.g., Schuller, 1968, pp. 116–119) and anthologized (e.g., Caffey, 1993).

"What a Wonderful World." By George David Weiss and Bob Thiele; rec. August 16, 1967, in New York City by Louis Armstrong's Orchestra and Chorus; CDs #4, #7, #14, #17, #23, #31, #39, #40, #61, #62, and #63. What became one of the most popular songs of the twentieth century was initially unappreciated, at least in the United States. Armstrong's recording did not please the ABC Records executives, who released it unpromoted. Only when "Wonderful World" became a big hit in **England** was Armstrong asked to make it the centerpiece of an album. He recorded it nine more times before 1970. Nevertheless, it took Barry Levinson's use of the original 1967 recording in the 1987 **movie *Good Morning, Vietnam*** to give "Wonderful World" the immense audience that it finally won. The song is heard about halfway through the film, and its affectionate, mystical quality contrasts starkly with scenes of war-ravaged Vietnam. Armstrong is not mentioned nor is his trumpet heard, but his delivery of the lyrics evokes everything good about America, even in the midst of the horrors depicted on the screen. This original recording was reissued and spent six weeks in 1988 on the ***Billboard*** Top 40.

"(What Did I Do to Be So) Black and Blue?" See "Black and Blue?, (What Did I Do to Be So)."

"What Is This Thing Called Swing?" By Louis Armstrong and **Horace Gerlach;** rec. January 18, 1939, in New York City by Louis Armstrong and His Orchestra; CD #18. This recording is energized by **Sid Catlett,** Armstrong's favorite drummer, who had just joined the big band and would stay until 1942.

"What Kind o' Man Is That?" By Richard M. Jones; rec. February 23, 1926, in Chicago with vocalist Baby Mack and pianist Richard M. Jones; CD #36. Armstrong recorded only two songs with blues singer

Mack, this and "You've Got to Go Home on Time."

"Whatcha Call 'em Blues." By Steve L. Roberts; rec. May 29, 1925, in New York City by **Fletcher Henderson** and His Orchestra. See comments on "Alabamy Bound."

"Whatcha Know, Joe?" Armstrong never recorded this traditional favorite, but he knew it well. In a letter to his friend **Leonard Feather,** he wrote about a command performance in 1941 at the Coast Guard's Fort Barrancas in Florida. After Armstrong had entertained the men, he was taken to the base hospital to continue his visit, enjoying the event at least as much as the patients. After playing "When the Saints Go Marching In," "one of the colored patients wanted a few bars of 'Whatcha Know, Joe.' So I laid it on him lightly before I departed" (Berrett, 1999, p. 117).

"Whatcha Say?" By Burton Lane and Ted Koehler; rec. August 9, 1944, in New York City by Louis Armstrong and His Orchestra. Armstrong performs this as a duet with Dorothy Dandridge in the 1945 **movie *Pillow to Post.*** The sequence was so highly sexually charged that it was cut by many southern censors.

"What's New?" By **Bob Haggart** and Johnny Burke; rec. October 14, 1957, in Los Angeles with the **Oscar Peterson** Quartet; CDs #28 and #37. Perhaps because fellow trumpeter **Billy Butterfield** owned this song (having introduced and popularized it under the title "I'm Free" with the Bob Crosby orchestra), Armstrong only sings here. See additional comments on "Blues in the Night."

"What's Your Hurry?" By Effie Kamman; rec. August 1945 in Los Angeles by Louis Armstrong and His Orchestra; CD #49.

"Whatta Ya Gonna Do?" By Sunny Skylar and Patrick Lewis; rec. April 27, 1946, in New York City by Louis Armstrong and His Orchestra; CDs #12, #17, and #21. Armstrong's fine trumpet solo inspires **Joe Garland**'s tenor sax solo on this otherwise so-so song.

"When Did You Leave Heaven?" By Richard A. Whiting and Walter Bullock; rec. January 29, 1957, in New York City by Louis Armstrong with the **Sy Oliver** Orchestra; CD #26. See comments on "And the Angels Sing."

"When I Grow Too Old to Dream." By Oscar Hammerstein II and Sigmund Romberg; rec. June 4, 1965, live at the Palais des Sports in Paris by **Louis Armstrong and the All Stars;** CDs #2 and #46. This was a feature number for All Stars pianist **Billy Kyle.**

"When It's Sleepy Time Down South." By Leon René, Otis René, and Clarence Muse; rec. April 20, 1931, in Chicago by Louis Armstrong and His Orchestra; CDs #2, #3, #4, #6, #12, #14, #16, #19, #20, #21, #22, #23, #24, #25, #28, #32, #39, #43, #44, #46, #48, #52, #53, #55, #57, #59, #61, and #63. Armstrong's signature song was written in 1931 by two New Orleans Creoles who had moved to Southern California. Armstrong immediately took it up at **Sebastian's New Cotton Club** just west of Los Angeles and recorded it when he got back to Chicago. He went on to record the song nearly a hundred times more, and he must have performed it several thousand times in concert. In 1942 it was made into a **soundie** (called simply ***Sleepy Time Down South***), a short film made for a coin-operated viewing machine, an ancestor of today's music video. "Sleepy Time" is about as nostalgic as a song can be, with its images of a pre-twentieth-century South. "Mammies" sing, "darkies" dance at the break of day, and there are "soft winds blowing through the pinewood trees." Armstrong eventually changed "darkies" to "folks," but only after considerable pressure. He used the song to introduce himself and his band and to put his audience into a pleasant mood. In a vaudeville-style intoductory dialogue between Armstrong and pianist **Charlie Alexander,** two old friends run into each other in an unnamed northern city. Their good-old-days conversation seques into a musical memoir of the mythical Old South.

"When Ruben Swings the Cuban." By Ted White, Leon Flatow, and Jack Meskill; rec. August 7, 1936, in Los Angeles with the **Jimmy Dorsey** Orchestra.

When the Boys Meet the Girls. Connie Francis and Harve Presnell star in this remake of the 1943 Judy Garland/Mickey Rooney film *Girl Crazy,* which was based on the Broadway show (music by George Gershwin) from 1930. As he does in ***High Society,*** Armstrong narrates the story. He is also featured in the songs "Throw It Out of Your Mind" (which he co-wrote) and "I Got Rhythm." M-G-M, 1965; color; 110 mins.; Dir. Alvin Ganzer.

"When the Red, Red, Robin Comes Bob, Bob, Bobbin' Along." By Harry MacGregor Woods; rec. January 24, 1956, in Los Angeles by **Louis Armstrong and the All Stars;** CDs #1 and #16. This 1926 song was originally introduced by Sophie Tucker.

"When the Saints Go Marching In." By James M. Black and Katherine E. Purvis; rec. May 13, 1938, in New York City by Louis Armstrong and His Orchestra; CDs #2, #6, #14, #19, #20, #22, #23, #45, #46, #61, and #63. Copyrighted in 1896, this spiritual seems to have been played at New Orleans funerals since around 1900. Gary Giddins reports that Armstrong's sister objected to his jazzing up a sacred song, but he countered that, well, she played bingo in church (1988, p. 140). In any case, Armstrong's recording was the first jazz version of a spiritual. It was a hit and became both a jazz standard and the signature tune of the traditional jazz movement. On this first of eventually fifty-eight recordings of "Saints" (second only to the ninety-eight times he recorded "When It's Sleepy Time Down South"), Armstrong lets his sidemen shine, and he himself takes two trumpet choruses as well as two vocal choruses. This is the format he would follow on this song in countless concerts for the next thirty years. **Louis Armstrong and the All Stars'** recording of "Saints" is one of the highlights of the 1960 documentary ***Jazz on a Summer's Day,*** and his duet version with **Danny Kaye** in the 1959 **movie *The Five Pennies*** is one of the best musical moments on film.

"When You Do What You Do." By Mitchell Parish and Georgy Johnsen; rec. April 18, 1925, in New York City by **Fletcher Henderson** and His Orchestra. See comments on "Alabamy Bound."

"When You Wish Upon a Star." By Ned Washington and Leigh Harline; rec. March 16, 1968, in Hollywood by **Louis Armstrong and the All Stars** with a studio orchestra and mixed choir; CD #15. One of the better numbers on the 1968 *Disney Songs the Satchmo Way* album, this song from the 1940 movie *Pinocchio* is a good example of Armstrong reaching out to the widest possible audience. Some might feel that the heavy-handed accompaniment and the lugubrious tempo sacrifice musical values, but there's no denying Armstrong's magic touch with his melodic liberties and fairy-dust sprinkling of **scat.** Armstrong also contributes a spritely trumpet solo, one of his last in the recording studio.

"When Your Lover Has Gone." By Einar A. Swan; rec. April 29, 1931, in Chicago by Louis Armstrong and His Orchestra; CD #48. Armstrong liked songs in minor keys and recorded many from the popular "St. James Infirmary" in 1928 to "Chim Chim Cher-ee" in 1968. Particularly remarkable about this recording of the Tin Pan Alley "When Your Lover Has Gone" is his rhythmic resetting of the first few notes of the melody at the piece's end.

"When Your Man Is Going to Put You Down, (You Never Can Tell)." By Leola B. "Coot" Grant; rec. October 1925, in New York City with vocalist Coot Grant, pianist **Fletcher Henderson,** and either Armstrong or **Joe Smith** playing cornet. There is some dispute as to who the cornetist is both here and on "Speak Now or Hereafter Hold Your Peace."

"When You're Smiling." By Mark Fisher, Joe Goodwin, and Larry Shay; rec. September 11, 1929, in New York City by Louis Armstrong and His Orchestra; CDs #6, #8, #12, #21, #24, #28, #39, #40, #48, and #52. Armstrong recorded this song numerous times, and even at this first session he recorded it twice, the second time for international distribution (i.e., without a vocal). Much has been made of the thrilling way he takes the melody up an octave in the last thirty-two measures. He was no doubt inspired by virtuoso cornetists of the day, example, B.A. Rolfe's "In Shadowland." This high-wire performance also highlights the song's subtext of forced optimism. An equally impressive though more subtle artistic achievement can be found at the beginning, when, after the **Lombardo**-like saxes, he makes his entrance. Here he turns the first three notes of the melody upside down and noodles around on them for sixteen measures. Armstrong develops this melodic-rhythmic cell in much the same way as would Beethoven or Brahms, with whom he can easily be ranked.

"Where Did You Stay Last Night?" By Louis Armstrong and **Lil Hardin;** rec. between June 22 and 29, 1923, in Chicago by **King Oliver**'s Jazz Band. See comments on "Alligator Hop."

"Where the Blues Were Born in New Orleans." By Cliff Dixon and Bob Carleton; rec. October 17, 1946, in Los Angeles by Louis Armstrong and His Dixieland Seven; CDs #12, #21, and #47. In this genial **Dixieland** number, Armstrong introduces band members in talking blues style, and each takes a brief solo. Armstrong rounds out the recording with a rousing solo of his own.

"Whiffenpoof Song, The." By Meade Minnigerode, George S. Pomeroy, Tod Galloway, and Rudy Vallee; rec. April 13, 1954, in New York City with the Gordon Jenkins Orchestra; CD #6. Armstrong turned the 1911 theme song of the Whiffenpoof Club of Yale University into a clever satire of the be**bop** style called "The Boppenpoof Song." Bop leader **Dizzy Gillespie** took it as a backhanded compliment, but the recording was withdrawn because of copyright problems.

"Whispering." By Vincent Rose, Richard Coburn, and John Schonberger; rec. July 6, 1956, live at the **Newport Jazz Festival** by **Louis Armstrong and the All Stars.** Paul Whiteman first made this 1920 song famous, and it was given a boost by Vivian Blaine in the 1944 film *Greenwich Village.* Armstrong's performance of it here (which was simultaneously broadcast on the **Voice of America**) took place during the Festival's celebration of what was thought to be his **birthday.**

"Whistle While You Work." By Larry Morey and Frank Churchill; rec. March 17, 1968, in Hollywood by **Louis Armstrong and the All Stars** with a studio orchestra and mixed choir; CD #15. One of the less successful numbers on Armstrong's 1968 *Disney Songs the Satchmo Way* album, this song from the 1937 movie *Snow White and the Seven Dwarfs* is almost buried under the thick orchestration. Armstrong, however, always finds his way through any kind of musical situation, and he both has fun with the words and takes a brief but memorable trumpet solo, one of his last on record.

"White Christmas." By **Irving Berlin;** rec. September 22, 1952, in Los Angeles by Louis Armstrong with the Gordon Jenkins Orchestra; CDs #7 and #33. Everyone seems to have recorded this 1942 Academy Award–winning song from the film *Holiday Inn,* and Armstrong's warmhearted version can be ranked with the best of them. See additional comments on "Christmas in New Orleans."

"Who's It?" By Richard M. Jones; rec. June 16, 1926, in Chicago by Louis Armstrong and His **Hot Five;** CD #10. Although one of the weaker Hot Five recordings, "Who's It?" features the curiosity of Armstrong playing the slide whistle. Also, **Johnny Dodds** does some nice low-register clarinet work that makes up somewhat for **Kid Ory**'s boozy trombone solo.

"Why Couldn't It Be Poor Little Me?" By Isham Jones and Gus Kahn; rec. mid-January 1925 in New York City by **Fletcher Henderson** and His Orchestra. See comments on "Alabamy Bound."

"Why Did Mrs. Murphy Leave Town?" Rec. August 1970 in New York City with the Nashville Group. See comments on "Almost Persuaded."

"Why Doubt My Love?" By Helen Mercer and Louis Armstrong; rec. March 12, 1947, in New York City by Louis Armstrong and His Orchestra; CD #12. This is one of a small batch of recordings (including "I Believe" and "It Takes Time") made on what turned out to be Armstrong's last big band session, and it demonstrates the appeal of that ensemble even as its popularity was waning. Armstrong opens with a spirited trumpet solo supported by a firm foundation of reeds and brasses and then sings in the crooner style. This tender song was not issued until after Armstrong's death.

"Wild Man Blues." Credited to Louis Armstrong and **Jelly Roll Morton,** although neither wrote it; rec. April 22, 1927, in Chicago by **Johnny Dodds**'s Black Bottom Stompers; CDs #5, #8, #10, #48, #52, and #61. In 1927 Melrose Music Company issued transcriptions of Armstrong solos including "Wild Man Blues" and erroneously attributed this piece to him and Morton. Armstrong, however, once said, "I never had a conversation with [Morton] until 1936" (Albertson, 1978, p. 36). The authorship of this piece remains a mystery. There's no question, however, that it is Armstrong playing here, although he was trying not to sound like himself since he was under exclusive contract to **Okeh Records** at the time. He doesn't succeed, playing even better than on a recording of the same piece made the following month with his own **Hot Seven.** The pianist here, **Earl Hines,** is also superior to the following month's **Lil Armstrong.** (This is the first recording Armstrong and Hines made together.) Notable, too, is Johnny Dodds's low clarinet solo. Armstrong rerecorded "Wild Man Blues" in 1957 for his *Satchmo: A Musical Autobiography* album (CD #52). This song gave its name to a 1998 documentary film of Armstrong admirer **Woody Allen**'s 1996 month-long tour of Europe with the New Orleans Jazz Band.

"Wild Man Moore." By **Duke Ellington;** rec. December 14, 1960, in Paris with Ellington and a French studio orchestra. Armstrong plays world-famous trumpeter Wild Man Moore in the 1961 **movie *Paris Blues.*** When greeted by local musicians playing this rousing number at the Gare St. Lazare, he joins in from the train window. Later in the film, he plays a reprise in the background as the protagonists walk through Paris at night.

"Will You, Won't You Be My Baby?" By John Nesbitt and Howdy Quicksell; rec. November 7, 1934, in Paris by Louis Armstrong and His Orchestra.

William Ransom Hogan Jazz Archive. Housed at Tulane University in New Orleans, the William Ransom Hogan Jazz Archive has an ample collection of Armstrong-related materials: sound recordings, photographs, newspaper clippings, correspondence, journal articles, and other ephemera and memorabilia, as well as transcribed oral histories and unpublished literary material. In the collection is the earliest surviving document written by Armstrong, a 300-word letter dated September 1, 1922 (reprinted in Brothers, p. 43), to alto horn player **Isidore Barbarin.** See also **archives.**

***William Tell* overture (Rossini).** See **Vendome Theater.**

Williams, "Black Benny" (c. 1890–1924). "Black Benny" was the most prominent of the many characters who held Armstrong "spellbound" during his youth (***Satchmo,*** 1954, p. 75 f). Although he played bass drum with the popular **Tuxedo Brass Band,** Williams was best known as a tough guy with a big heart. After the young Armstrong got out of the **Colored Waif's Home** in June 1914, Williams took him under his wing. **Kid Ory** recalled that "in the crowded places, Benny would handcuff Louis to himself with a handkerchief so Louis wouldn't get lost" (Shapiro and Hentoff, 1955, p. 49). Williams also helped Armstrong get gigs and gave him advice. For example, Armstrong always remembered what Williams said about how to succeed in life as a black man in a white man's world: "As long as you live, no matter where you may be—always have a *White Man* (who like you) and can + will put his Hand on your shoulder and say—*'This is "My" Nigger'* and, Can't Nobody Harm Ya" (this statement is from an August 2, 1955, letter to **Joe Glaser,** who, as Armstrong's manager from 1935 on, functioned in just this protective capacity; the letter, signed "From Your Boy," is reproduced in Brothers, pp. 158–163). Williams was stabbed to death by his wife.

Williams, Clarence (1893–1965). Pianist, composer, publisher, and promoter, Clarence Williams was all over the New York jazz scene in the 1920s and 1930s. He was born near New Orleans, traveled with a minstrel show, and left for Chicago with the mass migration of New Orleans musicians after the closing of **Storyville** in 1917. By the mid-1920s, he was a major musical entrepreneur in New York and frequently employed Armstrong, who had plenty of creative energy unused by the **Fletcher Henderson** band. Williams' group, the **Clarence Williams' Blue Five,** also included the excellent clarinetist **Sidney Bechet,** who challenged and thereby helped bring out the best in Armstrong, for example, in "Cake Walking Babies from Home" (1924). While Williams got along well with Armstrong and others, there was controversy over many of his authorship claims. Armstrong used to say that Williams had stolen his "I Wish I Could Shimmy Like My Sister Kate." However, Williams is at least the coauthor of such hits as "Royal Garden Blues," "I Ain't Gonna Give Nobody None of My Jelly Roll," and "Squeeze Me." See also **Eva Taylor,** Williams's wife.

"Willie the Weeper." By Walter Melrose, Grant V. Rymal, and Marty Bloom; rec. May 7, 1927, in Chicago by Louis Armstrong and His **Hot Seven;** CDs #10 and #44. New technology permitted the use of both drums and tuba on this recording, and the additions seem to give extra inspiration to Armstrong and his sidemen. After an ensemble statement of the tune of this popular 1920s song about someone whose dreams came true, there is a series of fine solos, **Johnny St. Cyr**'s guitar chorus in particular. At the end, Armstrong's superb playing, punctuated by **Baby Dodds**'s cymbal work, lead the ensemble in a collective improvisation that many consider the best ever recorded. Transcription in Kerman (p. 515).

"Willow Weep for Me." By Ann Ronell; rec. July 31, 1957, in Los Angeles with the **Oscar Peterson** Quartet; CDs #9 and #37. Armstrong's insouciant performance overrides much of the mournful quality of this tender song, first introduced in the 1932 movie *Love Happy.* See additional comments on "Blues in the Night."

Wilson, Lucille. See **Armstrong, Lucille Wilson.**

Wilson, Theodore Shaw "Teddy" (1912–1986). While Teddy Wilson, (whom some consider the most important pianist of the **swing** era) was coming up, he worked briefly in Chicago as a member of Armstrong's orchestra and helped make some excellent recordings. "I've Got the World on a String" and "Basin Street Blues" (both from January 1933) come to mind. On the first, Wilson plays the gracefully cascading piano introduction, and on the second he provides the opening celeste passage. On both and others he supplies **Earl Hines**–influenced percussive rhythms and trumpetlike melodic lines. Shortly after these sessions, Wilson left for New York, where he developed a distinctive legato and harmonic style in the **Benny Goodman** Trio. Although he went on to work with others and as a soloist, even serving as a Juilliard School instructor, he frequently participated in Goodman reunions.

"Winter Wonderland." By Felix Bernard and Dick Smith; rec. September 22, 1952, in Los Angeles with the Gordon Jenkins Orchestra; CDs #7 and #33. Armstrong loved **Christmas** (see comments on "Christmas in New Orleans"), and he presents this seasonal favorite with affectionate warmth.

wives. See **Armstrong, Alpha Smith; Armstrong, Daisy Parker; Armstrong, Lillian Hardin "Lil"; Armstrong, Lucille Wilson.**

"Wolverine Blues." By **Jelly Roll Morton;** rec. March 14, 1940, in New York City by Louis Armstrong and His Orchestra; CD #61. Armstrong's long (two-and-a-half choruses) and creative solo must have been overlooked by those who thought that he had earlier cashed in his muse. Unfortunately, the ensemble, having intonation problems in the saxophone section, is generally lackluster until Armstrong comes in at the fourth chorus.

"Wolverton Mountain." By Merle Kilgore and Claude King; rec. August 1970 in New York City with the Nashville Group. See comments on "Almost Persuaded."

"Woman Is a Sometime Thing, A." By George Gershwin, DuBose Heyward, and Ira Gershwin; rec. August 18, 1957, in Los Angeles with a studio orchestra and choir conducted by Russell Garcia; CDs #9 and #29. This popular number comes from Act I of *Porgy and Bess.* See additional comments on "Bess, You Is My Woman Now."

Woodward, Joanne (b. 1930). See ***Paris Blues.***

"Words." By Otis Spencer, Al Dubin, and Al Tucker; rec. October 30, 1924, in New York City by **Fletcher Henderson** and His Orchestra. See comments on "Alabamy Bound."

"Working Man Blues." By **Joe Oliver;** rec. between October 5 and 15, 1923, in Chicago by King Oliver's Jazz Band; CD #35. See comments on "Alligator Hop."

World War II (1939–1945). During World War II Armstrong performed on average once a week for GIs at army camps in the United States, and he frequently participated in war bond rallies.

World's Great Men of Color: 3000 B.C. to 1940 A.D. In his home library in **Corona,** Armstrong had numerous books (poetry, history, diet, biography, race relations, etc.), including this book by J.A. Rogers, published in 1946–1947. Scholar Joshua Berrett has pointed out that Armstrong seems to have read this two-volume work systematically, checking off each name as he worked his way through (1999, p. 103). Armstrong's copy of the book is available at the **Louis Armstrong House and Archives.**

"World's Jazz Crazy (and So Am I), The." By William H. Huff and Jimmy Blythe; rec. between March 16 and April 22, 1925, in New York City with vocalist **Trixie Smith** and her Down Home Syncopators; CD #36. See comments on "Mining Camp Blues."

"W.P.A. Blues." By J. Jones; rec. April 10, 1940, in New York City with the **Mills Brothers** and guitarist Norman Brown. Armstrong and the Mills Brothers usually recorded such old chestnuts as "Carry Me Back to Old Virginny" and "In the Shade of the Old Apple Tree," and they sometimes imbued them with double meanings (e.g., the sophisticated musical winks in "Old Folks at Home"). "W.P.A.," however, is direct social commentary, a searing if swinging indictment of the popular **Great Depression**-era work program. They leave no doubt as to how they and many others felt about the efficacy of the Work Projects Administration. The recording became hard to find when, at the request of First Lady Eleanor Roosevelt, it was withdrawn. The agency itself soon became the subject of a sharply critical Senate report, with the result that its appropriation was severely cut and many projects either curtailed or abolished.

"Wrap Your Troubles in Dreams." By Billy Moll, Ted Koehler, and Harry Barris; rec. November 4, 1931, in Chicago by Louis Armstrong and His Orchestra. Armstrong here covers a cheerful song that was introduced by **Bing Crosby** in 1931 and used in the 1952 movie *Rainbow Round My Shoulder.* Later in writing some notes for his biographer Robert Goffin, Armstrong ranked this as one of his finest recordings and felt that the band deserved more credit (Brothers, p. 108).

writer. Armstrong remains the most prolific musician-writer in the jazz world, having published two books and dozens of articles (see selected bibliography). One of the twenty-four pieces of luggage that he took on tours contained a typewriter, which he used backstage and in hotel rooms. Most of his writing was not meant for the public, that is, the hundreds of often rather lengthy letters to friends and fans. He also wrote hundreds more pages of **autobiography** fully intended for publication or posterity. Many of the writings in this latter category were either revised or heavily edited or rewritten by well-meaning associates, for example, **Robert Goffin**'s travesty *Horn of Plenty,* **Horace Gerlach**'s possible tampering with ***Swing That Music,*** and **Joe Glaser**'s wanting to suppress Armstrong's advocacy of **marijuana** in **"The Satchmo Story."**

Typically Armstrong the writer reflects Armstrong the man: open-hearted, eloquent, humorous, brash, and generous, though now and then he takes on an uncharacteristic brooding and pessimistic tone. ("Negroes *never* did stick together and they *never* will," he wrote while hospitalized in 1969. "They hold too much *malice—Jealousy* deep down in their hearts for the *few* Negroes who *tries.*") A good selection of his prose can be found in *Louis Armstrong, in His Own Words,* edited by Thomas Brothers. The quote above is on page 9 of that work.

Y

"Yeh!" By Bill Norvas; rec. April 25, 1955, in New York City by **Louis Armstrong and the All Stars;** CD #8. Armstrong and singer **Velma Middleton** developed a relaxed yet sexually charged style in "Mm-Mm," "Baby, It's Cold Outside," "Baby, Your Sleep Is Showing," as well as this cute number. Trombonist **Trummy Young** provides a genial introduction and accompaniment.

"Yellow Dog Blues." By W.C. Handy; rec. July 14, 1954, in Chicago by **Louis Armstrong and the All Stars;** CDs #38 and #46. Armstrong's recording of this 1928 number helped make it a jazz standard. Nat "King" Cole and Eartha Kitt later performed it in the 1958 film *St. Louis Blues.* See additional comments on "Atlanta Blues."

"Yes! I'm in the Barrel." By Louis Armstrong; rec. November 12, 1925, in Chicago by Louis Armstrong and His **Hot Five;** CD #10. The title of this instrumental refers to losing all one's money gambling and, having pawned one's clothes, wearing a barrel. It's the second of three numbers recorded on the very first session of the Hot Five. While the ensemble would go on to greater achievements, it is already functioning very well. All players except the pianist (Armstrong's wife, **Lil**) come from the same hometown—New Orleans—and all were well used to performing together in and around Chicago. Here one can witness jazz developing into a soloist's art, as clarinetist **Johnny Dodds** takes far more than just the two measures he might have been allowed in **Joe Oliver**'s band. In fact, Dodds takes more solo time than Armstrong, who nevertheless leads the ensemble strongly.

"Yes, Suh!" By Edgar Dowell and Andy Razaf; rec. April 11, 1941, in New York City by Louis Armstrong and His **Hot Seven.**

"Yes! Yes! My! My! (She's Mine)." By Sammy Cahn and Saul Chaplin; rec. February 4, 1936, in New York City by Louis Armstrong and His Orchestra; CD #51. This was the flip side of the more popular "I'm Putting All My Eggs in One Basket."

"You Are My Lucky Star." By Nacio Herb Brown and Arthur Freed; rec. October 3, 1935, in New York City by Louis Armstrong and His Orchestra; CDs #41 and #51. This recording from Armstrong's first session with his new band for his new record company (**Decca**) under his new manager (**Joe Glaser**) marks a career change for him from jazz innovator to popular performer. Nevertheless, his roots in jazz show through in his artful playing with both the tempo (in an arresting double-time passage) and the harmony (straying piquantly from prevailing chords). The song itself is from the movie *Broadway Melody of 1936.*

"You Are Woman, I Am Man." By **Bob Merrill** and Jule Styne; rec. April 18, 1964, in New York City by **Louis Armstrong and the All Stars.** Armstrong here covers the song that **Barbra Streisand** introduced in the 1964 Broadway musical *Funny Girl.*

"You Can Depend on Me." By Louis Dunlap, **Earl Hines,** and Charles Carpenter; rec. November 5, 1931, in Chicago by Louis Armstrong and His Orchestra; CDs #6, #28, and #58. Armstrong was good at performing well despite his backup band, but this one was truly a challenge. The players sound ill rehearsed, especially the saxophones, and there are wrong notes from every section. The steadfast Armstrong, however, delivers a fine vocal, and trumpeter **Zilner Randolph** (who assembled the players) provides him with an enjoyable accompaniment.

"You Can Have Her." By Bill Cook; rec. August 1970 in New York City with the Nashville Group. See comments on "Almost Persuaded."

"You Can Never Tell When Your Man Is Going to Put You Down." See "When Your Man Is Going to Put You Down, (You Can Never Tell)."

"You Can't Get Stuff in Your Cuff." Rec. early 1943 in Los Angeles by Louis Armstrong and His Orchestra; CD #49. Recorded from a radio broadcast in Los Angeles, this number features vocalists Ann Baker and **George Washington** (Armstrong's versatile trombonist).

"You Can't Lose a Broken Heart." By James Johnson and Flourney Miller; rec. September 30, 1949, in New York City with vocalist **Billie Holiday** and the **Sy Oliver** Orchestra; CDs #28, #40, and #61. See comments on "My Sweet Hunk o' Trash."

"You Can't Shush Katie (the Gabbiest Girl in Town)." By Harry White, Henry Creamer, and Harry Warren; rec. October 26, 1925, in New York City with vocalist **Eva Taylor** and **Clarence Williams' Blue Five;** CDs #36 and #48. See comments on "Cast Away."

"You Dirty Mistreater." By Wesley "Kid" Wilson; rec. October 1925 in New York City with vocalists Leola B. "Coot" Grant and Kid Wilson and **Fletcher Henderson**'s Orchestra; CD #36. Here Armstrong gets to shine briefly as a Henderson sideman in back of a popular duet act.

"You Don't Learn That in School." By Roy Alfred and Marvin Fisher; rec. March 12, 1947, in New York City by Louis Armstrong and His Orchestra; CDs #12 and #17. This is the last recording from Armstrong's last big band session before the **All Stars** era begins. It's hardly stuffy, however, showing both rhythm and blues influence and verve in the saxes and the brasses backing up Armstrong's two solos.

"You Go to My Head." By J. Fred Coots and Haven Gillespie; rec. October 14, 1957, in Los Angeles with the **Oscar Peterson** Quartet; CD #37. Armstrong usually recorded popular songs within a year or two of their coming out, but he did not get around to this one for nearly twenty years. Here he generously gives us six and a half minutes of singing and trumpet playing. See additional comments on "Blues in the Night."

"You Made Me Love You (When I Saw You Cry)." By Percy Venable and Louis Armstrong; rec. November 27, 1926, in Chicago by Louis Armstrong and His **Hot Five;** CDs #10 and #44. Armstrong introduces this song (a collaboration with the Chicago **Sunset Cafe** producer) with the kind of opening flourish that will eventually lead (by way of "Gully Low Blues" in 1927) to the "West End Blues" cadenza in 1928. Then, after trombonist Henry Clark's wobbily solo, he sings lustily to **Johnny St. Cyr**'s elegant banjo accompaniment. This recording is truly a neglected gem.

"(You Never Can Tell) When Your Man Is Going to Put You Down." See "When Your Man Is Going to Put You Down, (You Never Can Tell)."

"You Rascal, You (I'll Be Glad When You're Dead)." By Sam Theard; rec. April 28, 1931, in Chicago by Louis Armstrong and His Orchestra; CDs #3, #8, #12, #21, #24, #40, #52, and #61. Armstrong must have been attracted to the clever love triangle lyrics of this number, as well as the subtext of fighting back during **Great Depression** times. In 1932 it was the title song in a **Betty Boop** cartoon, and that same year he also played it in the **movie *A Rhapsody in Black and Blue.*** He recorded it again in 1942 for a **soundie,** a short film for use in a coin-operated viewing machine, an ancestor of today's music video. A sort of trademark number, the song was kept permanently in his repertory.

"You Run Your Mouth, I'll Run My Business." By Louis Armstrong; rec. May 31, 1940, in New York City by Louis Armstrong and His Orchestra; CD #18.

"You Swing, Baby" (a.k.a. "The Duke"). By **Dave Brubeck** and Iola Brubeck; rec. September 13, 1961, in New York City by **Louis Armstrong and the All Stars,** pianist Dave Brubeck, and guests; CD #50. This is one of the numbers from the jazz oratorio ***The Real Ambassadors*** that did not make the LP cut but that new technology found room for on the 1994 CD reissue. See additional comments on "Cultural Exchange."

"You Turned the Tables on Me." Louis Alter and Sydney Mitchell; rec. August 14, 1957, in Los Angeles with a studio orchestra conducted by arranger Russell Garcia.

"You Won't Be Satisfied (Until You Break My Heart)." By Freddy James and Larry Stock; rec. January 18, 1946, in New York City with vocalist **Ella Fitzgerald** and the **Bob Haggart** Orchestra; CD #9. Armstrong and Fitzgerald work so compatibly here that, thankfully, **Joe Glaser** (who managed both artists) got them together in the 1950s to make three LPs for Verve. See additional comments on "April in Paris."

"You'll Never Walk Alone." By Richard Rodgers/Oscar Hammerstein II; rec. September 1, 1954, in New York City by **Louis Armstrong and the All Stars;** CDs #2, #8, #19, and #28. Armstrong frequently transformed unlikely material into moving musical experiences, and this Broadway song (from the 1945 *Carousel*) is a good example. He frequently paired it with "Tenderly" in a slow dance medley. In his liner notes to both *The Great Chicago Concert* and *The Complete* **Decca** *Studio Recordings,* Dan Morgenstern relates Armstrong's story about a 1957 performance: "When we hit Savannah, we played 'I'll [*sic*] Never Walk Alone' and the whole house—all Negroes—started singing with us on their own. We ran through two choruses and they kept with us and later they asked for it again. Most touching damn thing I ever saw. I almost started crying right there on stage. We really hit something inside each person there."

"You'll Wish You'd Never Been Born." By Louis Armstrong; rec. December 8, 1932, in Camden, New Jersey, with the Chick Webb Orchestra (although the label reads "Louis Armstrong and His Orchestra"); CD #12. A companion to the 1931 hit "(I'll be Glad When You're Dead) You Rascal, You," this number features a similar patterlike lyric, whose hilarious mock-violent words keep even the singer in stitches. Armstrong opens with an awesome cadenza, and sidemen Pete Clark (clarinet) and Elmer Williams (tenor saxophone) contribute excellent solos.

Young, James Osborne "Trummy" (1912–1984). When at the end of 1951 the great trombonist **Jack Teagarden** reluctantly left **Louis Armstrong and the All Stars** to lead his own ensemble, Trummy Young not only filled his shoes but, like Teagarden, became Armstrong's friend. Young remained with the All Stars for twelve years, though many considered the group's repertory and style too restrictive for Young's considerable skills, which had been developed with **Earl Hines,** Jimmy Lunceford, **Benny Goodman,** and many others. Nevertheless, Young flourished with Armstrong, either playing in harmony to his melodic lines, inventing clever counterpoint, or adding those dramatic long glissandos that evoked the earlier New Orleans "tail gate" style (so called because on band wagons used for advertising the trombone had to stand on the tailgate to have room to extend his slide). He also did some singing (as Teagarden had). All these skills were put to use on "Rockin' Chair," which Young inherited as a feature number from Teagarden (and passed to *his* successor, **Tyree Glenn**). Elsewhere Young provides a beguiling obbligato in "When You're Smiling" (1956), a soulful ostinato on "The Beautiful American" (1961), and rollicking high spirits to many of the fifty-eight recordings of "When the Saints Go Marching In." In a wide-ranging 1976 interview with Patricia Willard, Young said that "over the long period of time I worked with [Armstrong], I picked up a lot. . . . He was a master of timing and phrasing and little innuendoes that he would put into things—I thought I knew something about the stage and all. I knew nothing. . . . He was a master" (Berrett, 1999, pp. 172–176). Young can be seen in ***The Glenn Miller Story*** and several other movies.

"Your Cheatin' Heart." By Hank Williams; rec. February 23, 1953, in Detroit, Michigan, with the **Sy Oliver** Orchestra; CD #40. Armstrong covered this country song shortly after the composer made it a hit.

"You're a Heavenly Thing." By Joe Young and Little Jack Little; rec. January 29, 1957, in New York City with the **Sy Oliver** Orchestra; CD #26. See comments on "And the Angels Sing."

"You're a Lucky Guy." By Saul Chaplin and Sammy Cahn; rec. December 18, 1939, in New York City by Louis Armstrong and His Orchestra; CDs #18 and #61. Here is an excellent example of the refined, elegant Armstrong, recorded during a period when he was also getting down and dirty with numbers such as "Bye and Bye" (which was recorded on the same day).

"You're a Real Sweetheart." By Irving Caesar and Cliff Friend; rec. June 26, 1928, in Chicago by vocalist **Lillie Delk Christian** with Louis Armstrong and His **Hot Four;** CDs #10 and #36. See comments on "Baby" and "I Must Have That Man."

"You're Blasé." By Ord Hamilton and Bruce Sivier; rec. August 14, 1957, in Los Angeles with a studio orchestra conducted by arranger Russell Garcia. Armstrong was always full of surprises, such as the obvious pleasure he feels here in working with a big studio orchestra (twenty-one strings!). It's hardly jazzy, but it's certainly musical. Armstrong is recorded particularly well by the Verve engineers, who frankly did not do as good a job two weeks earlier with **Oscar Peterson.** The song here dates from 1932, when it was introduced in the London musical *Bow Bells.*

"You're Driving Me Crazy." By Walter Donaldson; rec. December 23, 1930, in Los Angeles by Louis Armstrong and His **Sebastian New Cotton Club** Orchestra. This clever number opens with some amusing Armstrong–**Lionel Hampton** banter, a sample of the introductions that Armstrong would often provide at nightclubs.

"You're Just a No Account." By Sammy Cahn and Saul Chaplin; rec. December 18, 1939, in New York City by Louis Armstrong and His Orchestra; CD #18.

"You're Just in Love." By **Irving Berlin;** rec. February 6, 1951, in Los Angeles with the Gordon Jenkins Orchestra; CD #28. This song, first made popular by Ethel Merman in the 1950 Broadway musical *Call Me Madam,* is probably Armstrong's best collaboration with his singer **Velma Middleton.**

"You're Lucky to Me." By Eubie Blake and Andy Razaf; rec. October 16, 1930, in Los Angeles by Louis Armstrong and His **Sebastian New Cotton Club** Orchestra; CD #44.

"You're Next." By Louis Armstrong; rec. February 26, 1926, in Chicago by Louis Armstrong and His **Hot Five;** CD #10. Although **Lil Armstrong**'s piano playing here is more appropriate for vaudeville or a movie house than jazz, Armstrong's minor key improvisation and the ensemble's collective improvisation make this a memorable number.

"You're the Apple of My Eye." By Louis Armstrong, Fox, Al Trace, and Ben Trace; rec. April 23, 1951, in Los Angeles by **Louis Armstrong and the All Stars;** CD #8. This is a duet for Armstrong and his singer **Velma Middleton,** who fit with each other like well-worn jigsaw puzzle pieces.

"You're the Top." By **Cole Porter;** rec. August 14, 1957, in Los Angeles with a studio orchestra conducted by arranger Russell Garcia; CD #29. Armstrong did not get around to this song until well after Ethel Merman had introduced it in the 1934 Broadway musical *Anything Goes,* but as with his eight other Cole Porter recordings, he gives it a unique interpretation.

"Yours and Mine." By Arthur Freed and Nacio Herb Brown; rec. July 2, 1937, in New York City by Louis Armstrong and His Orchestra; CDs #18 and #34. Armstrong's bands were sometimes weak during the 1930s but not on this popular *Broadway Melody of 1938* number, where he gets plenty of call-and-response action from a trumpet section led by Shelton Hemphill and from trombones led by **J.C. Higginbotham.**

"You've Been a Good Ole Wagon." By **Bessie Smith** and Balcom; rec. January 14, 1925, in New York City with vocalist Bessie Smith and pianist Fred Longshaw; CD #36. Here is one of Armstrong's relatively rare uses of the wa-wa mute. See also "Careless Love Blues"; "Cold in Hand Blues"; "Reckless Blues."

"You've Got Me Voodoo'd." By Louis Armstrong, **Luis Russell,** and Neil Lawrence; rec. March 14, 1940, in New York City by Louis Armstrong and His Orchestra. Armstrong fan and scholar Gary Giddins points out that this witty number may constitute the first example of rap music (1988, p. 140).

"You've Got the Right Key But the Wrong Key Hole." By **Clarence Williams;** rec. October 17, 1924, in New York City with vocalist Virginia Liston and **Clarence Williams' Blue Five;** CD #36. See comments on "Early in the Morning."

"You've Got to Beat Me to Keep Me." By P. Grainger; rec. February 1925 in New York City with vocalist **Trixie Smith** and her Down Home Syncopators; CD #36. See comment on "Mining Camp Blues."

"You've Got to Go Home on Time." By Richard M. Jones; rec. February 23, 1926, in Chicago with vocalist Baby Mack and pianist Richard M. Jones; CD #36. Armstrong recorded only two songs—this and "What Kind o' Man Is That?"—with blues singer Mack.

Z

Zaire. See **Congo.**

" 'Zat You, Santa Claus?" By Jack Fox; rec. October 22, 1953, in New York City by Louis Armstrong and the Commanders; CDs #7 and #33. Having discovered the joys of **Christmas** late in life (see "Christmas in New Orleans"), Armstrong made up for lost time by recording "White Christmas," "Winter Wonderland," and others. The novelty number " 'Zat You, Santa Claus?" (despite its racial stereotyping) particularly suits his love of minor-key songs and clever lyrics. You can almost hear him winking as he sings, "We don't believe in no goblins today,/But I can't explain why I'm shaking that way."

"Zip-a-Dee-Doo-Dah." By Ray Gilbert and Allie Wrubel; rec. March 16, 1968, in Hollywood by **Louis Armstrong and the All Stars** with a studio orchestra and mixed choir; CD #15. This song from the 1946 **Disney** movie *Song of the South* finds a congenial interpreter in Armstrong, who gets a chance to add **scat** to an already scatlike text. Unlike other songs from this session, the accompaniment is basically an All Star **Dixieland** format, and Armstrong is quite at home. His brief trumpet solo, however, gets cluttered by the addition of a choir. After this studio session, his horn is never recorded again.

Zucker, Dr. Gary. Armstrong was very fond of this **Beth Israel Hospital** heart and lung specialist whom he met when he suffered with heart failure symptoms in September 1968. Dr. Zucker also saw Armstrong through several other life-threatening situations and was called to Armstrong's house early on that fateful morning of July 6, 1971. During one of Armstrong's extended stays at Beth Israel, Zucker inadvertently prompted the writing of the memoir **"Louis Armstrong + the Jewish Family in New Orleans, La., the Year of 1907"** when he sang a Russian lullaby that Armstrong had first learned in his early **childhood** in New Orleans from the **Karnofsky family** (this fascinating document is published in Brothers, pp. 3–36). Zucker's care may have added precious time and comfort to Armstrong's last few years by coaxing him into various medical procedures and teaching him to watch his diet more scientifically. Although Zucker wanted him to give up the now-strenuous music making, Armstrong said that he might as well be dead if he could not perform. In March 1971, before what would turn out to be his last engagement (two weeks at the **Waldorf Astoria,** where in 1939 he had played with **Benny Goodman** and in 1963 for President Kennedy), he told Zucker (who related the conversation to Armstrong biographer James Lincoln Collier): "My whole life, my whole soul, my whole spirit is to blow that horn. . . . Doc, I've got to do it" (Collier, 1983, p. 331). Zucker insisted that at least Armstrong stay at the Waldorf, leave his room only to perform, and then be admitted to the hospital at the end of the engagement. Armstrong carried out his part of the bargain, and Zucker helped him get well enough to return home on May 6, where he died peacefully in his sleep two months later.

Zulu Social Aid and Pleasure Club. Established in New Orleans early in the twentieth century as an African American social club/burial society that also participated in the annual Mardi Gras festivities, the Zulu Club chose Armstrong to be their King in 1949. Never before had a celebrity been chosen for the honor, and Armstrong was beside himself with pleasure. "It had been my life-long dream to be the **King of the Zulus,** as it was the dream of every kid in my neighborhood," Armstrong wrote in his **autobiography** (1954, p. 126). For the raucous parade the King wore heavy makeup (blackface with excessive white grease-paint around the eyes and lips) and an elaborate tribal costume (a wig, a red velvet gown, a grass skirt, and a feathered crown) and rode on a float on a throne (drinking champagne and tossing coconuts to the crowd). The event prompted a great deal of publicity, and newspapers around the country carried a picture of the outlandish Zulu King Louis. ***Time*** magazine even devoted its February 21, 1949, cover story to the event (the first such honor for a jazz musician). According to some, the occasion underscored Armstrong's status as a first-rank show business figure. Others criticized Armstrong for promoting an unsuitable racial image. He enjoyed himself thoroughly though, and his career took a quantum leap. By July 1, 1949, ***Down Beat*** noted that **Louis Armstrong and the All Stars** were "probably the highest paid unit of its size in existence" (p. 1). That summer he made four appearances on NBC-TV's *Eddie Condon Floor Show.* Now exclusively with **Decca,** his recording dates increased, and he had a big hit with his September recording of "Blueberry Hill." Finally, in the fall, he began a series of highly visible foreign tours.

"Zulu's Ball." By **Joe Oliver** and **Fred Robinson;** rec. October 5, 1923, in Richmond, Indiana, by King Oliver and His Creole Jazz Band; CD #35. See comments on "Alligator Hop."

APPENDIX 1

SATCHMO ON CD

Fortunately, most of Armstrong's music has been reissued on CD and is widely available. In the Armstrong centennial year, MUZE (that wonderfully useful electronic source of information on currently available recordings) listed over 327 Armstrong CDs. (Compare 61 for Barbra Streisand, 119 for The Beatles, 211 for Elvis, 233 for Ella Fitzgerald, and 281 for Frank Sinatra.) Listed here are 63 of the 327. Those CDs that didn't make the cut either repeated music available elsewhere, had poor sound quality, lacked informative liner notes, or were otherwise undistinguished. Nevertheless, what follows is a very full list, one that amply demonstrates that Satchmo is still very much on the charts. For an exhaustive list of Armstrong's recordings, see Hans Westerberg's *Boy from New Orleans,* which was published in 1981 and therefore does not include CD reissues. Other discographies can be found on various Armstrong Web sites (see Appendix 4). The best of these is Scott Johnson's (http://www.satchography.com/).

More information on many of the people, places, ensembles, terms, and films mentioned here, as well as the music itself, can be found in the encyclopedia.

1. *Ambassador Satch*
Columbia 471871
2003

Royal Garden Blues – Tin Roof Blues – The Faithful Hussar – Muskrat Ramble – All of Me – Twelfth Street Rag – Undecided – Dardanella – West End Blues – Tiger Rag

Performers: Louis Armstrong (trumpet and vocals) and the All Stars

Armstrong's career took a political turn when, after World War II, jazz became a symbol of freedom and liberation. As Felix Belair wrote on the front page of the November 6, 1955, *New York Times:* "America's secret weapon is a blue note in a minor key. Right now its most effective ambassador is Louis (Satchmo) Armstrong. American jazz has now become a universal language. It knows no national boundaries, but everyone knows where it comes from and where to look for more." These high-spirited concert recordings made on tour in Amsterdam and Milan in 1955 nicely illustrate Belair's point.

2. *The Best Live Concert*
Verve 440 013 030-2
2001

When It's Sleepy Time Down South – Indiana – Tiger Rag – When I Grow Too Old to Dream – Perdido – Hello Dolly! – On the

Alamo — Cabaret — A Kiss to Build a Dream On — Lover, Come Back to Me — Can't Help Lovin' Dat Man — Improvisation, Blueberry Hill — Muskrat Ramble — Volare — Mack the Knife — Tenderly/You'll Never Walk Alone — Mop Mop — I Left My Heart in San Francisco — My Man — Bill Bailey, Won't You Please Come Home? — When the Saints Go Marching In — Finale

Performers: Louis Armstrong (trumpet and vocals) and the All Stars—Billy Kyle (piano), Eddie Shu (clarinet), Tyree Glenn (trombone), Buddy Catlett (bass), Danny Barcelona (drums), and Jewel Brown (vocals)

Recorded live in Paris, at the Palais des Sports, on June 4, 1965, this CD illustrates a standard Armstrong and the All Stars concert from the 1950s and 1960s. He'd open with "Indiana" and close with "Sleepytime." In between, he'd oblige the audience with his signature songs, such as "Hello Dolly!" or "Mack the Knife," and always play some hometown music, such as "Muskrat Ramble" or "Tiger Rag." The sidemen and singer generally got specialty numbers, as Jewel Brown does here in "Can't Help Lovin' Dat Man." Perhaps because it was made late in his career and with improved technology, this is one of the better-recorded concerts.

3. *The Best of Louis Armstrong*

Intersound 4624
1998

St. Louis Blues — Mahogany Hall Stomp — Save It, Pretty Mama — Hobo, You Can't Ride This Train — West End Blues — I've Got the World on a String — Cornet Chop Suey — Heebie Jeebies — (I'll Be Glad When You're Dead) You Rascal, You — When It's Sleepy Time Down South — I Gotta Right to Sing the Blues — I'm Confessin' (That I Love You) — Star Dust

Performers: Louis Armstrong (trumpet and vocals) with various ensembles

"Best of" compilations can be disappointing, especially for such a multifaceted artist as Armstrong. Here the producer intelligently focuses on the early Hot Five and Hot Seven recordings that made Armstrong a star—"Mahogany Hall Stomp," "Cornet Chop Suey," and "Heebie Jeebies." This last was Armstrong's first hit, selling 40,000 copies in a few weeks, at a time when selling 5,000 copies of a record was excellent and 10,000 was astounding. Digitally remastered, these recordings have a slight touch of reverberation, which may offend purists.

4. *The Best of Louis Armstrong*

MCA Records 11940
1999

What a Wonderful World — Hello Dolly! — Dream a Little Dream of Me — Cabaret — That Lucky Old Sun — I Still Get Jealous — Blueberry Hill — A Kiss to Build a Dream On — Gone Fishin' — When It's Sleepy Time Down South

Performers: Louis Armstrong (vocals, trumpet), Bing Crosby (vocals), Gordon Jenkins Orchestra and Choir, Sy Oliver Orchestra, John Scott Trotter's Orchestra

This compilation focuses on only one period in Armstrong's long career, the later years (1949–1967), when his name became a household word and his voice and face were immediately recognizable. These are the megahit recordings, plus a few nice surprises like "Cabaret" and a "Blueberry Hill" that anticipates Fats Domino's 1955 hit by six years.

5. *The Best of the Decca Years, Vol. 2: The Composer*
MCA Records 10121
1990

Satchel Mouth Swing – Lazy 'Sippi Steamer – Old Man Mose – Hear Me Talkin' to Ya – Swing That Music – Brother Bill [live] – Back o' Town Blues [live] – Hobo, You Can't Ride This Train – Wild Man Blues – Someday You'll Be Sorry – Potato Head Blues – Gully Low Blues – Struttin' with Some Barbecue

Performers: Louis Armstrong (trumpet, vocals), Al Klink and Bud Freeman (tenor sax), Henry "Red" Allen and Billy Butterfield (trumpets), Trummy Young (trombone), Barney Bigard (clarinet), Billy Kyle (piano), George Barnes (guitar), Arvell Shaw and Pops Foster (bass), Barrett Deems and Sidney Catlett (drums)

This CD reminds us that Armstrong was a composer as well as a trumpet player and singer; in fact, he has some eighty copyrights to his credit. Here are some of his better-known titles. To "Gully Low Blues" he adds a genial spoken introduction about the origin of the tune. "Swing That Music" goes at the breakneck pace of 150 beats per minute and ends with a stratospheric "E-flat" after an unbelievable forty-two high Cs. In contrast is "Someday You'll Be Sorry," which a British radio journalist thought had a Noël Coward–like beauty. With characteristic modesty Armstrong responded, "Can't you name somebody a little lesser than Noël?" (Giddins, 1988, p. 105). Frankly though, one could instead take it up a notch and make a comparison with the great Viennese *Lieder* composer Franz Schubert, with whose songs of unrequited love, such as "Trockne Blumen" (Withered Flowers), Armstrong's "Someday" can favorably be compared.

6. *The California Concerts*
Decca Jazz 613, 4 CDs
1992

Disc 1: When It's Sleepy Time Down South – Indiana – Someday You'll Be Sorry – Back o' Town Blues – Way Down Yonder in New Orleans – Star Dust – The Hucklebuck – Honeysuckle Rose – How High the Moon – Just You, Just Me – Bugle Blues – A Monday Date – You Can Depend on Me

Disc 2: That's a Plenty – Body and Soul – Big Daddy Blues – Baby, It's Cold Outside – Muskrat Ramble – When It's Sleepy Time Down South – Indiana – The Gypsy – Someday You'll Be Sorry – Tin Roof Blues – My Bucket's Got a Hole in It – Tin Roof Blues – My Bucket's Got a Hole in It – Rose Room – Perdido – Blues for Bass – Me and Brother Bill

Disc 3: When You're Smiling (the Whole World Smiles With You) – 'Tain't What You Do (It's the Way That Cha Do It) – Lover, Come Back to Me – Don't Fence Me In – Basin Street Blues – When It's Sleepy Time Down South (closing theme) – Shadrack/When the Saints Go Marching In – C'est si bon – The Whiffenpoof Song – Rockin' Chair – Twelfth Street Rag – Muskrat Ramble – St. Louis Blues – The Man I Love – Back o' Town Blues – Old Man Mose

Disc 4: Jeepers Creepers – Margie – Big Mama's Back in Town – Big Butter and Egg Man – Stompin' at the Savoy – When It's Sleepy Time Down South – Struttin' with Some Barbecue – (Up a) Lazy River – Old Man Mose (with a false start) – My Bucket's Got a Hole in It – 'S Wonderful – Big Mama's Back in Town – Since I Fell for You – Mop Mop – When It's Sleepy Time Down South

Performers on discs 1–2: Louis Armstrong (trumpet and vocals) and the All Stars—Jack Teagarden (trombone and vocals), Barney Bigard (clarinet), Earl Hines (piano), Arvell Shaw (bass), Cozy Cole (drums), and Velma Middleton (vocals); on discs 3–4: Armstrong (trumpet and vocals) and the All Stars—Trummy Young (trombone and vocals), Barney Bigard (clarinet and vocals), Billy Kyle (piano), Arvell Shaw (bass), Barrett Deems (drums), and Velma Middleton (vocals)

This four-CD set generously offers two full Louis Armstrong and the All Stars concerts given in California, one recorded at Pasadena Civic Auditorium on January 30, 1951 (discs 1–2) and the other at the Crescendo Club in Los Angeles on January 21, 1955 (discs 3–4). High-spirited and diverse, there are not only the staples of nearly every concert ("When It's Sleepy Time Down South," "Indiana," and "Muskrat Ramble") but also some surprises, such as "The Whiffenpoof Song," a bebop satire sometimes called "The Boppenpoof Song." Armstrong liked to give his sidemen the spotlight now and then, and here, for example, trombonist Trummy Young turns in a memorable performance on " 'Tain't What You Do." Another bonus with this collection is a twenty-seven-page booklet of program notes by Dan Morgenstern.

7. *Christmas through the Years*

Delta 12774
1996

Cool Yule – White Christmas – 'Zat You, Santa Claus? – Christmas in New Orleans – Winter Wonderland – Christmas Night in Harlem – Baby, It's Cold Outside – Gone Fishin' – Joseph 'n' His Brudders – Santa Claus Blues – The Night before Christmas – What a Wonderful World

Performers: Louis Armstrong (trumpet and vocals) with various ensembles

Armstrong discovered Christmas late in life, in 1942 to be exact. He had recently married Lucille Wilson, and for their first Christmas together, she bought a small tree for their hotel room. This so entranced Louis that he made Lucille take it down and put it up in at least a dozen different hotels, night after night, until well after the New Year. His childlike response to the excitement of Christmas comes through on this compilation, as he makes "Cool Yule" swing and " 'Zat You, Santa Claus?" mock scary. Get out your handkerchief for "White Christmas" and hold on to it for his very last recording, a reading of "The Night before Christmas."

8. *The Complete Decca Studio Recordings of Louis Armstrong and the All Stars*

Mosaic Records MD6-146, 6 CDs
1993

Disc 1: Panama – New Orleans Function: Flee as a Bird/Oh, Didn't He Ramble? – Twelfth Street Rag – That's for Me – Bugle Call Rag/Ole Miss – I Surrender, Dear – Russian Lullaby – Baby, Won't You Please Come Home? – Fine and Dandy – My Bucket's Got a Hole in It

Disc 2: Unless – A Kiss to Build a Dream On – You're the Apple of My Eye – I'll Walk Alone – Kiss of Fire – April in Portugal – Ramona – Basin Street Blues – Otchi-tchor-ni-ya – Struttin' with Some Barbecue – Margie

Disc 3: Muskrat Ramble – Tenderly/You'll Never Walk Alone – Yeh! – Mm-mm – Baby, Your Sleep Is Showing – Tin Roof Blues – Pretty Little Missy – Easy Street – Lazy Bones – If I Could Be with You – Lazy River – I Can't Give You Anything But Love – On the Sunny Side of the Street – I Can't Believe That You're in Love with Me – Body and Soul

Disc 4: Mahogany Hall Stomp – When You're Smiling – Some of These Days – I Surrender, Dear – Georgia on My Mind – Exactly

Like You – High Society – Song of the Islands – That's My Home – Memories of You – Them There Eyes – This Younger Generation – In Pursuit of Happiness

Disc 5: Hotter Than That – Gut Bucket Blues – Weary Blues – Potato Head Blues – Cornet Chop Suey – Of All the Wrongs You've Done to Me – Two Deuces – Mandy, Make Up Your Mind – Wild Man Blues – Gully Low Blues – Everybody Loves My Baby – Heebie Jeebies – King of the Zulus – Froggie Moore Rag – Georgia Grind – Snag It – Dippermouth Blues – Canal Street Blues

Disc 6: (I'll Be Glad When You're Dead) You Rascal, You – Hobo, You Can't Ride This Train – Knockin' a Jug – Dear Old Southland – See See Rider – Reckless Blues – Trouble in Mind – Court House Blues – I Love Jazz – The Mardi Gras March – Basin Street Blues – Otchi-tchor-ni-ya

Performers: Louis Armstrong (trumpet and vocals) and the All Stars

This six-CD set is worth searching for since it has a full program by the 1950 version of the All Stars (which includes Jack Teagarden, Barney Bigard, and Earl Hines), the "Musical Autobiography" project (for which Armstrong revisited some of the numbers recorded in the 1920s and 1930s), and some odds and ends (including two vocal duets with Gary Crosby). The recordings were made between 1947 and 1957 and come with a twenty-four-page program booklet by Dan Morgenstern.

9. *The Complete Ella Fitzgerald and Louis Armstrong on Verve*

Verve Records 314537, 3 CDs
1997

Disc 1: Can't We Be Friends? – Isn't This a Lovely Day? – Moonlight in Vermont – They Can't Take That Away from Me – Under a Blanket of Blue – Tenderly – A Foggy Day – Stars Fell on Alabama – Cheek to Cheek – The Nearness of You – April in Paris – Don't Be That Way – Makin' Whoopee – They All Laughed – Comes Love – Autumn in New York

Disc 2: Let's Do It – Stompin' at the Savoy – I Won't Dance – Gee, Baby, Ain't I Good to You? – Let's Call the Whole Thing Off – These Foolish Things – I've Got My Love to Keep Me Warm – Willow Weep for Me – I'm Puttin' All My Eggs in One Basket – A Fine Romance – Ill Wind (You're Blowin' Me No Good) – (Our) Love Is Here to Stay – I Get a Kick Out of You – Learnin' the Blues – You Won't Be Satisfied (Until You Break My Heart) – Undecided

Disc 3 (*Porgy and Bess*): Overture – Summertime – I Wants to Stay Here – My Man's Gone Now – I Got Plenty of Nuttin' – Buzzard Song – Bess, You Is My Woman Now – It Ain't Necessarily So – What You Want Wid Bess? – A Woman Is a Sometime Thing – Oh, Doctor Jesus – Medley: Here Come de Honey Man/Crab Man/Oh, Dey's So Fresh and Fine – There's a Boat That's Leavin' Soon for New York – Oh, Bess, Oh Where's My Bess? – Oh, Lawd, I'm on My Way

Performers: Louis Armstrong (vocals and trumpet), Ella Fitzgerald (vocals), accompanied on various pieces by Oscar Peterson and Billy Kyle (piano), Herb Ellis (guitar), Ray Brown and Dale Jones (bass), Buddy Rich, Louie Bellson, and Barrett Deems (drums), Trummy Young (trombone), Edmond Hall (clarinet), and a studio orchestra directed by Russell Garcia

Armstrong and Fitzgerald recorded this material in Los Angeles between August 16, 1956, and October 14, 1957, and it was issued on three separate LPs between 1957 and 1958. While some critics have thought the performances a little on the stiff and formal side, others have enthusiastically hailed them as an instruction manual for aspiring jazz singers. Certainly there can be no question about the musicianship (phrasing, intonation, breath control, etc.). A bonus is the piquant contrast between Fitzgerald's polished voice and Armstrong's rugged voice. Particularly outstanding are their renditions of American songbook classics "April in Paris," "Autumn in New York," "Cheek to Cheek," "A Foggy Day," "Let's Call the Whole Thing Off," "The Nearness of You," and "They All Laughed." Their *Porgy and Bess* (by George Gershwin), recorded in a single day (August 18, 1957), is considered by many to be the best of dozens of adaptations of the opera.

A one-disc selection from this set was issued by Verve in 2000 in advance of the Armstrong centennial. (Can't We Be Friends? — Isn't This a Lovely Day? — Moonlight in Vermont — They Can't Take That Away from Me — Under a Blanket of Blue — Tenderly — A Foggy Day — Stars Fell on Alabama — Cheek to Cheek — The Nearness of You — April in Paris)

10. *The Complete Hot Five and Hot Seven Recordings*

Columbia/Legacy 63527, 4 CDs
2000

Disc 1: Gut Bucket Blues — My Heart — Yes! I'm in the Barrel — Come Back, Sweet Papa — Georgia Grind — Heebie Jeebies — Cornet Chop Suey [in F] — Oriental Strut — You're Next — Muskrat Ramble — Don't Forget to Mess Around — I'm Gonna Gitcha — Droppin' Shucks — Who's It? — King of the Zulus — Big Fat Ma and Skinny Pa — Lonesome Blues — Sweet Little Papa — Jazz Lips — Skid-Dat-De-Dat — Big Butter and Egg Man — Sunset Cafe Stomp — You Made Me Love You — Irish Black Bottom

Disc 2: Put 'em Down Blues — Ory's Creole Trombone — The Last Time — Struttin' with Some Barbecue — Got No Blues — Once in a While — I'm Not Rough — Hotter Than That — Savoy Blues — He Likes It Slow — Gambler's Dream — Sunshine Baby — Adam and Eve Had the Blues — Put It Where I Can Get It — Wash Woman Blues — I've Stopped My Man — Georgia Bo Bo — Drop That Sack — Cornet Chop Suey (in E-flat)

Disc 3: Willie the Weeper — Wild Man Blues — Alligator Crawl — Potato Head Blues — Melancholy — Weary Blues — Twelfth Street Rag — Keyhole Blues — S.O.L. Blues — Gully Low Blues — That's When I'll Come Back to You — Chicago Breakdown — Weary Blues — New Orleans Stomp — Wild Man Blues — Melancholy — You're a Real Sweetheart — Too Busy — Was It a Dream? — Last Night I Dreamed You Kissed Me

Disc 4: Fireworks — Skip the Gutter — A Monday Date — Don't Jive Me — West End Blues — Sugar Foot Stomp — Two Deuces — Squeeze Me — Knee Drops — No (Papa, No) — Basin Street Blues — No One Else But You — Beau Koo Jack — Save It, Pretty Mama — Muggles — Hear Me Talkin' to Ya — St. James Infirmary — Tight Like This — Weather Bird — I Can't Give You Anything But Love — Mahogany Hall Stomp — Knockin' a Jug

Performers: Louis Armstrong and His Hot Five, His Hot Seven, His Hot Four; also variously with the Savoy Ballroom Five, Lil's Hot Shots, Johnny Dodds's Black Bottom Stompers, and the Carroll Dickerson Orchestra

Between 1925 and 1929, Armstrong got together some groups simply to play standard blues and novelty tunes, but, as these eighty-seven tracks show, he created some of the most historically important recordings in jazz. This set contains every Hot Five and Hot Seven recording, including rarities and alternate takes. Sensibly organized, it groups recordings made by the 1925–1927 version of the Hot Five on the first two discs, the Hot Sevens on the third, and the 1928 version of the Hot Five on disc 4. Sprinkled here and there are some extra recordings, for example, an alternate take of "I Can't Give You Anything But Love." The originals have been remastered so that the music is at the same pitch as originally recorded. All this plus an informative eighty-three-page cloth-bound book makes it plain why this compilation won the 2000 Grammy for Best Historical Album.

11. *The Complete Louis Armstrong and Duke Ellington Sessions*
Roulette Records 24546, 2 CDs
2000

Disc 1: Duke's Place – I'm Just a Lucky So and So – Cottontail – Mood Indigo – Do Nothin' Till You Hear from Me – The Beautiful American – Black and Tan Fantasy – Drop Me Off in Harlem – The Mooche – In a Mellow Tone – It Don't Mean a Thing (If It Ain't Got That Swing) – Solitude – Don't Get Around Much Anymore – I'm Beginning to See the Light – Just Squeeze Me – I Got It Bad (And That Ain't Good) – Azalea

Disc 2: In a Mellow Tone – I'm Beginning to See the Light – Do Nothin' Till You Hear from Me [rehearsal/working out arrangement (take 1); discussion/complete take (take 2)] – Don't Get Around Much Anymore – Duke's Place [take 5, pianist Luckey Roberts intro/complete take] – Drop Me Off in Harlem – I'm Just a Lucky So and So – Azalea – Black and Tan Fantasy – Band discussion on Cottontail

Performers: Louis Armstrong (trumpet and vocals), Duke Ellington (piano), Barney Bigard (clarinet), Trummy Young (trombone), Mort Herbert (bass), Danny Barcelona (drums)

Armstrong spent December 1960 in Paris, where he played Ellington's music in the film *Paris Blues.* When he returned to New York, he and Ellington collaborated on two albums (*Together for the First Time* and *The Great Reunion*). Producer Bob Thiele helped the two jazz giants decide on content and personnel by persuading Armstrong to do Ellington songs with the All Stars, substituting Ellington for Billy Kyle on the piano. Even though these pieces were not in Armstrong's repertory, he gave them the Satchmo treatment, and the result was a memorable album, twice re-released on CD (1990 and 2000). An abbreviated, one-CD version was released by Roulette (#24547) in 2001. Armstrong's fresh approach to songs that Ellington had played for decades and recorded dozens of times delighted the composer. A good example is Armstrong's rambunctious solo, extra lyrics, and improvised scatting on "Cottontail," which make it almost a new creation. On Ellington's part, the small combo allowed his lean, suave piano style to be heard clearly, for example, on "Duke's Place." Both albums were recorded in just two days, April 3 and 4, 1961, at the RCA Studios in New York City. In this reissue, the second disc has conversations, false starts, and outtakes from the sessions. Dan Morgenstern provides program notes.

12. *The Complete RCA Victor Recordings*
RCA Victor 68682, 4 CDs
1997

Disc 1: That's My Home – Hobo, You Can't Ride This Train – I Hate to Leave You Now – You'll Wish You'd Never Been Born – (I'll Be Glad When You're Dead) You Rascal, You/When It's Sleepy Time Down South/Nobody's Sweetheart – When You're Smiling/St. James Infirmary/Dinah – I've Got the World on a String – I Gotta

Armstrong with neighborhood children at his home in Corona in the late 1960s. (Louis Armstrong House and Archives at Queens College/CUNY)

Right to Sing the Blues – Hustlin' and Bustlin' for Baby – Sittin' in the Dark – High Society – He's a Son of the South – Some Sweet Day – Basin Street Blues – Honey, Do! – Snowball – Mahogany Hall Stomp – Swing, You Cats

Disc 2: Honey, Don't You Love Me Anymore? – Mississippi Basin – Laughin' Louie – Tomorrow Night – Dusky Stevedore – There's a Cabin in the Pines – Mighty River – Sweet Sue, Just You – I Wonder Who – St. Louis Blues – Don't Play Me Cheap – That's My Home – Hobo, You Can't Ride This Train – I Hate to Leave You Now – You'll Wish You'd Never Been Born – When You're Smiling/St. James Infirmary/Dinah – Mississippi Basin – Laughin' Louie – Tomorrow Night – Blue Yodel No. 9 (Standing on the Corner)

Disc 3: Long, Long Journey – Snafu – Linger in My Arms a Little Longer – Whatta Ya Gonna Do? – No Variety Blues – Joseph 'n' His Brudders – Back o' Town Blues – I Want a Little Girl – Sugar – Blues for Yesterday – Blues in the South – Endie – The Blues Are Brewin' – Do You Know What It Means to Miss New Orleans? – Where the Blues Were Born in New Orleans – Mahogany Hall Stomp – I Wonder, I Wonder, I Wonder – I Believe – Why Doubt My Love?

Disc 4: It Takes Time – You Don't Learn That in School – Ain't Misbehavin' – Rockin' Chair – Back o' Town Blues – Pennies from Heaven – Save It, Pretty Mama – St. James Infirmary – Jack Armstrong Blues – Rockin' Chair – Someday You'll Be Sorry – Fifty-Fifty Blues – A Song Is Born – Please

Stop Playin' Those Blues, Boy – Before Long – Lovely Weather We're Having – Rain, Rain – Never Saw a Better Day

Performers: Louis Armstrong (trumpet and vocals), Jack Teagarden (trombone and vocals), Jimmie Rodgers (guitar and vocals), Edgar Sampson (alto saxophone and violin), Budd Johnson, Don Byas, and Peanuts Hucko (tenor saxophone and clarinet), Johnny Hodges (alto saxophone), Jimmy Hamilton (clarinet), Bobby Hackett (cornet), Charlie Shavers and Neal Hefti (trumpet), Kid Ory and Vic Dickenson (trombone), Barney Bigard (clarinet), Teddy Wilson, Billy Strayhorn, Leonard Feather, Duke Ellington, and Charlie Beal (piano), John Trueheart, Remo Palmieri, Allan Reuss (guitar), Mike McKendrick (banjo and dobro), Bill Oldham, Red Callender, Chubby Jackson, and Arvell Shaw (bass), Chick Webb, Zutty Singleton, Sonny Greer, Sid Catlett, and Yank Porter (drums)

This generous four-CD set covers Armstrong's recordings made with RCA between 1932 and 1956. The first two discs feature some outstanding work with his big band in the 1930s (e.g., "I've Got the World on a String"). The third and fourth discs include some of the earliest recordings by the All Stars (e.g., a rousing "St. James Infirmary"). These sessions, some of which are live, also feature Armstrong's sidemen, as well as guest appearances by Duke Ellington, Johnny Hodges, Kid Ory, and others. But wait, there's more: film tunes ("Pennies from Heaven"), Armstrong's own compositions ("Back o' Town Blues" and "Someday You'll Be Sorry"), and anomalies (such as "Blue Yodel No. 9" with country music star Jimmie Rodgers). Dan Morgenstern wrote the informative liner notes. A one-CD selection from this set (RCA 63636) was issued in 2000 for the Armstrong centennial.

13. *The Complete Town Hall Concert*
RCA Records 66541, 2 CDs
1992

Introduction by Fred Robbins – Cornet Chop Suey – A Monday Date – Dear Old Southland – Big Butter and Egg Man – Tiger Rag – Struttin' with Some Barbecue – Sweethearts on Parade – Saint Louis Blues – Pennies from Heaven – On the Sunny Side of the Street – I Can't Give You Anything But Love – Back o' Town Blues – Ain't Misbehavin' – Rockin' Chair – Muskrat Ramble – Save It, Pretty Mama – St. James Infirmary – Royal Garden Blues – Do You Know What It Means to Miss New Orleans? – Jack Armstrong Blues

Performers: Louis Armstrong (trumpet and vocals) and the All Stars—Peanuts Hucko (tenor saxophone and clarinet), Jack Teagarden (trombone and vocals), Bobby Hackett (trumpet), Dick Cary (piano), Bob Haggart (bass), and Sidney Catlett and George Wettling (drums)

Recorded live at Town Hall, New York City, on May 17, 1947, this concert marks a turning point in Armstrong's career. He had started out playing in small, New Orleans-style combos, but throughout the 1930s and 1940s he had been working with big bands. However, the big band era was now drawing to a close, a fact that was evident to nearly everyone at a Carnegie Hall concert earlier in 1947 (February 8, to be exact). On that occasion, Armstrong experimented by playing the first half of the show with a small group and the second half with a big one. Almost everyone preferred the former, and Armstrong decided to go with a small ensemble for the Town Hall concert. In the future he would work predominantly with the lithe, elite All Stars, which was born on this occasion. Although the recording quality is low, the musical magic is there for all who have ears to hear. Highlights of this twenty-one-piece collection include an evocative "Dear Old Southland," a daring "Cornet Chop Suey" (on which Armstrong is backed only by the rhythm section), and a memorable "St. James Infirmary," featuring sideman Jack Teagarden.

14. *The Definitive Louis Armstrong* [Ken Burns Jazz Collection]
Columbia/Legacy 61440
2000

King Oliver's Creole Jazz Band: Chimes Blues; Clarence Williams' Blue Five: Cake Walking Babies from Home; Louis Armstrong and His Hot Five: Heebie Jeebies – West End Blues – Tight Like This; Louis Armstrong and His Hot Seven: Potato Head Blues; Louis Armstrong and His Savoy Ballroom Five: Mahogany Hall Stomp; Louis Armstrong and His Orchestra: Ain't Misbehavin' – St. Louis Blues – When It's Sleepy Time Down South – Blue Again – Lazy River – Chinatown, My Chinatown – Star Dust – I Double Dare You – When the Saints Go Marching In; Louis Armstrong with the Murray Singers: Shadrack; Louis Armstrong and His All Stars: Rockin' Chair – Mack the Knife; Louis Armstrong with the Mills Brothers: Marie; Louis Armstrong with Gordon Jenkins' Orchestra and Choir: Blueberry Hill; Louis Armstrong with various ensembles: A Fine Romance – Hello Dolly! – What a Wonderful World

Performers: Louis Armstrong (cornet, trumpet, and vocals) with ensembles as noted above; additional performers include Ella Fitzgerald (vocals), Jack Teagarden (trombone), Kid Ory (trombone), King Oliver (cornet), Oscar Peterson (piano), Baby Dodds and Louis Bellson (drums)

Ken Burns's marvelous ten-part television documentary series *Jazz* spun off several "definitive" CDs that are really worthy of the adjective. Armstrong's is a good example—and appropriately so since he dominated the series. Here are the classics from his five-decade career, from "Potato Head Blues" (1927) to "What a Wonderful World" (1967). If you could have only one Armstrong CD (heaven forbid), this would be it. Included are excellent liner notes by Doug Ramsey.

15. *Disney Songs the Satchmo Way*
Disney 60920
2001

Zip-a-Dee-Doo-Dah – Ten Feet Off the Ground – Heigh-Ho – Whistle While You Work – Chim Chim Cher-ee – Bibbidi-Bobbidi-Boo – 'Bout Time – The Ballad of Davy Crockett – The Bare Necessities – When You Wish Upon a Star

Performers: Louis Armstrong (trumpet and vocals) with various vocal and instrumental ensembles

Armstrong liked children (though he had none of his own), and his affection for them along with his unique combination of playfulness and seriousness found a congenial outlet in these songs from Disney films. They were recorded in 1968 when he was in poor health, but one can hardly detect any fatigue in the performances. In "Zip-a-Dee-Doo-Dah" and "Bibbidi-Bobbidi-Boo," he delights in the kind of scat singing he'd popularized nearly half a century earlier. His "Chim Chim Cher-ee" brings out the dark side of the song, and his soulful "When You Wish Upon a Star" speaks to young and old alike. One hears his very last trumpet solos here, and they're memorable, especially on "The Ballad of Davy Crockett." Made available on CD in 1987, this popular item was reissued in 1996 and again for the Centennial in 2001.

16. ***The Essence of Louis Armstrong***
Columbia/Legacy 47916
1991

Mack the Knife – Back o' Town Blues – Six Foot Four – All of Me – When the Red, Red, Robin Comes Bob, Bob, Bobbin' Along – Blueberry Hill – Way Down Yonder in New Orleans – Do You Know What It Means to Miss New Orleans? – On the Sunny Side of the Street – When It's Sleepy Time Down South – Someday You'll Be Sorry – Cabaret

Performers: Louis Armstrong (trumpet and vocals) with various ensembles

"Essence" is not exactly the best word to describe this collection of only twelve of nearly a thousand songs from only two of five decades. "Some Pop Hits" would fit the material better. Here are the definitive versions of "Mack the Knife," "On the Sunny Side of the Street," and "When the Red, Red Robin Comes Bob, Bob, Bobbin' Along." The disc is a good start, though, and it's bound to whet the appetite for more. Included are excellent program notes by Will Friedwald.

17. ***The Fabulous Louis Armstrong***
RCA Victor 63488
1999

St. Louis Blues – Do You Know What It Means to Miss New Orleans? – That's My Home – He's a Son of the South – I Can't Give You Anything But Love – Basin Street Blues – Laughin' Louie – Mood Indigo – Whatta Ya Gonna Do? – Ain't Misbehavin' – Fifty-Fifty Blues – Swing, You Cats – Someday You'll Be Sorry – You Don't Learn That in School – Rockin' Chair (Concert Version) – Some Sweet Day – What a Wonderful World

Performers: Louis Armstrong (trumpet and vocals) with various ensembles

Armstrong was on the charts for an incredible sixty-two years. While most single-CD compilations focus on only one of his three broad periods (the early small groups, the middle big band, and the post-World War II popular star), this one offers seventeen tracks from throughout his career. Highlights are an energetic "That's My Home" from 1932 and a reflective "Mood Indigo" from 1970. As a valediction, the CD closes with his signature "What a Wonderful World."

18. ***The Glorious Big Band Years, 1937–1941***
EPM (import) 159752
2000

Public Melody Number 1 – Yours and Mine – Sun Showers – On the Sunny Side of the Street – I Double Dare You – Let That Be a Lesson – I Can't Give You Anything But Love – Ain't Misbehavin' – What Is This Thing Called Swing? – I'm Confessin' (That I Love You) – Baby, Won't You Please Come Home? – Shanty Boat on the Mississippi – You're a Lucky Guy – You're Just a No Account – Hep Cats' Ball – Lazy 'Sippi Steamer – You Run Your Mouth, I'll Run My Business – In the Gloaming – Now Do You Call That a Buddy?

Performers: Louis Armstrong (trumpet and vocals) and His Orchestra; some selections with His Hot Seven–John Thomas (trombone), Johnny Dodds (clarinet), Lillian Armstrong (piano), Johnny St. Cyr (banjo), Pete Briggs (tuba), and Baby Dodds (drums)

The selections on this CD come from the heyday of Armstrong's big band period, roughly 1929 to 1947. Highlights include the rowdy "Public Melody Number 1" (which was used in the 1937 film *Artists and Models)* and the tender "I'm Confessin' " (which demonstrates the influence of Bing Crosby on Armstrong).

19. *The Great Chicago Concert, 1956*
Columbia/Legacy 65119, 2 CDs
1997.

Disc 1: Flee as a Bird to the Mountain/Oh, Didn't He Ramble? – Memphis Blues/ Frankie and Johnny – Tiger Rag – Do You Know What It Means to Miss New Orleans? – Basin Street Blues – (What Did I Do to Be So) Black and Blue? – On the Sunny Side of the Street – Struttin' with Some Barbecue – When It's Sleepy Time Down South – Manhattan/When It's Sleepy Time Down South – Indiana – The Gypsy – The Faithful Hussar

Disc 2: Rockin' Chair – My Bucket's Got a Hole in It – Perdido – Clarinet Marmalade – Mack the Knife – Tenderly/You'll Never Walk Alone – Stompin' at the Savoy – Margie – Big Mama's Back in Town – That's My Desire – Ko Ko Mo (I Love You So) – When the Saints Go Marching In – The Star Spangled Banner

Performers: Louis Armstrong (trumpet and vocals) and the All Stars – Edmond Hall (clarinet and vocals), Trummy Young (trombone and vocals), Billy Kyle (piano), Dale Jones (bass), Barrett Deems (drums), and Velma Middleton (vocals)

Recorded live at Chicago's Medina Temple on June 1, 1956, and released the following year, this was an All Stars benefit for the Multiple Sclerosis Society. The excitement of a live concert shines through, along with the uneven sound quality (especially the first track, during which the band marches to the stage in New Orleans brass band style). The program included narration by actress Helen Hayes, but that has been edited out. What remains is a survey of fifty years of jazz, which in fact was the event's subtitle. Liner notes by Dan Morgenstern and producer George Avakian.

20. *Happy Birthday, Louis!*
Omega 3024
1994

Introduction by Willis Conover – When It's Sleepy Time Down South – Indiana – My Bucket's Got a Hole in It – Tiger Rag – Now You Has Jazz – High Society Calypso – Ole Miss – Girl of My Dreams – "C" Jam Blues – Blueberry Hill – Undecided – I'm Beginning to See the Light – Mack the Knife – Stompin' at the Savoy – St. Louis Blues – Ko Ko Mo (I Love You So) – After You've Gone – When the Saints Go Marching In – The Star Spangled Banner – Happy Birthday, Louis!

Performers: Louis Armstrong (trumpet) and the All Stars – Barney Bigard (clarinet), Trummy Young (trombone), Billy Kyle (piano), Mort Herbert (bass), Danny Barcelona (drums), and Velma Middleton (vocals)

Before it was discovered in the 1980s that Armstrong was born on August 4, 1901, he and everyone else thought his birthday was July 4, 1900, which would have been fitting for someone who became the most popular American musician of the twentieth century. This CD is a mixture of popular tunes, old standards, and New Orleans numbers that were played (and recorded) at a celebration of his "60th" birthday at the Newport Jazz Festival. Perhaps because the All Stars are tailor-made for the New Orleans style, "Ole Miss," "Tiger Rag," and "Stompin' at the Savoy" come off best. The Ellington and Porter numbers get spirited, up-tempo renditions, and Armstrong (ever the audience-pleaser) also plays "Blueberry Hill" and "Mack the Knife." "The Star Spangled Banner" and the requisite "Happy

Birthday" wrap up the disc with a salute both to the nation and to the man.

21. *A 100th Birthday Celebration*
RCA Victor 63694, 2 CDs
2000

I've Got the World on a String – He's a Son of the South – Whatta Ya Gonna Do? – Honey, Don't You Love Me Any More? – Blues for Yesterday – Honey, Do! – Sittin' in the Dark – Linger in My Arms a Little Longer – When You're Smiling/St. James Infirmary/Dinah – I Want a Little Girl – High Society – Hobo, You Can't Ride This Train – Laughin' Louie – Swing, You Cats – Do You Know What It Means to Miss New Orleans?

Disc 2: St. Louis Blues – That's My Home – Sweet Sue, Just You – There's a Cabin in the Pines – Hustlin' and Bustlin' for Baby – I Gotta Right to Sing the Blues – Mahogany Hall Stomp – (I'll Be Glad When You're Dead) You Rascal, You/When It's Sleepy Time Down South/Nobody's Sweetheart – Jack Armstrong Blues – Back o' Town Blues – Sugar – Joseph 'n' His Brudders – Where the Blues Were Born in New Orleans – Basin Street Blues – Rockin' Chair

Performers include: Louis Armstrong (trumpet and vocals), Louis Jordan (alto saxophone), Bobby Hackett (cornet), Jack Teagarden and Kid Ory (trombone), Barney Bigard (clarinet), Teddy Wilson (piano), and Chick Webb (drums)

To help celebrate what was thought to be Armstrong's one hundredth birthday, this collection of music recorded between 1932 and 1947 (i.e., Armstrong's big band period) presents classic versions of "St. Louis Blues," "Sweet Sue, Just You," and "I Gotta Right to Sing the Blues." The liner notes by Loren Schoenberg help explain why this music not only makes us smile but also makes us sometimes laugh out loud.

22. *In Concert, 1954*
Storyville 4095
1994

When It's Sleepy Time Down South – Indiana – Big Butter and Egg Man – High Society – Auld Lang Syne – Back o' Town Blues – Twelfth Street Rag – Shadrack/When the Saints Go Marching In – West End Blues – The Dummy Song – My Bucket's Got a Hole in It – Tin Roof Blues – When It's Sleepy Time Down South

Performers: Louis Armstrong (trumpet and vocals) and the All Stars – Velma Middleton (vocals), Trummy Young (trombone), Barney Bigard (clarinet), Billy Kyle (piano), Arvell Shaw and Milt Hinton (bass), and Barrett Deems and Kenny Jones (drums)

Although not widely available, this CD is well worth looking for. It consists of two 1954 radio broadcasts from the Club Hangover in San Francisco. The first part is from New Year's Eve and the rest from three weeks later. The tracks are the All Stars' usual repertory, plus some delightful surprises, such as Armstrong's scatting and joking with vocalist Velma Middleton on "Big Butter and Egg Man" and a down-and-dirty "Back o' Town Blues" driven by bassist Arvell Shaw. The sound quality is uneven, the crowd is rowdy, and songs often begin and end rather abruptly, but then this was a live event.

23. *The Katanga Concert*
Milan 35908, 2 CDs
2000

Disc 1: I Surrender, Dear – Blueberry Hill – Rockin' Chair – Stompin' at the Savoy – C'est si bon – La vie en rose – Undecided – Big Mama's Back in Town – That's My Desire – I Can't Give You Anything But Love – When It's Sleepy Time Down South

Disc 2: That's My Home – Struttin' with Some Barbecue – Jazz Me Blues – Basin

Street Blues — Margie — Mack the Knife — After You've Gone — What a Wonderful World — My Bucket's Got a Hole in It — Tiger Rag — Now You Have Jazz — High Society Calypso — Ole Miss — Perdido — St. Louis Blues — I Love You So — When the Saints Go Marching In

Performers: Louis Armstrong (trumpet and vocals) and the All Stars — including Trummy Young or Tyree Glenn (trombone), Barney Bigard, Joe Darensbourg, or Joe Muryani (clarinet), Billy Kyle or Marty Napoleon (piano), Arvell Shaw, Buddy Catlett, or Billy Cronk (bass), Danny Barcelona (drums), and Velma Middleton (vocals)

One of Armstrong's nicknames was "Ambassador Satch," and this CD helps prove why. His music represented America, and he generously took it all over the world. In the fall of 1960 the U.S. State Department sent him on a forty-five-concert tour of Africa (except for South Africa, where Prime Minister H.F. Verwoerd nixed the visit). In November he was in Katanga, Zaire, where the material on disc 1 was recorded. Tracks 8–17 of disc 2 were recorded in the Congo city of Elisabethville, and 1–7 were recorded in Nice, France. Armstrong here plays mostly the standard All Stars material of the 1950s and 1960s, but he also brought out some of his early music, such as "St. Louis Blues" and "Struttin' with Some Barbecue," first recorded, respectively, in 1925 and 1927. Particularly heartwarming is the audience response, which is nothing short of ecstatic.

24. *Laughin' Louie: Louis Armstrong and His Orchestra 1932–33*

RCA Bluebird ND 9759-2 RB

1989

That's My Home — Hobo, You Can't Ride This Train — When You're Smiling/St. James Infirmary/Dinah — (I'll Be Glad When You're Dead) You Rascal, You/When It's Sleepy Time Down South/Nobody's Sweetheart — I've Got the World on a String — I Gotta Right to Sing the Blues — Hustlin' and Bustlin' for Baby — High Society — He's a Son of the South — Some Sweet Day — Basin Street Blues — Honey, Do! — Mahogany Hall Stomp — Swing, You Cats — Laughin' Louie — Dusky Stevedore — There's a Cabin in the Pines — Sweet Sue, Just You — Don't Play Me Cheap — St. Louis Blues

Performers: Louis Armstrong (trumpet and vocals) and His Orchestra—Edgar Sampson (alto sax and violin), Louis Jordan and Arthur Davey (alto sax), Ellsworth Blake and Elmer Williams (tenor sax), Louis Bacon, Louis Hunt, and Billy Hicks (trumpet), Keg Johnson and Charlie Green (trombone), Ed Hayes (tuba), Elmer James (tuba and string bass), Bud Johnson (clarinet, tenor sax, and vocals), Teddy Wilson and Wesley Robinson (piano), John Trueheart (guitar), Mike McKendrick (banjo and guitar), Bill Oldham (bass, trombone, and tuba), Chick Webb and Benny Hill (drums), and Mezz Mezzrow (bells)

Among these recordings is the novelty title number in which Armstrong does a humorous ad-lib spoken part and plays a remarkable cadenza. Other memorable performances include "Hustlin' and Bustlin' for Baby" and a remake of "St. Louis Blues." A bonus is the rare alternate take of "Hobo, You Can't Ride This Train," Armstrong's depression-era composition that, ironically, was at first sold exclusively by Neiman Marcus. The informative liner notes are by Joe Muranyi, who was five or six years old when these recordings were made in 1932–1933 and who would later play clarinet with the All Stars from mid-1967 to the end in 1971.

25. ***Live at Winter Garden, NY and Blue Note, Chicago***
Storyville 8242
1997

Winter Garden, NY: Intro by Fred Murray – Way Down Yonder in New Orleans – Basin Street Blues – Muskrat Ramble – Dear Old Southland – Do You Know What It Means to Miss New Orleans? – Someday You'll Be Sorry – Tiger Rag

Blue Note, Chicago: Intro – When It's Sleepy Time Down South – Muskrat Ramble – A Song Is Born – Basin Street Blues – St. Louis Blues – High Society – Royal Garden Blues – I Gotta Right to Sing the Blues

Performers: Louis Armstrong (trumpet and vocals) and the All Stars–Jack Teagarden (trombone and vocals), Peanuts Hucko (tenor saxophone and clarinet), Ernie Caceres (baritone and bass saxophones), Bobby Hackett (cornet), Earl Hines and Dick Cary (piano), Jack Lesberg and Arvell Shaw (bass), and Sid Catlett and George Wettling (drums)

Here in two separate radio broadcasts we find Armstrong at a pivotal point in his career, as he turns from the big band format to the small New Orleans combo. In the first (from June 19, 1947) we can hear the recently organized All Stars play the kind of New Orleans music with which Armstrong grew up. The movie *New Orleans* had just come out, and the broadcast was part of its publicity. By the time of the second broadcast (December 11, 1948), the All Stars' routine has been pretty well set. Highlights include the standards ("Basin Street Blues" and "High Society") and Armstrong's own "Someday You'll Be Sorry."

26. ***Louis and the Angels***
Verve 549592
2001

When Did You Leave Heaven? – You're a Heavenly Thing – I Married an Angel – A Sinner Kissed an Angel – Angela Mia – Angel Child – And the Angels Sing – Fools Rush In – I'll String Along with You – Angel – The Prisoner's Song – Good Night, Angel

Performers: Louis Armstrong (trumpet and vocals) with studio chorus and orchestra directed by Sy Oliver

This is one of Armstrong's commercially oriented recordings, yet it has a strong appeal, if initially only to see what he might do with unpromising material. Made in January 1957, in New York City, this album presents a dozen songs, all with either "heaven" or "angel" in their title or lyrics. Ever the professional, Armstrong not only succeeds in making music but also has some fun, especially during "The Prisoner's Song" when he finally gets to the word "angel." Highlights include "I'll String Along with You," "I Married an Angel," and "When Did You Leave Heaven?" Will Friedwald wrote the liner notes.

27. ***Louis and the Good Book***
Universal B00005CDME
2001

Nobody Knows the Trouble I've Seen – Shadrack – Go Down, Moses – Rock My Soul (in the Bosom of Abraham) – Ezekiel Saw De Wheel – On My Way (Got on My Travelin' Shoes) – Down by the Riverside – Swing Low, Sweet Chariot – Sometimes I Feel Like a Motherless Child – Jonah and the Whale – Didn't It Rain – This Train – Sit Down, You're Rockin' the Boat – That's What the Man Said – Shadrack – Going to Shout All Over God's Heaven – Nobody

Knows the Trouble I've Seen – Jonah and the Whale – Elder Eatmore's Sermon on Throwing Stones – Elder Eatmore's Sermon on Generosity

Performers: Louis Armstrong (trumpet and vocals) and the All Stars with the Sy Oliver Choir

Recorded in New York in February 1958, this theme album doesn't offer typical All Stars fare. Not surprisingly, though, Armstrong performs spirituals with the same intimate knowledge as he does popular hits. Also not surprisingly, he gets them to swing. As a bonus this CD reissue includes four recordings (tracks 15–18) made in 1938, plus Armstrong's parodies of a hypocritical and pretentious preacher. Martin Williams's original liner notes are supplemented by Krin Gabbard's essay on Armstrong's religion. In its day, *Louis and the Good Book* was his bestselling LP.

28. *Louis Armstrong: An American Icon*
Hip-O Records 40138, 3 CDs
1998

Disc 1: Do You Know What It Means to Miss New Orleans? – Pennies from Heaven – Linger in My Arms a Little Longer – I Want a Little Girl – Sugar – (What Did I Do to Be So) Black and Blue? – That Lucky Old Sun – You Can't Lose a Broken Heart – That's for Me – My Bucket's Got a Hole in It – La vie en rose – Someday You'll Be Sorry – You Can Depend on Me – Baby, It's Cold Outside – You're Just in Love – If – Gone Fishin' – A Kiss to Build a Dream On – I Get Ideas – Kiss of Fire – Hesitating Blues

Disc 2: Tenderly/You'll Never Walk Alone – When It's Sleepy Time Down South – Basin Street Blues – C'est si bon – Rockin' Chair – Lazy River – Mack the Knife – The Gypsy – That's My Desire – Blueberry Hill – Stars Fell on Alabama – Can't We Be Friends? – If I Could Be with You – I Can't Give You Anything But Love – Body and Soul – On the Sunny Side of the Street – When You're Smiling – I Surrender, Dear

Disc 3: Georgia on My Mind – That's My Home – Memories of You – (Our) Love Is Here to Stay – Gee, Baby, Ain't I Good to You? – I Get a Kick Out of You – Summertime – That Old Feeling – I'll Never Be the Same – What's New? – Sweet Lorraine – Solitude – I Got It Bad – Mood Indigo – Azalea – Hello Dolly! – Mame – Cabaret – What a Wonderful World – Dream a Little Dream of Me – I Guess I'll Get the Papers and Go Home

Performers include: Louis Armstrong (vocals, trumpet), Billie Holiday, Ella Fitzgerald, and Bing Crosby (vocals), Jack Teagarden (trombone), Barney Bigard (clarinet), Earl Hines, Duke Ellington, and Oscar Peterson (piano), Herb Ellis (guitar), Ray Brown and Arvell Shaw (bass), Louis Bellson and Cozy Cole (drums)

These sixty carefully chosen tracks, handsomely packaged with a fifty-two-page booklet, amply document how and why Armstrong was so influential. Included are the signature pieces, such as "Sleepy Time Down South" (performed at virtually every concert), "Sweet Lorraine," "On the Sunny Side of the Street," "Lazy River," "Pennies from Heaven," and "I Can't Give You Anything But Love." There is also a generous sampling of his work with Ella Fitzgerald, Duke Ellington, Billie Holiday, and Oscar Peterson. Finally, there are his megahits, such as "Mack the Knife," "Hello Dolly!" and "What a Wonderful World." Except for the lack of pre-World War II material, this is a wonderful collection. It was included in *Vibe* magazine's 100 Essential Albums of the 20th Century (December 1999 issue, p. 156).

29. ***Louis Armstrong: An American Songbook***
Verve 843615
1991

Stormy Weather – Top Hat, White Tie, and Tails – Have You Met Miss Jones? – Don't Get Around Much Anymore – I Get a Kick Out of You – A Woman Is a Sometime Thing – You're the Top – I Gotta Right to Sing the Blues – Do Nothin' Till You Hear from Me – Little Girl Blue – Let's Do It (Let's Fall in Love) – There's a Boat Dat's Leavin' Soon for New York

Performers: Louis Armstrong (trumpet and vocals) with various artists and ensembles

Armstrong remains the only major figure in Western culture to influence the music of his time equally as an instrumentalist and as a singer, and this interactive CD makes the case. In addition to photographs, there are rare interview segments with Armstrong, along with visual profiles of Duke Ellington, George and Ira Gershwin, Cole Porter, and others. The audio portion is compatible with any CD player.

30. ***Louis Armstrong and Earl Hines***
Columbia/Legacy CK 45142
1989

Chicago Breakdown – Symphonic Raps – Savoyagers' Stomp – West End Blues – Sugar Foot Strut – Two Deuces – Squeeze Me – Knee Drops – No (Papa, No) – Basin Street Blues – No One Else But You – Beau Koo Jack – Save It, Pretty Mama – Weather Bird – Muggles – Hear Me Talkin' to Ya – St. James Infirmary – Tight Like This

Performers: Louis Armstrong (cornet, trumpet, and vocals) and Earl Hines (piano, celeste, and vocals) with various ensembles

In 1927–1928, Hines and Armstrong made around three dozen recordings together. Armstrong had at that time put together a new, more modern version of the Hot Five, and the felicitous results were soon noticeable in "West End Blues" and "Basin Street Blues." Although Hines contributes some sparkling passage work to the former and an evocative celeste solo to open the latter, his artistry can best be heard on "Two Deuces," "Save It, Pretty Mama," and a few others. "Weather Bird" is their most famous collaboration and some say the most famous recorded jazz duet.

31. ***Louis Armstrong and His Friends***
Bluebird 63961-2
2002

We Shall Overcome – Everybody's Talkin' – What a Wonderful World – Boy from New Orleans – The Creator Has a Master Plan – Give Peace a Chance – Mood Indigo – His Father Wore Long Hair – My One and Only Love – This Black Cat Has Nine Lives – Here Is My Heart for Christmas – The Creator Has a Master Plan (Peace) – The Creator Has a Master Plan (Peace)

Performers include: Louis Armstrong (vocals), Tony Bennett (vocals), Ruby Braff (trumpet), Eddie Condon (guitar), and Miles Davis (trumpet) with ensemble conducted by Oliver Nelson

Recorded in New York, May 26-29, 1970, this is Armstrong's penultimate album. (His last was a country and western production with Nashville artists, and his *very* last recording was a reading of Clement Moore's classic "The Night before Christmas.") It was a warm-hearted event featuring some jazz giants and issued on the occasion of Armstrong's birthday party at the Newport Jazz Festival in July. A large ensemble (including a full set of strings) backed him on "What a Wonderful World," and other classics, as well as some mediocre selections such as "His Father Wore Long Hair." On "We Shall Overcome," Armstrong was joined by horn players Ruby Braff, Miles Davis, and Bobby Hackett, singer Tony Bennett, and among many others singing as well, critic Stanley Dance and producer George Wein. Those involved recall it as a very moving occasion. This CD reissue adds three bonus tracks: "Here Is My Heart for Christmas" and two previously unissued alternate mixes/edits of "The Creator Has a Master Plan." Willard Jenkins and Stanley Dance both contribute liner notes.

32. *Louis Armstrong and His Friends*

GNP/Crescendo GNPD 11002
1993

When It's Sleepy Time Down South – Royal Garden Blues – Blueberry Hill – Way Down Yonder in New Orleans – Basin Street Blues – Baby, Won't You Please Come Home? – Rockin' Chair – Back o' Town Blues – Steak Face – I Gotta Right to Sing the Blues – I Get Ideas – Because of You – Lover's Leap

Performers: Louis Armstrong (trumpet and vocals), Jack Teagarden (trombone and vocals), Barney Bigard (clarinet), Charlie Lavere (piano), Morty Korb (bass), Nick Fatool (drums); the Les Brown Band in selections 11 and 13

Although recorded live (at the Pasadena Civic Auditorium, California, in 1951), this album has surprisingly good sound quality. Armstrong and friends play a mixture of classic hits, such as "Blueberry Hill" and lesser-known (at the time) gems, such as "Back o' Town Blues." The enthusiastic audience goes wild when the Les Brown Band joins in on "I Get Ideas" and "Lover's Leap." This generous CD includes liner notes by Dave Dexter, Jr.

33. *Louis Armstrong and Friends: What a Wonderful Christmas*

Hip-O Records 40065
1997

Christmas in New Orleans (Armstrong with the Benny Carter Orchestra) – White Christmas (Armstrong with the Gordon Jenkins Orchestra) – Silent Night (vocalist Dinah Washington) – The Christmas Song (vocalist Mel Torme) – Santa Baby (vocalist Eartha Kitt) – Christmas Night in Harlem (Armstrong with the Benny Carter Orchestra) – It's Christmas Time Again (vocalist Peggy Lee) – Cool Yule (Armstrong and the Commanders) – Merry Christmas, Baby (vocalist Sonny Parker) – 'Zat You, Santa Claus? (Armstrong and the Commanders) – Jingle Bells (Duke Ellington and His Orchestra) – Santa Claus Is Coming to Town (vocalist Lena Horne) – May Every Day Be Christmas (Louis Jordan and His Orchestra) – Winter Wonderland (Armstrong with Gordon Jenkins Orchestra)

Armstrong appears on only six of these fourteen tracks, but they are excellent performances, especially the playfully spooky " 'Zat You, Santa Claus?" and the tender "White Christmas." Outstanding among the other performances are Mel Tormé's "The Christmas Song," Eartha Kitt's "Santa Baby," and Peggy Lee's "It's Christmas Time Again." (Lee was called upon to sing "The Lord's Prayer" at Armstrong's funeral on July 9, 1971, at the Congregational Church in Corona.)

34. *Louis Armstrong and His Orchestra, Vol. 2 (1936–38): Heart Full of Rhythm*

Decca Jazz 620
1993

I Come from a Musical Family – Somebody Stole My Break – If We Never Meet Again – Lyin' to Myself – Ev'ntide – Swing That

Music – Mahogany Hall Stomp – The Skeleton in the Closet – Dippermouth Blues – Swing That Music – Public Melody Number One – Yours and Mine – Alexander's Ragtime Band – I've Got a Heart Full of Rhythm – Sun Showers – Once in a While – On the Sunny Side of the Street – Satchel Mouth Swing – Jubilee – Struttin' with Some Barbecue

Performers: Louis Armstrong (trumpet and vocals) and His Orchestra–Henry Jones, Charlie Holmes, and Pete Clark (alto saxophone), Bingie Madison and Albert Nicholas (tenor saxophone and clarinet), Greely Walton (tenor saxophone), Leonard Davis, Gus Aiken, Red Allen, and Shelton Hemphill (trumpet), Harry White, Snub Mosley, James Archey, J.C. Higginbotham, and Wilbur de Paris (trombone), Luis Russell (piano), Lee Blair (guitar), Pops Foster and Red Callender (bass), Paul Barbarin (drums); also Jimmy Dorsey and His Orchestra–Jimmy Dorsey and Jack Stacey (alto saxophone, clarinet), Fud Livingston and Skeets Hurfurt (tenor saxophone, clarinet), George Thow and Toots Camarata (trumpet), Bobby Byrne, Joe Yukl, and Don Mattison (trombone), Bobby Van Epps (piano), Roscoe Hillman (guitar), Jim Taft (bass), and Ray McKinley (drums)

Armstrong had recorded some of these numbers with a small, New Orleans–style ensemble during the previous decade, and by comparison he now plays in the more relaxed swing style. Having worked with Fletcher Henderson (one of the originators of the big band sound) in 1924–1925, Armstrong knew what dancers liked. There is some outstanding playing here by sidemen such as Albert Nicholas, Pops Foster, and J.C. Higginbotham. The fifteen-page program book is by Richard Sudhalter.

35. *Louis Armstrong and King Oliver*
Milestone Records 47017
1992

Just Gone – Canal Street Blues – Mandy Lee Blues – I'm Going Away to Wear You Off My Mind – Chimes Blues – Weather Bird Rag – Dippermouth Blues – Froggie Moore Rag – Snake Rag – Alligator Hop – Zulu's Ball – Working Man Blues – Krooked Blues – Mabel's Dream – Mabel's Dream (alternate take) – Southern Stomp – Southern Stomp (alternate take) – Riverside Blues – Texas Moaner Blues – Of All the Wrongs You've Done to Me – Terrible Blues – Santa Claus Blues – Nobody Knows the Way I Feel This Morning – Early Every Morn – Cake Walking Babies (from Home)

Performers: Louis Armstrong and King Oliver (cornet), Alberta Hunter and Clarence Todd (vocals), Stump Evans (C-melody saxophone), Charlie Johnson (bass saxophone), Charlie Irvis, Honore Dutrey, and Aaron Thompson (trombone), Sidney Bechet (clarinet and soprano saxophone), Buster Bailey and Johnny Dodds (clarinet), Lil Hardin Armstrong (piano), Buddy Christian, Johnny St. Cyr, and Bill Johnson (banjo), and Baby Dodds (drums)

Recorded between 1923 and 1925, these selections represent some of the first jazz masterpieces. Armstrong plays second cornet to his mentor, King Oliver, and generally stays in the background. This is literally as well as figuratively so, since Armstrong's sound was so big that he had to stand in the farthest corner of the recording studio. Other outstanding players here are Johnny Dodds and Sidney Bechet. On tracks 1–18, made in 1923, Oliver leads his Creole Jazz Band, and on tracks 19–25, made the following year, Armstrong leads the Red Onion Jazz Babies. This nicely engineered CD includes the original 1974 LP liner notes by Ralph J. Gleason.

36. ***Louis Armstrong and the Blues Singers***
Affinity AFS 1018, 6 CDs
1991

Disc 1: Ma Rainey and her Georgia Jazz Band: See See Rider – See See Rider (alternate take) – Jelly Bean Blues – Countin' the Blues – Countin' the Blues (alternate take); Virginia Liston with Clarence Williams' Blue Five: Early in the Morning – You've Got the Right Key But the Wrong Keyhole; Eva Taylor with Clarence Williams' Blue Five: Of All the Wrongs You've Done to Me – Everybody Loves My Baby (But My Baby Don't Love Nobody But Me); Alberta Hunter with The Red Onion Jazz Babies: Everybody Loves My Baby (But My Baby Don't Love Nobody But Me) – Texas Moaner Blues; Margaret Johnson with Clarence Williams' Blue Five: Papa, Mama's All Alone – Changeable Daddy of Mine; Sippie Wallace with Clarence Williams' Blue Five: Baby, I Can't Use You No More – Trouble Everywhere I Roam; Maggie Jones: Poor House Blues – Anybody Here Want to Try My Cabbage? – Thunderstorm Blues – If I Lose, Let Me Lose – Screamin' the Blues – Good Time Flat Blues

Disc 2: Eva Taylor with Clarence Williams' Blue Five: Mandy, Make Up Your Mind – I'm a Little Blackbird Looking for a Little Bluebird – Cake Walking Babies (from Home) – Pickin' on Your Baby – Cast Away – Papa De Da Da; Alberta Hunter with The Red Onion Jazz Babies: Nobody Knows the Way I Feel This Morning – Early Every Morn' – Cake Walking Babies (from Home); Clara Smith: Nobody Knows the Way I Feel 'Dis Morning – Broken Busted Blues; Bessie Smith: St. Louis Blues – Reckless Blues – Sobbin' Hearted Blues – Cold in Hand Blues – You've Been a Good Ole Wagon; Trixie Smith and her Down Home Sycopators: You've Got to Beat Me to Keep Me – Mining Camp Blues – Mining Camp Blues (alternate take)

Disc 3: Trixie Smith and her Down Home Syncopators: The World's Jazz Crazy (and So Am I) – The World's Jazz Crazy (and So Am I) (alternate take) – The Railroad Blues – The Railroad Blues (alternate take); Clara Smith: Shipwrecked Blues – Court House Blues – Court House Blues (alternate take) – My John Blues; Bessie Smith: Nashville Woman's Blues – Nashville Woman's Blues (alternate take) – Careless Love Blues – Careless Love Blues (alternate take) – J.C. Holmes Blues – I Ain't Gonna Play No Second Fiddle (If I Can Play the Lead); Billy Jones with the Southern Serenaders: I Miss My Swiss; Grant and Wilson with the Fletcher Henderson Orchestra: You Dirty Mistreater – Come on, Coot, Do That Thing – Have Your Chill, I'll Be Here When Your Fever Rises – Find Me at the Greasy Spoon (If You Miss Me Here) – Find Me at the Greasy Spoon (If You Miss Me Here) (alternate take)

Disc 4: Eva Taylor with Clarence Williams' Blue Five: Just Wait 'Til You See My Baby Do the Charleston – Livin' High – Coal Cart Blues – Santa Claus Blues – Squeeze Me – You Can't Shush Katie (the Gabbiest Girl in Town); Eva Taylor with Clarence Williams' Trio: Santa Claus Blues; Perry Bradford's Jazz Phools: Lucy Long – I Ain't Gonna Play No Second Fiddle (If I Can Play the Lead); Bertha "Chippie" Hill: Low Land Blues – Kid Man Blues – Lonesome, All Alone and Blue – Trouble in Mind – A Georgia Man; Blanche Calloway: Lazy Woman Blues – Lonesome Lovesick Blues; Hociel Thomas with Louis Armstrong's Jazz Four: Gambler's Dream – Sunshine Baby – Adam and Eve Had the Blues – Put It Where I Can Get It – Washwoman Blues – I've Stopped My Man

Disc 5: Baby Mack: You've Got to Go Home on Time – What Kind o' Man Is That?; Hociel Thomas: Deep Water Blues – G'wan, I Told You – Listen to Ma – Lonesome Hours; Sippie Wallace: A Jealous

Woman Like Me – Special Delivery Blues – Jack o'Diamond Blues – The Mail Train Blues – I Feel Good – A Man for Every Day in the Week; Nolan Welsh: The Bridwell Blues – St. Peter Blues; Butterbeans and Susie: He Likes It Slow; Bertha "Chippie" Hill: Pleadin' for the Blues – Pratt City Blues – Mess, Katie, Mess – Lovesick Blues – Lonesome Weary Blues

Disc 6: Sippie Wallace: Dead Drunk Blues – Have You Ever Been Down? – Lazy Man Blues – The Flood Blues; Lillie Delk Christian with Louis Armstrong's Hot Four: You're a Real Sweetheart – Too Busy – Was It a Dream? – Last Night I Dreamed You Kissed Me – I Can't Give You Anything But Love – Baby – Sweethearts on Parade – I Must Have That Man; Seger Ellis: S'posin' – To Be in Love – Ain't Misbehavin'; Victoria Spivey: Funny Feathers – How Do You Do It That Way?; Jimmie Rodgers: Blue Yodel No. 9 (Standin' on the Corner)

Armstrong's collaboration with Bessie Smith is well known (although it is not well known that she preferred trumpeter Joe Smith as an accompanist, perhaps feeling that Armstrong verged on outshining her), but he worked with many other singers when he was coming up in the 1920s. This excellent collection fills out the picture. Here are sessions with the other two Smiths, Clara and Trixie, as well as Chippie Hill, Alberta Hunter, and Ma Rainey. Also included are the vaudeville-oriented Butterbeans and Susie, Eva Taylor, and Lillie Delk Christian. With this last singer, Armstrong brings his Hot Four. One of the many bonuses is "Blue Yodel No. 9," made with country music pioneer Jimmie Rodgers. Nicely packaged with a lengthy booklet, this collection is well worth looking for.

37. *Louis Armstrong Meets Oscar Peterson*

Verve 825713-2
1997

That Old Feeling – Let's Fall in Love – I'll Never Be the Same – Blues in the Night (My Mama Done Tol' Me) – How Long Has This Been Going On? – I Was Doing All Right – What's New? – Moon Song – Just One of Those Things – There's No You – You Go to My Head – Sweet Lorraine – I Get a Kick Out of You – Makin' Whoopee – Willow Weep for Me – Let's Do It

Performers: Louis Armstrong (trumpet and vocals), Oscar Peterson (piano), Herb Ellis (guitar), Ray Brown (bass), and Louie Bellson (drums)

Recorded at the Capitol Studios in Hollywood on July 31 and October 14, 1957, this digitally remastered CD features the older Armstrong firmly supported by the strong playing of the young Peterson and his group. The slower songs ("You Go to My Head," "Sweet Lorraine") are the most successful, but the brisk, playful "Let's Fall in Love" is also a gem. As in other recordings of this period (e.g., the contemporaneous sessions with Ella Fitzgerald, accompanied by the same ensemble), the focus is on Armstrong's singing. Armstrong friend Leonard Feather supplies succinct, informative liner program notes.

38. *Louis Armstrong Plays W.C. Handy*

Columbia/Legacy CK 64925
1997

St. Louis Blues – Yellow Dog Blues – Loveless Love – Aunt Hagar's Blues – Long Gone (from Bowlin' Green) – The Memphis Blues – Beale Street Blues – Ole Miss Blues – Chantez les bas (Sing 'em Low) – Hesitating Blues – Atlanta Blues – George

Avakian's interview with W.C. Handy — Loveless Love (rehearsal sequence) — Hesitating Blues (rehearsal sequence) — Alligator Story — Long Gone (from Bowlin' Green) (rehearsal sequence)

Performers: Louis Armstrong (trumpet and vocals) and the All Stars—Trummy Young (trombone), Barney Bigard (clarinet), Billy Kyle (piano), Arvell Shaw (bass), Barrett Deems (drums), and Velma Middleton (vocals)

Originally released in October 1954, this CD reissue features three previously unreleased rehearsal sequences, an interview with Handy, and Armstrong telling his delightful alligator anecdote. However, what makes this recording a classic (and for many a desert island choice) is the playing and singing of the leader. Armstrong clearly had a profound admiration for Handy's compositions. At this time in the early to mid-1950s, Armstrong was overworked and often tired, but he nevertheless had the power to transcend. The original recording and CD reissue were both produced by George Avakian, who contributes the liner notes, which contain some excellent photographs.

39. ***Louis Armstrong's All Time Greatest Hits***

MCA Records 11032

1994

What a Wonderful World — Hello Dolly! — Sittin' in the Sun — Mack the Knife (theme from *Three Penny Opera*) — A Kiss to Build a Dream On — It Takes Two to Tango — That Lucky Old Sun — Kiss of Fire — I Get Ideas — Gone Fishin' (with Bing Crosby) — Skokiaan — La vie en rose — The Dummy Song — Chloe — I Still Get Jealous — When You're Smiling — Blueberry Hill — When It's Sleepy Time Down South

Performers: Louis Armstrong (trumpet and vocals) with various ensembles

This is one of the better "best of" Armstrong CDs. Although "Dippermouth Blues," "Struttin' with Some Barbecue," and "West End Blues" are missing, the commercially successful hits—"What a Wonderful World," "Hello Dolly!," "A Kiss to Build a Dream On," and "When You're Smiling"—are all here, nicely remastered, together with an essay by Will Friedwald and discographical information from Hans Westerberg's sourcebook.

40. ***Louis Armstrong Sings Back Through the Years***

MCA Records 112225, 2 CDs

2000

Disc 1: What a Wonderful World — Cabaret — Moon River — Hello Dolly! — Memories of You — Georgia on My Mind — When You're Smiling — Some of These Days — Exactly Like You — On the Sunny Side of the Street — Body and Soul — I Can't Give You Anything But Love — If I Could Be with You — Lazy River — I Can't Believe That You're in Love with Me — Basin Street Blues — The Gypsy — (I'll Be Glad When You're Dead) You Rascal, You — La vie en rose — I Surrender, Dear — You Can't Lose a Broken Heart — That Lucky Old Sun — Blueberry Hill — That's My Desire — I Wonder — I'm Confessin' (That I Love You) — Jeepers Creepers — Ain't Misbehavin' — The Song Is Ended

Disc 2: Someday You'll Be Sorry — Your Cheatin' Heart — A Kiss to Build a Dream On — Gone Fishin' — Dream a Little Dream of Me — (I'll Be Glad When You're Dead) You Rascal, You — La vie en rose — I Surrender, Dear — You Can't Lose a Broken Heart — That Lucky Old Sun — Blueberry Hill — That's My Desire — I Wonder — I'm Confessin' (That I Love You) — Jeepers Creepers — Ain't Misbehavin' — The Song Is Ended

Performers: Louis Armstrong (vocals and trumpet) with various vocalists, instrumentalists, and ensembles

This centennial collection focuses on Armstrong's vocals and his contribution to popular singing during thirty of his prime years (1938 to 1967). The producer has interestingly arranged these tracks in reverse chronological order, taking the album's title literally. Only the first four tracks are from the 1960s. These and the remaining thirty tracks amply demonstrate Armstrong's unique vocal style. For example, on "I Can't Give You Anything But Love," he sings key words such as "love" and especially "baby" with a rough coloring that brings out inner meanings. He also likes to recompose melodies, such as on "Basin Street Blues" when he delivers large portions of text on the same pitch. And everywhere, anywhere, and anytime, he creates that inimitable swing quality by singing either head of or behind (rarely on) the beat. Especially fun are Armstrong's duets with Bing Crosby, Billie Holiday, and Louis Jordan. This package features conscientiously remastered sound, a twenty-page booklet with rare photos, and detailed liner notes by Will Friedwald.

41. *Louis Sings, Armstrong Plays: 1935–1942*

Jasmine Records 2547
1998

I'm in the Mood for Love – You Are My Lucky Star – I've Got My Fingers Crossed – I'm Shooting High – Red Sails in the Sunset – On Treasure Island – Thanks a Million – Shoe Shine Boy – I'm Putting All My Eggs in One Basket – If We Never Meet Again – Pennies from Heaven (with Frances Langford and Bing Crosby) – Once in a While – On the Sunny Side of the Street – I Double Dare You – On the Sentimental Side – It's Wonderful – Love Walked In – I've Got a Pocketful of Dreams – I Can't Give You Anything But Love – Ain't Misbehavin' – Jeepers Creepers – I'm Confessin' (That I Love You) – I Cover the Waterfront – I Never Knew

Performers include: Louis Armstrong (vocals and trumpet), Frances Langford and Bing Crosby (vocals), Rupert Cole (alto saxophone and clarinet), Charlie Holmes and Phil Waltzer (alto saxophone), Bingie Madison and Albert Nicholas (tenor saxophone, clarinet), Greely Walton and Paul Ricci (tenor saxophone), Sid Trucker (baritone saxophone and clarinet), Prince Robinson (clarinet), Leonard Davis, Gus Aiken, Louis Bacon, Bunny Berigan, Bob Mayhew, Shelton Hemphill, and Red Allen (trumpet), Harry White, Jimmy Archey, Al Philburn, J.C. Higginbotham, and Wilbur De Paris (trombone), Paul Barbarin (vibraphone and drums), Luis Russell and Fulton McGrath (piano), Lee Blair, Dave Barbour, and Lawrence Lucie (guitar), Pops Foster, Pete Peterson, Red Callender, and John Simmons (bass), and Sidney Catlett (drums)

Recorded in New York and Los Angeles, the music on this CD represents Armstrong toward the end of his big band period and before the formation of the All Stars. Highlights include "I'm Putting All My Eggs in One Basket," "I Can't Give You Anything But Love," and "Pennies from Heaven." The result is a cross section of the American songbook. Included are liner notes by Paul Pelletier.

42. *Love Songs*

Columbia/Legacy CK62219
2000

I'm Crazy 'bout My Baby and My Baby's Crazy 'bout Me – Keepin' Out of Mischief Now – I Can't Give You Anything But Love – Squeeze Me – Body and Soul – I'm Confessin' (That I Love You) – Honeysuckle Rose – I've Got a Feeling I'm Falling – One

Moment Worth Years – My Sweet – I'm in the Market for You – If I Could Be with You – Ko Ko Mo (I Love You So) – All of Me – I Didn't Know Until You Told Me

Performers: Louis Armstrong (trumpet and vocals) with Carmen McRae (vocals), Dave Brubeck (piano), Lionel Hampton (vibraphone), Barney Bigard (clarinet), Velma Middleton (vocals), Eddie Condon (guitar), Billy Kyle (piano), Joe Turner (vocals), and others

What might have been an occasion for the repackaging of familiar material, this turns out to be a substantial CD of songs recorded between 1929 and 1961. "Honeysuckle Rose" and four other numbers come from the 1955 *Satch Plays Fats* album; "One Moment Worth Years" and "I Didn't Know Until You Told Me" come from the hard-to-find *The Real Ambassadors;* and Velma Middleton's "Ko Ko Mo (I Love You So)," previously unreleased, is from the 1958 Newport Jazz Festival.

43. *Mack the Knife*
Pablo Records 941
1991

When It's Sleepy Time Down South – Indiana – Now You Has Jazz – High Society Calypso – Mahogany Hall Stomp – Blue Moon – Sweet Georgia Brown – Riff Blues – Mack the Knife – Lazy River – Stompin' at the Savoy

Performers: Louis Armstrong (trumpet and vocals) and the All Stars—Trummy Young (trombone), Edmund Hall (clarinet), Velma Middleton (vocals), Billy Kyle (piano), Squire Gersh (bass), and Barrett Deems (drums)

One would never know from this enthusiastic recording from the July, 4, 1957, Newport Jazz Festival/Armstrong Birthday concert that there had been a major altercation back stage beforehand. The promoters wanted Armstrong to appear with a group of assorted musicians from his past rather than his regular All Stars, and they also wanted him to give his longtime vocalist Velma Middleton the night off. Always protective of his sidemen, Armstrong put his foot down. Hard. And he prevailed. However, consummate professional that he was, he does not admit a trace of storm and stress in his performance. He joyously goes through his usual program, highlighted on this occasion by "Now You Has Jazz" from the recently released movie *High Society* and his current hit "Mack the Knife." The package comes with notes by Stanley Dance.

44. *The Masters: Louis Armstrong*
Eagle Rock 397, 2 CDs
1997

Disc 1: Heebie Jeebies – Star Dust – Tight Like This – I'm Confessin' (That I Love You) – Dinah – St. Louis Blues – I'm a Ding Dong Daddy (from Dumas) – Hobo, You Can't Ride This Train – When It's Sleepy Time Down South – I Gotta Right to Sing the Blues – Basin Street Blues – Swing That Music – Jeepers Creepers – Down in Honky Tonk Town – I'm in the Mood for Love – Savoy Blues – That Rhythm Man – Body and Soul

Disc 2: Rockin' Chair – Keyhole Blues – I Ain't Got Nobody – Big Butter and Egg Man – You Made Me Love You – Potato Head Blues – Willie the Weeper – Jazz Lips – Muskrat Ramble – St. James Infirmary – I'm in the Market for You – Memories of You – You're Lucky to Me – I Hope Gabriel Likes My Music – Between the Devil and the Deep Blue Sea – That's My Home – Dippermouth Blues – Lawd, You Made the Night Too Long

Performers: Louis Armstrong (trumpet and vocals) with various ensembles

Armstrong compilations either focus on certain periods of his career or present highlights from the entire fifty-year span. This one tries to do the latter in thirty-six tracks, and the result is fairly successful. Although many of his best-known recordings are ignored (e.g., "West End Blues"), those included provide a detailed sketch if not a complete picture of his genius. The set also turns an occasional spotlight on Armstrong sidemen, such as clarinetist Barney Bigard, his singer Velma Middleton, and his trombonist/friend/foil Jack Teagarden. Included are liner notes by John Voysey.

45. *Now You Has Jazz: Louis Armstrong at M-G-M*

Rhino Records R2-72827
1997

From *The Strip* (1950): Ain't Misbehavin' – One o'Clock Jump – Ole Miss Blues – Basin Street Blues – I'm Coming, Virginia – A Kiss to Build a Dream On – Shadrack/When the Saints Go Marching In – That's a Plenty – Hines' Retreat – Fatha's Time – J.T. Jive; from *Cabin in the Sky* (1942): Ain't It the Truth?; from *Glory Alley* (1951): That's What the Man Said – Glory Alley – Oh, Didn't He Ramble? – South Rampart Street Parade – Flee as a Bird – It's a Most Unusual Day; from *High Society* (1956): High Society Calypso – Little One – I Love You, Samantha – Now You Has Jazz; from *When the Boys Meet the Girls* (1965): Throw It Out of Your Mind – I Got Rhythm

Performers: Louis Armstrong (trumpet and vocals), Jack Teagarden and Bing Crosby (vocals), and various ensembles

Armstrong was the first African American to be featured regularly (over two dozen credits) in major motion pictures. This collection focuses on the five musicals he made for MGM studios between 1942 and 1965. Along with hits such as the popular "High Society Calypso," here are several numbers that ended up on the cutting room floor (e.g., "Ain't It the Truth?" from *Cabin in the Sky*). While some fans might be embarrassed by Armstrong's clownish mugging, everyone can be proud that he was the first to bring real jazz to the silver screen. The package comes with twenty-four pages of informative liner notes by Will Friedwald.

46. *Paris Jazz Concert*

Malaco Jazz 1206
1999

When It's Sleepy Time Down South – Indiana – A Kiss to Build a Dream On – My Bucket's Got a Hole in It – Tiger Rag – Now You Has Jazz – High Society – Ole Miss – When I Grow Too Old to Dream – Tin Roof Blues – Yellow Dog Blues – When the Saints Go Marching In – Struttin' with Some Barbecue – Nobody Knows the Trouble I've Seen – Blueberry Hill – The Faithful Hussar – St. Louis Blues – After You've Gone – Mack the Knife

Performers: Louis Armstrong (trumpet and vocals) and the All Stars—Trummy Young (trombone), Joe Darensbourg (clarinet), Billy Kyle (piano), Billy Cronk (bass), Danny Barcelona (drums), and Jewel Brown (vocals)

Made in Paris on April 24, 1962, this is one of the better live concert recordings from the last decade of Armstrong's life. He and the All Stars offer the usual crowd-pleasing mixture of vintage gems such as "Struttin' with Some Barbecue," Hollywood hits such as "High Society," and signature numbers such as "Mack the Knife." There is some delightful interplay between Armstrong and trombonist Trummy Young, and other sidemen get a chance to shine too: Pianist Billy Kyle does a lengthy introduction to "When

I Grow Too Old to Dream" and vocalist Jewel Brown a passionate "St. Louis Blues." The liner notes are by Michel Laverdure.

47. *Pops: The 1940s Small Band Sides*
RCA Bluebird 6378-2-RB11
1987

I Want a Little Girl – Sugar – Blues for Yesterday – Blues in the South – Do You Know What It Means to Miss New Orleans? – Where the Blues Were Born in New Orleans – Mahogany Hall Stomp – Ain't Misbehavin' – Rockin' Chair – Back o' Town Blues – Save It, Pretty Mama – St. James Infirmary – Jack Armstrong Blues – Rockin' Chair – Someday You'll Be Sorry – Fifty-Fifty Blues – A Song Was Born – Please Stop Playing Those Blues, Boy – Before Long – Lovely Weather We're Having

Performers include: Louis Armstrong (trumpet and vocals) with various artists and ensembles

These twenty selections were all recorded right around the year 1947, when Armstrong was in the film *New Orleans,* broke up his big band, and formed the All Stars (with which he performed for the rest of his life). Five selections are from the landmark Town Hall concert of May 17. Armstrong is in top form, whether doing relaxed standards ("Ain't Misbehavin' ") or New Orleans gems ("Mahogany Hall Stomp"). He also teams up happily with his old boss, trombonist Kid Ory, and his good friend, trombonist Jack Teagarden. Dan Morgenstern contributed the liner notes.

48. *Portrait of the Artist as a Young Man: 1923–34*
Columbia/Legacy 57176, 4 CDs
1994

Disc 1: Chimes Blues – Snake Rag – Tears – Texas Moaner Blues – Everybody Loves My Baby – Naughty Man – Changeable Daddy of Mine – Anybody Here Want to Try My Cabbage? – Good Time Flat Blues – Cake Walking Babies (from Home) – Pickin' on Your Baby – St. Louis Blues – Sobbin' Hearted Blues – Papa De Da Da – Sugar Foot Stomp – Alone at Last – T.N.T. – You Can't Shush Katie (the Gabbiest Girl in Town) – Low Land Blues – Gut Bucket Blues

Disc 2: Listen to Ma – Heebie Jeebies – Cornet Chop Suey – Stomp Off, Let's Go – The Bridwell Blues – King of the Zulus – Skid-Dat-De-Dat – Big Butter and Egg Man – Pleadin' for the Blues – Wild Man Blues – Chicago Breakdown – Potato Head Blues – Weary Blues – Gully Low Blues – Put 'em Down Blues – Struttin' with Some Barbecue – Hotter Than That – Savoy Blues – Too Busy – Skip the Gutter

Disc 3: A Monday Date – West End Blues – Two Deuces – Symphonic Raps – Basin Street Blues – No One Else But You – Beau Koo Jack – Weather Bird – Muggles – I Must Have That Man – Tight Like This – Knockin' a Jug – I Can't Give You Anything But Love – Mahogany Hall Stomp – To Be in Love – Ain't Misbehavin' – (What Did I Do to Be So) Black and Blue? – That Rhythm Man – When You're Smiling – St. Louis Blues (alternate take)

Disc 4: Song of the Islands – My Sweet – I Can't Believe That You're in Love with Me – Blue Yodel No. 9 (Standin' on the Corner) – I'm a Ding Dong Daddy (from Dumas) – I'm Confessin' (That I Love You) – Memories of You – Sweethearts on Parade – When It's Sleepy Time Down South – Blue Again – When Your Lover Has Gone – Lazy River – Chinatown, My Chinatown – Star Dust – Star Dust (alternate take) – Between the Devil and the Deep Blue Sea – I've Got the World on a String – Basin Street Blues – On the Sunny Side of the Street – Song of the Vipers

Performers include: Louis Armstrong (cornet, trumpet, and vocals) with various artists and ensembles

With eighty-one well-chosen and well-engineered tracks, a chronological arrangement, and an illustrated eighty-page book of notes, it is not surprising that this collection was a 1995 Grammy nominee for Best Historical Album and the winner of the Grammy for Best Album Notes. Here is the first recorded decade of Armstrong's career, beginning with his work as a sideman with King Oliver, Fletcher Henderson, and Bessie Smith, then moving on to his leadership of the Hot Five, the Hot Seven, and finally the Louis Armstrong Orchestra. This set would be an excellent place to start an Armstrong collection, especially for those who only know the innovative "King of the Trumpet" from the work of his later, more commercial years.

49. *Radio Days*
Moon Records 8556
1995

Theme and Intro – Coquette – I've Got a Gal in Kalamazoo – Slender, Tender, and Tall – Dear Old Southland – Lazy River – You Can't Get Stuff in Your Cuff – Brother Bill – On the Sunny Side of the Street – Theme and Intro – Accentuate the Positive – Robin Hood – Sentimental Journey – On the Sunny Side of the Street – I Wonder – Saturday Night – Blue Skies – What's Your Hurry?

Performers: Louis Armstrong (trumpet and vocals) and His Orchestra–George Washington (vocals and trombone), Ann Baker (vocals), Rupert Cole and Carl Frye (alto saxophone), Prince Robinson and Joe Garland (tenor saxophone and clarinet), Frank Galbreath, Shelton Hemphill, and Bernard Flood (trumpet), James Whitney and Henderson Chambers (trombone), Luis Russell (piano), Lawrence Lucie (guitar), John Simmons (bass), and Sidney Catlett (drums); with Frank Sinatra and Ella Mae Morse (vocals) and Alvino Rey (steel guitar)

Recorded live in Los Angeles in 1943 and 1945, this CD is a time capsule consisting of two edited programs for the Armed Forces Radio Service. Between selections, emcee Ernie Whitmas makes announcements, Armstrong jokes with the guest vocalists, and everyone expresses support for the troops overseas. Outstanding are Armstrong's performances of "Lazy River," "Accentuate the Positive," and "I Wonder." He pairs up memorably with Sinatra on "Blue Skies." Guaranteed to inspire nostalgia, whether you were around to hear the original or not.

50. *The Real Ambassadors*
Columbia/Legacy CK 57663
1994

Everybody's Comin' – Cultural Exchange – Good Reviews – Remember Who You Are – My One Bad Habit – Lonesome – Summer Song – King for a Day – Blow Satchmo – The Real Ambassadors – Nomad – In the Lurch – One Moment Worth Years – You Swing, Baby (The Duke) – Summer Song – They Say I Look Like God – I Didn't Know Until You Told Me – Since Love Had Its Way – Easy as You Go – Swing Bells/Blow Satchmo/Finale

Performers: Louis Armstrong (trumpet and vocals), Dave Brubeck (piano), Carmen McRae, Dave Lambert, Jon Hendricks, and Annie Ross (vocals), Trummy Young (trombone, vocals), Joe Darensbourg (clarinet), Billy Kyle (piano), Gene Wright and Irving Manning (bass), Joe Morello and Danny Barcelona (drums)

Recorded in July and September 1961, and performed the following summer at the

Monterey Jazz Festival, this jazz oratorio was the brain child of Dave and Iola Brubeck, who originally set out to write a Broadway show. They had become incensed at how Armstrong, frequently an official jazz ambassador to the world, could still be refused service in his own country. Also, in 1960 both Brubeck and Armstrong had their southern U.S. tours canceled once the promoters discovered that their bands were racially mixed. Such discrimination was the inspiration for the work. Brubeck (who like Armstrong was represented by Joe Glaser) tells the full story to Chip Stern in the liner notes.

51. *Rhythm Saved the World*

Decca Jazz GRD-602
1991

I'm in the Mood for Love – You Are My Lucky Star – La Cucaracha – Got a Bran' New Suit – I've Got My Fingers Crossed – Old Man Mose – Old Man Mose (alternate take) – I'm Shooting High – Falling in Love with You – Red Sails in the Sunset – On Treasure Island – Thanks a Million – Shoe Shine Boy – Solitude – Solitude (alternate take) – I Hope Gabriel Likes My Music – The Music Goes Round and Round – Rhythm Saved the World – Yes! Yes! My! My! – I'm Putting All My Eggs in One Basket

Performers: Louis Armstrong (trumpet and vocals) and His Orchestra–Henry Jones and Charlie Holmes (alto saxophone), Greely Walton (tenor saxophone), Leonard Davis, Gus Aiken, Louis Bacon, Bunny Berigan, and Bob Mayhew (trumpet), Harry White, James Archey, and Al Philburn (trombone), Bingie Madison (clarinet and tenor saxophone), Sid Trucker, Phil Waltzer, and Paul Ricci (reeds), Luis Russell and Fulton McGrath (piano), Lee Blair and Dave Barbour (guitar), Pops Foster and Pete Peterson (bass), Paul Barbarin and Stan King (drums)

Recorded in New York City in 1935 and 1936, the music on this CD represents the middle-era, big band Armstrong, now more relaxed and popular music-oriented than the early jazz trail blazer of the 1920s. Particularly outstanding are his "I'm in the Mood for Love" and "I'm Putting All My Eggs in One Basket." Armstrong shows that he can do just about anything, even get "La Cucaracha" to swing. The liner notes are by clarinetist Joe Muranyi, who was a preteenager at the time of these recordings but from mid-1967 to 1971 a valued member of the All Stars.

52. *Satchmo: A Musical Autobiography*

Verve 314543, 3 CDs
2001

Disc 1: Dippermouth Blues – Canal Street Blues – High Society – Froggie Moore Rag – Of All the Wrongs You've Done to Me – Everybody Loves My Baby – Mandy, Make Up Your Mind – See See Rider – Reckless Blues – Court House Blues – Trouble in Mind – New Orleans Function: Flee as a Bird/Oh, Didn't He Ramble? – Gut Bucket Blues – Cornet Chop Suey – Heebie Jeebies – Georgia Grind – Muskrat Ramble – King of the Zulus – Snag It

Disc 2: Wild Man Blues – Potato Head Blues – Weary Blues – Gully Low Blues – Struttin' with Some Barbecue – Hotter Than That – Two Deuces – A Monday Date – Basin Street Blues – Knockin' a Jug – I Can't Give You Anything But Love – Mahogany Hall Stomp – Some of These Days – When You're Smiling – Song of the Islands – I Can't Believe That You're in Love with Me – Dear Old Southland – Exactly Like You

Disc 3: If I Could Be with You – Body and Soul – Memories of You – (I'll Be Glad When You're Dead) You Rascal, You – When It's Sleepy Time Down South – I Surrender, Dear – Them There Eyes – Lazy River – Georgia on My Mind – That's My Home – Hobo, You Can't Ride This Train – On the Sunny Side of the Street – A Monday Date

Performers: Louis Armstrong (trumpet and vocals), Sy Oliver and Bob Haggart (arranger, conductor), Trummy Young (vocals and trombone), Edmond Hall (vocals and clarinet), Velma Middleton (vocals), George Dorsey (alto saxophone and flute), Hilton Jefferson (alto saxophone), Lucky Thompson and Seldon Powell (tenor saxophone), Dave McRae (baritone and bass saxophone, bass clarinet), Yank Lawson (trumpet), Jack Teagarden (trombone), Barney Bigard (clarinet), Dick Carey, Earl Hines, and Billy Kyle (piano), Everett Barksdale and George Barnes (guitar), Arvell Shaw and Squire Gersh (bass), Sidney Catlett, Cozy Cole, Kenny John, and Barrett Deems (drums)

In addition to his two published volumes (and several lengthy manuscripts) of autobiography, Armstrong also recorded for producer **Milt Gabler** a musical autobiography between 1956 and 1957 with the All Stars (and some occasional supplementary personnel). On four LP discs, Armstrong recreated some of his earlier masterpieces of the 1920s and 1930s, reminiscing between cuts (to the accompaniment of pianist Billy Kyle). While the new versions hardly eclipse the originals, he seems to surpass some of the earlier cuts, such as "I Can't Give You Anything But Love," "King of the Zulus," and "When You're Smiling." Highlights of this set are Armstrong's storytelling and reminiscences. The three-CD reissue generously includes six tracks from 1927's legendary Hot Five sessions. Also included is an excellent forty-six-page booklet with original notes by Louis Untermeyer that have been augmented and updated by Joshua Berrett.

53. *Satchmo and the Dukes of Dixieland*

Leisure 1052
1988

Someday You'll Be Sorry – Washington and Lee Swing – Bye and Bye – Avalon – Sweethearts on Parade – New Orleans – Bourbon Street Parade – When It's Sleepy Time Down South – Dixie – Back o' Town Blues – Sheik of Araby – That's a Plenty – Limehouse Blues – Sweet Georgia Brown

Performers include: Louis Armstrong (trumpet and vocals) and the Dukes of Dixieland—Frank Assunto (trumpet), Fred Assunto (trombone), Jerry Fuller (clarinet), and "Papa Jac" Assunto (banjo, trombone)

Armstrong dropped in on a 1959 Dukes of Dixieland gig at the Preview Lounge in Chicago, and it went so well that they decided to record together. It probably should have happened before and later again, but we can be thankful for what there is. "They . . . were sensational from the first day that they left New Orleans," Armstrong wrote about the Dukes in 1969. "You can see how happy I am to know that I finally had a chance to *blow* with White Boys *at last*" (Brothers, p. 35). Unfortunately, this CD reissue includes only fourteen of the original twenty-seven numbers, and the liner notes are sketchy. Those with the three original Audio Fidelity LPs have a great treasure. Nevertheless, here are marvelous performances of "Avalon," "Sweethearts on Parade," "Bourbon Street Parade," and "Back o' Town Blues."

54. *Satchmo at Symphony Hall*

Decca Jazz 661
1996

Mahogany Hall Stomp – (What Did I Do to Be So) Black and Blue? – Royal Garden Blues – Lover – Body and Soul – Muskrat Ramble – Stars Fell on Alabama – Since I Fell for You – Tea for Two – Steak Face – On the Sunny Side of the Street – High Society – "C" Jam Blues – Baby, Won't You Please Come Home? – Boff Boff

Performers: Louis Armstrong (trumpet and vocals) and the All Stars—Jack Teagarden (vocals and trombone), Velma Middleton (vocals), Barney Bigard (clarinet), Dick Cary (piano), Arvell Shaw (bass), and Sidney Catlett (drums)

In 1947 Armstrong began the third and final phase of his career with the formation of the All Stars. After his triumph with a small, elite combo in New York in that year on February 8 at Carnegie Hall, Armstrong and the All Stars made their debut three months later on May 17 at Town Hall. On November 30 he took the All Stars to Symphony Hall in Boston with the same success. There in one of the bishoprics of classical music in America, Armstrong concentrated on the established repertory, such as "Mahogany Hall Stomp" and "Muskrat Ramble." He is in good voice on "Black and Blue" and "Sunny Side of the Street," but otherwise he sticks mostly to the trumpet. Other highlights include a rollicking "Royal Garden Blues" and sideman Jack Teagarden's "Lover." In making a CD from an eighteen-cut, two-LP album, the producers have unaccountably shuffled the concert order and left out a few numbers. However, the sound quality is fine, and the package includes liner notes by Ernest Anderson and Dan Morgenstern.

55. *Satchmo the Great*
Columbia/Legacy CK 62170
2000

Introduction by Edward R. Murrow – When It's Sleepy Time Down South – Indiana – Paris Interview with Edward R. Murrow – Flee as a Bird/Oh, Didn't He Ramble? – Mack the Knife – Mahogany Hall Stomp – All for You, Louis (Sly Mongoose) – (What Did I Do to Be So) Black and Blue? – St. Louis Blues (Concerto Grosso) – Royal Garden Blues – My Bucket's Got a Hole in It – On the Sunny Side of the Street

Performers: Louis Armstrong (trumpet and vocals) and the All Stars—Trummy Young (trombone), Edmond Hall (clarinet), Billy Kyle (piano), Arvell Shaw and Dale Jones (bass), Barrett Deems (drums); Leonard Bernstein and the Lewisohn Stadium Symphony Orchestra

In 1955–1956 CBS Television cameras followed Armstrong and the All Stars on a U.S. State Department tour of Africa and Europe. With the resulting footage, Edward R. Murrow and Fred Friendly made a half-hour profile for their popular *See It Now* program, but there was so much good material that they expanded it into an hour-long documentary titled *Satchmo the Great.* Here on this CD reissued soundtrack of that documentary is Armstrong jamming with local musicians in Africa, performing "(What Did I Do to Be So) Black and Blue?" for the prime minister of recently independent Ghana, delighting Princess Margaret with "Mahogany Hall Stomp," and other highlights of the tour. Also included are interview segments with Murrow, a musical welcome ("All for You, Louis") for Armstrong played by seven Gold Coast bands, and a triumphant homecoming concert with Leonard Bernstein conducting the Lewisohn Stadium Symphony Orchestra in "St. Louis Blues." The CD (with original LP liner notes by Nat Hentoff) underscores Armstrong's identity as a goodwill ambassador, dispensing jazz as a curative tonic around the world.

56. *Satch Plays Fats*
Columbia/Sony CK 64927
2000

Honeysuckle Rose – Blue Turning Grey Over You – I'm Crazy 'bout My Baby and My Baby's Crazy 'bout Me – Squeeze Me – Keepin' Out of Mischief Now – All That Meat and No Potatoes – I've Got a Feeling I'm Falling – (What Did I Do to Be So) Black and Blue? – Ain't Misbehavin' – (What Did I Do to Be So) Black and Blue? (edited alternate version) – I'm Crazy 'bout My Baby and My Baby's Crazy 'bout Me (edited alternate version) – Blue Turning Grey Over You (edited alternate version) – I've Got a Feeling I'm Falling (edited alternate version) – Squeeze Me – (What Did I Do to Be So) Black and Blue? (alternate take) – Ain't Misbehavin' (alternate take) – Blue Turning Grey Over You (alternate take) – Keepin' Out of Mischief Now – Sweet Savannah Sue – That Rhythm Man

Performers: Louis Armstrong (trumpet and vocals) and the All Stars—Trummy Young (trombone), Barney Bigard (clarinet), Billy Kyle (piano), Arvell Shaw (bass), Barrett Deems (drums), and Velma Middleton (vocals)

Armstrong spent most of April and May 1955 in New York where he and the All Stars recorded this album. The performers had a great affinity for Thomas "Fats" Waller's music, which they had been playing all their lives. Highlights include "Keepin' Out of Mischief Now," "All That Meat and No Potatoes," and "Honeysuckle Rose." Like *Louis Armstrong Plays W.C. Handy* (CD #38), *Satch Plays Fats* was that rarity, both a critical and a commercial success, charting at No. 10 on the *Billboard* Top 40 and charming such fastidious critics as Whitney Balliett (2000–2001, pp. 158–163). The tracks for this CD reissue were remastered directly from the original analog tapes, and the package includes liner notes by English Armstrong acolyte Humphrey Lyttelton.

57. *Sixteen Most Requested Songs*
Columbia/Legacy CD 57900
1994

Mack the Knife – Ain't Misbehavin' – All of Me – On the Sunny Side of the Street – Indiana – (What Did I Do to Be So) Black and Blue? – Honeysuckle Rose – Blueberry Hill – When It's Sleepy Time Down South – Back o' Town Blues – Do You Know What It Means to Miss New Orleans? – That's My Desire – Keeping Out of Mischief Now – St. Louis Blues – Rockin' Chair – Cabaret

Performers: Louis Armstrong (vocals, trumpet) and the All Stars—Velma Middleton (vocals), Jack Teagarden (vocals, trombone), Bobby Hackett (cornet), Trummy Young, Tyree Glenn (trombone), Edmond Hall, Barney Bigard, Peanuts Hucko, and Buster Bailey (clarinet), Billy Kyle and Marty Napoleon (piano), Arvell Shaw and Mort Herbert (bass), and Barrett Deems and Danny Barcelona (drums)

Among all the "All Time Masterpieces," "The Essential," "Greatest Hits of," "More Greatest Hits of," "Best of," "The Very Best of," and nearly a dozen "What a Wonderful World" CDs, this one ranks very high. These are not Armstrong's most important recordings but rather an admirable showcase that illustrates how Armstrong combined both art and entertainment. In addition to the dark "Mack the Knife," highlights include a bright "All of Me," a poignant "Black and Blue," and a rowdy "Indiana." Armstrong's sidemen kibitz good-naturedly on "Back o' Town Blues," and Armstrong sings two charming duets with Velma Middleton. Recorded between 1955 and 1966, most of the selections (all but "Rockin' Chair" and "Cabaret") are monophonic. Producer George Avakian wrote the liner notes.

58. ***Stardust***
Portrait Masters RK 44093
1990

Chinatown, My Chinatown – Star Dust – Star Dust (alternate take) – You Can Depend on Me – Georgia on My Mind – The Lonesome Road – I Got Rhythm – Between the Devil and the Deep Blue Sea – Kickin' the Gong Around – Home (When Shadows Fall) – All of Me – Love, You Funny Thing – Tiger Rag – Keepin' Out of Mischief – Lawd, You Made the Night Too Long

Performers: Louis Armstrong (trumpet and vocals) with various ensembles

Hoagy Carmichael (1899–1981) was already a fairly accomplished songwriter, singer, and pianist when he first heard Armstrong in the summer of 1923. "I dropped my cigarette and gulped my drink," he later wrote in his autobiography, *The Stardust Road.* "Something as unutterably stirring as that deserved to be heard by the world" (p. 53). The two eventually developed a close working relationship, sharing vocals on the first recording of "Rockin' Chair" (1931). Carmichael liked Armstrong's interpretation of "Star Dust" over all others, even if he took considerable liberties with the original. There is much more than just Carmichael's music, however, on this fine CD of recordings from 1930–1932, when Armstrong became a popular bandleader and vocalist. Highlights include the Harold Arlen/Ted Koehler "Between the Devil and the Deep Blue Sea." This digitally remastered package comes with liner notes by Nat Hentoff.

59. ***The Sullivan Years: Louis Armstrong***
TVT 9427
1992

When It's Sleepy Time Down South – Hello Dolly! – Lazy River – Ole Miss – Bill Bailey, Won't You Please Come Home? – Muskrat Ramble – Faithful Hussar – Stompin' at the Savoy – Basin Street Blues – Royal Garden Blues – That's My Home – Indiana – Blueberry Hill – Sunny Side of the Street – Nobody Knows the Trouble I've Seen – Mack the Knife – Cabaret – When It's Sleepy Time Down South

Performers include: Louis Armstrong (trumpet and vocals) and the All Stars—Trummy Young (trombone), Edmond Hall and Barney Bigard (clarinet), Billie Kyle (piano), Arvell Shaw (bass), and Danny Barcelona and Barrett Deems (drums).

Armstrong was a frequent and welcome guest on *The Ed Sullivan Show,* which was *the* prime-time variety show in its day, and here are eighteen tracks from nine appearances, 1956 to 1966. Armstrong the entertainer comes to the fore here in spirited performances of both hits and standards—"Hello Dolly!" to "Muskrat Ramble." The package includes liner notes by Stanley Crouch.

60. ***Swing That Music***
Drive Archive 41025
1994

Swing That Music – Jeepers Creepers – Dear Old Southland – Tiger Rag – Someday You'll Be Sorry – Heebie Jeebies – Storyville Blues – Brother Bill – Way Down Yonder in New Orleans – Rockin' Chair – Do You Know What It Means to Miss New Orleans? – Muskrat Ramble

Performers include: Louis Armstrong (trumpet and vocals), Bud Freeman (tenor saxophone), Ernie Caceres (baritone saxophone), Bobby Hackett (cornet), Jack Teagarden (trombone), Peanuts Hucko and Pee Wee Russell (clarinet), Fats Waller, Dick Cary, Earl Hines, and Joe Bushkin (piano), Al Casey and Eddie Condon (guitar), Jack Lesberg and Arvell Shaw (bass), and Slick Jones, George Wettling, Cozy Cole, and Sid Catlett (drums)

This CD offers selections from recordings made between 1947 and 1949, plus Armstrong's two 1938 collaborations with Fats Waller, "Jeepers Creepers" and "Tiger Rag." Not just another compilation of best-loved (i.e., sure to sell) numbers, it intelligently ranges widely in mood and tempo, from a wild "Swing That Music" to a delicate "Dear Old Southland." One highlight is the gospellike arrangement of "Someday You'll Be Sorry," a song that came to Armstrong in a dream. Included are intelligent liner notes by Scott Yanow.

61. *The Ultimate Collection*

Verve 543699, 3 CDs
2000

Disc 1: Copenhagen – Shanghai Shuffle – Stomp Off, Let's Go – Drop That Sack – Melancholy – I'm Goin' Huntin' – I'm in the Mood for Love – On Treasure Island – Thanks a Million – Ev'ntide – Dippermouth Blues – Swing That Music – Pennies from Heaven – On the Sunny Side of the Street – Once in a While – In the Shade of the Old Apple Tree – Jubilee – When the Saints Go Marching In – Shadrack – Ain't Misbehavin' – Jeepers Creepers

Disc 2: Rockin' Chair – West End Blues – Savoy Blues – Hear Me Talkin' to Ya – I'm Confessin' (That I Love You) – You're a Lucky Guy – Wolverine Blues – Sweethearts on Parade – Perdido Street Blues – 2:19 Blues – Coal Cart Blues – Groovin' – Royal Garden Blues – Mahogany Hall Stomp – Blueberry Hill – You Can't Lose a Broken Heart – My Bucket's Got a Hole in It – Panama – New Orleans Function: Flee as a Bird/Oh, Didn't He Ramble? – (I'll Be Glad When You're Dead) You Rascal, You – A Monday Date

Disc 3: A Kiss to Build a Dream On – It's All in the Game – Someday You'll Be Sorry – Basin Street Blues – When It's Sleepy Time Down South – I Can't Give You Anything But Love – Weary Blues – Wild Man Blues – Dippermouth Blues – Dear Old Southland – Stompin' at the Savoy – I Got a Right to Sing the Blues – Sweet Lorraine – Hello Dolly! – What a Wonderful World – Cabaret – Dream a Little Dream of Me

Performers: Louis Armstrong (trumpet, cornet, and vocals) with various artists and ensembles

Although an "ultimate" Armstrong collection should really include some of the Hot Five and Hot Seven recordings from the late 1920s, this one offers plenty of other recordings that Armstrong made with the Fletcher Henderson Orchestra (e.g., "Copenhagen"), with Billie Holliday ("You Can't Lose a Broken Heart"), Ella Fitzgerald ("A Kiss to Build a Dream On"), and others, including his own All Stars ("Hello Dolly!"). Chronologically arranged, the package includes excellent liner notes.

62. *What a Wonderful World*

GRP Records 656
1996

What a Wonderful World – Cabaret – The Home Fire – Dream a Little Dream of Me – Give Me Your Kisses – Sunshine of Love – Hello Brother – There Must Be a Way – Fantastic, That's You – I Guess I'll Get the Papers and Go Home – Hellzapoppin'

Performers: Louis Armstrong (trumpet and vocals) with various ensembles

Recorded in New York and Las Vegas between 1967 and 1968 (i.e., late in his life), this recording presents Armstrong the pop icon who can make big hits (e.g., the title song and "Cabaret") and who can also charm his way through relatively undistinguished material.

63. *"What a Wonderful World"—The Elisabethville Concert*
Milan 35686
1993

When It's Sleepy Time Down South – My Bucket's Got a Hole in It – Tiger Rag – Now You Has Jazz – High Society Calypso – Ole Miss – Perdido – St. Louis Blues – I Love You So – When the Saints Go Marching In – What a Wonderful World

Performers: Louis Armstrong (trumpet and vocals) and the All Stars—Velma Middleton (vocals), Trummy Young and Tyree Glenn (trombone), Barney Bigard and Joe Muryani (clarinet), Billy Kyle and Marty Napoleon (piano), Arvell Shaw and Buddy Catlett (bass), and Danny Barcelona (drums)

Recorded live in November 1960, while on a forty-five-concert U.S. State Department tour of Africa, this concert in the Congolese city of Elisabethville represents Armstrong the ambassador. Here are the All Stars' most popular numbers, starring, of course, the reflective title song. (See CD #23 for related material.)

APPENDIX 2

CHRONOLOGY

1901: Armstrong is born on August 4 to Mary ("Mayann") Albert and her common-law spouse William ("Willie") Armstrong in Jane Alley, between Poydras and Perdido Streets in the "Back o' Town" district of New Orleans. His father had already abandoned him by the time he was baptized a Catholic at the Church of the Sacred Heart of Jesus Christ when he was three weeks old, and Armstrong was raised primarily by his grandmother, Josephine Armstrong.

1906: Armstrong is returned to his ailing mother. He helps to care for her and his three-year-old sister, Beatrice ("Mama Lucy"), also born to Mayann and Willie after a short-lived reconciliation.... Armstrong hears Buddy Bolden playing cornet at Funky Butt Hall near his home, and there is "something about the instrument" that entrances him (Armstrong, *Satchmo,* 1952, p. 24). At this time Armstrong also begins following brass bands in parades, a practice known as "second lining."

1907: Armstrong begins attending the Fisk School for Boys and learns to read.... He sells newspapers and does odd jobs, trying to help his mother with whom he lives at 1303 Perdido Street.... As busy as he is, he forms a vocal quartet with friends.... Armstrong meets a Jewish family named Karnofsky with whom he works and who become dear friends. He helps them in their junk and coal businesses, and they help him buy his first instrument, a $5 pawnshop cornet. He teaches himself to play and learns Russian songs from the family.

1908–1911: Armstrong frequently visits Storyville, hearing Joe Oliver, Bunk Johnson, and others at various honky-tonks.

1912–1913: Dropping out of school in the fifth grade, Armstrong quits working for the Karnofskys but continues with others in the junk and rag business and doing odd jobs.... He joins a vocal quartet as tenor.... On December 31 he fires a pistol into the air to celebrate New Year's Eve and ends up arrested and locked up. The next day Armstrong is sent to the Colored Waif's Home for Boys, which is a significant turning point in his life ("[T]hat shot, I do believe, started my career" [Armstrong, 1936, p. 1]). Here he plays the tambourine, snare drum, alto horn, bass drum, bugle, and finally the cornet in the band. Band leader Peter Davis gives Armstrong cornet lessons and one day makes Armstrong the leader of the band. "I was in seventh heaven," he later recalled (Armstrong, *Satchmo,* 1954, p. 46).

1914: On June 16 Armstrong is released from the Colored Waif's Home and goes to live with his father and stepmother at Miro and Poydras Streets.... He helps take care of his two younger stepbrothers and also begins to play cornet around town for dances, picnics, funerals, and parades.... Later in the year Armstrong goes to live with his mother and sister at Liberty and Perdido Streets.... He begins sitting in with Kid Ory's band and playing regularly at Henry Ponce's honky-tonk.

1915: A hardworking lad, Armstrong tries his hand at being a milkman, delivering coal for a local company, selling second-hand clothes, hawking newspapers, and for a short time, acting as a pimp.... On August 8 Armstrong's mother's third cousin, Clarence Myles Hatfield, is born. Armstrong is the major source of income for his own mother, sister, and this new baby whose mother dies shortly after childbirth.... He is still playing for Kid Ory whose cornetist, Joe "King" Oliver, takes Armstrong under his wing, offering lessons in exchange for various errands.

1917: Storyville, viewed as a hotbed of immorality, is closed down by the U.S. Navy. Prostitution is declared illegal. As the honky-tonks are closed, many musicians are suddenly out of work.... Armstrong goes to Houma, Louisiana, to play with a funeral band but returns to New Orleans to live with his mother and play at Henry Matranga's tonk. Matranga buys him a cornet, paying himself back by fingering part of Armstrong's salary and tips.... Armstrong also continues to haul coal in and around town and with his earnings obtains a Victrola and jazz and opera recordings.

1918: Armstrong is still delivering coal, until Armistice Day (November 11), but the year is a big one for him musically.... When King Oliver leaves for Chicago in June, Armstrong takes his place in Kid Ory's band. He is called "Dippermouth," and his "I Wish I Could Shimmy Like My Sister Kate" is a tremendous hit at Pete Lala's club. Armstrong receives numerous invitations to play with other bands when Ory's isn't on.... Armstrong registers with his local draft board, putting down July 4, 1900, as his birthday.... Armstrong plays with Tom Anderson's New Cabaret house band, and he joins Oscar Celestin's sartorially splendid Tuxedo Brass Band with which many famous musicians (e.g., Jimmie Noone and Johnny Dodds) had played.... At Brick House, a dance hall in Gretna, Louisiana, where he plays on Saturday nights, he meets Daisy Parker, a Creole prostitute, whom he marries late in the year.

1919: Armstrong quits Anderson's when pianist and band leader Fate Marable hires him to play on the riverboat S.S. *Sidney* of the Streckfus Steamboat Line during its summer cruises from New Orleans to St. Louis. During intermissions Armstrong learned to read music better with help from mellophonist Davey Jones and from Marable himself. Armstrong later writes of this period, "I wanted to get away from New Orleans for another reason and that was because I was not happy there just then. Ten months before ... I got married.... In the seven months to come, I was to follow the Mississippi for nearly two thousand miles and visit many places. It was a handful of travelling ... for a kid who'd always been afraid to leave home before" (Armstrong, 1936, pp. 37–40).... Standing on the dock in New Orleans one day, Jack Teagarden first hears Armstrong play as the steamboat pulls in.

1920: Armstrong is busy performing in New Orleans but again spends June through September on the steamboat with Marable.... When the boat stops in Davenport, Iowa, he meets the young Bix Beiderbecke.

1921: In September Armstrong resigns from Marable's band because of artistic differences and takes the train back to New Orleans.... He returns to Tom Anderson's Cabaret. Here he attracts the attention of young bandleader Fletcher Henderson, who asks him to come to New York, but he does not go.... Armstrong also plays in a small band his friend Zutty Singleton has formed and becomes a regular member of Oscar Celestin's Tuxedo Brass Band.

Armstrong waves good night to one of his countless audiences. (Louis Armstrong House and Archives at Queens College/CUNY)

1922: Armstrong continues to play with Celestin and others. . . . In early August he receives a telegram from King "Papa Joe" Oliver inviting him to play second cornet in his Creole Jazz Band, which has a regular gig at Lincoln Gardens in Chicago. On August 8 he leaves his marriage to Daisy Parker Armstrong and New Orleans, which he will not see again for nine years. . . . "When I left New Orleans to go up north in 1922 the toughest Negro down there—his name is Slippers—he gave me a pep talk. . . . He came right over to me and said, 'When you go up north, Dipper, be sure and get yourself a white man that will put his hand on your shoulder and say "this is my nigger." ' Those were his exact words" (Jones and Chilton, pp. 16–17). . . . He lives at first with the Olivers at 459 East 31st Street. . . . Armstrong buys his first typewriter and begins to pursue his "hobbie" of writing letters and memoirs. Throughout his exhausting career of performing and touring, he writes wherever and whenever he can—in hotel rooms, backstage, between sets.

1923: Armstrong continues to play at Lincoln Gardens through late February with the Creole Jazz Band. . . . In March the band goes on tour through Illinois, Ohio, and Indiana. . . . Sometime during the winter Oliver suggests that he and Armstrong drop in at the Dreamland Café to meet the pianist, Lil Hardin, who soon joins the Creole Jazz Band. Hardin tells Armstrong that she was valedictorian of her class at Fisk University. It turns out that she was not even a graduate, having dropped out after no more than a year at the school. Armstrong, however, does not know the facts, begins falling in love with her, and during the summer begins taking musical and career advice from her. . . . On April 5 and 6 the band records nine historic tunes in Richmond, Indiana, for Gennett Records: "Just Gone," "Canal St. Blues," "Mandy Lee Blues," "I'm Going Away to Wear You Off My Mind," "Weather Bird Rag," "Dippermouth Blues," "Froggie Moore," and "Snake Rag." Armstrong records his first solo on Oliver's "Chimes Blues," going on later to make twenty-eight more recordings with Oliver and the Creole Jazz Band. Armstrong's playing is so strong that he has to stand behind the group at a considerable distance so as not to overwhelm them and the primitive recording equipment. . . . During this year Armstrong also records for Okeh, Columbia, and Paramount.

1924: On February 5 Armstrong marries Lil Hardin in Chicago. . . . February through early June Armstrong tours Illinois, Indiana, Pennsylvania, Ohio, Michigan, and Wisconsin with Oliver and the Creole Jazz Band. . . . He leaves Oliver's group in late June to join Ollie Powers's band, also in Chicago at the Dreamland Café. . . . In September bandleader Fletcher Henderson invites Armstrong to come to New York City and join his band at the Roseland Ballroom. Armstrong inspires awe in New York musicians such as Rex Stewart, Coleman Hawkins, and Duke Ellington. . . . In October Armstrong changes to the trumpet but continues to play cornet occasionally through 1927, especially when recording with blues singers. . . . In November he cuts "Everybody Loves My Baby," his debut recording as a singer. He was not, however, allowed by Henderson (who did not care for Armstrong's voice) to sing on stage or on any other recordings. . . . Beginning in October and continuing through May 1925, Armstrong accompanies many distinguished blues singers including Ma Rainey, Alberta Hunter, Margaret Johnson, Bessie Smith, and Clara Smith. . . . Also beginning in October and for about a year he records with pianist Clarence Williams' Blue Five on the Okeh label.

1925: Through May he continues to play with Fletcher Henderson at Roseland. . . . During the summer the band tours Connecticut, Maine, Maryland, Massachusetts, and Pennsylvania, and Armstrong begins to improvise more daringly in his solos.... Armstrong leaves Henderson (who would not let him sing) in November to join his wife's band at the Dreamland Café in Chicago for $75 per week. (Bix Beiderbecke is making $100 per week with the Goldkette band at the same time.) Trumpeter Doc Cheatham had vivid memories of Armstrong's return to Chicago: "Before Louis came, they had trucks with banners with Louis' name on them going all around Chicago: 'Louis Armstrong Coming Back to Chicago!' They had a record playing all of his things. You could hear it all over the South Side" (Deffaa, 1992, p. 18). On November 14 the *Chicago Defender* announced in an ad that Lil Armstrong's band was featuring "The World's Greatest Jazz Cornetist." ... Louis Armstrong puts together a studio band called the Hot Five, and they cut their first Okeh record (of sixty-five), "Gut Bucket Blues," on November 12 in Chicago.... Erskine Tate from the Vendome Theater hires Armstrong in December to join his symphony orchestra. Audiences come to hear Armstrong perform and sometimes leave as soon as he finishes, even before the movie. Armstrong and the orchestra play overtures, accompaniments to the silent films, operatic excerpts, and "Red Hot Numbers."

1926: In April Armstrong leaves the Dreamland Café and joins the Carroll Dickerson orchestra at the Sunset Club.... Also in April he first meets Joe Glaser, who will be his manager from 1935 on.... Armstong continues to play at the Vendome Theater with Erskine Tate.... The Hot Five recordings this year include such hits as "Muskrat Ramble," "Big Butter and Egg Man," "Sunset Cafe Stomp," and others, and on June 12 this recording group makes its only public appearance at the Chicago Coliseum. "Heebie Jeebies" is the Hot Five's first big hit and the first successful recording of scat singing.... Armstrong also records throughout the year with Sippie Wallace, Hociel Thomas, and other vocalists and with the Tate orchestra.... In August Armstrong takes a vacation with Lil on the lake in Idlewild, Michigan, where he buys some property.... During this year he also buys a home in Chicago on 44th Street.

1927: Early in the year Dickerson's orchestra leaves the Sunset Cafe. Joe Glaser, manager of the Sunset, hires Louis Armstrong and His [Sunset] Stompers (featuring Earl Hines on piano) to take its place.... Melrose Music publishes Armstrong's *125 Jazz Breaks for Cornet* and *50 Hot Choruses for Cornet*.... Through April Armstrong plays with Tate at the Vendome (often as many as four shows a night, finishing up at 11 P.M. before rushing to play at the Sunset), then he switches to the Metropolitan Theater to play with Clarence Jones's orchestra until December.... In May the Hot Five temporarily becomes the Hot Seven with the addition of tuba player Pete Briggs and drummer Baby Dodds. The Hot Five and Hot Seven record prolifically through the year.... In July Armstrong plays a two-week gig at the all-white Blackhawk Restaurant.... In the late summer, Armstrong's mother dies in Chicago.... In November Armstrong, Earl Hines, and drummer Zutty Singleton open their own dance hall, the Warwick Room, which closes after only a few weeks and is a financial disaster for all three.

1928: In January Armstrong, Hines, and Singleton are all scrounging around for work.... In March Armstrong rejoins Carroll Dickerson, this time at the newly opened Savoy Ballroom.... In May Armstrong plays (for $100 per day) to huge crowds on the S.S. *Saint Paul* in St. Louis. ... On July 5 for Okeh the Hot Five make their final recording. Kid Ory recalls that for a spell Okeh had given a photo of Armstrong to everyone who bought a record and sales skyrocketed.... Armstrong records throughout the year with many vocalists, such as Bertha "Chippie" Hill, Sippie Wallace, Eva Taylor, and Margaret Johnson. . . . The year is regarded by many as the zenith of Armstrong's recording career. Highlights are such masterpieces as "Fireworks," "Basin Street Blues," "St. James Infirmary," "No One Else But You," "Tight Like This," and perhaps the most famous jazz recording of all, "West End Blues."

1929: From January through May Armstrong fronts the Carroll Dickerson Orchestra at the Savoy and at clubs in Detroit and St. Louis. . . . In March Armstrong makes a trip to New York to work briefly with the Luis Russell Orchestra and cut "I Can't Give You Anything But Love" and "Mahogany Hall Stomp." . . . In May he returns to New York at the request of his new manager, Tommy Rockwell, and rehearses in Philadelphia for the new Vincent Youmans show "Great Day." Armstrong doesn't make it to Broadway with the show, which flops after 36 performances. . . . After a brief stint at the Savoy in Harlem, on June 24 Armstrong begins a four-month stay at Connie's Inn, also in Harlem. The same month he begins appearing in *Connie's Hot Chocolates* on Broadway at the Hudson Theater. The show runs over 200 performances, right up to the end of the year. . . . In July Armstrong records "Ain't Misbehavin'" and "(What Did I Do to Be So) Black and Blue?" (both from *Hot Chocolates*). . . . Late in the year, after Black Friday, the Connie's Inn band is sent packing by owner Immerman and breaks up. . . . Armstrong's career takes a turn from jazz to popular and theater works, and he begins performing and recording (beginning in July) exclusively with big band backing, which he will continue until the mid-1940s.

1930: During January and February Armstrong plays with Luis Russell's band in Washington, D.C., Baltimore, and Chicago. . . . In February he begins playing with the Mills Blue Rhythm Band at the Coconut Grove in New York and (through May) in Detroit, Baltimore, Philadelphia, Pittsburgh, and Chicago. . . . In July Armstrong, troubled by his deteriorating friendship with old pal Zutty Singleton and marital problems with Lil, makes the transcontinental trip to Los Angeles. He settles in at Frank Sebastian's New Cotton Club in Culver City as a soloist with a band, at first led by Leon Elkins but later by saxophonist Les Hite (with whom he made some fine recordings). In the band are drummer Lionel Hampton (whom Armstrong eventually persuades to take up the vibraphone) and trombonist Lawrence Brown. . . . Late in the summer Armstrong makes his first film appearance in *Ex-Flame,* now lost. . . . Through radio he quickly becomes a favorite of Hollywood and packs them in at the New Cotton Club. . . . Beginning in October of this year and continuing through March of 1931, Armstrong records a number of popular hits such as "Body and Soul," "Memories of You," "You're Lucky to Me," "Shine," "The Peanut Vendor," and "Just a Gigolo."

1931: Early in the year Lil Hardin Armstrong comes out to California to see her husband and realizes their marriage is doomed. . . . Shortly thereafter, Alpha Smith, a woman he met in Chicago at the Vendome Theater in 1925 (and later to become his third wife), also comes to visit him. . . . In early March Armstrong and drummer Vic Berton are arrested in the New Cotton Club parking lot for smoking marijuana (a habit that Armstrong had acquired early in his career in Chicago). Armstrong spends nine days in jail, eventually receiving a suspended sentence, due mainly to the efforts of his new manager, Johnny Collins, who was sent to Los Angeles by Tommy Rockwell. Armstrong's popularity is not dented by the notoriety. . . . April finds Armstrong back in Chicago with a band he forms with trumpeter Zilner Randolph to play briefly at the Regal Theater and then at the Showboat nightclub. This group is together for about a year and records some two dozen numbers.... In May Armstrong and the band begin a tour of Illinois, Kentucky, Ohio, Michigan, Virginia, and West Virginia.... On the eve of the Kentucky Derby, Armstrong makes history in Louisville by leading the first African American band ever to play the Roof Garden of the Kentucky Hotel.... In June the tour takes Armstrong back to his hometown for the first time in nine years. He is given a hero's welcome and visits the Colored Waif's Home. He stays three months, playing for an all-white audience at the Suburban Gardens where Armstrong is a hit despite an announcer who refuses to introduce an African American on the radio broadcast. He sponsors a local baseball team, "Armstrong's Secret Nine," made up mostly of members of the Zulu Social Aid and Pleasure Club (an African American social club and burial society).... Armstrong and Lil permanently separate in August, although they are not officially divorced until 1938.... In September the band strikes out on the road again, this time touring Texas, Oklahoma, Tennessee, Missouri, and Ohio. Despite the Great Depression, they draw huge crowds.... On October 10 Armstrong and the whole band are arrested in Memphis, apparently for simply arriving as a group of well-dressed black men with a white woman, Mrs. Johnny Collins, in their bus.... The end of the year finds the band on the East Coast, touring Baltimore, Washington, D.C., and finally Philadelphia.... A cigar, the Louis Armstrong Special, is named after him.

1932: In January Armstrong and the band play in New Haven, Jersey City, Boston, and New York.... Soon thereafter the band splits up due to the Depression's effect on the entertainment industry and Armstrong's own restlessness.... In February he begins a three-month stint at Frank Sebastian's New Cotton Club in Los Angeles.... In the spring while in Los Angeles, Armstrong appears (in leopard skins, no less) in the short film *A Rhapsody in Black and Blue* and singing with cartoon character Betty Boop in "You Rascal, You."... For his first European tour, Armstrong applies for a passport and describes himself as "actor and musician." Accompanied by Johnny Collins and Alpha Smith, he sets sail on the S.S. *Majestic* on July 9 for England. His most famous and enduring nickname is acquired upon arrival as he is met by Percy Brooks of *Melody Maker* magazine, who fumbles over "Satchelmouth" and says, "Hello, Satchmo!" Armstrong opens a two-week run at the London Palladium on July 18 and mesmerizes audiences. He tours the United Kingdom, visits Paris in October, and returns to New York in November.... Through December 2 he is featured in a new version of *Hot Chocolates* at the Lafayette Theater with drummer Chick Webb and his orchestra.... Although he is having trouble with his lip, Armstrong records some (now with Victor Records) and plays with the Chick Webb group in Philadelphia and Washington, D.C., in December.

1933: Back in Chicago, Armstrong fronts the new band Zilner Randolph has pulled together. Although his lip is still hurting, Armstrong and the group tour Illinois, Kentucky, Indiana, and Nebraska.... On March 31 rumors of Armstrong's death are greatly exaggerated on the front page of the London *Daily Express.* A correction is issued, but the news has spread around the world.... In July, after an engagement in Philadelphia, Armstrong sets sail from New York on the S.S. *Homeric* with Alpha Smith and Johnny Collins. During the voyage he fires his "slave driver" manager Collins, taking on in his place English bandleader and impressario Jack Hylton in September.... Armstrong opens his European tour at the Holborn Empire in London on August 5 before touring the United Kingdom.... On

August 17 Armstrong's father Willie dies in New Orleans of gastroenteritis and pneumonia.... Late fall finds Armstrong touring Denmark, Norway, Sweden, and Holland. In Denmark, where thousands greet him upon his arrival and present him with a trumpet made of flowers, he appears in the musical revue film *København, Kalundborg Og?*... December is spent in London.

1934: January is spent in England while Armstrong rests his lip.... He moves to Paris in April for an extended vacation. During his stay he gets to know critic Hugues Panassié, guitarist Django Reinhardt, and violinist Stephane Grappelli.... Under contract with new manager Jacques Canetti, Armstrong records some ("Sunny Side of the Street," "Song of the Vipers," and others) in October for Brunswick with a newly formed band.... In November he plays twice at the famous Salle Pleyel and makes a forty-minute French radio appearance.... Later in the month and into December he tours Belgium, Switzerland, and Italy. Armstrong recalls in *Swing That Music* playing for the Crown Princess of Italy in Turin before crossing the Alps to spend New Year's Eve in Lausanne, Switzerland (1936, p. 114).

1935: Breaking his contract with Canetti and suffering with embouchure problems, Armstrong returns to New York with Alpha Smith in late January.... He moves back to Chicago and does not play his trumpet much at all until the spring.... He sings with the Duke Ellington Orchestra on Valentine's Day.... In the spring Lil Armstrong (who is doing well in her own career as bandleader) sues for $6,000 "maintenance."... In May Armstrong begins a thirty-four-year association with his new manager, Joe Glaser.... Zilner Randolph puts together for Armstrong an orchestra, which opens in Indianapolis on July 1 before a tour of the Midwest and the South (including New Orleans). They wind through Pittsburgh, Detroit, and Washington, D.C., before disbanding in New York City in September after an engagement at the Apollo Theater.... In the fall, Glaser gets Armstrong a contract with the new Decca Records, with whom he records upwards of 120 sides during the next seven years.... On October 29 he opens at Connie's Inn with the Luis Russell band (billed as "Louis Armstrong and His Orchestra"). The stint lasts four months, and Armstrong is frequently heard over CBS radio. Although some critics feel Russell's is the worst band Armstrong ever fronted and that his years with it (most of the 1930s) represent a low point in his career, he stays with them (but not exclusively) until well into the 1940s.... Late in the year both *Esquire* (October) and *Vanity Fair* (November) publish major articles about Armstrong. He is now firmly established as a major figure in American cultural history.

1936: In February Armstrong again appears in the pages of *Vanity Fair,* this time in a fictional dialogue with classical violinist and composer Fritz Kreisler.... March is spent playing a week at the Apollo Theater in New York, then at the Metropolitan in Boston.... In May Armstrong begins a long tour with the band to Pittsburgh, Detroit, St. Louis, Chicago, and Kansas City. His only rest comes when he has a tonsillectomy in May.... In California in August, Armstrong makes the Columbia film *Pennies from Heaven* with Bing Crosby. He is the first African American to appear in a feature film. He plays "Skeleton in the Closet" with the Jimmy Dorsey Band, including Lionel Hampton on drums.... Back on the road again from September through the end of the year with his orchestra, Armstrong plays in Texas, Pennsylvania, West Virginia, Illinois, Washington, D.C., Georgia, New York, Missouri, Ohio, and finally Illinois (Chicago) for Christmas and the end of the year. Both Armstrong's health and the quality of his orchestra are greatly improved by now....

On November 7, *Swing That Music* (his first autobiographical volume) is published with a foreword by Rudy Vallee.

1937: In January Armstrong has surgery at Provident Hospital in Chicago for vocal nodes, then begins a tour that includes Nebraska, Massachusetts, and Pennsylvania and ends in New York City in April. . . . On April 9 Armstrong becomes the first African American to host a national radio show when he replaces Rudy Vallee on *The Fleischmann's Yeast Hour* at the Paramount in New York. . . . He appears in Chicago and New York in May, before heading to California the same month to film *Artists and Models* (with Jack Benny). . . . Back on the road in June, Armstrong performs in Connecticut; then in Pittsburgh and Washington, D.C. in July; in Boston and throughout the South in September. His orchestra is considerably stronger now with the addition of Henry "Red" Allen on trumpet, Albert Nicholas on clarinet, and J.C. Higginbotham on trombone. . . . Armstrong returns to California in October to finish out the year performing there and to make Paramount's *Everyday's a Holiday* (with Mae West) and *Doctor Rhythm* (with Bing Crosby). His only contribution to the latter movie is scrapped on the cutting room floor and lost.

1938: After a monthlong stay at the New Cotton Club in Culver City, Armstrong heads to Chicago for a residency at the Grand Terrace through March 9. During this time he also plays dates in Indianapolis, Pittsburgh, New York, and Cincinnati. . . . On April 10 King Oliver dies in Savannah, Georgia. His funeral in New York is attended by stellar musicians, and Armstrong writes that he "is desperate at the idea" that Oliver "has left this earth" (*Jazz-Hot,* Apr.–May 1938, p. 9). . . . In May Armstrong records the first jazz version of a spiritual, "When the Saints Go Marching In," for Decca in New York. He would go on to record this standard fifty-seven more times. . . . Back on the road June through September, Armstrong tours the South, including New Orleans. . . . Flying to Hollywood on August 27 for a few days to film *Going Places* (with Dick Powell for Warner Brothers), he rejoins the band to continue touring the South through mid-October. . . . On September 30 his divorce from Lil Hardin is final. . . . On October 11 while on tour he marries Alpha Smith in Houston, Texas. . . . Later in October, Armstrong plays at the Cotton Club in New York, where he meets chorus girl Lucille Wilson, who will become his fourth (and final) wife. . . . December is spent playing and recording in New York. . . . On Christmas Eve he is guest vocalist at a Paul Whiteman concert at Carnegie Hall. . . . In general, 1938 was a bit lackluster for Armstrong since the hot swing craze blossomed this year with Benny Goodman's famous January 16 Carnegie Hall concert and with hoards of new swing bands. Although there was burgeoning interest in traditional jazz as well at this time, Armstrong was thought by many to be old-fashioned.

1939: Armstrong spent much of the year as he did all the years from 1935 to 1971: in hotel rooms and dressing rooms, on busses, planes, and stages all over the United States. . . . Manager Joe Glaser puts him on the same bill as his idol Bill "Bojangles" Robinson. (Robinson was Armstrong's favorite entertainer. "That man was so sharp he was bleeding," Armstrong wrote in the 1970 "Open Letter to Fans," reprinted in Brothers, pp. 179–188.) . . . In October Armstrong appears with the Benny Goodman Orchestra at the Waldorf Astoria in New York. . . . Also in October Armstrong begins a six-month residency at New York's Cotton Club. . . . On November 29 he opens on Broadway at the Rockefeller Center Theater as Bottom in *Swingin' the Dream,* a jazz version of *A Midsummer Night's Dream.* The show folds after sixteen days. . . . On December 18 Armstrong broadcasts from the Cotton Club. . . . Generally in the late 1930s Armstrong rerecords many of his previous hits (e.g., "Struttin' with Some Barbecue").

1940: On April 5 Armstrong finishes his gig at the Cotton Club. . . . On April 10 and 11 he records with the Mills Brothers, including the satirical "W.P.A. Blues," which is later withdrawn at the request of First Lady Eleanor Roosevelt. . . . On May 27 he teams up again with buddies clarinetist Sydney Bechet and drummer Zutty Singleton for some traditional, small group jazz recordings for Decca. The session, however, is not a huge success and not without personality conflicts. . . . In June Armstrong plays in Chicago. . . . July sees him in New York at the Apollo and Paramount Theaters. . . . From August to December he and the band tour Alabama, Georgia, South Carolina, Iowa, California, Mississippi, and Florida.

1941: The year is spent crisscrossing the country on tour, with stops at many military bases and a June stay in Toronto. During World War II Armstrong and his orchestra toured almost nonstop. . . . The traditional jazz movement continued to gain strength since all things American were especially important now. . . . Regarding his visit in September to Fort Barrancas in Florida (near Panama City), Armstrong wrote to his friend, the jazz figure Leonard Feather, that when they pinned the official Coast Guard insignia on his lapel, "I was almost in tears. It was really a touching moment" (Berrett, 1999, p. 117).

1942: March and April find Armstrong in Los Angeles, playing at Casa Mañana in Culver City. . . . He makes several recordings ("Coquette," "Among My Souvenirs," "I Never Knew," and "Cash for Your Trash") in April before an American Federation of Musicians strike that cripples the industry for two years. . . . In April he also records four "soundies" (three-minute films rather like music videos). . . . In September he films *Cabin in the Sky* for MGM with director Vincent Minnelli. . . . On October 2 his divorce from Alpha Smith is final, and on October 12 he marries Lucille Wilson in St. Louis, Missouri. Armstrong says that this time it's serious. . . . Lucille buys a house at 34-56 107th Street in Corona (a section of Queens), New York. This is the Armstrongs' home for the rest of their lives. . . . On Christmas Day he performs at Fort Benning in Georgia.

1943: Armstrong returns to New York in March after a long tour and is delighted with the new home in Queens. . . . In April he contributes "I Can't Give You Anything But Love" to the film musical *Jam Session* for Columbia Studios. . . . In November he performs with Duke Ellington and Benny Goodman over NBC radio on a national broadcast. . . . Throughout the year he continues to tour and does numerous programs for the Armed Forces Radio Service.

1944: On January 18 Armstrong plays in a jam session with other winners of the first *Esquire* jazz poll at the Metropolitan Opera House in New York City. Armstrong, voted "musician of the year," performs with Coleman Hawkins, Jack Teagarden, Barney Bigard, Art Tatum, Lionel Hampton, Red Norvo, Sidney Catlett, Roy Eldridge, Billie Holliday, and others. . . . Throughout the year he tours and performs on many military bases and for the Armed Forces Radio Service. . . . In May and June he makes *Atlantic City* with Dorothy Dandridge and Constance Moore for Republic Films. . . . In August the recording strike is finally over, and Armstrong gets back into the studio in Los Angeles to cut three tunes, working with Dorothy Dandridge and his big band (including the young Dexter Gordon on tenor sax). Curiously, these titles are not issued until they come out on LP years later. . . . August and part of September are spent in California, where he cuts records and films *Pillow to Post* with Ida Lupino for Warner Brothers. . . . In September at

Camp Reynolds in Pennsylvania Armstrong records "Perdido" and "Is You Is or Is You Ain't My Baby?"—his first of many recorded duets with vocalist Velma Middleton. . . . On December 7 Armstrong participates with other stellar musicians (such as Jack Teagarden, Bobby Hackett, and Cozy Cole) in recording V-discs ("Victory discs" for the military).

1945: Armstrong does Armed Forces Radio Service broadcasts throughout the year. . . . "I Wonder," recorded for Decca in January, reaches No. 3 on the *Billboard* rhythm and blues chart. Some of Armstrong's fans are dismayed by the crossover. . . . While booked at the Club Zanzibar in New York from December (1944) to March, on January 17 he plays in the second *Esquire* All-American Jazz Concert in New Orleans and on February 11 on the WNEW Fats Waller Memorial program in New York. . . . The rest of the year is spent getting on and off the tour bus.

1946: On January 10 Armstrong performs at the third annual *Esquire* All-American Jazz Concert in New York along with Johnny Hodges, Duke Ellington, and Billy Strayhorn. . . . Also in January he records with Ella Fitzgerald "The Frim Fram Sauce," which reaches No. 4 on the *Billboard* rhythm and blues chart. . . . In New York he plays at the Aquarium in April and May and at the Apollo in June. . . . In Chicago he appears at the Regal in June and at the Savoy Ballroom in August. . . . Armstrong is back in Los Angeles in late August to play and record. While there in September he makes the film *New Orleans* for United Artists with many other jazz greats like Kid Ory, Barney Bigard, Red Callender, Zutty Singleton, and Billie Holliday.

1947: On February 8 in Carnegie Hall Armstrong plays with the Edmond Hall sextet on the first half of the program and with his own big band on the second half. The smaller group is such an overwhelming success that the course of Armstrong's career is changed. His big band is about to dissolve after its last recording session on May 12. . . . A Town Hall concert in New York on May 17 with a small combo put together by Bobby Hackett underscores the demise of the big band. . . . On June 19 the premiere of the film *New Orleans* at the Winter Garden Theater in New York is followed by a concert (broadcast over NBC radio) with Armstrong and the All Stars. . . . July sees him playing at the Apollo in New York before going the next month to Hollywood to film *A Song Is Born* with Danny Kaye for RKO Studios. . . . On August 9 Armstrong plays at the Giants of Jazz concert with Tommy Dorsey, Benny Goodman, and others in Los Angeles. . . . On August 13 in Los Angeles the new All Stars (Jack Teagarden, Barney Bigard, Dick Cary, Arvell Shaw, Sid Catlett, and singer Velma Middleton) make their official debut at Billy Berg's Club. This small combo will endure through many personnel changes and will be Armstrong's vehicle for three dozen years. . . . The All Stars move on to Chicago in the fall to play and record, with gigs following in Boston and New York. The Boston concert of November 30 is one of the first boxed sets of jazz recordings, although it is not released for four years. . . . Two books about Armstrong are published: Robert Goffin's *Horn of Plenty* and Hugues Panassié's *Louis Armstrong*.

1948: Throughout the year Armstrong speaks out against bebop music. "You get all them weird chords which don't mean nothing . . . and you got no melody to remember and no beat to dance to," he is quoted in the April 7, 1948, issue of *Down Beat* (p. 2). . . . After a gig at Billy Berg's in Los Angeles and a couple of dates in New York in January, Armstrong and the All Stars are off to Europe. February 22–28 they participate in the Nice Jazz Festival in France. . . . In March they appear in Paris at the Salle Pleyel and then later in the month broadcast from Switzerland. . . . Returning to the United States in May, they play at Carnegie Hall. . . . June 2–12 is spent in Philadelphia, broadcasting from Ciro's. . . . Armstrong's back on the West Coast in the fall. . . . On November 21 he makes his first appearance on television on CBS's *Toast of the Town.* He will be on television more than 150 times during his career.

1949: Armstrong and the All Stars are nearly always on the road (up to 300 nights a year) during the late 1940s and early 1950s in auditoriums and clubs, in cities and small towns, and on college campuses. . . . In January he plays at Governor Adlai Stevenson's inaugural ball in Illinois. . . . Later in January and into February the All Stars perform in Vancouver, British Columbia. . . . On February 21 Armstrong is in San Francisco for Bing Crosby's radio show when he makes the cover of *Time* magazine on the occasion of his coronation as "King of the Zulus" for New Orleans' annual Mardi Gras. Armstrong, who is drawn with a crown of trumpets, is the first jazz musician to make the cover. . . . Between June 11 and September 10 he makes four appearances on the *Eddie Condon Floor Show* on NBC-TV in New York. . . . Now exclusively with Decca, Armstrong records with various studio bands. His "Blueberry Hill" with Gordon Jenkins's band, for example, is a hit. . . . In October and November Armstrong and the All Stars are back in Europe, though manager Joe Glaser had doubts about the financial success of another European tour. However, Armstrong is practically revered in Europe and Scandinavia, and the All Stars play to sold-out houses in Switzerland, France, Italy, and all over Scandinavia. . . . In Rome Armstrong films *La botta e risposta* in October, and he and his wife Lucille have an audience with Pope Pius XII.

1950: The year is spent very successfully touring and recording with the All Stars. Armstrong also begins working on the second volume of his autobiography. . . . In San Francisco on January 18 he appears on Bing Crosby's television show. . . . In July Armstrong's supposed fiftieth birthday is celebrated, and *Down Beat* magazine devotes most of an issue to him. . . . In August Armstrong records with Louis Jordan and His Tympany Five (a new version of "You Rascal, You" with a trumpet intro that amazes musicians) and with Ella Fitzgerald ("Can Anyone Explain?" and "Dream a Little Dream of Me"). . . . Early in December in Los Angeles Armstrong makes the Paramount picture *Here Comes the Groom* with Bing Crosby and Dorothy Lamour. . . . Late in December he and the All Stars film *The Strip* for MGM. They receive $20,000 for seven days' work. . . . From this year on, the new 33-rpm microgroove technology provides better-quality, longer-playing recordings.

1951: Touring with the All Stars continues almost nonstop throughout the whole year, but Armstrong pauses to film *Glory Alley* with Leslie Caron and Gilbert Roland for MGM in November and to make five television appearances at various times. . . . He records with the All Stars some during the year and also with other vocalists and groups, for example, Bing Crosby ("Gone Fishin' ") in April and Ella Fitzgerald in November.

1952: Throughout the year Armstrong makes numerous television appearances, beginning on January 1 with Frank Sinatra on CBS. . . . February and March are spent touring California, Colorado, Hawaii, and generally the West Coast, including Vancouver, British Columbia. . . . In the spring *Down Beat* readers select Armstrong "the most important musical figure of all time." He beats out Duke Ellington (number two) and J.S. Bach (number six). . . . The All Stars are on the road in April and May, from Arizona to Canada, and many stops in between. . . . In June and July Armstrong and the band spend four weeks at the Blue Note in Chicago and then go to New York to play at the Paramount. . . . It's back to Europe in October and November, where they play in Germany, Switzerland, Italy, Belgium, France, Scandinavia, and North Africa, returning to the United States at the end of the year. . . . *Satchmo: My Life in New Orleans* by Armstrong, which covers the years 1900–1922, is first published in France as *Ma Nouvelle Orléans.* The book comes out two years later in the United States.

1953: After a gig in February with Sy Oliver's orchestra in Detroit, Armstrong takes the All Stars back on the road. . . . Manager Joe Glaser arranges what was to have been a six-week tour beginning in April with Benny Goodman. Advance sales are excellent, but Goodman and Armstrong clash, and in Boston Goodman is admitted to a hospital (for possible heart problems) and further engagements are canceled. . . . In early June Armstrong with the All Stars films *The Glenn Miller Story* for Universal-International with Jimmy Stewart. Armstrong plays himself, performing "Basin Street Blues." . . . The All Stars play at the Blue Note in Chicago in July and August. . . . In December and on into early January Armstrong and the band tour Japan most successfully.

1954: Armstrong no longer records exclusively for Decca but is a free agent, and Joe Glaser successfully moves him from label to label. . . . Between July 12 and 14 Armstrong and the All Stars record an LP of the music of W.C. Handy in Chicago for Columbia. According to clarinetist Barney Bigard, this album is Armstrong's favorite record. . . . Armstrong and the All Stars continue touring all over the country. . . . In August *Ebony* magazine publishes Armstrong's article "Why I Like Dark Women." . . . In November he and the band tour Australia, doing twenty sold-out concerts in ten days. . . . *Satchmo: My Life in New Orleans,* the second volume of Armstrong's autobiography, is published by Prentice-Hall.

1955: Armstrong appears on national television broadcasts seven times throughout the year. . . . On January 21 Decca records Armstrong and the All Stars in Los Angeles at the Crescendo Club and releases a double LP including many of his hits, both old and new. . . . In February Armstrong plays at the Absinthe House in New Orleans. . . . Most of April and May are spent in New York where he records the album *Satch Plays Fats,* which charts at No. 10 on the *Billboard* top 40. Included on the LP are such Fats Waller favorites as "Ain't Misbehavin' " and "Honeysuckle Rose." . . . On September 28 Armstrong records one of his biggest hits, "Mack the Knife" from Brecht and Weill's *Threepenny Opera.* . . . Jeanette Eaton's book for young people, *Trumpeter's Tale: The Story of Young Louis Armstrong,* is published. . . . From October through December Armstrong and the All Stars are in Europe on a U.S. State Department tour playing in Scandinavia, Germany, Holland, Belgium, Switzerland, and Italy. They cut some records while they are there this time, and the LP *Ambassador Satch* is issued by Columbia the following year. When they play in West Berlin, fans from the East Zone sneak over to hear them. "Hardly any of them could speak any English, but that didn't bother them or us. The music did all the talking for both sides" (Jones and Chilton, p. 31). . . . On December 13 Armstrong is the subject of Edward R. Murrow's popular *See It Now* television show, including film footage from the All Stars' recent European tour.

1956: In January Armstrong and the All Stars are playing in Los Angeles. While there they film *High Society* with Bing Crosby and Grace Kelly for MGM. . . . In the spring they go on another foreign tour sponsored by the U.S. State Department. The itinerary includes Australia, the Far East, and then England, Scotland, and Ireland, before heading to Africa where 10,000 fans turn out to greet Armstrong on May 24 at Accra Airport in Ghana. He is struck by the resemblance between himself and the Ghanians. His first performance there (May 25) draws a crowd of 100,000. Another highlight of the tour is his performance for Kwame Nkruma, the prime minister of Ghana. A news crew from CBS television again follows the All Stars, and their footage (combined with that of the previous year's European tour) later becomes an hour-long documentary called *Satchmo the Great,* which premieres on September 5 the following year.... On July 6 Armstrong does a Voice of America broadcast from the Newport Jazz Festival.... He performs with the Lewisohn Stadium Symphony Orchestra and Leonard Bernstein in New York on July 14.... In mid-August he and Ella Fitzgerald record with the Oscar Peterson Quartet in Los Angeles.... Armstrong plays the role of the leader of a circus band in September in an NBC ninety-minute musical called *The Lord Don't Play Favorites,* also starring Kay Starr, Robert Stack, Dick Haymes, and Buster Keaton.... On December 18 Armstrong performs with the Royal Philharmonic Orchestra in Royal Festival Hall in London to benefit the Hungarian and Central Europe Relief Fund.

1957: On January 28 Armstrong finishes recording a four-LP set for Decca titled *Satchmo: A Musical Autobiography* with recreations of many of his masterworks from the 1920s and 1930s.... On February 19 in Knoxville, Tennessee, someone throws a stick of dynamite from a car at the theater where Armstrong is giving a concert for an integrated audience. Armstrong tells them not to worry ("It's only the telephone"), diplomatically downplaying the incident.... In May Armstrong and the All Stars perform before an audience of 100,000 in Kingston, Jamaica, before a tour of the East Coast of the United States.... In July they headline the Newport Jazz Festival.... Later in the month Armstrong plays at Lewisohn Stadium in New York, then in Atlantic City with Lionel Hampton's band.... On July 31 and on October 14 Armstrong records with Oscar Peterson and his trio in Los Angeles.... Also in Los Angeles, Armstrong and Ella Fitzgerald cut *Ella and Louis Again* on July 23 and August 13. On August 18 the two record *Porgy and Bess*.... On September 5 in New York the hour-long documentary *Satchmo the Great* (an expanded version of Edward R. Murrow and Fred Friendly's *See It Now* television show about Armstrong) is premiered.... On September 18, while on tour in Grand Forks, North Dakota, Armstrong speaks out against the U.S. government, Eisenhower, and Governor Faubus of Arkansas after the school integration incident in Little Rock. Armstrong decides to cancel a State Department–sponsored tour of the USSR. ("The people over there ask me what's wrong with my country. What am I supposed to say?" [*New York Herald-Tribune,* Sept. 19, 1957, p. A3]) ... In October he and the All Stars are on tour (as usual).... Late in the month he begins a tour of South America with the All Stars. They receive a triumphant welcome especially in Brazil, also playing in Argentina, Uruguay, and Venezuela. In Caracas Armstrong and All Star trombonist Trummy Young stage a mock bullfight to much applause.... It's back to New York to spend Christmas at home and appear with the All Stars on December 30 on NBC on a musical extravaganza, the first of many *Timex All Star Shows*.

1958: Early in the year Armstrong and the All Stars are on the road all over the Midwest.... On February 4 with Sy Oliver's choir and orchestra in New York, Armstrong records a gospel album for Decca, *Louis and the Good Book,* his bestselling LP to date.... In May the All Stars continue touring and play in Montreal.... On July 7 they appear at the Newport Jazz Festival again where they are filmed for director

Bert Stern's documentary about the Festival, *Jazz on a Summer's Day* (Union Films). ... Later in July Armstrong plays again at Lewisohn Stadium.... September and October are spent in Los Angeles playing and filming *The Five Pennies* at Paramount with Danny Kaye and also *The Beat Generation* for MGM.... Late in the year he and the All Stars tour the East Coast.

1959: On January 7 Armstrong and Dizzy Gillespie appear on CBS television on the *Timex All-Star Jazz Show* in New York to play "Umbrella Man."... From mid-January through late June Armstrong and the All Stars make an exhausting but profitable tour of Denmark (where he appears in the film *Kaerlighedens Melodi*), Sweden, Holland, Germany (where he makes the films *Die Nacht vor der Premiere* and *La paloma*), Switzerland, Austria, England, Belgium, Greece, Turkey, France, and Italy. While in Italy he suffers a heart attack in Spoleto on June 23 and is hospitalized until the end of the month.... On his ceremonial birthday, July 4, at Lewisohn Stadium in New York, Armstrong makes a surprise appearance and plays for fifteen minutes to wild applause.... In August in Chicago he is recording with the Dukes of Dixieland and performing with the All Stars at the Playboy Jazz Festival.... From September on he is back on the road for limited engagements, making recordings, and appearing on various television shows.

1960: On New Year's Day Armstrong appears on NBC-TV's *Bell Telephone Hour* in New York.... Early in the year Armstrong goes back on the road with the All Stars.... In May he records with the Dukes of Dixieland in New York.... In June there are gigs at Madison Square Garden in New York and in Canada.... Armstrong hits the Newport Jazz Festival again in July with the All Stars.... He and pal Bing Crosby record *Bing and Satchmo,* with full studio orchestra and choir, for MGM Records on July 5 in New York.... October finds Armstrong and the All Stars back in Africa on a U.S. State Department tour of forty-five concerts seemingly all over the continent, except for South Africa, where the prime minister nixes a visit.... Armstrong spends December in Paris where he plays several concerts and films *Paris Blues* for United Artists starring Paul Newman, Joanne Woodward, and Sidney Poitier, with music by Duke Ellington.

1961: During the year Armstrong and the All Stars appear five times on CBS-TV's popular *Ed Sullivan Show* and tour widely as usual.... In February there is more international travel for the All Stars with concerts in Europe and Africa. Singer Velma Middleton, who has been with Armstrong since 1942, has a fatal stroke in Sierra Leone on February 10.... On April 3 and 4 Armstrong collaborates with Duke Ellington in New York on an album for Roulette Records.... During the summer Armstrong makes his annual appearance at the Newport Jazz Festival.... For several days in mid-September Armstrong, pianist Dave Brubeck, singer Carmen McRae, and a small jazz ensemble record Dave and Iola Brubeck's jazz oratorio *The Real Ambassadors* in New York. The work get its first concert performance the following year in September at the Monterey Jazz Festival.... On September 30 Armstrong plays in the Dixieland at Disneyland Festival in Anaheim, California, with Kid Ory and Johnny St. Cyr from the original Hot Five. Their performance of four tunes (including "Muskrat Ramble" and "Bourbon Street Parade") is recorded for the short promotional film *Disneyland after Dark,* which is premiered on television during the following April.... At home in New York for the holidays, Armstrong plays in December at Basin Street East.

1962: From February through May Armstrong and the All Stars tour Europe, performing in Germany, Austria, France, Switzerland, Italy, England, Spain, Portugal, and Holland. . . . On July 7 it's back to the Newport Jazz Festival. . . . The rest of the year is spent on the tour bus. . . . On December 14 the All Stars play on *The Ed Sullivan Show* from Guantanamo Naval Base in Cuba. . . . New Year's Eve finds Armstrong playing at the Cocoanut Grove in Los Angeles.

1963: March through May Armstrong and the All Stars tour New Zealand, Australia, South Korea, Japan, Hong Kong, and Manila. . . . On May 22 Armstrong plays in New York at the Waldorf Astoria at a dinner for President John F. Kennedy. . . . For the rest of the year Armstrong tours with the All Stars throughout the United States. . . . On July 2 it's time again for the Newport Jazz Festival. . . . On December 3 Armstrong and the All Stars, plus a string section and a banjo, record "Hello Dolly!" in New York for Kapp Records. The song is from a new Broadway musical and becomes an incredible hit. By May 1964 it is, as the *New York Post* estimates, played 10,000 times a day in North America. . . . On December 1, at the end of a concert at Smith College in Massachusetts, Armstrong plays "God Bless America," unaccompanied and alone on stage, in homage to President Kennedy, who was assassinated nine days earlier.

1964: In January Armstrong co-hosts the daily *Mike Douglas Show* for a week in Philadelphia. The All Stars play, and he sings (with Douglas at times) but does not pick up his horn. . . . Armstrong spends a week in March at Beth Israel Hospital in New York for acute edema in the lower right leg. His health is beginning to flag seriously. . . . On March 22 he is the mystery guest on the popular *What's My Line?* TV show on NBC and sings a chorus of "Hello Dolly!" when begged by panelist Arlene Francis. . . . Early in May Armstrong's recording of "Hello Dolly!" of the previous year reaches the No. 1 spot (bumping the Beatles) on *Billboard*'s Top 40 list where it stays for six weeks. . . . July 2 is "Louis Armstrong Day" at the World's Fair in New York, and Armstrong is on hand to receive a medal. . . . The rest of the year is spent playing and recording as much as his health will allow.

1965: January is busy with such varied gigs as playing at San Quentin prison in California, touring Minnesota, and appearing at President Lyndon Johnson's inaugural ball in Washington, D.C. . . . In February Armstrong plays in Nova Scotia, Iceland, the West Indies, and Miami. . . . March finds the All Stars on a tour of Eastern Europe. . . . Back in the States, Armstrong takes six weeks off beginning in April for dental surgery. . . . Late in May it's back to Europe for a tour including England, France (including the Antibes Festival on the French Riviera), Scandinavia, and Hungary. While in Copenhagen he reads of the race riots in Selma, Alabama, and remarks, "They would beat Jesus if he was black and marched" (Giddins, 1988, p. 165). . . . On July 4 (his unofficial sixty-fifth birthday) Armstrong begins a two-week engagement at the Steel Pier in Atlantic City. . . . Later in July he is in Hollywood to make a short film for television (*Solo*) and *When the Boys Meet the Girls* with Connie Francis and Paul Anka for MGM. . . . On September 17 Armstrong and the All Stars broadcast from the Monterey Jazz Festival for Voice of American radio. . . . Armstrong and the band return to New Orleans in October for the first time in twelve years. They give a benefit concert for a New Orleans jazz museum, and Armstrong is presented with a key to the city. . . . In New York in late November and early December Armstrong films *A Man Called Adam* with Sammy Davis, Jr., for Embassy Pictures. . . . On December 27 Armstrong is the celebrity guest on NBC's popular *I've Got a Secret* television show.

1966: Although suffering minor ailments, Armstrong keeps playing, recording, and singing. He sings more and plays less during the late 1960s, but he is still much in demand and has become a legend.... *Life* magazine runs a fifteen-page cover story about Armstrong titled "An American Genius" in its April 15 issue.... In May Armstrong sings for Prince Philip in Los Angeles and does a brief stint with his "inspirator" Guy Lombardo and his Royal Canadians.... July through September Armstrong and the All Stars play at the Jones Beach Marine Theater in New York.... The rest of the year is spent touring and making television appearances.

1967: On April 24 Armstrong and the All Stars play for the Grammy Awards television show on NBC in New York.... In late May and June Armstrong struggles with a bout of pneumonia.... He is on the road again in July with stops in Ohio and Atlantic City, before taking off for Dublin, St. Tropez, Majorca, Copenhagen, and Juan-les-Pins (France) with the All Stars.... Back in the States, on August 16 he records his hit song "What a Wonderful World."... Armstrong is ill again in September and spends some time recuperating at home in Corona.... He finishes out the year making television appearances and a few recordings.

1968: New Year's Day Armstrong and the All Stars play at the Tropicana Hotel in Las Vegas on the NBC television show "All Star Parade of Bands."... In Italy with the All Stars in early February, Armstrong appears at the San Remo Festival and also has an audience with Pope Paul VI.... In late February and March there are gigs in Pennsylvania, Maine, and Mexico City, and then it's back to New York.... On three dates in February and March Armstrong and the All Stars plus strings and choir record *Disney Songs the Satchmo Way.* This is the last recording of Armstrong playing the trumpet.... In the spring he refuses to appear on the Oscar awards telecast out of respect for the recently assassinated Martin Luther King, Jr. Other performers such as Diahann Carroll, Sammy Davis, Jr., and Sidney Poitier do the same.... In May Armstrong makes his last appearance in a feature film, *Hello Dolly!,* in Hollywood with Barbra Streisand for 20th-Century Fox Studios.... In June he appears at the New Orleans Jazz Festival, then is off to England (through much of July) to tour and appear on BBC television and radio.... Complaining of shortness of breath in September, Armstrong spends the next seven months in and out of Beth Israel Hospital in New York and at home convalescing. Acute heart and kidney failure is the diagnosis.

1969: Released from the hospital briefly in January, Armstrong has to return in February for more heart problems and a kidney infection. He undergoes a tracheotomy and is hospitalized until April. Dr. Gary Zucker, his longtime physician, tells him that he should no longer play the trumpet. Zucker reports that Armstrong "made it abundantly clear that the only thing that was important to him was to continue to make music. If he couldn't make music then he was through, and life wasn't worth anything" (Collier, 1983, p. 328).... Armstrong's longtime manager Joe Glaser, who had been comatose following a stroke, dies on June 6.... On October 28 Armstrong is in London to record "We Have All the Time in the World," the theme song for the new James Bond movie *On Her Majesty's Secret Service.* It is his only recording of the year.... Also in October Armstrong is interviewed in his home in Corona for a French documentary titled *L'Aventure du Jazz.*

1970: While he is in a generally weakened condition and now plays much less than he sings, Armstrong makes some twenty television appearances throughout the year.... In April he attends a New Orleans jazz festival that is dedicated to him as the "town's most famous son."... In late May in New York he records the album *Louis Armstrong and His Friends* for the Flying

Dutchman label, singing a variety of songs from "Mood Indigo" to "We Shall Overcome." . . . On July 3, the eve of his unofficial birthday, Armstrong is guest of honor at a concert at the Shrine Auditorium in Los Angeles. Hoagy Carmichael is on hand to present him with a gigantic birthday cake. . . . On July 10 the Newport Jazz Festival opens and is billed as a tribute to Louis Armstrong. Dizzy Gillespie, Bobby Hackett, Joe Newman, Wild Bill Davidson, Jimmy Owens, and Ray Nance each play an Armstrong favorite from different points in his career. Armstrong sings a bit on two numbers. The evening's performance becomes the subject of three documentaries: *The Antiquarians, Finale,* and *Trumpet Players' Tribute.* Another film, *Anatomy of a Performance,* is made of footage from preconcert rehearsals and features some narration by Armstrong. . . . In August he records an album, his last, with the country and western Nashville Rhythm Section in New York. . . . Armstrong and the All Stars play a two-week stint in Las Vegas in September. . . . In October he both plays and sings at a charity event in London. . . . Right after Christmas Armstrong begins a two-week gig in Las Vegas.

1971: In late January the ailing Armstrong appears at the National Press Club in Washington, D.C., with trombonist Tyree Glenn. . . . In all Armstrong makes eight television appearances this year. His last is on May 11 with Bing Crosby on *The David Frost Show.* . . . Armstrong makes his last recording in his home in Corona on February 26: Over a musical background he reads "The Night before Christmas." . . . In early March Armstrong, against his doctors' advice, plays a two-week gig at the Waldorf Astoria's Empire Room in New York with the All Stars. . . . On March 15 he suffers a heart attack and is admitted to Beth Israel Hospital, where he is in intensive care until mid-April. On May 6 he leaves the hospital and returns to his home in Corona. . . . On July 4, his supposed birthday, Armstrong does a television interview from his home. . . . The next day he makes plans to bring the All Stars back together for a rehearsal. . . . On July 6 around 5 A.M. Armstrong dies in his sleep at home from kidney and heart failure. . . . On July 8 approximately 25,000 mourners file past his open casket at the Seventh Regiment Armory on Park Avenue and 66th Street in New York. He is buried on July 9 after a funeral (which is broadcast to sixteen countries) at the Congregational Church of Corona. Many musicians and celebrities are in attendance, including Duke Ellington, Ella Fitzgerald, Benny Goodman, Lionel Hampton, Dizzy Gillespie, Earl Hines, Bing Crosby, Frank Sinatra, Gene Krupa, Guy Lombardo, and others. Peggy Lee sings "The Lord's Prayer," and Al Hibbler sings "Nobody Knows the Trouble I've Seen" and, to conclude the service, "When the Saints Go Marching In." After a eulogy by longtime friend and New York television and radio personality Fred Robbins, and a few words from musician and unoffical jazz spokesman Dr. Billy Taylor, Armstrong is buried in Flushing Cemetery in Corona. . . . On July 11 a traditionally boisterous jazz funeral is held in Armstrong's hometown. Many bands play, and as many as 15,000 fans convene. The Onward Brass Band, which Armstrong used to second line as a small boy, winds through the streets of his childhood.

Posthumously: On August 28, 1971, Lil Hardin Armstrong suffers a heart attack and dies while playing the piano on a televised Armstrong memorial concert in Chicago. . . . On July 4, 1973, Lucille Armstrong is on hand in New York to rename the Singer Bowl the Louis Armstrong Memorial Stadium. Fifty musicians play a tribute to Louis Armstrong. . . . In 1974 a bust of Armstrong is dedicated in the Jardins de Cimiez in Nice, France, in the presence of Lucille Armstrong and Princess Grace of Monaco.... In May 1977 the name of the Meadow School (a.k.a. PS 143) in Queens, New York, is changed to Louis Armstrong School. Later a Queens middle school (a.k.a. IS 227) also takes the name Armstrong.... On July 4, 1976, an eleven-foot-tall bronze statue of Armstrong by Elizabeth Catlett (financed by Bing Crosby, other performers, and the public) is dedicated in Jackson Square in New Orleans. Four years later (April 1980) the statue is moved to the new Louis Armstrong Park, which is near the French Quarter on the site of the old Congo Square and within a mile of Armstrong's birthplace.... Lucille Armstrong dies suddenly on October 5, 1983, in Boston where she has gone to attend a fundraising concert to honor her husband at Brandeis University. She is buried in Flushing beside her husband.... In 1987 Armstrong is back in the Top 40 on the charts for six weeks with "What a Wonderful World," which is featured in the current popular film *Good Morning, Vietnam*.... On September 7, 1995, the U.S. Postal Service issues the Louis Armstrong commemorative stamp.... In the thirteenth arrondissement of Paris, near the old Polydor recording studios where Armstrong had worked in the 1930s, a square is named in his honor, Place Louis Armstrong.... On July 13, 2001, in advance of what would have been Armstrong's one hundredth birthday on August 4, the New Orleans airport becomes the Louis Armstrong New Orleans International Airport. It is the first major airport named after a musician, jazz or otherwise, black or white.

APPENDIX 3

MOVIES

When the film version of *Hello Dolly!* came out in 1969, it was common in movie theaters for audiences to burst into spontaneous applause when the camera moved to Armstrong performing the theme song. While he didn't have this effect in all of his twenty-eight full-length feature films, his contribution was inevitably beneficial, and it frequently saved the day. In addition to movies, he also appeared in cartoons, documentaries, "soundies" (short films intended for use in coin-operated viewing machines), and televised broadcasts. For details on plot, stars, directors, music played, and special features, please consult the encyclopedia. An analytical essay appears under "movies." Under "television" is an entry on Armstrong's approximately 150 appearances on the small screen.

The following list includes most of his work in the film studio. Not listed are the many movies in which he may have been heard but was not himself present on the set. Examples are *Good Morning, Vietnam* (1987) and many Woody Allen films. For an incredibly detailed, all-inclusive study of this subject, see Klaus Stratemann's *Louis Armstrong on the Screen* (JazzMedia, 1996). Full-length feature films are marked with an asterisk.

Anatomy of a Performance, 1970
Antiquarians, The, 1970
**Artists and Models,* 1937
**Atlantic City,* 1944
Aventure du jazz, 1970
**Beat Generation, The,* 1959
**botta e risposta, La,* 1951
Boy from New Orleans, The, 1970
**Cabin in the Sky,* 1943
Disneyland after Dark, 1962
**Every Day's a Holiday,* 1938
**Ex-Flame,* 1930
Finale, 1970
**Five Pennies, The,* 1959
**Glenn Miller Story, The,* 1954
**Glory Alley,* 1952
**Going Places,* 1938
Goodyear Jazz Concert: Louis Armstrong, 1962
**Hello Dolly!,* 1969
**Here Comes the Groom,* 1951
**High Society,* 1956
I'll Be Glad When You're Dead, You Rascal, You, 1932 and 1942
**Jam Session,* 1944
Jazz, 2000
Jazz Legends, The, 1985
Jazz on a Summer's Day, 1960
**Kaerlighedens Melodi,* 1959
**København, Kalundborg Og?,* 1933
**Man Called Adam, A,* 1966
**Nacht vor der Premiere, Die,* 1959
**New Orleans,* 1947

**paloma, La,* 1959
**Paris Blues,* 1961
**Pennies from Heaven,* 1936
**Pillow to Post,* 1945
Rhapsody in Black and Blue, A, 1932
**route du bonheur, La,* 1953
Satchmo: Louis Armstrong, 1989
Satchmo the Great, 1957
Shine, 1942
Solo, 1965
**Song Is Born, A* 1948
**Strip, The,* 1951
Studio Visit, 1946
Swingin' on Nothing, 1942
Swing Wedding/Minnie the Moocher's Wedding Day, 1937
Trumpet Kings, 1985
Trumpet Players' Tribute, 1970
When It's Sleepy Time Down South, 1942
**When the Boys Meet the Girls,* 1965

APPENDIX 4

ON THE WEB

A wealth of information (including many fine photos and illustrations of interest) can be found about Armstrong and his music on the Web. While naturally some sites are more complete and accurate than others, the following are for the most part, as Armstrong might have said, solid.

All About Jazz. http://www.allaboutjazz.com/larmstrong.htm. This general source for the jazz fan may not be as accurate as it could be, but it has a well-organized, uncluttered home page. Browsers can join in on discussions and submit short articles, as well as CD and book reviews. Other features include a timeline and links to related sites.

All-Music Guide, The. http://www.allmusic.com/. Some feel that this is the best Web source of information on jazz of all kinds. Organized by albums and CDs, many of which are out of print, one finds enough detailed biographies, professional reviews, videographies, and bibliographies to make this a reference worth consulting.

Armstrong Lyrics. http://www.lyricsconnection.com/. This and the Louis Armstrong Tribute Site below are the two best (i.e., consistently reliable) sources for lyrics to many of the songs that Armstrong sang.

Downbeat.com. http://www.downbeat.com/. The home office of jazz offers a well-organized and informative Armstrong page, complete with a photo gallery, bibliography, discography, MP3 downloads, and links to related sites.

Jazz Roots. http://www.jass.com/. This site provides an excellent overview of early jazz musicians, with an essay on jazz's formative years, portraits of musicians, a timeline, and some fun features such as an early jazz quiz and e-postcards.

Louis Armstrong: A Cultural Legacy. http://www. npg. si. edu/exh/ armstrong/ index.htm. Between 1994 and 1997, an exhibition titled *Louis Armstrong: A Cultural Legacy* (curated by Marc H. Miller) toured the United States, stopping in eight cities. This site contains downloadable samples of the visual material from that exhibition, along with a fairly detailed essay on Armstrong's life. Like the traveling exhibit, this Web site is the work of the Smithsonian Institution.

Louis Armstrong Discography, The. http://www.satchography.com/. A labor of love by super fan Scott Johnson, this discography is accurate, user-friendly, and very detailed.

Louis Armstrong Odyssey, The. http://www.louissatchmoarmstrong.com/. This extensive site has many sections, the best of which are the lengthy biography, the generous "slideshow," and a batch of helpful album reviews. Most ambitiously, the site creators have even included a basic guide to the trumpet and instructions on how to play it.

Louis Armstrong Online. http://www.satchmo.net. This learned and professional official site of the Louis Armstrong House and Archives is both inviting and gratifying. Curator Michael Cogswell and his staff provide valuable information about books, exhibits, recordings, and Armstrong's life. Richly illustrated with items from the Archives' holdings, the site features a bulletin board that sees many a lively discussion. No wonder it gets some 8,000 hits a day from ninety different countries.

Louis Armstrong Tribute Site, The. http://www.members.fortunecity.com/ kybhr_enterprizes/. Another labor of love by a super fan, this lively site includes information about Armstrong history, quotations, photos, lyrics, and links to other sites.

PBS Jazz Biographies: Louis Armstrong. http://www. pbs. org/ jazz/ biography/ artist _id_armstrong_louis. htm. Based on the Ken Burns documentary *Jazz,* this site has a generous sample of audio clips, both the music of Armstrong and excerpts from National Public Radio broadcasts, including some of Armstrong himself speaking. There are also a biographical essay and a few photographs.

Red Hot Jazz Archive, The. http://www.redhotjazz.com/. This excellent site focuses on jazz before 1930. It offers essays, discographies, bibliographies, and some downloadable recordings of artists and bands to the early 1930s.

Satchmo.com. http://www.satchmo.com/. Begun in 1995 to disseminate information about the music of Louisiana in general and New Orleans in particular, this site features a "Louis Armstrong Centennial" section with current news of Armstrong-related events, a photo gallery, a discussion forum, quotes and tributes, and additional links. Several places on the site offer Armstrong merchandise.

Schomburg Video Oral History Gallery: Louis Armstrong. http://www.nypl.org/research/sc/scl/MULTIMED/JAZZHIST/jazzhist. html. Under the aegis of the New York Public Library, the Schomburg Center for Research in Black Culture has collected oral histories from those who knew Armstrong. The site offers photos of the interviewees, audio snippets from the histories, video clip transcripts, and full catalog descriptions of the materials. Among those who have something to say about Armstrong are Jon Faddis, Doc Cheatham, Art Farmer, Milt Hinton, Marian McPartland, and Clark Terry.

Time 100: Artists & Entertainers—Louis Armstrong. http://www.time.com/time/time100 / artists / profile / armstrong.html. This site features a genial essay by Armstrong expert Stanley Crouch, a reprint of the Armstrong cover story from the February 21, 1949, issue of *Time,* a video clip from *High Society,* a brief timeline, and a quiz.

Welcome to Cape Cod, Massachusetts. http://www.libertyhall.com / stamp / 1971.html. This oddly named site features a wonderful collection of Louis Armstrong postage stamps. It wasn't until 1995 that the United States put Armstrong's visage on a stamp and thereby became the tenth nation to do so. You can download images of favorite stamps for your own site.

SELECTED BIBLIOGRAPHY

The Armstrong literature is predictably vast, and no one has contributed to it more than Armstrong himself. The following is a selection of essential items, many of which may be hard to find but some of which, fortunately, have been either reprinted or excerpted in Thomas Brothers's *Louis Armstrong, in His Own Words* or Joshua Berrett's *The Louis Armstrong Companion*. These happy duplications are indicated by brackets, as are the eight books intended for juvenile readers. Additional information on many of the authors, subjects, places, music, and ensembles mentioned here can be found in the encyclopedia. The "CD" number after some items refers to the numbered recordings listed in Appendix 1.

Albert, Richard N., ed. *From Blues to Bop*. Baton Rouge: Louisiana State University Press, 1990.

Albertson, Chris. *Bessie*. Rev. ed. New Haven, CT: Yale University Press, 2003.

——. *Giants of Jazz: Louis Armstrong*. Alexandria, VA: Time-Life Books, 1978.

Alexios, T. "Armstrong Gets Stamp of Approval." *Down Beat* 63 (June 1995), p. 13.

Allen, Walter C. *Hendersonia*. Highland Park, NJ: Jazz Monographs No. 4, 1973.

Allen, Walter C., and Brian A.L. Rust. *"King" Oliver*. Rev. ed. by Laurie Wright. Chigwell, England: Storyville Publications, 1987.

Anderson, Gene H. *Louis Armstrong's Original Hot Five*. Hillsdale, NY: Pendragon Press, 2004.

Armstrong, Lillian Hardin. *Satchmo and Me*. Liner notes. Riverside 12-120, LP recording. [Excerpted in Berrett, 1999, pp. 36–42]

Armstrong, Louis. *50 Hot Choruses for Cornet*. Transcribed by Elmer Schoebel. Chicago: Melrose Bros., 1927. Rpt. as part of *Louis Armstrong's 44 Trumpet Solos and 125 Jazz Breaks*. New York: Charles Hansen, 1951.

——. *125 Jazz Breaks for Cornet*. Transcribed by Elmer Schoebel. Chicago: Melrose Bros., 1927. Rpt. as part of *Louis Armstrong's 44 Trumpet Solos and 125 Jazz Breaks*. New York: Charles Hansen, 1951.

——. "Berigan Can't Do No Wrong." *Down Beat* 8 (Sept. 1, 1941), p. 7.

——. "Bop—That's Ju-Jitsu Music." *Melody Maker* 28 (Aug. 16, 1952), p. 9.

——. "Bunk Didn't Teach Me." *The Record Changer* 9 (July–Aug. 1950), p. 30. [Rpt. Brothers, pp. 40–41]

——. "Care of the Lip." *The Record Changer* 9 (July–Aug. 1950), p. 30.

——. " 'Chicago, Chicago, That Toddlin' Town': How King and Ol' Satch Dug It in the Twenties." *Esquire's 1947 Jazz Book*, 1946, pp. 40–43.

——. "Daddy, How the Country Has

Changed! [interview with David Dachs]." *Ebony,* May 1961, p. 81.

——. *Dixieland Jazz Classics for the Cornet.* New York: Melrose Music Corp., 1951.

——. "Europe—with Kicks." *Holiday* 7 (June 1950), p. 3.

——. "Good-bye to All of You." *Esquire,* Dec. 1969, p. 158. [Rpt. Brothers, pp. 189–190]

——. "It's Tough to Top a Million." *Our World,* Aug. 1954, p. 22.

——. *A Jazz Master* [20 solos transcribed by Lee Castle and edited by Ronny Schiff]. Melville, NY: MCA Music, 1975.

——. "Jazz on a High Note." *Esquire,* Dec. 1951, pp. 85-86+. [Rpt. Brothers, pp. 127–136]

——. "Joe Oliver Is Still King." *The Record Changer* 9 (July–Aug. 1950), pp. 10–11. [Rpt. Brothers, pp. 37–39]

——. "King Oliver Is Dead." *Jazz-hot,* April–May 1938, p. 9.

——. "Les Hite et son Orchestre." *Jazz-hot,* Dec.-Jan. 1938, p. 7.

——. "Lombardo Grooves Louis! [interview with Leonard Feather]." *Metronome* 65 (Sept. 1949), p. 18. [Rpt. Brothers, pp. 165–166]

——. "Louis Armstrong, Who Tells You about Storyville, Where the Blues Were Born." *True: The Man's Magazine* 21 (No. 126, Nov. 1947), pp. 100–105.

——. *Louis Armstrong's Own Original Tunes.* New York: Clarence Williams, 1938.

——. "Louis on the Spot." *The Record Changer* 9 (July–Aug. 1950), pp. 23–24+.

——. "My Kicks in Europe." *Melody Maker* 28 (June 28, July 5, July 12, July 19, July 26, Aug. 2, Aug. 9, Aug. 16, Aug. 23, Aug. 30, 1952), all on p. 9.

——. "Pops Pops Top on Sloppy Bop [interview with Leonard Feather]." *Metronome* 65 (Oct. 1949), p. 18+.

——. "Red Beans and Rice: One of the Only Birthmarks I Can Remember." *Melody Maker* 28 (July 26, 1952), p. 9.

——. *Satchmo: My Life in New Orleans.* New York: Prentice-Hall, 1954; rpt. New York: Da Capo Press, 1986.

——. "Satchmo—My Life in New Orleans." *Saga,* Nov. 1954, p. 18.

——. "Scanning the History of Jazz." *The Jazz Review* 3 (July 1960), p. 7. [Rpt. *Esquire,* Dec. 1971, p. 184, and Brothers, pp. 173–175]

——. "Special Jive." *Harlem Tatler,* July 2 and July 19, 1940, p. 7.

——. *Swing That Music.* Intro. by Rudy Vallee. New York: Longmans, Green, 1936; rpt. New York: Da Capo Press, 1993.

——. "That Italian Boy Could Sing Jazz Like We Did!" *Melody Maker* 28 (July 19, 1952), p. 9.

——. "That Roman Jazz Took Me Back to the Riverboats!" *Melody Maker* 28 (Aug. 2, 1952), p. 9.

——. "Them Glasses Cost a Load of Loaf." *Melody Maker* 28 (Aug. 9, 1952), p. 9.

——. "There Were Three Encores to That Spaghetti!" *Melody Maker* 28 (July 5, 1952), p. 9.

——. "They Cross Iron Curtain to Hear American Jazz [interview]." *U.S. News and World Report,* Dec. 2, 1955, p. 54.

——. "They'll Never Come Back—the Good Old Days." *Melody Maker* 27 (Sept. 15, 1951), p. 3.

——. "A Toast to Mezzrow and Joe Oliver." *Melody Maker* 29 (Jan. 10, 1953), p. 3.

——. *Trumpet Method.* Munich: Chappell, 1961.

——. "Ulceratedly Yours." *Down Beat* 17 (July 14, 1950), p. 1.

——. "Why I Like Dark Women." *Ebony,* Aug. 1954, p. 61.

Asbury, Herbert. *The French Quarter: An Informal History of the New Orleans Underworld.* New York: Knopf, 1936.

——. *Gem of the Prairie.* New York: Knopf, 1940.

Ashmore, Harry S. *Arkansas: A History.* New York: W.W. Norton, 1978.

Austin, William W. *Music in the 20th Century: From Debussy through Stravinsky.* New York: W.W. Norton, 1966.

Balliett, Whitney. "A Hostile Land." *The New Yorker,* Sept. 11, 1989, pp. 106–107.

——. "King Louis." *The New Yorker,* Aug. 8, 1970, p. 70.

——. "Louis, Miles, and the Duke [review of Ken Burns' *Jazz*]." *The New Yorker,* Dec. 25, 2000–Jan. 1, 2001, pp. 158–163.

Baraka, Amiri. *Blues People.* New York: Morrow, 1963.

Barker, Danny. *A Life in Jazz.* Ed. by Alyn Shipton. London: Macmillan, 1986.

" 'Beat' Readers Elect Louis to Hall of Fame." *Down Beat* 19 (Dec. 1952), p. 1.

Bechet, Sidney. *Treat It Gentle.* New York: Hill and Wang, 1960; rpt. New York: Da Capo Press, 1975.

[Belair, Felix.] "United States Has Secret Sonic Weapon—Jazz." *New York Times,* Nov. 6, 1955, p. 1.

Bergreen, Laurence. *Louis Armstrong: An Extravagant Life.* New York: Broadway Books, 1997.

Berrett, Joshua. "Louis Armstrong and Opera." *Musical Quarterly* 76 (No. 2, 1992), pp. 216–240. [Excerpted in Berrett, 1999, pp. 24–29]

——, ed. *The Louis Armstrong Companion: Eight Decades of Commentary.* New York: Schirmer Books, 1999.

Berton, Ralph. *Remembering Bix.* London: W.H. Allen, 1974.

Bigard, Barney, with Barry Martyn. *With Louis and the Duke: The Autobiography of a Jazz Clarinetist.* New York: Oxford University Press, 1986.

Blassingame, John W. *Black New Orleans.* Chicago: University of Chicago Press, 1973.

Blesh, Rudi. *Shining Trumpets.* New York: Knopf, 1946; rev. 1958; rpt. New York: Da Capo Press, 1976.

Blesh, Rudi, and Harriet Janis. *They All Played Ragtime.* New York: Oak Publications, 1971.

Bogle, Donald. *Blacks in American Films and Television: An Illustrated Encyclopedia.* New York: Fireside, 1989.

——. *Toms, Coons, Mulattos, Mammies, and Bucks: An Interpretive History of Blacks in American Films.* New York: Continuum, 1989; rpt. New York: Viking Press, 1992.

Bordman, Gerald. *American Musical Theatre: A Chronicle.* New York: Oxford University Press, 1986.

Borneman, Ernest. " 'Bop Will Kill Business Unless It Kills Itself First'—Louis Armstrong." *Down Beat* 15 (April 7, 1948), p. 2. [Rpt. Berrett, 1999, pp. 144–151]

Boujut, Michel. *Louis Armstrong.* Trans. by Charles Penwarden. New York: Rizzoli, 1998.

Bradbury, David. *Armstrong.* London: Haus, 2003.

Bradbury, Ray. "Satchmo Saved." *International Trumpet Guild Journal* 19 (No. 3, Feb. 1983), p. 19.

——. "Satchmo's Syndrome." *International Trumpet Guild Journal* 23 (No. 3, Feb. 1987), p. 6.

Brask, Ole, and Dan Morgenstern. *Jazz People.* New York: H.N. Abrams, 1960.

Bricktop [Ada Smith], with James Haskins. *Bricktop.* New York: Atheneum, 1983; rpt. New York: Welcome Rain Publishers, 2000.

Brooks, Edward. *Influence and Assimilation in Louis Armstrong's Cornet and Trumpet Work, 1923–1928.* Lewiston, NY: Edwin Mellen Press, 2000.

——. *The Young Louis Armstrong on Records: A Critical Survey of the Early Recordings (1923–1928).* Lanham, MD: Scarecrow Press, 2002.

Brothers, Thomas, ed. *Louis Armstrong, in His Own Words.* Annotated index by Charles Kinzer. New York: Oxford University Press, 1999.

Brun, H.O. *The Story of the Original Dixieland Jazz Band.* Baton Rouge: Louisiana State University Press, 1960.

Buerkle, Jack V., and Danny Barker. *Bourbon Street Black.* New York: Oxford University Press, 1973.

Caffey, H. David. "The Musical Style of Louis Armstrong, 1925–1929." *Journal of Jazz Studies* 3 (No. 1, Fall 1975), pp. 72–96.

——. " 'West End Blues' [transcription]." In *Anthology for Musical Analysis,* 5th ed. Ed. by Charles Burkhart. New York: Holt, Rinehart and Winston, 1993.

Carmichael, Hoagy. *The Stardust Road.* Bloomington: Indiana University Press, 1946.

Carner, Gary. "The Agony and the Agony:

James Lincoln Collier's Jazz Writing." *Annual Review of Jazz Studies* 5 (1991), pp. 81–89.

Castle, Lee. *Louis Satchmo Armstrong's Immortal Trumpet Solos.* Transcribed by Lee Castle. New York: Leeds Music Co., 1947; rpt. 1961 in 2 vols.

Charters, Samuel B., and Leonard Kunstadt. *Jazz: A History of the New York Scene.* New York: Da Capo Press, 1981.

Chevan, David. "A List of Compositions with a Copyright Assigned to Louis Armstrong." Ms., Library of Congress.

——. *Written Music in Early Jazz.* Ph.D. dissertation, City University of New York, 1997.

Chilton, John. *A Jazz Nursery.* London: Bloomsbury Book Shop, 1980.

——. *Sidney Bechet: The Wizard of Jazz.* New York: Oxford University Press, 1987.

Chilton, John, and Max Jones. *Louis: The Louis Armstrong Story 1900–1971.* Boston: Little, Brown, 1971; rev. ed. New York: Da Capo Press, 1988.

Clayton, Buck, with Nancy Miller Elliott. *Buck Clayton's Jazz World.* New York: Oxford University Press, 1987.

Cogswell, Michael. "Armstrong, Louis." In *The New Grove Dictionary of Jazz,* 2nd ed. Ed. by Barry Kernfeld. London and New York: Macmillan/Grove, 2002.

——. "The Armstrong Collection." *Humanities* 21 (No. 4, July–Aug. 2000), pp. 10–14.

——. *Louis Armstrong: The Offstage Story of Satchmo.* Foreword by Dan Morgenstern. Portland, OR: Collectors Press, 2003.

Collier, Geoffrey L., and James Lincoln Collier. "A Study of Timing in Two Louis Armstrong Solos." *Music Perception* 19 (No. 3, Spring 2002), pp. 463–483.

Collier, James Lincoln. "Armstrong, Louis." In *The New Grove Dictionary of Jazz.* Ed. by Barry Kernfeld. London and New York: Macmillan/Grove, 1988.

——. *Louis Armstrong: An American Genius.* New York: Oxford University Press, 1983.

——. *The Making of Jazz.* Boston: Houghton Mifflin, 1978.

——. *The Reception of Jazz in America: A New View.* Brooklyn, NY: Institute for Studies in American Music, 1988.

Collins, Lee. *Oh, Didn't He Ramble.* Urbana: University of Illinois Press, 1974.

Condon, Eddie. *We Called It Music: A Generation of Jazz.* New York: Henry Holt, 1947.

Covarrubias, Miguel. Caricature accompanying anonymous "Impossible Interview: Fritz Kreisler vs. Louis Armstrong." *Vanity Fair* 40 (No. 6, Feb. 1936), p. 33.

Cripps, Thomas. *Slow Fade to Black: The Negro in American Film, 1900–1942.* New York: Oxford University Press, 1977.

Crouch, Stanley. "Laughin' Louis." *The Village Voice,* Aug. 14, 1978, p. 45; rpt. *The Village Voice,* Nov. 14, 1995, p. 43.

Crow, Bill. *Jazz Anecdotes.* New York: Oxford University Press, 1990.

Dance, Stanley. *The Complete Louis Armstrong and Duke Ellington Sessions.* Liner notes. Roulette Records 24546, 2 CDs, 2000. (CD #11)

——. *The World of Duke Ellington.* New York: Scribner's, 1970.

——. *The World of Earl Hines.* New York: Scribner's, 1977.

——. *The World of Swing.* New York: Scribner's, 1974; rpt. New York: Da Capo Press, 2001.

Dapogny, James. "Louis Armstrong." In *New Grove Dictionary of Music and Musicians,* 2nd ed. Ed. by Stanley Sadie. New York: Macmillan/Grove, 2001.

Darensbourg, Joe, with Peter Vacher. *Jazz Odyssey.* Baton Rouge: Louisiana State University Press, 1988.

Daver, Manek. *Jazz Graphics—David Stone Martin.* Tokyo: Gurafikkusha, 1991.

Davis, F. James. *Who Is Black?: One Nation's Definition.* University Park: Pennsylvania State University Press, 1991.

Davis, Miles, and Quincy Troupe. *Miles: The Autobiography.* New York: Simon and Schuster, 1989.

Deffaa, Chip. *In the Mainstream: Eighteen Portraits in Jazz.* Metuchen, NY: Scarecrow Press, 1992.

——. *Swing Legacy.* Metuchen, NY: Scarecrow Press, 1989.

——. *Traditionalists and Revivalists in Jazz.* Metuchen, NY: Scarecrow Press, 1993.

——. *Voices of the Jazz Age.* Urbana: University of Illinois Press, 1990.

DeVeaux, Scott. *The Birth of Bebop: A Social and Musical History.* Berkeley: University of California Press, 1997.

Dickerson, James L. *Just for a Thrill: Lil Hardin Armstrong, First Lady of Jazz.* New York: Cooper Square, 2003.

Dodds, Baby, with Larry Gara. *The Baby Dodds Story.* Baton Rouge: Louisiana State University Press, 1992.

Douglas, Ann. *Terrible Honesty: Mongrel Manhattan in the 1920s.* New York: Farrar, Straus, and Giroux, 1995.

Driggs, Frank, and Harris Lewine. *Black Beauty, White Heat: A Pictorial History of Classic Jazz.* New York: Morrow, 1982.

Duberman, Martin. *Paul Robeson.* New York: New Press, 1989.

Early, Gerald. *Tuxedo Junction: Essays on American Culture.* New York: Ecco Press, 1989.

Eaton, Jeanette. *Trumpeter's Tale: The Story of Young Louis Armstrong* [juvenile literature]. New York: Morrow, 1955.

Ecklund, Peter. " 'Louis Licks' and Nineteenth-Century Cornet Etudes: The Roots of Melodic Improvisation as Seen in the Jazz Style of Louis Armstrong." *Historic Brass Society Journal* 13 (2001), pp. 90–101.

Edwards, Brent Hayes. "Louis Armstrong and the Syntax of Scat." *Critical Inquiry* 28 (No. 3, Spring 2002), pp. 618–650.

Eldridge, Roy. "Jim Crow Is Killing Jazz." *Negro Digest* 8 (No. 12, 1950), pp. 44–49.

Ellington, Edward Kennedy "Duke." *Music Is My Mistress.* Garden City, NY: Doubleday, 1973.

Ellison, Ralph. *Invisible Man.* New York: Random House, 1952.

——. *Shadow and Act.* New York: Random House, 1964.

Englund, Björn. "A Louis Armstrong Filmography." *Coda* 12 (No. 3, 1975), pp. 5–6; additions and corrections by Klaus Stratemann in Vol. 12, No. 4, pp. 32–33.

Enstice, Wayne, and Paul Rubin. *Jazz Spoken Here: Conversations with Twenty-two Musicians.* Baton Rouge: Louisiana State University Press, 1992.

Fahlenkamp-Merrell, Kindle. *Louis Armstrong* [juvenile literature]. Chanhassen, MN: Child's World, 2002.

Feather, Leonard. *The Book of Jazz.* New York: Horizon Press, 1965.

——. *From Satchmo to Miles.* New York: Stein and Day, 1972; rpt. New York: Da Capo Press, 1984.

——. *Louis Armstrong Meets Oscar Peterson.* Liner notes. Verve 825713-2, 1997. (CD #37)

——. "The Three Armstrongs." *Melody Maker* 34 (Aug. 22, 1959), pp. 2–3.

Ferguson, Otis. *The Otis Ferguson Reader.* Highland Park, IL: December Press, 1982.

Fiehrer, Thomas Marc. *Louisiana's Black Heritage.* New Orleans: Louisiana State Museum, 1979.

Finkelstein, Sidney. *Jazz: A People's Music.* New York: Citadel, 1948; rpt. New York: Da Capo Press, 1975; New York: International Publishers, 1988.

Firestone, Ross. *Swing, Swing, Swing: The Life and Times of Benny Goodman.* New York: Norton, 1993.

Foster, George "Pops," with Tom Stoddard. *The Autobiography of George "Pops" Foster.* Berkeley: University of California Press, 1971.

Fox, Stephen. *Blood and Power: Organized Crime in Twentieth-Century America.* New York: Penguin Books, 1990.

Freeman, Bud. *You Don't Look Like a Musician.* Detroit: Balamp, 1974.

Friedwald, Will. *Jazz Singing.* New York: Collier Books, 1990. [Excerpted in Berrett, 1999, pp. 191–200]

Fuld, James J. *The Book of World-Famous Music: Classical, Popular, and Folk,* 4th ed. New York: Dover, 1995.

Gabbard, Krin. *Jammin' at the Margins: Jazz and the American Cinema.* Chicago: University of Chicago Press, 1996. [Excerpts in Berrett, 1999, pp. 201–233]

Garner, Gary. *The Miles Davis Companion: Four Decades of Commentary.* New York: Schirmer Books, 1996.

Garrett, Charles Hiroshi. "Louis Armstrong and the Sound of Migration." In *Playing Changes: New Jazz Studies.* Ed. by Robert Walser. Durham, NC: Duke University Press, forthcoming.

Gelatt, Roland. *The Fabulous Phonograph.* New York: Collier Books, 1977.

Giddins, Gary. *Bing Crosby: A Pocketful of Dreams. The Early Years, 1903–1940.* Boston: Little, Brown, 2001.

——. *Rhythm-a-ning: Jazz Tradition and Innovation in the '80s.* New York: Oxford University Press, 1985.

——. *Satchmo.* New York: Doubleday, 1988; rpt. New York: Da Capo Press, 1998 and (text only) 2001.

——. "Satchuated: Running Down the Rabbit Hole at the Louis Armstrong Archive." *The Village Voice,* April 16–22, 2003, p. 58.

Giddins, Gary, Dan Morgenstern, and Stanley Crouch. "Armstrong at Eighty-five." *The Village Voice,* Aug. 27, 1985, p. 79+.

Gillespie, Dizzy, with Al Fraser. *To Be or Not to Bop.* Garden City, NY: Doubleday, 1979.

Gitler, Ira. *Swing to Bop.* New York: Oxford University Press, 1985.

Gleason, Ralph J. *Celebrating the Duke and Louis, Bessie, Billie, Bird, Carmen, Miles, Dizzy, and Other Heroes.* Boston: Little, Brown, 1975.

——. *Jam Session: An Anthology of Jazz.* New York: G.P. Putnam's Sons, 1958.

——. "Perspectives [remarks about the Little Rock school integration issue]." *Down Beat* 25 (Feb. 6, 1958), p. 33.

Goddard, Chris. *Jazz Away from Home.* London: Paddington Press, 1979.

Godwin, Joscelyn, ed. *Schirmer Scores: A Repertory of Western Music.* New York: Schirmer Books, 1975.

Goffin, Robert. *Horn of Plenty: The Story of Louis Armstrong.* New York: Allen, Towne and Heath, 1947.

——. *Jazz: From the Congo to the Metropolitan.* Garden City, NY: Doubleday, 1944; rpt. New York: Da Capo Press, 1975.

Goldblatt, Burt. *Newport Jazz Festival: The Illustrated History.* New York: Dial Press, 1977.

Gordon, Max. *Live at the Village Vanguard.* New York: St. Martin's Press, 1980.

Gosnell, Harold F. *Negro Politicians.* Chicago: University of Chicago Press, 1935.

Gourse, Leslie. *Louis' Children: American Jazz Singers.* New York: Quill, 1984.

Gridley, Mark C. "Jazz History: Why Is Louis Armstrong So Important?" *Jazz Educators Journal* 16 (No. 3, 1984), pp. 71–72.

Grigson, Lionel. *A Louis Armstrong Study Album.* London: Novello, 1992.

Gushee, Lawrence. "The Improvisation of Louis Armstrong." In *In the Course of Performance: Studies in the World of Musical Improvisation.* Ed. by Bruno Nettl and Melinda Russell. Chicago: University of Chicago Press, 1998.

——. "Oliver, King." In *The New Grove Dictionary of Jazz,* 2nd ed. Ed. by Barry Kernfeld. London and New York: Macmillan/Grove, 2002.

Hadler, Mona. "Jazz and the Visual Arts." *Arts Magazine* 57 (No. 10, June 1983), pp. 91–101.

Hadlock, Richard B. *Jazz Masters of the Twenties.* New York: Macmillan, 1965.

Hair, William Ivy. *Carnival of Fury.* Baton Rouge: Louisiana State University Press, 1976.

Hammond, John, with Irving Townsend. *John Hammond on Record: An Autobiography.* New York: Ridge Press, 1977.

Harker, Brian Cameron. *The Early Musical Development of Louis Armstrong, 1901–1928.* Ph.D. dissertation, Columbia University, 1998.

——. "Louis Armstrong and the Clarinet." *American Music* 21 (No. 2, Summer 2003), pp. 137–158.

——. " 'Telling a Story': Louis Armstrong and Coherence in Early Jazz." *Current Musicology* 63 (1999), pp. 46–83.

Harrison, Daphne Duval. *Black Pearls: Blues Queens of the 1920s.* New Brunswick, NJ: Rutgers University Press, 1988.

Harrison, Max, Charles Fox, and Eric Thacker. *The Essential Jazz Records.* Westport, CT: Greenwood Press, 1984.

Henderson, Mary. *Broadway Ballyhoo: The American Theatre in Posters, Photographs, Magazines, Caricatures, and Programs.* New York: Abrams, 1989.

Hentoff, Nat. *Jazz Is.* New York: Random House, 1976.

——. *The Jazz Life.* New York: Dial Press, 1961; rpt. New York: Da Capo Press, 1985.

Hentoff, Nat, and Albert J. McCarthy, eds. *Jazz: New Perspectives on the History of Jazz by Twelve of the World's Foremost Jazz Critics and Scholars.* New York: Da Capo Press, 1974.

Hillman, Christopher. *Bunk Johnson: His Life and Times.* New York: Universe Books, 1988.

Hinton, Milt, and D.G. Berger. *Bass Lines: The Stories and Photographs of Milt Hinton.* Philadelphia: Temple University Press, 1988.

Hobson, Wilder. *American Jazz Music.* New York: W.W. Norton, 1939.

Hodes, Arthur, and Chadwick Hansen. *Selections from the Gutter: Jazz Portraits from "The Jazz Record."* Berkeley: University of California Press, 1977.

Hodier, André. *Hommes et problèmes du jazz.* Paris: Au Portulan, 1954.

——. *Jazz: Its Evolution and Essence.* New York: Grove Press, 1956.

Holiday, Billie. *Lady Sings the Blues.* Garden City, NY: Doubleday, 1956.

Hughes, Langston, and Milton Meltzer. *Black Magic: A Pictorial History of the Negro in Entertainment.* Englewood Cliffs, NJ: Prentice-Hall, 1967.

Ingman, Dan S. "England's Welcome to Louis Armstrong." *Melody Maker* 7 (Aug. 1932), p. 9. [Rpt. Berrett, 1999, pp. 50–55]

January, Brendan, and François Roca. *Louis Armstrong: Jazz Musician* [juvenile literature]. Philadelphia: Mason Crest Publishers, 2003.

Jepsen, Jørgen Grunnet. *A Discography of Louis Armstrong, 1923–1971.* Copenhagen: Knudsen, 1973.

Jones, Max. "Lil Armstrong, Royalties, and the Old Songs." *Melody Maker* 42 (April 8, 1967), p. 8. [Rpt. Berrett, 1999, pp. 42–45]

——. "Louis Blasts Jim Crow." *Melody Maker* 34 (Dec. 12, 1959), p. 11.

——. *Talking Jazz.* New York: W.W. Norton, 1988.

Jones, Max, and John Chilton. *Louis: The Louis Armstrong Story 1900–1971.* Boston: Little, Brown, 1971; rev. ed. New York: Da Capo Press, 1988.

Kael, Pauline. *5001 Nights at the Movies.* New York: Holt, 1985.

Kaminsky, Max. "Louis Is Not an Uncle Tom." *Melody Maker* 32 (Oct. 12, 1957), p. 5.

Kaminsky, Max, with V.E. Hughes. *My Life in Jazz.* New York: Harper and Row, 1963.

Kellner, Bruce, ed. *The Harlem Renaissance: A Historical Dictionary for the Era.* Westport, CT: Greenwood Press, 1984.

Kennedy, Rick. *Jelly Roll, Bix, and Hoagy: Gennett Studios and the Birth of Recorded Jazz.* Bloomington: Indiana University Press, 1994.

Kenney, William Howland. *Chicago Jazz: A Cultural History 1904–1930.* New York: Oxford University Press, 1993.

——. " 'Going to Meet the Man': Louis Armstrong's Autobiographies." *Melus* 15 (No. 2, Summer 1988), pp. 27–48.

——. "Negotiating the Color Line: Louis Armstrong's Autobiographies." In *Jazz in Mind: Essays on the History and Meanings of Jazz.* Ed. by Reginald T. Buckner and Steven Weiland. Detroit: Wayne State University Press, 1991.

Kerman, Joseph. *Listen,* 3rd ed. New York: Worth Publishers, 1980.

Kernfeld, Barry, ed. *The New Grove Dictionary of Jazz.* London and New York: Macmillan/Grove, 1988.

——. *The New Grove Dictionary of Jazz,* 2nd ed. London and New York: Macmillan/Grove, 2002.

Kernfeld, Barry, and Leonard Feather. "Singing." In *The New Grove Dictionary of Jazz,* 2nd ed. Ed. by Barry Kernfeld. London and New York: Macmillan/Grove, 2002.

Kisch, John, and Edward Mapp. *A Separate Cinema: Fifty Years of Black Cast Posters.* New York: Farrar, Straus, and Giroux, 1992.

Kmen, Henry. *The Music of New Orleans.* Baton Rouge: Louisiana State University Press, 1966.

Laverdure, Michel. *Louis Armstrong.* Paris: Vade Rétro, 1997.

Lemann, Nicholas. *The Promised Land: The Great Black Migration and How It Changed America.* New York: Alfred A. Knopf, 1991.

Lewis, David Levering. *When Harlem Was in Vogue.* New York: Knopf, 1981.

Locke, Alain. *The New Negro: An Interpretation.* New York: Boni, 1925; rpt. New York: Atheneum, 1968.

Lomax, Alan. *Mr. Jelly Roll: The Fortunes of Jelly Roll Morton, New Orleans Creole and "Inventor" of Jazz.* New York: Duell, Sloane, and Pearce, 1950; rpt. Berkeley: University of California Press, 1973.

Long, Richard. *African Americans: A Portrait.* New York: Crescent Books, 1993.

"Louis the First." *Time* 53 (No. 8, Feb. 21, 1949), pp. 52–58.

Lyttelton, Humphrey. *The Best of Jazz II.* New York: Taplinger, 1982.

MacDonald, J. Fred. *Blacks and White TV: Afro-Americans in Television since 1948.* Chicago: Nelson-Hall Publishers, 1983.

Marquis, Donald. *The Search for Buddy Bolden.* Baton Rouge: Louisiana State University Press, 1978.

McCarthy, Albert J. *Louis Armstrong.* New York: Barnes, 1959.

McElroy, Guy C. *Facing History: The Black Image in American Art, 1710–1940.* San Francisco and Washington, DC: Bedford Arts and the Corcoran Gallery of Art, 1990.

Meckna, Michael. "After Louis Armstrong Played, the Jazz World Changed Forever." *The Instrumentalist* 56 (No. 1, Aug. 2001), pp. 12–16.

——. "Louis Armstrong Blasts Little Rock, Arkansas." In *Perspectives on American Music since 1950.* Ed. by James R. Heintze. New York: Garland, 1998.

——. "Satchmo Lives! The Legacy of Louis Armstrong." *Brass Player,* Fall 2000, p. 1+.

——. *Twentieth-Century Brass Soloists.* Westport, CT: Greenwood Press, 1994.

Meeker, David. *Jazz in the Movies: A Guide to Jazz Musicians, 1917–1977.* New Rochelle, NY: Arlington House, 1977.

Mellers, Wilfrid. *Music in a New Found Land.* London: Barrie and Rockliff, 1964.

Meryman, Richard. "An Interview with Louis Armstrong." *Life* 60 (No. 15, April 15, 1966), pp. 92–116.

——. *Louis Armstrong—a Self-Portrait.* New York: Eakins, 1971.

Mezzrow, Mezz, with Bernard Wolfe. *Really the Blues.* New York: Random House, 1946; rev. ed. Garden City, NY: Doubleday, 1972.

Miller, Marc H., ed. *Louis Armstrong: A Cultural Legacy.* New York and Seattle: Queens Museum of Art and the University of Washington Press, 1994.

Monceaux, Morgan. *Jazz: My Music, My People.* New York: Knopf, 1994.

Morgenstern, Dan. "The Armstrong I Knew." *Annual Review of Jazz Studies* 10 (1999), pp. 127–133.

——. *The Complete Decca Studio Recordings of Louis Armstrong and the All Stars.* Program booklet. Mosaic Records MD6-146, 6 CDs, 1993. (CD #8)

——. *The Complete RCA Victor Recordings.* Program booklet. RCA Victor 68682, 4 CDs, 1997. (CD #12)

——. *The Great Chicago Concert, 1956.* Liner notes. Columbia/Legacy 65119, 2 CDs, 1997. (CD #19)

——. "Louis Armstrong 1901-1971: Satchmo and the Critics." *The Village Voice,* June 6, 2001-June 12, 2001, pp. 102–103.

——. "Louis Armstrong and the Development and Diffusion of Jazz." In *Louis Armstrong: A Cultural Legacy.* Ed. by Marc Miller. New York and Seattle: Queens Museum of Art and the University of Washington Press, 1994.

——. *Portrait of the Artist as a Young Man: 1923–34.* Program booklet. Columbia/Legacy 57176, 4 CDs, 1994. (CD #48)

——. "Roses for Satchmo [birthday tributes from some eighty musicians]." *Down Beat* 37 (July 9, 1970), pp. 14–19.

——. "Yesterday, Today and Tomorrow: An Interview with Louis Armstrong." *Down Beat* 32 (July 15, 1965), pp. 15–18.

——, ed. "[Louis Armstrong, obituaries]." *Down Beat* 38 (Sept. 16, 1971), pp. 12–14.

Morgenstern, Dan, and Ole Brask. *Jazz People.* New York: Abrams, 1976; rpt. New York: Da Capo Press, 1993.

Muse for Music. Serial CD ROM. New York: Muze Inc., 1994–.

Napoleon, Art. "A Conversation with Bobby Hackett." *Jazz Journal* 26 (No. 1, Jan. 1973), pp. 2–6.

North Carolina Museum of Art. *Riffs and Takes: Music in the Art of Romare Bearden.* Raleigh: North Carolina Museum of Art, 1988.

Ondaatje, Michael. *Coming Through Slaughter.* New York: Vintage International, 1976.

Orgill, Roxane. *If I Only Had a Horn: Young Louis Armstrong* [juvenile literature]. Boston: Houghton Mifflin, 1997.

——. "Satchmo's Stamp of Approval." *Wall Street Journal,* Sept. 27, 1995, p. A13. [Rpt. Berrett, 1999, pp. 243–246]

Osofsky, Gilbert. *Harlem: The Making of a Ghetto.* New York: Harper and Row, 1963.

Ostransky, Leroy. *Jazz City: The Impact of Our Cities on the Development of Jazz.* Englewood Cliffs, NJ: Prentice-Hall, 1978.

Panassié, Hugues. *Douze années de jazz (1927–1938): Souvenirs.* Paris: Editions Corréa, 1946. [The chapter "Louis Armstrong at the Salle Pleyel" appears in Berrett, 1999, pp. 60–73.]

——. *Hot Jazz: The Guide to Swing Music.* New York: M. Witmark, 1936.

——. *Louis Armstrong.* Paris: Editions du Belvédère, 1947. Rev. ed. New York: Scribner's, 1971.

Pinfold, Mike. *Louis Armstrong.* New York: Universe Books, 1987.

Planas, Jaime, and Bernard L. Kaye. "Rupture of the Orbicularis Oris in Trumpet Players (Satchmo's Syndrome)." *International Trumpet Guild Journal* 19 (No. 2, Dec. 1982), pp. 12–14.

Pleasants, Henry. *The Great American Popular Singers.* New York: Simon and Schuster, 1974.

Porter, Lewis. *Louis Armstrong and Sidney Bechet in New York, 1923–1925.* Liner notes. Smithsonian Recordings R 026, 1981. [Excerpted in Berrett, 1999, pp. 33–36]

Porter, Susan. "Events of Interest [opening of the Louis Armstrong Archive at Queens College]." *Sonneck Society Bulletin* 17 (No. 3, Fall 1991), p. 121.

Powell, Richard J. *The Blues Aesthetic: Black Culture and Modernism.* Washington, DC: Washington Project for the Arts, 1989.

Ramsey, Frederick, Jr., and Charles Edward Smith, eds. *Jazzmen: The Story of Hot Jazz Told in the Lives of the Men Who Created It.* New York: Harcourt, Brace, 1939; rpt. New York: Limelight, 1985.

Richards, Kenneth G. *People of Destiny: Louis Armstrong* [juvenile literature]. Chicago: Childrens Press, 1967.

Rose, Al. *Storyville, New Orleans.* Tuscaloosa: University of Alabama Press, 1974.

Rose, Al, and Edmond Souchon. *New Orleans Jazz: A Family Album.* Baton Rouge: Louisiana State University Press, 1967.

Rusch, Robert D. *Jazztalk: The "Cadence" Interviews.* Secaucus, NJ: Lyle Stuart, 1984.

Russell, Bill. *New Orleans Style.* New Orleans: Jazzology Press, 1994.

Rust, Brian. *The American Record Label Book.* New Rochelle, NY: Arlington House, 1978.

——. *Jazz Records, 1897–1942,* 4th ed. New Rochelle, NY: Arlington House, 1978.

Sadie, Stanley. *Stanley Sadie's Music Guide.* New York: Prentice-Hall, 1986.

Sanders, Ruby Wilson. *Jazz Ambassador: Louis Armstrong* [juvenile literature]. Chicago: Childrens Press, 1973.

Schuller, Gunther. *Early Jazz: Its Roots and Musical Development.* New York: Oxford University Press, 1968.

——. *The Swing Era: The Development of Jazz.* New York: Oxford University Press, 1989.

Shapiro, Nat, and Nat Hentoff. *Hear Me Talkin' to Ya: The Story of Jazz as Told by the Men Who Made It.* New York: Rinehart, 1955; rpt. New York: Dover, 1986.

——. *The Jazz Makers.* New York: Rinehart, 1957.

Shaw, Arnold. *Black Popular Music in America.* New York: Macmillan, 1985.

Smith, Jay D., and Len Guttridge. *Jack Teagarden: The Story of a Jazz Maverick.* New York: Da Capo Press, 1976.

Spear, Allan H. *Black Chicago: The Making of a Negro Ghetto.* Chicago: University of Chicago Press, 1967.

Starr, S. Frederick. *Red and Hot: The Fate of Jazz in the Soviet Union.* New York: Oxford University Press, 1983.

Starrex, A.V. "An Adventure in Discography: Louis Armstrong Discoveries." *Coda* 249 (May-June 1993), pp. 32–33.

St. Cyr, Johnny. "The Original Hot Five." *The Second Line,* Sept. 1954, pp. 1–2.

Stearns, Marshall W. *The Story of Jazz.* New York: Oxford University Press, 1956.

Stewart, Milton L. "Earl Hines' 'Trumpet' Piano Style: The Influence of Louis Armstrong." *Annual Review of Jazz Studies* 4 (1988), pp. 189–195.

Stewart, Rex. *Boy Meets Horn.* Ed. by Claire Gordon. Ann Arbor: University of Michigan Press, 1991.

——. *Jazz Masters of the Thirty's.* New York: Macmillan, 1972.

Storb, Ilse. *Louis Armstrong: Mit Selbstzeugnissen und Bilddokumenten.* Reinbek bei Hamburg, Germany: Rowohlt, 1989.

Stratemann, Klaus. "Louis Armstrong: A Filmo-Discography." *International Association of Jazz Record Collectors Journal* 10 (Autumn 1977), pp. 28–30; and 11 (Autumn 1978), pp. 10–11.

——. *Louis Armstrong on the Screen.* Copenhagen: JazzMedia, 1996.

Sudhalter, Richard M., and Philip R. Evans. *Bix: Man and Legend.* New Rochelle, NY: Arlington House, 1974.

Tanenhaus, Sam. *Louis Armstrong: Musician* [juvenile literature]. New York: Chelsea House, 1989.

Taylor, Jeffrey. "Doctor Jazz [Doc Cheatham]." *Institute for Studies in American Music Newsletter* 27 (No. 2, Spring 1998), p. 11.

——. *Louis Armstrong and Earl Hines, 1928.* Liner notes. Smithsonian Recordings R 002, 1975.

——. "Louis Armstrong, Earl Hines, and 'Weather Bird.'" *The Musical Quarterly* 82 (No. 1, Spring 1998), pp. 1–40.

Terkel, Studs. *Giants of Jazz.* New York: Thomas Y. Crowell, 1957.

Theile, Bob, and Bob Golden. *What a Wonderful World: A Lifetime of Recordings.* New York: Oxford University Press, 1995.

Thompson, Kay C. "Louis and the Waif's Home." *The Record Changer* 9 (July-Aug. 1950), p. 8+.

Thomson, Virgil. *A Virgil Thomson Reader.* New York: Dutton, 1981.

Thrasher, Frederic M. *The Gang.* Chicago: University of Chicago Press, 1936.

Tinker, Edward Laroque. *Creole City.* New York: Longmans, Green, 1953.

Tirro, Frank. *Jazz: A History,* 2nd ed. New York: Norton, 1993.

Tomkins, Les. "The Classic Interview: Louis Armstrong." *Crescendo International* 24 (No. 5, 1987), pp. 26–27.

Traill, Sinclair. "Back o' Louis." *Jazz Journal* 23 (No. 7, 1970), pp. 24–25.

Travis, Dempsey J. *An Autobiography of Black Jazz.* Chicago: Urban Research Institute, 1983.

——. *The Louis Armstrong Odyssey: From Jane Alley to America's Jazz Ambassador.* Chicago: Urban Research Press, 1997.

Tucker, Mark. *Ellington: The Early Years.* Urbana: University of Illinois Press, 1991.

——, ed. *The Duke Ellington Reader.* New York: Oxford University Press, 1993.

Ullman, Michael. *Jazz Lives.* Washington, DC: New Republic Books, 1980.

Voce, Steve. "Clark Terry." *Jazz Journal International* 40 (No. 1, 1987), pp. 16–17.

Waller, Erle. *Chicago Uncensored.* New York: Exposition Press, 1965.

Walser, Robert, ed. *Keeping Time: Readings in Jazz History.* New York: Oxford University Press, 1999.

——. *Playing Changes: New Jazz Studies.* Durham, NC: Duke University Press, forthcoming.

Wells, Dicky, and Stanley Dance. *The Night People.* Boston: Crescendo Publishing, 1971.

Wentworth, Harold, and Stuart Berg Flexner. *Dictionary of American Slang.* New York: Crowell, 1967.

Westerberg, Hans. *Boy from New Orleans: A Discography of Louis "Satchmo" Armstrong.* Copenhagen: JazzMedia, 1981.

Whitehead, K. "Satch, Smack, and Swing." *Down Beat* 62 (Jan. 1995), p. 47.

Willems, Jos. *"All of Me": The Complete Musical Legacy of Louis Armstrong.* Copenhagen: JazzMedia, 2004.

Williams, Martin. *Jazz Masters of New Orleans.* New York: Macmillan, 1967; rpt. New York: Da Capo Press, 1979.

——. *The Jazz Tradition,* rev. ed. New York: Oxford University Press, 1983.

——, ed. *Jazz Panorama: From the Pages of "The Jazz Review."* New York: Crowell-Collier Press, 1962.

Wolbert, Klaus. *That's Jazz: Der Sound des 20. Jahrhunderts.* Darmstadt, Germany: Ausstellunghallen Mathildenhohe, 1989.

Wood, Berta. "Don't Blame Louis." *Jazz Journal* 10 (April 1957), p. 13.

Woog, Adam. *Louis Armstrong* [juvenile literature]. San Diego, CA: Lucent Books, 1995.

Wright, John S., and Tracy E. Smith. *A Stronger Soul within a Finer Frame: Portraying African-Americans in the Black Renaissance.* Minneapolis: University of Minnesota Press, 1990.

INDEX

Boldface page numbers indicate main entries, and ***boldface italics*** indicate photographs.

About the Author

MICHAEL MECKNA is Professor of Music History at Texas Christian Unviersity. He is also the author of *Twentieth-Century Brass Soloists* (Greenwood, 1994).

DATE DUE

781.65092 A736M

DISCARD

Meckna, Michael.
Satchmo :the Louis
Armstrong encyclopedia /
Central NONFICTION
07/19

R
781
.6509
2
A736M

HOUSTON PUBLIC LIBRARY
CENTRAL LIBRARY

MLA Bibliography

DUCKLES

3/06